Lynn Picknett is a writer, broadcaster, television presenter and lecturer on the paranormal, secret societies and religious and historical mysteries.

Clive Prince is a writer and researcher on the subject of religious and historical mysteries and conspiracies. One of his main areas of interest is the influence of esoteric societies on political ideologies, including the origins and growth of Nazism.

Picknett and Prince are the co-authors of *Turin Shroud: In Whose Image?*, *The Templar Revelation*, *The Stargate Conspiracy*, *The Sion Revelation* and *The Masks of Christ*.

Stephen Prior is a theologian and political historian who has had an interest in Rudolf Hess since 1969. He has spent five years extensively researching the truth behind the enigma, with assistance from contacts within the intelligence communities on both sides of the Atlantic, some of whom appeared in the ITV and History Channel documentary based on this book.

Robert Brydon is a miliatary historian who has researched numerous film treatments and scripts for US and UK documentaries, including preliminary scripts for the Occult Reich series. He has been researching the Rudolf Hess mystery for over fifteen years.

DOUBLE STANDARDS

The Rudolf Hess Cover-up

Lynn Picknett, Clive Prince
and
Stephen Prior

with additional research by
Robert Brydon

sphere

SPHERE

First published in Great Britain in 2001
by Little, Brown and Company
This edition published by Time Warner Paperbacks in 2002
Reprinted by Time Warner Books in 2006
Reprinted by Sphere in 2009, 2010

A CIP catalogue record for this book
is available from the British Library.

ISBN 978-0-7515-3220-3

Typeset in Goudy by M Rules
Printed and bound in Great Britain by
Clays Ltd, St Ives plc

Papers used by Sphere are natural, renewable and
recyclable products sourced from well-managed forests and certified
in accordance with the rules of the Forest Stewardship Council.

Mixed Sources
Product group from well-managed
forests and other controlled sources
www.fsc.org   Cert no. SGS-COC-004081
© 1996 Forest Stewardship Council
FSC

Sphere
An imprint of
Little, Brown Book Group
100 Victoria Embankment
London EC4Y 0DY

An Hachette UK Company
www.hachette.co.uk

www.littlebrown.co.uk

This book is dedicated in general to those men who despaired of the change of command from Officers and Gentlemen to the Technocrats of Total War.

In particular to one man of peace,
His Royal Highness Prince George, Duke of Kent
K.G. K.T. G.C.M.G. G.C.V.O.

b. 20–12–02   d. 25–08–42

'A Gallant and Handsome Prince'
W. S. CHURCHILL, SEPTEMBER 1942

Contents

Illustrations

9, 10, 11   Although the Duke of Windsor has been vilified as a Nazi sympathiser (seen here as the guest of Hitler in 1937), other members of the Royal Family were also impressed by the Führer's economic success and his determination to destroy Bolshevism. Certainly, the King and Queen were utterly opposed to a war with Germany, treating Prime Minister Neville Chamberlain to a hero's welcome on the balcony at Buckingham Palace after he made the ill-fated announcement of 'peace in our time' as a result of meeting Hitler in Munich. George VI and Queen Elizabeth were anxious that the pro-appeasement Lord Halifax should succeed Chamberlain as Prime Minister, being opposed to Winston Churchill whom they regarded as a maverick and warmonger. Royal approval of appeasement was, until recently, carefully airbrushed out of history.

12, 13   Press baron Lord Beaverbrook whose pro-peace
& 14   sympathies were cleverly pressed into service by Churchill as the Hess saga unfolded. Sir Samuel Hoare, whose attempts to broker peace between Britain and Germany extended, secretly, beyond the outbreak of hostilities.

15   The map purporting to show his route to Scotland, drawn by Hess while imprisoned at Mytchett Place. Note the handwritten date of '8.8.41'.

16, 17 &   Servicemen remove the wreckage of Hess's Me-110.
18   Mrs Annie McLean in the kitchen at Floors Farm, Eaglesham, near Glasgow, where she offered the Deputy Führer – who claimed to be Hauptmann Alfred Horn – a cup of tea after he parachuted into a nearby field on 10 May 1941. Hess claimed to have come to meet with the Duke of Hamilton – who denied all knowledge of such an arrangement.

19 & 20   The airstrip and outbuildings (known as the 'Kennels') at Dungavel House, the Hamilton family residence. Although Hamilton had moved out for the duration, evidence suggests that highly placed persons, including a royal duke, *were* there that night waiting for Hess.

what was the 'special mission'? The last photograph of the Duke, taken in August 1942. An Air Commodore, he was on a morale-boosting visit to an air force base.

32 & 33   21 September 1946: Hess rambles incoherently in the dock during the Nuremberg War Trials. His behaviour was so bizarre that it amused and embarrassed his fellow Nazis (Göring, on the left, barely suppresses his laughter). Certainly, his demeanour was by no means normal, but was this because 'Hess' was – as the evidence may indicate – a double, controlled and bewildered by mind-altering drugs administered by British psychiatrists? Was his 'amnesia' a convenient cover for the double's ignorance of the real Hess's past?

34, 35   The last inmate of Spandau, aged ninety-three, walks in
& 36   the grounds shortly before his death, allegedly from suicide, on 17 August 1987. Wolf Rüdiger Hess and lawyer Dr Alfred Seidl wait outside the prison, hoping to see the body of Prisoner Number Seven. They were denied permission. The memorial erected by the Rudolf Hess Society at Eaglesham. Widely deemed an affront to decent feeling, it was soon destroyed. It has not been replaced.

Acknowledgements

We would like to thank the following people for their help, support and encouragement in the writing of this book:

Francesca Norton-Prior and Lyndsay Brydon for their unstinting – and largely uncomplaining – support over many years for their respective menfolk.

Richard Taylor, Keith Prince, Ben Prior and Stephen J. W. Prior for their substantial research. Thanks, too, to Keith for the maps and diagrams.

Their Graces the Duke and Duchess of Hamilton, for putting up with endless enquiries and allowing us access to the family archives.

Wolf Rüdiger and Andrea Hess, for generously giving us their time, important information and for their hospitality.

Niven Sinclair, the catalyst whose curious role in bringing us together led indirectly to this book.

The late Michael Bentine, for inspiration, invaluable introductions and countless hours of discussion and analysis.

Michelle Norton, whose timely nagging helped ensure that this book became a reality. And Joanne Norton and Alice Prior for their understanding and for keeping us going.

Craig Oakley, for help with the research and his continuing support and encouragement.

Our agents, Lavinia Trevor and Jeffrey Simmons, for their hard work on behalf of this book.

At Little, Brown UK: Alan Samson, Jim Cochrane, Viv Redman and Linda Silverman.

For generously giving us their time and the benefit of their research and expertise: Anthony Cave Brown; Iain Gray; John Harris; Tony Marczan; Robin Macwhirter; Professor Scott Newton; Andrew Rosthorn; Lord James Douglas-Hamilton, the Earl of Selkirk, MSP; Alfred Smith; Eric Taylor; Dr Hugh Thomas.

For sharing their memories, experiences and information:

In the UK: Elizabeth Adam; Theresa Anderson; Dr Paul Aronow; Jean Auld; Will Bethune; Baron St Clair Bonde; Herbert Bushke; the late Elizabeth Byrd; Evelyn Criddle; the late Kenneth de Courcy; Lady 'Bunty' Gunn; Dr Robert Hancock, RAMC retd.; Alec Kennedy; Louise Kennedy; Ivor Lewis; Wing Commander Hector MacLean, RAF retd.; Brigadier Desmond Murphy, RAMC retd.; the late Trevor Ravenscroft; Professor Robert Shaw; Lieutenant-Colonel Eric Sturdy, RAMC retd.; the late 2nd Viscount Thurso (Robin Sinclair); Gwynn Watkins; – and 'Alexander', and all those who have helped us but who for various reasons prefer not to be named.

In the United States: Ralph de Toledano; Father Durkin, S. J.; Howard Massey; George P. Morse; Walter Pforzheimer; Howard Sartori; Nicholas Sheetz; John Taylor; John Waller; Ward Warren.

For their help in many different ways: Clementina Bentine; Irwin Bruckner; Gordon Cato; Leon Ellenport; Sir David Frost; Willi Henderson; Bob Kingdon; Tina Metz; Mary Neilson; Chris Ogilvie-Herald; Trevor Poots; the late Archie Prior; John Ritchie; Pane Talev; Sheila Taylor; Piroshka Torkoly.

The staff of the following archives and libraries: British Library, London; Bundesarchiv, Koblenz; Cambridge University Library; Edinburgh Castle; Edinburgh City Library; Georgetown University Library, Washington, DC; House of Lords Record Office; Imperial War Museum; International Committee of the Red Cross, Archive Division, Geneva; National Library of Scotland, Edinburgh; Public Record Office, Kew; Royal Air Force Museums, Hendon and Duxford; Royal Archives, Windsor; Royal Corps of Signals Archive, Blandford Forum; Scottish Record Office, Edinburgh; Sikorski Museum and Historical Archive, London and Glasgow; 602 Squadron Museum Association, Glasgow; US National Archives, Washington, DC; OSS, CIC and CIG archives at the US National Archives, Maryland.

About five years ago at the request of the Imperial War Museum I gave their representative a taped interview about my war time memories. They agreed to let me have a duplicate tape which duly arrived from London. Much to my surprise the tape came suddenly to an abrupt end when I began my description of Hess's arrival. This has made me wonder whether there is someone in authority, either with instructions or acting on his or her own initiative, who is giving orders to keep the lid on information connected with the Hess affair. If so it is high time that the lid was taken off. Should there still be an unrevealed secret the British people, and particularly those of us who spent six years of our young lives containing the aspirations of the German tyranny, have a right to know it.

Wing Commander C. Hector MacLean, 1999
602 (City of Glasgow) Squadron

Introduction

This book grew out of the chance meeting of four people: Stephen Prior, Robert Brydon, Lynn Picknett and Clive Prince, whose paths crossed over a period of several years, and whose individual enthusiasm for the Rudolf Hess mystery fuelled a joint ambition to discover – and make known – what really happened to the Deputy Führer of the Third Reich after he flew to Scotland in 1941.

Stephen Prior

My interest in the Hess affair began in a uniquely personal way. Having worked on the fringes of the intelligence communities of three countries, I know from personal experience what it feels like to be – in the jargon of that murky world – a 'deniable asset', having been imprisoned on terrorist charges in 1969 while working as an *agent provocateur* for one of the security services. Suffering solitary confinement for three months, I experienced the surreality of having to live with just my own thoughts and four blank walls, day in and day out. After that experience, I had a certain amount of fellow feeling for the old man condemned to rattle around in the great fortress of Spandau Prison for decades, the man known to the world as Rudolf Hess, who began his life sentence in 1946, only being released by death – officially suicide – in 1987.

My own imprisonment coincided with the time when Hess, having already suffered twenty-five years in Spandau, briefly returned to the headlines because of a life-threatening illness that had prompted his first reunion with his wife and son since 1941. Comparing this with my own considerably briefer period of enforced isolation, I became fascinated by the whole story of the Deputy Führer's historic flight to Britain and the dark mysteries surrounding his imprisonment.

Back in the outside world in the early 1970s, I became involved in co-ordinating a secret project with some remarkable men: Michael Bentine, the famous British comic and man of many roles, including intelligence work; Trevor Ravenscroft, author of the controversial *Spear of Destiny*, which centred on Hitler's fascination with the occult, and a member of the team sent to assassinate Rommel in 1941; Dr Andrija Puharich, the controversial American experimental psychologist who often worked closely with the Pentagon, and had been a colleague of Dr Donald Ewen Cameron, a key figure in unravelling the Hess mystery; and Dr Christopher Bird, co-author of *The Secret Life of Plants* (1974). During this period I had ample opportunity to discuss my growing interest in the Hess affair with Bentine and Ravenscroft, both of whom had connections with it. Bentine had become intrigued with the mystery through his friend, the Conservative MP Airey Neave, who as an army officer had served the indictment papers on Hess in his cell at Nuremberg, but who later campaigned for his release. Ravenscroft, apart from his research into the Nazis and the occult, also had some interesting things to say as a friend of Lord Beaverbrook, a crucial player in the wartime Hess drama.

Another landmark in the history of this book came when I had a conversation with a remarkable Latvian I met in 1973. Introduced by a mutual friend – who was, ironically perhaps, Jewish – this man turned out to have joined the SS in a moment of youthful enthusiasm but, soon regretting it, succeeded in smuggling a middle-aged couple out of the Riga ghetto. After the war, this atypical SS officer became a refugee, finally settling in England and making friends with a relative of the couple he had helped escape. The former SS officer made an astonishing, and seemingly incredible, remark. He said there was considerable doubt that the prisoner in Spandau was the real Rudolf Hess. I was frankly sceptical. How could a double keep up the pretence for all that time? Perhaps even more to the point, why would a double agree to serve another man's life sentence in the harshest of conditions? The idea seemed preposterous.

It was to be six years before the idea resurfaced, in the form of a book by a Welsh ex-army surgeon, Dr Hugh Thomas. Like my Latvian acquaintance, he claimed that the old man in Spandau was not Rudolf Hess – but unlike the former SS man's revelation, this appeared to be much more than a sensational rumour. Dr Thomas backed up his extraordinary claim with evidence, having had the opportunity to examine the prisoner for himself. In his expert medical opinion, the old man in Spandau, believed by the world to be Hitler's Deputy, was a double.

In 1990 I was introduced to Robert Brydon through our mutual interest in Rosslyn Chapel, that strangely decorated fifteenth-century edifice not far from Edinburgh, which has long been an almost magical focus for both Freemasons and the Knights Templar. Robert is a respected historical researcher, often working as a consultant for television documentaries, such as the acclaimed *Occult Reich* series.

Since the mid 1980s Bob had also researched another great aviation enigma of the Second World War, one that seemed completely separate from the Hess story, but which was to provide the missing key. This was the mystery of the plane crash in 1942 that killed King George VI's brother, George, Duke of Kent, a tragedy that has always been shrouded in the deepest secrecy for reasons that have never been satisfactorily explained. While officialdom has never encouraged independent investigators into the Hess affair – quite the contrary – if anything their attitude towards Kent crash researchers is even more unhelpful, to the point of being obstructive. Delving further, and putting the two mysteries together, it soon became obvious why officialdom is so nervous. Revelations about either of the investigations can certainly stir up a hornets' nest, but using one as the key to the other effectively threatens much of what the Establishment is sworn to uphold.

Lynn Picknett and Clive Prince

At the time when we first met – in 1989 – questions were being asked about the nature of Hess's death in Spandau prison almost two years previously. It seemed to us, even then, that something was being covered up: in any case, both of us had already come to the conclusion that something other than a desire for either justice or revenge lay behind the draconian regime of his incarceration for over forty years. It could only be that he held some secret that the authorities were afraid to let him reveal. And if he had been murdered, this only reinforced that suspicion.

Over a ten-year period we had produced several books on controversial historical mysteries, including *Turin Shroud: In Whose Image?* (1994), which presented new evidence that artist and hoaxer Leonardo da Vinci was responsible for faking Christendom's greatest relic, and *The Templar Revelation: Secret Guardians of the True Identity of Christ* (1997), which revealed the existence of a heretical Church of John the Baptist. Our most recent book, *The Stargate Conspiracy* (1999), explored the political subtext behind 'alternative' theories about the ancient world and certain New Age cults. Rudolf Hess – whose story we continued to research for years – makes a cameo appearance in *The Stargate Conspiracy* in a discussion about the politico-occult roots of Nazism. We had come to realise that, despite the almost universal dismissal of the Deputy Führer as a powerless has-been, he was the most important man in the Nazi empire after – perhaps even including – Adolf Hitler. This made his flight to Britain in the middle of the war an act of supreme significance.

We met Stephen and Robert in 1998 when Stephen organised the launch of the paperback edition of *The Templar Revelation* at the hotel he manages, the aptly named Templar Lodge Hotel, in the seaside village of Gullane, not far from Rosslyn Chapel. Also long bitten by the Hess mystery bug, we were intrigued and excited to hear about Stephen and Robert's research. After many long days of deep discussion, in the end the four of us agreed that we had no choice but to collaborate on a book.

We all pooled our material – amassed over a decade – and set ourselves the task of looking behind the propaganda and half-truths that obscured the story of Rudolf Hess. We were fired by the same question President Roosevelt asked when he first heard of it: 'I wonder what is really behind this story.'

The challenge

When Rudolf Hess flew to Scotland, alone and unarmed in the early stages of the Second World War, Hitler denounced him as a delusional madman who had stolen a plane with the crazy notion of brokering a peace deal with the enemy. The Germans also claimed that he had sought to negotiate with the Duke of Hamilton, Scotland's premier peer. Officially disowned by his own side, he was confined by the British until immediately after the war, when he was tried at Nuremberg and sentenced to life imprisonment in Spandau, where he died, apparently by his own hand, aged ninety-three, in 1987. To most people in Britain who have heard of Rudolf Hess, he was just 'that mad Nazi who flew over and was put away by our lot – and good riddance'.

Although there are plenty who accept the official history of Rudolf Hess, even a cursory glance at the details is enough to thrill any researchers. Questions scream out from virtually every official statement about that strangely fated man. Was he really the lone madman, acting on delusions, as both Hitler and Churchill claimed? If he was mad, then why was he not repatriated in accordance with the Geneva and Hague Conventions and why did the British deem him fit to stand trial at Nuremberg? If he really was a peace envoy, why was he imprisoned by the British? The more the subject is studied, the more the questions accumulate, and the more contradictory and even outrageous the official line becomes.

It soon becomes apparent that the whole Hess affair, from 1941 onwards, is riddled with so many contradictions and anomalies that it is obvious that the British authorities were desperate to conceal something. Judging by the fact that they are still desperate to conceal it, common sense dictates that they deem this secret to be unsuitable for public consumption, even after sixty years. But why? What could be so unacceptable to Britain, or the Allies, in the early twenty-first century? What does the Rudolf Hess story conceal that would in some way shock even today's cynical world?

Faced with such a massive wall of official denial, we set out to answers these questions:

- What were Hess's true motives when he flew to Scotland?
- Who else – if anyone – knew about it?

- Did he bring peace proposals, and if so, what were their terms? Were they the rantings of a madman, or the realistic proposals of a seasoned politician? Did they offer threats or some kind of compromise scenario that Britain could have seriously considered?
- Why did the British government keep Hess's peace proposals secret – and why do they maintain a wall of silence about them even now? What was there about Hess's peace plan that is still too explosive to make public?
- Was there, as Hess clearly believed, an influential peace lobby in Britain in 1941 and if so, how far up the social ladder did it reach?
- Is Dr Hugh Thomas right about the old man in Spandau being a Hess double? If the real Hess had been replaced by a lookalike, what happened to the Deputy Führer? Why was such an elaborate ruse necessary? And how did the British authorities pull it off?
- Why was Spandau's Prisoner Number Seven incarcerated for so long?
- Was he murdered and if so, was it because even at the age of ninety-three he still represented some kind of a threat to the authorities?

Many other researchers, including Peter Padfield and the late John Costello, have made their own conclusions based on the evidence at their disposal. However, we have been exceptionally fortunate in having key information made exclusively available to us – through new witnesses and files opened for us both in Britain and the United States. In particular, the family archives of the Duke of Hamilton threw significant light on many of these questions, and in some cases answered them with a measure of finality.

Because of the massive political reverberations of this story, throughout our investigation it was sometimes difficult to remember that it is essentially about just one man – and an unlikely 'hero' at that. Intense, bushy-eyebrowed, with very little in the way of wit or charm, Rudolf Hess fails to ignite any emotion in non-Nazis, except perhaps, in the end, compassion. Even as an anti-hero – it must be remembered that he was an unrepentant Nazi – he fails to excite, although his story and its implications are other matters entirely.

Utterly absorbed by a story that would shame the most dramatic

Greek tragedy, we had to discover the truth about Rudolf Hess, what made him what he was, what drove him, and what really drew him to Britain on that fateful night long ago.

LYNN PICKNETT
CLIVE PRINCE
STEPHEN PRIOR

CHAPTER ONE

Judgement Day

In October 1945 there were fewer more desolate places on earth than Nuremberg. Of the once beautiful old city there was little trace: the Allies had virtually flattened it as the Second World War drew to its close, leaving mounds of rubble as far as the eye could see. In the last months of the war, eleven major air raids had destroyed more than 90 per cent of the city.[1] Only 17,000 houses out of the original 130,000 remained and for those who clung to a kind of life, stunned and hesitant spectres among the ruins, it must have seemed like eking out an existence in hell. There was no electricity or water and no communications: the telephone system no longer worked – and as for the post, where was there left to deliver it? Yet in the last months of 1945, all eyes were focused on this terrible place, for now the apocalypse was over, it was Judgement Day.

There was – in Allied eyes – no more fitting place to hold the war crimes trials than the spiritual home of Nazism, scene of the most flamboyantly sinister calls to arms on behalf of Adolf Hitler, the Nuremberg Rallies. But now the Nazi leaders were coming to their reckoning, and although all eyes would be on every last one of them, there was a special curiosity reserved for the man who was once closest to Hitler, the Deputy Führer in the glory days of the rise of the Nazi Party, who had already been a prisoner of the British since 1941. Rudolf Hess, who had been so instrumental in organising the Nuremberg Rallies, in whipping the faithful into a fanatical frenzy, was being brought back to this bleak place to account for himself.

But there was another element to the world's fascination with

Rudolf Hess. By then he had an almost mythical status because of the mystery that still clung to him after his flight to Scotland in 1941, the 'peace mission' that was to end his life as a free man for ever. It had been an extraordinary exploit by anyone's standards, and even the most virulent anti-Nazi had to admit that, in one sense at least, the man who undertook to fly to an enemy country in the middle of a war to endeavour to make peace must be extraordinary. Most believed he would appear in court only briefly before meeting his end on the gallows, but, as events would prove, this was by no means the end of the Rudolf Hess story.

Surely few were prepared for the human wreckage that answered to the name of Rudolf Hess. The newsreel footage of the Nuremberg Trials shows a terribly gaunt, darkly intense man in a pitiable state, both mentally and physically, clutching his stomach, weaving about in his seat and staring with a dreadful blankness out of sunken eyes. He seems to be genuinely confused, sometimes half asleep, sometimes gazing at others without a hint of recognition or comprehension. The man with strangely burning eyes in the dock bore little resemblance to the high-ranking Nazi who had left Germany on his fateful mission four years before. But although fit, Hess was no longer a young man when he had set off to fly to Scotland. Fourteen days previously he had celebrated his forty-seventh birthday, and, in a unique display of respect and affection for a public figure other than the Führer himself, so had the German people. Encouraged from the highest levels to express their regard for Hess, ordinary Nazis listened to speeches that praised him to the skies. Little did they realise that it was to be the last celebration for the Deputy – indeed, the last birthday he was in any real sense to celebrate at all.

The great mission

The Deputy Führer took off from an airfield at Augsburg shortly before 6 p.m. on Saturday, 10 May 1941, in a Messerschmitt Bf110 (Me-110) – a fighter–bomber normally crewed by two airmen. Even for such an experienced aviator, this solo flight had to be arduous, nerve-racking and, of course, highly dangerous. According to the standard account, he had to fly and navigate alone from Augsburg to the countryside near Glasgow – a journey of 1,200 miles and five long hours. If spotted and chased by the RAF he had no means of defending himself, being totally unarmed. The Me-110 was fitted with auxiliary fuel tanks under its wings, because his destination was well beyond the normal range of the aircraft. There was no fuel for a return trip.

Hess crossed the British coast over Northumberland just before 10.30 p.m. At about 11.10, he parachuted from his plane near the village of Eaglesham, south of Glasgow, just in time to see the Me-110 crash a quarter of a mile up the road, close to Eaglesham House. Having damaged his ankle as he baled out, his landing must have been painful. It is astonishing that he was not more seriously injured – this was his first ever parachute jump. But Hess came down to earth with a bump in more ways than one: the end of this heroic journey was an ignominious arrest by the local Home Guard, who failed to recognise him. He gave his name as Hauptmann (Captain) Alfred Horn, asking to be taken to the Duke of Hamilton, whose family seat, Dungavel House, lay some eight miles away.

Not unnaturally, the arrival of Hitler's Deputy on enemy soil was a sensation. The news broke two days after his flight – Monday, 12 May – prompting intense speculation about his motives and intentions. Had he, of all people, fled from the Third Reich? Was his flight a sign that the evil empire was disintegrating? Or had he genuinely come to offer peace? The public's excited curiosity was never to be satisfied. Apart from a brief official statement confirming that the Deputy Führer had indeed arrived in Scotland, no more details were forthcoming. In fact, the British government did not make any public statement on Hess's motives until two years later, when, in September 1943, in a reply to a question in the House of Commons, Foreign Secretary Anthony Eden finally announced that Hess had come to try to negotiate a peace settlement, but that he refused to negotiate with the Churchill government.

Hitler was not so slow to respond to Hess's flight and subsequent imprisonment by the British, issuing an official statement claiming that his former Deputy was mentally unbalanced and had stolen the Me-110. The clear message was that he, Hitler, knew nothing of the flight, had never known of it, and did not wish to hear of it again. He had washed his hands of the Hess mission and Hess the man completely. Where Hitler led, the German nation followed, so the reputation of the man whose birthday had so recently been a cause of national rejoicing was abruptly plunged into the cesspool of history.

The official position – decided upon, in a rare example of agreement, by both Britain and Germany – was that Hess had acted on his own initiative, alone and as the result of a delusion. Hitler had effectively disowned his one-time best friend and Deputy as swiftly as possible, while the British agreed that he was not to be taken seriously – ever, if they could help it. The problem of what to do with this delusional Nazi remained, however.

Brought to trial

Now Hess and his fellow Nazis were to be brought to trial at the Palace of Justice in Nuremberg, once the central court of Bavaria. It was a large, barrack-like three-storey building with a separate block of cell accommodation for 1,200 prisoners. Having been reduced to a windowless and fire-blackened shell of its former self, the Allies virtually had to rebuild it before the trial could begin. No expense would be spared in exploiting the symbolic value of Nuremberg for the war crimes trial.

There was to be no jury. Guilt or innocence was to be decided by a panel of judges appointed by the 'four victorious powers': two judges each from the USA, Great Britain, the USSR and the provisional government of France, making up the International Military Tribunal (IMT). Its president was the British Lord Justice Sir Geoffrey Lawrence. Each of the four powers sent its own team of prosecutors. The accused were to be defended by German lawyers appointed by the victors.

Taken to Nuremberg by plane, Hess finally returned to Germany on 19 October 1945. For the next year he lived in a cell in the prison block attached to the courts, watched night and day by American guards. He had lost a considerable amount of weight: by that time – when he was photographed for the first time in four and a half years – he was gaunt and hollow-cheeked, a shadow of his former self. But was this the only reason he had written from his cell a strange warning to his wife Ilse, whom he had not seen since May 1941? He wrote: 'Do not let yourself be taken in by bad flashlight photographs or tendentious reports. I am still exactly the same man, inwardly and outwardly, as my comrades have recognised with joy.'[2]

Despite their years apart, he refused to allow her to visit him in Nuremberg, claiming that he did not want her to see him in such a degraded situation.

At Nuremberg Hess claimed to be suffering from total amnesia, remembering nothing of his life in Germany. When he was reunited with his fellow defendants, he claimed not to recognise them. In an effort to stimulate his memory – or perhaps to catch him out – he was confronted with close friends such as Professor General Karl Haushofer, his old political mentor and 'second father', and Ernst Bohle, who had run Hess's special agency, the Auslandorganisation (AO or Foreign Organisation). Hess not only claimed not to recognise Haushofer, but seemed not to react to the name of the professor's son, his friend of twenty years, Albrecht Haushofer, or even to the news that he had been killed by the SS a few weeks before the end of the war. Hess's amnesia seemed so complete that, although he remembered his wife, he told Haushofer he had no memory of his son Wolf (nicknamed 'Buz'), who had been three and a half when he last saw him, and whom he had adored.

Hess's apparent amnesia led to some bizarre exchanges. When he came face to face with Hermann Göring, the flamboyant Reichsmarschall who was in charge of the Luftwaffe and – until a few days before the very end – Hitler's designated successor, his first response was: 'Who are you?'[3]

Loss of memory was not the only bizarre symptom that Hess exhibited at Nuremberg. As Major Douglas M. Kelley, the American psychiatrist who was responsible for Hess during the trials, recorded: 'Hess's suspiciousness has been manifested during his entire stay in the prison by countless little actions. One of the most interesting was his refusal to sign his name to anything.'[4] Kelley goes on to tell how Hess had even refused to give an example of his signature to the French psychiatrist Dr Jean Delay. There was also an American guard who was collecting all the signatures of the defendants on a dollar bill as a somewhat grisly souvenir of the trials. When it was Hess's turn, he signed it amenably enough, but then immediately tore it into pieces and threw it out of his cell window, saying, 'Our German signatures are precious.'[5]

This was not the first time that Hess's state of mind had been called into question. Although the British made no public statements about Hess's mental condition, it was reported soon after the

Nuremberg Trials – in a book by Brigadier John Rawlings Rees, the army psychiatrist who had been responsible for him – that he had been suffering from various psychological abnormalities almost from the moment of his arrival in Britain. He was said to have had paranoid delusions in the early months of his confinement, and hysterical amnesia towards the end, although others who dealt with him reported that they saw no such signs. Confidential statements from the British government to other Allied powers had also been contradictory. Churchill told Roosevelt a few days after Hess's capture that he showed no signs of psychiatric disorder, but later in the war informed the Soviet government that Hess was mentally ill, but that this information was being withheld because otherwise – under the Geneva Convention – he would have to be repatriated.

Although the official British line was that Hess was mentally unbalanced, curiously, when he came to stand trial, they agreed he was competent enough to do so. And when his defence counsel requested that he should be examined by a psychiatrist from neutral Switzerland, the tribunal responded with a peremptory: 'This application is denied.'[6] No reason was given. Instead, it was decreed that Hess was to be examined by psychiatrists from all four victorious powers to establish whether he was fit to plead. In the end he was examined by eight doctors – three British, three Soviet, one American and one French. The British representatives were Brigadier Rees, Dr George Riddoch and Churchill's personal physician, Lord Moran. According to Rees, it was not a long examination: together with discussion and decision-making, it took only a matter of hours. The British doctors were in Nuremberg for less than a day.[7]

Although they were unable to agree on whether his amnesia was real or feigned, or even exactly what his mental condition was, they did agree that he was fit to stand trial. There was only one dissenting voice: Lord Moran.[8] This is interesting for several reasons. Why Churchill's doctor – who was not a psychiatrist – was even involved is a puzzle. Had he been sent there with some specific purpose in mind? And why was he the only medical man there who appeared to want Hess to escape trial (which would have released him back into British custody)? The British team reported that:

His mental state is of a mixed type. He is an unstable man, and what is technically called a psychopathic personality. The evidence of his illness in the past four years, as presented by one of us who had him under his care in England [Rees], indicates that he has had a delusion of poisoning, and other similar paranoid ideas . . . Partly as a reaction to the failure of his mission, these abnormalities got worse, and led to suicidal attempts . . . At the moment he is not insane in the strict sense. His loss of memory will not entirely interfere with his comprehension of the proceedings, but it will interfere with his ability to make his defence and to understand details of the past, which arise in evidence.[9]

The report, signed jointly by the American and French psychiatrists, concluded that, although his symptoms were genuine, he was deliberately exaggerating them and that he was 'not insane'. Interestingly, the American, Soviet and French delegates saw none of the signs of paranoia that had been reported of Hess in his early captivity in Britain. In fact, the Soviet report specifically states that: 'In the psychological personality of Hess there are no changes typical of the progressive schizophrenia disease, and therefore the delusions from which he suffered periodically while in England cannot be considered as manifestations of a schizophrenic paranoia . . .'[10]

Only the British team reported both paranoid and hysterical behaviour – and even then their 'paranoid' diagnosis was only based on what Brigadier Rees told them about the prisoner's behaviour in Britain. The failure of the other psychiatrists to spot any signs of paranoid delusions is particularly significant. Even a year after the Nuremberg Trials Rees was still maintaining that Hess was suffering from paranoid schizophrenia.[11]

Not one of the doctors thought Hess was feigning his mental symptoms – although he later stood up in court and said he was! Ten days into the trial, Hess's defence counsel, Dr Günther von Rohrscheidt – against his client's wishes – asked that the case against him be quashed because of his mental state. But Hess insisted on making a statement on his own behalf to the court, stating:

In order to anticipate any possibility of my being declared incapable of pleading, although I am willing to take part in the rest of the proceedings with the rest of them, I would like to give the tribunal the following declaration, although I originally intended not to make this declaration until a later point in the proceedings:

My memory is again in order. The reasons why I simulated loss of memory were tactical. In fact, it is only that my capacity for concentration is slightly reduced. But in consequence of that, my capacity to follow the trial, my capacity to defend myself, to put questions to witnesses or even to answer questions – these, my capacities, are not influenced by that.

I emphasise the fact that I bear the full responsibility for everything that I have done or signed as signatory or co-signatory. My attitude, in principle . . . that the tribunal is not competent, is not affected by the statement I have just made. Hitherto in conversations with my official defence counsel I have maintained my loss of memory. He was, therefore, in good faith when he asserted I lost my memory.[12]

What was Hess up to? If he was pretending to be mad in order to get off on a plea of insanity, why, when given such a golden opportunity, did he declare that he had been play-acting?

Despite this statement, however, within a few days Hess began to claim once more that he had lost his memory. The psychologist assigned to the IMT, Dr G. M. Gilbert, records that:

As the time for Hess's defence approached, there was consternation in the prisoners' dock as they realised that Hess was in fact losing his memory. They had been taking it for granted that he had been malingering in the beginning after his apparently complete recovery. But those for whom Hess was supposed to give supporting testimony, as former Deputy Party Leader, were greatly disconcerted to find that Hess no longer remembered what they were talking about when they reminded him of the questions he was supposed to answer for them.[13]

Gilbert is referring mainly to Baldur von Schirach, the former Hitler Youth leader, for whose defence Hess was supposed to answer two questions on the witness stand. When von Schirach originally discussed this with Hess, the latter told him that he could remember the occasions in question and even the dates on which they occurred. But eight days later von Schirach complained that Hess was now saying he didn't know what von Schirach was talking about, and had no memory even of their earlier conversation.[14]

An extraordinary suggestion

However, perhaps the most telling episode at Nuremberg happened when Hess was examined by the American psychiatrist Dr Donald Ewen Cameron as part of the assessment of his fitness to stand trial. Before his examination of the prisoner, Cameron was called to see US spy chief Allen Welsh Dulles – who was later instrumental in creating the CIA, of which he was to become director. In the words of Gordon Thomas, in his study of the military and intelligence uses of psychiatry and psychology, *Journey into Madness* (1993):

> Dulles first swore Dr Cameron to secrecy, and then told him an astounding story. He had reason to believe that the man Dr Cameron was to examine was not Rudolf Hess but an impostor; that the real Deputy Führer had been secretly executed on Churchill's orders. Dulles had explained that Dr Cameron could prove the point by a simple physical examination of the man's torso. If he was the genuine Hess, there should be scar tissue over his left lung, a legacy from the day the young Hess had been wounded in the First World War. Dr Cameron had agreed to try to examine the prisoner.[15]

He was never to make that examination. The next day, when Hess was brought to him, he was handcuffed to a British Military Police sergeant, who refused point blank to remove the handcuffs so that Cameron could take the prisoner's shirt off – or even unbutton it – to look at his chest.[16] It is reasonable to assume that a British Military Police sergeant would only have refused a request from a senior doctor like Cameron if he had been specifically ordered not to permit him to examine the prisoner under any circumstances.

How did Dulles – a well-informed man if there ever was one – arrive at the notion that the Hess in Nuremberg was a double, and that the real Hess had been killed on Churchill's orders? And why was Cameron refused permission to make the examination that would confirm the prisoner's identity?

As we have seen, Dulles was not the only person who seriously questioned the true identity of the man on trial – and later imprisoned – as Rudolf Hess. In 1973 a former SS officer had told one of us that there was some doubt about whether the prisoner in Berlin's Spandau Prison was the former Deputy Führer. Most famously, the

British army surgeon Dr Hugh Thomas also made the claim, but to a much wider audience, through his books *The Murder of Rudolf Hess* (1979) and *Rudolf Hess: A Tale of Two Murders* (1988). He had personally examined the prisoner during a tour of duty in Berlin in 1973 and noted that he did not bear the chest scars from the First World War.

There were numerous other strange episodes during Hess's imprisonment at Nuremberg which cumulatively seem suspicious. For example, according to Airey Neave (who had served the indictments on the Nuremberg defendants), on one occasion Hess answered an officer who called his name: 'There is no Rudolf Hess here. But if you are looking for Convict Number 125, then I'm your man!'[17]

Seen in the context of a possible double, the whole question of the prisoner's alleged amnesia takes on an entirely different complexion. What better way to avoid potentially damaging revelations than to pretend you have lost your memory, especially if you are supposed to give evidence for the defence of your former colleagues?

Some of the other prisoners seemed to hint heavily that they had their own suspicions about 'Hess'. The former Nazi Foreign Minister Joachim von Ribbentrop, when told that Hess was denying all knowledge of certain events because he had lost his memory, said: 'Hess? You mean *our* Hess? The Hess we have here? He said that?'[18]

Göring, too, appeared to have his suspicions, taking great delight in needling Hess when the prisoners were herded into a room together during recess. He said that Hess had some 'great secret' that he should reveal. Even in the dock, during a break in the proceedings, Göring wasted no time in mischievously needling the Deputy Führer, saying:

'By the way, Hess, when are you going to let us in on your great secret? . . . I make a motion Hess tell us his big secret in the recess. How about it, Hess?'[19]

Does the emphasis on Hess's name suggest that Göring already suspected what the 'big secret' was? (Of all the prisoners who were sentenced to death, only Göring cheated the hangman by taking poison in his cell, before he could make a final statement to the waiting world.)

The trial

Some have suggested that it seems a strange form of justice in which the victors act as hanging judges, and that a fairer trial might have resulted if the judges had been drawn from neutral powers. Yet it seemed that the victors wanted to be seen to use the rule of law, while extracting the utmost revenge on those they had vanquished.

The trial of the major German war criminals began on 20 November 1945 and lasted for just over a year. Hess was charged on all four counts, which were:

- Count One: 'Common plan or conspiracy' to commit the crimes covered in the other three counts. (That is, even if the accused did not participate in the crimes themselves, the fact that they were part of the regime that perpetrated them rendered them culpable.)
- Count Two: Crimes against peace, specifically in waging war in contravention of international treaties and agreements.
- Count Three: War crimes, such as actions against civilians, massacres of prisoners of war, and so on.
- Count Four: Crimes against humanity. This comprised the atrocities carried out against Germany's own citizens, which would not be covered under war crimes as such.

Hess was one of twenty-one defendants, including Göring, von Ribbentrop and Alfred Rosenberg, the Nazi ideologue. Martin Bormann, who had disappeared, was tried *in absentia*.

The indictment against Hess read:

The defendant Hess between 1921 and 1941 was: a member of the Nazi Party, Deputy to the Führer, Reich Minister without Portfolio, member of the Reichstag, member of the Council of Ministers for the Defence of the Reich, member of the Secret Cabinet Council, Successor Designate to the Führer after the defendant Göring, a General in the SS and a General in the SA.

The defendant Hess used the foregoing positions, his personal influence and his intimate connection with the Führer in such a manner that: he promoted the accession to power of the Nazi conspirators and the consolidation of their control over Germany set forth in Count One of the Indictment; he promoted the military, economic and psychological preparations for war set forth in Count One of the Indictment; he participated in the political planning and preparation for Wars of Aggression and Wars in Violation of International Treaties, Agreements and Assurances set forth in Counts One and Two of the Indictment; he participated in the preparation and planning of foreign policy of the Nazi conspirators set forth in Count One of the Indictment; he authorised, directed and participated in the War Crimes set forth in Count Three of the Indictment and the Crimes against Humanity set forth in Count Four of the Indictment, including a wide variety of crimes against persons and property.[20]

When the indictment was read out, and Hess was asked to plead, he simply said, '*Nein*'. The president of the tribunal said that this would be taken as a plea of not guilty, which caused some laughter in court, including from fellow defendant Hermann Göring.[21]

The case against the other Nazis was largely concerned with their ordering and organisation of the death camps, slave labour and the brutalities committed in Eastern Europe. Little of this could be laid at Hess's door, since the worst excesses were carried out after he had flown to Britain. The plans for the Final Solution, for example, were made at the Wannsee Conference in January 1942 – nine months after Hess became a prisoner of the British – but the prosecution argued that, as he had been one of the original members of the Nazi Party and one of the main architects of its rise to power, he should still be regarded as one of the main conspirators under Count One. It also pointed out the extent of his powers as Deputy Führer. The prosecutor, Lieutenant-Colonel Mervyn Griffith-Jones stated: 'My Lord, it will be my submission that it is sufficient to justify and bring home the conviction of this man and his colleagues, to produce simply evidence of their positions in the Nazi State and the control of the State, and also the general evidence of the crimes which were committed by the German people.'[22]

Other points brought up against Hess were his signing of laws depriving Germany's Jewish citizens of their civil rights and the decree for compulsory military service – regarded by the prosecution as evidence of conspiracy to wage war. The prosecution also argued that the Auslandorganisation was a fifth column, and that, as its head, Hess had helped lay the ground for the illegal annexation of Austria and Czechoslovakia.

Throughout the prosecution the emphasis remorselessly lay not only on Hess's culpability, but on his power within the Third Reich up to 1941. The prosecution spent a great deal of time and effort establishing the extent of his responsibility and the fact that nothing could happen in Germany without his knowledge and approval, specifically drawing attention to his signature on all laws passed. This was the basis of charging him with Counts One and Two (conspiracy against peace and organising and preparing an illegal war).

Almost without exception, post-war historians have dismissed Rudolf Hess as an ineffective yes-man, no more than Hitler's poodle, who had become an embarrassment to the leadership. The general image of him is of someone who had no initiative of his own – and certainly no power. This Hess would have found it hard to tie his own shoelaces without a direct order from his beloved Führer. But the whole point of the prosecution at Nuremberg was that he had genuine power and influence, that he was an initiator who should be brought to book for his deeds, and that he was a major force behind the rise of Hitlerism in Germany. So which was the real Rudolf Hess – the sycophantic nonentity or a power to be reckoned with?

When it came to the flight to Scotland, the prosecution argued that far from revealing Hess's peace-making intentions, it was further evidence of a conspiracy to wage war, since it was intended to make a deal with Britain in order to increase Germany's chances of success in its coming conflict with the Soviet Union. Griffith-Jones added: 'My Lord, my submission, therefore, is that the only reason he came to England was not humanitarian at all, but purely, as I say, to allow Germany to fight her battle against Russia on one front only.'[23]

This raises another of the crucial questions about the flight of Rudolf Hess. Historians have generally agreed with Hitler's statement that Hess, having lost his grip on reality, had made a sincere but misguided solo flight to broker peace and that Hitler knew nothing of it until the British had his Deputy in their clutches. But if, as the prosecution alleged, this was merely a calculated move in a much wider game, it is reasonable to assume that Hitler *did* know about the flight, and that only when it had obviously gone disastrously wrong did he think it expedient to deny all knowledge and disown both the plan and its executor.

Dr Günther von Rohrscheidt, who had been appointed by the tribunal, was Hess's original defence counsel but the prisoner dismissed him during the course of the trial. He subsequently asked Dr Alfred Seidl, who was representing Hans Frank, Hitler's lawyer and the former Nazi Governor-General of Poland, to defend him. Seidl had two main lines of defence. The first was an attempt to contradict the idea that the Nazi leaders were involved in a conspiracy to wage war from the very beginning in contravention of international treaties, specifically the Treaty of Versailles. Seidl argued that although it might be technically true that from the start the major aim of the Nazi Party had been to reverse the humiliations inflicted on the German people at Versailles, the treaty itself was unfair, against natural justice and had been accepted by Germany only under duress. Perhaps unsurprisingly, the tribunal ruled this inadmissible.[24]

Seidl's other main line of defence was more ingenious and courageous, or perhaps foolhardy. He had learned through Dr Friedrich Gauss, the chief of the Legal Department of the German Foreign Ministry, that there had been a secret deal between Germany and the USSR that had resulted in Poland being divided between the two nations in September 1939.[25] He argued that the Soviet government was therefore equally guilty of conspiracy to wage war, and that the presence of a Soviet judge on the tribunal rendered the whole trial unjust.

To prove his point, Seidl presented an affidavit sworn by Gauss, (the only two copies of the agreement being in Russian hands). After considerable prevarication by the tribunal, and in the face of Soviet opposition – the Soviet prosecutor, Roman Rudenko, went so far as to call it 'an act of provocation' – the affidavit was admitted, but was totally ignored by the judges.[26]

Hess himself showed very little interest in his own defence. His attitude was one of indifference to – sometimes seeming incomprehension of – what was going on around him. Whereas the other defendants listened intently to the translation of the proceedings, he refused to wear his headphones (although Hess had good English, Russian, French and other languages were spoken in the court) and studiously read a novel while his life hung in the balance. However, through Seidl, he stated that he refused to acknowledge the authority of the court in any area except war crimes, and freely admitted responsibility for all the laws and decrees he had signed or issued in his time as Deputy Führer.[27] Then, at last, all eyes were on him as he was called to the stand to make a speech in his own defence.

Hess delivered a rambling and bizarre speech. Perhaps with more justice than he has been given credit for, he compared the proceedings with the Moscow show trials of the 1930s, pointing out that the defendants there appeared to have been under the influence of drugs or hypnosis. Then he launched into a diatribe in which he argued that virtually everyone involved in the war had been under the same kind of hypnotic influence: the witnesses at the trial, his captors in Britain, the guards at the German concentration camps, and even Hitler. As we will see, his words, although apparently crazily paranoid, appear to have been carefully chosen in order to convey a significant subtext.

Eventually the president of the tribunal cut him short, saying that he had reached the end of his allotted twenty minutes. Hess said he would forgo the rest of the statement he intended to make, and then, suddenly coherent and lucidly passionate, finished with this carefully worded declaration:

> I was permitted to work for many years of my life under the greatest son my people has brought forth in its thousand-year history. Even if I could, I would not want to erase this period of time from my existence. I am happy to know that I have done my duty to my people – my duty as a German, as a National Socialist, as a loyal follower of my Führer. I regret nothing.
>
> If I were to begin again, I would act as I have acted. Even if I knew that in the end I should meet a fiery death on the pyre. No matter what human beings do, some day I shall stand before the judgement of the Eternal. I shall answer to Him, and I know He will judge me innocent.[28]

The verdict

After a month's deliberation, all the judgements were handed down on 1 October 1946. As far as Hess was concerned, because of his position in the Nazi government – particularly because all legislation had to be approved by him – it was held that he had conspired to wage war. The fact that he had signed the decree introducing conscription in 1935 was singled out. The judgement declared:

It is true that between 1933 and 1937 Hess made speeches in which he expressed a desire for peace and advocated international economic co-operation. But nothing which they contained can alter the fact that of all the defendants none knew better than Hess how determined Hitler was to realise his ambitions, how fanatical and violent a man he was, and how little he was to refrain from resort to force.[29]

The judgement declared Hess to be a 'willing and informed participant' in the events of 1938–9 that were the prelude to world war: the annexation of Austria and the invasions of Czechoslovakia and Poland. Of his mission to Britain, the judgement drew attention to the fact that his flight took place just ten days after Hitler had fixed the date for the launch of the offensive against Russia (Operation Barbarossa), explicitly connecting the two events. However, the tribunal found insufficient evidence to convict Hess on war crimes or crimes against humanity, and sentenced him to life imprisonment.

The Soviet judge dissented, believing that there were sufficient grounds for a guilty verdict on all counts, and that Hess should be sentenced to death, declaring: 'The mission undertaken by Hess in flying to England should be considered as the last of these crimes, as it was undertaken in the hope of facilitating the realisation of aggression against the Soviet Union by temporarily restraining England from fighting.'[30] He also argued that although Hess might have been out of action by the time the worst atrocities were committed, he had helped to prepare the ground for them and was therefore guilty of complicity.

While his life hung in the balance, Hess stared around him, not even bothering to don his headphones to hear the verdict. After being led from the dock he said he had not listened and was surprised to discover he was not to face the gallows. In fact, he had escaped the death sentence by a whisker. Although all four powers agreed on his guilt on Counts One and Two, it was a two–two tie on the other Counts – the United States and France voted 'Not Guilty', while Britain and the USSR voted 'Guilty' – and as it had been agreed that a tie would mean acquittal, the 'Not Guilty' verdict won the day.[31] However, when it came to sentencing, even though he had only been convicted on two counts, the Soviet judges still stuck out for 'death', but were outvoted. It was notable that the British judges had found Hess guilty on all four counts, obviously intending him to hang and be done with it.

Now, whether he was Rudolf Hess or someone completely different, the shambling, hollow-eyed man in Nuremberg Prison was shortly to receive another title. For the rest of his life, the man who had been known, tried and sentenced as Rudolf Hess was to be known, day in, day out, simply as Prisoner Number Seven in the great fortress of Spandau in Berlin.

The Old Man of Spandau has spawned numerous books, both during and after his long life. The first, published within weeks of the judgements being given at Nuremberg, was E. N. Dzelepy's *Le Mystère Hess*, in which the author expressed his disappointment that there were no great revelations about Hess's mission during the trials: 'the Nuremberg Trial has not shed any light on the "Hess Mystery". Hess himself has not departed from his great "discretion" which has lasted for five years. He has refused to tell "the whole truth" about his case. His testimony brought nothing new, only a little more mystery.'[32] Dzelepy believed that Hess flew to Scotland on a genuine peace mission, backed by Hitler, to meet with the highest members of the British Establishment who were opposed to Churchill. Yet, like many other Hess researchers since, Dzelepy confessed to feelings of profound frustration because he believed the British authorities were keeping back the truth – in the form of black-and-white archival material – from the public.

Years later, and indeed after many of the Hess archives have been released into the public domain, we can only sympathise with Dzelepy's frustration. It seems that the British authorities have no intention of making certain details of the Hess affair widely known, presumably for reasons connected with national security. Yet after all this time, how can that possibly be the case? How can the details of an abortive mission undertaken sixty years ago even begin to threaten today's Britain in any way?

CHAPTER TWO

Behind the Myth

Everything written about Rudolf Hess since 1941 is coloured by the great mystery of his flight. But we soon came to realise that focusing almost exclusively on that tiny window of history means that many crucial elements of the story are ignored. Most books about Hess concentrate on the years between 1941 and 1987, largely ignoring the fact that the man who arrived in Scotland was already forty-seven years old, bringing half a lifetime of experience and a fully formed character to bear on what was to happen. In order to begin to understand the flight, we had to ask certain questions about his background. Although the mission was undoubtedly the culmination of his life so far, what had brought him to that point? What drove the man who became an object of derision, disowned by the Nazi regime and yet seen as its face by the victorious powers? Who was Rudolf Hess?

As we have seen, there is a major discrepancy between the historians' view of Hess and that of the prosecutors and judges at Nuremberg. He was tried and found guilty because of his authority and his role in organising and bringing to power the most single-minded and deadly politico-military machine of the twentieth century. Yet as far as most post-war historians are concerned, Hess was an ineffective yes-man to Hitler, whom he literally idolised. The standard image is that of a rather dim-witted, hysterical and deluded character, with no real power except to embarrass, as typified by this damning entry from Robert S. Wistrich's book, *Who's Who in Nazi Germany* (1982):

From 1925 to 1932 Hess had no official rank in the Nazi Party but acted as Hitler's private secretary, his confidant and blindly loyal follower. Introverted, shy, deeply insecure and dependent on an idealized father-figure, Hess made up for his lack of intelligence, oratorical ability or capacity for political intrigue by a dogged subservience and devotion to Hitler which was as naïve as it was sincere.[1]

This, the party line, is rarely challenged: when it is, a very different Hess emerges. When we examined Hess's pre-war career, and the testimony of those who knew or met him, we concluded that nearly every one of Wistrich's statements concerning Hess was based on a misreading of the facts.

As we will see, Hess was considerably more than Hitler's private secretary during the Nazis' climb to power – and even more than his confidant, the man who shared his most soul-searching moments. And although undoubtedly loyal and utterly devoted to Hitler, he was fully aware of the Führer's weaknesses. Indeed, far from being Hitler's poodle, cowed into submission, Hess was so sure of himself that from time to time he took the radical – and, for most people, utterly terrifying – step of arguing with him. In fact, the Deputy's apparently slavish and unquestioning devotion was in many respects an act, for public consumption only, deliberately assumed in order to set an example – at first for the relatively small band of Hitler's followers, but later for the entire German people. Rather than a brow-beaten lackey, the real Rudolf Hess was the power behind the throne, the shrewd, efficient and highly effective image-maker, watching from the shadows.

It is often said that while Hess was the more educated of the two, the Führer was the more intelligent. However, this is an oversimplification: Hitler had the sharper native wit, the ability to think on his feet – and, of course, a charisma and mastery of dramatic timing that made him only too memorable as a leader – but Hess was a more profound thinker, a cautious planner, a considered adviser. Hitler was action; Hess was strategy. Together they made a formidable team – but not as master and slave: at least at the beginning they were more or less equals.

The quiet Nazi

Many who met Hess in the pre-war days – including those who were hardly admirers of Nazism – agreed that he could be very impressive, in his quiet, watchful way. In 1934 Group Captain Frederick W. Winterbotham, head of the Air Department of MI6, on a fact-finding mission to assess the build up of the Luftwaffe, had the dubious honour of meeting many of the leading Nazis, including Hitler and Hess. Before his first meeting with the Deputy Führer, Winterbotham had been briefed by his contact in Berlin, Baron William de Ropp, who had made a special study of the character of the Nazi leaders:

> Bill [de Ropp] had warned me that he was a well-educated and highly intelligent man who, as deputy to Hitler, always backed him up in a rather quiet, self-effacing way. Hess was, when required to be, a force-ful speaker, but I too was to gain the impression that he was more concerned with the well-being of his country than the conquest of others.[2]

Over the course of several months, Winterbotham met Hess several times, even going with him to the theatre to see a production of Shakespeare's *Coriolanus*, which revealed a telling side to the Deputy's character. The MI6 man was amused to note that the play seemed to have been chosen specifically to allow for repeated oppor-tunities to give the Nazi salute, masquerading as the Roman greeting. The audience loved it, going wild every time a 'Hail Caesar!' became a '*Heil Hitler!*' but Hess became increasingly uncomfortable with the rising hysteria. Finally, he leaned over and whispered to his English guest, 'It's not really necessary, you know.'[3] It seems quite incon-ceivable that the Deputy Führer of all people was embarrassed by this – after all, it was part of his own job to whip the masses into a frenzy. But it was almost as if he were seeing the production through the eyes of his guest, with all the distaste of a civilised man. Over the course of several meetings, Winterbotham found that the initially reserved – and never less than totally punctilious and correct – Deputy gradually thawed out, allowing himself little jokes. His final assessment of Hess's character was: 'I . . . found a certain depth of character and level of intelligence which was often missing in other

Nazi leaders. There was a latent sensitivity in place of the ruthless efficiency of the Görings and the Himmlers. His poise increased but always seemed tinged with diffidence.'[4]

Winterbotham's account makes it clear that Rudolf Hess was no mere cipher. Naturally reserved and quiet, he was happier to work from the wings than to seek centre stage – but if so, what exactly was his role? Was he waiting to be thrust into the limelight, however unwillingly, to stammer out his part when the time came? Already he was a power to be reckoned with, as Hitler's prompter, scriptwriter, stage-manager, producer, director – and muse. While he may not have harboured an ambition for personal stardom, he had a clearly defined set of ambitions for his beloved Germany. Tellingly, on the eve of Nazi success in finally taking power, he wrote scathingly to his parents about 'career-makers' – those who worked for personal gain rather than from a sense of patriotism or duty:

> The career-maker is often not far removed from a career-racketeer. He more resembles a phoney than an able man . . . The man rising on the strength of his own ability comes up against the career-makers. He does his duty without thinking about his career . . . rising upwards, assured and erect – the career-maker tries to get hold of a free seat in the cable car.'[5]

Hess was no hypocrite. Other Nazi leaders may have used and abused their positions in order to feather their own nests, living lives of unbridled luxury and debauchery – Hermann Göring's drug-fuelled excesses were already notorious – but Hess continued to live modestly, his conscience not even permitting him to fiddle trivial expenses. Unlike all the other Nazi officials, he refused to use petrol from the government petrol station for his private car (a Mercedes sports model) because it was against the rules.[6] Far from decorating his walls with valuable paintings at the party's expense, not so much as a government paperclip found its way on to his desk at home. Of course, an anal-retentive passion for petty rules does not make a man either honourable or attractive, but Hess's opinions could be surprising. Although he was usually in agreement with the inflexible sexism of the Nazi regime, there was one subject on which he was willing to oppose the established morality – even, if necessary, taking on Hitler himself. Hess had no qualms about standing up to be counted as the champion of single mothers, attacking those who ostracised them, and actively campaigning to remove the stigma of illegitimacy. He even offered to act as godfather for illegitimate children whose fathers had been lost in the war[7] – hardly the act of a man incapable of thinking for himself or of someone too easily intimidated ever to challenge the status quo.

Hess the man

It may be difficult to assess the role of the Deputy Führer with any objectivity, but it is even harder to discern Rudolf Hess the man. Those who met him regularly often remarked that he seemed only a little more relaxed after months of encounters than at the first meeting – although, as we have seen, Winterbotham did mention a slight thawing towards the end of their acquaintance. And, as the MI6 man and others noted with surprise, Hess was not a typical Nazi leader. Whereas his peers tended to be little more than thugs, he tried hard to instil a sense of honour into those who worked for the cause, always seeking to present his own conduct as the perfect example for them to follow. Unlike many of those who bludgeoned their way into the bully boys' club of the Third Reich, he was an intelligent, cultivated man, with strong artistic and musical instincts – he wrote romantic poetry and was particularly fond of Beethoven. (He would never agree with Hitler about the superiority of Wagner.)

Hess was by nature refined and – like all true *éminences grises* – essentially unobtrusive, although with his height and dark, intense looks he would rarely go unnoticed in a crowd. In his youth he was known as 'handsome Rudi', although, being always shy and reticent with girls, he never capitalised on his good looks. As time passed and life became hard and earnest, full of life-or-death decisions and fanatical obsessions, his face took on a strangely haunted look. Gradually he developed from the glamorous flying ace with the chiselled jaw into a somewhat wild-eyed middle-aged man, whose most memorable features were his enormous bushy eyebrows, adding to an image of driven intensity. By the time he parachuted into Scotland his face had already set into a permanent look of profound anxiety – as well it might, given the circumstances.

Sometimes the unattractive intensity prevents the real Hess shining through. He does seem to have had a sense of humour, and was known to laugh and behave spontaneously, but mostly he is seen as a rather dour, proper man who exercised extreme control over his emotions. His private secretaries, who knew him well, claimed they never saw him lose control no matter what the provocation. He was always – apparently – cool and collected, although they knew only too well what this almost superhuman control cost him in terms of health. Hess's nervous system was notoriously oversensitive, causing a host of psychosomatic ailments that mimicked, among other manifestations, attacks of gall-bladder disease and stomach ulcers. However, there was one thing over which he seemed to have no control: he was an incorrigible – and profoundly irritating – whistler, driving his staff to distraction with the endless ear-numbing racket of which he himself was rarely aware.

On the whole his colleagues in the Nazi hierarchy found him not to their taste, treating him with caution at first – after all, he was Hitler's intimate friend – then with increasing derision. The feeling was mutual. Even in the early days, they were rarely encouraged to put their relationship on a friendlier basis: in any case, Hess ensured that his home life was kept strictly apart from his party duties. Although he and Ilse did entertain, their preferred guests tended to be artists, musicians and philosophers rather than jackbooted colleagues from the office with their coarse language and empty minds.

Not all Nazi leaders were blind to Hess's good points. Goebbels wrote in his diary after their first meeting in 1926: 'Hess: the most decent person, quiet, friendly, reserved,'[8] while another of his colleagues, Kurt Ludecke, commented in 1933: 'To me, he was masculinity personified,' adding that he was 'very cool, very polite – too polite'.[9] This endorsement of Hess's masculinity seems rather oddly abrupt and uncalled for, perhaps being intended to deflect the persistent rumours that the Deputy Führer was homosexual. In reality there were many gays in the Nazi hierarchy, even though officially it was *verboten*: indeed, homosexuals were among the first victims of the concentration camps. But there is no evidence that Hess was gay, despite the rather sad comment by Ilse Hess that their marriage made her feel like a 'convent pupil'.[10] Clearly Hess was hardly a great lover: although he was genuinely drawn to Ilse's personality and intellect, the thought of marrying her never seemed to have crossed his mind until he was virtually ordered to do so by

Hitler. His detractors also gleefully pointed out the ten-year gap between the dates of their marriage and the birth of their only child in 1937, and even then there were rumours that Hess was not the father (although he clearly adored little Wolf). There is no evidence that he was anything but a virgin on his wedding night, and none that he had any kind of relationship outside of his marriage. He seemed to reserve his passion for Germany and his dedication for Hitler. Although every German was supposed to show blind obedience to the Führer, Hess's devotion was considered so extreme as to earn him the nickname of 'the Fraulein' – but this seems less a comment on his sexuality than on his supportive role in Hitler's life. Frederick Winterbotham commented on this:

> Hess, unlike his master, was ever content to be the shadow. He avoided the limelight and I think few people knew him intimately. His brown shirt also lacked any form of decoration but, like the rest of his clothes, was extremely well cut. His flared breeches could not have been improved upon by Savile Row; he was tall and slim, with a good leg for a boot; indeed, his boots were the envy of the Party. Not only were they real leather but they fitted him well, and the shine on the black leather would have done justice to a cavalry batman. I could not make up my mind at first whether he was shy of foreigners, not quite sure of himself, or just plain eccentric. He was certainly fastidious.[11]

The comment about Savile Row would have been music to Hess's ears, because he was a devoted Anglophile. Trying very hard to model himself on the 'stiff upper lip' Briton, he kept his emotions in check, and his craving to look the part extended to wearing tweed jackets at weekends. Perhaps his Anglophilia stemmed at least in part from the peculiar quirk of fate that had brought Rudolf Hess into the world in the British protectorate of nineteenth-century Egypt.

The Egyptian

Born to Fritz and Klara Hess in Alexandria on 26 April 1894, the young Rudolf grew up in a very Victorian atmosphere. His mother took the intense, intelligent little child under her wing, showing him the glittering constellations in the Egyptian night sky, inspiring him with a fascination for the mystical and spiritual, and giving him a lifelong love of astronomy and astrology, in addition to a great belief in homoeopathic remedies. His father, however, was not nearly so approachable. Fritz Hess, a successful importer–exporter, was very much in the mould of the typical Victorian paterfamilias: Rudolf and his siblings tiptoed around – both literally and figuratively – in constant terror of disturbing him. Mealtimes were silent. The children only dared play when he had gone to work. His attitude to his wife also left a lot to be desired: he slept through the birth of one of his brood, not even rousing himself when the tiny – and rather brave – Rudolf tried to wake him with the momentous news of a new addition to the family, his brother Alfred.

The Hess family lived in a large, pleasant villa on the Mediterranean coast, spending the summer holidays at their country house in the mountains of Bavaria. Apart from the families of expatriate Germans, Alexandria also had a thriving British community, although Fritz Hess rarely mixed with them or permitted his family to do so. They were not great socialisers, and any parties they gave tended to be for the benefit of stolid German worthies like themselves, with few, if any, foreign guests.

Rudolf's father wanted him to go into the family business, but the young Hess's interests lay in other directions – he always showed a marked aptitude for the sciences, particularly physics, chemistry and mathematics. There are indications of some tension between father and son over this, but perhaps not enough to affect Hess's fundamental psychological development. He was always the dutiful son. However, there was something that almost certainly *did* affect him to a large extent, perhaps inspiring his fanatical devotion to German nationalism, something that may have seemed trivial enough at the time: a school nickname.

After attending the German Protestant School in Alexandria, his education shifted to Germany, where he became a boarder between the ages of fourteen and seventeen. It was there that he was shocked to the core to be taunted with the nickname 'the Egyptian' because of his background and rather swarthy features. He, who had always thought of himself as quintessentially German, was being treated as a foreigner in his own land! One can imagine that this was not only traumatic, but profoundly catalytic for the young Hess, to whom establishing his credentials as a German nationalist became an obsession. After this rude awakening, he attended the Ecole Supérieur de Commerce in Neuchâtel, Switzerland, before going on to an apprenticeship in a Hamburg trading company. He was eagerly looking forward to becoming a student at Oxford – the culmination of both his academic ambitions and his burgeoning Anglophilia – when the First World War intervened. (As fate would have it, he was only ever to see England as a prisoner, although perhaps there was a certain perverse cause for pride in the fact that he was to be locked up in that great British institution, the Tower of London.)

Like all good Germans, Hess obeyed the call to arms, volunteering for the Bavarian infantry. He fought amid the horrors of Ypres, knowing terrible hunger, deprivation and the trauma of witnessing human carnage from close quarters, once being trapped in a trench for a day with half a dead Frenchman. Like all those who fought in the Great War, he returned home radically changed. It was a baptism of fire from which a phoenix Hess was to rise, cleansed of childish hopes and fears, with iron in his soul. He was also to emerge a hero, having been awarded the Iron Cross, Second Class, for bravery under fire, and rising to the rank of *Vizefeldwebel* (vice-sergeant). He was described by a comrade-in-arms – rather chillingly, perhaps – as a brave soldier, 'exemplary in his cold-bloodedness and self-sacrifice'.[12]

In June 1916, at Verdun, he was hospitalised because of a wound in the left arm and hand caused by shrapnel, although his injuries were not serious and he recovered rapidly, being promoted to lieutenant. Posted to fight in Romania, it was there that he sustained a much more serious injury, one that was to assume enormous significance in the controversy over the identity of the prisoner in Spandau. In June 1917 he was shot through the chest, the bullet travelling through his left lung and exiting through his back. He spent four months in hospital and another month convalescing at home on leave, finally being declared medically unfit to return to the infantry. As it happened, by then it suited him perfectly, for he had a new ambition, having already set his sights on joining the fledgling Flying Corps. To his great joy he was accepted, but before he took up his new duties he was given one last assignment as an infantryman – to provide an escort for a unit to the List Regiment at the Western Front. Here he had a fateful encounter. According to the anti-Nazi commentator Konrad Heiden, writing shortly after Hess's flight to Britain:

> On a certain occasion he had to report to the regimental commander . . . Lieutenant-Colonel von Tubeuf. At Tubeuf's side stood his dispatch-runner, a corporal. Hess and the corporal looked into each other's eyes, two survivors of the holocaust. How could they have had any inkling of the improbable future? Later they recalled the scene. Both were convinced that destiny had singled them out for some special purpose, since it had led them unharmed through the mass slaughter that overwhelmed most of the List Regiment. The name of the corporal was Adolf Hitler.[13]

By the time Hess had completed his training as a pilot in October 1918, the war was almost over. He flew some missions in Fokker biplanes over Belgium, but never saw any serious aerial action. It was all good experience for a novice airman. Now at least he knew what he really wanted to do: all his instincts cried out that he was destined for aviation glory, and it was not long before those instincts proved to be correct.

The legacy of defeat

Any euphoria Hess might have felt over finally finding his niche as an aviator was obliterated by the stark fact of his beloved Germany's defeat in the First World War. He returned home from the front to a demoralised, impoverished and bleak land peopled with broken soldiers and starving families. Germany had been shattered, politically, economically and socially. The victorious powers – Britain, the USA, France and Belgium – did their worst to wreak vengeance for the protracted horrors of the Great War, making defeat as punitive, humiliating and painful as possible. They sought to disarm Germany, to castrate its military might once and for all, and also to destroy its economy.

Because of a blockade by the victors – which continued for some months after the Armistice – the German nation was literally starving to death. The infant mortality rate was appallingly high: as much as 60 per cent in some areas.[14] And while the lowest echelons of society struggled to stay alive, the highest in the land found themselves facing an anxious future. Kaiser Wilhelm II had been forced to abdicate, going into exile in Holland, in the château of Count Godard Bentinck; his heir had renounced his rights to the German throne, and, by doing so, signed the death warrant for the monarchy in Germany. The Social Democrats had been chosen – not elected – by the Allies to govern the post-war wasteland that had once been proud, affluent Germany. It was a very different world from the overconfident superpower of just four years before, and everyone who lived through that time felt it keenly, especially with the edge of desperation that hunger, humiliation and despair brought. To cap it all, the Treaty of Versailles of June 1919 placed the blame for the entire nightmare conflict squarely at the door of the Germans and their allies.

The war not only changed Germany beyond recognition: it brought sweeping changes to the whole of Europe. New or revived states – such as Poland, Czechoslovakia and Yugoslavia – were created out of splinters of the former Austro-Hungarian, Russian and Ottoman empires. Slices of German and Austrian territory – with predominantly German-speaking populations – were carved off and given to other countries. Hundreds of thousands of German citizens awoke to find themselves with another nationality, and no say in the matter. The principle followed by the victors in creating the new states was that of a people's right to self-determination – except in the case of Germany, where this rule did not apply. Austria's request for a plebiscite to determine whether it should unite with Germany was specifically denied.[15]

The treaty also took drastic steps to prevent any future military build up in Germany by reducing the armed forces and forbidding the number of personnel in the national standing army (the Reichswehr) and navy to rise above 100,000 and 15,000, respectively. This effectively prevented Germany not only from waging an aggressive war, but from defending itself. It is easy to understand how the harsh revenge exacted by the Treaty of Versailles was to fester in the souls of millions of Germans for many years to come. Aside from preventing Germany from defending itself, the treaty had specified that it should pay exorbitant reparations to the victorious countries. In 1921 the amount was finally fixed at the phenomenal, almost mythical, sum of 132 billion gold marks. This was so enormous that, if the Second World War had not intervened, it would not have been paid off before the 1970s.

Politically, too, the country was in chaos. The new Weimar government (named after the town where its constitution was drawn up) was mistrusted by Germans and blamed for selling Germany out to the Allies. Germany was still a federation of largely autonomous states, which bitterly resented this new centralised government. But it hardly mattered, for that government had virtually ceased to function. The army had been largely disbanded, and the bulk of the men sent home – where there was no work, food or hope.

In this tense and explosive atmosphere of profound resentment and fear, it was inevitable that there would be a surge of activity, a new way forward, at least a hope of light at the end of the tunnel. The energy of oppressed pride and humiliation had to find an outlet. Encouraged by the success of the Russian Revolution in 1917, German Communists – known as the Spartakus League – began to agitate for revolution. (It should be remembered that when Karl Marx wrote *Das Kapital*, calling for a workers' revolution, he had Germany, not Russia, in mind.) It was not a popular movement in official quarters: the authorities responded by setting up 'unofficial' volunteer groups of ex-servicemen, called Freikorps, to fight the communist menace. Less than two months after the Armistice, there were bloody riots on the streets of Berlin and other cities throughout Germany. Across the whole tortured land there were marches, riots and political assassinations. In Bavaria the monarchy was overthrown and in February 1919 the capital, Munich, was seized by pro-Russian Communists, who proclaimed it a Soviet republic. (To add to the confusion, these Communists were also opposed by the Spartakus League.) It was into this volatile situation that the twenty-four-year-old Rudolf Hess was demobilised, arriving in Munich a few days before the Communist takeover.

Less sensitive souls than Hess by far had been severely and lastingly traumatised by the war, but his personal torment was intensified by the realisation that he and his compatriots had endured such suffering for nothing. He wrote to a cousin in 1927:

I have fought for the honour of our flag where a man of my age had of course to fight, where conditions were at their worst, in dirt and mud, in the hell of Verdun, Artois and elsewhere. I have witnessed the horror of death in all its forms, been battered for days under heavy bombardment, slept in a dugout in which lay half a

Frenchman. I have hungered and suffered, as indeed have all front-line soldiers. And is all this to be in vain, the suffering of the good people at home all for nothing? . . . No, if all this was in vain I would still today regret that I did not put a bullet through my brain on the day the monstrous armistice conditions and their acceptance were published. I did not do it at the time solely in the hope that in one way or another I might still be able to do something to reverse fate.[16]

Hess also viewed with the cold horror of a true-blue nationalist the internal divisions in the new Germany, in particular what he perceived as the Communist threat. He had gone into hell to fight his country's enemies and returned only to find an even more monstrous enemy – this time considerably closer to home. What made it worse was that these were not foreign foes, but fellow Germans, traitors seeking to fly the Red Flag over their country in defeat. His whole soul was revolted; he had to fight them.

The British having expropriated the family business in Alexandria, Fritz Hess was slowly building it up again with characteristic determination. Hess took a job as a salesman for a cheap furniture store to help finance his studies at Munich University, although he also had a small bursary, having been selected to benefit from a Bavarian government scheme for ex-servicemen. Abandoning his favourite scientific subjects, he chose to study politics and economics, feeling they would be more useful in the prevailing climate of the day.

Students living under any less-than-perfect political regime can always be relied upon to make their anger and frustration felt, and even the quiet and studious Rudolf Hess was no exception. He soon threw himself with fanatical enthusiasm into the resistance movement against the newly imposed Communist regime in Munich. It was here that he was to meet one of the two major influences on his life, and, as we shall see, a key player in the drama of the flight: Professor General Karl Haushofer.

The great inspiration

Karl Haushofer was to become Hess's teacher, mentor, friend, father-figure and great inspiration, the powerful not-so-grey eminence behind the future Deputy Führer. Destined to die by his own hand in the aftermath of the Second World War, Professor Haushofer was born in Bavaria in 1869, rising to become a distinguished figure in two areas that do not always sit comfortably with each other – the army and the world of academia. He became the German Military Attaché to Tokyo between 1908 and 1911, serving three years later at the front as a major general. After the war he settled down to life as Professor of Geography at Munich University, keeping up his many contacts abroad. (His pre-war quest had taken him to exotic and mystical locations such as the Himalayas and the Far East, where he developed a lifelong fascination with the occult and the more arcane forms of spirituality. Becoming a highly respected expert in the mystical arts, he was the only European member of a Japanese secret society, the esoteric Order of the Green Dragon.) Haushofer's urbane sophistication and wide knowledge of both the material and invisible worlds gave him an irresistible mystique compared to the more stolid Bavarian lecturers on the campus. Of all his hero-worshipping students, however, none was more avidly devoted than Rudolf Hess, who was particularly attracted to the professor's *idée fixe* – the concept of 'geopolitics', the relationship between a nation, its politics, economics, natural resources and position on the map. In this, Haushofer had been heavily influenced by the pioneering British geographer Sir Halford Mackinder, MP (1861–1947), founder of Reading University and the first person to climb Mount Kenya. Haushofer had studied the cultures and politics of other nations, becoming an expert in international relations, on which he was later to be a key adviser to the Nazi Party. One reason why he found such favour with them was his concept of *Lebensraum* ('living space') – the idea that if Germany was to become an important global power, it had to expand eastwards.

Another geopolitical idea advocated – but not invented – by Haushofer which was equally central to Nazi foreign policy was that of *Alldeutscher*, or Pan-Germanism. This is the apparently reasonable belief that all German-speaking peoples should be part of one nation – Greater Germany. Unfortunately, partly due to the Allies' redrawing of the map of Europe after the First World War, German-speakers were now scattered, boxed in here and there by inconvenient wedges of other countries. In order to create Greater Germany, the Nazis would have to acquire and overrun the surrounding areas.

The professor also supported the idea of a United States of Europe – indeed, he thought it was essential if the individual nations were to survive in the new global economy. He saw that world finance had been fundamentally altered by the rise of the USA as the great economic power in the West and that of Japan in the East. Like Hess – and Hitler – Haushofer was a great admirer of Britain and its empire, which he believed played a vital role in world geopolitics. Indeed, he saw the British Empire as playing a parallel role in the world to Germany's dominance of Europe.

However, Haushofer parted company with the Nazis over one major issue: he was no racist. Although his geopolitics was to shape the Third Reich's ideology and help inspire the greatest military mobilisation the world has ever known, in the matter of race he refused to lead them. Perhaps the reason for his dangerous defiance was the fact that his wife Martha – for whom Hess developed great respect and liking – was half-Jewish.

Although Hess met Haushofer at Munich University, he had already moved in similar circles for some time. He had trained for the Flying Corps with a former member of Haushofer's military staff, Max Hofweber, who later introduced the idealistic young man to his superior. It was also Hofweber who set Hess up with the job as furniture salesman – in a company owned by another former member of Haushofer's staff. It was inevitable that Hess would be drawn into Haushofer's inner circle. Soon the professor became a second father, and the Haushofer family's open affection and mutual respect were revelations to him. Here mealtimes – far from being conducted in the repressive silence of Fritz Hess's displeasure – usually erupted into loud and lively discussions, with everyone having their say on a multitude of topics. Hess was particularly struck by the way in which the professor listened to his wife's views with the same courtesy and interest he reserved for any other speaker – Klara Hess had been bullied just as much as her children, emphatically relegated to a non-speaking role. This was an ambience in which the young Hess, suddenly free from the shackles of his own upbringing, could blossom and grow.

Hess also struck up a close friendship with one of Haushofer's sons, Albrecht, who was only sixteen when they first met, but intellectually advanced and very accomplished. Hess particularly admired Albrecht's English accent, trying to emulate it on their long walks together. It makes a quaint picture: two earnest young Germans in their quasi-Savile Row tweeds, marching along side by side, correcting each other's English. But there was far more to Albrecht Haushofer than an enviable accent. Later, having travelled widely, building up contacts for his father around the world, he struck up a friendship that was to have particularly far-reaching consequences – with a young British nobleman, the then Marquess of Clydesdale. This scion of Scotland's premier dynasty was later to become the Duke of Hamilton, perhaps the single most significant person in the confused – and suspicious – flurry of activity surrounding the Hess flight. After all, it was Hamilton whom Hess claimed he had flown into enemy territory specifically to meet.

Significantly, while on a visit to the Hamiltons' family home, Dungavel House, in 1938, Albrecht Haushofer drew the extent of the territory he passionately believed should become part of Greater Germany on an atlas.[17] Clearly, Albrecht held similar views to those of his father, the pioneer of geopolitics. The attitude of his hosts at Dungavel House towards the concept that underpinned the whole of Nazi Germany's foreign policy is more difficult to ascertain. (Although it is known that Hamilton supported the German claim to South Tyrol, one of the components of a Greater Germany.[18]) Three years later Karl and Albrecht Haushofer were to play key roles in arranging Hess's flight to meet the Duke of Hamilton. Hess even took their visiting cards with him.

The occult imperative

The full extent of the Haushofers' influence on Rudolf Hess and his life was astounding. It percolated through on every level, from the political (and geopolitical) to the spiritual and mystical, effectively ensuring that he was totally their man – heart, mind and soul. It was even a former member of Karl Haushofer's staff, then Hess's boss at the furniture company, who took him to the first of his many meetings of an organisation called the Thulegesellschaft (the Thule Society). This seminal group was officially registered as a 'study group for German antiquity' – certainly one way of describing it. To some extent, it *was* concerned with discussion of German mythology, folklore and literature, but this was largely a cover for political fomentation and intrigue. The German biographer of Hess and

Hitler, Wulf Schwarzwäller, describes the Thule Society as 'a secret organisation of conspiring right-wing radicals with rigorous anti-Marxist, anti-liberal, anti-democratic and anti-Semitic opinions'.[19] This is a formidable list of what it was against: what it was *for*, of course, was the creation of a Greater Germany.

At the time when Rudolf Hess first encountered the Thule Society, it had another less obvious but at least equally potent agenda. Founded in 1918 by, among others, a well-known occultist, the self-styled Baron Rudolf von Sebottendorff, the Thule Society had a markedly mystical character, which may well have been highly influential in determining both Hitler's and Hess's sense of personal destiny, the concept of their roles as chosen ones in shaping Germany's future glory. The fake aristocrat von Sebottendorff (real name Adam Glauer, 1875–1945) was an established member of another occult society, the Germanenorden (founded in 1912), which advocated two ideas that were to become central to the Nazis.[20] The first is the concept of the 'mystical purity' of German blood, and the other is the belief in a global conspiracy for world domination by the Freemasons and Jews. It was von Sebottendorff who inculcated both concepts into the Thule Society – which began as the Munich lodge of the Germanenorden – where they were seized upon excitedly by the future lords of the Third Reich.

Although the Thule Society included known occultists such as von Sebottendorff, there is no evidence that it was an active occult organisation itself – it certainly never carried out recognisably magical rituals *en masse*. The society was more concerned with its own mystical interpretation of the legends and folklore of the German people, and the search for particularly potent symbols that they could adopt. Soon the original myths had become virtually unrecognisable under the Thulists' heavy hand. By overenthusiastically imposing their quasi-mystical interpretation of the ancient Teutonic legends, they inadvertently created a pagan past that had never really existed. Their research did, however, give the fledgling Nazi Party a hugely important symbol that was either to inspire or strike terror into the hearts of millions – the swastika.

Another leading light of the Thule Society was the poet Dietrich Eckart, a vociferous anti-Semite who was to wield great influence over Hess, Hitler and the Nazi movement as a whole. Eckart, like von Sebottendorff, believed that Germany's future lay in the emergence of a new leader who, like a timely Teutonic messiah, would galvanise the people into making their dream of greatness a reality. The new leader, he argued, would not arise from the shattered ranks of the old order, nor would he come from the defeated officer class. The German messiah, the *Führer*, would rise from the people themselves. He would be an ordinary man made superhuman by the fact of his destiny.

Whether Professor Haushofer was a member of the Thule Society is open to question. Certainly, he had many friends who were, and he shared many – though not all – of their ideals. It is possible that, with a half-Jewish wife, he thought it advisable to distance himself from that vociferously anti-Semitic organisation. However, Hess's involvement in the Thule Society brings up the vexed question of the Nazis and the occult. It is now widely known that some of the Nazi leaders' belief in the paranormal powers of holy talismans and sacred objects, together with other mystical ideas, had a powerful influence on Nazism as a whole. What is debatable is whether any of the Nazi leaders were actively involved in the occult, as initiates in specific secret societies or cults, or whether they merely paid lip service to more generalised mystical ideas that served their purpose – such as the concept of a pure Aryan bloodline, for example. It is true that many of the top Nazis were interested in subjects and practices that were deemed cranky in their day. Hitler, Hess and Himmler were vegetarians, refusing meat – with an irony that is not lost on today's pro-meat lobby – on moral grounds. They and many of their colleagues were also advocates of alternative medicine, particularly homoeopathy. Hess, particularly, was a great believer in homoeopathic remedies, carrying several with him at all times, and he, Himmler and, for a while at least, Hitler were all firm believers in astrology. The late Airey Neave, who was part of the British team at the Nuremberg Trials, told the British comic, parapsychologist and ballistics expert Michael Bentine that the Allied governments were well aware of the Nazis' interest in the occult, but had deliberately suppressed the details in case they were used as the basis for a plea of insanity.[21]

On the available evidence, however, it seems that the Nazi leadership did not constitute an order of black magicians, although individuals may well have practised some form of the dark arts. It is more accurate to say that certain ideas originating in nineteenth-century occult circles had a profound influence on Hitler, Hess and other Nazi leaders, especially Heinrich Himmler. Combined with their own – often highly idiosyncratic – interpretations of the myths, legends and folklore of the Nordic and German peoples, these occult concepts were then fed back into the ideology of the Nazi movement as a whole. Two concepts in particular were to fire Nazi imaginations: the idea of a lost homeland of the Teutonic people in the form of the fabled island Ultima Thule – linked to Atlantis – and the belief in 'root races', the idea that certain races were predestined to rule the earth. This Age, according to that theory, belongs to the blond, blue-eyed Aryans.

It is uncertain how far Hitler himself bothered to study the esoteric ideas that lay behind the Thule Society. His own ideas of German mythology were culled from the wild and stirring music of Richard Wagner, with which he was obsessed. Indeed, it was the musician's son-in-law who was to provide another curious link with the idea of the Master Race. This was the British-born naturalised German Houston Stewart Chamberlain (1855–1927), whose life's work, *The Foundations of the Nineteenth Century*, extolled the superiority of the Aryan race as exemplified to perfection in the German people. He wrote: 'Physically and spiritually, the Aryans stand out among all men; hence they are by right the lords of the world.'[22] Chamberlain sent a copy of his book to Kaiser Wilhelm II, who became an enthusiastic disciple, even awarding him an Iron Cross – and it soon became required reading for officers of the elite Guards Corps. His Teutonic credentials established, Chamberlain settled in Bayreuth, marrying Eva Wagner, the composer's daughter. The myth of Aryan supremacy was now firmly wedded to the music of Wagner. After Germany's catastrophic defeat in the First World War, Chamberlain became a prime mover in the search for the longed-for Aryan messiah who would destroy democracy and establish Germany in its rightful place as master of the world. Although Chamberlain's ideas were, unsurprisingly, very popular in Germany, particularly among the officer class and aristocracy, they reached Hitler only through an intermediary, the Nazi ideologue Alfred Rosenberg, to whom they became the gospel truth.

Born of German parents in Estonia, then under Russian control, Rosenberg attended Moscow University, where in 1917, as a twenty-four-year-old student, he was given a copy of the now-notorious *Protocols of the Elders of Zion*, a document purporting to originate from a meeting of Jews in Basle, Switzerland, in 1897 that inaugurated the Zionist Movement. It was, as Rosenberg, the Nazis and many others, including the London *Times*, firmly believed, a blueprint for world domination by international Jewry, but it has since been unmasked as a forgery by the Tsar's secret police, whose aim was to stir up anti-Semitic hatred.

Rosenberg fled the Russian Revolution and settled in Munich, where – by then a disciple of Houston Stewart Chamberlain – he became a keen member of the Thule Society. In 1930 he published a book that is second only to Hitler's *Mein Kampf* as the 'bible' of Nazism, *Mythus der XX Jahrhunderts* (*The Myth of the Twentieth Century*), in which he identified the legendary land of Atlantis with Ultima Thule, placing it in the far north. It also announced the supremacy of the Aryan race. From the first, Hitler was entranced by Rosenberg's ideas: in October 1923 he took him on a pilgrimage to Bayreuth to meet their hero Chamberlain – whose funeral in 1927 would also be attended by Adolf Hitler, the only public figure there.

There is a frequent misapprehension that, in the 1920s and 1930s, the Germans in general and the Nazis in particular held the monopoly on anti-Semitism. Unfortunately, life was not that simple. Anti-Semitism was rife throughout Europe: a glance through English literature of the period is evidence enough that, while nowhere near as brutal as the German version, British anti-Semitism was insidious and almost ubiquitous. Neville Chamberlain expressed the prevailing attitude when he wrote in a private letter in 1939: 'No doubt Jews aren't a loveable people. I don't care about them myself. But that is not sufficient to explain a pogrom.'[23] In today's atmosphere of political correctness and heightened sensitivity it is easy to forget that not so very long ago it was quite the done thing to profess a sly anti-Semitism. Poland was one of the most anti-Semitic countries in Europe at that time – 'pogrom' is a Polish word – yet it was the occupation of Poland by the Nazis that was to trigger the Second World War.

Hess was undoubtedly anti-Semitic. He happily swallowed the idea of an evil Jewish conspiracy for world domination, and the 'fact' that Jews were behind the rise of the hated Bolshevism. But did Rudolf Hess also share the quasi-mystical beliefs that underpinned the myth of Aryan supremacy? As a member of the Thule Society, he accepted many of the racial and historical concepts that derived from occult circles, developing a personal interest in subjects such as astrology (although his mother had sown the seeds long before in Egypt) and unorthodox methods of healing. He also practised a form of meditation for relaxation and enhancing mental focus, which he may have learned as a child from the Arabs in the Egyptian desert. But there is no evidence that his interest went any deeper than that – there is certainly no suggestion that he was an initiate of any explicitly occult order; nor does he seem to have practised any ritual or ceremonial magic. However, Hess was certainly fascinated with the more arcane myths associated with the Wagnerian cycle, and was particularly intrigued by the mystical elements of that culture that pertained to Scotland. Like many another 'seeker' after the elusive wisdom of the ages both before his day and since, Hess was drawn to the mysteries of Rosslyn Chapel, that strangely compelling fifteenth-century building long associated with both the Freemasons and the Knights Templar, situated close to the village of Roslin, near Edinburgh. Many have gone so far as to link Rosslyn Chapel with the Holy Grail itself, most relevantly the occult scholar Walter Johannes Stein, who was very influential in the 1930s and became Churchill's adviser on the occult and secret intermediary with King Leopold of the Belgians. According to Andrew Sinclair in his book about Rosslyn Chapel and its builders, the ancient St Clair family, *The Sword and the Grail* (1992):

> Stein was approached by Hitler through Rudolf Hess to help find the Grail . . . A belief that the Grail was, indeed, in Scotland may have been another inducement for the deluded Hess to fly there during the Second World War . . . An intimate of Hess and member of the secret Nazi Thule society, Hans Fuchs, visited Rosslyn Chapel in May 1930 and signed the Visitors' Book and told members of the Edinburgh Theosophical Society that Hess identified with Parsifal – his nickname in Nazi circles – and believed Rosslyn was a Grail chapel or the Grail chapel.[24]

There is also a certain amount of evidence that Hess was active in circles best described as 'politico-occult', those that promoted political agendas inspired by occult ideas. The Thule Society was one such group, but there are suggestions that it was only part of a much wider network.[25] Allied to the Thule Society was a paramilitary organisation called Oberland, which was organised along similar lines to the Freikorps, but had certain significant differences. While most Freikorps units were made up of ex-soldiers looking for a good fight, Oberland was much more disciplined and organised, with an extensive underground network throughout Germany and Austria.[26] Of all the early Nazi leaders, it was Rudolf Hess who had the closest relationship with this shadowy, and extremely powerful, organisation.

The Communist overthrow

After his first visit, Hess became an enthusiastic member of the Thule Society, which was soon playing a leading part in conspiring to overthrow the Soviet Republic of Bavaria. His particular task was to procure weapons – with so many out-of-work soldiers they were in plentiful supply, and very cheap. It was possible to buy a hand grenade for just one mark, and boxes of ammunition and rifles for not much more. He also showed a remarkable talent for organising the infiltration of Thule members into the Bavarian Communist Party.

Although a law-abiding and sensitive man like Hess naturally recoiled from violence, he rapidly came to believe that it was a necessary evil if they were to overthrow the Communist regime in Bavaria and restore Germany's honour. The Thule Society was itself a target of violence: on 26 April 1919 Hess himself – probably because it was his birthday – escaped a Communist round-up of Thulists, who were all summarily executed. It was a terrible shock: they were his friends and comrades; one of them was Countess Heila von Westarp, the beautiful young secretary of the Thule Society and, according to some, Hess's first love. In addition, six of his other friends, including Prince Gustav von Thurn und Taxis and Baron von Seydlitz, were killed. It was surely time to fight fire with fire.

Chaos ruled. Although the Bavarian army accepted the change of government and the orders of the new Communist regime, its commanders fled. Senior officers, including Major General Franz Ritter von Epp – a close friend of Haushofer – plotted the overthrow of the new regime, using the Reichswehr, veterans and 'fifth columnists' who, in Munich, included the whole of the Thule Society. Hess joined one of the Freikorps squads organised by von Epp and only too soon received a minor battle honour, being shot in the leg during a successful attempt by the Reichswehr troops and the Freikorps to capture Munich from the Communists.

Once again, the respective destinies of Rudolf Hess and Adolf Hitler appear to circle round each other fatefully like the opposite poles of a magnet. At this time, Hitler, then a young infantryman, was technically on the opposite side to Hess, but was almost certainly also working as an informant and *agent provocateur* on behalf of von Epp.

Cometh the time, cometh the Man

In 1921 Hess won a prize in a University of Munich competition for an essay with the ponderous title of 'How Must the Man be Constituted who Will Lead Germany Back to her Old Heights?' In it he described 'the Man' in these words:

> For the sake of national salvation the dictator does not shun to use the weapons of his enemy, demagogy, slogans, street parades, etc. Where all authority has vanished, only a man of the people can establish authority . . . He himself has nothing in common with the mass; like every great man, he is all personality . . .
>
> Parliament may go babbling, or not – the man acts. It transpires that despite his many speeches, he knows how to keep silent . . . In order to reach his goal, he is prepared to trample on his closest friends . . . For the sake of a great ultimate goal, he must even be willing temporarily to appear a traitor against the nation in the eyes of the majority... As the need arises, he can trample them [the people] with the boots of a grenadier, or with cautious and sensitive fingers spin threads reaching as far as the Pacific Ocean . . . One day we will have our new, Greater Germany, embracing all those who are of German blood.[27]

The phrase 'willing temporarily to appear a traitor' has an extra significance in the light of Hess's flight.

However, the image of the expected leader in Hess's essay also included one much more surprising characteristic:

The work must not be tailored to the towering proportions of its builder, else the whole will totter when he passes away, as did the states of Frederick the Great and Bismarck. New and independent personalities, who might in the future lead the steed of the remounted Germania, do not thrive under a dictator. That is why he achieves the last great deed: instead of savouring his power to the dregs, he lays it down, standing aside as counsellor and mentor.[28]

As Konrad Heiden wrote in 1941, commenting on this passage: 'In truth, Hess can be said to have remained more loyal to Hitler than Hitler himself. For these thoughts of Hess about voluntary abdication were once shared by Hitler.'[29]

Hess's ideal leader will be a consummate rabble-rouser who will inspire the passions and loyalty of the masses, assume dictatorial powers and act ruthlessly – or, when necessary, subtly – to suppress opposition and create the Greater Germany. All of this is unsurprising, coming from Rudolf Hess, but what is less predictable is his theoretical requirement that this messianic figure will also stand down in favour of a non-dictatorial government once the great goal has been reached. If a personality cult grows up around this messiah, however, all will be lost when he dies . . . Of course, all this describes Hitler's career and its effect on Germany only too accurately; there is some evidence that, in the 1930s, he *was* planning to stand aside once his objectives had been achieved. But although Germany *did* fall apart after Hitler's death, it was what happened during his life that truly ruined his country.

While it is true that Hess wrote the essay a year after meeting Hitler – perhaps tailoring his requirements to the man – he had been thinking in those terms months before that meeting. He wrote to his parents: 'A great part of the people cry for strong government, for a dictator who will create order, oppose the Jewish economy, put an end to graft and profiteering.'[30] Within a short time, he and Haushofer had found that man.

After the overthrow of the Communists, Hess had continued to frequent political meetings in Munich during the remainder of 1919, including the gatherings of a group of army officers called the Eiserne Faust (Iron Fist), the leader of whom was Captain Ernst Röhm, General von Epp's chief of staff.

In the early months of 1920 Hess briefly saw more action as a pilot, this time flying with the Air Corps against the Spartakus uprisings in the Ruhr region. He was discharged from military service at the end of April 1920. Barely a month later, a bright, feisty and politically minded nineteen-year-old student named Ilse Pröhl moved into the same lodging house in Munich. Very soon she became his constant companion, supporting him untiringly throughout the years of the Nazi struggle for power. A few weeks after first meeting his future wife Hess was to have another encounter with enormous repercussions that were to extend far beyond their intimate circle, for the fates finally allowed him again to meet Adolf Hitler. This time their destinies became inseparably entwined.

Ironically for two such abstemious men, their first encounter was in a room attached to a Munich brewery. They had attended a meeting of the Deutscher Arbeiterpartei (DAP, or German Workers' Party), a small and disorganised political group which was, under Hitler's leadership, to become the Nazi Party. The DAP had such close connections with the Thule Society that some even regard it as Thule's political wing. Founded by locksmith Anton Drexler and journalist Karl Harrer, with just forty members, at first it showed no signs of becoming a force to be reckoned with. Its somewhat chaotic gatherings have been described by one commentator as 'a mixture of a secret society and drinking club'.[31] The DAP boasted a string of serious speakers, including Alfred Rosenberg, who lectured on the evils of *The Protocols of the Elders of Zion*, whipping his audience into a fury of self-righteous anti-Semitism, as he hammered home the point that the Jews were behind all of Germany's ills – from the defeat in the Great War to the economic and social problems – and the Bolshevik Revolution. That other prime mover in the Thule Society, Dietrich Eckart, also frequented the DAP.

A week or so after first meeting Ilse Pröhl, Hess, together with Karl Haushofer, heard Hitler speak for the first time at the DAP. Next day Hess excitedly told Ilse that 'if anyone can free us from [the Treaty of] Versailles it is this man'.[32] Unfortunately, however, he had forgotten 'this man's' name, although he added, 'This unknown man will restore our honour', insisting that Ilse went with him that evening to hear the saviour speak again. It was their first date.

Professor Haushofer never totally agreed with Hess's view of Hitler. He acknowledged his potential as a leader, as the man who could fulfil his great dream of Pan-Germanism, but the Austrian's strange self-absorption disturbed him and he could never bring himself to join in the upsurge of Hitler worship. Haushofer was not used to biting his tongue, and often spoke very forthrightly to Hitler (to the awe and amazement of onlookers), which ensured that their relationship was continually marred by friction. On one occasion, when Haushofer had inadvertently lapsed into lecturing mode, Hitler – after reacting with astonishment to the old man's daring to lecture him – simply got up and walked out, leaving the distinguished academic in mid-sentence. Of course, this was a relatively mild reaction – even in the early days, it could have been much worse. (Perhaps the fact that the professor continued to live, and even flourish, after this incident speaks volumes for Haushofer's influence, or maybe for Hess's power over Hitler. Haushofer himself, when interviewed by the Americans in November 1945, confirmed that his ideas had influenced Hitler, but more significantly: 'I was only able to influence him through Hess.' In the same interview he described Hitler, interestingly, as 'an angry man with excited eyes whom only Hess could calm'.[33]) And, of course, Haushofer refused to agree with Hitler's anti-Semitism. Yet even with all his reservations, the inventor of geopolitics had to admit that an astounding thing seemed to have happened: the longed-for messianic leader had arrived at precisely the right moment. Or perhaps it is more accurate to say that a man with all the potential for such a job had arrived in their circle, someone they could mould to fit the role. Either way, Hitler was their man.

The making of the Führer

The son of a customs official, Adolfus Hitler (née Schicklgruber – his father used his mother's maiden name for most of his life) was born on 20 April 1889 at Braunau am Inn, just 250 metres from the Austrian–German border. His family moved to Linz six years later. The school reports of the future colossus were, on the whole, lukewarm, describing his performance in most subjects as 'adequate' or 'satisfactory', although he was 'excellent' in drawing and – somewhat surprisingly – gymnastics.

Hitler longed to be a great artist, and as soon as he had finished with the three Rs, he attended a private art school in Munich for a few months, before enrolling at Vienna's Academy of Fine Arts

School of Painting, where he distinguished himself by failing the entrance examination twice. This was a bleak, but undoubtedly formative, phase for Hitler, in which he eked out a precarious living with a few drawing commissions, painting postcards for sale and starving in a basement. He became an active member of the Christian Social Party, which appealed to sectors of the lower middle class with its bluntly anti-Semitic message.

When the First World War broke out, Hitler, enthusiastic about the Kaiser's cause, joined the Bavarian army, although as a foreigner (he became a German citizen only in 1932) he had to obtain special permission to do so. As a corporal in the List Regiment he was a runner, carrying messages to and from the front line, a hazardous job in which he acquitted himself with bravery, being awarded the Iron Cross and the Iron Cross First Class – an extraordinary honour for someone of the lower ranks. Perhaps it is significant that one of his superior officers was one Lieutenant Horn (the name Hess assumed in 1941), who won Hitler's gratitude by testifying on his behalf in a libel case in 1932.[34]

When the Armistice finally came, Corporal Hitler was in hospital after having been temporarily blinded in a British gas attack near Ypres. The gas also injured his larynx and lungs, although, judging by his infamous histrionic performances before mass rallies in later years, it did no lasting damage. After the Armistice he remained in the Bavarian army until the end of the short-lived Communist regime.

When the Communists were overthrown in May 1919, the Bavarian soldiers who had continued to serve under them were treated as mutineers and brutally decimated – every tenth man was shot without question. According to Konrad Heiden, an ardent anti-Nazi who wrote the first biography of Hitler in 1936, only one soldier was excluded from this round-up: Adolf Hitler, who had been left in the barracks at Munich to spy for Major General von Epp and the other infantry commanders when they fled the Communist takeover.[35] Although Hitler glosses over this episode in *Mein Kampf*, Heiden is almost certainly correct: the future Führer appears to have informed on his colleagues during the months of Communist rule – successfully, it seems. Several infantrymen were executed as a direct result of his testimony. A clue to the real nature of his job is the fact that he then went to work for the euphemistically named Press and

News Bureau of the District Army Command – a covert operation that kept watch on subversives in Munich. Working under Captain Ernst Röhm, Major General von Epp's chief of staff, part of his job was to spy on political meetings and report back to the army. Ironically, it was as an undercover agent that he first attended a meeting of the DAP – the future Nazi Party – in 1919.

However, Hitler found nothing reprehensible to report about the DAP – quite the reverse. He was so impressed that he threw in his lot with them, joining the movement on 16 September 1919, and being immediately put in charge of organising meetings, recruiting new members, and disseminating propaganda. His first organisational success – hard won after a big row – was to persuade the committee to buy three rubber stamps.[36] As so often before and afterwards, Hitler played a double game, acting as informant against the political party he was helping to create. As Len Deighton put it, he was both 'spy against the Party and its most active member'.[37]

Hitler made his first public speech at a DAP meeting on 24 February 1920. On this occasion he was not the star speaker, the top of the bill being one Johannes Dingfelder, a homoeopathic doctor. But even so, it was Hitler's speech that stuck in the memory, if only because even then he had with him a band of what were called 'faithful supporters', whose idea of dealing with hecklers consisted of brandishing firearms and throwing opponents bodily out of the hall. That night, in the intervals between punch-ups in the audience, Hitler managed to outline a twenty-five-point programme drawn up by himself, Drexler, Eckart and an engineer named Gottfried Feder. The first point, written by Hitler himself, was: 'We demand that all Germans be gathered together in a Greater Germany on the basis of the right of all peoples to self-determination.'[38]

Dietrich Eckart was a particularly strong influence on the emergent Führer at this time, becoming, in the words of one early Nazi Party member, Hitler's 'spiritual father'.[39] The second volume of *Mein Kampf* is dedicated to him. It was Eckart who provided the Nazi Party with its emotive, rabble-rousing slogan: '*Deutschland Erwache!*' ('Germany awake!'), which soon began to reverberate throughout the land – a strident wake-up call to national pride.

Under the influence of the DAP and Eckart, Hitler's still-vag political ideas began to take a more concrete form, althou were always to remain visceral and emotional – fuelled monstrously inflated, patriotism – as opposed to Rudolf Hess's more intellectual and considered approach. Yet Hitler was also in his own way a visionary with large-scale plans: one of his main aims was the creation of the Third Reich, or the third historical union of the German states. (The first being the Holy Roman Empire in the Middle Ages and the second Bismarck's Reich of 1871, which finally collapsed in the First World War.) Hitler's master plan for a Greater Germany was to incorporate Austria and the German-speaking regions of neighbouring countries – and finally to reverse the Treaty of Versailles.

Genesis of the Nazi Party

The full effects of the Nazi phenomenon were still in the future when Hitler resigned his position as a political informant in March 1920, although he continued to be supported by the army. Major General von Epp and Captain Ernst Röhm were Hitler's – and the fledgling Nazi Party's – major supporters. Von Epp even bought the failing weekly newspaper owned by the Thule Society, the *Völkischer Beobachter* (*People's Observer*) and gave it to the DAP as their official organ, which installed Alfred Rosenberg as its editor.[40] Röhm's invaluable contribution was to ensure that the Nazis were plentifully furnished with arms and protection squads. (When they finally came to power Major General von Epp was rewarded with the governorship of Bavaria, a post he held throughout the war. He died in an American internment camp in January 1947.)

In 1920, under Hitler's influence, the DAP changed its name to the characteristically unwieldy Nationalsozialistische Deutsche Arbeiterpartei (the National Socialist German Workers' Party) or simply the NSDAP – the Nazi Party – for short. The party also drew up a new constitution and adopted the Thule Society's symbol – the swastika – as its own. The Nazi flag was designed by a Thulist, a dentist called Dr Friedrich Krohn, although his swastika was upright and turned in the normal, counter-clockwise direction. It was on Hitler's specific orders that it was reversed and placed edgeways on. It is possible, as some esotericists believe, that the intrinsically positive symbol of the swastika was deliberately perverted into a talisman of evil by this reversal. The rest of the design of the flag included the Red Flag of socialism, while the white circle represented nationhood and the swastika the struggle of the Aryan race.

It was against this background of fanatical nationalism, half-baked mystical ideas, anti-Semitism and the rising influence of Adolf Hitler that Rudolf Hess joined the DAP in June 1920, supported by Ilse. (But her organisational talents were to be wasted: women were forbidden by the NSDAP constitution to be anything other than helpers. Their real job, according to Nazism, was to stay at home, breed large families of blond-haired, blue-eyed Aryans and look after their menfolk.) Hess rapidly became Hitler's political adviser, although as he was still a student at the time, it is likely that he was more of a conduit for Haushofer's ideas. Already, however, there is a noticeable discrepancy between the modern image of Hess as a nonentity in the background, Hitler's rather embarrassing yes-man, and his role as a key player in the Nazi story.

At Hitler's request, Hess organised a National Socialist group among the students at Munich University, and it was Hess who was entrusted with writing the important articles in the *Völkischer Beobachter* that first outlined the NSDAP's programme.[41] It was also in his capacity as Hitler's adviser that he accompanied the latter to a meeting with the Bavarian President, Gustav Ritter von Kahr, in May 1921.[42]

In July 1921 Hitler found himself faced with opposition – the first of several titanic power struggles for control of the Nazi Party. During his absence in Berlin, Anton Drexler plotted with the head of the German Socialist Party, Julius Streicher, to unite the two parties under Streicher's leadership. As soon as this crisis blew up, Hitler was abruptly summoned back to Munich by a telegram signed by Eckart and Hess. Immediately on his return Hitler locked himself away with Hess for a long meeting, emerging with the first of a series of 'all or nothing' moves intended to increase his power; he resigned from the party, knowing that his oratorial skills had made him such a force to be reckoned with that Drexler would have no option but to cave in and ask him back. The plan worked beautifully: Drexler begged him to return, very much on Hitler's own terms. But before making his comeback, Hitler once again closeted himself with Hess, emerging this time to demand total leadership of the party, and the abolition of the committee that ran it. With Hess ever on hand to advise, Hitler took sole charge of the Nazi Party and Drexler was left impotent to challenge him.[43]

At that time the movement was only effective in Bavaria,

although similar groups, also espousing National Socialist ideals, were beginning to flourish in other German states. It made sense to Hitler to unite them all under his leadership, but when he demanded this at a congress of these groups in January 1922 he was soundly rebuffed. In those early days of struggle, opposition was common: on 4 November the previous year, Hitler's bodyguard, Emil Maurice, and Rudolf Hess had been involved in a brawl in which they successfully protected their leader. As a result, Hess received a nasty wound on the back of his head, leaving him with a permanent bald spot.

The party's private army at the time was the formidable Sturmabteilung (the Storm Section or SA), otherwise known, prosaically, as the Brown Shirts. Their talent lay in breaking up opposition to the Nazis so emphatically that those particular enemies would not be keen to raise so much as their voices again. Although Hess, the quiet middle-class intellectual, had nothing in common with the yobs of the SA, he was utterly devoted both to the cause and to his leader. With his fundamental sensitivity on the back burner, he threw himself into the new challenge, commanding his personal unit of the SA – the 11th Division – made up of students from Munich University. However, young intellectuals were hardly the norm, for by 1923 the 15,000-strong SA was largely made up of demobilised members of the Freikorps, under the command of Captain Ernst Röhm. In those early days Röhm was one of Hitler's closest allies and friends. Later, apart from Hess, he was the only Nazi leader to be allowed to use the familiar *du* with the Führer. This intimacy was not to last.

At the end of the First World War, Röhm had been entrusted by the army with hiding secret arms dumps throughout Bavaria, which he then made available to Hitler and the Nazi Party, along with street-fighters culled from the ranks of ex-soldiers. Known originally with a grim euphemism as the party's 'Sports Section' (Sportabteilung), their name was changed in 1921 to the more honestly evocative Storm Section. An organised rabble, essentially in it for the fight, they were not known for their political sensibilities (Röhm wrote a memo to Hitler in 1923 insisting that 'Party politics will not be tolerated in the SA';[44] the irony seems to have escaped him). They were intended to beat the Communists at their own game, seizing mastery of the streets – which was fine as far as it went – but soon the leaders realised that they needed a more disciplined and ideologically committed force. To serve that end, in 1922 the elite group that was to become the SS (Schutzstaffel or Guard Squadron) was created, made up of Nazi fanatics. At first a small and select band, drawn exclusively from the ranks of the securely employed – and easy to control – it eventually succeeded the SA in the 1934 purge of the Night of the Long Knives.

In the early days of the party, Hess was responsible for Hitler's personal intelligence section, not only gathering information about opponents, but keeping fellow party members under surveillance.[45] To him it was perfectly acceptable to keep secret dossiers on friends and colleagues, and indeed for others to do the same where he was concerned. (Later, when Ilse wrote a semi-ironic letter to Himmler complaining about their telephone being tapped, Hess was uncharacteristically furious. How dare she complain about such a matter! She must understand it was a necessity![46])

Although in public Hess was careful to embody the perfect example of blind obedience to Hitler, in private it was quite another story. He and Hitler certainly did not always see eye to eye. One source of disagreement in particular was telling: the two men clashed over the whole subject of Nazi thuggery, especially the increasingly unbridled 'Jew baiting'.[47] Although Hess believed ruthlessness and violence were essential in the struggle for power, he also made it clear that he saw them only as a means to an end, not an end in themselves. He firmly believed that there should be limits to brutality, and deplored the conduct of Nazis and SA members who indulged in violence and intimidation for their own sake.

The Beer Hall Putsch

In 1921 began the nightmare hyper-inflation that was to grip Germany for the next two years. By November 1923 money was virtually worthless: a single copy of the *Völkischer Beobachter* cost 8 billion marks. (The emergent Nazi Party was able to survive the economic crisis because of donations in foreign currency from supporters in other countries, principally the USA, Switzerland and Czechoslovakia.)

When the Weimar government in Berlin declared a state of emergency at the end of September 1923, the Bavarian government rebelled, attempting to break away from the German union. It was a critical time for Germany: the former monarchist President of Bavaria, Gustav Ritter von Kahr, was appointed State Commissioner with dictatorial powers, and a junta made up of the Reichswehr commander and the head of the Bavarian State Police was poised to take control. Hitler believed that the Nazi Party had arrived at its moment of truth: a moment he had been planning for some months. He could not let Bavaria leave the German union, for this would effectively put his plans for a Greater Germany into reverse. He had to act before it was too late.

Von Kahr and other senior members of the Bavarian government were scheduled to speak at a beer hall in Munich called the Bürgerbräukeller on the evening of 8 November: Hitler suspected he was about to announce Bavaria's independence and possibly even the restoration of the monarchy. Plans were hastily made for a coup – or *putsch* ('push') – to sweep the Nazis to power in Bavaria, with Hitler at their head. He had managed to secure a psychological advantage in the form of the endorsement and support of the elderly General Erich Ludendorff, one of the greatest generals of the First World War, widely regarded as a war hero. Although now drifting towards senility, his reputation alone made him a powerful figurehead for the imminent revolution.

The Beer Hall Putsch is universally described as a complete debacle – as, in every way but one, it was. The standard accounts fail to mention its one small triumph, the one part that went according to plan – the role played by Rudolf Hess. That night, Hitler, Hess and the SA broke in on the packed hall in the middle of von Kahr's speech. Hitler was flanked by Hess on one side and his bodyguard, Ulrich Graf, on the other – all three armed with pistols. Melodramatically stopping the proceedings dead by firing at the ceiling, Hitler announced that the hall was surrounded and that von Kahr and his ministers were all under arrest, his intention being to compel them to recognise the Nazi Party as the dominant force in Bavaria. He seemed to have succeeded at first. During the long night in the beer hall, von Kahr appeared to capitulate but, bizarrely, no celebrations or proclamations greeted this significant change of heart. Uncharacteristically, Hitler failed to capitalise on it, immediately lapsing into indecision, even failing to issue new orders. No one knew what to do next. Things became yet more uncertain the next morning, while Hitler was not even present. The farce intensified when, naïvely taking the surrender of the von Kahr faction at face value, Göring and Ludendorff released them. Somewhat predictably, as soon as the captives were out of sight, they changed their minds.

Everything was disastrously falling apart. In desperation Hitler – with Ludendorff at the forefront – led a march of SA men and other supporters on the Feldherrnhall in the middle of Munich, but their way was barred by von Kahr's armed police, who opened fire, killing fourteen Nazi demonstrators and three policemen. Hitler dislocated a shoulder and Göring was shot in the leg. Their flag, drenched in the blood of what came to be seen as Nazi martyrs, became the Third Reich's most revered relic, the 'Blood Flag'. In the later days of glory, all other flags were consecrated by touching it. (The current location of the banner is a closely guarded secret.)

Subsequent events were to prove more spiritually trying for the future head of the Luftwaffe: two Nazis helped Göring to shelter in a nearby bank, where he was given first aid by the owner. This Good Samaritan turned out to be Jewish.[48] Göring's two comrades resigned from the party in shame, but Göring, whose prime concern was always for his own aggrandisement, did not. He had ambitions in which the Nazi Party played the central part.

This Rabelaisian mountain of a man, who was to cheat the Allies' hangman at Nuremberg by taking poison in his cell, already had a heroic reputation. In 1922, as a famous First World War flying ace, Göring had been recruited into Hitler's Deutscher Kampfbund, the group that planned the putsch, which also included Friedrich Weber, head of the Freikorps Oberland (the Thule Society's paramilitary wing). As the new leader of the SA, Göring was Hitler's lieutenant on the night of the putsch, while Hess was not even a member of the Kampfbund – a matter often taken as proof of his political insignificance. However, although Hitler had appointed Göring as his lieutenant, he gave secret orders to Hess that covered the most sensitive parts of the plan.[49] It is clear why he did this: both men knew that the coup could easily get out of hand – the SA and the rabble would be hard to control once the fighting got under way with a vengeance. Some aspects of the takeover would need discipline, a cool head in the midst of riot, and it was these matters that were entrusted to Hess. This was to become a recurring pattern. Hitler and Hess needed the mob to help them to power, but could not afford to let them seize the upper hand. Hess contributed the control, his role deliberately not made obvious. He would be much more effective when working from the shadows.

On the night of the Beer Hall Putsch Hess's first job was to round up the senior ministers, taking them as hostages to a secret location out of the way of the mob. His second task, the following morning, was to lead an assault with his own SA unit on Munich City Hall to convey Jewish and Social Democrat councillors forcefully to the beer hall. They, too, had to be kept well protected from the angry mob. No doubt with an enormous sense of pride, Hess paused at City Hall just long enough to fly the swastika flag over the building.[50]

When he realised that the coup had failed, Hess – after first seeking the advice of Karl Haushofer – took two of the ministers as hostages and, accompanied by a couple of SA men, drove into the mountains, intending to take them into Austria. At this point some suggestive anomalies creep into the story. According to Hess's own account, given at his trial some months later, a snowstorm cut short their journey, so he stopped at a country house to ask if the owner could put them up for the night.[51] (Surely a somewhat bizarre scenario, with two hostages being held at gunpoint.) Hess claimed that when he came out of the house, he discovered that the SA men had driven back to Munich, leaving him stranded. However, their version was rather different: they claimed that Hess had ordered them to take the hostages back to Munich, which makes much more sense.[52] Whatever the truth of the matter, Hess went on to Austria alone, where he was sheltered by members of the shadowy Oberland group for the next five months.[53] It seems probable that Hess's rather unlikely version of events was a cover story. (Presumably the friendly house owner was a member of the Oberland network, playing his part in an escape plan.) This shows that Hess had a particularly close relationship with the Oberland network. Originally created as the paramilitary wing of the Thule Society, it worked closely with the SA, although it guarded its independence jealously, remaining under the command of Fritz Weber. It may be significant that when Hess arrived at the beer hall that night he was admitted as Weber's adjutant.[54]

After the debacle of the putsch, Göring fled to Sweden, ending up in a mental home where he became addicted to morphine (only being broken of it by his doctors at Nuremberg just before taking poison). Both the Nazi Party and the SA were declared illegal and banned. Hitler, Ludendorff, Weber, Röhm and five other leaders were charged with high treason and leading an armed uprising. Ludendorff was acquitted and, despite the gravity of their crimes, the others were given astonishingly light sentences: Röhm was put on probation, Weber got five years. Hitler was also sentenced to five years' imprisonment, but in the event served less than nine months. And although the law demanded that – as an Austrian citizen – he should be deported, he only got as far as the fortress in Landsberg am Lech, where he served his time in relative comfort. Unlike other prisoners, he and his compatriots were allowed to rise late, see visitors and hold meetings in each other's cells. There seems little doubt as to where their jailers' sympathies lay.

Hess returned from Austria and gave himself up, after reading in the newspapers about Hitler's light sentence. He was sentenced to eighteen months, of which he served just six.

The Landsberg watershed

Landsberg proved to be a landmark in the relationship between Hess and Hitler. Given adjoining rooms, and requesting – and being granted – another room to use as a study, the two men worked hard together, designing the blueprint for the Third Reich. One of their most frequent visitors was Professor Karl Haushofer.

Until that time, Hess was the efficient, reliable and trusted lieutenant, particularly useful when disciplined and discreet action was needed – as in capturing hostages and dealing with the mob during the putsch. But Landsberg redefined his role, establishing him as Hitler's confidant, muse and mentor. There was no question of his being Hitler's lackey. If anything, at least at this time, the reverse was true. Far from being kept in the dark about Hitler's plans, Hess himself shaped many of them. The two men were their own charmed inner circle, from which the likes of Hermann Göring were excluded. A visitor to Landsberg commented on Hess's manifestly growing influence over Hitler and their deepening friendship: 'Hitler enjoyed repeating his friend's slogans. [It is interesting that they were *Hess*'s slogans, not his own.] It was obvious to everyone that a very close relationship existed between the two of them. For the first time I heard them use *du*.'[55] Hitler had taken to calling his friend by the affectionate diminutive 'Rudi' or 'Hesserl'.

At Landsberg, Hitler embarked on *Mein Kampf*. The accepted story is that Hess was little more than Hitler's amanuensis at this time, but Rudolf Hess's contribution to *Mein Kampf* was much more significant than that. Pierre van Paassen, a Canadian journalist who covered the Nazis' rise to power, wrote shortly after Hess's flight: 'There is no doubt that Hess is the author of whole passages in the work.'[56] This is underlined by James Murphy, who translated *Mein Kampf* into English and worked in Berlin before the war as a translator for Hess's Foreign Department of the Ministry of Propaganda:

> Those chapters of *Mein Kampf* which deal with the propaganda and organization of the Nazi movement owe their inspiration to Rudolf Hess and most of the actual composition was done by him. He was also responsible for the chapters dealing with *Lebensraum* and the function of the British Empire in the history of the world. His younger brother, Alfred, often assured me of this. For a time we used to see each other almost daily in Berlin.[57]

Even Karl Haushofer admitted, during his interrogation by the Allies in 1945, that Hess had done more than act as Hitler's secretary, saying: 'As far as I know Hess actually dictated many chapters of that book.'[58] Wulf Schwarzwäller goes further, saying: 'He [Hess] helped organize Hitler's train of thought, he advised, edited, rearranged and introduced some ideas. It is no exaggeration to call Hess the co-author.'[59] Ilse Hess said that her husband edited Hitler's words, often taking a tough line with the new author, ordering rewrites and strongly advising other major changes.[60] According to Brigadier Rees, Hess himself told his British captors that he regarded *Mein Kampf* 'as a definite collaboration'.[61]

Between them, Hitler and Hess managed to write two chapters in Landsberg, finishing the book after their release in December 1924 in a house in Obersalzburg in Austria, which had been lent to them by a Hamburg merchant. The first volume came out in June 1925, the second a year later. Even Hitler's most ardent supporters thought it was dreadful. Originally, Hitler had wanted to call it *Four and a Half Years of Struggle against Lies, Stupidity and Cowardice*. Hess and his publishers insisted that he change it to *Mein Kampf* (*My Struggle*), which at least had the virtue of brevity.

In this turgid and at times almost unreadable work, Hitler expounds his political ideas, outlining their development in a rambling autobiographical narrative. There are long digressions, about such diverse topics as architecture, prostitution and venereal disease – and, more predictably, lengthy rants about the Jews and other 'inferior' races, drawn from the ideas of Alfred Rosenberg and Houston Stewart Chamberlain. The most cogently argued sections are those that deal with geopolitics, presumably because they derived from Hess and Haushofer, and may even be their own words.

Landsberg, then, was Hitler's political finishing school. On his emergence as a free man once more, his objectives and approach had changed radically. Until Landsberg he had been content to aim, at least initially, for the leadership of Bavaria, but afterwards his mind became set upon seizing control of the whole of Germany. There was another radical change that may be the result of Hess's influence: Hitler was now determined to achieve his ambitions not through street-fighting or revolution, but through the ballot box, even though it was clear that, once he had won, he would abolish democracy and assume dictatorial powers. Hitler had long accepted the Pan-Germanic ideal, but it was only now that it began to dominate his thinking. He was obsessed with creating *Lebensraum*.

He also made it his policy to attract support from those members of the middle class now completely disenchanted with the Weimar government and ruined by hyper-inflation. Hitler wanted to make Germany great again, a cry that was music to German ears after the humiliations of the Treaty of Versailles. And, in a grand gesture that swept away the mistakes of the past, the Nazi Party for the moment officially severed all ties with the SA (although they were later to be re-established). It is no accident that the new Hitler took shape while under the intensive influence of Rudolf Hess and Professor General Karl Haushofer.

As for the newly freed Hess himself, the professor offered him a post as his assistant at the Deutsche Akademie, whose aim was to study the culture of Germans abroad (although it is likely it was also used for gathering information on behalf of the Pan-German cause). However, Hess soon chose instead to become Hitler's private secretary, explaining explicitly why he had made the decision in a letter to his parents:

it was important to him [Hitler] from the outset that I am not a party employee, and that my position is quite independent of the party. This is necessary because of the authority located there.

I have been in the movement since the time when it consisted of less than a hundred members. I am therefore aware of the external build-up, the external effects, and I know the Tribune's [his nickname for Hitler] innermost thought, his attitude towards all questions, his whole nature. He knows me; our mutual trust to the very utmost [*sic*]; we understand one another.

I am qualified to act as a link between the mass movement and the intelligentsia. On the other hand, I am far too convinced of the necessity of the often unpleasant methods and nature of the struggle in terms of mass psychology to allow this to frighten me away from the participation in this movement, as are so many other members of the intelligentsia. I am convinced that by exerting influence in many directions I can do some good in *that* respect. After all, it doesn't bind me for ever to the Tribune.[62]

The last sentence is particularly illuminating about Hess's relationship with Hitler. This is hardly the slavish devotion most historians would have us believe characterised Hess's attitude towards his leader: if anything, Hess reveals a cynical and manipulative side to his nature. Clearly, he knew only too well what others were saying about his relationship with Hitler, and mocked them for it.

The Nazis' rise to power

With the spectacular failure of the Munich putsch, Hitler and his Nazi Party had gone into an immediate decline: in fact, the party's fortunes waxed and waned in inverse proportion to Germany's. Hitler's message needed the uncertainty of economic chaos to be successful in attracting the masses, but the years between 1924 and 1928 saw a marked recovery in Germany's economy. The government ban on the NSDAP was lifted at the beginning of 1925 (although some restrictions remained on its activities). On 27 February Hitler formally announced the relaunching of the party, perhaps with a deliberate tempting of providence, in the Munich Bürgerbräukeller. This time there was no debacle and by August 1927 20,000 supporters turned up at the first of the Nuremberg Party

Days, where they heard Hitler say (in a transparent attempt to whip up disaffection in the increasingly complacent population): 'Credulous optimism has befogged hundreds of thousands, in fact millions, of our people.'[63] Perhaps to establish himself as a gritty realist, Hitler then declared that he envisioned it would take 'twenty or even a hundred years' to establish the National Socialists as the ruling party of Germany.[64]

Seeking power through the ballot box rather than revolution, the new strategy was slow to bear fruit. In the elections of May 1928 the Nazis won only 12 seats out of 491 in the Reichstag, with less than 3 per cent of the vote. Then something unforeseen happened that almost magically hastened the rise of the Nazi star: in October 1929 the Wall Street Crash brought about the near collapse of the West's economy – and once again, Germany suffered badly. Unemployment soared virtually overnight, standing at 7 million by the end of 1932. A time of high anxiety returned, and with it a sudden eagerness to listen to Hitler's promises to restore German greatness.

September 1930 saw a volte-face on the part of the German electorate. The Nazis' share of the vote climbed to just over 18 per cent, winning them 107 seats out of 577, and making them the second largest party after the Social Democrats. In the next election, in July 1932, their share of the vote went up to over 37 per cent, giving them 230 seats. And although, as ever, the voters' minds were perhaps aided in their decision by Nazi thugs, there is no doubt that these results were, by and large, the true voice of the German electorate. Even so, the Nazi Party still had no overall majority, and the next few months saw various negotiations with other parties in attempts to form a coalition with Hitler as Chancellor, although there was a formidable obstacle in their path in the form of the elderly President, Paul Ludwig von Hindenburg.

An upright German field marshal of the old school, von Hindenburg thoroughly disapproved of the upstart Hitler and his street-fighting supporters. Left to himself he could never have approved the Nazi leader's chancellorship. However, a group of financiers and industrialists led by the economic genius Hjalmar Schacht, former president of the Reichsbank (a position to which he was reappointed by Hitler), and Kurt von Schröder of the famous banking family, pressured the old man to accept Hitler and his party. Such people saw a golden economic future for Germany if Hitler came to power, particularly because of two of his pledges to build up the armed forces and to abolish democracy. Invaluable to the wooing of this highly influential cabal was Rudolf Hess, who together with Himmler had several top-level meetings with von Schröder – particularly during the crisis following the 1932 elections when this circle threatened to withdraw its financial support. Hess won them over.[65] Urbane, charming, controlled and with all relevant facts and figures at his fingertips, Hess's style appealed to the bankers considerably more than the wild-eyed rantings of Hitler. Hess was reassuringly polite, businesslike and *normal*. If someone like him could obey Hitler to the letter, then clearly there was not much wrong with Nazism. So once again we find Hess managing a vital event in the Nazis' rise to power.

Finally, at the end of January 1933, von Hindenburg agreed to accept Hitler as Chancellor: he took up the position on 30 January. The first person to congratulate Hitler as Chancellor when he returned from the President's palace was Rudolf Hess. It was a defining moment for both of them: after the long years of struggle, reversals of fortune and even imprisonment, they had reached a position of real power from which they could begin to impose the Hitler/Hess vision of a new, more strident Germany – first on their own desperate country, and then on Europe.

Hitler called new elections for 5 March 1933, but on 17 February the Reichstag was burned down in an arson attack. A mentally unbalanced young Dutch Communist was arrested, but the debate continues as to whether the Nazis themselves were responsible. Whatever the truth, Hitler exploited the incident with great shrewdness: the day after the Reichstag fire President von Hindenburg signed a decree declaring a state of emergency, suspending the constitution, and giving Hitler and his government unprecedented powers to restrict civil liberties. Some 4,000 Communists were arrested and interned in the newly created concentration camps (Hitler persuading the President to authorise them). The alleged ringleaders of the Reichstag plot were executed. In one night, democracy had gone up in flames.

There was one last obstacle to be overcome. Despite a campaign of intimidation, in which more than fifty anti-Nazis were murdered, and despite gaining 44 per cent of the popular vote, the Nazis failed to gain an overall majority on 5 March. But now, with many left-wing deputies under arrest or in hiding – and the NSA 'guard' posted intimidatingly inside and outside the Kroll Opera House (where parliament was temporarily convened) – Hitler had no trouble in securing an Enabling Act. This granted him dictatorial powers for a period of four years.

The Nazi machine, now legally unhindered by such inconveniences as civil liberties and democracy, swung fully into action. But before Hitler could enjoy supreme power he had to ensure the way was clear. No actual or potential rivals could be allowed to survive. On 30 June 1934 came the Night of the Long Knives, in which his former friend and close ally Ernst Röhm and all the SA leadership were purged in a two-day bloodbath. Fate added a bonus: on 2 August President von Hindenburg died. The old order had gone. A day of army parades to celebrate the twentieth anniversary of the mobilisation for the First World War had been planned for 2 August, but at the last minute it was changed to a memorial service for the esteemed President. However, in all but name, this was Hitler's day. Now he assumed presidential powers – although he never bothered to take the title officially – taking supreme command of the armed forces. That evening, every army unit held a quasi-religious ceremony during which they took an oath of loyalty to Hitler personally, swearing 'unconditional obedience' and declaring their willingness to lay down their lives for him. The army's chief of staff, Walther von Reichenau, played an important role in organising this event. (With their usual genius for emotive ritual, the team of Hitler, Hess and Himmler had adapted the ancient custom wherein the army swore loyalty to the monarch.)

As the new dictator and his henchmen settled into their roles, they were, on the whole, greeted enthusiastically by the majority of the weary and battered population. (Although there were dissenting voices, they were not too loud, and even they fell silent soon enough.) Others, beside Germans, were excited and impressed by the rise of Hitler. Lord Rothermere, publisher of the *Daily Mail*, went to Munich to meet the new Chancellor, and afterwards penned a glowing tribute that was published simultaneously in the *Mail* and the *Völkischer Beobachter*. It enthused:

Enlightened opinion in England [presumably he meant Great Britain] and France should therefore give the National Socialists full recognition for the services which they have performed in Western Europe.

Under Hitler's supervision, German youth is actually organised against the corruption of communism . . . It would be the best thing for the welfare of Western civilisation if Germany were to have a Government imbued with the same healthy principles by which Mussolini in the last eight years has renewed Italy. And I see no need for Great Britain and France to maintain an unfriendly attitude towards the efforts of the National Socialists in the field of foreign affairs.[66]

Rothermere ended this paean with an appeal for the relaxation of the terms of the Treaty of Versailles.

Hitler was the most popular leader in German history. A plebiscite to discover the level of his support among the public resulted in a 'yes' vote of 90 per cent, on a turnout of 95 per cent of the population.[67] This is hardly surprising: between 1933 and 1938 Germany rose from the depths of a crippling and destabilising economic depression to the highest standard of living in Europe, almost matching that of the United States. There was zero unemployment, no good Aryan went hungry, and the country developed an impressive network of autobahns. This economic miracle was largely the work of Hjalmar Schacht, president of the Reichsbank and Minister of Economics from 1934 to 1937, who had succeeded in attracting foreign investment into Germany on a massive scale. But to the masses this miracle was brought about by only one man –Adolf Hitler – and it was to him that they looked for a yet more golden tomorrow.

During these years, repudiating the conditions of the Treaty of Versailles, the Nazis poured resources into rebuilding the navy, army and air force. Now in complete control of the country, Hitler turned towards his ultimate objective – the creation of a Greater Germany.

Hero of the air

Despite the claims upon his time and energy resulting from his role in the rise of Hitler, during that period Hess's personal life also progressed by leaps and bounds. Passionate about flying, he had continued to take to the air as often as possible – much to Hitler's disapproval. For a while it looked as if Hess would be grounded completely, but he had an idea. Shrewdly turning the situation to his advantage, he offered to use his flying skills for party propaganda: he had persuaded the publishers of the *Völkischer Beobachter* to buy a Messerschmitt light aircraft 'for publicity purposes', which he then flew over rallies.

In 1927 the whole world had suddenly became wildly enthusiastic about aviation, as millions followed the pioneering transatlantic flight of Charles Lindbergh with their hearts in their mouths. No one was more inspired by this gripping tale of heroism than Rudolf Hess, perhaps because Lindbergh was a fervent (and, as it turned out, lifelong) Nazi supporter. Hess's great ambition was to be the first to do the Lindbergh journey in reverse, from France to the USA. It came as a great disappointment when his plans came to nothing because no insurance company would take him on. But he won personal triumph when he came second in the prestigious Zugspitze race in 1932. Two years later – by then a government minister – he won it.

Another achievement that impressed his aviator's soul deeply was that of the Houston–Everest expedition's first flight over Everest in 1933. One of the leading figures in the British aviation team's heroic exploit was another flying pioneer, the young Marquess of Clydesdale – later the Duke of Hamilton.

In December 1927, Hess had finally married Ilse, who was by then his constant companion. Left to himself, almost certainly their relationship would have remained intensely intellectual, but – according to Ilse – Hitler himself stirred Hess into action by acting as matchmaker. One night in their favourite Munich café, Hitler took her hand, placed it in Hess's and asked, 'Haven't you ever thought of marrying this man?'[68] Hess was quick to take the hint: Hitler and Karl Haushofer were witnesses at their wedding.

The newly-weds bought a villa in the well-to-do Munich suburb of Harlaching in 1933, settling down to domestic life. Then, in 1937 – after ten years of marriage – they had their only child, Wolf Adolf Karl Rüdiger Hess. 'Wolf' had been Hitler's codename in the early days of the Nazi Party, 'Adolf' is self-explanatory, and, of course, he was named 'Karl' after Professor Haushofer. Both men after whom the baby was named acted as his godfathers.

Hess in office

Until he was appointed to public office in 1932, the name of Rudolf Hess was virtually unknown to the wider German public. In that year, although he was runner-up in the Zugspitze flying race, nowhere in the attendant publicity was his connection with Hitler or the Nazi Party mentioned, for the simple reason that the German press did not know about it.[69] Hess might have been Hitler's private secretary, but through his own express wish he had never been a party employee. However, it is important to realise that, although not employed by the party, he was its de facto leader. Hitler was now Führer of the state, his role as head of the Nazi Party nominal. Hitler ran the country, but Hess ran the party, even though he had assiduously been kept in the background. Now it was deemed to be the right time to allow him to emerge from the shadows.

In 1932 Himmler appointed Hess Gruppenführer (Lieutenant General) of the SS, but this was almost as nothing compared to his appointment as head of the newly created Central Political Commission of the Nazi Party, which co-ordinated the policy of all German government and regional departments – an extremely powerful position. Then, in April 1933, he became Deputy Führer of the Nazi Party – or rather, the *Stellvertreter* – which has no precise translation in English. James Murphy, who worked as a translator for the Nazi Propaganda Ministry in Berlin between 1934 and 1938, and who produced the first English translation of *Mein Kampf*, gave the closest definition: '[He is] Hitler's proxy, with plenipotentiary authority. This means that when he speaks officially he is *ipso facto* speaking for Hitler.'[70] Hess is known to have carried a document in Hitler's own hand, in Heiden's words: 'vesting him with blanket authority and stating that his orders were to be obeyed as though they issued from the Führer himself'.[71] Hess was also known, perhaps with more accuracy than was intended, as 'the party's conscience'.[72]

Around this time there are some curious gaps in Hess's biography. It is known, however, that in the autumn of 1933 he travelled abroad incognito, using a false passport. According to his son, he used the alias 'Alfred Horn' – the name he was to use on his ill-fated mission to Scotland.[73] But where Herr Horn went on these mysterious trips remains a mystery.

The real power of Rudolf Hess

On 1 December 1933 Hitler appointed Hess as Minister without Portfolio, which is often taken to mean that the Führer had failed to find a suitable job for him. However, this ignores the fact that Ministers without Portfolio, freed of the responsibilities of running any one government department and able to cross departmental boundaries at will, are often far more powerful than their more restricted colleagues. It is usually an assignment given by a party leader who wants to keep his other ministers under control – as in Peter Mandelson's reign as Minister without Portfolio in the Blair administration of late 1990s Britain. Hess's new job gave him supreme authority over all aspects of government except foreign policy and the armed forces. His brief was to ensure that all legislation conformed to Nazi ideology: every law proposed by any government department had to be approved by him. Essentially, nothing could be done without Hess's signature.

A neat summary of the common misrepresentation of Hess's role in the Hitler regime can be found in Robert S. Wistrich's *Who's Who in Nazi Germany*:

> In this position [as Deputy Führer] he largely exercised subordinate representative functions and supervised charitable duties, acting as the Führer's shadow but proving incapable and unwilling to take any initiatives of his own. His most important privilege was to announce Hitler from the tribunal at mass meetings, with the wide-eyed, ecstatic enthusiasm of the true believer. Hess masked his lack of independence, his clumsiness in thought and deed, by an unrestrained cult of the Führer that exceeded even the most sycophantic eulogies of the Nazi elite.[74]

Like a great many other dismissive accounts of Rudolf Hess, this is nonsense. That it is a far cry from the reality can be seen from the description of his duties and responsibilities as listed in the *Nazi Party Year Book* for 1941, which was cited by the prosecution at Nuremberg:

> By decree of the Führer of 21 April 1933, the Deputy of the Führer received full power to decide in the name of the Führer on all matters concerning Party leadership. Thus, the Deputy of the Führer is the representative of the Führer, with full power over the entire leadership of the National Socialist German Workers' Party . . . All the threads of the Party work are gathered together by the Deputy of the

Führer. He gives the final Party word on all intra-Party plans and all questions vital for the existence of the German people.[75]

The *Year Book* goes on to list his duties in the framing of all legislation, approval of all appointments of government officials, and his specific roles. Besides being chief of the Auslandorganisation, Hess was Commissar for Foreign Policy, Commissar for All Technological Matters and Organisation, Commissar for All University Matters and University Policy, and head of the Office for Racial Policy. One of his most important roles was to settle disputes between Nazi ministers: even being officially excluded from interfering in matters of foreign policy failed to lessen his influence in that area. It helped to have a constant supply of inside information from his own foreign intelligence department, the Auslandorganisation, which was responsible for co-ordinating Nazi Party activities in German communities abroad. The head of the AO was Ernst Bohle, who had been born in Bradford, West Yorkshire, and brought up in South Africa, and whose deputy was Hess's younger brother, Alfred. Many have tried to dismiss the AO as either incompetent or unimportant, but this is a mistake. In 1945 Bohle admitted to his Allied interrogators that information about foreign developments often reached Hess ahead of anyone else in the Nazi government.[76]

Hess also created the People's League for Germans Abroad (the Volkstum für das Deutschen im Ausland or VDA) – ostensibly a cultural organisation for German minorities in neighbouring countries, but that was merely a cover for yet more intelligence gathering, also ensuring that expatriates were kept up to date with what was going on in Berlin. It was no accident that Hess appointed Karl Haushofer, the godfather of Pan-Germanism, as its head. Haushofer's son Albrecht was also one of Hess's chief agents, travelling extensively – particularly in Britain and the USA – to build up valuable contacts and reporting back on political developments.

Often Hess had control over a specific department in a ministry under the overall auspices of another Nazi leader: although Joseph Goebbels infamously ran the Ministry of Propaganda, Hess had complete control over its internal Foreign Department – and, indeed, much else. He ran offices dealing with the law, the press, public finances and taxation, education, public works, employment, industry and technology – in fact, every aspect of government. There were more than twenty such offices in all, a veritable empire.

Also under his personal control was the Verbindungsstab ('liaison staff'), which acted as a monitoring centre for intelligence gathered by all the various intelligence organisations, such as the Abwehr (army intelligence), the Gestapo and the SD (Sicherheitsdienst, the security service).[77] Obviously, this was supremely important work, which put Hess in a uniquely powerful position in Germany at that time. The Verbindungsstab also included intelligence networks that were under Hess's personal control, such as the AO, and another, more anonymous, political intelligence unit of some significance. This was a network of agents and informants that had been set up during the First World War to gather intelligence from diplomatic circles abroad, and although it was supposed to have been disbanded on Germany's defeat it had been kept operational by an army colonel and Freikorps member, Walther von Reichenau (later a general and Hitler's most ardent supporter in the army leadership), using mysterious secret funding.[78] When the Nazis came to power this network (now run by Franz Pfeffer von Saloman) was placed under Hess's personal control – and both the network in general and von Reichenau in particular were to be highly useful in Hess's peace-making venture.

Just a few months after Hess's flight to Scotland the Canadian journalist Pierre van Paassen summed up his role in the Third Reich as follows:

> Through his position in the party and its elaborate spy system, which stretched its antennae and tentacles into every nook and corner of the various state departments, Rudolf Hess knew, therefore, more about the real state of feeling in Germany than anybody else, including Hitler himself. He also knew, more than any other man, the innermost thoughts of his master. There was no major military plan and secret of the Third Reich of which he was unaware.[79]

One of Hess's most important roles was to keep his finger on the pulse of public opinion in Germany. He sternly specified to the local officials charged with gathering information for him that they must not doctor it. He must always know the unvarnished truth.[80]

Some matters presented the 'conscience of the party' with a particularly intractable moral dilemma. Between 1933 and 1938 a series of laws was passed depriving German Jews of their civil rights and banning them from practising certain professions such as the civil service, law and medicine. The 'Nuremberg Laws' of 1935 forbade intermarriage or sexual relations between 'Aryan' Germans and Jews. As with all legislation, these acts were signed by Rudolf Hess, who clearly approved of them. But as late as 1940 he ordered that 'under no circumstances may Jews be denied any social security rights which are due to them'.[81] He also made it clear that, as Jews were forbidden to own businesses, and therefore had to sell them to 'Aryans', this should not be taken as an opportunity for plunder. He instructed that Jewish property should be assessed at the current market value, and that the buyers should not be prejudiced by 'anti-Jewish feeling'.[82]

The moral dichotomy revealed in Hess's treatment of the Jews is perhaps not surprising in such a devoted student of Karl Haushofer; although, of course, Hess was vehemently anti-Semitic, his intrinsic sense of honour – and orderliness – prevented him from approving of the excesses of the mob. On 8 November 1938 there was a wave of attacks on Jewish businesses, homes and synagogues across Germany, which became known as Kristallnacht ('Night of [Broken] Glass'). Hess was shaken and upset by this mass outburst. As always, mob violence – especially in what was supposed to be an orderly nation – disturbed him profoundly. The day after Kristallnacht Hess issued an order (Ordnance No. 174/38) to all Gauleiters (regional administrators), which read: 'On explicit orders from the highest level, no incendiary actions against Jewish businesses or similar are to be taken for any reason.'[83]

This order can be open to other interpretations, as was seen during the David Irving libel trial in London in spring 2000, when it was suggested that the Nazi hierarchy was dismayed by the arson attacks on Jewish property because – and only because – they endangered adjacent 'Aryan' properties. Besides, it was claimed that the Nazi leaders were only concerned with the firing of Jewish businesses because Germans were taking them over. While this interpretation may be valid where some, if not most, of the Nazi hierarchy were concerned, it does not appear to have applied in the case of Rudolf Hess. After Kristallnacht he complained to friends: 'Pillages and desecrations of places of cultural interest are unworthy of a German citizen.'[84] This view is completely in keeping with a speech he gave to the SA in 1933, in which he declared that it was 'unworthy' of a National Socialist to harass those of a 'Jewish-Bolshevistic [sic] persuasion'.[85]

It would be naïve and misleading to portray Rudolf Hess as the Reich's reluctant anti-Semite. He was a Nazi through and through. But while by no means condoning the attitudes that lay behind the Nuremberg Laws, it must be remembered that such attitudes were not confined to Germany at that time – similar laws in Poland had previously banned Jews from becoming civil servants. Hess has also been condemned for signing new statutes that permitted the enforced sterilisation of those least likely to produce good Aryan stock, such as mental patients. The Nazis' sterilisation programme was modelled on those already in force in Switzerland,[86] and it is now known not only that such policies were adopted in countries such as Sweden and Canada, but that in some cases they outlived those of the Nazis (Sweden's scheme continuing until 1976). Winston Churchill himself – who, although not an anti-Semite, subscribed to the racism of the era[87] – was a great advocate of eugenics. In 1906 he had proclaimed:

> The unnatural and increasingly rapid growth of the feeble-minded and insane classes, coupled as it is with steady restriction among all the thrifty, energetic and superior stocks, constitutes a national and race danger which it is impossible to exaggerate. I feel that the source from which the stream of madness is fed should be cut off and sealed before another year has passed.[88]

Six years later he went so far as to draft a bill that, for the 'good' of the race, would have had people of 'weak intellects' forcibly confined, the price of their freedom being sterilisation.[89] Churchill was a Liberal at this time, and the unpalatable truth is that such views were commonplace in Liberal and even in socialist circles in the early twentieth century.

In 1940 the terrible holocaust of the 'Final Solution' was still two years away. Until the beginning of 1942, the Nazis' preferred answer to the 'Jewish Question' was one of mass deportation: initially the island of Madagascar was a serious contender for the new Jewish settlement, an idea first put forward in Bismarck's day.[90] After Operation Barbarossa and the expansion to the east, mass deportations took place to the Baltic states. It is impossible to know how

Hess would have reacted to the atrociously euphemistic 'Final Solution' – although he had signed many of the laws that made it possible. It was not until after his flight that the orders for the mass extermination camps were given.

Hess and the Hitler cult

Wulf Schwarzwäller describes Hess as 'High Priest of the Hitler Cult'. In fact, it was Hess who created the 'cult of the Führer', intending to set an example to every other German of how to submit totally to the dictator. He was the first person to call Hitler '*Mein Führer*' and it was he who dreamed up the '*Heil Hitler!*' greeting.[91] He also invented the slogan: 'Adolf Hitler is Germany and Germany is Adolf Hitler.'[92] It was always Hess who stepped forward to introduce the Führer to the faithful at the mass rallies at Nuremberg – or, as they were properly known, the Reichs Party Day Congresses. (And contrary to the image portrayed by the likes of Wistrich, Hess gave regular speeches at a multitude of public meetings and radio broadcasts to the German nation.) Distasteful though they may be today, it is generally acknowledged that the Nuremberg Rallies were masterpieces of psychological manipulation, moulding the masses out of a single plastic emotion into a giant slavish machine. They were organised, down to the last detail, by Rudolf Hess.[93] But his influence went much further even than that.

There is little point in trying to find the truth about the Hess of this time in accounts written after the end of the war, when too many vested interests combined to squeeze the real Hess out in favour of another man altogether – a weakling who had never had any real power or authority. But examine the pre-flight accounts and such a different picture emerges that one might be forgiven for imagining they are describing another Hess entirely. For example, the translator James Murphy wrote in a booklet published within weeks of Hess's arrival in Scotland: 'Originally Hitler was his [Hess's] pupil and protégé.'[94] Konrad Heiden, writing in 1936, went further, describing him as Hitler's 'alter ego', summing up their relationship as follows: 'Hitler knew that his boundless imagination sometimes prompted him to irresistible follies, and he expected Hess to protect him against himself at uncontrolled moments.'[95]

The idea that Hess was Hitler's 'alter ego' was also used by Pierre van Paassen[96] who, as European correspondent for the Canadian newspaper *Evening World* between 1924 and 1940, closely followed the Nazis' rise to power and had many opportunities to observe their leaders at first hand. It must be remembered that Murphy, van Paassen and Heiden – unlike post-war historians – had personally observed Hess and Hitler.

Hess also had another role in his complex relationship with Adolf Hitler: not only had he schooled the Führer in etiquette in the early days but he remained his drama coach and stage director, spending long hours helping him hone his idiosyncratic speech-making style, with the trademark gestures and voice rising to an impassioned scream. Rather than being spontaneous, every last phrase, look and gesture was rehearsed under the eagle-eye of Rudolf Hess, until Hitler had perfected a towering performance that could wring every last vestige of devotion out of his audience. Hitler implicitly trusted Hess's judgement in other ways, too: whenever the Führer had to meet important visitors, such as representatives of a foreign government, Hess would sound them out first. Then, tailoring his advice to their foibles, he would school Hitler on how to act when he met them. Konrad Heiden describes such a tutorial:

HITLER: Fire away, Hess! Can he be used or not?

HESS: He can be used. But he's the silent type.

HITLER (*suspiciously*): Critical?

HESS: No, embarrassed. Would be terribly glad to admire, but he's embarrassed.

HITLER: They are all prepared. For ten years they have heard of me, for the last year they have heard of nothing else but me. What does he expect?

HESS: Authority, of course. You can speak at length. Your will is unshakeable. You give laws to the age.

HITLER: Then I'll speak with the firm voice, without yelling.

HESS: Of course.

Hitler utters a few sentences. Hess, the human tuning fork, listens: 'No, not like that, quiet – no passion, commanding. You want nothing of him. It is destiny that speaks . . .'

At length the adviser falls silent. Hitler is in the swing and speaks evenly for several minutes, with the 'firm voice' . . . After six or seven minutes he breaks off, already moved by his own words. 'Good, now I think we have it,' he concludes. Then the time and the place for the reception are set.[97]

The degree to which Hitler relied on Hess for help in crafting his 'performances' is remarkable. Hess's views were not merely welcomed by the Führer, they were of paramount importance – Hitler made no opening move without them. He saw Hess as a particularly incisive judge of character, a shrewd diplomat and politician, and a trustworthy ally who came over not as a sycophant, pitifully hoping for scraps of encouragement from the table of the great man, but – at least – as an equal. Heiden goes on:

> Suddenly, in the midst of a conversation, Hitler's face grows tense as with inner vision; these are the moments in which the humanly repulsive falls away from him and the unfathomable is intensified until it becomes truly terrible. His eyes peer into the distance, as though he were reading or gazing at something which no one else sees; and if the observer follows the direction of his gaze, sometimes, it has been claimed, Rudolf Hess can be seen in the far corner, with his eyes glued to his Führer, apparently speaking to him with closed lips.[98]
>
> . . . it is certain that in the decisive years of his career Hitler used his younger friend as a necessary complement to his own personality; as a stage director or spiritual ballet master who helped him shape his own powerful but formless and uncertain nature into whatever image he momentarily wanted.[99]

Hess's relationship with Hitler was more than merely remarkable: for Hitler, it was essential. Heiden wrote in an article entitled 'Hitler's Better Half' for the American journal *Foreign Affairs* a few months after Hess's flight: 'Rudolf Hess was the intellectual creator of Adolf Hitler to the extent that a piano creates music.'[100]

The myth of the fall from grace

The intensity of the friendship between the Führer and his Deputy was universally acknowledged among the leadership in the early days of Nazi supremacy – but was it too good to last?

Many believe that the relationship had already disintegrated significantly before Hess made his flight: indeed, they surmise that it was for this reason that he undertook such a mammoth, and apparently foolhardy, task. What better way to impress his Führer than to change the course of the war with one superbly heroic gesture? Superficially, this interpretation, which is the standard line, appears to make sense, but there is very little evidence to support it – and a good deal against it.

One of the major events cited to demonstrate the growing rift between Hess and Hitler is the Night of the Long Knives. Although Hess helped organise the purge and largely supported Hitler's actions, it has been argued that the bloodbath marked the beginning of a split between Deputy and Führer. After all, he did disagree with Hitler over the details, demanding that certain names be removed from the list of those to be executed.[101]

On 30 June 1934 SS commanders throughout Germany were ordered to open sealed orders at precisely the same time. The instructions were to arrest all the SA leaders in their area. Over the next few days many of them were executed – along with others, as people took advantage of the turmoil to settle old scores. Hitler personally arrested Röhm who, after refusing an offer to shoot himself, was shot dead in his cell. The reason given to the German people was that Hitler had discovered that Röhm was planning an SA coup to overthrow him – but the truth was that Hitler was taking pre-emptive action to rid himself of a dangerous rival. Röhm's command of the SA, which now numbered several hundred thousand men (it was larger than the army), simply gave him too much power. Rather illadvisedly, he had clashed with Hitler about his ambitions for the SA, which he thought should now replace the army.

Another major reason for the purge was that the SA had outlived its usefulness and was an embarrassment. It had been needed during the Nazis' strife-torn climb to power as a means of intimidating rivals and 'encouraging' the electorate to vote for the 'correct' party. Now that Hitler was in power, there was no further need for such an unruly organisation: the more disciplined and Hitler-loyal SS were to be given the task of keeping order in Germany.

Several authors – such as Wulf Schwarzwäller[102] – have concluded that Hess was kept in the dark about the planned purge, which Hitler arranged with Himmler and Göring. If true, it would have been the first time that Hess had been excluded from an important decision. Others claim that Hess was so deeply shocked by the events – during which several former friends and colleagues were murdered – that the inner conflict triggered his subsequent mental instability.[103]

There is no doubt that Hess played his part in the purge, at least at the beginning. When Hans Frank, Bavaria's Minister of Justice, disputed the legality of Hitler's 'hit-list' (on the grounds that martial law had not yet been declared) it was Hess who telephoned him to insist he accept the Führer's orders.[104] And five days beforehand, on 25 June, he had made a radio broadcast in which he warned party members to be cautious of those who 'try to agitate the comrades against one another and to disguise this criminal act by giving it the honourable name of a "second revolution" '.[105] He also said, in his usual declamatory style, 'Woe to him who breaks faith, and thinks to serve the revolution by rebellion!' Clearly setting the scene for the fall of Röhm and the SA, these were hardly the words of someone who knew nothing about it.

After personally arresting Röhm in Munich on the night of 30 June, even Hitler began to have scruples about executing his old comrade and protector from the earliest days of the DAP, the man who had stood in the dock with him after the 1923 putsch. But now, when one party leader, the head of the Reich Press Chamber, Max Amann, stated that Röhm must die (offering to do the job himself), it was Rudolf Hess who stepped forward briskly, saying, 'No, that's my duty, even if I should be shot afterwards.'[106] In the event, however, Röhm's execution was carried out by an SS officer.

Even more tellingly, afterwards, on 13 July 1934, Hitler made a speech to the Reichstag in which he singled out Hess's role: 'I started having my doubts [about Röhm's loyalty] due to warnings – especially from my Deputy Rudolf Hess – which I just couldn't ignore any more.'[107] Far from not knowing about the purge, it seems that Hess might even have inspired it.

The SA survived as an organisation – just – but was no longer armed, its primary function being to look impressive on ceremonial occasions. The once formidable fighting force was emasculated under its new head Viktor Lutze, previously one of Hess's agents inside the SA.[108] Once again, Hess was a key influence.

Descriptions of Hess's reaction to Hitler's announcement of the names of the SA leaders to be executed vary widely. Some record that he became visibly distressed at seeing friends' names on the list, although we are also told that he argued heatedly with Hitler about them, succeeding in having many of them removed. Hess's adjutant, Alfred Leitgen, said after the war, 'There were many, it will never be known how many, he saved.'[109]

Many years before, in his seminal essay, Hess had written of the necessity to be ruthless in the climb to power, but that such methods should be discarded once the objective had been reached. Therefore, he may well have been in total agreement with the measures taken against the SA and the passing of civil power to the SS – even if the process sickened him as a man. It seems that the bloodbath literally turned his stomach: around this time he began to suffer from a variety of ailments that were probably psychosomatic in origin, ranging from stomach trouble and kidney pains to insomnia and other nervous problems, which he tried to treat with a variety of alternative therapies. (He was deeply committed to alternative medicine, even finding the funding for several homoeopathic and naturopathic clinics, nicknamed the 'Rudolf Hess hospitals'. Unfortunately, they were never established.) It has been argued that his various ailments were the physical manifestations of a profound inner confusion and turmoil, caused either by his distress at the bloodletting or by the deterioration in his relationship with Hitler and an increasing sense of isolation. While it is likely that his symptoms were signs of inner tension, the idea that this was due to a rift with Hitler, or to any form of mental breakdown, is pure speculation. After all, such ailments could just as easily have been caused by overwork. And perhaps it is significant that both Heinrich Himmler and Hitler himself also suffered from similar health problems – headaches and stomach cramps – probably for the same reasons. If Hess's symptoms are to be taken as evidence of secret doubts about the Nazi cause, what did they mean in Hitler's case?

But what of the rift with Hitler? It is true that after the flight to Scotland rumours began to circulate in Germany of a breakdown in the relationship between the two men. Frequently quoted is the following account, taken from the memoirs of Armaments Minister Albert Speer, written after his release from Spandau in the 1960s:

Hess was a regular dinner guest of Hitler's at the Chancellery. However, one day Hitler discovered that he brought his own

vegetarian food with him, which he had heated up in the kitchen.
When Hitler remonstrated, Hess explained that he was on a special
diet of 'biologically dynamic' food. Hitler told him that, in that case,
he should eat his meals at home. After this Hess was a much less frequent dinner guest.'[110]

Is this strong evidence of a serious rift? Perhaps more significant is
the fact that this story is repeated so often because it is the *only* such
evidence.

In virtually every analysis of the Hess affair, a connection is made
between his flight and the 'fact' that on the outbreak of war he was
'demoted' to second in line behind Göring in the leadership of Nazi
Germany. It is true that on 1 September 1939, when war with Britain
and France seemed inevitable, Hitler did announce publicly that, if
anything happened to him, Göring would take over as Germany's
Führer, and that if anything happened to Göring, Hess would be next
in line to lead the country. But was this proof of a demotion? This was
the arrangement for the succession as leader of the state, not of the
Nazi Party. Hess had never been Deputy Führer of Germany, but of the
NSDAP. In any case, he had been made third in command of the
country as far back as December 1934, an appointment confirmed by
a secret decree on 23 April 1938: the 1939 announcement was merely
the first time it had been made public.[111] Perhaps because of the threat
of a successful assassination attempt shortly after first coming to power,
Hitler had set out what was to happen in the event of his death or serious incapacity. As well as naming Hess as his executor, he appointed
Göring as his successor. Both men had long known about this
arrangement. It was not, and had never been intended as, a demotion
for Rudolf Hess, nor was it a surprise. Hess's flight was not a desperate
bid to restore his standing in the eyes of the Führer: he had no need to
do so. There is no evidence that he was excluded from anything –
quite the reverse was true. In 1938, as plans for war were already far
advanced, Hess was elevated to the Secret Cabinet Council, and when
war broke out he was one of the six-member Ministerial Council for
Defence of the Reich in charge of planning the whole Nazi war effort.
Even a British government document – a briefing prepared after Hess's
arrival by the Foreign Research and Press Service at Balliol College,
Oxford – states that on both these councils Hess 'represented the
Führer who was not himself a member'.[112]

This, then, was the real Rudolf Hess, whose extraordinary influence over Adolf Hitler was undiminished at the time of the flight. Hess's role in Hitler's Germany has been radically – and shamelessly – rewritten because the powers that be deemed it essential to portray the mission as a badly conceived, ill-planned and impulsive act undertaken by someone who had little grasp of the realities of British politics or the course of the war. But if this were true, it would have been absolutely out of character – Hess was a meticulous organiser, cautious and methodical, with a detailed knowledge of foreign affairs, gleaned from his own intelligence network, and of Germany's plans for the war. To make the official version work, his personality, role and status have been rewritten to make his flight appear in character. After all, the crazy flight of a has-been is less suggestive – and considerably less disturbing in its implications – than the story of a carefully planned mission by the man who made Adolf Hitler.

CHAPTER THREE

Journey into Conflict

The accepted interpretation of Rudolf Hess's mission to Scotland is that he was in the grip of a great delusion. He believed wholeheartedly that there was a highly influential peace party waiting for him in Britain, who could join him to halt the war. This, claim historians, is proof of the Deputy Führer's delusional state of mind: there never was such a peace party. His mission therefore was always doomed. But what if there *was* such a powerful British cabal?

There is a danger in assessing history with the benefit of hindsight – what has been described as 'writing history backwards' (or, using the magnificent German word for it, *Hineininterpretierung*). Today we know what happened next in those far-off days, but it is important to remember that the people at the time had no idea how things were going to work out. Historians tend to judge historical figures – especially politicians – too harshly because they think they should have known better, that they should have seen what was coming. How they treated Neville Chamberlain is a case in point. He has gone down in history as weak and ineffective because of his attempts to appease Hitler in 1938. But this is only because we know that he failed to avert the war. At the time things were rather different: not only was his an honourable attempt at 'jaw-jaw' rather than 'war-war', his actions were supported by his cabinet, the King and the vast majority of the British public, who had no desire for another round of carnage. On his return from Munich on 30 September 1938, when Chamberlain announced a deal with Hitler that would bring –

in that much-ridiculed phrase – 'peace in our time', he was given a hero's welcome. He took his place on the balcony of Buckingham Palace with the Royal Family to receive the cheers of the people, the first Prime Minister to be accorded this honour. Yet today we would be forgiven for believing that Chamberlain was despised the moment he waved his bit of paper and was the only man in Britain who failed to see the futility of his negotiations.

It is now tactfully forgotten that many important people in Britain – leading politicians and even royalty – took a keen interest in the political philosophy and methods of Hitler and his men. In the mid-1930s, however, it was not thought so terrible to confess to an interest in Nazism. After all, it was a system that had succeeded beyond anyone's wildest dreams: massive unemployment was a thing of the past in Germany; virtually overnight, almost everyone had a job. It was a country that had climbed from the depths of terrifying economic depression to enviable affluence in just a few years. And not only had Hitler appeared to solve the same social problems that were threatening to destabilise the old order in Britain, but he had done so while at the same time effectively suppressing Communism. Many movers and shakers of British society – including the Prince of Wales (later Edward VIII and subsequently the Duke of Windsor) and the Duke of Kent – were keen to discover the Nazis' secret so they could work a similar magic on Britain's lumbering economy.

There is no denying that as far as many Britons in those days were concerned, Hitler had worked miracles. When Germany became the enemy in 1939 most of those who had been actively pro-German took the patriotic course, effectively being seen to change sides, no matter what they still believed in private. Those who remained unrepentant pro-Germans were interned – even shot as traitors in some extreme cases. This did not mean that the desire for peace with Germany had been totally subsumed in the war effort and simplistic jingoism. Many of the mysteries and anomalies surrounding Rudolf Hess's flight are due to the reluctance of certain crucial players to be labelled as pro-German.

Between the wars

After the brutal awakening of the killing fields of the Great War, the old certainties of the social hierarchy were being questioned in every country. Now the ordinary man in the street had a voice and finally he dared asked what – and for whom – he had been fighting. The working classes found a new confidence, and the old rule of privilege and the inequalities of birth were beginning to be overturned. Although it was to be a slow process in some countries – the feudalism of the landed gentry and their complete hold over their 'tied' workers was to continue for years in Britain – there was, however, one echelon of society already seriously undermined. The Great War had seen a sudden and dramatic reduction of the power of the ruling classes – and, in particular, the absolute power of the many inter-related monarchies of Europe.

Until the end of the First World War, most of Europe (with the major exception of France) had been ruled by relatively few royal and aristocratic dynasties – in effect, a 'royal club'. There was the Kaiser in Germany, the King in Britain, the Habsburg Emperor in the Austro-Hungarian Empire, the Tsar in Russia and so on, most of whom were related, largely thanks to the proliferation of Queen Victoria's brood. Where it was not owned directly by the crown, most of the land was owned by counts, dukes, barons and lords. Incredibly, even by the 1940s one-third of all land in Britain was owned by a few noble families whose pedigree went back many centuries. But by 1920, after the Great War, the royal club was considerably diminished. Many families who had ruled without question for centuries found themselves dispersed, dispossessed or – as with the Tsar and his family – looking down the barrel of Bolshevik guns. The Austro-Hungarian Empire had been broken, and new and revived republics such as those of Poland and Czechoslovakia set up in their place. The Kaiser had been forced into exile and his son renounced the throne, marking the end of the monarchy in Germany. In countries where royal rulers did survive – such as in Britain, Holland and Belgium – their political influence had been greatly reduced. It was not a good time to be royal, especially as many of the remaining families were related to the murdered Tsar. Images of the last moments of his family, imprisoned, taunted and executed by the Bolsheviks, must have been constantly at the backs of their minds, together with the dread question: might it happen to us?

As if to drown out the screams of the dying Russian royals, the younger generations of old elite families threw themselves with vigour into a very different world. Out went the starched collars and whalebone corsets of regal respectability, and in came cocktails, fast cars, cocaine and hobnobbing with the new twentieth-century royalty – the glitterati of Hollywood. Although kings since time immemorial had frequently, and often notoriously, drunk deep of the world of excess, this was the true beginning of the era of the playboy prince as we know it today. It was to prove a popular and persistent trend.

Like many young men of means, Edward, Prince of Wales exorcised the nightmares of the Western Front – where, if he was not allowed to take part in the action, he certainly witnessed the traumas of war – with obsessive partying. The plaintive wail of the crooner and the jagged syncopation of the jazz band drowned out the memory of whistling shells and the crimson shrieks of the dying. There was, as ever, solace in sex: Edward and his brother Prince George (later the Duke of Kent) were the most sought-after young men of their day, and – except where marriage was concerned – they were happy not to do too much running from the flappers who crowded round them. They, and many of their generation, liked to link themselves to the new stars of the celluloid world such as Douglas Fairbanks, Charlie Chaplin and the rising British luminary of the musical comedy stage, Noel Coward. There was magic in their unreal world and the members of the young generation of the royal club were eager to lose themselves in its enchantments.

Britain was overflowing with dispossessed royalty, and by 1940, when Hitler had already cut a swathe through Europe, virtually all the remaining heads of the royal houses were in exile in Britain, including the royal families of Norway, the Netherlands, Albania, Yugoslavia and Luxembourg. Huddled together in Britain as if for comfort, the great dynasties of Europe realised that another lengthy war would only erode their power, prestige and ultimately their wealth further. If ever there was a reason to pursue the possibility of peace to the eleventh hour and beyond, this was it.

Hitler and the British Empire

The Führer never intended to have a war with Britain. Under the influence of Hess, Haushofer and Rosenberg, while his detestation of certain other nations remained as robust as ever, Hitler always saw the British as worthy of a respect that almost amounted to awe. Yet in the 1920s and 30s, this was hardly a common view in Germany. To the war-weary, defeated population, the British must have been seen not only as shrewd businessmen but also the nation that tried to starve them to death. When Hitler expressed a much more favourable view of the former enemy, he was certainly not pandering to the masses on the subject of Britain. He summed up his projection of Britain's value as a nation in *Mein Kampf*:

> The British nation will therefore be considered as the most valuable ally in the world as long as it can be counted on to show that brutality and tenacity in its government, as well as in the spirit of the broad masses, which enables it to carry through to victory any struggle that it once enters upon, no matter how long such a struggle may last, or however great the sacrifice that may be necessary or whatever the means that have to be employed; and all this even though the actual military equipment at hand may be utterly inadequate when compared with that of other nations.[1]

Hitler saw that the Second Reich had failed because, in trying to expand its overseas colonies, it had come into direct competition with the British Empire. In his view Germany should have made an alliance with Britain and expanded at the expense of Russia: 'No sacrifice should have been considered too great if it was a necessary means of gaining England's friendship. Colonial and naval ambitions should have been abandoned and attempts should not have been made to compete against British industries.'[2] But Hitler was determined not to make the old mistake again, declaring: 'Only by alliance with England was it possible to safeguard the rear of the new German crusade.'[3] (The theme of alliance with Britain also appears in the 'sequel' to *Mein Kampf*, which remained unpublished until a manuscript, found by the Americans in Berlin in 1945, was finally published in 1961 as *Hitler's Secret Book*. This has a chapter entitled 'England as an Ally', and shows distinct signs of Hess's influence.)

Hitler's attitude to Britain was to remain much the same even when war between the two countries became inevitable and then finally erupted. While not willing to compromise his territorial ambitions or his desire to make Germany the dominant nation in Europe, he regarded war with – to his way of thinking – the other great Aryan nation as a tragedy, and was baffled when Churchill insisted on continuing the fight even when Britain stood alone, with apparently no hope of ever winning. As late as the autumn of 1943, Hitler was writing: 'England for the good of the world must remain unchanged in her present form . . . Consequently, after final victory, we must effect a reconciliation.'[4]

Before he came to power in 1933 Hitler was keen to strengthen Anglo-German relations and reassure Britain that his well-publicised desire to rebuild Germany and reverse the Treaty of Versailles posed no threat to British interests. As a public relations exercise he invited several prominent British politicians and businessmen – including former Prime Minister David Lloyd George – to Germany to meet him. They were duly impressed. Hess sent influential Nazis such as Alfred Rosenberg to London to cultivate the friendship of British society. This was also a great success. While Nazi diplomat Joachim von Ribbentrop (Germany's Ambassador to London between 1936 and 1938) may have been a laughing stock, Rosenberg soon became an admired and fêted guest at some of the best dining tables in the capital, becoming the perfect unofficial ambassador for the Nazi regime.

But what of British attitudes to Hitler? The coming to power of the Nazi regime prompted some very hard thinking in Britain. Would Hitler alter the balance of power in Europe? People were beginning to feel nervous – after all, he had been elected on a promise to re-establish Germany as a major political and economic force. Britain had to come to terms with the spectre of a united, prosperous and expanding Germany, with its rebuilt industry and growing armed forces. Many in Britain viewed Hitler's ambitions with increasing anxiety. There were some – notably Winston Churchill, then a backbencher – who saw a strong and unified Germany of any political persuasion as a threat. To them, automatically recalling the horrors of the trenches, Germany would always be the enemy. Some considered that a strong Germany would inevitably lead to a decline in Britain's influence in Europe, while of course those on the left were ideologically opposed to Nazism. But there was another set of attitudes to Hitler's Germany, and here it might be possible to find the origins of the 'peace group' that Hess claimed he flew to Britain to meet.

The peace group

Hess's contention that a British peace group existed has always been treated with derision, because it is assumed that although there were a few Hitlerites in Britain – such as Oswald Mosley's British Union of Fascists – they constituted a small minority, lacking any real power or influence. However, recent studies reveal that, before the outbreak of war, a substantial number of the British Establishment – prime movers in political, aristocratic and financial circles – were totally opposed to the escalating conflict. And when, despite their best efforts, war had finally broken out, these people continued to believe that it should be resolved as soon as possible through a negotiated peace. This belief did not necessarily make them pro-Nazi. Many, perhaps most, were totally opposed to Hitler and his brutal regime, but still fervently believed that it was not in Britain's best interests to become embroiled in a costly war (unless it was to stem the tide of Bolshevism). And there were many others, including leading figures in the armed forces, who were simply appalled at the prospect of another war, and felt it should be avoided at any cost.

Dr Scott Newton, Professor of History at the University of Cardiff, has made a detailed study of the pro-peace grouping in Britain before and during the Second World War. His findings – published in *Profits of Peace* (1996) – reveal conclusively that a substantial sector of the British Establishment was opposed to the outbreak of war and thus, once war had begun, was in favour of an early compromise peace with Germany.

During the 1930s, several groups were founded to foster closer Anglo-German ties, among which the Right Club, founded on the very brink of war in 1939 by Conservative MP Captain Archibald Ramsay, was the most pro-Nazi, anti-Bolshevik and anti-Semitic – and the most closely monitored by MI5. Its members included the Duke of Wellington, Baron Redesdale (father of the Mitford sisters), several other prominent peers of the realm and William Joyce, later the notorious 'Lord Haw-Haw', whose wartime broadcasts on behalf of Hitler were to earn him a traitor's death in 1946.[5]

Another peace group active at this time was the Link, whose membership ranged from those who merely supported closer ties with Germany to staunch pro-Nazis, including a number of peers, army and navy officers and MPs. Between March 1938 and June

1939 the Link more than doubled its membership to around 4,300 – a sign, perhaps, of rising anxiety among the ruling classes about the coming conflict. One of its founding members was Admiral Sir Barry Domvile, director of naval intelligence, and a committed believer in the existence of a Jewish–Masonic conspiracy. (Domvile was later detained as a threat to national security.) On the eve of war, Britain's largest landowner, the Duke of Westminster, also joined the Link.[6]

Another major organisation committed to fostering better relations between Britain and Germany was the Anglo-German Fellowship. It is particularly important to this investigation because of an enduring controversy over whether the Duke of Hamilton (then the Marquess of Clydesdale) was a member. New evidence has emerged about his status vis-à-vis the Fellowship, which will be dealt with in the next chapter, and which sheds important new light on the matter.

There were, of course, some who did not want a war with Germany because they agreed with Hitler and the ideals of Nazism. Apart from Mosley's Fascists, there were many in the upper echelons of British society who admired the Führer: Lord McGowan, chairman of ICI, General Sir Ian Hamilton, head of the British Legion, and Montagu Norman, governor of the Bank of England. Others who saw Hitler as a saviour were the anti-Bolsheviks, who perceived Nazism as a line of defence against Soviet expansion into Europe – both geographically and ideologically. As the war progressed, and the Soviet Union became one of the Allies, this group was shaken to the core because, as they saw it, the British were on the wrong side. (Of course, this is how Hitler himself viewed the situation, boasting when interviewed by Pierre van Paassen in 1928 of his aim of destroying the Soviet Union 'to the applause of the whole civilised world'.[7])

There were other reasons to be pro-German in those unsettled and anxious days. Many industrialists and financiers had invested heavily in German industry during the 1930s, often encouraged by Montagu Norman. There were several major banking concerns that were Anglo-German ventures. It is no exaggeration to say that, almost to a man, the City was opposed to a war with Germany, and, once it had begun, desired Britain to extricate itself as soon as possible. As the US Military Attaché in London reported to Washington as late as December 1940, the City 'was ready for appeasement at any time'.[8] Some industrialists – such as Lord McGowan, who had attended the 1938 Nuremberg Rally – were ideologically committed to peace as staunch supporters of Hitler, but most were against war because of its devastating effect on economic and social stability. Many industrialists feared that a war would encourage the working classes to move to the left and increase the power of the unions – it had happened after the First World War and it was likely that, even if Britain won this war, the same would happen again, but even more radically. Of course, their worst nightmares came true: not only did trade union membership increase from 6.25 million to 8 million during the Second World War[9] – a rise of 30 per cent – but the first elections held after VE Day saw a Labour landslide. (A case in point is what happened to the fortunes of the Duke of Hamilton: the nationalisation of the mining industry meant that the Hamiltons lost their coal mines to the government virtually overnight.)

There were other fears that ran particularly deep with the old order, especially among the imperialists who feared that Britain would have to incur another massive war debt, increasing its dependence on the United States. They foresaw that this chain of events would ultimately lead to the breakup of the British Empire – and once again, in most respects, their fears were justified. The monarchy and some of the most ancient noble houses feared that the old order would be undermined and their own power with it. Most of these great dynasties had German branches, and shared the view that Bolshevism was the real enemy – especially after what it had done to the Tsar and his family, to whom many of them were related. Because of such concerns, most members of the House of Lords also desired a settled peace, and as the landowning classes also had a significant presence in the Commons, so did many members of the lower house. A study in 1938 showed that 238 Conservative MPs came from the nobility or landed gentry.[10] (Clydesdale was an MP before becoming the Duke of Hamilton and being elevated to the Lords.)

Britain's leading landowner, the Duke of Westminster, organised the anti-war peers into a group that would lobby the government for peace.[11] This highly influential body included the former Conservative MP Henry Drummond-Wolff (who believed that the war was being encouraged by the USA, the USSR and a Jewish-dominated press), Lord Aberconway, the Labour peer Lord Buxton and the Duke of Buccleuch, whose sister Alice was married to the Duke of Gloucester, the King's younger brother. From 1937 Buccleuch was Keeper of His Majesty's Household – a prestigious appointment that also automatically made him a Privy Councillor, one of the King's hand-picked advisers. By virtue of his high office, he was also the monarch's 'liaison' with the House of Lords, which meant that all messages from the King to the upper house went through him. Perhaps it is significant that, even as late as 1937, George VI should have appointed such a well-known and contro-versial pro-German to this position. Even more significantly, the role was removed from Buccleuch by Churchill in 1940 because of his then arguably treacherous pro-German sentiments (although he continued to be a Privy Councillor).[12] The title was given instead to the Duke of Hamilton. It is also interesting that the standing that Buccleuch retained in the eyes of the Royal Family is demonstrated by the fact that George VI wanted the Duke's son and heir, Johnny Dalkeith, to marry Princess Margaret. Indeed, according to Lord Glenconner, had the King not died when he did he would have insisted on the match.[13]

Buccleuch was a particularly vocal pro-German even after war broke out, which is presumably why he was also placed under close surveillance by MI5. In February 1940 he stated publicly that the war would 'play into the hands of Soviet Russia, Jews and Americans',[14] and would also destroy the empire. Another peer who argued vocif-erously for peace with Germany was the Duke of Bedford, who produced a lengthy series of pamphlets throughout the war – at one stage even making overtures to the German Embassy in neutral Dublin. Bedford proposed that one of the terms of settlement between the warring countries should be the setting up of a com-mission to find a Jewish homeland. (Ironically, part of Bedford's stately home, Woburn Abbey, was given over to the Headquarters of the Special Operations Executive (SOE) for the duration of the war.)

While the official line on the war was hawkish and jingoistic, foreign observers could see quite another side to the British. In August 1940 President Roosevelt, for example, following a report from journalist Fulton Oursler, expressed his amazement that 'some of the greatest people in the British Empire, men of the so-called upper classes, men of the highest rank, secretly want to appease

Hitler and stop the war'.[15] But how far did this desire for peace reach up the social ladder? What were the Royal Family's true sentiments about the war?

Although the Duke of Windsor, the former Edward VIII, is usually singled out for his support of Germany and his ill-advised visits to Hitler after his abdication – recently earning him the title of the 'Traitor King' – he was by no means the only member of the Royal Family to be opposed to the war. Perhaps British royalty was naturally predisposed towards Germany because their roots were solidly Hanoverian. However, all the royal houses of Europe shared a kinship with the German aristocracy (the Kaiser had been George VI's 'Uncle Willi'), and the House of Windsor's wartime matriarch, Queen Mary, was of German blood and upbringing. As wife of George V and mother of Edward VIII and George VI, the former Princess Victoria Mary ('May') of Teck had enormous influence both within her own large family and in the wider society of the aristocracy. Dr John Charmley, writing in the *Sunday Telegraph* in December 1996, stated:

> George V, Edward VIII and George VI all deplored the prospect of another Anglo-German war, which, given their ancestry, they all had reason to regard as something akin to an internecine conflict: the first threatened to 'wave a red flag' in Trafalgar Square, if that was what it took to avoid a war; the second certainly expressed admiration for the Nazi regime, and after his abdication met Hitler; but only the last actually offered positive support for appeasement.[16]

The sadly diminished former King, the Duke of Windsor, has become something of a convenient scapegoat for more revered members of the Royal Family. Recently it has been stated that Queen Elizabeth (now the Queen Mother) was very much in favour of appeasement and a fervent supporter of both Neville Chamberlain and Lord Halifax[17] – and there is no doubt that the rest of the Royal Family agreed with her position to a greater or lesser degree.

In February 1939, just four months after the violence of Kristallnacht, George VI became concerned that unauthorised Jewish refugees from Germany and Austria were surreptitiously entering Palestine. He asked his private secretary to write to his close friend the Foreign Secretary, Lord Halifax, urging him to take steps to stop it. Two days later the British Ambassador in Berlin was instructed to urge the German government to do what it could to stop the emigration.[18]

Charmley points out that an important factor in Churchill's political insecurity – which lasted at least until late 1942 – was the lack of confidence and support he received from the King and Queen. He says: 'Like most of those who supported appeasement, the Royal Family quietly changed sides and rewrote history.'[19]

Key men and kingmakers

Although Chamberlain rapidly became the scapegoat for the failed peace attempt of 1938, his policies were firmly supported by his cabinet, several members of which were to become key figures in this investigation. One name that repeatedly surfaces is Sir Samuel Hoare, whose role in the run-up to Hess's flight was considerable. As a Quaker, Hoare – who became Viscount Templewood in 1944 – held strong views on the iniquities of war and the necessity to seek any and every means of avoiding it. During the Great War he was a secret service officer stationed in Moscow, where he built up contacts with the Swedish aristocracy and Royal Family, and where he saw the evils of the Russian Revolution at first hand.[20] Later in 1917 he became chief of military intelligence in Italy, using his influence to get to know the then newspaper editor Benito Mussolini, actively encouraging him in his anti-Communist activities. After this he entered politics, becoming a Conservative MP in 1920, progressing to several ministerial posts, including Secretary of State for Air (1922–9) and eventually rising to the post of Foreign Secretary in 1935. He was regarded by many as a Prime Minister in waiting.[21]

On 3 October 1935 Mussolini's Italian army invaded Abyssinia (Ethiopia). Then Foreign Secretary in the newly elected government of Stanley Baldwin, Hoare tried to negotiate a compromise peace, together with the French Prime Minister Pierre Laval, eventually devising what is known as the Hoare–Laval Pact. Under this arrangement, Italy could keep a large part of Abyssinia – a foretaste of Chamberlain's later appeasement policy at Munich. When news of the plan leaked out there was uproar in the House, especially from the opposition. Although Baldwin and the cabinet had approved the pact, Hoare himself became the scapegoat and, in order to protect the new Prime Minister in his first major crisis, he did the honourable thing and resigned. This was not the end of his influence, however: during the abdication crisis he was chosen by Edward VIII as one of his closest advisers, becoming great friends with the embattled monarch. Still very much a force to be reckoned with politically, he held the post of Home Secretary between 1937 and 1939.

Hoare believed in exploring every possible avenue to settle disputes peacefully. As Foreign Secretary in 1935 he made a speech in the Commons in which he stated that the search for peace would be the centrepiece of Britain's foreign policy[22] – a sentiment that earned him several enemies. Sir Alexander Cadogan, the permanent undersecretary to the Foreign Office – never an admirer of Sir Samuel – wrote uncompromisingly of Hoare and his wife Maud in his diary in May 1940: 'The sooner we get them out of the country the better. I'd rather send them to a penal colony. He'll be the Quisling of England when Germany conquers us and I'm dead.'[23]

Two other central figures were Lord Halifax, Foreign Secretary from 1938 until November 1940, and his under-secretary, R. A. (Richard Austen – 'Rab') Butler. Halifax, although a minister, was a peer and therefore in the House of Lords, whereas Butler was the Foreign Office's representative in the Commons, so it proved particularly useful for them to work as a team. Both men were staunch supporters of Chamberlain's policies, continuing to explore ways of bringing about peace even after the outbreak of war. Halifax described Churchill and his supporters as 'gangsters'[24] – an epithet gleefully seized upon by the Nazi propaganda machine. Halifax not only disliked and distrusted Churchill, but was his chief rival for the job of Prime Minister after Chamberlain's resignation. Professor Scott Newton writes:

> Halifax and Butler's profound misgivings about continuing the war if there was any chance of escape with dignity placed them at the centre of a peace movement which was connected to all the core institutions of the Conservative Party. The presence within it of Queen Mary, the Dukes of Westminster and Buccleuch, Lords Aberconway, Bearsted, Brockett, Buckmaster, Harmsworth, Londonderry, Mansfield and Rushcliffe, as well as of at least thirty MPs, demonstrated the enduring nature of the lobby's links to the

court, the City, large-scale industry and to the landowning aristocracy . . .

All its members shared a profound fear that the domestic and
international order which had sustained liberal-imperialist Britain
was about to be irrevocably changed . . . With some justification it
was believed that total war meant the socialization of Britain and a
ruinous conflict in the heart of Europe from which only the Soviet
Union could benefit.[25]

Another major figure in the events surrounding Hess's arrival was
the flamboyant tycoon-turned-politician Lord Beaverbrook. Born
William Maxwell Aitken in Ontario, Canada, of Scottish emigrant
parents in 1864, he made a fortune in financial deals, went to Britain
in July 1910 – and within four months of arriving was an MP (at that
time, Canadians enjoyed full British citizenship). The cornerstone of
Beaverbrook's political beliefs was empire free trade, or what he
called 'splendid isolation', based on the idea that Britain's best economic interest lay in the resources of its empire.[26] He rejected
increasing monetary ties with Europe, being adamant that Britain
should keep out of continental European affairs. Anti-American to
his back teeth, Beaverbrook was a lifelong friend of Sir Samuel
Hoare, and enjoyed above all the role of behind-the-scenes mediator – in the words of his biographer and close friend A. J. P Taylor,
'the go-between, the man who tried to arrange compromise between
the contending political leaders'.[27] Beaverbrook delighted in arranging secret meetings, either between rival party leaders or outright
enemies, playing this role in the 1913 talks over Irish Home Rule
and even acting as secret adviser to Sinn Féin in the negotiations of
October 1921. But it was his acquisition of the *Daily Express* in 1916,
and the part this played in the downfall of a wartime Prime Minister,
that was to prove most significant to our investigation.

At the time, Prime Minister Herbert Asquith headed a strong
coalition and seemed to sail serenely on calm waters, secure in his
position. But suddenly, in the course of just a few days in late
November and early December 1916, he was swept from power –
being forced to resign on 5 December – to be replaced by David
Lloyd George. This abrupt change at the top was the result of a
'palace coup' orchestrated by a small group of conspirators and
power-brokers, one of them being Beaverbrook. His plotting did not

go unrewarded: four days after coming to power, Lloyd George gave him his peerage, and two months later he took his seat in the House of Lords. All this happened so swiftly largely because he had used the *Express* to set the wheels in motion by criticising Asquith; although he had bought the newspaper just a few weeks before, he later suppressed the date to disguise its connection with the coup.[28] Twenty years later, when asked what he considered to be the 'biggest thing' he'd ever done, he replied: 'The destruction of the Asquith government which was brought about by honest intrigue.'[29] Beaverbrook soon established himself as a formidable kingmaker, a role that he played with aplomb and great personal delight.

In 1940 his relish for power-broking was undiminished. As his biographers Anne Chisholm and Michael Davie write: 'Having thought that the war could have been prevented by giving Hitler a free hand in Europe, Beaverbrook thought after it started it could and should be stopped.'[30] In January that year he met with the Duke of Windsor during one of his visits to London. Royal adviser Walter Monckton, who was present, reported: 'Both found themselves in agreement that the war should be ended at once by a peace offer to Germany.'[31]

Keeping the slogan 'There Will Be No War' in his newspapers until the very brink of hostilities, Beaverbrook wrote as part of his 'creed': 'I Believe [*sic*] that the pursuit of Peace is the highest and most moral task before civilisation.'[32] As Taylor said, he made no bones about considering Britain's entry into the war as 'mistaken and unnecessary'.[33] He had been 'reluctant to enter the first world war. He was resolutely opposed to entering the second.'[34] As war loomed, Beaverbrook declared his belief that British Jews were pushing the country into an unnecessary war[35] – although to the end of his days he maintained he was anti-Zionist, not anti-Semitic.

Other key players in the assembled dramatis personae include another former Foreign and Home Secretary, Sir John Simon, Chamberlain's Chancellor of the Exchequer – and very much a supporter of appeasement. Simon would be one of those Churchill chose to interview Hess after the flight. Then there is David Lloyd George, the former Prime Minister and, by 1939, a much-respected elder statesman. Having sampled Hitler's hospitality at his mountaintop retreat, the Berghof at Berchtesgaden, he returned with nothing but praise for the Führer and was more firmly than ever convinced of the desirability of averting war. When Germany invaded Poland in September 1939, Lloyd George – who had opposed giving Upper Silesia to Poland in 1919 – declared that that country 'deserved its fate'.[36] When Churchill became Prime Minister in May 1940, the Commons' opposition to his leadership focused on Lloyd George as the most suitable candidate for getting them out of the mess.

Meanwhile, as always, the intelligence agencies followed their own agendas. MI6 in particular worked diligently behind the scenes to change the course of the war, being mainly concerned with the threat from Soviet Communism – to them, the real enemy. The head of MI6, Sir Stewart Menzies – whose identity was a state secret, hidden under the customary codename of 'C' – was himself a prominent member of the peace group. Significantly, his elevation from deputy to head of the department (after the death of his predecessor) was strenuously opposed by Churchill, then First Lord of the Admiralty and a member of the War Cabinet, precisely because of his anti-war stance.[37] Like many of his peers, Menzies advocated making peace with Germany in order to allow it to turn its full attention on Soviet Russia. Whoever won that conflict, both would be greatly weakened – to Britain's advantage.

Menzies' influence should not be underestimated. As head of MI6 he had the right of access at any time of the day or night to the King, Prime Minister and Foreign Secretary, making him one of the most powerful men in the country.[38] According to Scott Newton, he was at the very centre of the disparate sections of the Establishment who wanted peace:

Menzies . . . had a network of connections in the City and multinational industry as well as in the Royal Court. This network was dominated by those who had espoused 'imperial isolationism' during the 1930s. It included the Duke of Buccleuch, Lord Steward of the Royal Household, and a governor of the Royal Bank of Scotland, Lieutenant-Colonel W. S. Pilcher of the Coldstream Guards [*sic* – he was in the Grenadier Guards], Lord Bearsted, founder of Samuel's (the merchant bank) and chairman of the Nineteen Twenty-Eight Investment Trust as well as of Shell Transport and Trading, the British holding company for Dutch Shell; Lord Londonderry, like Lothian a member of the Anglo-German Fellowship; Baldwin Raper, the managing director of Shell-Mex; and Sir Robert Renwick, the stockbroker and industrialist who had met Göring shortly before the war.[39]

Knights of the air

There is one group whose key role in the attempts to strengthen Anglo-German relations in the 1930s is barely recognised today, yet its influence was crucial, certainly in events surrounding the Hess affair. This is what we call the 'aviation group', which consisted of senior officers of the RAF and officials of the Air Ministry, particularly centring on the RAF Club. This circle was targeted by the Nazis even before they came to power, as can be seen from a report drawn up for Hitler by Alfred Rosenberg in 1935:

> The attempts to find people in England who were eager to comprehend the German movement date back to 1929. Our English agent R. [Baron William de Ropp] in Berlin then made possible my first journey to London in 1931. There it was possible to make a number of contacts which worked out well for Anglo-German understanding. In the forefront here was Squadron Leader W. [Frederick W. Winterbotham], a member of the Air General Staff, who was entirely convinced that Germany and England must move together to ward off the Bolshevik danger. The outcome of the various discussions was the widening of the group amongst the Air General Staff, and the Royal Air Force Club became a centre for fostering Anglo-German understanding.[40]

Winterbotham was the RAF officer who was made head of MI6's new Air Intelligence Section in 1930. In the First World War he had been Baron de Ropp's commanding officer in the Royal Flying Corps, maintaining close contact with him afterwards. De Ropp was from a noble Baltic family but settled in Britain in 1910, becoming a naturalised British citizen and marrying an Englishwoman. In 1920 he went to live in Berlin, where he became a close friend of Alfred Rosenberg – who introduced him to Hitler and Hess – and his liaison with pro-German circles in Britain. Underlying the intrigues of Winterbotham and de Ropp was their shared membership of the 'aviation group', an exclusive fraternity whose bonds crossed national boundaries. They saw themselves as something like an order of chivalry, fighting according to a code of honourable conduct. This can be seen in the way German airmen – as opposed to German soldiers or sailors – were portrayed during the war. For example, the British propaganda weekly *War Illustrated* (which appeared as soon as war was declared) depicted the German army and navy as ruthless, brutal louts, but – at least before the Blitz – portrayed aerial combat as a duel between 'knights of the air'. It seems incredible now, but the first Luftwaffe crews who were shot down and killed over Britain were buried with full military honours. It is disconcerting to come across newspaper photographs of coffins draped with swastika flags and flanked by a guard of honour made up of respectfully saluting British bobbies, either lying in solemn state in a church or being driven on carriages through the streets. What was it about the airmen that prompted such awe and respect in their enemies? Perhaps it had some connection with the fact that in the air force it was the officers, from good middle- and upper-class families, who did the fighting, while it was the lower classes who serviced and maintained their glamorous flying machines – just like the squires of old whose job it was to look after the knights' horses and their armour.

This noble ideal also found expression in the Guild of Air Pilots and Air Navigators, which was and is mainly concerned with air safety. But that, too, was organised on quasi-Masonic lines, their Grand Master in the late 1930s and early 1940s being none other than the Grand Master of English Freemasons, the Duke of Kent. (The Guild's Grand Master is now the Duke of Edinburgh.) As we were to discover, it would be a serious mistake to overlook the significance of Kent's oath of loyalty to his fellow airmen – irrespective of their nationality or political persuasion.

Prime movers

These, then, are the disparate elements that made up the peace group – clearly an enormously powerful upswelling of opinion that was by no means as unpopular in its day as some historians would have us believe. We have the King, the Queen, the mother of the King, a former Prime Minister and two potential Premiers, a large part of the aristocracy and many of the country's leading industrialists and financiers all sharing the same desire to make peace with

Germany. However, although all these different parties wanted to negotiate with the enemy, it was not to be peace at any price. Although they firmly believed that it was either in Britain's or their own best interests not to become embroiled in a war, they were not advocating surrender. The terms would have to be acceptable, but what could they have been? Obviously they would have varied from group to group. Halifax and Butler, for example, wanted Hitler to be removed from power, whereas others insisted that the safety of German Jews was part of the deal. Others still would probably simply have been happy for Britain to get out of the war in one piece, without giving anything up to Germany. Yet although they had their different variants on the same theme, together they formed one great organic whole, a large and powerful body of opinion highly receptive to offers of negotiations.

Their power can be illustrated by Churchill's riposte, when on 8 June 1940 – his premiership just a month old – there were calls for an inquiry into the 'appeasement party' with a view to prosecuting its members. He replied that this would be 'foolish' as 'There are too many in it'.[41] (Ironically, we came across the record of this exchange in the Hamilton Muniments, the family archive within the Scottish Record Office.)

The road to war

While the rest of Europe – by and large – dithered and flapped, Hitler set about fulfilling the ambitions he had originally outlined in *Mein Kampf*. Like many fanatics, he was remarkably focused and consistent, sticking to a rigid agenda for the creation of the Greater Germany. First came his annexation of Austria in the *Anschluss* (connection, or union) of May 1938, which was essentially a response to one of the more controversial decisions of the Allies after the First World War. In direct contravention of the avowed principle of a people's right to self-determination, Austrians were denied a plebiscite to decide whether they wanted to unite with Germany. Of course, Hitler of all people was hardly going to offer them a referendum: he simply told the Austrian Chancellor, Kurt von Schuschnigg, that Austria was now to be one with Germany. Not surprisingly, von Schuschnigg resigned. He had little choice: on 12 May 1938 Hitler marched in his troops, adding a note of finality to the proceedings. (However, it must be said that an overwhelming majority of Austrians supported the union.)

The rest of Europe was aghast, particularly at the speed with which Hitler had moved. As historian Robert Shepherd says: 'An independent country had disappeared within a weekend, and with scarcely a shot fired.'[42] For his part, Hitler had taken some account of other countries' sensibilities, although his choice of adviser was somewhat unfortunate: according to James Murphy, von Ribbentrop had reassured him by showing him letters from supporters in the 'British nobility' that there would be no British intervention if he annexed Austria.[43]

Against a backdrop of rising international tension, Hitler then demanded the return of the ethnically German part of Czechoslovakia – the Sudetenland. His path was smoothed by the agitation of the local Nazis, whose strikes and demonstrations roused their fellow Germans to a state of righteous fury, aided by Hess's foreign organisations, principally the AO. As Hitler made it clear that he intended to take the Sudetenland by force if necessary, Britain and France were faced with a stark question: was it worth going to war over? While the crisis deepened, the British prepared for the worst-case scenario by issuing gas masks and digging air-raid shelters. Meanwhile, the politicians wrestled with the problem. On 27 September 1938 Neville Chamberlain made what is now considered to be one of his more embarrassing gaffes during a radio broadcast. He wondered whether it was worth going to war over 'a quarrel in a faraway country between people of whom we know nothing'.[44] Often quoted as a prime example of Chamberlain's lily-livered attitude to foreign policy – not to mention his insensitivity – his words accurately reflected the views of the majority of the people at the time. Then there was the problem of Germany's ultimate threat. Even if the Sudetenland crisis were somehow averted, was a war with Germany still inevitable? Should Britain face the situation and make a tough stand now? Chamberlain – and the majority of his cabinet and party – took one view of this, while others, notably Winston Churchill, took another. As the crisis deepened, Chamberlain offered to meet Hitler to try to find a compromise. While the elderly statesman made three visits to the Berghof, Godesberg and Munich (the first time he had ever flown), Britain held its breath. When Chamberlain announced to the Commons that Hitler had agreed to the third meeting, in Munich, wild cheering broke out (witnessed, from the public gallery, by Queen Mary and the Duke and Duchess of Kent[45]). The result was the now-infamous Munich Agreement, signed by the Prime Minister and the Führer on 29 September 1938 – the 'piece of paper' waved so triumphantly on the plane steps that proved to be utterly worthless.

Chamberlain was mobbed when he arrived at Downing Street and the cabinet meeting at which he was trying to brief his ministers was interrupted by the strains of 'For He's a Jolly Good Fellow' drifting in from outside. There was even something of a merchandising madness: special souvenir photographs of the Prime Minister were produced and Neville Chamberlain dolls and sugar umbrellas with his name picked out in icing were sold on street corners.[46] The Poet Laureate, John Masefield, contributed a poem in his honour, which appeared in *The Times*. None of this seemed like a deeply humiliating folly at the time. The royal invitation to Chamberlain to appear alongside them on the Palace balcony had a deeper purpose than a simple celebration that war had been averted. By according the Prime Minister this exceptional honour, and publicly showing their approval of the agreement *before* he took it to the Cabinet or Parliament for endorsement, the King and Queen had effectively made it impossible for those bodies to do anything else than rubber stamp it.

We now know, of course, that it was Hitler who benefited from the Munich Agreement, although it is less well remembered that it also handed over parts of Czechoslovakia to Poland and Hungary. Six months later his troops occupied Bohemia and Moravia, including the capital Prague. Once again, it was more or less a bloodless operation, the Czech President Emil Hacha having been personally bullied by the Führer into ordering his troops not to resist.

Hitler now turned his attention to the matter of Poland. Although once an independent nation, it had been swallowed up by the Tsars, but at the negotiations that led to the Treaty of Versailles the Poles pressed and won their claim to become independent again. They did more than that: the newly acknowledged state of Poland, a landlocked country, had asked for access to the Baltic – and had been given a strip of German land leading to the coast, which became known as the 'Polish Corridor', but which separated East Prussia from the rest of Germany. Matters escalated when the port of

Danzig – with a 90 per cent German population – at the end of the Corridor, was declared a free port under the administration of the League of Nations. This arrangement was detestable to many Germans and especially to Hitler. He wanted both the Corridor as a whole and Danzig in particular back. If they were not forthcoming, he would take them back by force. Once again, ethnic Germans in the disputed area began to agitate, while back at home stories circulated in the German press about discrimination against ethnic Germans, often including outright violence.

Hitler knew that after his reneging on the Munich deal there was no chance that Chamberlain would offer to engage in talks over Poland. It was clear to everyone that a world war hovered in the shadows, and so the situation became an intense diplomatic game among Germany, Poland, Britain, France and the Soviet Union. But within Britain there was a certain embarrassment. As the British Ambassador to Berlin, Sir Nevile Henderson, wrote: 'The Corridor and Danzig were a real German national grievance, and some equitable settlement had got to be found in respect of these questions if there was ever to be genuine peace in the future between Germany and Poland. This was, in reality, fully appreciated by His Majesty's Government . . .'[47] On the other hand, there was the fear that Danzig might not represent the end of Hitler's ambitions. Even if a settlement were found, would he honour it – or, as with Czechoslovakia, would it prove only a temporary respite? This time Chamberlain made it clear that if Germany resorted to the use of force, Britain would come to Poland's aid. France made the same promise. So when Poland cried out for help, Britain could hardly turn its back. Although Britain's military capability was by no means strong enough to defend Poland, Chamberlain had no choice but to commit Britain to its defence against the Nazis. Under the circumstances, to break his word would be to commit personal political suicide, not to mention terminally damaging Britain's standing on the international stage.

Yet there is a mystery concerning the outbreak of war. We know that Hitler had no wish to become Britain's enemy – quite the reverse, in fact – so why did he persist in embarking on a course of action that could have no other outcome? High-ranking Nazis have since testified that Hitler was utterly convinced that – when it came to the crunch – Chamberlain would not take the ultimate step that led to war. The Führer may have been overconfident because of the pact he had just made with the Soviet Union, but it is more likely that he had put his trust in the advice of von Ribbentrop to the effect that Britain would back down. Many Germans, such as the Haushofers, blamed the war on von Ribbentrop. As the German Ambassador to the Court of St James – although widely considered to be a bumbling fool – he did have friends in high places and might have been fatally misled by their private opinion of the way the government would go. He often dined with Edward VIII and Mrs Simpson and the Kents, for example.

There may not have been too many overt or official overtures to Germany at that time, but there were frantic efforts behind the scenes to avert the coming catastrophe, which were backed up by Chamberlain and his supporters, especially Lord Halifax. And the diplomatic efforts were not all from the British side: in June 1939 Göring's representative, Helmut Wohltat, used his position as a delegate to the International Whaling Commission to have meetings in London with Chamberlain's chief industrial adviser, Sir Horace Wilson, to discuss ways of avoiding the war through negotiation.[48] Unfortunately, a press leak spelled the end of that idea, but there were other attempts, some more promising.

In early August 1939 a delegation of seven British businessmen met Göring in order to offer concessions that could prevent the outbreak of hostilities. The existence of this mission has been known for a long time, and largely dismissed – in the words of historian Donald Cameron Watt, writing in 1989 – as being made up of 'well-meaning amateurs'.[49] The group consisted of Lord Aberconway (then chairman of the shipbuilders John Brown & Co. and Westland Aircraft); Sir Edward Mortimer Mountain (chairman of Eagle Star Insurance, among other companies); Charles F. Spencer (chairman of Edison Swan Cables); and the prominent stockbroker Sir Robert Renwick. But in 1999 the last surviving member of the delegation, Lord Aberconway, finally revealed that far from being an ad hoc group, it had been sanctioned by Lord Halifax and very probably by Chamberlain himself. The delegation was acting on behalf of the British government, with the aim of persuading Hitler to make the offer of peace talks, which Chamberlain would argue it was his moral obligation to accept.

The meeting had been arranged by a friend of Göring, Birger

Dahlerus, a Swedish businessman with interests in Britain – he was managing director of Electrolux – who was also in contact with Lord Halifax. Dahlerus was assisted on the British side by Electrolux's chairman, Sir Harold Wernher.[50] At a preliminary meeting in London's Constitutional Club in early July, Charles Spencer read from a prepared document that if Hitler had not broken the Munich Agreement he 'would have been considered the greatest German leader of all time'.[51]

The meeting with Göring and several high-level advisers took place on 7–8 August in a farmhouse – with the wonderful name of Soonke Nissen Koog – belonging to Dahlerus's wife near the German–Danish border. Though keeping to the party line about standing by Poland, the British delegation offered Germany 'financial and industrial prosperity and the *Lebensraum* she had been seeking' if she did not invade Poland. They proposed a four-power conference with Chamberlain, Hitler, Mussolini and French Prime Minister Edouard Daladier to negotiate a solution to the Danzig crisis. They had come prepared with answers to questions Göring might ask: it is particularly interesting to note their planned response to a question about why Britain continued to support the Jews: 'In the past England has never been preyed upon by the Jews to the extent Germany has.' In the event, however, the question was never asked. In turn, Göring promised that Germany would never attack Britain, which has been taken as a prime example of his – and Hitler's – duplicity. But the fact is that they had no intention of waging war with Britain – unless Britain declared war first.

Obviously this mission failed, probably because Hitler took it as a sign that Britain would not take up arms to defend Poland (despite the delegates' lip service to the party line). However, there was another last-ditch attempt to broker a peace deal: Labour peer Lord Charles Roden Buxton went to Munich, where he met Rudolf Hess on 17 August 1939. Documents in the Public Record Office show that, although this was ostensibly an unofficial, personal mission, Buxton had the backing of Lord Halifax and that, apart from Buxton's brother Noel, the only other people aware of the plan were Chamberlain and Sir Samuel Hoare.[52]

Birger Dahlerus also persisted in his efforts to avert war. On 31 August 1939 – the day before Germany invaded Poland – he had an eleventh-hour meeting with Göring in Berlin, after which he tele-phoned Chamberlain in person from the British Embassy.[53]

Russian roulette

Were there other ways of dissuading Hitler from waging all-out war? Chamberlain decided to add the Soviet Union to the exist-ing alliance between France and Britain in order to build up the Allies' muscle power. A team of British and French diplomats were duly dispatched to Moscow to try to work out a mutually acceptable deal – but it was doomed from the start. Stalin had no reason to trust the British. He had offered a defence pact with Britain and France as early as March 1939, following the German seizure of Prague. But the British and French governments were distinctly lukewarm about the offer – the British in particular pro-crastinated, largely because of Chamberlain's personal hatred of Bolshevism. Stalin already feared that Britain and France were trying to provoke a German–Soviet war, and their lack of enthu-siasm for his plan only increased his suspicions. He decided to turn the tables by making his own pact with Germany, effectively slamming the door on the prospect of peace and ensuring a war, which could only assist the expansion of Bolshevism in Europe. While the Anglo-French team were immersed in long-drawn-out talks with representatives of the Soviet Foreign Ministry in Moscow, a secret agreement was already being drawn up between Germany and the USSR. On 23 August, Germany's Foreign Minster, von Ribbentrop, abruptly appeared in Moscow to sign a pact of non-aggression with his Russian counterpart, Vyacheslav Molotov.

The pact gave Stalin an immediate advantage. There was also a secret protocol – which has only become known since the war – which set out the parts of Poland that Germany and Russia would each take in the event of a 'territorial and political rearrangement' of the country.[54] (It was this that Hess's defence counsel sought to invoke at Nuremberg.) The two countries would, if circumstances dictated, further discuss the 'question of whether the interests of both parties make desirable the maintenance of an independent Polish state'. In other words, Hitler and Stalin had already divided up Poland between them – at least in principle.

This joint arrangement was so secret that even Hitler's commanders were unaware of it as the Polish offensive began. The German army's Chief of Operations, General Alfred Jodl, reacted with alarm when told that the Russian army had entered Poland, asking: 'Against whom?'[55]

The unaskable question

Recently historians have begun to ask what was for sixty years the great unaskable question: should Britain ever have got involved in this conflict at all? Although the propaganda of over half a century can weigh heavy from time to time, it should be possible to come up with an objective answer, even if it is not one that many people want to hear.

Britain's avowed reason for entering the conflict was to protect the sovereignty of Poland – to defend the principle that one state should not take parts of another by force. Britain and France had a mutual defence pact with Poland, so both countries were simply fulfilling their obligations in coming to the defence of the underdog. However, there is a glaring inconsistency: Poland was invaded by two aggressors – Germany from the west and, seventeen days later, the Soviet Union from the east, as a result of their secret deal. The Polish government went into exile, and its nation ceased to exist.

A new Polish government was set up in Paris on 30 September, with General Władysław Sikorski as Prime Minister. He had been Chief of Staff to the Polish armed forces between 1919 and 1925. When France fell in June 1940 he was in London for talks with Churchill, and shortly afterwards he moved the Polish government in exile to Scotland, where it remained for the duration of the war.

Michael Bentine, who acted as a liaison officer with the Free Polish forces, made an important point to one of us: whereas many Poles hated the Germans, all of them hated the Russians. To them – Sikorski included – Russia was the real and enduring enemy. This is important because the Poles in exile were very deeply involved in the Hess affair, and it must be remembered that they were open to the idea of a settlement with Germany, and in favour of a war between the Nazis and Soviets if it would get the Russians out of Poland.

So if Britain's reason for declaring war was the principle of sovereignty, why did it only declare war on one of Poland's aggressors?

Why Germany and not Russia? Immediately on hearing of the invasion of Poland by Russia, the British government pointed out that their treaty with Poland only applied to an attack by Germany, so therefore Britain was not obliged to declare war on the Soviet Union. Although this is correct where the letter of the law is concerned, it certainly begs the question about the spirit.

The British Ambassador in Moscow, Sir William Seeds, sent a message to London saying that 'Soviet invasion is not without advantage to us in the long run'[56] while Sir Alexander Cadogan stated: 'It would be unwise to proclaim that we stand for the old boundaries of Poland. Such an attitude would render inevitable a conflict with Russia.'[57] And a Foreign Office minute of 6 December 1939 took pains to note that 'We have been very careful to avoid committing ourselves to any guarantee to restore Polish frontiers.'[58] There is another great 'unthinkable' involved. Although Britain and her Allies may have 'won' the war, the fact is that they failed dismally to achieve their original objectives. Although Britain went to war to defend Poland's sovereign rights, six long years of carnage later she agreed, at the Yalta Conference, to accept the Soviet Union's occupation of that same country. Poland simply exchanged one brutal foreign master for another.

The problem was that Britain's history where the issue of sovereignty was concerned was not very impressive. Britain had refused to support Poland in its war with the Soviet Union in 1919–20 in spite of its clear obligation to do so under the Treaty of Versailles.[59] And when France occupied the Ruhr region of Germany in the 1920s, the British government contented itself with a written protest – a slap on the wrist, no more.[60] Nor did Britain honour its obligations to China when Nanking was invaded by Japan in 1937. For that matter, the principle of sovereignty was hardly mentioned when Poland itself annexed part of Czechoslovakia in 1938, nor when Yugoslavia invaded the southern parts of that country a year later. It seemed some countries were fair game, while others were only useful as pawns in a much wider strategy. The principles involved were, it seems, optional.

The second reason most often cited for the war starting is purely moral, not political. Many people believe that the Second World War – although terrible and tragic – was a necessary evil in order to fight Nazism, particularly to take arms against what Hitler was doing to the Jews. Although in the final analysis this is a just cause, it was not the reason why Britain went to war.

Hitler's policies towards the Jews attracted criticism in Britain, although – as we have seen – the atrocities of the Holocaust were still unimaginable in 1939. The Nazis may have made no secret of their wish to rid the Greater Germany of all Jews, but they planned to do so by mass deportation: an odious idea, of course, but a far cry from the death camps.

In any case, a long hard look at the regime Britain allegedly went to war to defend makes one wonder just what the moral principles were. Re-emerging as an independent nation after the First World War, Poland was set up as a parliamentary democracy, but only managed to maintain this veneer of democracy for eight years. In May 1926 Marshal Józef Piłsudski, the original architect of the democratic Polish constitution, led a military coup and became Poland's dictator in all but name. Although elections continued, they were shams: faced with possible defeat in 1930, Piłsudski's Sanacja regime ensured victory by having its opponents arrested. And when a coalition of opposition parties complained about the 'actual dictatorship of Józef Piłsudski', he had its leaders arrested too.[61] After his death in 1935 (coincidentally on the anniversary of his coup), the army continued to govern, forming a movement called the Camp of National Unity, which – in the words of historian Norman M. Davies – was a 'much more disciplined and exclusive organisation on the military model'.[62] Opponents of the new regime were summarily rounded up and interned in concentration camps – as were many Jewish currency speculators, who were blamed for a financial crisis in 1937.[63]

Apart from its internal strife, Poland was hardly peaceful towards its neighbours between the wars, fighting six campaigns against the Ukraine, Lithuania, Czechoslovakia, and most seriously against the Soviet Union from February 1919 until October 1920. And until mid-1921 there were also frequent outbreaks of fighting along the German–Silesian border, mostly against Freikorps groups. Most ironically, however, in 1934 Piłsudski had considered declaring war on Germany, but failed to get the support of Britain and France.[64]

There is another grave irony. Just as the Nazis have become the byword for anti-Semitism since the war, the Poles were renowned for their persecution of the Jews before it. When Poland was formally recognised by the Treaty of Versailles, the British economist J. M.

Keynes declared it to be 'an economic impossibility whose only industry is Jew-baiting'.[65] Since the Middle Ages Poland had been the Jewish heartland of Europe – by the nineteenth century, 80 per cent of the world's Jews lived there. This was clearly not to the liking of many Poles, who invented the word 'pogrom' to describe their preferred way of dealing with them. In 1919 a congress of the Association of Poles of the Jewish Faith issued a plea that their situation might improve: 'The Congress addresses the whole of Polish society . . . the request to declare their disapproval of the "pogroms" . . . and to prevent in the future in the eyes of the democracies of the whole civilised world the staining of Poland's flag with the blood of Jewish citizens.'[66]

Polish anti-Semitism ran deep. While Poland and Lithuania were part of the Tsarist Russian Empire in the nineteenth century, special laws were enacted forbidding Jews from holding senior ranks in the civil service and army, or from buying land. There were even certain towns that Jews could not enter without a permit. In the twenty years of Poland's independent existence, the lot of its Jewish citizens greatly deteriorated. Although there were no longer laws to prevent the Jews from entering certain professions, the laws were not needed, since anti-Semitism created an unofficial apartheid anyway. The 'Jewish Question' was a regular feature of political debate in Poland long before it entered the German vocabulary with the Nazis' rise to power. Outbreaks of anti-Semitic violence – similar to the German Kristallnacht that for whatever reason so appalled Rudolf Hess – were common in Poland. And, just as in Germany, the Jews became the scapegoat for all the country's economic problems. *The Times*' Polish correspondent, describing the situation of the Jews as a 'nightmare', reported on 18 September 1937 that the 'sudden wave of animosity against the Jews that started last year has affected even the most cultured and reasonable people'. He continued:

> The peasantry, which has no active race hatred, has been lately made to believe that all its economic struggles can be solved if the small village retail trade is taken away from its present sole representative, the Jew; hence the minor pogroms on market-days which the newspapers report daily.
>
> The upper classes and the Roman Catholic Church take at best a

passive attitude and maintain that although brutal and illegal methods of fighting the Jew are most reprehensible, nevertheless the Jew
always stands behind every immoral publication, that it is he who
teaches the Civil Servant how to take bribes and undermines all traditional forms of social decency, and is responsible for Communist
unrest.

Jews were explicitly barred from the government's Camp of National
Unity with the logic that since Zionism would not let Poles join,
then Jews would be excluded from their movement. *The Times* of 23
April 1937 reported on the Polish Jews' fears about where this would
lead: 'by the Jewish community as a whole it is regarded as tantamount to the disenfranchisement of over 3,000,000 Jews, as the
course of events clearly indicates that failure to enter the Camp of
National Unity will sooner or later mean the loss of all political
rights'. In other words, in 1939 there was little to choose between
Poland and Germany where their attitudes to the Jews were concerned. Even during the Nazi occupation of Poland, bands of
partisans hiding in the forests would casually massacre any groups of
Jewish fugitives they came across.[67]

Of course, this is not some kind of grim contest to see which of the
two regimes was the worst, but in this respect Britain took up arms to
defend one anti-Semitic dictatorship against another. Indeed, alle-
viating the plight of Jews under Nazism was not a conspicuous part
of Britain's agenda. As late as November 1944, Foreign Secretary
Anthony Eden rejected an American plan to exchange Jewish
inmates of Bergen-Belsen who had South American passports for
German citizens who had been interned in South America.[68] Eden
feared that these Jews might emigrate to Palestine and add to
Britain's problems there. (The documents relating to this were not
due to be made public until 2021, but were released in July 1999.)

The invasion of Poland

Without declaration of war and on a fictitious claim that Poland was
infringing German territory, Hitler's forces invaded on the morning
of 1 September 1939. The *Schleswig Holstein*, a German warship in
the harbour at Danzig, began shelling the Polish navy's arsenal in
what were the opening shots of the Second World War. German

tanks rolled over the border and headed towards Warsaw, and bombers began to rain their weapons of terror upon the city. The British and French governments issued a last-minute ultimatum to Germany, demanding that it withdraw its troops or face war.

Several people who were with Hitler when the final British ultimatum was handed to him have testified to his utter dismay. Von Ribbentrop was incorrect– the British *would* fight if he attacked Poland. It was all going badly wrong. But neither Chamberlain nor Hitler could back down at that late stage.

The tragedy of the situation is underscored by the sheer hollowness of the British and French assurances to Poland, which could never have been met. As Norman M. Davies says:

> Both Gamelin and Ironside, the French and British Chiefs-of-Staff, gave precise, and as it proved, fraudulent assurances of their proposed action in the event of German aggression. Gamelin formally undertook to throw 'the bulk of the French army' across the Maginot Line. Ironside said that the RAF would match any German air raids on Poland with similar raids on Germany.[69]

In the event, the RAF did not bomb Germany at that time; France made no more than tentative moves across the Maginot Line, and then withdrew. Poland was therefore left to be dismembered by both the German and Russian armies. By the end of September it had ceased to exist, with its allies scarcely lifting a finger in its defence.

The continuing peace moves

Having been dragged into a war it never wanted, Chamberlain's government now sought a way out of it as soon as was possible without losing face. Although Chamberlain appointed Churchill as First Sea Lord and gave him and his ardent supporter Anthony Eden places in the War Cabinet, these were mere sops to the pro-war elements in the House of Commons. Chamberlain's cabinet remained resolutely composed of appeasers such as Halifax, Hoare and Simon. Astoundingly, on 2 September 1939 – the day before Britain declared war – Hoare told a German journalist: 'Although we cannot in the circumstances avoid declaring war, we can always fulfil the letter of a declaration without immediately going all out.'[70]

It was the Chamberlain government's undeclared policy to fight a short and strictly limited war with a negotiated peace being made as soon as possible – in other words, the whole campaign would be merely a face-saving exercise.[71] This was the strange nervy period known as the 'Phoney War', which lasted from September 1939 until April 1940. While Germany and the Soviet Union looted Poland, Britain and France geared up for military action, training troops and manufacturing weapons. Most of the action at this time took the form of grappling for command of the North Sea, with the RAF bombing German warships and U-boats attacking British vessels.

Even after war broke out, certain groups continued to put out peace feelers, many through neutral mediators. On 12 January 1940, Sir Francis D'Arcy Osborne – British Ambassador to the Vatican – had a meeting with Pope Pius XII, later reporting on it to Lord Halifax (a devout Catholic).[72] The Pope said he was 'speaking for certain German army chiefs, whose names he knew but would prefer not to give', and that they had warned of a 'Grand German offensive' that would soon begin. These anonymous German generals proposed that – if they were assured that Britain was willing to make favourable terms – they would overthrow Hitler and establish an interim military government. Under their new regime, Germany would restore Poland and Czechoslovakia, but remain united with Austria. The Pope made it clear that he was acting only as an intermediary: he would not take it upon himself to 'endorse or recommend' anything. The generals' proposal was seriously considered by the Foreign Office over the following months, but, unconvinced by the Germans' promises to oust Hitler, the matter was allowed to slide. But many of the other peace feelers were at least semi-official, made with the blessing of British ministers – chiefly Lord Halifax and Rab Butler.

In 1965, Bjorn Prytz, Swedish Ambassador to London during the Second World War, revealed on Swedish radio that he had discussed the possibility of a negotiated peace between Britain and Germany with the Halifax/Butler team in June 1940. The first meeting with Butler was on 17 June, the day that France surrendered to the Nazis. Butler told Prytz that Churchill was indecisive, and assured him that 'no occasion would be missed to reach a compromise peace if reasonable conditions could be obtained'.[74] According to Prytz, Butler also said that 'diehards like Churchill would not be allowed to prevent Britain making a compromise peace with Germany'. During their meeting, Butler was telephoned by Halifax, who asked him to assure Prytz that Britain's actions would be guided by 'common sense and not bravado'. After this Prytz sent a telegram to his superiors in Stockholm, the details of which were withheld by the Swedish government from the public until the 1990s 'because of British objections'.[74]

It is interesting that when Churchill (not yet Prime Minister) made a vehement attack on Hitler on 19 November 1939 – calculated to anger the dictator and effectively scupper any chance of making peace – Butler hurriedly assured the Italian Ambassador that the speech 'was in conflict with the government's views'.[75] At this stage at least, Churchill's bellicose attitude was widely seen as an embarrassment and a major stumbling block to peace.

One of the most puzzling attempts to broker peace after war had broken out was the notorious 'Venlo Incident', which came to a head on 8 November 1939. Two MI6 agents in Holland, Major Richard Stevens and Captain Sigismund Payne-Best, had several meetings with a German agent – the chief of foreign counter-intelligence, Walther Schellenberg (although he used a false name). He claimed to represent a group of German generals who were planning to depose Hitler, at one point even discussing the possibility of Schellenberg's flying to Britain to meet Lord Halifax. Chamberlain was kept informed, reporting on the meetings to the War Cabinet on 1 November.[76] A week later, Stevens and Payne-Best were invited to a meeting at a café in Venlo, close to the German border. But it was a trap: a squad of SS men crashed through the border barrier and captured the two British agents, who languished in Nazi prisons for the rest of the war. It may or may not be a coincidence that earlier that evening there had been an attempt to blow up Hitler at the Bürgerbräukeller in Munich, where he had been making a speech on the anniversary of the 1923 putsch. (Incidentally, Hess was initially wrongly reported as having been killed by the bomb.) Hitler had cut his speech short and left early.

Was the Venlo Incident a hoax, set up simply to lure the two British agents into a trap? Or was there a genuine peace movement in Germany that had been discovered and destroyed? Much about the affair remains obscure to this day. But when he came to office six months later, Churchill was not slow to use it as a cautionary tale, ordering that no further peace feelers be either made or responded to.

At the same time – although it was apparently unconnected with the Venlo Incident – a British businessman recruited by MI6, Group Captain Malcolm Christie, had several meetings at his house in Venlo with Prince Max von Hohenlohe.[77] A Sudeten Czech aristocrat who became a citizen of Liechtenstein (and therefore neutral), von Hohenlohe claimed to be acting for Göring, although it emerged that he was Himmler's agent. He made the suggestion that Göring would become head of an interim government who would negotiate for peace. According to Scott Newton, as a result of this Himmler received 'a Royal invitation to parley'[78] A very popular figure in international society, von Hohenlohe turned up in Madrid in late February or early March 1941, where he made contact with Sir Samuel Hoare (by then Ambassador to Spain), offering to go to London to try to open peace talks with Hoare's contacts. Although Hoare sent a report of their meeting to the Foreign Office, concluding pessimistically that he 'saw not the least chance of finding any basis for a peace discussion',[79] this was not quite the whole picture. A report by the Italian Ambassador stated that Hoare had told von Hohenlohe that Churchill was in trouble politically, and that he, Hoare, expected to be 'called back to London to take over the Government with the precise task of concluding a compromise peace'.[80] Hoare also said that he planned to replace Eden as Foreign Secretary with Rab Butler – which, although it was to prove rather overconfident, does reveal that there was a serious peace movement working behind the scenes in Britain, of which Hoare himself was a key member.

The peace camp was very busy in the early months of the war. Goebbels records in his diary that, in June 1940, Hitler told him that peace negotiations were under way, through Sweden.[81] Three days after Goebbels confided this to his diary, a Swedish banker named Marcus Wallenberg approached British Embassy officials in Stockholm. He told them that the Germans were prepared to negotiate – but only with Lord Halifax.[82]

Another Swede who earnestly tried to broker a peace was the diplomat Baron Knut Bonde. Married to a Scotswoman, he had a home and business interests in Scotland, and was a keen supporter of British interests. Bonde was also a close friend of Count Eric Rosen, the brother-in-law of Göring's first – Swedish – wife, which gave him ample opportunities to get to know the Reichsmarschall. He had made several attempts to interest the British Foreign Office in his unusually good contacts – to the point where the FO regarded him as, in Peter Padfield's words, a 'considerable nuisance'[83] – and was certainly engaged in putting out peace feelers in late 1939. In January 1941 he met with Göring to discuss a possible compromise offer, and although the meeting was inconclusive, Bonde wrote to his contact in Britain, Lady Barlow, that she should tell Lloyd George that he, Bonde, could 'see Göring at any time and nobody outside will know'.[84] It is significant that Lady Barlow was instructed to contact Lloyd George, who is reported to have been holding himself in readiness to form a government once peace terms had been offered.

Another Swedish businessman who acted as middleman for the August 1939 meeting between British businessmen and Göring was Birger Dahlerus, who also made several attempts to interest the British in Göring's overtures after the war had begun. And in the aftermath of Dunkirk other offers to broker peace between Britain and Germany came from the Swedish King – who made his offer directly to George VI – the Portuguese dictator Salazar and the Finnish Prime Minister.

The real imperative

Despite the failure of his appeasement policies, Neville Chamberlain had continued as Prime Minister, leading the Conservative government. His downfall came as a result of a disaster caused by Winston Churchill, then First Lord of the Admiralty; yet even though he was to blame, he managed to come out on top.

Norway was a neutral country but of strategic importance especially because Germany's essential iron ore from Sweden was shipped through the port of Narvik. In April 1940 Churchill's plan was to capture the town and cut off the Nazis' supply – though in doing so he was, of course, invading a neutral country. But the operation was bungled. The British expedition was easily repulsed by German forces which had anticipated the move and invaded earlier. A puppet government was set up under Vidkun Quisling, and the British had to abandon Norway. Not only was the Germans' supply of iron ore not cut off, but the whole debacle had handed over Norway to the Nazis and even, for a time, threatened Swedish neutrality in favour of Hitler. It was a terrible blunder, with appalling repercussions, recalling the other great military disaster masterminded by Churchill, the Dardanelles campaign of 1915, which resulted in his resignation from his previous incarnation as First Lord of the Admiralty. Memories of the Dardanelles disaster prompted many to doubt Churchill's abilities as a leader in 1940. Ironically, however, this new fiasco led to renewed criticism of Chamberlain's leadership, clearing the way for Churchill's date with destiny.

On the night of 7–8 May 1940 Chamberlain faced attacks from all sides of the House of Commons: even former friends and allies called for his resignation. A stormy session ended with a vote of no confidence, which he won by an unconvincing majority (282 against 200). Chamberlain had to concede that the only way forward was to form a coalition government, but even this avenue was closed as the Labour Party refused to serve under him. It was then the custom for an outgoing Conservative Prime Minister to name his successor. This time there were only two candidates: Lord Halifax and Winston Churchill. Halifax was the favourite of both the Conservative Party and the Establishment. He was a close friend of George VI, and his wife was one of Queen Elizabeth's ladies-in-waiting. If anything he was even more of a supporter of a negotiated peace than Chamberlain, continuing to press for talks even after war had broken out. Churchill, on the other hand, was widely regarded as a maverick – and one with a dubious track record as a leader of men – but he did have the support of Tory rebels (and of the Labour Party) and was enormously popular among the people.

The momentous decision was made behind closed doors on 9 and 10 May 1940, and it is by no means clear exactly what went on. When they emerged it was announced that Halifax had declined the offer of becoming Prime Minister, claiming that as he was a peer he doubted whether he could govern adequately from the House of Lords. That left Winston Churchill as Prime Minister. The outsider had won. Clearly something unexpected had happened in that meeting, but nobody knows exactly what it was. Perhaps there is a clue, however, in the diary of John Colville, the private secretary to both Chamberlain and Churchill, in his entry for 10 May: 'Nothing can stop him [Churchill] having his way – because of his powers of black-mail – unless the King makes full use of his prerogative and sends for another man: unfortunately there is only one other, the unpersuad-able Halifax.'[85]

Churchill's triumph was a terrible blow for the King. He was said to be 'bitterly opposed' to Churchill becoming Prime Minister, trying to persuade Chamberlain to change his mind and to think up ways of overcoming Halifax's objections – even suggesting a temporary sus-pension of his peerage.[86] When Chamberlain stood by his decision, such was George VI's fury that he delivered an unprecedented snub, refusing to send the customary message of regret at his resignation.[87] A broken man, Chamberlain did not last long: ill health prompted his retirement from politics in November 1940, and he died just two months afterwards.

It seems likely that Churchill had some kind of hold over Chamberlain or Halifax – note Colville's reference to his 'powers of blackmail' – and had not hesitated to use it as a threat. Despite all the odds being in Halifax's favour, the maverick ex-journalist had clawed his way to the top. And there he had every intention of stay-ing. Yet it seems that the cabinet accepted Churchill – however grudgingly – only because they regarded him as a 'stop-gap' Prime Minister who would do until peace negotiations became practicable. The extravagant post-war mythologising of Churchill has obscured the fact that he remained in a very insecure position politically for at least the first two years of his premiership, largely because it was well known that he did not – to put it mildly – enjoy the support and confidence of the King. As one commentator writes: 'the Court and Royal Family had been opposed to Churchill as Prime Minister, pre-ferring Halifax; and Churchill now depended on the support of his former opponents – and none more than the King.'[88]

'Walking with destiny'

Summoned to Buckingham Palace on the evening of 10 May 1940, according to the ancient custom, Churchill was formally (if reluc-tantly) requested by the King to form a government. As he put it in his now famous words: 'I felt as if I were walking with destiny, and that all my past life had been but a preparation for this hour and this trial.'[89] These were characteristically memorable words – Churchill's rhetorical genius alone may have earned him a place in history – and it seems they were genuine. One of his schoolfellows recorded a conversation with the sixteen-year-old Churchill in 1891 when the future Prime Minister had said: 'I see further ahead than you do. I see into the future. This country will be subjected to a tremendous invasion, by what means I do not know, but I tell you I shall be in command of the defences of London and I shall save London and England from disaster.'[90] Was this truly a premonition of the future? Or was it a role he imposed upon himself, a self-fulfilling prophecy – even if, as some believe, he had to create the menace from which Britain had to be saved?

Churchill had always had a *Boy's Own* attitude to war, from his earliest encounter with it as a war correspondent (and military intelligence agent) in the Spanish war in Cuba in 1895. But it was his exploits in South Africa – and particularly his heroic escape from a Boer prison – that made him a household name. The public lapped up each instalment of his adventure with every new edition of the newspapers. The name Winston Churchill became synonymous with dash and courage. Politically, however, he displayed quite a different character. It has been said that he was wrong about everything in his political career except for one thing – his recognition of the threat from Germany. Until becoming Prime Minister in 1940, Churchill had had a very unsatisfactory career. Regarded as self-seeking, unreliable and something of an opportunist – he had switched from the Conservative to the Liberal Party and then back again – by 1930 he was believed to be past his heyday. He had held most of the higher positions in government, including Home Secretary (1910–11) and Chancellor of the Exchequer (1924–9), but all that seemed a very long time ago. Even though his background – as the third son of the Duke of Marlborough – placed him resolutely in the ranks of the Establishment, there was always something about Winston Churchill that unsettled his fellow members of the upper classes. Perhaps it was the legacy of his beloved American mother, the beautiful and forthright Jennie Jerome, that itself manifested in his unashamed passion for the United States and his promotion of American interests. Whatever it was, he was always regarded in certain quarters as something akin to a buzz-bomb: you heard it roaring towards you in the distance but once its noise stopped you never knew where it was going to explode.

Perhaps it was his own unusually developed sense of destiny that made Churchill aware of the implications of the rise to power of 'That Man' in Germany. Almost as soon as Hitler took control, Churchill – then a backbencher – began to issue dire warnings and predictions, calling for an alliance with Stalin and pressuring the government to step up its output of armaments. Of course, this had the effect of thoroughly alarming the peace movement.

He was also a great advocate of the use of intelligence-gathering – in which he was somewhat ahead of his time. As a twenty-one-year-old he had gone to Cuba as a correspondent for the *Daily Graphic* to cover the war with Spain but was also acting for British military intelligence, being personally briefed by its director, Colonel Edward Chapman, before his departure.[91] Later he played a key role in the formalisation of the various intelligence services in the 1910s which resulted in the basic structure that still exists today.[92] As Home Secretary, MI5 had been his responsibility, and when heading the Admiralty he had worked closely with MI6. But – like Rudolf Hess – he took his interest in intelligence much further. According to historian David Stafford: 'During the 1930s he established a private intelligence network to track Nazi rearmament which rivalled that of the official government.'[93] He also had 'moles' in government departments and the armed forces who supplied him with a constant stream of secrets.

A central figure in Churchill's personal spy network was Major Desmond Morton, head of a new MI6 department the Industrial Intelligence Centre (IIC), created in 1931. Morton would leak IIC reports to Churchill, who then 'with proper discretion' would use their contents in speeches in the Commons.[94] In the Second World War Morton became Churchill's personal intelligence adviser, playing a major role in the aftermath of Hess's arrival.

Churchill takes over

Churchill began his administration by appointing himself the first ever Minister of Defence. As Lord Beaverbrook famously remarked, there was no point in him giving anyone else the role, since if they disagreed with him they would be sacked, and if they agreed with him they would be superfluous. Churchill also immediately purged his War Cabinet of all pro-peace sympathisers: Sir John Simon was moved out to become Lord Chancellor; Sir Samuel Hoare was dispatched to Spain as Ambassador 'on a special mission', although this was not quite the insult some have claimed it to be. It was a very sensitive posting: Hoare's job was to try to ensure that Franco's Spain remained neutral – after all, it was hardly difficult to work out whose side it would take if it did not. Besides, in the early months of his Spanish posting, the Duke and Duchess of Windsor were temporarily living in Madrid, and Hoare was tasked with making sure that the Nazis failed to use them to their advantage (Hoare was an old friend and adviser of the Duke). But even so, the Spanish posting still removed Hoare from Westminster and Whitehall. It was there that he would have posed a real threat to Churchill.

Determined to fight the war 'to the bitter end', Churchill immediately turned his attention to rounding up the enemies within the realm. On 1 September 1939, Defence of the Realm Regulation 18b had been approved, which provided for the detention without trial of suspected Nazi sympathisers, but it went nowhere near far enough for Churchill. Originally it required an individual to have committed a 'prejudicial act' before the Home Secretary could issue a warrant for his or her arrest – under Churchill its powers were immediately extended so that he could order the detention of any member of an organisation that was in any way connected with, or sympathised with, the enemy. As John Costello writes: '"Sympathize" was the catch-all word that permitted the government to detain without trial, indefinitely, members not only of Fascist organizations but of any group that the Home Secretary judged sympathetic to the Germans – including those who advocated negotiations with Hitler.'[95] Armed with this formidable weapon, Churchill was not slow to use it. Among the many detained under the new regulation were Oswald Mosley and his wife Diana, Captain Ramsay (founder of the Right Club) and Sir Barry Domvile, former director of naval intelligence. Others must have wondered when the authorities would knock at their door, especially as Churchill made it clear that rank would be no deterrent with the action taken against the Duke of Buccleuch. Although there were a few who posed a genuine threat to national security among those put away under Regulation 18b, there is little doubt that Churchill used it as an implicit threat against his old opponents.

Within weeks of taking office he had also created the Special

Operations Executive – specifically in order to remove 'special operations' from Menzies' MI6, which the new Premier clearly did not trust.[96] SOE came under Hugh Dalton's Ministry of Economic Warfare, and recruited from outside the intelligence community as a matter of policy.

The simmering feud between the foreign intelligence department MI6 and the clandestine operations organisation SOE continued throughout the war, but the tensions between the two agencies went considerably deeper than mere interdepartmental rivalry: in most cases it seemed to be a matter of fundamental ideology. Not only had SOE been created specifically to fight the Nazis, it is now recognised that it was deeply infiltrated by the Soviet NKVD. It was so riddled with Russian agents that, after the war, the Americans refused to have anything to do with it, and the entire organisation was closed down.[97] During the war, with the USSR as an ally, this did not seem so much of a problem, since although it was true that the agents were reporting back to Moscow, they were not trying to subvert the organisation. On the other hand, MI6 has always seen itself as an anti-Communist outfit and, like Menzies himself, regarded the USSR as the real enemy. The policies of the two agencies were therefore entirely different: SOE was primarily anti-Nazi and supported the alliance with the USSR, while MI6 was nervous about such an alliance, preferring – if such a thing were possible – Britain to be fighting the Communists, not the Nazis. With such diametrically opposed *raisons d'être*, no wonder there were infighting and skullduggery between the two organisations.

Leo Marks, head of SOE's Agents' Codes, said of MI6: 'They did everything they could to close us down, to discredit us, to make our existence as difficult as possible, to minimise our priorities.'[98]

The 'miracle' of Dunkirk

On the very day that the mysterious behind-the-scenes deals took place that brought Churchill so unexpectedly to power – 10 May 1940 – the Germans launched their blitzkrieg attack on Holland, Belgium and Luxembourg. Their armoured divisions, supported by the Luftwaffe's dive-bombers, seared their way through the Low Countries within days. Then they invaded France, outflanking the Maginot Line by means of a surprise attack through the Ardennes

Forest, regarded as impassable by French and British strategists. One observer who had predicted such a move, however, was the Duke of Windsor, who had tried to warn the authorities in a detailed report – but to no avail.[99]

The British Expeditionary Force, together with the French army, was beaten back by the advancing German forces, which began enclosing them in a pincer movement. The retreating British force was gradually forced back to the coast around Dunkirk. By 22 May 1940 some 250 German Panzers were advancing along the French coast towards Dunkirk, threatening to seal off the British escape route. Then, just six miles from the town, at around 11.30 a.m., they abruptly stopped dead in their tracks. Something astonishing had happened: Hitler had personally ordered all German forces to hold their positions for three days. Literally they had to stop where they were, just miles from the enemy. Even more remarkably, this order was sent uncoded and was picked up by the British. The order to stop the German army's advance – the *Haltbefehl* ('Halt Order') – said: 'By the order of the Führer . . . attack northwest of Arras is to be limited to the general line Lens–Béthune–Aire–St Omer–Gravelines. The canal will not be crossed.'[100]

Hitler's generals were astounded by this. Ewald von Kleist said after the war that, because the order seemed so nonsensical, 'I decided to ignore it, and to push on across the [Aire–St Omer] Canal. My armoured cars actually entered Hazebrouck, and cut off the British lines of retreat . . . But then came a more emphatic order that I was to withdraw behind the canal. My tanks were kept there for three days.'[101] Another general, Thoma, literally begged for permission for his tanks to advance – but Hitler was adamant that they should wait.[102]

The order was lifted three days later, but even then the German tanks were ordered south to deal with a French counter-offensive across the Somme, reducing the pressure on the British and French defenders. Those three days gave them the vital time they needed to set up defences around Dunkirk to keep the Germans at bay long enough for the evacuation.

Although the mythology views the evacuation – the armada of fishing boats and private yachts, in addition to naval vessels, that took the retreating troops to safety – as little less than a miracle, it is easy to see where the real miracle lay: quite deliberately, Hitler had given the British a chance to save their army. The evacuation of 338,000 Allied troops, of whom more than 200,000 were British, was complete by 3 June – and it was a genuine testament to the courage and determination of the British people. Yet the fact remains that without the Halt Order from Hitler, there would have been either a massacre that would have outdone even the carnage of the First World War or an ignominious mass surrender. So why did the Führer let them go when he had virtually the entire British army at his mercy?

In 1948 the military historian and strategist Colonel Basil Liddell Hart – after interviewing many of the German generals involved – concluded that Hitler *had* wanted the British army to escape. It transpires that in the days before the Halt Order was issued he had told some of his generals that he anticipated – after France had fallen and Britain been isolated – that he could make peace with Britain. General Günther Blumentritt, the Army Chief of Staff, went on record as having been astonished when Hitler suddenly waxed lyrical about the British Empire and its vital role in world affairs[103] (although anyone who had read Mein Kampf would not have been so amazed). Perhaps more tellingly, another general told Hart that Hitler aimed to make peace with Britain 'on a basis that was compatible with her honour to accept'.[104] Hart concluded that: 'The escape of the British Expeditionary Force in 1940 was largely due to Hitler's personal intervention.'[105]

According to Ilse Hess, the most violent argument her husband ever had with Hitler was over Dunkirk and the best option for using it to make peace with Britain. Hess was in favour of smashing the British forces totally, while the Führer believed that massacring or capturing – in any case, humiliating – the British army would make such negotiations harder, because of the bitterness and resentment it would cause.[106]

Churchill could not face the thought that Hitler – of all people – had shown mercy towards the British, so he always maintained that the Halt Order was given by Field Marshal Gerd von Rundstedt, Commander-in-Chief of the German armies in the West.[107] Churchill was wrong: it was Hitler who gave the order. But, in any case, what general would have dared to take it upon himself to give such an unprecedented advantage to the enemy? After the war, Churchill even claimed the credit himself for taking the action that saved the British army, by ordering a diversionary attack by the garrison at Calais,[108] but this is also untrue.

Dunkirk might have given the British army a second chance, but it spelled the end of a free France. With its forces defeated and the British withdrawn across the Channel, France surrendered on 17 June. The fall of France had a tremendous psychological effect. The idea that a civilised country, and one so very close, could fall prey to the Nazis with such relative ease sent shudders throughout Britain, and even prompted one of the architects of France's doom, Rudolf Hess, to consider the long-term effects of the Nazi domination of Europe.

With France under the jackboot, and Britain licking its wounds, Hitler could now turn his attention to his real goal, the war with the Soviet Union. Under the circumstances, he now fully expected the British to want to talk peace, especially after the feelers that had been extended before June 1940. Unable to believe that Britain would seek to continue the war, he revealed his intentions at a conference of the Axis leaders in Munich on 18 June. The Italian Foreign Minister, Count Galeazzo Ciano, outlined Hitler's attitude in his diary:

> If London wants war it will be a total war, complete, pitiless. But Hitler makes many reservations on the desirability of demolishing the British Empire, which, he considers, even today, to be an important factor in world equilibrium. I ask von Ribbentrop a clear-cut question: 'Do you prefer the continuation of the war, or peace?' He does not hesitate for a moment. 'Peace.' He also alludes to vague contacts between London and Berlin by means of Sweden.[109]

A month later, Hitler gave the order for the preparation for the invasion of Britain, but even then added 'if it should become necessary'.[110] Three days after this, on 19 July, in a speech at the Reichstag in what he called his 'last appeal to reason', he called for Britain to come to the peace table. Significantly, however, he did not address his words to Churchill – whom he denounced as a warmonger – but to the British people as a whole: 'Mr Churchill ought perhaps, for once, to believe me when I prophesy that a great empire will be destroyed – an empire which it was never my intention to destroy or even to harm . . . I see no reason why this war must go on.'[111]

Here we see the basic idea behind Hess's mission – the belief that Churchill was out of tune with the British public, and that they could be persuaded to turn against him if an honourable settlement could be made. Copies of this speech were dropped by the Luftwaffe over Britain. Of course, one result of this was that Churchill himself was in no doubt where he stood, receiving a forewarning of probable plots to overthrow him as he took Britain deeper into war.

Three days later the British government roundly rejected Hitler's offer, and dug itself in for what it firmly believed would come next – a German invasion. All over Britain communities braced themselves, forming invasion committees to plan their last-ditch stand against the Nazis. Old men, women and even children steeled themselves for hand-to-hand fighting with the Nazis on the village greens and in the streets. Villages invented elaborate codes for sending messages to the army, and fleets of cycle messengers were organised, while church bells were silenced: orders were given that they were only to be rung to signal the first sight of the enemy coming up the beaches. (The next time they were heard was on VE Day.) Many families solemnly agreed on what they would do when the Nazis arrived: some planned on hiding, some on fighting, some on 'muddling through', while others made quiet arrangements to say goodbye to their children with a bottle of aspirins dissolved in a final glass of milk, rather than let their loved ones fall into enemy hands. They had seen what had happened to Belgium, Holland and France. There seemed no doubt that Britain would be next.

In the event, however, they need not have worried.

Operation Sea Lion

Ordering the preparations for the invasion of Britain, known as Operation Sea Lion (*Fall Seelöwe*), on 16 July, Hitler demanded that they be finished by the middle of August. Preparations duly went ahead, but Sea Lion was first postponed in the middle of September 1940, and quietly cancelled on 12 October. This is generally believed to be the result of the Battle of Britain, in which the RAF beat back the Luftwaffe, denying Hitler the air supremacy needed to allow his invasion force across the Channel. But there is a simpler reason for Sea Lion's cancellation. Hitler was never serious about invading Britain in the first place: Sea Lion was a sham right from the beginning. This was the conclusion reached by, among others, the German military historian Egbert Kieser, after studying the documents relating to it in the German archives. He concluded that Sea Lion was effectively a bluff.[112]

Of course, Hitler's Chiefs of Staff did not know this – he had to make it seem a reality, and the best way of ensuring this was to have everyone concerned believe it was real. But the naval command noticed that the resources allocated to the operation were woefully inadequate. One of the most telling points – discussed by Kieser – was that although Hitler was customarily a complete nuisance to his generals, constantly interfering and overruling them with respect to the smallest details, where Sea Lion was concerned he showed no interest in their planning at all.[113]

There is overwhelming evidence that Sea Lion was only ever part of a massive campaign of deception aimed at the Russians. Hitler had to make the Soviets believe that he would turn the might of his armies on them only when he had fully dealt with Britain. Because he had hardly kept his ambition to destroy the Soviets to himself in his early days, Stalin was well aware that the Nazi attack was not a question of if, but of when. But with the deception of Sea Lion in place, it seemed that Hitler was still pushing westwards. Even when Panzer divisions were deployed to the East, Stalin fell for the explanation that they were being kept out of the way of the RAF, so that when Barbarossa finally came, in June 1941, it took him utterly by surprise. Without a single Nazi having scrambled up the White Cliffs of Dover, Operation Sea Lion could be considered – from the Führer's point of view – a complete success. Documents captured by the Allies at the end of the war show that from at least the beginning of 1941 invasion of Britain was off the agenda, but the belief that it was about to happen was an important part of the smokescreen around Barbarossa. This can be most clearly seen from a top-secret instruction from the Führer's headquarters to senior officers, dated 15 February 1941, which stresses the strategy of: 'Strengthening the existing impression of a coming *invasion* [original emphasis] of England.' It continues: 'In spite of the further relaxation of the preparation for SEA LION, everything should be done to maintain the impression that the landing in England is being prepared.'[114] On 9 December 1940, the naval diary of the German High Command recorded that Sea Lion was to be maintained as a deception until the launch of Barbarossa, while as late as 4 February 1941 Hitler was telling Grand Admiral Erich Raeder that 'Sea Lion must be maintained as a deception'.[115] Clearly, Sea Lion no longer existed as a serious military operation, but was it *ever* meant to be?

As early as 31 July 1940 – just two weeks after initiating Sea Lion – Hitler was talking about feigned operations against Britain being used as a diversion for the Soviets.[116] In August Grand Admiral Raeder (who had not then been initiated into the Barbarossa plan) learned that troops were being transferred to the East, and – astounded – asked Hitler why. The Führer told him that this was part of a deception to camouflage Sea Lion by tricking the British into thinking that Germany was about to attack Russia.[117] Although we now know that the deception was the other way round, this shows that Hitler was already linking Sea Lion with a campaign of military deception. It is also interesting to note the way Hitler's mind worked: even the commander of his navy was being deceived into thinking that the invasion of Britain was the top priority.

There are indications that Churchill – who had an uncanny knack of second-guessing Hitler – suspected that the invasion would never come. In June 1940 he wrote to the South African Prime Minister Jan Smuts: 'If Hitler fails to beat us here, he will probably recoil eastward. Indeed, he may do this even without trying invasion.'[118] And on 8 July he informed Lord Beaverbrook, then Minister of Aircraft Production:

> Should he [Hitler] be repulsed here *or not try invasion* [our italics], he will recoil eastward, and we have nothing to stop him. But there is one thing that will bring him back and bring him down, and that is an absolutely devastating, exterminating attack by very heavy bombers from this country upon the Nazi homeland.[119]

Yet there *was* the Battle of Britain – the air battles between the RAF and the Luftwaffe over Britain between 10 July and 31 October 1941 – to consider. If the Luftwaffe's attack was not a prelude to invasion, what was it?

After Dunkirk, Britain was contained in its island fortress, and did not have the capability to launch a military offensive across the Channel, but the RAF was still a threat to continental Europe. The

German raids aimed to destroy RAF bases and command centres as well as other military and industrial targets. Although the heroism of the RAF pilots – 'the Few', as Churchill memorably called them – in tackling the German planes cannot be overestimated, ultimately the Luftwaffe failed because it spread its resources too thinly, being sidetracked into attacking civilian targets. In the end – ironically – it was the Blitz that destroyed Göring's finest.

Churchill tightens his hold

If the War Cabinet did harbour the idea that Churchill would be a stop-gap leader they were to become sorely disappointed. The German invasion of France and the Dunkirk debacle strengthened his position, giving him golden opportunities for employing his extraordinary talent for inspiring rhetoric. His famous speech about how 'we will fight them on the beaches . . . we will never surrender' had an astonishing impact on the morale of the British people – although, according to Lloyd George, it was received less rapturously by the Commons[120] – instantly stiffening resolve where the propaganda campaigns of a dozen spin doctors would have failed.

While Hitler's great and abiding ambition was to crush the Soviet Union under his heel, Churchill never lost sight of his own burning ambition, which was to achieve much the same where Hitler and Germany were concerned. He had no qualms about waging total war, and would stop at nothing to destroy Germany utterly. But he knew that Britain was in an extremely precarious position. It simply did not have the resources to beat the might of the Nazi war machine. The Prime Minister was fully aware that victory depended upon two things: the United States coming into the war, and Germany striking at the Soviet Union, making Stalin a British ally. (Ironically, that great anti-Bolshevik of the 1920s, Winston Churchill, had been calling for an alliance with Stalin from at least the beginning of 1939.[121])

As Churchill dug himself yet deeper into his Prime Ministerial role, Hitler faced a few problems of his own. Although incredibly popular with the mesmerised German public, he was not without opponents – some of them highly influential. Many of the military commanders, professional soldiers of the officer caste, were secretly against him. Although they were patriotic Germans, these men were not Nazis and privately deplored Hitlerism. They might have supported the Führer in reversing the Treaty of Versailles, but now that the Reich had been restored and the Greater Germany created, some of these generals and admirals had reservations about where Hitler's leadership was taking their country. As for the man himself, they considered him to be a vulgar upstart with little talent for military planning and, increasingly, a madman.

Besides this cabal, several Nazi leaders harboured their own ambitions to lead Germany, if Hitler could be removed. He knew he had to watch his back constantly. And there was also a broad underground network – a German resistance – made up of those opposed to Hitler and the Nazi ideology, working behind the scenes to bring about the downfall of the regime.

There was one Nazi leader, however, whose personal ambitions have always been seen as being inseparable from Hitler's, and who had yet to play his hand – trying to broker a peace with Britain before Europe was blown apart by the cataclysm of total war and Britain itself had been utterly destroyed. It was an enormous personal risk, but he felt it was his destiny to take it. As all the other peace initiatives failed one by one, Deputy Führer Rudolf Hess began to plan his flight.

CHAPTER FOUR

The Network is Activated

According to Hess's testimony while in British custody after his flight, the idea of the peace mission came to him soon after the fall of France, when the full horror of what one civilised neighbour could inflict on another finally dawned on him. Another major factor in galvanising him into action was Britain's out-of-hand rejection of Hitler's peace offer of July 1940, which must have seemed to him like a catastrophic waste of a golden opportunity by the British (confirming his argument about Dunkirk). However, although it was one thing to conceive intellectually of a peace mission, it was quite another matter to put it into action. For a cautious, meticulous man like Hess this meant leaving nothing, as far as humanly possible, to chance – that is, as far as the dictates of security would allow. He had to be very careful who else he involved, knowing full well that if the plan backfired it would blow up in the faces of everyone concerned.

The planning began during a walk in the Bavarian woods on 31 August 1940 with his mentor Karl Haushofer, who – because they shared almost identical visions and ideals – was one of the very few people to whom he could have confided such an undertaking. The ensuing plotting can be traced from surviving correspondence between Hess and the two Haushofers, Karl and Albrecht,[1] although some of the material has to be treated with caution because they were aware that their letters might be intercepted. For this reason, they often employed codenames – for example, Hess is referred to as 'Tomo', short for Tomodachi, a sixteenth-century

Japanese warrior king. They also seem to have covered themselves in case the mission went awry. For example, Albrecht was careful to portray himself as a pessimist. Should the mission fail, over-enthusiasm and blind optimism would do him no favours in the eyes of posterity, not to mention the immediate political fallout that would come his way.

The Lisbon connection

Hess's initial idea is discussed in a letter from Karl to Albrecht Haushofer dated 10 September 1940. After discussing family news and gossip, Karl describes his recent visit to the Bavarian Alps, launching into what amounts to a clear admission of his own role at the centre of an international network of intrigue:

> it [the visit to the Alps] brought me a meeting with Tomo from 5 o'clock in the afternoon until 2 o'clock in the morning, which included a 3-hour walk in the Grünwalder Forest, at which we conversed a good deal about serious matters. I have really got to tell you about a part of it now.
>
> As you know, everything is so prepared for a very hard and severe attack on the island in question [Britain], that the highest-ranking person [Hitler] only has to press a button to set it off. But before this decision, which is perhaps inevitable, the thought once more occurs as to whether there really is no way of stopping something which would have such infinitely momentous consequences. There is a line of reasoning in connection with this which I must absolutely pass on to you because it was obviously communicated to me with this intention. Do you, too, see no way in which such possibilities could be discussed at a third [i.e. neutral] place with a middleman, possibly the old Ian Hamilton or the other Hamilton?
>
> I replied to these suggestions that there would perhaps have been an excellent opportunity for this in Lisbon at the Centennial, if, instead of harmless figureheads, it had been possible to send well-disguised political persons there. In this connection it seems to me a stroke of fate that our old friend, Missis [sic] V. R., evidently, though after a long delay, finally found a way of sending a note with cordial and gracious words of good wishes not only for your mother, but also for Heinz and me, and added the address.

Address your reply to Miss V. Roberts, c/o Post Box 506, Lisbon, Portugal. I have the feeling that no good opportunity should be overlooked; at least it should be considered.[2]

The letter implies that 'Miss' (actually Mrs) Roberts had initiated the contact herself, although there is reason to doubt this. (see below). Her letter has not survived: it is known to have existed solely because of this reference. The Lisbon address was simply a means of communicating via neutral Portugal: Box 506 was owned by Thomas Cook & Co., the travel agency, and was used by anyone who wanted to send and receive letters from Germany. Naturally, it was very carefully monitored by the British security services.

The 'old Ian Hamilton' to whom Haushofer refers was the redoubtable General Sir Ian Hamilton (1853–1947), leader of the British forces at Gallipoli, by this time retired and head of the British Legion, an organisation that strove assiduously to avert the war,[3] and of which Karl Haushofer was an honary member.[4] Robustly and unashamedly a leading light of the extreme right wing, he was a staunch supporter of Hitler and had met Hess on several occasions before the war – even, in 1938, inviting him to stay at his home, Lennoxlove House in East Lothian, Scotland.[5] (By one of the stranger coincidences, although the families of General Sir Ian Hamilton and the Dukes of Hamilton are unconnected, Lennoxlove became the home of the Duke of Hamilton after the war.) 'The other Hamilton' mentioned in Haushofer's letter clearly refers to the Duke, while the 'Centennial' was the joint celebrations of the 800th anniversary of the founding of the Portuguese state and the 300th anniversary of the restoration of its independence from Spain that were held on St John the Baptist's Day (24 June) 1940 in Lisbon.

One of the most important points in the Haushofer letter is the fact that it is Rudolf Hess who first suggests they approach certain friendly contacts in Britain, including – by implication – General Sir Ian Hamilton or the Duke of Hamilton as middlemen. And the use of the word 'middleman' in itself is very significant, implying that their ultimate target is somebody else – but who is the mysterious final link in the chain?

The secrets of Mrs Roberts

The widow of a Cambridge University lecturer, Mrs Mary Violet Roberts and her late husband had met Karl and Martha Haushofer before the First World War. Together with their son Patrick (then serving at the British Embassy in Berlin), they enjoyed the hospitality of their new German friends. They all got on famously – or perhaps infamously, if John Harris and M. J. Trow, authors of *Hess: The British Conspiracy* (1999), have their way. They argue that the letter was the opening move in a conspiracy of the British intelligence agencies to lure Hess to Britain, using Violet Roberts' connection with the Haushofers.

They base their hypothesis on the fact that her nephew, Walter Roberts, worked for the Special Operations Executive (SOE). However, Walter Roberts was no James Bond – although he worked for SO1, the section that dealt with propaganda and misinformation, he was its Establishment and Finance Director. But did the fact that her nephew was in charge of SO1's accounts make Violet Roberts a stooge for British intelligence? Harris and Trow seem to think so, although they produce no conclusive evidence. Perhaps, though, Walter Roberts could still have tipped off his colleagues about his aunt's relationship with the Haushofers – presumably they would have jumped at the opportunities it presented. There may have been another way in which Walter Roberts could have been instrumental in a plot to lure Hess over. As a fellow Old Etonian he may well have kept in touch with his old schoolmate Sir Stewart Menzies, head of MI6. Or maybe the initial contact came from the Duke of Hamilton – after all, Violet Roberts clearly knew him. She was one of the Hall-Maxwells, prominent landowners whose family seat was in Renfrewshire.[6] It is unlikely that she did not know the county's most prestigious family, the Douglas-Hamiltons. On purely logistical grounds it is unlikely that SOE had initiated the plan because SOE itself had only been set up in July – its recruits were not fully trained and operational until October – and a letter coming through neutral Portugal would have taken some time to reach Haushofer, who had it by the end of August.

Karl Haushofer's letter of 10 September 1940 makes it clear that it was Hess himself, during their walk in the Grünwalder Forest on 31 August, who had first brought up the idea of contacting the Duke of

Hamilton. Haushofer had recently received the letter from Mrs Roberts that gave him the idea of using her as a go-between – the mission was not initiated by that letter, and therefore not by either SOE or MI6. But why did she suddenly get in touch with old friends at that particular time? There may be a mundane explanation: the Thomas Cook mailbox in Lisbon was only established in July 1940, so she had no means of getting a letter to them until that date.[7] On the other hand, Violet Roberts must have had a motive for reviving her contacts in Germany. Although it does seem rather too much of a coincidence to send her note just as Hess was planning his mission, perhaps it was only natural that peace-makers on both sides would be prompted to open lines of communication after Dunkirk and the fall of France.

Karl Haushofer's words also make it clear that Violet Roberts' letter was addressed to Albrecht – he says that she passed on good wishes to himself, his wife and Heinz, but not Albrecht, and he asks Albrecht to 'address *your* reply' to the Lisbon address. This is significant because, whereas Violet Roberts was a pre-war friend of the senior Haushofers, Albrecht was a close friend of the Duke of Hamilton, which suggests that she had written it at the Duke's request.

Summoned by Hess

Before Albrecht received his father's letter about the walk in the Grünwalder Forest, he had already had an opportunity to discuss matters with Hess. He wrote a note of his meeting:

> On 8 September, I was summoned to Bad G [Godesburg] to report to the Deputy of the Führer on the subject discussed in this memorandum. The conversation which the two of us had alone lasted 2 hours. I had the opportunity to speak in all frankness.
>
> I was immediately asked about the possibilities of making known to persons of importance in England Hitler's serious desire for peace. It is quite clear that the continuance of the war was suicidal for the white race. Even with complete peace in Europe, Germany was not in a position to take over the inheritance of the [British] Empire. The Führer had not wanted to see the empire destroyed and did not want it even today. Was there not somebody in England who was ready for peace?[8]

Haushofer realised that the core of the problem was that the British government simply did not trust Adolf Hitler. He developed his argument forcefully (and, considering the post-war situation, prophetically):

> If the worst came to the worst, the English would rather transfer their whole empire bit by bit to the Americans than sign a peace that left to National Socialist Germany the mastery of Europe. The present war, I am convinced, shows that Europe has become too small for its previous anarchic form of existence; it is only through close German–English co-operation that it can achieve a true federative order . . . while maintaining a part of its world position and having a security against Soviet Russian Eurasia.

Haushofer then summed up the likely scenario if peace were not made: whatever else might happen, Germany would always distrust the strength of the British navy and Britain would be suspicious of the strength of the Luftwaffe. He went on, outlining an astonishing vision: 'There is only one way out of this dilemma: friendship intensified to fusion, with a joint fleet, a joint air force and joint defence of possessions in the world – just what the English are now about to conclude with the United States.'

To Haushofer, the fact that Churchill himself was half-American was of some significance. After discussing the Prime Minister's pro-American views, he goes on: 'In fact, I am of the opinion that those Englishmen who have property to lose, that is, precisely the portions of the so-called plutocracy that count, are those who would be readiest to talk peace. But even they regard peace as an armistice.' He then blames von Ribbentrop for starting the war. Deeply unpopular among British society, the former champagne salesman had authoritatively reported to Hitler that the British would not declare war on Germany if Poland was invaded. Clearly, his sojourn in London had taught von Ribbentrop nothing about the British in general and Churchill in particular. (Incredibly, when caught by the Allies in 1945, the former Ambassador to the Court of St James had a letter on his person addressed to 'Mr Vincent [sic] Churchill'. This was the man on whose advice Hitler effectively began the war.)

Hess had asked Haushofer to name Britons who might be open to peace overtures – despite the awkward fact of Hitler's dictatorship:

I mentioned among diplomats, Minister O'Malley[9] in Budapest . . . Sir Samuel Hoare, who is half-shelved and half on the watch in Madrid, whom I do not know well personally, but to whom I can at any time open a personal path; as the most promising, the Washington Ambassador, Lothian,[10] with whom I have had close personal connections for years . . .

As the final possibility I then mentioned that of a personal meeting on neutral soil with the closest of my English friends, the young Duke of Hamilton who had access at all times to all important persons in London, even to Churchill and the King. I stressed in this case the inevitable difficulty of making contact and again repeated my conviction of the impossibility of its succeeding – whatever approach we took.

The upshot of the conversation was H's statement that he would consider the whole matter once more and send me word in case I was to take steps. For this extremely ticklish case, and in the event I might possibly have to make a trip alone, I asked for very precise directions from the highest authority. From the whole conversation I had the strong impression that it was not conducted without the prior knowledge of the Führer, and that I probably would not hear any more about the matter unless a new understanding had been reached between him and his Deputy.

The last two paragraphs reveal that Albrecht Haushofer was under the impression that Hitler had sanctioned the meeting, and – not unnaturally – that the plan would only proceed if the Führer approved it.

The plan proceeds

With or without Hitler's approval Hess proceeded with his plan. On 10 September 1940 he wrote to the professor (addressing him as *Hochverehrter und lieber Freund!* – 'Highly respected and dear friend'), referring to their walk in the woods of a few weeks previously, and to his later meeting with Albrecht. He goes on, momentously:

Albrecht will have told you about our conversation, which beside *volksdeutschen* [Germanic peoples'] matters, above all touched on the other matter, which is so close to the hearts of us both. I have reconsidered the latter carefully once more and have arrived at the following conclusion:

Under no condition must we disregard the contact or allow it to die aborning. I consider it best that you or Albrecht write to the old lady [Mrs Roberts], who is a friend of your family, suggesting that she try to ask Albrecht's friend [clearly Hamilton] whether he would be prepared if necessary to come to the neutral territory in which she resides, or at any rate has an address through which she can be reached [Lisbon], just to talk with Albrecht.

If he could not do this just now, he might, in any case, send word through her where he expected to be in the near future. Possibly a neutral acquaintance, who had some business to attend to over there anyway, might look him up and make some communication to him, using you or Albrecht as reference . . .

You thought that knowing about his whereabouts had no military importance at all; if necessary, you would also pledge yourselves not to make use of it with regard to any quarter which might profit from it. What the neutral person would have to transmit would be of such great importance that his having made known his whereabouts would be by comparison insignificant.

The prerequisite naturally was that the inquiry in question and the reply would not go through official channels, for you would not in any case want to cause your friends over there any trouble.

It would be the best route to have the letter to the old lady with whom you are acquainted delivered through a confidential agent of the AO to the address that is known to you. For this purpose Albrecht would have to speak either to Bohle [head of the AO] or my brother. At the same time the lady would have to be given the address of this agent in L. [Lisbon] or if the latter does not live there permanently, of another agent of the AO who does live there permanently, to which the reply can in turn be delivered.

As for the neutral I have in mind, I would like to speak to you orally about it some time. There is no hurry about that since, in any case, there would first have to be a reply received from over there.[11]

This letter clearly gives the go-ahead for contact with Hamilton. But why would Hess, with all his Auslandorganisation contacts, have gone to the trouble of trying to make contact with Hamilton through the intermediary of Mrs Violet Roberts? And why did he choose to contact Hamilton rather than the better-known pro-German members of the British aristocracy such as the Duke of Buccleuch or Lord Londonderry, who had much greater overt influence? And why should Hess pursue this particularly roundabout link when he could have made plenty of much more direct contacts through neutral territories? Albrecht Haushofer himself had listed more promising contacts – Lothian, Hoare and O'Malley – during his meeting with Hess on 8 September 1940. Hoare and Lothian in particular were closer to the heart of British politics, had more support and were then living in safer, neutral territories, Spain and the United States, respectively. Why neglect such attractive channels in favour of an apparently much more dangerous and tenuous link? Surely it could not be simply because Hamilton was, as Albrecht described him, 'the closest of my English friends'.

The only answer is that Hamilton was in a position to offer something that the others did not possess. Haushofer's note spells out what this 'something' was, suggesting Hamilton for the task because he 'had access at any time to all important persons in London, even to Churchill and the King'.

The premier peer

It is well known that Rudolf Hess arrived in Scotland and asked for the Duke of Hamilton, whom he believed would help broker a peace deal with Germany. There is a huge amount of confusion about Hamilton's true role in the Hess affair – much of it a deliberate smokescreen.

Douglas Douglas-Hamilton, the Duke of Hamilton and Brandon (the 14th of the former and 11th of the latter) had inherited his title at the age of thirty-seven, on the death of his father in 1940. He also held no fewer than ten other titles. The Hamiltons were, and still are, the premier peers of Scotland, theirs being the oldest surviving dukedom, established in 1643. Every Duke of Hamilton always has precedence over all the other Scottish nobility, a position that naturally bestows certain privileges, but also brings with it specific responsibilities, the most significant being the role of hereditary Keeper of the Palace of Holyroodhouse. (The current Duke was first in the procession of the historic opening of the Scottish Parliament in Edinburgh in 1999.) By what might be considered – up to a point – an ironic twist of fate, the 14th Duke also held the title of Lord Steward of His Majesty's Household, having been granted it after it was stripped from the Duke of Buccleuch for his pro-German sympathies in 1940. Moreover, the Duke of Hamilton – besides being a Privy Councillor – was, by virtue of his inherited rank, effectively no less than the King's representative in Scotland.

By the time of Hess's flight, Douglas Douglas-Hamilton already had a lifetime of adventure behind him. As is customary for the heir to the Hamilton dukedom, he had previously held the title of Marquess of Clydesdale, and it was in that name, as a younger man, that he became famed as a boxing champion. He boxed for Eton and Oxford and won the Scottish amateur middleweight championship. Even in 1941 he was still known as the 'Boxing Marquis'.

His other great passion was flying. As the Marquess of Clydesdale he became one of the elite aviators in Europe at that time, a member of the two-plane team that was the first to fly over Everest – which greatly impressed fellow flying ace Rudolf Hess. With Group Captain D. F. McIntyre he wrote a book about their great Everest adventure, *The Pilot's Book of Everest* (1936). Clydesdale was also a valued flying instructor for the Auxiliary Air Force, and as the much-revered commander of Glasgow's 602 Squadron he gave young men from right across the social spectrum the chance to become qualified pilots in an age when the RAF was particularly riddled with snobbery. Because of his passion for flying, he had an airstrip built at the family seat at Dungavel which was to figure prominently in the mystery of Hess's flight.

In 1930 Clydesdale became Unionist (Conservative) MP for East Renfrewshire – the youngest MP in the House of Commons at the time – only leaving when he was elevated to the House of Lords on inheriting his dukedom. Then he joined the RAF as a wing commander, and by 1941 had become the commanding officer at RAF Turnhouse (now Edinburgh Airport).

The hidden strategy

Hess's mission was not merely a committed Anglophile's last-ditch attempt to save the nation he so admired from being blasted to pieces: there was a sharp strategic purpose behind it, too. It must be remembered that Hitler's invasion of the Low Countries – necessitated, as far

as he was concerned, by Britain and France's declarations of war –
was, for him, a distraction from his real ambition: the fulfilment of the
geopolitical and ideological objectives set out in *Mein Kampf*. With
the invasion of Poland he had in effect completed the creation of the
Greater Germany. Now he was turning his attention to the matter of
Lebensraum – the expansion of Germany to the east, which meant
war with his hated ideological enemy: the Soviet Union.

Operation Barbarossa was an awe-inspiring objective, one about
which neither Hitler nor his advisers had any illusions. The sheer
scale of the enterprise made it unlike anything in Hitler's experience.
The logistics of maintaining a vast army thousands of miles from
Germany – ammunition, medical supplies and food would all be
needed in massive quantities – seemed like a nightmare, as indeed it
was to prove. With hindsight it may seem obvious that Barbarossa
was an act of lunacy, but to Hitler this was his most urgent task, one
that he had ached to undertake since the Communist takeover in
Bavaria. But he needed to concentrate as much of his firepower on
the invasion of Russia as possible, knowing that his chances of success would be greatly increased if significant military resources were
not tied up in an ongoing war with Britain.

Hess's view, expressed forcibly to Hitler, was that it would be folly
to launch an attack on the USSR without first at least concluding an
armistice with Britain. And despite attempts to play down this aspect
of Hess's mission, it is clear from the timing alone that there was a
strong connection between his flight and Operation Barbarossa:
Hitler ordered his generals to start planning the offensive in late July
or early August 1940. The original date set for Barbarossa was 15
May 1941, but he postponed the operation in January 1941, then on
30 April, eleven days before the flight, he set the new date of the
offensive at 22 June.[12] Could this have been a deliberate ploy to
allow time for Hess to negotiate with the British?

The union that never was

Another major concern for the Nazis at this time was the possibility
of the United States coming into the war on Britain's side, which
would have spelled disaster for them, especially if they were in the
thick of taking on Russia at the same time. However, there appears
to have been another fear which, if it has any basis in fact, has quite

staggering implications. This was the idea that not only would Britain and the United States become allies against the Nazis for the duration of the war, but they would then join forces permanently, with a full act of union between the two countries. Whether this astonishing scenario was ever likely to happen, it was certainly a factor in Hess and Haushofer's calculations. A letter Albrecht sent to his father on 19 September, enclosing the draft of the letter he was about to send to the Duke of Hamilton, ends: 'The whole thing is a fool's errand [he uses the English phrase], but we cannot do anything about that. According to the latest reports, the treaties of union between the [British] Empire and the United States are about to be signed.'[13] Albrecht might have believed that Hess's mission was a 'fool's errand' but he seemed convinced that it had to be attempted because of a reported imminent union of Britain and the USA. Astonishingly, there is evidence that such a union was being seriously contemplated at that time – and that its timing was directly related to Hess's flight. According to White House spokesmen, President Roosevelt was to make a speech to the Pan-American Conference on 14 May 1941 of a 'historic' nature. The White House leaks left the media buzzing with speculation, mostly about the possibility that the President was going to announce the union of Britain and the USA. The respected Washington-based journalist Leonard Engel, wrote:

I have strong reason to believe Roosevelt will come out in favour of a union of the United States and Britain. He will probably specify the end of the war as the occasion for such a merger of the two great English-speaking nations, but I believe he will suggest an earlier date.

I am making a guess, but that guess is supported by a considerable amount of evidence.[14]

Because virtually no one seems to know about this proposal, it is tempting to deny that such a thing was even a possibility. But after the fall of France and before its armistice with Germany, the British government seriously proposed an Act of Union between Britain and France.[15] Not surprisingly, this peculiarly unrealistic notion was rejected out of hand by the French cabinet.

In the event, two days before Roosevelt was scheduled to give his momentous speech – and two days after Hess's arrival – he cancelled it. (As we will see, when the speech was finally delivered, the President's position had changed radically.)

Preventing a world war

At this stage the conflict was still largely confined within the boundaries of Europe: it was not yet a world war. But it was clear that if the conflict did escalate – as it most certainly would if Germany found itself fighting on two fronts and against the USA – it would be a 'total war', even bloodier and more catastrophic than the 1914–18 conflict. Hess was appalled at the prospect of such a war – especially because he of all people knew about the scale of the destruction the German war machine could unleash. Besides, he had his own traumatic memories of what war was like, which he had expressed in a particularly impassioned speech on 8 July 1934. After talking of the camaraderie of soldiers and the heroism of war, he went on:

> But let us be honest. The smell of death was always in our nostrils. We have seen death in more fearful and mangled shapes than any men before our time. We squatted and crouched in our dug-outs, waiting to be crushed to pieces. We listened with stilled breath as our trained ear heard the hiss of the shell above us, as the mine exploded before our feet. Our hearts throbbed as if they would break to pieces when we sought cover in vain against the deadly rattle of the machine-gun. With our gas masks on we felt ourselves suffocating to death in the midst of the gas clouds. We stumbled along in the water-logged trenches. We lay out in shell craters through the freezing nights. For days and weeks together the horror of battle passed over us. We were frozen and hungry and often on the verge of madness. The cries of the heavily wounded men were in our ears. We met blinded men staggering back and we heard the death rattle in the throats of the dying. Among the heaped-up corpses of our dead comrades we lost all hope of life. We saw the misery of the refugees behind the lines. We saw the widows and the orphans, the cripples and the suffering, the sick children and the hungry women at home.
>
> Let us be honest. Did not each one of us then and there often ask: 'Why all this? Must it be? Can humanity not be spared this in the future?'[16]

He also said:

> Those who took part in the [First] World War had a presentation
> of what a modern war would signify today with more fully perfected
> weapons.[17]

In the same vein in July 1941 Hess told the Lord Chancellor, Lord
Simon: 'I do not think I could have arrived at my final choice unless
I had continually kept before my eyes the vision of an endless line of
children's coffins with weeping mothers behind them, both English
and German; and another line of coffins of mothers with mourning
children.'[18]

Whatever the political reasons for Hess's mission, there is no denying that he also had a humanitarian aim, which was to prevent the
most ferocious possible attack on Britain – as Karl Haushofer stressed
in his report on the walk in the Grünwalder Forest. On the same day
that Albrecht finally sent his letter to the Duke of Hamilton on
Hess's behalf, he also wrote to his father: 'If there is the "total victory"
for our wild people from Glasgow to Capetown that is envisaged,
then the drunken sergeants and the corrupt profiteers will set the
tone anyway; experts with quiet manners will not be needed then.'[19]

Hess had been living for some time with the possibility of another
nightmare. As the Commissar of All Technological Matters and
Organisation, he was ultimately responsible for the Nazis' atom
bomb project, the chillingly codenamed 'Virus House'. At that time
there was no clear leader in the race to develop the atom bomb and
there was a good chance that Germany would win. Some of Hess's
later statements to his British captors about the imminent emergence of 'new and more terrible weapons' could have been referring
to the atom bomb. For example, he told Lord Simon, 'one day sooner
or later this weapon will be in our hand and I don't say it will be
decisive, that it will win the war, I only say that it will be more terrible than anything that has gone before'.[20]

Behind the scenes

Much of the controversy surrounding the flight centres on the Duke
of Hamilton's actions and the true extent of his knowledge about
Hess's mission. Obviously, if the Deputy Führer really did come to

make contact with the British peace group, Hamilton would surely have been the intermediary. The official line is that the Duke was more surprised than anybody when Hess turned up to see him, a line also taken by books seeking to debunk any claims of collusion, especially Lord James Douglas-Hamilton's (the Duke's second son) *The Truth about Rudolf Hess* (first published as *Motive for a Mission* in 1971, and revised in 1993) and Roy Conyers Nesbit's *The Flight of Rudolf Hess: Myths and Reality* (co-written with Georges van Acker, 1999). Both books dismiss any notion that Hamilton had met Hess before the war or knew he was coming, but our own research was to turn up some very challenging information. Ironically, much of this was to come from the family archive, the Hamilton Muniments, held in the Scottish Record Office in Edinburgh, which the current Duke kindly gave us permission to access.[21] To our knowledge, only Lord James Douglas-Hamilton has had unrestricted access to the Muniments.

Sceptics about Hamilton's importance argue that by May 1941, no longer an MP and serving in the RAF, he had no political power or influence, and that alone demonstrates the folly of Hess's mission. Why make such a dangerous journey specifically to see a man who was essentially powerless to help? Critics also point out that, although Hamilton and Churchill had once been close friends, they had fallen out over certain Scottish issues and no longer had any significant contact with each other. But the sceptics fail to mention that Hamilton was, by virtue of his rank, a Privy Councillor and Keeper of the Royal Household, both of which roles gave him direct access to the King and Court. Far from being an inconsequential sinecure, Hamilton's sphere of influence was extremely impressive and the Haushofers knew it, as their letters show. Indeed, if anybody knew the true extent of Hamilton's influence it was Albrecht Haushofer, because he and the Duke had been close friends for several years. According to Lord James Douglas-Hamilton, the German had met the then Marquess of Clydesdale when he attended the 1936 Berlin Olympics in a party of MPs.[22] The two men met again in Munich in January 1937, when Albrecht introduced Clydesdale to his father Karl.[23] Clydesdale then arranged for Albrecht to speak to the Royal Institute of International Affairs at Chatham House, London, in early 1938 and by the end of April he had been a guest for a week at Dungavel.[24] It was during this visit that he drew the outlines of the Greater Germany on an atlas (see page 33).

A few weeks before the outbreak of war, in July 1939, while on a cruise along the coast of Norway, Albrecht Haushofer wrote to his Scottish friend, expressing his fear that war was unavoidable, and discussing what could be done to make it as short as possible. Beginning the letter with Clydesdale's nickname, 'My Dear Douglo', Albrecht explained that he had deliberately kept a low profile for a few months since the Munich Agreement, not wishing his unpopular views to ruin his career in the diplomatic service:

> We have had more than one talk on the Versailles Treaty and its aftermath. You know how I feel about it. I have always regarded it as a failure on the side of British farsightedness – to put it mildly – (but you may blame the French!) that concessions and revisions mostly came too late.
>
> After the National Socialist advent to power there remained one hope: that – after having done away with most (if not all) of the Versailles grievances by rather violent and one-sided methods – the great man of the regime would be prepared to slow down, to accept an important (though not an all-dominating) position in 'the Concert of Europe' . . . Now – I cannot entertain that hope any longer; and that is my reason for writing and posting this letter somewhere on the coast of western Norway, where I am taking a few short weeks of rest.

After expressing the hope that his friend might survive the conflict, Albrecht states that although 'there is not yet a definite timetable' for the invasion of Poland 'any date after the middle of August might prove to be the fatal one'. He added that his major concern was to stop the conflict over Poland escalating into a world war: 'I am very much convinced that Germany cannot win a short war and that she cannot stand a long one.'[25]

Haushofer goes on to suggest that Britain adopt the strategy of putting diplomatic pressure on Mussolini (or 'the big man in Rome', as he guardedly calls him) adding: 'What Europe needs is a real British peace plan on the basis of full equality and with considerable safeguards . . . on the military side.' Diplomatically admitting that the British had been provoked by the Führer, Haushofer urges Clydesdale to remind the British public of the unfair treatment of Germany over the plebiscites in the Polish Corridor and Upper

Silesia. He adds, significantly, 'if you can do anything to promote a general British peace and armaments control plan – I am sure you would do something useful'. Haushofer ends by drawing his friend's attention to the risk he is running in sending such a letter, asking him to destroy it 'most carefully' after reading it. (Obviously, Clydesdale did no such thing.) But curiously, Haushofer does give his permission – at Clydesdale's discretion – to show it first to 'Lord H and to his under-secretary Mr B', that is, Halifax and Butler. Then he initiates a code: to confirm he has received the letter, Clydesdale is to send an innocent picture postcard to Haushofer in Munich. If he has shown the letter to Halifax and Butler the message is to include some news of Clydesdale's family. The letter is simply signed 'A'.

Although suggesting a compromise peace, Haushofer's letter primarily establishes him in Clydesdale's eyes as someone in Germany who could be trusted once war breaks out, someone moreover who is not a Hitlerite. He also sought to make contact with Halifax and Butler, the two members of the British government likely to be most supportive of a negotiated peace.

Clydesdale did, as requested, show the letter to Halifax. But, according to his son Lord James, he also showed it to one other person for whom Albrecht had not given him permission: Winston Churchill.[26] It is far from clear why he did this. Churchill was just emerging from his 'wilderness years' as a backbencher, so his potential influence on any future peace negotiations was virtually nil at that time. And although he and Churchill had been old friends, Clydesdale had many friends in the Commons with considerably more clout. Why involve Churchill? Did he somehow suspect that his star would soon be in the ascendant?

However, the Hamilton family archives reveal that the Duke showed the letter to yet another person: Prime Minister Neville Chamberlain.[27] This simple fact demonstrates conclusively the fallacy of the official line about Hamilton's political ineffectuality.

The meeting that never was

Hamilton always denied that he had ever met the Deputy Führer before his arrival in Scotland – a line that has been maintained by Lord James Douglas-Hamilton. He claims that during the 1936 Berlin Olympics his father attended a dinner given by Hitler at which Hess was present, and that on this occasion Hess 'may have seen Clydesdale across the room',[28] but he denies that they ever met face to face. However, he did say that another MP in the party – Kenneth Lindsay – met Hess and reported back to him on the meeting.[29] But there is plenty of evidence that Hamilton *did* meet Hess, on that occasion at least.

Common sense dictates that two such famous aviators – members, as it were, of an elite club – would have been keen to meet, especially given Hess's admiration for Clydesdale's Everest triumph. After all, Hess had specifically invited his other great hero, Charles Lindbergh, to a meeting when he visited Germany in 1938. It is inconceivable that he could have dined in the same room as Clydesdale and not asked to be introduced. Albrecht Haushofer made a special point of introducing his Scottish friend to Göring specifically because of their shared passion for flying,[30] so why not also introduce him to Rudolf Hess?

Two of the other MPs on the trip and even Clydesdale's younger brother, Lord Malcolm Douglas-Hamilton,[31] had no qualms about stating unequivocally that they met Hess on that occasion. One of the MPs, Henry 'Chips' Channon – later famous as a chronicler of the day – wrote in his diary that both he and Clydesdale had been invited to lunch by Hess, and although he himself had declined, Clydesdale had accepted.[32] Indeed, Kenneth Lindsay stated that he was with the Marquess when he met Hess[33] . . . And Brendan Bracken, Churchill's Minister of Information, who was with the Prime Minister on the night that Hess arrived in Britain, stated publicly in New York in August 1943 that the Deputy and Hamilton had met before the war.[34]

There is more evidence – some of it very telling. In an extract from Churchill's later book *The Second World War* in the *Daily Telegraph* in March 1950 there was the clear statement that Hamilton had met Hess at the Berlin Olympics. However, after a request from the Duke, the statement was 'corrected' before the book appeared.[35]

Finally, the strongest indication that the two men had met can be found in the Hamilton papers themselves. These include the Duke's own handwritten account of his statement addressing this question, for which he obviously had considerable difficulty in finding the right words. He first writes (about one of the receptions in Berlin):

'During this time and at no time thereafter was I introduced to Hess.'
This was crossed out, to be replaced with: 'As far as I know he was
not present.' This, too, was crossed out, and the final version reads:
'It is possible that he was at one of the large parties which I attended
but I did not recall his name or consider him a person in particular I
wanted to see.'[36] Hamilton was saying, 'Yes, I met Hess,' then, 'No,
I didn't,' before settling on 'Well, we might have met but I can't
remember'. This was to become the official version.

Why, then, the obsessive denial that the two had ever done more
than exchange glances across a crowded reception in Berlin? The
first official announcements after Hess's arrival in Scotland did say
that the two had met at the Olympics, but because this fuelled
rumours that Hamilton was a Nazi sympathiser, a blanket denial was
deemed to be more prudent. The problem was that once denied, it
could never be admitted without calling the rest of the Duke's testimony into question, so from 1941 to the present day the official
line has remained that Hamilton and Hess never met.

Whether the two men had ever talked face to face is almost
immaterial because they shared one very close friend, Albrecht
Haushofer. The important point is that it seems Hamilton was at the
very least extremely evasive, calling into question the credibility of
his testimony.

'To the bitter end'?

On 6 October 1939 – just over a month after war had been
declared – *The Times* published a letter from the Marquess of
Clydesdale in which he expressed his views on the escalating conflict
in no uncertain terms. Because of its importance to this investigation, it is reproduced in full:

Sir,
Many, like yourself, have had the opportunity of hearing a great deal
of what the men and women of my generation are thinking. There is
no doubt in any quarter, irrespective of any party, that this country
had no choice but to accept the challenge of Hitler's aggression
against one country in Europe after another. If Hitler is right when he
claims that the whole of the German nation is with him in his cruel-
ties and treacheries, both within Germany and without, then this war

must be fought to the bitter end. It may well last for many years, but the people of the British Empire will not falter in their determination to see it through.

But I believe that the moment the menace of aggression and bad faith has been removed, war against Germany becomes wrong and meaningless. This generation is conscious that injustices were done to the German people in the era after the last war. There must be no repetition of that. To seek anything but a just and comprehensive peace to lay at rest the fears and discords in Europe would be a betrayal of our fallen.

I look forward to the day when a trusted Germany will again come into her own and believe that there is such a Germany, which would be loath to inflict wrongs on other nations such as she would not like to suffer herself. That day may be far off, but when it comes, then hostilities could and should cease, and all efforts be concentrated on righting the wrongs in Europe by free negotiations between the disputing parties, all parties binding themselves to submit their disputes to an impartial equity tribunal in case they cannot reach agreement.

We do not grudge Germany *Lebensraum*, provided that *Lebensraum* is not made the grave of other nations. We should be ready to search for and find a colonial settlement, just to all peoples concerned, as soon as there exist effective guarantees that no race will be exposed to being treated as Hitler treated the Jews on 9 November last year [Kristallnacht]. We shall, I trust, live to see the day when such a healing peace is negotiated between honourable men and the bitter memories of twenty-five years of unhappy tension between Germany and the Western democracies are wiped away in their responsible co-operation for building a better Europe.

Yours truly,
Clydesdale

Clydesdale's conscience would not allow him to accept a war that would destroy Germany. However, his war record speaks for itself: once war was declared he carried out his duties to King and country gallantly – including his duty to attempt to secure a just peace. His position was clear: he believed that Hitler's tyrannies should be fought, but all efforts should also be made for a negotiated settlement – provided it could be done with 'honourable men'. Clydesdale also becomes one of the first people to link the idea of a settlement with the plight of German Jews, something that had not featured conspicuously in any other official or unofficial peace moves.

One of the other major controversies about Clydesdale is whether he was a member of the Anglo-German Fellowship, the organisation established to foster relations and trade between the two countries. Several authors have stated this as a fact, but we found their evidence to be inconclusive. Certainly, according to Lord James Douglas-Hamilton, his name does not appear on the Fellowship's list of members, although there was a blank application form found in his papers.[37] On the other hand, a report on the Anglo-German Fellowship in the London *Evening Standard* on 28 November 1935 named the Marquess of Clydesdale as a member, as did the *Daily Telegraph* in 1939, neither of which resulted in a complaint from him. However, we discovered that the answer to this perennial question can be found in the Hamilton archives, which contain a receipt for a year's subscription to the Anglo-German Fellowship (one guinea), dated 29 June 1936.[38] So finally the controversy is over, with proof positive that he was a member. (It is interesting that the names of two of the Duke's three brothers also appeared on a membership list of the Fellowship, the significance of which will become apparent.)

The centre of the web

The fact that there was a hidden subtext to Hamilton's pre-war activities can be clearly seen from the statement about why he visited the 1936 Berlin Olympics which he prepared for his lawyers in a libel case in 1942. He states: 'My sole object in being interested in Germany at this time was to obtain information I might be given which would be open to me in the interests of my country as I was an officer of the Auxiliary Air Force'.[39] This is the closest he could get to admitting that he was working for air intelligence, which links him with Group Captain Winterbotham and MI6 (which was responsible for air intelligence). This may seem to suggest that he was part of an intelligence plot to lure Hess over, but, as we have seen, the RAF Club and the chivalric brotherhood of the 'knights of the air' were at the heart of the movement for closer ties with Germany in order to confront the Soviet Union. In any case, his claim that this was the 'sole object' of his interest in Germany is manifestly untrue. The Hamilton archives show beyond question that during the 1930s he was at the forefront of moves to improve Anglo-German relations, and that, as war approached, he was a key player in moves to avert it. We have seen that he showed Albrecht Haushofer's 1939 letter to Neville Chamberlain, bringing the existence of this extremely influential German intermediary to the notice of the British Prime Minister. But his role had even deeper roots: on 27 June 1935 he had been invited to join a German study group set up by the then Prince of Wales (later King Edward VIII and then the Duke of Windsor), proof at least that his interest in such matters was well known in royal circles.[40]

In May 1938 Clydesdale received a personal invitation to visit Germany from Adolf Hitler as guest of honour at the annual Nuremberg Rally. This reached him via the Anglo-German Fellowship: there is a letter dated 11 May 1938 in the Hamilton archives from the Fellowship's secretary, D. Conwell Evans, advising Clydesdale that, as it was the custom that an invitation from a head of state could not be refused, it was coming to him via a third party to allow him the opportunity to do so.[41] The real significance of this invitation, however, is that not only did Hitler clearly recognise Clydesdale's importance, but the Anglo-German Fellowship – and not the German Embassy – was acting as the Führer's agent in this (and presumably in much else). Could it be that there was a close link between the Anglo-German Fellowship and Rudolf Hess's intelligence-gathering organisation, the Auslandorganisation?

Also in his submission to his libel-case lawyers, Hamilton explicitly denies he was ever a member of the Anglo-German Fellowship, but adds a note that he did dine with von Ribbentrop (he gives no date for this) and as a result his brother Lord Nigel briefed the RAF on the details of their conversation.[42]

On 14 August 1939 Clydesdale received a letter from a Mr Hurd of the Anglo-German Fellowship, and with it was enclosed a memorandum, dated 31 July 1939, written by one of the founders of the Fellowship who is not identified.[43] The writer describes how he had spent the afternoon and evening of 26 July with von Ribbentrop at his lakeside castle and the following day had travelled with him in his private railway carriage to Berlin. The memorandum is a briefing on what the two men discussed: von Ribbentrop stressed that Hitler did not want a war with Britain and was keen to know why Britain insisted on backing Poland, expressing anger at the British attempts to negotiate a pact with the Soviet Union. (Was this a major historical turning point? Was this when von Ribbentrop decided to make his own deal with Stalin in the form of the Molotov–Ribbentrop Pact?) The memo also contains this very telling statement: 'Hitler much admires the British Empire, and in his visionary view of the future he regards it as a most important and necessary asset in world development.'

Although there was nothing new in that report, it is significant because it was sent to Clydesdale, who was clearly being kept up to date with developments.

Stripping away all the evasions and economical half-truths, it appears clear that Clydesdale was not just Albrecht Haushofer's friend: he was effectively his sponsor – as Haushofer was his in Germany – putting him in touch with key figures in the British Establishment. There is a letter to Clydesdale from Lord Halifax dated 3 May 1938, when Haushofer was staying at Clydesdale's London flat. In it Halifax thanks Clydesdale for letting him know that the German was in town, but regrets he has no time to meet him. Halifax ends by saying: 'I am glad to say, however, that Dr Haushofer is in touch with the Foreign Office and I shall therefore have an opportunity of hearing his views.'[44]

The Hamilton archives contain equally telling material dating from after the war broke out, including a letter of 9 November 1939 from Hamilton's brother Lord Malcolm, who was stationed at RAF Grantham in Lincolnshire. It also encloses a letter from one 'Mac' Hamilton, sent from Stockholm on 30 October, saying that Britain and Germany should stop fighting each other and concentrate on attacking their common enemy, Bolshevism, adding that he was convinced the Germans were willing to make peace. He also talks candidly about a Swede – a doctor of philosophy and 'world-known explorer' – who would be willing to go to London to act as mediator, providing the way was smoothed for him first. There is no mystery about the identity of this individual because, as the Hamilton archives reveal, Clydesdale had written his name on the letter: Sven Hedin, a famous Swedish explorer of distinctly pro-Nazi sympathies. (When he arrived in Scotland, Hess stated that some of the medicines he had brought with him – rare Tibetan curatives – had been given to him by Hedin when he had visited him in Munich in November 1940.[45])

Lord Malcolm Douglas-Hamilton had passed this letter on to Clydesdale, suggesting that he bring it to the attention of 'the I of the Air Ministry' – that is, the intelligence branch – and to 'Van', presumably Sir Robert Vansittart (chief diplomatic adviser to the Foreign Office) or anybody else at the Foreign Office whom Clydesdale thought would be interested.[46]

It is clear that German peace feelers were being fed to key people in Britain through contacts in Sweden and then through the Douglas-Hamiltons. One major point which has gone unnoticed by other researchers is that 'Douglo's' brothers were surely involved in these machinations. It seemed at that time to be very much a family affair. Lords Malcolm, Nigel and David Douglas-Hamilton served in the RAF – David was killed on active service in 1944. Both Malcolm and David were certainly members of the Anglo-German Fellowship and, significantly, in his own notes, Hamilton states that although he first met Albrecht Haushofer in 1936, he had already heard a lot about him from his brother David.[47] When Clydesdale went to the Olympics, he was accompanied by Nigel – something that is rarely mentioned.[48]

During the 1930s Lord David and his wife – the formidable Prunella Stack – were both known for their interest in the social programmes of the Nazis. Lord David visited the German labour camps 'for experience', seeing them as a possible solution for the problem of unemployment at home in Glasgow.[49] Prunella Stack was head of the Women's League of Health and Beauty, modelled on the pioneering regime of Gertrud Scholtz-Klink, whose programme of physical jerks was designed to create an army of Aryan amazons, fanatically fit mothers of the next generation of Hitler Youth.[50] Even Clydesdale's mother made a pro-peace speech in Edinburgh in June 1936.[51]

Also significant is that Clydesdale's letter to *The Times* (reprinted above) was originally intended to be a *group* letter, signed by many people as a clear signal to the Germans that there was a powerful peace lobby in Britain. Correspondence in the Hamilton archives shows that the letter was to be signed by several MPs who had become serving officers in the armed forces, and it was to contain the following statement: 'We are Members of Parliament, representing all parties and at the same time serving officers in the Royal Navy, Army and Royal Air Force. We believe that we speak for the young men and women of the Empire in saying that Britain has no choice but to accept the challenge of Hitler's aggression.'[52] It then continues as published in *The Times*. This discovery also changes the picture in other ways. The correspondence in the archives makes it absolutely clear not only that Lord Halifax had assisted in drafting the letter and had approved it, but that it had been shown in advance (by Lord Dunglass, later Tory Prime Minister Sir Alec Douglas-Home) to Neville Chamberlain, who had also approved it. However, Chamberlain later ruled that the other MPs should not sign it because it might create the wrong impression in the armed services. This is confirmed in a letter from Clydesdale to Halifax dated 30 September 1939.[53]

A letter of 22 September 1939 from Lord David discusses the drafting of *The Times* letter, stating that it was originally drafted by 'Hahn and Brooke', and it 'has the merit of lacking any whine for peace and is bold enough to convey a definite policy'.[54] It also says that Hahn was making sure that the BBC would give full publicity to the letter in Germany: indeed, later correspondence confirms that the German service of the BBC did broadcast the text of the letter on the same day as it was published in *The Times*.[55] This was clearly a very carefully orchestrated move – backed by Chamberlain and Halifax and using Clydesdale as the front man – to tell the Nazi government that there were prominent figures, both in the political sphere and in the armed forces, who would back peace with Germany. There is another important subtext, however. They were looking forward to a time when they could make peace with 'honourable men' – in which category the peace lobby did not include Hitler. The implication is that they were only willing to discuss peace if he was replaced as leader. The letter also makes it clear that a settlement must take account of the plight of Germany's Jews, but the most important message being sent is that Clydesdale is to be the contact within the peace group. Should anyone in Germany be willing to discuss these terms they should talk to him. It is therefore clearly aimed at those in Germany who opposed Hitler, into which camp both Haushofers fell.

The involvement of 'Hahn' is interesting. This was Dr Kurt Hahn (1886–1974), the influential educationalist and founder of Gordonstoun School in the wilds of Scotland, a school later much favoured by the Royal Family (and attended by Karl Haushofer's grandson, whose guardian was Lord Malcolm Douglas-Hamilton, after the war[56]). A Rhodes Scholar at Oxford, Hahn was a German Jew who had established a well-known school in Germany before fleeing from the rise of Nazism in 1934, bringing some of his schoolmasters with him, and founding Gordonstoun in the same year.

We were also to make a discovery that finally gives the lie to the idea that Clydesdale had no real political power: in the Hamilton archives we found a particularly intriguing seating plan for a major meeting, virtually a summit, on 9 June 1939 at the Foreign Office.[57] The meeting was chaired by Lord Halifax (Foreign Secretary) and includes delegates from various countries, including Spain, Italy and Germany. The leader of the German delegation – which also included Prince Adolf zu Mecklenburg – was General Walther von Reichenau. Of all the German army generals – who by and large were not devoted Hitlerites – von Reichenau was the staunchest adherent to the Führer and the Nazi cause.[58] (Responsible for ensuring that the army swore allegiance to Hitler on the Nazis' rise to power, he would eventually be promoted to field marshal after the success of the French campaign and was finally put in charge of the Russian campaign before dying mysteriously on 17 January 1942.) As we have seen, von Reichenau played a key role in Hess's diplomatic intelligence network, being described by Peter Padfield as 'Hess's secret political intelligence collaborator'.[59] Undoubtedly, because he controlled this network, von Reichenau was also part of the Hess/Rosenberg group that worked to foster good relations with Britain via the RAF Club, being one of Group Captain Winterbotham's circle.[60] For von Reichenau of all people to be present at a meeting chaired by Lord Halifax at the Foreign Office less than three months before the outbreak of war is nothing less than staggering.

Although the seating plan is the only mention of this round-table meeting in the archive, it is headed 'Seating Plan for a Meeting *Held* on 9 June . . .', indicating that it had taken place. But there is something even more interesting about it, at least as far as this investigation is concerned. At the centre of the table, apart from Lord Halifax and Sir Robert Vansittart (chief diplomatic adviser to the Foreign Office), was the name The Marquess of Clydesdale. Such an important gathering was hardly the place for someone on the sidelines of politics. Also present was Kenneth Lindsay MP (who had reported to Clydesdale on his meeting with Hess in 1936) and also a curiously incongruous figure, who was seated facing General von Reichenau: Group Captain Sir Louis Leisler Greig. Although a year later he was to become the private secretary to Sir Archibald Sinclair, Minister for Air, at that time he held no special political position. However, his presence was to prove particularly significant.

A flurry of correspondence

Hess and the Haushofers had agreed that Albrecht would write to Hamilton, via Violet Roberts' mailbox address in Lisbon. Albrecht wrote to his parents soon after this arrangement was agreed:

> It won't really go the way he thinks it will. However, I could formulate a letter to D. H. [Hamilton] in such a way that the transmission of it will in no way endanger our lady friend; above all, I must make it clear to T. ['Tomo' – Hess] once again that my ducal friend of course can't write to me without the permission of his highest authority.[61]

Then he wrote directly to Hess on 19 September:

> H [Hamilton] . . . cannot fly to Lisbon – any more than I can! – unless he is given leave, that is unless at least Air Minister [Sir Archibald] Sinclair and Foreign Minister Halifax know about it. If, however, he receives permission to reply or to go, there is no need of indicating any place in England; if he does not receive it, then any attempt through a neutral mediator would also have little success.[62]

Contained here is a very important point: Hamilton needed permission 'to *reply* or to go'. Most researchers pick up on the fact that he would have needed permission to travel to Lisbon, but here Albrecht anticipates that Hamilton would need to seek permission even to answer the letter. Clearly, Hess and the Haushofers expected other senior figures to know about the contact – specifically Sir Archibald Sinclair and Lord Halifax. This changes the picture radically. Halifax's pro-peace sentiments have already been discussed, but where did Sir Archibald Sinclair stand? Sinclair (1890–1970, later

Viscount Thurso) was the confrontational and controversial leader of the Liberal Party who had refused to bring his party into a coalition under Chamberlain, but did so with Churchill. As a reward for this he was appointed Secretary of State for Air in 1940. Although he was Churchill's personal secretary when the latter (then a Liberal) was in the War Office between 1919 and 1921 – often enjoying the odd day on the grouse moors with him – the two men continued to clash over many issues.

Sinclair aroused the suspicions of several other highly placed politicians of the day. Chamberlain distrusted him, and John ('Jock') Colville – private secretary to both Chamberlain and Churchill – wrote in his diary that Sinclair was considered 'an untrustworthy person',[63] which seems to have resulted in his being placed under surveillance. On 3 May 1940 (a week before Churchill came to power) Sinclair had written to Chamberlain complaining that his telephone was being tapped.[64]

Sinclair is one of the major figures in this story and yet his sympathies are among the hardest to pin down. At times he seems a staunch Churchill man, but at others he seems to share the aims of the anti-Churchill peace group. Sinclair's views were those of the traditional aristocratic Liberal. He had been a member of the Anglo-German Association,[65] which had been disbanded after Hitler's rise to power, but had declined to join the Anglo-German Fellowship that had been formed to foster relations with Nazi Germany. The important point here, however, is that the Haushofers and Hess clearly had no problem with Sinclair knowing about their approach.

These, then, were two of the major British politicians that Albrecht Haushofer singled out as the best contacts to help arrange Hamilton's trip to Lisbon. But did Haushofer really believe such public figures would put their reputations on the line in this way? It seems he was far from convinced of a successful outcome, ending his letter of 19 September to Hess on a characteristic note of pessimism: 'I already tried to explain to you not long ago that, for the reasons I gave, the possibilities of successful efforts at a settlement between the Führer and the British upper classes seem to me – to my extreme regret – so infinitesimally small.'[66] Of course, as always with his letters, there is the possibility that he was covering himself against the day when the plot, and all its correspondence, might be discovered by the wrong people, although equally he may truly have believed it was a lost cause. But there is an important detail, often overlooked in that small extract, which shows that Hess's mission is to reach a settlement 'between the Führer and the British upper classes' – not Churchill or the government. It is a direct appeal to the aristocracy. The letter can also be read as meaning that Haushofer believed that the chances of a peace being made while Hitler was still in power were 'infinitesimally small'.

On the same day Albrecht wrote to his parents about his misgivings, taking care to add: 'I have now made it clear enough that in the action involved I did not take the initiative.'[67]

The fateful letter

Having first sent a draft to Hess – who made a few changes with the help of his brother Alfred – Albrecht posted the letter to Mrs Roberts care of the mailbox in Lisbon, addressing it to 'the Duke of Hamilton and Brandon' at the House of Lords. He enclosed a short covering note asking Mrs Roberts to forward it.

Dated 23 September 1940, the letter reads, in full:

My dear Douglo,
Even if there is only a slight chance that this letter should reach you in good time, there is a chance, and I am determined to make use of it.

First of all, to give you my personal greeting.

I am sure you know that my attachment to you remains unaltered and unalterable, whatever the circumstances may be.

I have heard of your father's death.

I do hope he did not suffer too much after so long a life of permanent pain.

I heard that your brother-in-law [the Duke of] Northumberland lost his life near Dunkirk. Even modern times must allow us to share grief across all boundaries.

But it is not only the story of death that should find its place in this letter.

If you remember some of my last communications in July 1939, you and your friends in high places may find some significance in the fact that I am able to ask you whether you could find time to have a talk with me somewhere on the outskirts of Europe, perhaps in Portugal.

I could reach Lisbon any time within a few days after receiving news from you.

Of course I do not know whether you can make your authorities understand so much, that they give you leave.

But at least you may be able to answer my question.

Letters will reach me (fairly quickly; they would take some four or five days from Lisbon at the utmost) in the following way: double closed envelope: inside address 'Dr A.H.' Nothing more!

Outside address: 'Minero Silricola Ltd, Rua do Cais de Santarem, 32/1, Lisbon, Portugal.

My father and mother add their wishes for your personal welfare to my own . . .

Yours ever,

A.[68]

The arrangements

The official story is that nothing happened on the British side between the initial contact with Hamilton on 23 September 1940 and Hess turning up out of the blue on 10 May 1941. If there had been further communications in the intervening months, it would radically alter the picture, although it would also raise other questions about Hess's true objectives and why it was necessary for him to come in person. But had there been any further contact between the German and the British sides? There are even problems about the first letter, if one believes the official version, according to which it never even reached its destination, being intercepted by the censors en route. At least, this is what Hamilton and the Churchill government claimed. However, in the Hess–Haushofer correspondence there is mention of a contingency plan: if no reply is forthcoming, they should attempt to contact Hamilton through a citizen of a neutral country. Perhaps this happened via individuals such as Sven Hedin or the Swedish diplomat Baron Knut Bonde.

The censors certainly *did* intercept the letter because their report on it still exists.[69] (Which argues against the hypothesis that the original Roberts letter was part of an intelligence plot: SOE or MI6 would have issued instructions that all her mail should go straight to them – thus sidestepping the censors.) In the event, however, the censors' office passed photographed copies on to the relevant intelligence departments: MI5 and the Foreign Office (and from there to MI6) and the Inter-Services Research Bureau (IRB) – the cover name for SOE. What happened to the original letter is uncertain, although – despite official denials and his own protestations – it seems that Hamilton did receive it. There is a memo dated 22 November 1940 from MI5 to the Foreign Office,[70] that asks whether they had any objection to sending the original letter to the Duke, and a reply dated 7 December confirming that the Foreign Office had none.[71] There is another telling piece of circumstantial evidence that is frequently overlooked. A few days after Hess's arrival, when it was admitted that he had come specifically to meet Hamilton, the Ministry of Information, as reported, for example, in the *Bulletin and Scots Pictorial*, announced: 'Hess made an attempt to communicate with the Duke some months ago. The Duke immediately placed the letter in the hands of the security authorities, and no reply was sent.'[72]

The government subsequently condemned itself out of its own mouth in a report on the Hess affair in November 1942 that it compiled for the Russian government. It reads: 'The Duke of Hamilton had in fact *received* [our italics] a letter dated 23 September from Haushofer suggesting a meeting in Lisbon but without any reference to the presence of Hess. The letter was brought to the attention of His Majesty's Government at the time of its arrival.'[73]

Surprisingly, given his later denials, Hamilton – in his briefing to his solicitors in 1942 – states that although the original of Haushofer's letter seems to have been lost, he received a copy on 19 February 1941 'and on 26 February had to see the Provost Marshal', seeming to imply that he was required to take the letter with him.[74] (The Provost Marshal is chief of the RAF Military Police – why Hamilton connected their meeting with the letter is unclear.)

So there seems little doubt that Hamilton *did* receive the letter. Assuming this to be the case – or that he was contacted, in accordance with 'plan B', by an operative from a neutral country – how did he respond, if at all? Although he appears not to have answered the letter, we know – thanks to the research of Peter Padfield – that he does seem to have taken some action immediately after receiving it. Apparently, without either warning or explanation, Hamilton abruptly took ten days' leave, beginning on 12 November 1940, although what he did during this time or where he went is unrecorded.[75] The mystery is compounded by the fact that he then took another ten days' leave between 26 January and 4 February 1941. Until now his whereabouts were a matter for speculation, but the current Duke permitted us to see his father's diary for 1941, in which he states that he spent this period of leave at Lesbury, on the estate of his brother-in-law, the Duke of Northumberland, near the Northumberlands' family seat at Alnwick. Peter Padfield has suggested a connection between Hamilton's leave and Albrecht Haushofer's visit to Stockholm during the same days.[76] This does suggest that plans relating to Hess's mission were being made on both sides – significantly, the normally crammed Hamilton diary shows only the single word 'Lesbury' for these days. (The Duke's diary for 1940, covering the earlier period of leave, has reportedly been lost.) As the commanding officer of an important RAF base, it would have been unthinkable for Hamilton to have disappeared from base like this without permission from his superiors – but it must be remembered that one of them was Sir Archibald Sinclair.

Whatever happened to the original letter, the cat was out of the bag. The real question is what action the authorities took: did they, as some believe, initiate an intelligence operation by forging Hamilton's replies in order to capture Rudolf Hess? Certainly, one of the copies ended up with RAF intelligence and the XX ('double-cross') Committee, also known as the Twenty Committee, of MI5 – the section that handled German agents who had been 'turned' and other forms of misinformation. The machinery swung into action: on 26 February 1941 Group Captain F. G. Stammers of air intelligence wrote to Hamilton requesting a meeting at the Air Ministry in London.[77] Apparently in response, the Duke then took another ten days' leave in the middle of March, during which he called in on Stammers, who showed him a copy of Haushofer's letter and asked what he had done with the original. According to Hamilton's postwar account, this was the first time he was aware that Albrecht had written to him since July 1939. But we have seen that he told his solicitors he received a copy on 19 February, nearly a month before this meeting and a week before Stammers' invitation. (And Stammers clearly believed the original letter had reached its destination.)

On 28 March, Stammers wrote to Hamilton mildly rebuking him for not having sent him a copy of Albrecht Haushofer's July 1939 letter as he had promised, and reminding him to do so. In reply, Hamilton said that he would be in London at some point in the next three weeks and would bring a copy with him then – apparently playing for time.[78]

So far civilities had been respected. But then on 18 April Hamilton received a telegram from air intelligence *ordering* him to report to a meeting in London on 25 April.[79]

Accordingly, the Duke reported to the men from the ministry – this time meeting Group Captain D. L. Blackford of RAF intelligence and Major T. A. ('Tar') Robertson of the XX Committee. The presence of Robertson, an MI5 officer responsible for the handling of double agents on behalf of the XX Committee, suggests that the meeting was initiated by them. At this meeting Hamilton was asked if he would travel to Lisbon to see Haushofer – after all, it could be very valuable for intelligence-gathering. But the Duke was unenthusiastic, replying that he would only go if ordered to do so. He was told that they preferred volunteers for that kind of mission.[80] Three days later, the Duke sent a letter agreeing to go but imposing certain conditions of his own: that the British Ambassador in Portugal be informed; and that he must be allowed to brief Sir Alexander Cadogan, the Foreign Office permanent under-secretary, before he went. Hamilton also demanded that they supply him with a convincing cover story for his seven-month delay in replying and asked for certain information that would help him concoct an excuse for Haushofer, saying: 'May I therefore have an explanation of the circumstances in which the letter was withheld from me last autumn.'[81]

This was a very shrewd move. It suggests that he was suspicious: first he wanted to be reassured that the Foreign Office and British officials in Portugal knew of the plan – presumably because he was afraid of being set up in some way. Then, by asking where the letter had been for six months – which was hardly necessary for dreaming up an excuse for Albrecht – he was trying to find out who else knew about it. He added that if he met Haushofer in Lisbon, it might be misinterpreted by the Germans as a sign that Britain's resolve was weakening and they wanted to sue for peace!

However, on 3 May – exactly a week before Hess's flight – Group

Captain Blackford wrote to Hamilton and said they had just realised that such an operation could not go ahead without cabinet approval, and that it was therefore being held 'in abeyance'.[82] By the time Hamilton replied to Blackford's letter his attitude had undergone a sea change. Gone were the extreme caution and the attempts to cover himself: suddenly he was enthusiastic about the projected trip to Lisbon, promising that he would be ready the moment it was approved, and even coming up with his own excuse to offer Albrecht about the delay in replying.[83] (Perhaps the marked change in tone had something to do with the fact that this letter was dated 10 May, the day of Hess's flight: he may have believed that within a very short time everything would be different.)

In the Hamilton archives there is a letter dated 29 April 1941 – between the London meeting and Blackford's letter of 3 May – signed 'Eustace' and written from The Rector's Lodge, King's College, Newcastle-upon-Tyne.[84] The writer is easy to identify: Lord Eustace Percy, Hamilton's wife's uncle, younger brother of the 8th Duke of Northumberland. In this letter he tells 'Dear Douglo' that in the bath that morning he had thought of 'a better procedure' for dealing with the approaches made to him by RAF intelligence, and proceeds to outline his suggestions. Surprisingly, they appear, word for word, in Hamilton's reply to Blackford; he simply copied them out.

One of the important implications here is that Hamilton was taking advice – perhaps even instruction – from others. But the other major implication is even more telling: Hamilton was clearly unhappy with the pressure being put upon him by RAF intelligence, so he could not have been a willing part of an intelligence lure himself.

The fact that Lord Eustace Percy was involved reveals another significant connection. It was the 9th Duke of Northumberland, his nephew – and Hamilton's brother-in-law – whose death in 1940 was referred to by Albrecht Haushofer in his letter of 23 September 1940. And, as we will see, the Northumberland family seat, Alnwick Castle, was to play a curious role in Hess's flight.

Was there an intelligence trap?

This series of meetings between Hamilton, Blackford and Robertson is taken by some as evidence that MI5's XX Committee was responsible for luring Hess to Britain, although why the interception of a letter that made no mention of Hess should have inspired a plan to entrap him is unclear. But the first meeting did not take place until March 1941 and by that time the plan was already well advanced: Hess himself had conceived of the mission long before – in the previous August. Moreover, if the XX Committee had kept up a correspondence with Haushofer in Hamilton's name, surely it would have put him in the picture about it when they met face-to-face, having the perfect opportunity to explain and elicit his involvement when he asked for an excuse about the delay in replying. Finally, if a trap had already been set for Hess, why was it still deemed necessary to involve Hamilton? (The Duke had already taken two periods of leave, but he could not have been working for an intelligence operation during this time; had he been, the meetings with Blackford and Robertson would have been unnecessary.)

Hamilton had previously worked for air intelligence in 1936, so he was known to be reliable and had been considered to be useful for intelligence operations. Seen in this context, there seems to be no direct connection between the meeting at which they attempted to set up a rendezvous with Haushofer in Lisbon and the arrival of Hess a few weeks later. The evidence – given in official statements at the time – suggests that Hamilton had received the letter, but had 'placed it in the hands of the authorities'. But these are clearly not RAF intelligence or MI5's XX Committee, who seemed totally unaware that Hamilton had done this.

Then there is the question of the abrupt shelving of the Lisbon operation – apparently on the sudden realisation that higher clearance was needed – just a week before Hess's flight. This seems too much of a coincidence. Were Stammers, Blackford and Robertson really not aware from the beginning that cabinet approval would be needed?

One document in the Public Record Office confounds all attempts to link Hamilton's meeting with Blackford and Robertson to Hess's capture. This is a memorandum from Robertson to his superior, Air Vice-Marshal Medhurst, dated 13 May 1941 – three days after Hess's arrival – which makes it clear that Robertson was as taken aback as everyone else by the Deputy Führer's appearance in Scotland. Indeed, initially he did not even know the identity of the German airman who had asked for the Duke.[85]

One important factor that previous attempts to explain this

episode fail to take into account is that the Hess–Haushofer plan anticipated that Hamilton would show the letter to his superiors before taking any other step, including even replying to it. They expected him to show the letter at least to the Air Minister, Sir Archibald Sinclair, and the Foreign Secretary, Lord Halifax. More to the point, Hess and the Haushofers clearly had no problem with those two gentlemen knowing about it.

So what is the truth about Hamilton and Albrecht Haushofer's letter? The scenario we believe to be most consistent with the evidence, either direct or circumstantial, is as follows.

Hamilton received the letter, and, as expected, showed it to both Halifax and Sinclair. Both of these ministers were supportive of the peace initiative, which had to be kept officially secret and distant from Churchill. So while it is true to say that Hamilton showed the letter to his superiors, what is omitted is the fact that *they* kept quiet about it.

Hamilton then went on leave to make the arrangements for Hess's flight. Then, unexpectedly, a copy of the letter arrived at RAF intelligence, probably from MI5. They – together with the XX Committee – considered it was worth following up, and contacted Hamilton. They were unaware of the Hess plan, which their inadvertent interference threatened to expose. When confronted with the letter in Stammers' office, Hamilton had no choice but to deny all knowledge of it.

Knowing that Hess's flight was fixed for early May, the Duke played for time and, worried that the plan had been discovered, tried to find out from Blackford and Robertson what had been done with the letter, and who else knew about it. Evidently he was reassured that the surfacing of the copy was simply a coincidence. The Lisbon operation was then killed by pressure from above, with Blackford and Robertson being made aware that authorisation from the War Cabinet was needed. This would have stalled the operation without giving anything away to them about Hess's flight.

Assuming that Hamilton had shown the letter to Halifax and Sinclair, was it one of them who stepped in to put a stop to the Blackford–Robertson initiative? If so, it must have been Sinclair, as Halifax was no longer Foreign Secretary – Churchill having found a very adroit way of removing him from Britain. Lord Lothian,

British Ambassador to Washington, had died suddenly in December 1940, and the Prime Minister had seized the opportunity to remove one of the main supporters of peace negotiations from his cabinet by appointing Halifax as Lothian's successor. (Halifax was Churchill's second choice: he had first offered the post to Lloyd George for exactly the same reason, but the wily old Welshman had refused to go as he was holding himself in readiness to become Prime Minister when, as he was utterly convinced, Churchill would be ousted at the start of negotiations with Germany.[86]) With Halifax gone, Churchill filled the post of Foreign Secretary with Anthony Eden, a loyal supporter of his own policy of fighting 'to the bitter end'.

It is clear that Hamilton was up to something in the months between Haushofer's letter and Hess's arrival. But, of course, this is only the British side of the story.

The German preparations

Naturally there appears to have been a considerable amount of preparation and preliminary negotiations for Hess's mission. Yet the accepted line is still that as he failed to receive a reply from Hamilton via Albrecht, the Deputy Führer had decided to take a more direct approach and drop in on the Duke unannounced. If this scenario were correct, then we would expect – apart from Hess's own preparations for his mission – to find no evidence of any other flurry of activity. Instead, however, there was a great deal of it. Particularly of interest is the fact that, between October 1940 and February 1941, Ernst Bohle, head of the AO, was kept busy translating documents relating to the mission into English. In 1945 he told his interrogators: 'I did all the translation work for this trip to England. I didn't know he was going to England. I thought he was going to Switzerland.'[87] This is confirmed by Goebbels' diary, in which he recorded a meeting with Bohle a few days after Hess's flight, in which the AO boss told him that he had translated the documents that Hess took with him.[88]

Albrecht Haushofer made several visits to neutral countries in the early months of 1941. Between 2 and 5 February, he was in Sweden, although why he was there is a mystery.[89] However, as mentioned above, this coincides with one of Hamilton's mysterious periods of leave (26 January–5 February). And, at Hess's express bidding, Albrecht also opened up the way for negotiations with Sir Samuel Hoare in Madrid. Haushofer's agent was a German diplomat named Heinrich Stahmer, a former student of his who approached Hoare through the Swedish Embassy in Spain.[90] According to Scott Newton, 'The upshot was agreement by Hoare and Haushofer that no armistice could proceed without the removal from power of both Hitler and Churchill.'[91] We have already seen that Hoare was involved in various meetings with mediators for the Germans.

On 28 April 1941 Albrecht was in Switzerland for a meeting with another influential middleman for peace negotiations, Carl Jacob Burckhardt, a member (and later president) of the International Committee of the Red Cross.[92] (His involvement is hardly accidental: he had been High Commissioner to the Port of Danzig – where the war started – between 1937 and 1939, having been recommended for the post by Rudolf Hess.[93]) Burckhardt had been in communication with an unnamed British contact 'close to leading Conservative and City circles' who had 'expressed the wish of important English circles for an examination of peace'.[94] In fact, although some believe that Burckhardt's mysterious contact could have been Montagu Norman, governor of the Bank of England, from the testimony of Karl Haushofer there is – as we shall see – a strong suggestion that it was Sir Samuel Hoare.[95]

The triple agent

Although by training a musician, Albrecht Haushofer was very much his father's son, being secretary of the German Geographical Society and the editor of the journal *Geopolitik*. Almost certainly because of these roles in the 1930s he made a number of trips to many countries, including Britain, the USA, Japan and China. In 1936 he was dispatched to London to make preparations for Lloyd George's – extremely positive – meeting with Hitler.[96] He was deemed sufficiently important in Britain to receive an invitation to the coronation of George VI in 1937.[97]

Naturally Haushofer was under surveillance. A report by British intelligence in 1937 stated: 'He is not a man of means and it is believed that his frequent visits to this country were paid for by some government department . . . The source who reported this considered that Haushofer was probably engaged in the collection of intelligence in the United Kingdom.'[98] But for whom did Haushofer gather this intelligence? Not only was he acting as Hess's intermediary vis-à-vis the peace plans, but he was simultaneously an agent for Himmler's peace initiatives.[99] Then again, he was also involved in the conservative German opposition to Hitler, the Mittwochgesellschaft (Wednesday Group), undertaking missions on their behalf.[100] He is even known to have been in contact with members of the Soviet spy ring in Nazi Germany, the Rote Kappelle (Red Orchestra).[101] At his meetings with Carl Burckhardt in Switzerland Haushofer was acting not just for Hess, but for Himmler *and* the Wednesday Group.[102] It must have taken immense concentration to remember what to report to whom.

(Inevitably, Albrecht Haushofer's subversive activities caught up with him: he was eventually imprisoned after the bomb plot against Hitler of July 1944, and was executed, allegedly by the SS, in April 1945, shortly before the German surrender.)

With all his varied and apparently conflicting interests, how can we be sure that Haushofer's many trips to neutral countries during this period were related to Hess's mission? It is clear that at least some of them were: both the Spanish and Swiss trips were authorised by Hess himself, and it is rather telling that in both cases he reported to Hess immediately afterwards. Besides, Karl Haushofer went on record during his interrogation by the Allies in October 1945 as saying:

It is my firm conviction that the reason for that [Hess's flight] was his own sense of honour and his desperation about the murders going on in Germany. It was his firm belief that if he sacrificed himself and went to England, he might be able to do something to stop it . . . At that time Hess initiated peace feelers to be put forward and the responsible man in dealing with these peace feelers was my murdered son. He was in Switzerland and talked with Burckhardt, and Burckhardt told him to come back again to Switzerland and then he would be flown to Madrid and would there have a conference with Lord Templewood [the title Sir Samuel Hoare was given in 1944]. When my son returned from Switzerland Hess spoke to him again, and it was after that that he flew to England. I don't know what he spoke to him about at this discussion.[103]

However, a few days earlier, Haushofer had told officers from the American intelligence department, the Office of Strategic Services (OSS), that his son had *met* Hoare in Switzerland. (Unlike the interview given above, this was not shared with the other Allies. We were able to obtain a copy from the OSS archive.)

> In 1941 Germany put out peace feelers to Great Britain through Switzerland. Albrecht was sent to Switzerland. There he met a British confidential agent – a Lord Templewood, I believe. In this peace proposal we offered to relinquish Norway, Denmark and France. A larger meeting was to be held in Madrid. When my son returned, he was immediately called to Augsburg by Hess. A few days later Hess flew to England.[104]

Further confirmation of the train of events comes from Karl Haushofer's reaction to a story that appeared in the American newspaper *Stars and Stripes* in January 1946, which stated:

> Peace feelers from 'important English circles' were conveyed to a representative of Rudolf Hess a month before Hess flew to England and captivity in May 1941, a 1400-word confidential report included in Adolf Hitler's secret papers revealed last night. Within 48 hours after Hess' departure, his intimate adviser, Dr Albrecht Haushofer, sat down at Obersalzburg and wrote the Führer a full admission of his own role in the peace overtures which he said used a prominent Swiss official of the International Red Cross as intermediary.

In a letter to Father Edmund A. Walsh, the American Jesuit who acted as a special consultant to the American prosecutor at Nuremberg, and with whom Karl Haushofer struck up a relationship based on mutual respect, Haushofer sent a copy of this article with the comment: 'it states the complete truth – a thing that happens but seldom in newspaper reports.'[105]

So we see that Albrecht's trips abroad were intimately connected with Hess's mission, and that there was a definite – if unclear – connection between the talks in Switzerland with Burckhardt, those with Hoare in Spain and the flight of Rudolf Hess. It is also apparent that a key figure on the British side was that high-flying politician-turned-diplomat Sir Samuel Hoare. Albrecht returned from the last of these meetings in such an unusually upbeat frame of mind that it was recorded in his mother's diary. Martha Haushofer notes a phone call from him in Switzerland at the time of his meetings with Burckhardt, adding that his mission 'hasn't been without success'.[106] On his return to Germany on 5 May, she writes that 'the conversations of Albrecht have been fruitful'.[107] Seven months before, his tone had been considerably more pessimistic, as we have seen, so presumably his meetings had given him every reason to suppose that there was real hope of imminently negotiating a peace with Britain. But was Haushofer the lone German representative at these meetings, or was Rudolf Hess also present?

There is a claim that the Deputy himself travelled to Spain to meet with the members of the British pro-peace party around 20–2 April 1941 – just three weeks before his flight. Heinrich Stahmer (Albrecht's agent in Spain) claimed in 1959 that there was a plan for a meeting between Hoare and Lord Halifax on one side, and Hess and Albrecht Haushofer on the other, in either Spain or Portugal in February or March 1941.[108] Tantalisingly he failed to clinch matters by saying whether such a meeting took place, but, fortunately, Scott Newton has clarified the matter, presenting a strong, if circumstantial, case.[109] He reveals that Hess's presence in Spain was reported in the Vichy French press (although the German press took pains to issue a denial). The British Foreign Office contacted King Carol of Romania – then exiled in Seville – for details. He confirmed that Hess had visited Madrid. Puzzled by Hoare's silence on the presence of such a high-ranking Nazi, the Foreign Office demanded to know if this was true: Sir Samuel's reply is a masterpiece of diplomatic – but curiously transparent – evasion. He said that if Hess were in Spain 'his arrival has been kept remarkably secret and his presence in town is not even rumoured yet'.[110] Most telling of all is that, although the files of correspondence between the Madrid Embassy and the Foreign Office were routinely released to the Public Record Office after fifty years, all the documents relating to the weekend of 20–2 April 1941 have been held back until 2017.[111] Clearly, something highly sensitive happened at that time, something that the Foreign Office still wants to keep secret. The evidence points to Hess personally meeting with British representatives – presumably including Sir Samuel Hoare – in Spain shortly before his flight.

We conclude that Albrecht's trips were intended to follow up the

proach to Hamilton, which had not gone cold since the
23 September 1940. In the circumstances they could have
for only one purpose: to co-ordinate the preparations for Hess's
flight with the British pro-peace group.

One major question remains: if Hess, in person or through
Haushofer, was able to meet British representatives on neutral
ground, why did he still think it necessary to make a foolhardy solo
flight into enemy territory? It would seem to be particularly pointless
in the light of Albrecht's firm belief that the talks were very promising. Hess began preparations for his flight in September 1940,
around the time that Albrecht sent his letter to Hamilton, so the
flight must have been part and parcel of the overall plan from the
very beginning. If Hess really had been the lone idealist of the standard story, fired with the idea of the grand gesture, nobody in Britain
would know he was coming. However, if Hess had met Sir Samuel
Hoare or other British representatives in Madrid in April, and if
preparations had been made on the British side, there is no way that
this version can be true. Hess clearly believed that he was going to a
two-day secret meeting, fully expecting to return safely to Germany
without anyone knowing he had ever been away. We know for certain that he did not intend his flight to be seen as a grand public
gesture because one of the first things he did on his arrival was to ask
that his presence be kept from the press.[112] So why did he fly over to
Scotland? Why not continue to negotiate through a neutral country?

Churchill's spies had ensured that the Prime Minister knew all
about the peace-plan network abroad, effectively nipping its activities in the bud. Following Halifax's departure as Foreign Secretary all
diplomatic initiatives now came directly under the scrutiny of Eden,
who was nothing if not a Churchill man through and through. The
flight would be a much more direct approach to British peace circles – effectively cutting out the middleman. Even so, it has to be
admitted that the flight was an enormous risk. Why undertake such
a dangerous venture if it were not essential?

The only answer that makes sense is that Hess had to meet someone who could not leave Britain. The time for talking through
intermediaries was over; the principals had to come face-to-face.
And since this mysterious British principal was unable to leave the
country, Hess had to go to him.

CHAPTER FIVE

Into the Unknown

When war broke out Hess had asked Hitler for permission to join the Luftwaffe. Not surprisingly, the Führer, horrified at the thought of losing his Deputy in a dogfight, refused, and tried to extract a promise that he would remain grounded for the duration of the war. Hess argued, and as a compromise it was agreed that he would not even attempt to fly for one year.[1] That pledge expired in September 1940: Hess wasted no time. He began training for his flight immediately.

One of the most hotly debated questions about the whole affair is whether Hitler knew in advance about Hess's flight. Although both Hitler and Hess repeatedly stated that the Führer had no prior knowledge of his Deputy's mission to Scotland, there is compelling evidence that he did know, and even approved.

Hess's line to his captors was that his mission was in accordance with Hitler's wishes, but was carried out without his knowledge. But surely it is extremely unlikely that Hess would have told the British that Hitler knew, it would have given them far too much of an advantage in the propaganda war: the British could then claim that Hitler was suing for peace. It made sense to keep Hitler's name out of it from the first in order to give him 'plausible denial' in case the whole thing blew up.

On the other hand, it is clear from the way Hess organised his mission that it was not an officially sanctioned operation, and – even if Hitler did know about it – that there were good reasons to keep it from the rest of the Nazi hierarchy. As it was, Hess had to make all the arrangements for the provision and modification of the plane in Augsburg personally. Although it would have been far easier to take off from an airfield in France or Holland, rather than fly across the expanse of Germany single-handedly, this way he kept the number of people who knew about it to the minimum. (There is some evidence that Göring knew of the mission, although it is unclear whether he was initiated into the plan or had discovered it through his own informers in Hess's staff.[2])

Perhaps Hitler disowned Hess because he was anxious to prevent his Axis partners from thinking Germany was trying to negotiate a peace behind their backs. Germany's relations with Italy were particularly strained at that time: von Ribbentrop, when he heard of Hess's flight, specifically feared that this might finish them off. And if the Russians saw that it was German strategy to make peace with Britain they would have realised that they could expect the Nazis on their doorstep at any moment. Hitler's whole strategy for lulling Stalin into a false sense of security was based on convincing him that all his efforts were directed at the invasion of Britain. This may not prove that Hitler knew about the flight, but it does show that he would not have admitted it if he did.

Most informed commentators at the time assumed that Hess must have come with Hitler's blessing. Just two months after the flight, James Murphy produced a pamphlet called *Who Sent Rudolf Hess?* in which he wrote: 'It wasn't a stunt on Hess's part, nor was it a breakaway from his country. It was part of a policy that had been thought out months ahead. The dramatic method of the approach was quite in Hitler's Wagnerian style. And undoubtedly Hitler was a party to it.'[3]

Hitler's denial of all knowledge of the flight is entirely in keeping with his style of leadership. Throughout his career he maintained power by keeping even the most senior Nazis in the dark when he deemed it necessary, adopting a 'divide and rule' approach. He knew he was surrounded by ambitious men who, despite their oaths of loyalty, might eventually conspire against him in an attempt to rule Germany themselves. With the exception of Rudolf Hess, all the other Nazi leaders were permanently engaged in a power struggle, spying on each other, trying to take over each other's territories. Shrewdly, Hitler used this very ambition to maintain his own supreme position. Keeping the leaders fighting among themselves

November 1918: Second Lieutenant of the Reserve Flying Corps. Hess in front of a Fokker Dr. 1 Triplane close to the Western Front. He was to become an acknowledged aviation ace: like the Duke of Hamilton and the Duke of Kent, one of the elite international pilots who saw themselves as 'knights of the air'.

HULTON GETTY

General Karl Haushofer, Professor of
Geopolitics at Munich University, who
became Hess's mentor. He was a moderating influence on Hess – and, through
him, even on the Führer himself in the
early days.

BRIGADIER D. MURPHY

Rudolf Hess at the height of his power as
Hitler's Deputy.

Left: Hitler becomes a German citizen in 1932, with Hess's sponsorship. Always by Hitler's side (*below*), and a central figure in whipping up pro-Nazi hysteria (*bottom*), Hess was considerably more important than history has allowed.

Hess after winning the Zugspitze
Air Race with his wife Ilse.

A very private man, Hess
enjoyed family life: he adored
his only child, Wolf Rüdiger
whom he nicknamed 'Buz'.
The boy was still a toddler
when his father left for Britain.

Although the Duke of Windsor has been vilified as a Nazi sympathiser (*top left*) (seen here, as the guest of Hitler in 1937), other members of the Royal Family were also impressed by the Führer. Certainly, the King and Queen were utterly opposed to a war with Germany, treating Prime Minister Neville Chamberlain to a hero's welcome on the balcony at Buckingham Palace (*above*) after he made the ill-fated announcement of 'peace in our time'. George VI and Queen Elizabeth were anxious that the pro-appeasement Lord Halifax (*top right*) should succeed Chamberlain as Prime Minister, being opposed to Winston Churchill.

Above left: Press baron Lord Beaverbrook, whose pro-peace sympathies were cleverly pressed into service by Churchill (*above right*) as the Hess saga unfolded. *Left:* Sir Samuel Hoare, whose attempts to broker peace between Britain and Germany extended, secretly, beyond the outbreak of hostilities.

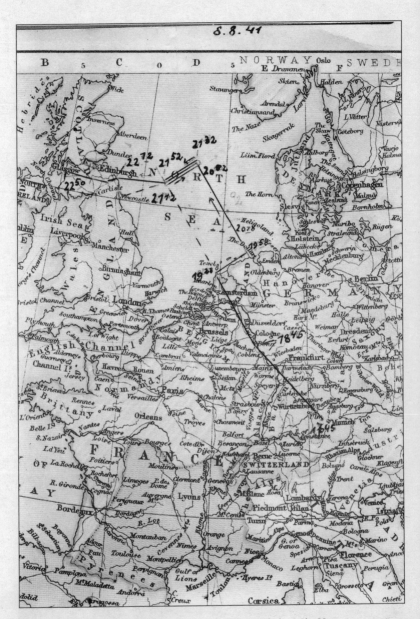

The map purporting to show his route to Scotland, drawn by Hess while imprisoned at Mytchett Place. Note his handwritten date of '8.8.41'.

Top left: servicemen remove the wreckage of Hess's Me-110. *Top right*: Mrs Annie McLean in the kitchen at Floors Farm, Eaglesham, near Glasgow, where she offered the Deputy Führer – who claimed to be Hauptmann Alfred Horn – a cup of tea after he parachuted into a nearby field on 10 May 1941. Hess claimed to have come to meet with the Duke of Hamilton (*right*) – who denied all knowledge of such an arrangement.

not only prevented them from building up an effective power base, but strengthened his overall authority. Only he could settle their disputes.

Many others were convinced that Hitler knew about – or had even sanctioned – Hess's mission, disowning him when it failed as part of a pre-arranged plan. Colonel Armando Bernal, the Mexican Military Attaché in Berlin, stated that the Führer had authorised the flight but concocted the story of Hess's madness when it became clear that it was a debacle.[4] And Ernst Bohle, the AO chief who had helped Hess translate letters to the Duke of Hamilton, was convinced that Hitler knew all about it. He said during his interrogation by the Allies in September 1945:

> . . . it was my firm opinion at the time, which I cannot prove today, that Hitler knew all about it because it seemed impossible to me that Hess would do anything of such importance without asking Hitler . . . It was my opinion that only three people in Germany knew anything about it, Hitler, Hess and myself . . . I had orders to speak to nobody, not even to his own brother, who was in my own office, not even to his secretary.[5]

Four days after Hess's flight, a cable was intercepted from the Japanese Embassy in Rome to Tokyo, reporting on the visit of von Ribbentrop, who had hurried to reassure Mussolini of Germany's commitment to the Axis agreement. According to the cable, von Ribbentrop told Mussolini and Count Ciano that, although Hess's flight required the Führer's 'patronage', he had 'made the flight on his own account'. The report confirms that Hess had met Hamilton before the war but adds that 'the only thing he did not allow for was the fact that Hamilton had changed sides'.[6]

Preparations for the mission

After initially trying out a Messerschmitt Bf109, Hess finally settled on an Me-110, a twin-engined fighter–bomber that usually required a crew of two (pilot and navigator/bomb aimer) because of its superior speed and range. The plane came from the Messerschmitt factory at Augsburg – some forty miles from Hess's home – under the direct auspices of Dr Willi Messerschmitt, its owner, who had been a friend since the First World War. He was also known to be in favour of peace with Britain.[7] Because the plane was larger and more complicated than the light aircraft that Hess usually flew, he needed intensive training from Messerschmitt's chief test pilot, initially Willi Stör, later Helmut Kaden. Despite the burden of his public duties, he still managed to have practice flights a couple of times a week – around thirty sessions in all. It is interesting that on his first flight he was accompanied by Hitler's personal pilot, Hans Baur – who also supplied him with updated maps for his journey showing the zones over which flying was forbidden for military purposes.[8] It seems highly unlikely that Baur was so involved without the full knowledge of the Führer, who may even have offered his personal pilot's services.

In a lecture to the Rudolf Hess Society in Munich in 1989 Helmut Kaden – who after the war became managing director of Augsburg Airport – gave a detailed account of the preparations for Hess's flight.[9] (Although Kaden was instrumental in preparing for the flight and modifying the plane, at no stage did he know the reasons for Hess's mission.) Kaden stated that both he and Stör suggested that Hess should take the twin-engined Me-110 because they thought it safer than a single-engined aircraft – and there was also room for an instructor during the training flights. Kaden described Hess as a 'first-class pilot'. Hess began the training in September 1940 and flew several Me-110s until he found one that he particularly liked. At his request this plane – serial number 3869, identification code VJ-0Q – became his reserved machine, being kept under a special guard in a factory hangar.

In October 1940 Hess asked for special radio equipment to be fitted. This was too large and cumbersome to fit into the cockpit, and was instead installed in the navigator's seat, with a device that enabled him to operate it from the pilot's position. Also at this time he asked for drop tanks for extra fuel to be fitted, which made Kaden and his colleagues wonder what he was up to, but they were afraid to ask.

Kaden's account also sheds some light on another enduring question about the flight – namely whether Hess had made any previous attempts, or whether his flight to Scotland on 10 May 1941 was the first. Members of Hess's staff gave contradictory accounts of how many earlier attempts there were and different dates on which they happened, as did Hess himself, telling the Duke of Hamilton that he had made two earlier attempts, but claiming to Lord Simon that the 10 May flight was his 'first attempt'.[10]

According to Kaden, on Saturday, 21 December 1940 one of Hess's staff telephoned the airfield and asked for the plane to be fully fuelled, including the drop tanks – 3,000 litres of fuel in all. This was the first time that Kaden and his team had been required to fill the tanks completely. This gave fuel for ten hours in the air with a range of 2,500 kilometres (1,560 miles); clearly Kaden realised that this was no usual training flight.

Hess arrived at the airfield and changed into his flying suit while one of his adjutants made a telephone call. Kaden asked the adjutant whom he was calling and was told it was the naval meteorological office in Hamburg. Hess then walked to the plane with his adjutant, carrying two briefcases, one of which – Kaden says – contained a Thermos flask and food, the other being full of documents. Kaden asked the adjutant what was going on, and was told that 'maybe' Hess was flying to the English Channel to test the plane and while there was going to broadcast his annual Christmas message from the front. Hess took off at about 1.30 p.m. but returned three hours later, making the difficult and dangerous landing with the wing tanks still attached on the snow-covered airfield. He explained he had been forced to return because one of the flaps had stuck. Was this an aborted attempt to fly to Dungavel, or merely a rehearsal for landing with drop tanks?

On Saturday, 18 January 1941 Hess went through the same process once more, again with briefcases, again taking off at 1.30 p.m., only to return about three and a half hours later. This time he said he had returned because he had been unable to pick up the radio signal he was expecting from the radio station at Kalundborg in Denmark. Josef Blumel, Messerschmitt's radio specialist, said that the signal was too weak and so a more powerful radio receiver was installed. A radio compass was also fitted. Again, was this just a test of the technology – in this case the radio equipment – or a serious attempt to fly to Scotland?

Hess's next attempt, on 30 April 1941, seems to have been a genuine one. Four days before, on 26 April, Hess had celebrated his forty-seventh birthday, but this birthday was rather different. For the first time, dozens of column inches and several radio broadcasts were devoted to the admirable qualities of the Deputy Führer, particularly stressing – intriguingly – his glorious triumphs in the air.[11] There is the strong whiff of the spin doctor about it, suggesting that his profile was deliberately being built up in preparation for a special mission: the German people were being primed to welcome him back as a great hero.

Five days after Hess's birthday Hitler himself was due at the Messerschmitt factory, from where he was going to make his annual May Day speech to the Reich. This was a huge break with tradition. Every year since taking power in 1933 he had made the speech at the Tempelhofer Feld in Berlin, but suddenly he had decided to do it from an aircraft factory, specifically the Messerschmitt factory in Augsburg.

The day before, 30 April, Kaden was again requested to fuel up Hess's Me-110. This time Hess sat in the plane with the engines running, as one of his adjutants made a telephone call – Kaden presumed for instructions. After making the call, the adjutant signalled to Hess to turn off the engines, after which he exchanged a few words with him. Hess then called Kaden over, saying: 'I have just been informed that the Führer will not be coming to Augsburg to give his speech. I will be doing it instead.' It is difficult to exaggerate how unusual this was, and the magnitude of the honour it bestowed on him.

It is hard to avoid the conclusion that the adjutant had telephoned the Führer's headquarters in Berlin, and that he had been given the word for Hess not to go ahead with his flight. Therefore, Hitler knew. One might go further: was it his plan to link one of the major speeches in the Nazi calendar with Hess's flight? And is it significant that it was also on 30 April that Hitler set the date for the attack on Russia, Operation Barbarossa?

Evidence of the war correspondent

Until recently, the most persuasive evidence that Hitler knew about Hess's plans to fly to Britain came from the French war correspondent André Guerber who, according to the *Sunday Dispatch* of September 1945, had discovered documents in the Berlin Chancellery that proved this to be the case. (Perhaps not surprisingly, the documents have since disappeared.) According to the

Sunday Dispatch, these consisted of minutes of meetings between Hitler, Hess and Göring at the Berghof at Berchtesgaden on 4 May 1941, at which the Deputy Führer reported on his visit to Madrid in April to contact British representatives. (As we have seen, there is evidence that such a visit did take place.) Hess stated that, as a result, he was convinced that some influential individuals in Britain were willing to negotiate for peace. Hitler responded that he wanted the war with Britain to end, adding ominously: 'I have reached the solemn decision to go to war with Russia this autumn.'[12]

Later the same day Hitler called Hess back for another meeting, specifically for a briefing on the British mentality and the state of public morale in Britain at the time. Hess told him: 'We must show the British we are sincere. If we do that the British people will rise up and compel Churchill to make peace.' They then devised a series of peace proposals – a four-point plan – which they called Plan S 274K ABCD. Its aims were:

A. To convince the British that they would eventually lose the war.
B. To delineate the British and German spheres of influence: Britain would rule its empire, while Germany would govern Europe.
C. To offer a twenty-five-year alliance. (Apparently, this was Hess's suggestion.) Significantly, an alliance for exactly that period is believed to have been required by Neville Chamberlain in his secret attempts to avert war in the summer of 1939.[13]
D. To demand that Britain should adopt an attitude of 'benevolent neutrality' to Germany in its coming war with the Soviet Union.

Because the documents have vanished, it is impossible to be certain they were genuine – or even existed at all. Although much of the detail dovetails with evidence from other sources, there is one error. Hitler, Hess and Göring were not at Berchtesgaden on 4 May, but in Berlin. However, it is not clear from the *Dispatch* report whether this comes from the document or was merely an assumption on the part of either Guerber or the reporter. If the report is true, it shows that Göring, too, was aware of the plan.[14]

More recently, new evidence has emerged that more persuasively reveals the truth behind Hess's flight.

The Gestapo reports

New light is shed on the days immediately before the flight by the reports of the later Gestapo interrogations of members of Hess's staff.[15] (Interestingly, all of them were released and their subsequent careers do not appear to have suffered from their dealings with Hess – except at the hands of Bormann in 1943.) The reports of their interrogations, which took place between 18 and 22 May 1941, were unearthed in America and copies are now lodged in the Institut für Zeitgeschicht (Institute for Contemporary History) in Munich. The story they have to tell changes the standard version of Hess's flight radically, because they provide proof that Hitler knew and that yet another attempt was made – this time on Monday, 5 May 1941. (Kaden makes no mention of it, but then he might not have been on duty that day.) That such an attempt was intended for that date is supported by the fact that when ordering modifications to the plane, Hess instructed that they be completed by 5 May.[16]

Those interrogated were Hess's security man, Kriminalrat Franz Lutz, adjutant Günther Sorof and driver Rudolf Lippert – all SS officers. Perhaps it is significant that Karl-Heinz Pintsch, the adjutant who seems to have been more privy to Hess's plans than the rest of his staff and who, after the war, became the main disseminator of information about the days immediately preceding the flight, was not among those interrogated.

Sorof told his questioners that Hess had flown to Berlin to see Hitler on 3 May. According to Lutz, Hess took his new, specially made Luftwaffe uniform with him. A few minutes before the plane took off from Munich, he had a meeting with Karl Haushofer at the airport. Sorof was ordered to wait behind in Munich so that he could relay an important message that Haushofer would telephone through either that evening or the next morning. As it happened, he phoned that evening, with the message 'On a scale of one to six, things stand at around three or four and more needs doing', and that Albrecht Haushofer (who was then in Switzerland) would report as soon as he returned to Germany.

According to Lutz, who was with Hess in Berlin, when the latter received this message he took it straight to Hitler. (Lutz says he was told this by Pintsch.) He added that he believed the message originated from Portugal.

The following day – 4 May – Hitler was due to give a speech in the Reichstag, but, according to Lutz, the enigmatic message made him and Hess revise the wording, although we do not know which parts were changed. After they had agreed the text of the speech, Hess instructed Ernst Bohle to translate it into English and to have several copies – in a small typeface – printed. (It seems likely that he intended to take them with him on his flight.) The theme of Hitler's speech is very significant in the light of Hess's mission. Very similar to the one he made on the fall of France – this was the first time that Hitler had addressed the Reichstag since then – it stressed that he had never wanted a war with Britain, claiming that he had been forced into it by the Chamberlain government's intransigence over Poland and compelled to continue it by Churchill's refusal to consider a negotiated peace. He declared that: 'All my endeavours to come to an understanding with Britain were wrecked by the determination of a small clique which, whether from motives of hate or for the sake of material gain, rejected every German proposal for an understanding due to their resolve, which they never concealed, to resort to war, whatever happened.'[17] The clear implication is that it was not the British people but the Churchill government that he blamed, and that he would still have preferred not to be fighting Britain. Although Hitler did not make a direct offer of peace talks (such an offer would perhaps have been taken as a sign of weakness by the German people, and would warn Stalin of the impending offensive against Russia), such an offer was certainly implied. It fits so well with the message that Hess brought that, especially in the light of the testimony in the Gestapo reports, it is hard to credit that there was no connection between the two events.

But of even greater importance in the light of Hess's mission is a statement that Hitler made early in the speech: 'On 6 October 1939 I therefore once more publicly stated that Germany had neither demanded nor intended to demand anything either from Britain or from France, that it was madness to continue the war and, above all, that the scourge of modern weapons of warfare, once they were brought into action, would inevitably ravage vast territories.'[18] Not only are the sentiments expressed pure Hess, but the mention of the specific date of 6 October 1939 – the date of Clydesdale's letter to *The Times* – like the offer itself, seems intended as a further signal to the peace group in Britain. Presumably this was the part rewritten in the light of Albrecht Haushofer's message from Switzerland: the British had asked for coded reassurance that Hitler backed the plan. Here it was.

Lutz also says that Pintsch specifically told him that Hess had discussed his plan with Hitler that night and that Hess had said, 'The Führer was not averse to it.' This is especially significant because after the war Pintsch always maintained – even when tortured by the Russians – that Hitler had not known of Hess's plans.[19]

Although Pintsch may have continued to obey orders long after the war had ended, there was another witness to the last meeting between Hess and his Führer: one of Hitler's aides at the Chancellery. According to this source, the two men were closeted away for four hours in intense discussion – which seemed to erupt into argument at one point, for voices were raised, followed by a period of silence. When Hess and Hitler emerged, however, any anger had disappeared: the Führer had his arm affectionately around the Deputy's shoulders, and his parting words were: 'Hess, you are and always were a terribly stubborn person.'[20]

According to the Gestapo reports, after the Reichstag speech Hess and his entourage left Berlin by overnight train for Augsburg. When they arrived the next morning, Hess booked into the Hotel Drei Mohren, going immediately into a meeting with Albrecht Haushofer, who – as we know from other sources – had just returned from his meeting with Carl Burckhardt in Switzerland. That afternoon, dressed in his Luftwaffe uniform underneath his leather flying suit, Hess drove to the Messerschmitt works where his Me-110 was ready waiting.

He took off around 5 p.m., but some time later he returned, having to circle the field for over an hour in order to lose fuel before landing. Apparently – according to Lippert – a radio fault had forced him to return. (Whether this was a fault in the equipment or, once again, a failure to pick up the radio signal is uncertain.)

From this new material it is quite clear that there was an extraordinary flurry of activity surrounding Hess's flight, and several previous attempts – most, if not all, with Hitler's knowledge and support. And there is every reason to believe that the testimony of Hess's staff is genuine – if they were not telling the truth, they were contradicting the Führer's overt position to their Gestapo interrogators.

The tension builds

On 9 May Hess telephoned Alfred Rosenberg in Berlin to summon him to an urgent meeting the next day – even laying on a special plane for him.[21] Then, on the morning of 10 May he took a final walk with his son 'Buz' and their German shepherd dog and her pups. This was the last time he was to enjoy domesticity, have his family around him or even walk the earth as a free man.

Rosenberg arrived and the two leading Nazis took lunch together (Ilse, who was unwell, stayed in bed). Unusually, the staff were given strict instructions not to disturb the men's meal. Rosenberg did not return to Berlin immediately afterwards, but was driven straight to Hitler's weekend retreat at Berchtesgaden. After Rosenberg's departure, Hess had a short nap, then, dressing in a new Luftwaffe captain's uniform – tailor-made for this occasion – he went to say goodbye to Ilse. Although she always maintained she knew nothing of her husband's plans, the fact that she was reading *The Pilot's Book of Everest* by the Marquess of Clydesdale does seem to stretch coincidence rather too far. Indeed, there is something of a mystery about this book: according to Ilse, it had been given to them by 'English friends' before the war.[22] It was inscribed: 'With all good wishes and the hope that out of personal friendships a real and lasting understanding may grow between our two countries' and was signed by the 'English friends'. Hess picked it up, turned to a photograph of Clydesdale, looked at it for a few seconds and remarked: 'He's very good looking.' He and Ilse had tea together and then said what was to be a much more final goodbye than they ever intended. She asked when he was coming back. Hess replied, seriously tempting fate: 'I don't know exactly – perhaps tomorrow, perhaps not, but I'll certainly be back by Monday evening.' After saying goodbye to his wife and little son, Hess drove off with Pintsch and his detective, Franz Lutz, on the forty-mile journey to Augsburg and the Me-110, stopping for a walk in the woods on the way.

The flight

Hess took off from the Messerschmitt factory at 5.45 p.m. Probably on the Deputy's personal orders, the Me-110's guns were packed in grease to disable them and it carried no bombs or ammunition. Hess himself was unarmed, as befits a peace envoy. The specially fitted drop tanks contained an extra 1,800 litres of fuel, extending the range of the plane to a maximum of around 1,560 miles.

The map Hess used to navigate across Britain – a German reproduction of a British Ordnance Survey map – is now on display at Lennoxlove House, the home of the current Duke of Hamilton. Dungavel and several useful landmarks had been marked. The map had been strapped to Hess's thigh to enable him to consult it with relative ease during the flight (which is how it survived the crash). After his capture Hess maintained that he navigated entirely by himself, using compass bearings until reaching the British coast and then relying on the map, together with visual sightings of landmarks that he had memorised.

All reconstructions of the flight up to his approach to the Northumberland coast are based on Hess's own testimony given while in custody, particularly a map showing his route that he drew on an atlas in August 1941 and a description in a letter to his son written the previous month. (British radar and Royal Observer Corps records cover his flight path towards and after he crossed the coast.)

Hess claimed he had flown northwest across Germany and Holland, but after leaving the Dutch coast behind he took a very curious, almost box-shaped route (see diagram), so that he approached the Northumberland coast from the east. He said that he then realised he had an hour to kill because at this more northerly latitude the sun set later and obviously he wanted to be flying over-land at dusk.[23] He turned 180 degrees and flew back the way he had come for about twenty minutes. Then he did another 180-degree turn back towards the British coast. He marked this complicated manoeuvre clearly on the map he drew for his captors.

However, there are very good reasons for believing that this was not the route that Hess took, and that the journey he described was a deliberate deception on his part. After months of meticulous planning it seems improbable that Hess would have overlooked such an elementary matter as the fact that the sun sets later in more northerly latitudes. In his 1989 lecture to the Rudolf Hess Society, Helmut Kaden pointed out that Hess could not have taken the route he claimed – northwest across Germany – because it would have taken him over the Ruhr Valley. This industrial area was so heavily defended that even a German aircraft flying without authorisation would have been a target.[24] Kaden recalls that after circling the airfield, Hess flew off exactly due north.

Further suspicions are aroused by the killing-time manoeuvres over the North Sea. Hess carefully and precisely noted the changes of course and their exact times on the map he drew while in custody. He claims he reached the Dutch coast at 19.28, but instead of continuing out over the North Sea, he turned 90 degrees to starboard – northeast – and flew parallel with the coast for some seventy miles before turning northwest again (at 19.58) and following a track parallel with his original course. At 20.52, over the middle of the North Sea, he made another 90-degree turn to port to begin his approach to Britain. Then, at 21.12, came the realisation that he had to kill time, the doubling-back manoeuvres, and, finally, the crossing of the British coast. If all this really happened as he claimed, then Hess should be congratulated on a quite astonishing feat of navigation. This zigzagging over the North Sea was achieved – according to Hess – by compass alone, and yet still brought him in at exactly the right spot. Just half a degree's error on any of the turns would have taken him many miles out of his way.

Had these manoeuvres been invented to cover up the fact that Hess's journey took an hour longer than it should have done?[25] The most glaring problem with Hess's version of events centres on the radar question. At that time, long-range British radar – the Chain Home network – extended some 150 miles out into the North Sea (up to 200 miles in good conditions[26]) and it was at approximately 150 miles that it first detected Hess's plane.[27] Felicity Ashbee, the WAAF who plotted Hess's flight at the Filter and Operations Room at RAF Leighton Buzzard, notes that 'reception was extremely good that night'. According to Hess's map, at least part of his zigzagging had taken place within the range of the British radar: he was about 140 miles from the coast when he doubled back and about 210 miles out when he began his second approach. But the British records show that he came straight in: there was no zigzagging. Had Hess invented the story of a considerably more complex and difficult flight? If so, why?

The only logical reason is that revealing details of his real course to the British would have given away some secret information, presumably connected with German radio navigation systems. Helmut

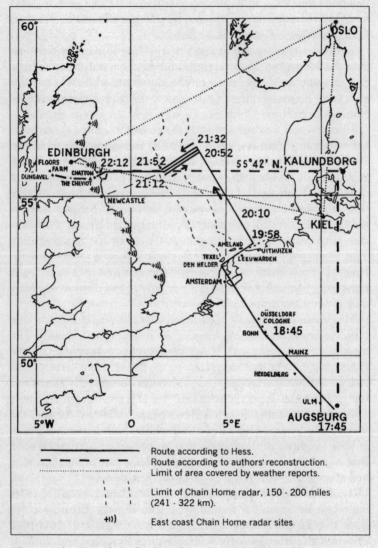

The route that Hess claimed to have flown from Augsburg to Glasgow, compared with the route according to the authors' reconstruction. The dotted line shows the area for which Hess received daily weather reports while preparing for his flight.

Kaden mentioned a radio station at Kalundborg in Denmark, and described Hess's plane as being fitted with special radio equipment, while Ilse Hess – in her 1951 book *Prisoner of Peace* – said Hess had brought new radio equipment into the house, which was tuned to the Kalundborg station. She also said that she learned after the flight that Hess had used the signals from Kalundborg and had asked the station to broadcast one of his favourite tunes at various intervals that day.[28]

Kalundborg is on the west coast of Zeeland in Denmark, and the radio station – then known as Kastanie Y, but now the home of Denmark's Radio One – is on a peninsula outside the town. Judging by its position on the map, it is in a remarkably suitable location for Hess, exactly due north of Augsburg and precisely due east of both Hess's intended destination, Dungavel House, and the point where he crossed the British coast. Therefore, if he had made use of this station, his simplest course of action would be to fly directly north until he reached Kalundborg – Kaden, it will be recalled, said he departed in a northerly direction – and then turn west, following a directional beam until he reached the British coast. No navigational skill whatsoever would have been needed beyond the ability to locate north and west: once on the beam, he would just use the radio signal to keep on a straight course. If this is what happened, it would have added about 250 miles to his journey, which is one hour's flying time.[29] In order to keep the use of this transmitter secret he had invented the tale of three twenty-minute doubling-back manoeuvres.

More evidence for this comes from the post-war testimony of one of the meteorologists at the Central Weather Group in Potsdam. In 1993 this individual – who did not want to be identified – told Belgian researcher Georges Van Acker that, every morning for several months before the flight, one of Hess's secretaries had telephoned for a weather forecast for the area falling within the triangle of Oslo, Kiel and Edinburgh.[30] Hess's version of the flight would require a different area forecast, whereas if he had flown from Kalundborg this forecast would have been correct.

His true route is confirmed by the Gestapo reports of the interrogation of Hess's staff. Listed among the documents he left behind were letters to Hitler, Himmler, Director Hensen of the Messerschmitt works, his sister-in-law Ingeborg Pröhl – and a 'map with the flight-route with several zigzags' (*Richtungsänderungen*), which would appear to tally with the map he drew for the British.[31] But why leave a map of his route when all he needed to tell them was his destination? And why did this map already show the 'zigzags' that he later claimed he only decided to make when he realised he would have to kill time? The most obvious answer is that he left the map to show the course that he would pretend to have followed. Essentially, he was reassuring the people he was leaving behind that the secret of the Kalundborg transmitter was safe with him.

Now we can understand why Hess showed such amusement in letters to people in Germany about the British admiration for his navigational skills. Without Kalundborg they certainly would have been remarkable.

Inside the special mission

There are other intriguing questions about his long and arduous journey. Did he fly alone as he claimed or did he have an escort, at least for part of the journey? If Hitler was involved in the plan, it is extremely unlikely that Hess would not have been provided with protection for the dangerous North Sea crossing, when his unarmed plane could well have fallen foul of a British patrol. On the other hand, if only a few 'need to know' people were in on the secret, it is unlikely that the escort would be entrusted to ordinary airmen. Perhaps significantly, there is evidence that Reinhard Heydrich, head of the SS's intelligence branch, the Sicherheitsdienst (SD), and a few hand-picked companions were flying Me-109 fighters over the Channel and North Sea that evening.[32] There is also evidence – although not conclusive – from British radar that Hess's plane was accompanied by perhaps as many as three others, all of which turned back before he reached the coast.

Having successfully navigated the North Sea, the Me-110 was followed visually by the Royal Observer Corps' network. The tracking of the flight was co-ordinated by Fighter Command Headquarters at Bentley Priory in Middlesex, which kept other RAF bases informed – including RAF Turnhouse, where the progress of Hess's aircraft was being closely followed by Wing Commander the Duke of Hamilton.

The British response to the flight requires close examination, since it has been argued that it reveals prior knowledge of Hess's arrival, and – much more controversially – that he was even protected for much of the journey over Britain. The Me-110 was picked up by the radar station at Ottercops Moss on the Northumberland coast, but this splendidly named station had a reputation for false alarms, so there was some disbelief at Fighter Command HQ when it made its report.[33] Did Hess know that this was the weakest link in the chain of coastal radar? If so, he could only have learned this from someone in Britain who had inside information.

On this occasion, however, Ottercops Moss's reputation was unsullied, even when its radar tracks suggested there was more than one aircraft and that the others turned back before reaching the coast. Other radar stations soon confirmed this, suggesting that Hess had been given an escort and that someone very high up in the German military command not only knew about the mission, but had gone out of their way to facilitate it. But it must be admitted that the reports from the different radar stations are frustratingly contradictory: some claim that the accompanying aircraft turned back towards the east, while others report that there was only ever the one plane.[34] On balance, the evidence points to the existence of escorting planes that peeled off some way from the English coast. This is suggested by the designations given to the radar track: initially it was 'X42', 'X' standing for unidentified aircraft; but later it became 'Raid 42J', 'J' standing for a raid that had split up, showing that those who gave the designation believed there to have been more than one aircraft to begin with.

Another anomaly of the flight was an apparently pointless detour as Hess crossed the Northumberland coast. As we have seen, he came in on a precisely westerly direction on the same latitude as Dungavel, but as soon as he approached the coast he briefly deviated from his strictly straight course for about fifteen miles (see diagram). The only possible reason for making this detour was to fly close to some place of significance: in sight because of the change of course was Alnwick Castle, the family seat of the Duke of Northumberland, whose sister was married to the Duke of Hamilton. (And, of course, Northumberland's uncle was Lord Eustace Percy, who, only days before, had advised Hamilton on his dealings with air intelligence.) Indeed, one of the official notes made on the radar tracking of Hess's plane gives his landfall specifically as Alnwick.[35]

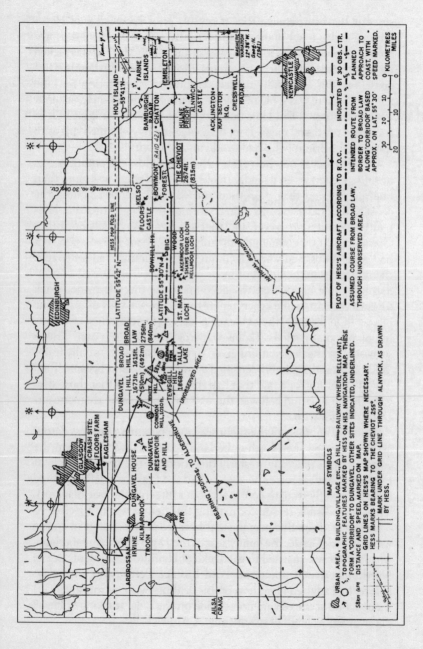

It is no coincidence that both Alnwick Castle and Dungavel were the homes of high-ranking individuals who were related by marriage and were at some level involved with the peace lobby. Moreover, as Alnwick Castle is situated on the coast just a few miles off the same latitude as Dungavel and Kalundborg, could it have been transmitting a radio signal to guide Rudolf Hess's flight? Is this why such powerful radio equipment had been specially installed in the Me-110? Or, on the other hand, could somebody at Alnwick have been receiving the same signal as Hess from Kalundborg, and was the specific piece of music a code for Hess's approach?

The reaction of the RAF

After crossing the coast the course of the lone Messerschmitt was tracked over Northumberland and into Scotland by the Royal Observer Corps' eagle eyes. They noted that the pilot flew as low as fifty feet from the ground at some points.[36] (This was characteristic of Hess's barnstorming style in his young days as a dashing pilot.)

It is not true, as various commentators have suggested, that the RAF did nothing, but what little they did do seems suspiciously like a token response. The official record shows that four aircraft were, at various stages, sent up to try to intercept the intruder. The scrambling of so few fighters might seem a mild response to an enemy aircraft heading towards the city of Glasgow, but in the circumstances it was not particularly surprising. By then 'Raid 42J' was known to be a single plane, and it was a common occurrence for the Luftwaffe to send lone aircraft to lure British fighters away from a Blitz hotspot. Besides, precious resources would not be wasted on chasing a single fast-moving plane. Curiously, however, that is not the impression given after the event by the Duke of Hamilton, who described whole squadrons of Spitfires being scrambled to intercept

Hess's flight across Britain: from the coast this is based on Royal Observer Corps observations, compared to his intended course as marked on his own map. Hess used the fold line – which indicates the latitude of Kalundborg – to disguise the direction of his approach to the British coast. He marked his diversion from this route to Alnwick with a series of speed and distance indicators, joined up here for clarity. Also note the 250 degree bearing from the 'abort point' to RAF Aldergrove.

Hess's flight.[37] According to him, the Deputy Führer was lucky to have got through. The same impression was given by Sir Archibald Sinclair to the House of Commons on 22 May, when he stated that Hess's plane 'was in imminent danger of being shot down' at the time he baled out.[38] This could not have been true: not a single British fighter even got close. On the other hand, there does seem to have been a curious degree of ineptitude on the night of 10 May – almost as if those co-ordinating the interception did not really want the plane to be captured. First, two Spitfires from RAF Acklington that were already on patrol were ordered to intercept the intruder. They failed to find the Me-110: at one point they were even vectored on to each other by radar operators![39] Secondly, a Spitfire piloted by Sergeant Maurice Pocock was scrambled from RAF Acklington. According to John Costello, Pocock later admitted he had been given the order far too late realistically to expect to see – let alone catch – the Me-110.[40] Finally, a Boulton Paul Defiant night fighter flown by Pilot Officer William A. Cuddie of 141 Squadron was sent up from RAF Ayr. That, too, failed to locate the Nazi intruder.

Another very suggestive piece of evidence that the RAF gave Hess a degree of protection in his flight over Britain emerged in 1999, in the form of claims by two Czech pilots, flying Hurricanes for 245 Squadron based at RAF Aldergrove in Northern Ireland. The two pilots concerned – both now dead – were Sergeant Vaclav 'Felix' Bauman and Sergeant Leopold 'Polda' Srom. After the war they returned home to Czechoslovakia and lived under Soviet rule where they remained unaware of the post-war controversy about the flight of Rudolf Hess. But in the early 1990s, after the downfall of the Communist regime, the Prague-based military archivist Jiri Rajlich was researching a book about the exploits of Czech airmen who had flown for the RAF in the Second World War and interviewed Bauman and Srom. They told how they had been scrambled to intercept a single German plane that was heading towards the Firth of Clyde, some forty miles from RAF Aldergrove. But as they came within range, the order came through on their radio: 'Stop action and return.' When Bauman said that they were within range to shoot it down he was told, 'Sorry, Felix, old boy. It is not possible. You must return. Now.'[41] The pilots' story remained unknown to the West for several years – Rajlich's book *Stihaci Pilot (Fighter Pilot)* was published only in Czech – until it was discovered by a translator working on Hugh Thomas's book about Hess. In turn, the story was passed on to a British researcher of Czech descent, Tony Marczan, who – already bitten by the Hess bug – delved further. Happy to co-operate, Rajlich gave him a copy of Srom's log book for the evening of Hess's flight, which was countersigned by his commanding officer and contains the entry for the scramble of 10 May. But there is no time noted, and no record of any such scramble in RAF Aldergrove's operation records book for that day. (Although it must be said that the ORBs of fighter stations were notoriously slapdash at that time.) The pilots' squadron leader, J. W. C. Simpson, asked Fighter Command for an explanation and was told that the two Czechs were called off because they had crossed into another RAF squadron's sector. Simpson told Bauman that he found this explanation 'very strange'.[42]

Tony Marczan placed an advertisement in the RAF Association's magazine asking for information from veterans of 245 Squadron and he was duly contacted by former Leading Aircraftsman David McCormack. When Marczan asked him vaguely about a scramble by two Czech pilots on 10 May 1941, McCormack volunteered: 'I know what you're on about. They're the two guys that could have shot down Rudolf Hess, if they hadn't been recalled.' McCormack went on to say that he remembered the events of that night very well, and had listened in to the conversation between the pilots and their controller on the radio.[43]

Rajlich's book also describes how

> The excitement reached its peak when, after dark, a liaison Avro Anson landed with several strange [unknown] RAF officers on board. They immediately summoned both Czech sergeants. The sergeants were separately subjected to intensive interrogation. The officers asked for impossible details and urged both pilots to recall the German plane's markings and in particular whether they both saw a pilot and a gunner on the plane.
>
> The Czechs couldn't help much and 'Polda' [Srom] lost his patience with the officers, but buttoned his lip when he noticed their coolness and high rank.[44]

There is an intriguing postscript to the Aldergrove connection. Hess's route across Britain can be reconstructed from the Royal

Observer Corps plots (although there are some slight discrepancies between them), but the most important document is Hess's own map, on which he had indicated the landmarks he intended to use. One very significant marking, however, has gone completely unremarked. At a point just past a prominent landmark, Broad Hill, some twenty miles from his destination, Hess drew a line on a bearing of 250 degrees. The line makes no sense in terms of navigation, but the bearing and the point at which he makes it are extraordinarily intriguing: it was the first point on his journey when he would have been able to see Dungavel House – and when the line is extended it passes exactly through RAF Aldergrove. The most logical explanation is that this was the 'abort point' at which, if he did not receive a signal from Dungavel, he would change course and head for Aldergrove. This implies that he was expecting such a signal and that, having not aborted the mission at that point, he must have received it. (As we will see, this is confirmed by witnesses on the ground.) It also explains why the two fighters were scrambled from Aldergrove when Hess's plane passed over the west coast later, but were recalled when it turned back towards Dungavel.

There are two pieces of corroboration for this. The first comes from Hess himself, who told some of those who arrested him that he had seen two Hurricanes closing in on him.[45] This has been explained by his mistaking Defiants for Hurricanes, although only one Defiant is recorded as having been in his immediate vicinity. The second comes from an article published in America in 1943, based on alleged inside information on the Hess affair (and which will be discussed more fully in the next chapter), which states that 'two Hurricanes took off to trail the mystery plane with orders to force it down *but under no conditions to shoot at it*'.[46] (Emphasis in original.)

Some have found it significant that Hamilton's command at RAF Turnhouse, which controlled a number of other airfields in the east of Scotland, failed to send up any fighters at all. Tempting though it is to read between the lines, the fact remains that Hess's plane did not fly over any of the sectors for which Hamilton was responsible. But in a sense the RAF's action – or lack of action– that night is a red herring because by the time Hess arrived near Glasgow it was dark and fighters were only used to defend British airspace during the day. At night, the island was defended by the anti-aircraft units on the ground. And the action that they took is rather more significant.

Hess gets closer

As the Me-110 was tracked across the north of England and into Scotland, crossing the border at about 10.30 p.m. – it was apparent that it was heading towards Glasgow. Even so, no air siren sounded that night in the city: there was no air-raid alert. This anomaly was commented on by Sergeant Daniel McBride, who was on duty with the Royal Corps of Signals unit based at Eaglesham House.[47] (Among their other duties, they were responsible for relaying air-raid alerts.) When the Me-110 appeared over Eaglesham, McBride first thought it was a captured German aircraft being test flown by a British pilot, for the simple reason that no alert had sounded. Officially, no enemy plane was approaching Glasgow.

This is baffling. Hess's plane had been misidentified as a Dornier 17,[48] which – unlike the Me-110 (a fighter–bomber) – was an aircraft designed for reconnaissance or dropping bombs, so the British should have pulled out all the stops to prevent it getting through. That area of Scotland already knew to its cost the devastating potential of single bombers,[49] so why was this one ignored? Even more significantly, as the plane approached Glasgow, some of the anti-aircraft units around the city, in the absence of an alert, urgently requested permission to open fire – only to be refused. This included AA units under the direct command of RAF Turnhouse.[50] An explanation for this apparent dereliction of duty was given later: because there was a dispute over whether the plane was a Messerschmitt or a Dornier, it was considered to be 'unidentified', and obviously the procedure was that unidentified aircraft were not fired at.[51] Of course, this is ludicrous: Hess's plane had at least been positively identified as *German*.

The official accounts claim that some of the confusion was due to disbelief that the plane could have been an Me-110: later, the government's announcement of Hess's arrival specifically made this point. But this is ridiculous. At least two ROC posts identified the plane correctly, although one did report that it 'might be' a Dornier 215 bomber.[52] Fighter Command believed it could have been a Dornier 17 because they were sceptical that an Me-110 could have got so far with enough fuel to make the return journey. The Duke of Hamilton's later remark that the identification of the plane as an Me-110 was greeted with 'hoots of derision'[53] in the Operations Room at RAF Turnhouse is often quoted. However, it was known that Me-110s could and did get as far as the airspace over Glasgow. Just two months before – on 14 March 1941, the day after the massive air raid known as the Clydeside Blitz – an Me-110 was positively identified over the city in broad daylight and assumed to be a German reconnaissance flight checking the damage inflicted in the raid.[54] Fighters tried to intercept it, but it outran them. The fact that an Me-110 had penetrated so far caused quite a stir: the episode was well known to the Royal Observer Corps and others who were responsible for identifying and tracking aircraft. So why were there allegedly 'hoots of derision' when the men at Turnhouse knew that Me-110s with drop tanks could easily reach as far as Glasgow?

It was at this point that the Duty Section Controller at RAF Ayr, Squadron Leader Hector MacLean, ordered two Defiant night fighters to search for and destroy the intruder. His action is cited by supporters of the official version of events as proof that there was no conspiracy to let Hess in. However, MacLean's own account clashes head-on with this interpretation.

First, MacLean makes it clear that the Defiants 'by chance' were already airborne on practice flights when his Ops Room detected the 'hostile' approaching – and that, having not been warned of its approach by other RAF stations, he ordered the Defiants to hunt for it *on his own initiative*. Moreover, he states that, having no direct link to the Section covering the Northumberland coast, news of the approaching Me-110 should have been relayed to Ayr *through RAF Turnhouse* (whose commanding officer, the Duke of Hamilton, was also in command of Ayr) – but they had failed to do so.[55]

The progress of the Me-110 was also being monitored at the Royal Observer Corps' Group Centre based in New Temperance House in Glasgow. The Assistant Group Observer, Major Graham Donald – who was to become a key player in the extraordinary events of that night – believed, 'because of its speed', that it was an Me-110, although his report could have been coloured by hindsight (or perhaps foreknowledge).[56]

Soon afterwards, the ROC post near Eaglesham, also confirming that the intruder was an Me-110, reported that it had crashed, one crewman baling out. Major Donald leapt into action: joking to colleagues at the Group Centre that if the RAF couldn't bring down an Me-110 with Spitfires he was going to bring one back in his Vauxhall, he roared off in the direction of the crash site.

The destination

As he readily admitted when captured, Hess's destination was Dungavel House, the family seat of the Dukes of Hamilton, south of Glasgow. This distinctive building – now a prison – rears up out of the woodland, almost like a German *Schloss* with its many spires and turrets. Hess had memorised Dungavel's appearance to use it as a landmark to enable him to land on the estate. There was an airstrip – built by the Duke for his own light aircraft – in the fields to the front of the house, close to a group of outbuildings known as the Kennels. Some have claimed that the airstrip at Dungavel was unsuitable for an Me-110 to land, but this is incorrect: it was listed as an Emergency Landing Ground (ELG) for RAF crews,[57] showing that it was at least robust enough for most operational planes, and John Harris found in RAF Turnhouse's records that there is a reference to a Bristol Beaufighter landing there in April 1941.[58] The Beaufighter was very similar to an Me-110 in size and weight. (Indeed, this could have been a dummy run for Hess's arrival.) Also, the airstrip at Dungavel was even longer than RAF Turnhouse's runway at that time.

It has been suggested that Hess proved his folly by aiming for Dungavel, because the Duke was not there that night, being on duty at RAF Turnhouse. However, given the meticulous planning that had gone into the flight, surely it is unlikely that Hess would aim for the wrong place. But since Hamilton was at Turnhouse maybe Hess was expecting to find someone else at Dungavel House.

Flying over land without navigational aids, Hess was in trouble. He overflew Dungavel but did not land, then went over the coast at West Kilbride, jettisoning his drop tanks, before turning back towards his destination. The probable reason for this is that an approach from the west is the correct direction for landing on the airship. However, on his second approach he failed to find Dungavel again, and so eventually had to bale out. What went wrong?

It could be that when called upon to navigate for himself he simply made an error by taking a wrong bearing from a prominent landmark – perhaps the pyramid-shaped island of Ailsa Craig. He must have known that even a small error could have meant missing Dungavel, unless there was some kind of pre-arranged signal to guide him in. From the various eye-witness accounts by people on the ground at Eaglesham that night,[59] who describe the Me-110 making at least two passes over the area as if the pilot was looking for something he expected to find there, it is clear that Hess believed he was at Dungavel. Obviously, when he realised he had lost his bearings, and failed to find the airstrip, he had no alternative but to bale out.

It was his first parachute jump: nerve-racking enough at any time, but for a forty-seven-year-old at the end of a long, arduous and dangerous flight – not to mention jumping into the unknown in enemy territory – it was a considerable achievement. He had nothing to guide him except the memory of verbal instructions. Finding it impossible to pull himself out of the plane because the air pressure was pressing him back, he remembered that the best way was to turn the plane upside down and literally fall out – hardly the perfect end to a historic flight. In the event, he was lucky not to sustain a much more serious injury, having blacked out briefly during the jump and chipping an ankle bone on the tail of the plane as he fell.

He bailed out over Bonnyton Moor at 11.09 p.m., as was witnessed and recorded by the nearby ROC post at Eaglesham. (They were subsequently ordered to erase the entry in their log.) The plane crashed in a field, bursting into flames – killing, as one newspaper reported with sublime bathos, a young hare. Hess himself came to rest in a field near Floors Farm, not far from Eaglesham House. At about the same time as he was landing in a Scottish field in the dark, the heaviest air raid of the Blitz on London was just beginning. But it was also to be the last, as if the cessation of the Blitz was meant to be taken as some kind of sign, or almost as if the Deputy Führer's arrival on British soil signalled the beginning of an armistice.

CHAPTER SIX

The Capture of Alfred Horn

In reconstructing the events following Hess's landing in Scotland the main sources are eye-witnesses and official reports from the various military units involved, which – with two very significant exceptions – are found in a single file in the Public Record Office at Kew in south London.[1] However, the picture that emerges is, to say the least, somewhat confused. Even allowing for the passage of time, bad reporting and the very human desire to make rather too much of inconsequential roles in the Hess affair, this is a peculiarly difficult story to reconstruct with any clarity. It is understandable that the arrival of Hitler's Deputy should have generated excitement and confusion, but it must be remembered that no one on the ground that night was supposed to have known the identity of the lone Nazi airman. It should have been a routine operation, but it rapidly became something of a fiasco.

From the reactions of the people on the ground, one could be forgiven for thinking this was the only German airman to have landed by parachute in that area during the entire war up to that point. But Glasgow had had more than its fair share of air raids: several planes had been shot down and their crews had baled out and been captured by the locals. Yet right from the start it seems to have been implicitly understood by those involved that there was something special about this pilot.

In the events surrounding Hess's capture people whose presence is largely unexplained slip in and out of the action, yet they seem to play some kind of important, if elusive, role. The official accounts often seem suspiciously evasive about certain issues, and there are many major departures from standard military procedures.

The accepted story is that Hess came to earth in a field near Floors Farm, was found by a ploughman who held him in his cottage until he was taken into custody by the local Home Guard and, after some shuttling about between scout huts, ended up under guard in Glasgow's Maryhill Barracks. Throughout these events, the Nazi airman's true identity remained unknown: he insisted that he was Hauptmann Alfred Horn and that he had flown to Scotland to see the Duke of Hamilton. (The 'Horn' alias was a composite: Alfred was after Hess's brother and the surname was inspired by the family name of Ilse's stepfather. The 'A. H.', of course, may be a reference to Adolf Hitler, although it is more likely to be Albrecht Haushofer, who signed his letter to Hamilton simply 'A. H.')

Hess certainly landed in a field belonging to Floors Farm (owned by Basil Baird, of the same family as television pioneer John Logie Baird) just outside Eaglesham. A couple of hundred yards away was the cottage home of ploughman David McLean, his sister and their sixty-four-year-old mother Annie. Their account of what happened next is compiled from various interviews they gave afterwards. McLean described hearing the plane roar alarmingly low over the farm, then crash. Rushing outside, he saw the wreckage in flames and a man in a parachute descending from the night sky:

> I immediately concluded that it was a German airman baling out and raced back to the house for help. They were all asleep, however. I looked round hastily for some weapon, but could find nothing except a hayfork. Fearing I might lose the airman, I hurried round by myself again to the back of the house and in the field there I saw the man lying on the ground with his parachute near by.[2]
>
> He rolled over and I helped him to unloose his harness and get on his feet, and I asked him whether there were any more in the plane besides himself, and he said no, and he had no bombs or arms or anything.[3]

Note that Hess's virtually first voluntary statement emphasises the fact that he is unarmed. But his very first words to McLean were 'Am I on the estate of the Duke of Hamilton?'[4] (As Hamilton's connection with Hess's arrival was hushed up until announced by German radio several days later, the Deputy's real opening words did not appear in the first newspaper reports.) An American report is considerably more telling. It gives Hess's first words as 'My name is Alfred Horn. Please tell the Duke of Hamilton I have arrived.'[5] It is interesting to compare this with the official account of the events of that night (which was attached to the Duke of Hamilton's account of his meeting with Hess the next morning), which summarises Hess's request in what were to prove very significant words: 'The German prisoner gave his name as Alfred Horn and stated to the Home Guard and Police that he was on a "Special Mission" to see the Duke of Hamilton and had intended to land at Dungavel.'[6]

The fact that the airman, although German, asked for the Duke of Hamilton and claimed to know him personally probably accounts for the respect accorded him by some of the local people. Not only was Hamilton Scotland's premier peer, but he had been their MP for nine years and – because of his boxing and flying triumphs – was something of a hero to the people around Eaglesham.

McLean helped the injured airman to hobble across the field to his cottage. We do not know what they said during what must have been a relatively lengthy exercise – Hess was a big man and must have been difficult to assist across uneven ground – or even if the two men spoke at all. McLean said: 'He was a thorough gentleman. I could tell that by his bearing and by the way he spoke. He sat down in an easy chair by the fireside, and my mother got up out of bed, dressed, and came through to the kitchen to see our unusual visitor.'[7] With typical Scottish understatement, Mrs McLean asked, 'Will you have a cup of tea?' thus providing history will one of its more incongruous moments. Hess's reply – 'No, thank you. I do not drink tea at night, thank you' – is usually reported without comment, but it does carry an interesting subtext. Presumably Hess did not want tea in case it would interfere with a good night's sleep, which he seemed sure of at that stage.

McLean continued: 'He was the calmest of the party and I could see from the way he spoke that he was a man of culture. His English, although it had a foreign accent, was very clear, and he understood every word we said to him.'[8] Hess then asked for a glass of water. At this point, according to the report in the *Scots Pictorial and Bulletin* on 13 May, based on McLean's account, one of 'two young soldiers who had been attracted to the farm by the sound of the plane crashing' jocularly remarked: 'It's beer we drink in Britain.' To which Hess replied: 'Oh yes, we drink plenty of beer, too, in Munich where I come from.'[9] Suddenly, two soldiers have appeared from nowhere. In the early accounts, their presence in the McLean kitchen is not explained, although their identities are now known: they were Sergeants Daniel McBride and Emyr Morris. And, as we will see, the apparently innocent banter about beer may be more significant than it appears.

According to McLean's later accounts, the two soldiers – who were themselves unarmed – searched the prisoner for weapons. After their conversation about beer, 'Horn' wrote his name on a piece of paper and gave it to McBride.[10] A Home Guard soldier, Gordon Stewart, who arrived at the cottage a few minutes later, was told by the occupants of the cottage that when the two soldiers had entered, Hess had said immediately: 'British soldiers – are you friends of the Duke of Hamilton? I have an important message for him.'[11]

If the standard story is correct, this makes no sense. Why should Hess think that ordinary soldiers would be friends of a duke? Does this imply that he expected the Duke to have sent a search party out to look for him? If so, he must have been on tenterhooks, anxiously interpreting the sound of any new arrivals at the cottage as heralding his salvation. His hopes must have been almost continually raised that night, only to be shattered every time.

The next people to arrive on the scene were Lieutenant John Clarke of the Home Guard, who arrived with Special (part-time) Constable Robert Williamson. Clarke was armed with a revolver. Both were off duty that evening, but lived near by, had seen the plane crash and hurried to the scene in Williamson's car. It is Clarke and Williamson who are generally – but incorrectly – credited with the arrest of Rudolf Hess. Shortly after their arrival on the scene, another car arrived carrying the local Home Guard unit's duty officer, a Lieutenant Cameron, in the company of an off-duty regular army officer, Lieutenant A. R. Gibson, who was in civilian clothes. They were accompanied by two privates in the Home Guard, one of whom was Gordon Stewart.

A third car arrived at roughly the same time, carrying Major Donald of the Royal Observer Corps. After finding out where they were planning to take the airman, Donald (according to his own later account) went off to inspect the wreckage of the Me-110.

David McLean recalled that Hess seemed unbothered by the

influx of military men: 'When the officials came on the scene he greeted them with a smile and assured them that he was unarmed. He was then taken away.'[12] His mother agreed, adding: 'There was some excitement in the kitchen when the military people came to take him away, but he was the coolest of the lot.'[13]

David McLean went on to describe Hess's behaviour on his departure from their cottage:

> He was most gentlemanly in his attitude to my old mother and my sister, and stiffly bowed to them when he came in and before he left. He thanked us profusely for what we had done for him.
>
> He was anxious about only one thing, and that was his parachute. He said to me, 'I should like to keep that parachute, for I think I owe my life to it.'[14]

Hess did not get his wish: it was cut into pieces as souvenirs by the soldiers who cleared the wreck.

The impression that all this was taking place at a near-deserted remote farmhouse is dispelled by the report of Inspector Thomas Hyslop of the Renfrewshire Constabulary, who stated that, when he arrived at Floors Farm about half an hour after the parachutist's arrival, he found some two hundred people milling about. They included local people and members of several military units.[15]

The mystery of the two soldiers

We have seen that in some of the initial press reports David McLean referred to the presence of 'two young soldiers' – Emyr Morris and Daniel McBride – who searched the prisoner for arms, but he gives no explanation of when or how they arrived. However, they were already there when Home Guard Lieutenant Clarke and Special Constable Williamson reached the cottage, so those two mysterious soldiers were the first to arrive on the scene.

McBride and Morris came from the top-secret signals unit up the road at Eaglesham House. One of the main anti-aircraft signals stations for the area, its real business was classified. Even the local people were told it was a searchlight station. That is ostensibly the reason why the press either gave no details about the two men or, in many cases, ignored their presence.

One of the official reports states that Lieutenant Clarke had collected the two (unnamed) soldiers from Eaglesham House before setting out to find the parachutist.[16] As this is manifestly untrue, why did the report lie? The only purpose appears to be to play down the fact that Morris and McBride were the first to arrive at Floors Farm. As these were secret reports, destined not to be released into the public domain for many years after the war, there was no need to protect either the identity of the soldiers or the real function of their unit, so why is there this deliberate obfuscation?

Adding to the suspicion that something is being suppressed is the fact that of all the reports made by military personnel of the events of that night, only McBride's and Morris's are still withheld from the public. All the others were released to the PRO in the 1970s, but, although they are referred to in the file,[17] and are listed in the file's index, the signallers' reports are absent.

J. Bernard Hutton, in *Hess: The Man and His Mission* (1970), mentions the presence of McBride and Morris without naming them, but he describes them as 'two young [McBride was thirty-nine] Army signallers wearing battledress with blue and white flashes of the Signal Corps'. He adds: 'McLean was surprised the Signallers were not armed with rifles.'[18] Hutton's version, based on McLean's account, explicitly states that McBride and Morris arrived *before* Lieutenant Clarke and Special Constable Williamson. He explains the slight air of mystery about their presence by the fact that 'The detachment of the Royal Signals that was billeted in Eaglesham House was under orders not to betray the nature of its activities. But the two Signallers could not reveal their orders and could only refuse to accommodate the prisoner.'[19] In other words, the Home Guard had wanted McBride and Morris as regular soldiers to take charge of the prisoner, but they had to refuse because of the secret signals station at Eaglesham House. This appears to be perfectly reasonable, but McBride's own post-war account, which has been largely ignored, contradicts this position. Although it has received some, mainly local, publicity from time to time, the full story has only ever been published in the foreign press, the first time being in the *Hongkong Telegraph* of 6 May 1947. (When he was demobilised at the end of the war, McBride lived in Hong Kong for some years before returning to his native Glasgow.)

McBride always felt a bond with the Deputy Führer after their paths crossed so historically at Floors Farm, and during Hess's years of imprisonment, the signaller often tried to write to him. He sent him a Christmas card every year, although it is doubtful that the famous prisoner ever received them. (In Spandau, Prisoner Number Seven was only allowed communications from immediate family.) McBride also corresponded with Ilse and Wolf Rüdiger Hess, and in the 1970s became active in the campaign for the release of the former Deputy. McBride's daughter, Daniella Royland, in a letter to Ilse Hess informing her of her father's death, stated that McBride had 'spent the last days of his life trying to free him, night and day' and that Hess's freedom was 'his greatest wish'.[20] (Clearly the Deputy had made a great impression in a very short time, something hardly in keeping with the image of the rather absurd figure promoted by the official version.) Throughout McBride seems to have been motivated by the belief that Hess had been unfairly treated and that there was more to his flight than was officially acknowledged. Did McBride know something about what really happened that night that was kept from the public?

Daniel McBride died on 7 March 1978, and his papers and memorabilia passed to Daniella Royland. She continued to work tirelessly on behalf of the Free Rudolf Hess Campaign until its work was no longer necessary due to the abrupt death of Prisoner Number Seven in August 1987. In 1996 she and her family sold her father's collection through Bonham's, the London auctioneers – where we were fortunate to acquire these illuminating documents and, as we will see, an object of particular interest.

McBride's own story intrigued us the most. The original typewritten account was adapted for the *Hongkong Telegraph* of 6 March 1947, and it has also been featured in the German press. The *Hongkong Telegraph* story begins as follows:

Now that I am under no further obligation to HM Forces and Rudolph [sic] Hess has been sentenced at the Nuremberg Trials, the true story of Hess's apprehension after he landed at Eaglesham, Scotland, can be told for the first time.

The purpose of the former Deputy Führer's visit to Britain is still a mystery to the general public, but I say, and with confidence too, that high-ranking Government officials were aware of his coming. No air-raid warning was given that night, although the plane must have been distinguished during his flight over the city of Glasgow. Nor was the plane plotted at the anti-aircraft control room for the west of Scotland.

I was the man who apprehended Rudolph Hess, although the name he gave me was Alfred Horn.[21]

Note that McBride says he knows 'with confidence' that 'high-ranking Government officials' knew in advance about Hess's flight. What made him so sure? His own written account gives the background to the drama: 'On Saturday, May 10th 1941, I was in West of Scotland Signals Operations Room [in Eaglesham House] anxiously awaiting 1800 hours and my relief. Came six o'clock, my relief and a blow! All leave had been cancelled.'[22] This is one of many hints that there was a flap on in the area of Eaglesham that night. McBride's account continues:

Later that evening, I was lying in bed lost in reverie and my companions asleep, when I heard the unmistakable drone of a low flying aircraft increasing rapidly to a nerve-racking roar, which brought me to earth with a jolt. The sleepers woke, jumped out of bed and were outside in no time. We were standing in various stages of undress as the plane zoomed low overhead. We saw it plainly, but owing to the fading daylight we could not make out the markings. From the noise of the engine and the design of the plane, we guessed it was not one of ours. Like a giant moth it circled HQ and went off in the direction of the city. The drone diminished and finally died away.

Scarcely had the last man climbed into bed again when the plane was heard returning. Out we dashed and the machine was clearly to be seen. Twice the pilot circled HQ.

The engine cut out and they watched as the plane crashed. McBride rushed to where he saw the parachutist descend. He makes the telling comment: 'I thought it must be one of our own boys come to grief while trying out a German machine, more especially as there had been no anti-aircraft fire directed at him and no sirens sounded.'

McBride claims that he was the first to reach Hess, and that he helped him into the McLeans' cottage. Of course, this contradicts the familiar version in which it is David McLean himself who found the injured Hess in the field, with McBride and his companion arriving later. It seems clear, therefore, that all references to McBride's and Morris's presence were forbidden at the time. However, if McBride's version is correct, the new picture that emerges poses some interesting questions. If McBride and his companion did get to Hess first, why was it kept secret? Either McBride must have asked McLean not to mention his initial presence or the newspapers were forbidden to mention it.

When the signallers were in McLean's cottage, according to McBride, 'I said to him [Hess]: "I am not in uniform, but I am a soldier." I must confess I did not look much like a soldier as my rig-out consisted of a pair of slacks, a vest and army boots. My mate was similarly dressed.' Once again, this contradicts David McLean, who described them as being in battledress but unarmed. (McBride does not draw attention to their being unarmed in his own account.) We should also remember Gordon Stewart's version of events, in which he says that Hess had asked the two soldiers if they were friends of the Duke of Hamilton.

McBride continues:

> His reply, given in good English, gave me a nasty jar, for certain intonations betrayed that he was a foreigner.
>
> 'Huh,' he grunted dryly. 'A soldier!'
>
> I stared at him, wondering whether he could really be a German. The answer to my next question settled any doubt I might have had as to his nationality.
>
> 'Where have you come from?' I asked.
>
> 'Munich.'
>
> To open up the conversation I remarked: 'They make good beer in Munich, don't they?'
>
> His keen eyes sparkled beneath his dark, bushy eyebrows as he replied: 'Why yes. Have you been to Munich?'
>
> 'No,' I said, 'but I have drank [sic] Munich beer in Hamburg.'
>
> My answer evidently amused him, for he laughed so heartily that I had to join in.

McBride then asked the airman if there was anybody else on the plane, to which he replied that he was alone. The signaller then asked: 'Have you any arms?'

With a grin, he raised his arms saying: 'These are the only arms I possess.'

'Was your plane armed?'

At this point the farmer's wife [*sic*] came in to ask if we would like a cup of tea. I accepted her kind offer without hesitation, as I felt I needed something to steady my nerves, but the airman expressed a preference for water. I offered him a cigarette but he declined it with thanks. From the doorway my companion [Morris], a young lad, was watching the proceedings with interest.

Under the steadying influence of the hot tea, my mind began to function more or less normally. I realised that I had to report the incident to my HQ, asking them to send an escort and transport for the injured airman.

Fortunately there was a telephone in the farmhouse and I put through a call.

I went back to the stranger, guarded by my companion. He was staring into the fire deeply immersed in thoughts which were evidently not too pleasant, judging by the grim expression on his tired face.

Satisfied that he was all right, I went back to the telephone. I was friendly with the news editor of a national newspaper and I realised that here, at this lonely farmhouse, was news and my friend might as well have the first option on it.

He listened to my story and said: 'OK, Mac. I'll send someone right away to cover it. Thanks for the tip.'

Having – rather unwisely – alerted the media, McBride whiled away the time before the escort arrived by talking to the airman. He explains: 'The escort was long overdue and I wondered when it would arrive.'

While McBride and the airman were talking, the signaller began to notice something familiar about his prisoner.

I remember reading in some report the mention of an identity disc on his wrist, but I did not see it; otherwise I should certainly have inspected it. I asked his name.

He replied, 'Horn, Alfred Horn.'

. . . Producing a scrap of paper and a pencil, I asked him to write his name down.

He wrote distinctly: 'Alfred Horn'.

Rummaging in his pockets, he brought out a photograph of his wife and young son and showed it to me with pride.

'Did you come to bomb us?' I asked.

'My plane was not fitted to carry bombs,' he replied indignantly. 'I came to see the Duke of Hamilton.'

He asked me to take him to the Duke's home, which, he said, was not far away. To this I could only reply that I had no power to do so but my superiors would probably do so later on.

Shortly afterwards there was a commotion outside. The door was flung open and a Home Guard officer rushed in, followed by a number of his men.

The pilot said to the officer: 'I wish to see the Duke of Hamilton. Will you take me to him?'

'You can save all that for the people concerned,' said the officer. 'At present you are coming with me.'

I resented this attitude and protested to the officer that the prisoner was in my charge awaiting an escort from my HQ.

'Are you questioning my authority?' demanded the officer truculently.

'I cannot leave my prisoner, sir,' I said. 'If you take him I must go with you.'

The officer glared furiously at me and the men behind him crowded into the room. I was unceremoniously bundled to one side while the officer and his men marched out with my prisoner.

This, presumably, was the 'excitement' referred to by Mrs McLean. Concluding the story, McBride says:

When I reported to the Operations Room the next morning – Sunday – for duty, the Brigade intelligence officer was there and I had to recount the story of the previous night. He asked me for the slip of paper bearing the signature: 'Alfred Horn'. As he was leaving he whispered: 'Don't be surprised if your prisoner turns out to be Rudolph Hess.'

Like a flash it came to me that this was the reason that the airman's face had seemed so familiar.

If true, this is significant because it shows that 'Horn's' true identity was known by individuals apart from Hamilton early the following morning, although the official version has it that it was not known until Hess revealed it to Hamilton later that morning. Hamilton also claimed that he had not revealed it to anyone before contacting London in the afternoon.

Should we take McBride's version of events seriously? After all, it might have simply been fabricated for self-aggrandisement – tall stories tend to mushroom in wartime. But McBride's version of the events of 10 May 1941 does stand up to closer scrutiny.

Clearly it was McBride who arrested Rudolf Hess, but his prize was taken from him by the Home Guard, and the official reports were then adjusted to diminish his role. On the surface, this seems highly unlikely – logically, if any tinkering with the facts had gone on one might expect the outcome to be in favour of the regular soldier, not the Home Guard. It could not have been a matter of McBride being outranked and overruled by the over-officious Home Guard lieutenant (there is even some question of whether Lieutenant Clarke was in uniform). And, according to an account by Hess that he sent to his wife later, Clarke was manifestly drunk and reeking of whisky, while the way he was brandishing his revolver gave serious cause for alarm.

As Clarke and McBride argued about whose prisoner it was, Lieutenant Cameron – the *on-duty* officer in charge of the local Home Guard – arrived accompanied by a regular army officer, Lieutenant A. R. Gibson (who was in 'civvies'). The story is that they had been out in Gibson's car doing the rounds of Home Guard posts when they saw the plane come down. Two privates from the Home Guard unit they were with at the time (one of whom was Gordon Stewart) were ordered into the car as they headed for the scene.[23]

Clearly it should have been Cameron who made the decision to take the airman into Home Guard custody. The puzzle is why Lieutenant Clarke – especially if drunkenly waving a revolver around – was allowed to keep charge of the prisoner.

McBride says he reported his arrest of the airman to his HQ – Eaglesham House – and requested an escort. Before this could arrive the Home Guard were allowed to take Hess into custody. But thanks to McBride's account, we now know that the first military facility to be informed of the airman's capture was Eaglesham House, although

The signature that Rudolf Hess gave to Sergeant Daniel McBride on 10 May 1941, with McBride's own note.

this did not emerge in any of the official reports. It raises the question of what action they took in response.

McBride's claim to have informed a friend at a national newspaper may appear an odd response for a soldier when faced with a matter of national security – but some of the Scottish newspapers (to a Scot they would be 'national') do seem to have got wind of the story before any official announcement. In particular, the *Daily Record* already had the story of Hess's arrival on its presses on Sunday night, ready for the Monday morning edition, when the official announcement confirming his identity came through.[24] The *Record*'s reporters seem to have been convinced from their first sniff of the story that there was more to it than met the eye. Fortunately for McBride's army career, however, they took care to protect their source – he could otherwise have found himself in very hot water.

The paper on which Hess had written his alias – together with two other mementoes, a box of Bengal matches and a flash lamp – were sent to London for examination, but remarkably were returned to McBride and Morris a few days later because they asked to keep them as souvenirs.[25] The signed paper is still among McBride's papers, with a handwritten note that says: 'The signature given to me by Rudolph Hess when I apprehended him on 10th May 1941.' A recently opened MI5 file includes a letter, written by McBride in 1946 during his voyage to Hong Kong, obviously in response to an official query, saying that he had lodged the paper with a Glasgow solicitor for safekeeping.[26]

There are strong reasons for suspecting that McBride is not telling the whole story about that night. His intention in making his story public was clearly to receive due credit for having arrested Rudolf Hess, but he still seems reluctant to reveal certain elements. Something else was either said or done in the cottage at Floors Farm that the authorities wanted to remain secret – and which McBride seems to have hinted at in his latter years.

Among his papers is an intriguing letter from his former superior at Eaglesham, W. B. Howieson, dated 8 May 1974, advising McBride to 'drop this Hess business'. Howieson goes on to give his reasons: that official records state that Hess was found by McLean and handed over to the Home Guard, and 'that is something that you cannot argue against'. However, he then states 'We know what really happened' – but he reminds McBride that they are still subject to the Official Secrets Act. The letter ends on a rather cautionary note, suggesting that if he were to pursue his investigations further he could 'stir up a hornets' nest.'[27]

How could this story 'stir up a hornets' nest' in 1974? Howieson's letter implies that if the seemingly minor point of who captured Hess is admitted, other – much more damaging – information will somehow naturally flow from it, which is presumably why McBride's official report is still withheld. It seems that Howieson knew that something passed between McBride and Hess that night that is not even mentioned in the signaller's papers, but which he seems to have been about to make public. Presumably Howieson's words of caution persuaded McBride not to do so. But something significant must have passed between the two, *because Rudolf Hess gave McBride his Iron Cross that night*. This fact is not mentioned in McBride's account, tempting one at first to dismiss it. In fact, it was in McBride's collection, which we now own. He could, of course, have bought any old Iron Cross from a memorabilia shop and tried to pass it off as the Deputy Führer's. Yet McBride never revealed until just before his death (and then only to his family) that he owned this historic artefact. He seems to have been curiously reticent about the Iron Cross from beginning to end, quietly lodging it with a Glasgow solicitor. More recently, its provenance has been confirmed by Wolf Rüdiger Hess, who never had any doubt that the Iron Cross was his father's. After the death of Prisoner Number Seven in 1987, he tried, without success, to recover it from McBride's daughter and son-in-law.[28]

Of course, Hess would have been wearing his Iron Cross for his flight – after all, he had dressed with a sense of occasion in his specially tailored uniform, presumably in order to look the part for his meeting with the Duke of Hamilton and, as he believed, other distinguished figures. Yet there is no mention of the medal in any of the records of his capture, which supports McBride's claim that Hess gave it to him. But why should Rudolf Hess have handed over such a personal and precious item to an enemy, and an ordinary soldier at that? It suggests that he trusted McBride on sight or came to trust him very quickly for some reason. It also raises the question of whether the Iron Cross was intended to be delivered to someone as proof of his arrival.

Descent into farce

Even when no Duke of Hamilton had stepped from the shadows to welcome him, perhaps Rudolf Hess continued to imagine that his night would end in civilised banter amid ducal splendour, sitting by a roaring fire and cracking jokes about parachute jumps and being offered tea by the elderly mother of a local ploughman. It was certainly the stuff to dine out on, both with Hamilton and – perhaps in a few days' time – back home with Hitler, and of course with Ilse. The Haushofers would love it. However, as the night wore on it soon became apparent that the operation had gone badly wrong. Far from being invited into the lap of luxury as an honoured guest, he was driven to the headquarters of the local Home Guard – a scout hut in the village of Busby. It was farce not fête for Rudolf Hess, but he was hardly in the mood to see the funny side: he was exhausted, had an injured ankle and his initial bewilderment must by now have become tinged with an increasing panic.

The farce escalated. Home Guard volunteers poured out of the scout hut, then, seeing him, ground to a halt. They stared at the prisoner, who coolly stared back. This went on for some time, until the prisoner himself, used to giving orders, said, 'Do we go inside?'[29]

The spell was broken, and – grateful for some leadership – they took the German airman into the scout hut.

Gordon Stewart, the last surviving member of that Home Guard unit, writing in January 1999, said of the prisoner: 'He gave his name as Alfred Horn and said he had flown without permission from Munich.'[30] The Deputy Führer seems suspiciously quick off the mark to offer the gratuitous piece of information that his flight was unsanctioned, as if wanting to establish the point in the minds of his captors as quickly as possible.

Then Lieutenant Clarke telephoned his battalion (the 3rd Battalion Renfrewshire Home Guards) headquarters in the nearby village of Giffnock to tell them about their prisoner – although at this stage they believed the Nazi to be merely the unimportant Luftwaffe officer Alfred Horn. Following the proper procedure, the Giffnock Home Guard battalion commander then attempted to telephone the HQ of the regular army in the neighbourhood, the Argyll and Sutherland Highlanders, to request an escort for the prisoner. He had enormous difficulty getting through as all the lines were busy – another sign that there was a major flap on in the area that night. By the time he was connected, Giffnock had already dispatched some of its own Home Guards to fetch the prisoner, and they solemnly escorted him to their HQ. This time Hess did not find himself in a humble scout hut as in Busby, but in a scout *hall*. The Deputy Führer was going up in the world.

There he suffered the further ignominy of being searched and having an inventory made of his belongings, which included the visiting cards of both Karl and Albrecht Haushofer, packets of homoeopathic medicines and a hypodermic syringe, a Leica camera (borrowed from Ilse, as his own was broken), plus photographs of himself and his wife and son. This inventory has never been made public, almost certainly because it included a letter, probably to the Duke of Hamilton, the contents of which are obviously still deemed too sensitive to be made public.[31] Throughout all of this activity 'Alfred Horn' kept repeating his request that the Duke of Hamilton be informed of his arrival.

At some point in these proceedings, Inspector Hyslop arrived at the Giffnock scout hall accompanied by what is described mysteriously as 'a group of army and RAF officers'.[32] Who they were and what they were doing there have never been explained.

The role of Major Donald

All the indications are that there is more to Major Graham Donald's role than meets the eye. He already has one major claim to fame: he is generally credited as the person who identified 'Alfred Horn' as Rudolf Hess. A veteran pilot from the First World War, Major Donald was Assistant Group Observer in No. 34 Group of the Royal Observer Corps. He was also one of the directors of a Glasgow machine-tool company, Graham & Donald Ltd, and was well connected: a week after Hess's arrival he wrote about the incident to a friend in London, the former Conservative MP Sir Harry Greer.[33] Major Donald – although this is not apparent from his own account – also knew the Duke of Hamilton, if only because his ROC duties meant he had many dealings with RAF Turnhouse.[34] But did he also know Rudolf Hess before his arrival in Scotland? It seems likely that he would at least know him by sight, as he had lived in Hess's home town of Munich for some time before the war.[35]

Major Donald's account of meeting Hess on the night of 10 May 1941 contains some astonishing statements. Written a year and a half after Hess's arrival, in October 1942, Donald's account appeared in the *Journal of the Royal Observer Corps*, and claims that, after being informed that the Me-110 had crashed, he alerted the Home Guard in the Eaglesham area (although this is not mentioned in any of their own reports about that night), and then set out for the scene himself. He arrived at Floors Farm just a few minutes after the Home Guard had arrested the German airman. Donald asked the volunteers where they were taking the prisoner, and then inspected the wreckage, together with an RAF officer – one Flying Officer Malcolm – who was home on leave in the area. The two men then went to the Home Guard HQ in Giffnock to question the prisoner, who seemed to cheer up when they arrived. Hess stood, with difficulty on his injured ankle, and bowed to Major Donald. There was, Donald reported, a distinct tension in the air, which the major blamed on the presence of a Pole who was trying to 'interpret for the police' and the Home Guard in the midst of great confusion.

Donald, who spoke some German, and who happened to be carrying a pocket German dictionary with him that night, offered to talk to the prisoner. Hess informed him that he had come with an urgent message for the Duke of Hamilton, whom he must see at once. He declared he was on a 'special mission' to Britain, adding that his intended destination was Dungavel House. The German then showed Donald his map, on which the Hamilton residence was clearly ringed in red. This is where Donald's account begins to become absurd. Finding the man rather familiar, he turned the conversation to Munich: 'I then said, "Yes, and very good beer too! The good old Lowenbrau!" . . . unlike a good German, he did not agree with me. He looked as disapproving as a maiden aunt. He was a teetotaller. I had only heard of two German teetotallers, one being Hitler and the other Hess. This one wasn't Hitler.'[36]

Donald then asked the prisoner to sign his name on an aircraft identification card – appropriately, as it happened, for an Me-110. The airman obediently wrote: 'Alfred Horn, 10.5.41'. This is astonishing. For the second time that night Hess is involved in a stilted conversation about German beer (although, unlike the previous exchange with McBride, this one failed to raise a smile from him), after which he obligingly writes his name – or rather, alias – on a piece of paper. Then on the basis of the prisoner being a teetotaller, not being Adolf Hitler but calling himself Alfred Horn, Donald triumphantly identifies the German as Rudolf Hess! Donald then digs himself in deeper with this extremely unlikely explanation: '"Alfred" is simply an old Anglo-Saxon rendering of Alf, or Olf, the Red. German should be Rot Olf, or latterly, Rudolf.'[37] As a result of this expert deduction, he told the prisoner: 'I shall see that your message is conveyed to the Duke. I shall also tell him, on my authority, that your true name is Rudolf Hess.' He reports that the prisoner responded by jumping about fifteen inches into the air and uttering a forced laugh, thus moving the proceedings from farce to melodrama. Donald left with one final flourish, bidding the airman: 'Gute Nacht, Herr Hess.' Back at the ROC Centre, he phoned the duty controller of the sector, asking him to relay the message to the Duke at RAF Turnhouse, and stressing that he believed the man to be Rudolf Hess.

The suspicion that Donald's published account is deliberately distorted is compounded by his own official report, which is in a file that was due to be closed until 2019, but which was released in 1992. In his report, written on 11 May – significantly, before any public announcement in either Britain or Germany about Hess's flight – he is adamant that he recognised Hess, writing:

I studied his face, while conversing, for a few minutes. I then remembered it. I am not expecting to be believed immediately, that our prisoner is actually No. 3 in the Nazi hierarchy. He may be one of his 'professional doubles'. Personally I think not. The name may be *Alfred Horn*, but the face is the face of *Rudolf Hess* [Donald's emphasis].[38]

There are more contradictions in other statements made by Donald over the years, the most glaring in an interview for the *Sunday Dispatch* in April 1950, in which he stated: 'I finally managed to get the Duke of Hamilton to come over and see the fellow. He took just one look and said, "Heavens above! It is Rudolf Hess."'[39]

Another puzzle concerns the identity of the RAF officer who was with Major Donald when he arrived at the Home Guard headquarters. We have seen that in his 1942 article he named this person as a Pilot Officer Malcolm (although in his official report he fails to mention such a person at all). The Home Guards' report has Donald arriving with another – unnamed – ROC officer. But the most significant version appears in the manuscript of James Leasor's 1962 book about the Hess affair,which was sent to the Hamilton family for approval, and which is now in the Hamilton archives.[40] Leasor states that Donald arrived with an RAF wing commander, who agreed that the prisoner was Hess. More mysteriously, this passage was deleted from the published version of Leasor's book, which makes no mention of a second person and says that Donald did not even speak to the prisoner (contradicting all other accounts, including Donald's own). Obviously something is being covered up about the identity of Donald's companion. In the light of Leasor's original statement that he was an RAF wing commander, and Donald's 1942 version that he was 'Pilot Officer Malcolm', perhaps it is significant that one of the Duke of Hamilton's brothers, Lord Malcolm Douglas-Hamilton, was a wing commander. In fact, during the Second World War, Lord Malcolm was stationed in Rhodesia, but according to one of his post-war secretaries he was home in Scotland at the time of Hess's arrival. So although the Duke was at RAF Turnhouse when Hess was captured, at least one of his brothers was in the area.

One of the many mysteries about that night concerns the presence of the Pole who, as Donald recorded, interrogated Hess in German in a markedly tense atmosphere. Donald does not name him, but other reports identify him as Roman Battaglia, a clerk at the

Polish Consulate in Glasgow. The Foreign Office file contains Battaglia's account of his session with Hess, but adds little to the overall picture. 'Alfred Horn' said that he had flown from Augsburg, and that he had an important message for the Duke of Hamilton which was 'in the highest interest of the British Air Force [*sic*]'.[41] This is a peculiarly brief summary considering that the Pole spoke with the airman for some two hours, but it still contains something of interest. The last remark is very similar to the one Hess made to David McLean about the importance of his mission to the RAF. Perhaps this was an agreed contingency plan: if he had failed to make the expected contact and had fallen into the wrong British hands, he was to claim he had vital information for the RAF that he would only disclose to the Duke. However, the major mystery is why Battaglia was there at all. It has been assumed that he had been summoned by the police or Home Guard to interpret for them in their interrogation of the airman. But the standard procedure was to call in a specially trained German-speaking RAF interrogator. In any case, Hess spoke very good English, as McLean pointed out, and the awkward fact remains that nobody seems to have sent for Battaglia: certainly nobody admits doing so.

The Pole's presence was even a puzzle to MI5: files released in January 1999 show that they were concerned to find out how Battaglia came to be there, but were unable to come up with a satisfactory explanation. In a memo of 17 May 1941, Major Perfect of MI5 Edinburgh reported angrily to his senior colleagues in Oxford: 'How on Earth he got to know of Hess's arrival, and, furthermore, went out and interrogated him for over two hours, I simply cannot conceive.'[42]

MI5 sent another officer, Lieutenant John Mair, to interview Battaglia at Glasgow Police's headquarters on 29 May. He described the Pole as 'extremely shrewd' and reported his impression that 'far better acquaintance with him would be necessary before trusting him completely'. Battaglia expressly requested that his name should not be made public. He denied knowing the identity of the German airman, although he did offer his reaction that 'the circumstances were so fantastic, that the prisoner must have come on some special mission'. Remarkably, there is nothing in Mair's report to answer the most pressing question of all: how Battaglia came to be there on 10 May 1941.[43]

Mair's report also fills in some of the background of this mysterious 'consular official'. Battaglia had been at the Polish Consulate in Danzig between 1935 and 1937. (From other documents in the PRO we know that he was posted to Washington before joining the Polish Consulate in Glasgow in 1940.) More intriguing is the fact that he admitted to Mair that, during his time in Danzig, he had been trained in interrogation techniques, as he dealt with 'political suspects' there, raising the suspicion that Battaglia was rather more than a simple clerk. This suspicion was confirmed by Polish sources, who told us that, certainly later in the war, Battaglia served as one of General Sikorski's intelligence officers, and that his name featured on a list drawn up by the Soviet NKVD of Poles who were to be executed should they return to their country after the war. It is therefore hard to avoid the conclusion that Battaglia was working for Polish intelligence in May 1941, and that his presence at Giffnock – where he was the first person to interrogate Hess – was no coincidence. It is more accurate to say that Battaglia *spoke* to Hess for two hours, and as they were speaking in German – which, until the arrival of Major Donald, no one else present understood – anything could have passed between them without the others having any idea what was said.

A final anomaly – which was to assume greater significance in the light of testimony to be revealed in the next chapter – concerns the role of the 14th Argyll and Sutherland Highlanders. As we have seen, the Home Guard reported their capture of the airman to the Argylls' headquarters at Paisley. Standing instructions specified that the Home Guard should report such incidents to the nearest regular army unit (excepting anti-aircraft and signals units) so that they could take charge of the prisoner. And yet it was not the Argylls, but the 11th Cameronians (Scottish Rifles) from Glasgow who came to fetch Hess. This anomaly is commented on in the report by the head of Scottish Command's intelligence section, Colonel Firebrace.[44] The reason is given in other reports: when the Argylls' duty officer informed Clyde Sub-Area Command that they were sending an escort, Sub-Area *ordered* them not to go, instead arranging for the Cameronians to do it.[45] A squad of Cameronians was duly dispatched to Giffnock. By now it was realised that the prisoner was somebody of importance, so as 'an extra measure of courtesy'[46] he was driven in a private car to Maryhill Barracks in Glasgow, where he was put in the hospital wing so that his injured ankle could be treated. It was now 2.30 a.m.

Questions, anomalies, subtexts

As Peter Padfield has noted, there is something to be said for the principle employed by Sherlock Holmes concerning the mystery of the 'dog that didn't bark in the night' – always be alert for the one thing that should have happened but didn't. On 10 May 1941 there were several dogs with inexplicable laryngitis.

Despite initial confusion in identifying the plane, by the time it was flying over Dungavel and Eaglesham it had been positively identified. In any case, when it crashed it became obvious what kind of plane it was. So before or after it hit the ground, the Home Guards and the Royal Observer Corps knew it was an Me-110, and the first question they should have asked was 'Where is the second crewman?' Planes of that type always carried a crew of two. And yet, in all the official reports of events on the ground that night there is no mention of a search for the second airman. That is curious enough, but what is even more perplexing is the fact that the official accounts imply that this was because Hess had assured his captors that he had been alone in the plane. This beggars belief. Was it customary for Home Guard units and the Royal Observer Corps to take the word of an enemy airman that he had arrived alone? Did they really harbour no niggling thoughts that a second airman might have parachuted out elsewhere, equipped with a clandestine radio in the vicinity of a top secret signals base?

In his account of October 1942 Major Donald does admit that he was puzzled when examining the wreckage by the fact that only one crewman was reported to have baled out, but there is no mention of this in his official report of 11 May, which went into meticulous detail about everything else to do with the plane.[47] The official reports try to cover up this rather glaring anomaly, but – in their clumsy way – only succeed in drawing attention to it. For example, one of the reports says: 'Lieut. Clarke took him [the prisoner] in his car from the farm to Company Headquarters and advised Lieut. Gibson on the way that he had the German parachutist in charge. Lieut. Gibson was satisfied that no other parachutist had come from the Plane and then returned to his Coy. [Company] Headquarters.'[48]

How could Gibson – the off-duty army officer in civilian clothes – possibly have been 'satisfied' there was no other parachutist? He had arrived by car with Home Guard Lieutenant Cameron just a few minutes after the airman's descent. Everybody appears to have taken Hess's word that he was alone. The blood runs cold at the thought that Britain's defences were in the hands of such unprofessional soldiers – unless, of course, they already knew that there was no point in scouring the neighbourhood for a second Nazi airman.

Another major anomaly is the fact that two RAF bases refused to interrogate the prisoner that night. After being informed of the airman's capture by the Home Guard, the Argyll and Sutherland Highlanders' duty officer had properly asked the nearest RAF base, Abbotsinch near Glasgow, to send over an interrogation officer. But RAF Abbotsinch told them to hold the prisoner overnight in police cells, saying he would be interrogated in the morning.[49] This was totally against standard procedure. All captured airmen were to be interrogated as soon as possible, preferably while still disoriented or in shock – after all, in that state they could well be caught out and reveal invaluable details of an imminent raid, which might save countless lives. RAF Abbotsinch's departure from this procedure has never been explained, but when a second RAF base also departed from the regulations in the same way the situation becomes even more suspicious – particularly when the captured airman has made such a point of claiming to have 'important information' for the RAF.

The telephone lines were certainly busy that night. Calls were soon put through to RAF Turnhouse to inform its commanding officer – Hamilton – that a captured German airman named Alfred Horn, who claimed to know him, was saying he had important information to give him personally. We know that at least four calls were made to Hamilton that night, as various military and civilian authorities learned the news and quickly passed it on. The first was from RAF Ayr (which had been informed by Eaglesham Police Station).[50] Their duty officer, Squadron Leader Hector MacLean – who had vectored the Defiant in on 'Raid 42J' earlier – reported that he had difficulty convincing those at Turnhouse to wake the Duke, who had already gone off duty. The second call came from the Royal Observer Corps, although who made it and how they knew about 'Horn' is unknown. The most obvious explanation – that it came from Major Donald – is not borne out by his own account, which puts his call much later. The third call was from Glasgow Area Command, some time before 1.30 a.m. on 11 May, who were informed that the message had already been received from RAF Ayr and from the ROC.[51] (This is how we know that there was a call from the ROC.) The last was from Major Donald, according to his own testimony, at around 2 a.m.[52] He added that he believed the airman to be Rudolf Hess.

What with the flurry of excited calls, all the activity and the demands of the prisoner to see the Duke of Hamilton – especially when he had been identified as Hitler's Deputy – one might be forgiven for imagining that the Duke got out of his pyjamas to go off to see the enemy VIP pretty quickly. However, according to the official records, nothing could be further from the truth. They claim that the Duke of Hamilton not only failed to move a muscle in Hess's direction that night but failed to send RAF Turnhouse's interrogation officer, Flight Lieutenant Benson. Both men – officially, that is – waited until the next morning. This astonishing breach of regulations was the subject of an angry memo from Colonel Firebrace:

> If it is true that the RAF authorities were informed before 0100/11th that an important prisoner was anxious to make a statement to them, their laxity is most unfortunate as the prisoner might have had urgent operational information to divulge. It can only be assumed that the decision to do nothing until the morning was taken by Wing Commander the Duke of Hamilton and that in consequence Flt/Lt Benson could not go posthaste to the spot as he should normally have done.[53]

The same point was made by the Clyde Sub-Area Command duty officer, Captain Anthony White, in his report on that night.

In other words, Hamilton had ordered Benson not to go. In addition to standard procedure dictating that the prisoner should have been interviewed immediately, there is an extra reason why Hamilton should have seen Hess as soon as possible. At one point in the chaos of that night a message became garbled to the effect that the prisoner required medical attention because he was 'seriously injured' and might not last the night.[54] The Argylls' duty officer who made this call – Lieutenant Cowie – specifically pointed out the urgency of questioning the prisoner to Glasgow Area Command, who then called RAF Turnhouse to ask for Flight Lieutenant Benson to come out for the interrogation. They were amazed to be told that it had already been decided that Benson would wait until the morning![55]

It is interesting to note that Major Donald was mildly rebuked by his commanding officer for questioning Hess specifically because he should have left it to the RAF, in these words: 'As you are probably aware there is a special organisation of officers to interrogate prisoners as soon as possible after capture and they are anxious that no one else should do so before their arrival as it tends to make the prisoner more careful in what he says.'[56] To have shown such a flagrant disregard for standing orders, Hamilton must have realised that something was going on. And it must be remembered that he had written a letter to air intelligence just that morning concerning an approach by a German closely associated with Rudolf Hess, and who signed himself 'A. H.'.

On the road to Glasgow

The casual fashion in which the various parties – especially Hamilton himself – appeared to react to the arrival of Rudolf Hess was presumably designed to conceal quite the reverse. The indifference was just an act: the sensational news of the arrival of Hitler's Deputy was not really greeted with a shrug and a wave of an aristocratic hand. Presumably plans were immediately put into action under the cover of all that suspiciously unprofessional inertia. It is even conceivable that Hamilton *did* meet Hess that night, while he was supposedly fast asleep at RAF Turnhouse.

According to his own later accounts, Hamilton had gone off duty soon after receiving the report that the Me-110 had crashed near Eaglesham – at around 11.15 p.m. He went to bed in the house that he and the Duchess kept near the base, only to be roused later when the first of the calls about 'Alfred Horn' came through. Perhaps it is significant that all the official accounts stress the fact – even though it is to the Duke's detriment – that he took no action until the next morning, when he went to see the prisoner at Maryhill Barracks, arriving at around 10 a.m. It was only then, it is said, that the airman revealed himself to be Rudolf Hess.

However, on 16 May, after it was finally announced that Hess had flown to Britain intending to meet the Duke of Hamilton, a very odd newspaper report appeared in the *Glasgow Herald*. This stated matter-of-factly that the two men had met *on the night Hess had arrived*: 'The meeting between the Duke and Hess took place at a point on the road to the hospital to which Hess was removed [i.e. between Giffnock and Maryhill Barracks], and it is understood that representatives of the Intelligence Service and the Foreign Office were present.'[57] Is this simply poor reporting, or had something very important slipped past the censor? As the article appeared in a Glasgow newspaper the reporters would have had the benefit of local knowledge. And at that stage the official version of events had yet to appear, so the *Herald* had no way of knowing that it had inadvertently committed a serious gaffe. More significantly, however, there is independent evidence to back up its story of a meeting between the Duke of Hamilton and Rudolf Hess on the night of his arrival, several hours before they were supposed to have had their encounter.

Hector MacLean reports the following exchange with the Duke when he telephoned him with the German's request:

> 'What do you think I should do?' said the Duke. 'I think you should go and see him.' 'Yes, I think I will.' He put the phone down and I told Ops B to warn the Police he was coming.[58]

Peter Padfield, in the research for *Hess: Flight for the Führer* (1991, updated 1995) interviewed Hamilton's widow, today's Dowager Duchess, and several of the people who had been on duty in RAF Turnhouse's Operations Room that night, and the picture that emerges from their accounts is completely different from the party line. Remarkably, the Dowager Duchess told Padfield that, after the second of the calls had come through in the middle of the night (presumably the somewhat mysterious one from the ROC), her husband left the house and she did not see him again until the following afternoon.[59] Since his account claims that he went back to bed, he should have been at breakfast, but clearly he was not.

Revisiting the reports about that night by the various units involved reveals suspicious discrepancies that do allow for a meeting to have taken place on the road between Giffnock and Glasgow. The report by the duty officer at Glasgow Area Command, Captain White, states that he put in a request to Sub-Area Command for an escort before making two other calls.[60] The first was to RAF Turnhouse to try (unsuccessfully, as it turned out) to get Flight Lieutenant Benson to see the prisoner, and the second to Maryhill Barracks to alert them about Hess's imminent arrival. He timed the last of these calls at approximately 12.45 a.m – his call requesting an escort must therefore have been earlier. But the report from the unit that provided the escort, the Cameronians, states that they received the call at 1.10,[61] while Maryhill Barracks gave the time they were informed as 1.30.[62] The Home Guard report states that Hess was picked up from Giffnock at 2.12[63] – which, if true, means that it took the escort over an hour to make the journey from Glasgow. Yet in 1987, Denis C. Bateman, asked to reconstruct the journey for a magazine article, took just fifteen minutes.[64] What happened in the missing three-quarters of an hour?

Hamilton seems to have spent the night trying to find out what was going on or what he should do. But, as we will see, there is evidence that he informed key figures in London – including Churchill – of Hess's arrival during the night of 10–11 May and not, as stated in the later official accounts, the following afternoon.

There are more significant departures from the official line. Two WAAFs on duty in the Operations Room at RAF Turnhouse that night told Peter Padfield that when Hamilton was recalled to duty to take the call – at about 11.45 – reporting 'Horn's' arrival, his reaction was most interesting. According to one of the former WAAFs, Nancy Moore, Hamilton looked 'extremely horrified'.[65] This is hardly the puzzled indifference of the usual story.

Nancy Moore's testimony contains another particularly telling memory of that night. She was the daughter of the deputy commander of the Scottish Command of the Royal Observer Corps, Squadron Leader W. Geoffrey Moore. When Nancy went home that night she mentioned the odd incident of the crashed German airman to her father. In Padfield's words: 'He replied that he was going to breach confidence, and if she absolutely promised not to tell anyone he would tell her who the pilot was: Rudolf Hess.'[66] This confirms that some people in the military – certainly in the Royal Observer Corps – were aware that Hess was expected that night.

Assessing the debacle

From start to finish the story of Hess's arrival and capture looks like one of the most serious indictments of British military – and intelligence – incompetence ever recorded. It is littered with bungling, indifference and blatant dereliction of duty, often by top men, and in a crisis – a matter of national security. If that is a fair summary, then perhaps it is understandable why the authorities should try to bury the whole thing and forget it ever happened. But if it isn't a case of wide-ranging ineptitude, we can only understand all the anomalies in terms of quite another scenario.

Hess's arrival was expected by a small elite group who were in a position to assist his flight – and ultimately his mission. Despite Hamilton's later denials, he must have been part of this group: this is supported by the eye-witness accounts of his reaction to the news of 'Horn's' capture – as opposed to his own, carefully worded version – and by the testimony of his widow. But the mission had gone calamitously wrong. Hess had been forced to bale out over Eaglesham, rather than land safely – and secretly – at Dungavel. 'Outsiders', such as the Home Guard and the police, became involved, effectively pre-empting any attempt to resurrect the plan by setting procedures in motion that resulted in various military units and command posts that were not in the conspiracy becoming aware of the airman's arrival. Hess himself attempted to retrieve the situation by trying to get word to the Duke of Hamilton, and even by trying to persuade his captors to take him to Dungavel, but to no avail.

This scenario makes sense of certain particularly puzzling features about that night: if Hess knew he was expected, he would also realise that efforts would be made to find and take him to Dungavel. This would explain his otherwise rather odd question to the out-of-uniform McBride and Morris about whether they were 'friends' of the Duke of Hamilton. It is also reasonable to assume that those who awaited him had a contingency plan in place to find him if he did not land as planned at Dungavel. Hess would have been viewing each new arrival on the scene as a potential ally, but how was he to tell a friend from a foe? Presumably some form of password would have been pre-arranged, which would account for the surreal rerun of the conversation about German beer, followed by his scribbling the name 'Alfred Horn' on bits of paper twice. It was apparently as a result of this that Donald identified the airman as Hess, and informed the Duke of Hamilton accordingly. This may explain why McBride's account is so obviously incomplete – and why Hess gave him his Iron Cross, perhaps as evidence of his arrival to give to Hamilton.

The Duke and his confederates had to try to retrieve what was rapidly becoming a hopeless situation. They had to wrest control of the prisoner from the Home Guard, or at least get word to Hess. At this point the mysterious Polish diplomat, whom nobody sent for, appears on the scene and talks to the prisoner for a full two hours in a language understood by no one else in the room. And, of course, there is the meeting on the road to Glasgow between Hess and Hamilton that never took place, according to the official story. By the time Hess arrived in Maryhill Barracks, at least he knew the full extent of the debacle, although he may still have been given reason for hope.

This version of events also raises more questions. Hess appears to have been expected – but by whom? If this was, as some have argued, part of a plot by British intelligence to lure him over, was there a 'welcoming committee' awaiting him in Dungavel? Or was that welcoming committee composed, as Hess himself believed, of representatives of an anti-Churchill group, a peace party? Given the seniority and influence of some of those involved, how did Hess come to remain so long in the custody of the Home Guard? Even though others had already become involved, surely Hamilton of all people could have pulled rank enough to take charge of Hess. But the fact is that he did not. This suggests that those involved were not acting with the official sanction of the government or any of the military or intelligence services. Those expecting Hess were now engaged on a damage-limitation exercise: too many people were now aware of the mystery airman who kept asking for the Duke of Hamilton. Sooner or later questions would be asked, and Churchill would get to hear of it.

Certainly Battaglia could only have arrived on the scene because of prior Polish knowledge of Hess's arrival. Did he spend two hours reassuring Hess and telling him to 'sit tight until we can assess the situation'? Is that what Hamilton told him on the road to Glasgow? He also needed to agree a story with Hess, since their original plans had been so rudely interrupted and the Nazi emissary was in 'enemy' hands.

There is, however, another possibility: perhaps Churchill himself had uncovered the plan. Is it possible that there were two opposing factions out looking for Hess that night?

CHAPTER SEVEN

The Aftermath

Those involved in the Hess plan were not alone in busily concocting a story. Officialdom was scrabbling around trying to
construct a version of events that would cover its tracks,
finally settling on the following:

The Duke of Hamilton, as arranged the night before, went to see
the captured airman at Maryhill Barracks on the morning of Sunday,
11 May. The prisoner revealed himself to be Rudolf Hess. He said he
had come on a 'mission of humanity' to try to end the war between
Britain and Germany. Hamilton contacted senior officials in London
in order to inform Churchill about this astounding development,
and to arrange to brief the Prime Minister in person. He then flew to
the south of England and was taken to Churchill, who was staying at
a country house called Ditchley Hall. (For security reasons, it was his
custom to stay at Ditchley, the home of Sir Ronald and Lady Tree,
rather than at his official country residence of Chequers.) The Duke
briefed the Prime Minister on the situation after dinner that night.

After meetings with Foreign Office officials the next day, Churchill
dispatched a senior Foreign Office man, Ivone Kirkpatrick – who
had served at the British Embassy in Berlin before the war and knew
Hess personally – to Scotland to confirm the identity of the prisoner.

However, if the evidence given in Chapter 6 of this book is correct, the official story omits certain key facts and conceals the real
motives.

There are good reasons to believe that the standard story of

Hamilton's so-called initial meeting with Hess is inaccurate. At this stage the Duke was allegedly working on his own initiative, and until he arrived at Maryhill Barracks at 10 a.m. on 11 May he was supposed to have been unaware of the airman's true identity. But a statement written – but not given to the Commons – by Churchill on 12 May says: 'When the unidentified German airman, who afterwards turned out to be the Deputy Führer, asked for the Duke of Hamilton, the Duke who is serving as a Station Commander in the RAF was ordered to go to the hospital and receive any statement he might make.'[1] Later in the war, in November 1942, a document prepared by the British government for the Soviet Union summarising the Hess affair – authorised by Churchill and the War Cabinet – includes the statement: 'On 11th May the Duke was ordered by his superior officer in the Royal Air Force to see Hess, then under confinement in Maryhill Barracks, Glasgow.'[2] Both statements contradict Hamilton's account. Far from acting on his own initiative when he first visited Hess, we now see that he was under orders to do so. There is also the implication that Hamilton had already discussed the arrival of the airman with others – who then gave him his orders. Also significant in the report to the Russians is the use of the term 'superior officer' rather than 'commanding officer'. Although this may appear to the non-military person to be splitting hairs, in this kind of statement every term is always very precise; here the implication is that whoever gave Hamilton this order might have been of higher rank in the RAF but was not his immediate superior.

What happened at Hamilton's alleged first meeting with Hess on the morning of 11 May must remain a matter of speculation. We know that the Duke was accompanied by Flight Lieutenant Benson, RAF Turnhouse's interrogation officer, but when the prisoner asked to speak to Hamilton in private, Benson withdrew and left the two together. Hamilton's report about their meeting reads:

The German opened by saying that he had seen me in Berlin at the Olympic Games in 1936 and that I had lunched in his house. He said 'I do not know if you recognise me, but I am Rudolf Hess.' He went on to say that he was on a mission of humanity and that the Führer did not want to defeat England and wished to stop fighting. His friend Albrecht Haushofer told him that I was an Englishman who he thought would understand his (Hess's) point of view. He had consequently tried to arrange a meeting with me in Lisbon (see Haushofer's letter to me dated September 23rd 1940). Hess went on to say that he had tried to fly to Dungavel and this was the fourth time he had set out, the first time being in December. On the three previous occasions he had turned back owing to bad weather. He had not attempted to make this journey during the time when Britain was gaining victories in Libya, as he thought his mission then might be interpreted as weakness, but now that Germany had gained successes in North Africa and Greece, he was glad to come.

The fact that Reich Minister Hess had come to this country in person would, he stated, show his sincerity and Germany's willingness for peace. He then went on to say that the Führer was convinced that Germany would win the war, possibly soon but certainly in one, two or three years. He wanted to stop the unnecessary slaughter that would otherwise inevitably take place. He asked me if I could get together leading members of my party to talk over things with a view to peace proposals. I replied that there was now only one party in this country.

He then said he could tell me what Hitler's peace terms would be. First he would insist on an arrangement whereby our two countries would never go to war again. I questioned him as to how that arrangement could be brought about and he replied that one of his conditions, of course, was that Britain would give up her traditional policy of always opposing the strongest power in Europe.

He requested me to ask the King to give him 'parole' as he had come unarmed and of his own free will.

He further asked if he could inform his family that he was safe by sending a telegram to Rothacker, Herzog Str., 17, Zürich [Emma Rothacker was Hess's aunt] stating that Alfred Horn was in good health. He also asked that his identity should not be disclosed to the Press . . . From Press photographs and Albrecht Haushofer's description of Hess, I believed that this prisoner was indeed Hess himself. Until this interview I had no idea that the invitation in Haushofer's letter to meet him (Haushofer) in Lisbon had any connection with Hess.[3]

After this interview, Hamilton instructed the garrison commander that they had an important prisoner who should be moved out of

Glasgow and placed under tight security. That afternoon Hess was taken to the Drymen Military Hospital in Buchanan Castle, on the shores of Loch Lomond.

We have seen that Hess asked Hamilton to send a telegram to his aunt, Emma Rothacker in Zurich – obviously a signal that he had arrived safely. Clearly she was expected to pass this message on to someone in Germany – later, Wolf Rüdiger Hess was told by his mother that it was intended for her and that she would have passed the information on to Hitler.[4] More significantly, however, according to the testimony of Günther Sorof when interrogated by the Gestapo a few days after Hess's departure, a letter was received from Frau Rothacker to Hess on the morning of 10 May itself, which refers to his earlier request to receive an important telegram on his behalf – obviously the 'Alfred Horn' message.[5] She was concerned that it had failed to arrive – probably because the mission was planned for 5 May, so she had expected to have received it around that time. Apparently she did not realise that he was about to make a historic flight: all she knew was that she would be sent a telegram. But what is very significant is that if all had gone well she was to have received the message from the Red Cross.

Reactions in high places

According to Hamilton, he made no call to London until the afternoon of 11 May. After seeing Hess at Maryhill, he visited the crash site, then returned to RAF Turnhouse in order to collect Albrecht Haushofer's letter of July 1939. Then, with the permission of his immediate superior, he telephoned the Foreign Office, demanding to speak to the permanent under-secretary, Sir Alexander Cadogan (who was staying in his country cottage that weekend). The official who took the call, John Addis, had a heated argument with Hamilton because the latter refused to tell him the reason for the urgency in contacting Cadogan. Just as the two men were about to reach boiling point, John Colville, Churchill's private secretary, appeared in the office, and the telephone was passed over to him. Both Hamilton and Colville wrote accounts of this incident – the former in a report about the Hess affair produced at the Nuremberg Trials, and the latter in his diaries, published in 1985. Lord James Douglas-Hamilton also quotes Colville's description in his book about the Hess affair. The two versions make somewhat odd reading, not least because of the extraordinary discrepancies between them.

According to Colville's version, his first words to Hamilton were: 'Has somebody arrived?'[6] Having blurted out what was tantamount to a state secret, he attempted to explain it away so clumsily as to call to mind Major Donald's gobbledygook about German teetotallers. Of course, like Donald's, Colville's verbal gymnastics only succeeded in drawing attention to the matter he wished to obfuscate. He claimed that he had woken that morning 'thinking unaccountably of Peter Fleming's book *Flying Visit*'.[7] Written by the brother of the more famous Ian Fleming, creator of James Bond, this was a short comic novel, published in 1940, in which Hitler is forced to parachute into England, where he becomes involved in various unlikely adventures (including winning first prize in a village fête fancy-dress competition). Claiming that he had blurted out 'Has somebody arrived?' when told Hamilton was on the phone because Fleming's book had just come 'unaccountably' to mind, Colville had to place the conversation on the *morning* of 11 May to make this tale work (in a rider added to his diary in 1985, Colville explicitly states that it was shortly after breakfast[8]) – but in doing so only succeeds in clashing head-on with Hamilton's account. He also names the official who passed the phone over to him as Nicholas Lawford, not John Addis – but this was untrue as Lawford was at home on leave in Hertfordshire that weekend.[9] So we can reasonably conclude that Colville concocted this tale to cover the fact that his question – 'Has somebody arrived?' – gave the game away. It seems that he, at least, was expecting a certain 'somebody'. Hamilton's account states that Colville said: 'This is the Prime Minister's secretary speaking. The Prime Minister sent me over to the Foreign Office as he is informed that you have some interesting information.'[10]

As this goes so obviously against the party line, Hamilton is unlikely to have invented it or made a mistake, but why would he invite suspicion by including such inflammatory material in his statement in the first place? The answer is that he was effectively under oath, having written this report to be used in the war crimes trials; and as his behaviour at a later libel case reveals, Hamilton might have chosen his words carefully, but his principles did not allow him to commit perjury.

In his account of the events of that day – drawn up for his later libel action – Hamilton states: 'I telephoned the Foreign Office and got hold of Sir Alex Cadogan's secretary but the PM's secretary took charge of the telephone and started speaking to me for the PM had heard that the German had asked for me.'[11] Colville's diary entry makes it clear that he was told about a German airman asking for Hamilton when he called Churchill at Ditchley Hall to report on the bomb damage during the *morning* of 11 May. Clearly, Churchill had been advised of the airman's arrival during the night, possibly via the Air Minister, Sinclair, who was also staying at Ditchley Hall – even if he was still in the dark about his identity. The story was later rewritten to make Churchill first hear of it in the afternoon. It seems likely that the night before, Hamilton was instructed to telephone Sir Alexander Cadogan on the morning of the 11th. But when it was realised that Cadogan had gone to his country residence, Colville was told to get over to Cadogan's office fast to make sure that he picked up the call.

In fact, this is confirmed by Churchill's own account of the events of that weekend. He states that on the evening of Sunday, 11 May, he was watching a Marx Brothers film in the private cinema at Ditchley, occasionally going out to ask for the latest news on the heavy raid on London (which, of course, took place on the *previous* night). He was then interrupted by a secretary, who informed him of a telephone call from someone who wanted to speak to him 'on behalf of' the Duke of Hamilton about a matter of 'Cabinet importance'. The Prime Minister asked Brendan Bracken to take the call, and Bracken reported that the Duke had 'an amazing piece of information' to convey. Churchill then gave the order for Hamilton to fly down to brief him.

Clearly this episode took place on the night of 10–11 May, not the following evening, as demonstrated by the air raid on London and the fact that by the evening of 11 May Hamilton was already at Ditchley.[12]

Added to this, Churchill's hostess at Ditchley – Nancy, Lady Tree – recalls that the Prime Minister informed her on Sunday *morning* that Hamilton would be staying that night.[13] This evidence completely undermines the official line, which has always been that the Duke himself did not realise the significance of 'Horn's' arrival until he saw the prisoner late that morning.

Hamilton briefs Churchill

A car was waiting at RAF Northolt to take Hamilton straight to Ditchley Hall, arriving just as dinner was being served. Characteristically, perhaps, the arch trencherman Winston Churchill insisted that they should dine before Hamilton told his story, although it does seem extremely odd that even he should put the satisfaction of his stomach before the arrival of Scotland's premier peer with urgent news of the greatest importance – unless he already knew what it was. After dinner, Churchill and Sinclair withdrew to a separate room where the Duke briefed them, being invited to do so with the idiosyncratic Churchillian words: 'Now tell us this funny story of yours.'

At the end of Hamilton's briefing, Churchill uttered words that have become the stuff of legend: 'Well, Hess or no Hess, I'm going to see the Marx Brothers.'[14] This insouciance is usually taken to show the true bulldog spirit at its best. Deputy Führers may fall out of planes, but old Winnie is so unimpressed that he calmly watches Groucho and the gang as planned. However, as with much else in this story, Churchill's words might not have meant quite what they seemed.

The next morning Churchill, accompanied by Hamilton, was driven to London where they had urgent top-level meetings with various ministers and officials – the most important being Sir Stewart Menzies, head of MI6. Churchill also sought the advice of Lord Beaverbrook, then the Minister for Aircraft Production. At Number 10 Downing Street on the afternoon of 12 May, the Prime Minister showed him the photographs of the airman that Hess had given to Hamilton: Beaverbrook, who had met Hess on many occasions before the war, confirmed they were of the Deputy Führer.[15]

It was decided to send Ivone Kirkpatrick, a close friend of Menzies – whose official title of Controller of European Services at the BBC concealed the fact that he was working for the Political Warfare Executive – to Scotland with Hamilton to see the prisoner. Ostensibly this was to confirm the airman's identity. (As Kirkpatrick had been one of the interpreters at the Munich talks of 1938, his knowledge of German and of the Nazi leaders was extremely useful.) However, as Beaverbrook had already positively identified the photographs, and since the first announcement of Hess's arrival was made at 11.20 that night – while Kirkpatrick and Hamilton were still en route to Buchanan

Castle – this could hardly be the real reason for Kirkpatrick's trip to Scotland. It is more likely that he had been dispatched to discover exactly why Hess had come. A party of what were euphemistically described as 'guardians' – officers supplied by MI6 – were sent to Buchanan Castle, relieving its regular guards the next day.[16]

Another government department whose role would prove vital in the coming days was the Ministry of Information, under the leadership of its minister, Alfred Duff Cooper, and director general, Walter Monckton. One puzzling aspect of their involvement was, as Peter Padfield put it, that Monckton 'knew more about the Hess affair than his Minister, Duff Cooper'.[17] During the following week he leaked to the press that Hess had tried to contact Hamilton, via Haushofer's letter, in September 1940 – which was not mentioned in either the British or German announcements, and had not figured in any cabinet discussions. This unofficial statement included the detail that Hamilton had 'immediately placed the letter in the hands of our security services'. So Walter Monckton at least had no doubt that Hamilton had received the letter.

This was not one of the Ministry of Information's successes. Although the information was leaked to protect the Duke, it backfired badly, intensifying rumours that he had been in collusion with Hess for months. This and other aspects of the Ministry of Information's handling of the affair attracted so much criticism that Monckton tendered his resignation on 27 May, but Churchill refused to accept it.

Clearly, Monckton had inside information – hardly surprising for someone in his position, with his wide scattering of contacts within intelligence, political and Court circles. Just the evening before he leaked the information that he had had separate meetings with J. C. Masterman, head of the XX Committee (in itself highly suggestive), and with the King's private secretary, Sir Alexander Hardinge.[18] (Previously, Monckton had played a major role in royal intrigue as one of the main advisers to Edward VIII during the abdication crisis of 1936.)

Plausible denial

Meanwhile, what was happening in Germany in the wake of Hess's failed mission? Hess had left several letters behind, in the keeping of his adjutant Pintsch, to be delivered when he had gone: among them were explanatory notes to Ilse, to Willi Messerschmitt – and, of course, to Adolf Hitler.[19] If, as seems likely, the Führer knew all about his Deputy's mission, this letter was designed to help enable the 'plausible denial' that Hitler needed if something went terribly wrong for Hess.

The failure of Hess's mission had created a highly volatile situation, which had to be handled with great care. Hitler needed to cover himself as rapidly and thoroughly as possible because Stalin would view any suggestion that Germany was trying to negotiate peace with Britain with considerable suspicion. Despite the fact that Germany and the USSR were still officially allies at that time, Stalin must have had reservations about the Führer: *Mein Kampf* made no secret of Hitler's hatred of Communism and the need for *Lebensraum* that would inevitably bring the two nations into conflict. He might guess, correctly, that a bid for peace with Britain was a prelude to an attack on Russia. Besides, Hitler did not want his Axis partners, particularly Mussolini, to think that he was negotiating behind their backs. It was essential to win back confidence by disowning Rudolf Hess and his mission.

It is not known exactly when Hitler 'officially' found out. If Hess had told Rosenberg of his plans at lunch on 10 May, perhaps the ideologue told Hitler when he joined him immediately afterwards at his retreat at the Berghof. Or perhaps it was the unfortunate adjutant, Pintsch, who had the dubious honour of handing over Hess's letter when he arrived at the Berghof at about 7.30 the next morning. At first the adjutant must have been enormously relieved at Hitler's reaction to the bad tidings: after reading the note, the Führer asked him to stay to lunch. But Pintsch's luck lasted no longer than the meal – afterwards Hitler calmly ordered that he be arrested, together with Hess's driver and bodyguard.[20] (According to the driver, Rudolf Lippert, they were arrested at 5.30 a.m. on 11 May[21] – two hours before Pintsch arrived at the Berghof, which effectively demolishes Pintsch's story.)

Hitler immediately sent for the Nazi leaders and flew into one of his infamously spectacular rages. He spat out the news of Hess's flight to Britain to try to negotiate a peace and made sure they were in no doubt where he stood: it was outrageous; it was unthinkable; it was treason. It seems that this vein-throbbing reaction was, at least in part, genuine. But was Hitler really beside himself because of Hess's defection – or was there quite another reason? Perhaps the melodramatic rage covered up a secret fear for his close friend and guide – after all, at this stage nobody in Germany had received any sign of Hess's safe arrival in Britain. Anything could have happened to him. Or was Hitler appalled because he already knew that the peace initiative with Britain had failed, and ignominiously so?

That evening a crisis meeting took place at the Berghof. Most of the leading Nazis believed that Hess had perished somewhere in the North Sea, but Hitler insisted that this was not possible: Hess, he said, was far too skilful a pilot. Therefore, he argued, his Deputy must be in British hands, and his mission had failed – but in that case, it was very odd that the British had said nothing.

Even without having precise knowledge of the situation, the Nazi High Command knew they had to act swiftly. Just fifty hours after Hess's departure – at 8 p.m. on 12 May – they broadcast this statement on German radio:

It is officially announced by the National Socialist Party that party member Rudolf Hess who, as he was suffering from an illness of some years' standing, had been strictly forbidden to embark on any further flying activity, was able, contrary to this command, again to come into possession of an aeroplane.

On Saturday, 10 May, at about 6 p.m., Rudolf Hess again set off on a flight from Augsburg, from which he has so far not returned.

A letter which he left behind unfortunately shows by its distractedness traces of a mental disorder, and it is feared he was a victim of hallucinations.

The Führer at once ordered the arrest of the adjutants of party member Hess, who alone had any cognisance of these flights, and did not, contrary to the Führer's orders, of which they were fully aware, either prevent or report the flight.

In these circumstances, it must be considered that party member Hess either jumped out of his plane or has met with an accident.[22]

In the two days since Hess's departure, there had been total silence from the British, and the Nazis had not received the message that 'Alfred Horn was safe' from Emma Rothacker in Switzerland. Therefore, at least the uncertainty about whether he had been captured or had met with an accident was genuine. The radio announcement was clearly designed to prepare the public for either eventuality – otherwise the emphasis on his alleged mental state was completely unnecessary. Both possibilities meant the ruin of 'party member' Hess in the eyes of the German public.

The first British announcement

During 12 May Churchill had also been wrestling with the problem of what to tell the public, finally calling in Eden and Cadogan to agree on a statement. The Prime Minister wanted to include an explanation of why Hess had come, a statement that he had declared that 'he had come to England in the name of humanity hoping that a peace might be made between Great Britain and Germany',[23] but after a heated exchange of views, Eden and Cadogan persuaded him to drop it in favour of a simple announcement of Hess's arrival.[24] Cadogan proposed that they should also suggest that Hess had fled Germany as a result of a split in the Nazi leadership. There was to be no mention of a peace initiative, which might have proved dangerously appealing to Blitz-weary Britons.

The final statement – giving only the bare bones of the story, without any mention of Hamilton's involvement – was issued at a press conference called by the Ministry of Information and presided over by Duff Cooper and Monckton at 11.20 p.m., some three hours after Berlin's announcement. Not to be outdone, the Nazis responded the next day with:

A perusal of the papers left behind by Rudolf Hess discloses that he laboured under the delusion that a step taken on his personal initiative with Englishmen whom he formerly knew would lead to an understanding being reached between Germany and Britain. He had, indeed, as had been confirmed by a report from London, landed in Scotland by parachute near the place he wished to visit, and was presumably picked up there injured.

Rudolf Hess, it was known to the Party, has for years suffered physically and increasingly took refuge in various forms of hypnotism and astrology etc. Attempts to elucidate to what extent this is responsible for causing Hess the mental disturbance which led him to take this step are also being made.

It is also conceivable that Hess in the end was intentionally led into a trap by the British.[25]

The last sentence is particularly interesting because it contradicts the Germans' official line that Hess had acted merely on impulse. It suggests that there had been some form of prior communication with people in Britain.

The statement went on to say that Hess's ideas that he could broker a peace between Germany and Britain were misguided but well intentioned. It added that Hitler's resolve to prosecute the war was as strong as ever – and, significantly, that he had announced that the war would be continued 'until the British leaders have been overthrown or are ready for peace'. (Even then Hitler was still not talking in terms of invading Britain, clearly expecting the British leaders to be overthrown from within the country.) It ends with a warning that 'Churchill and his clique will abuse the whole affair for the vilest purposes of propaganda'. While this might seem a reasonable supposition, it never happened – to the great puzzlement of Goebbels, who would never have let such a golden opportunity slip through his hands.

That same day Hitler also announced that Hess was to be succeeded by Martin Bormann, who was to assume the role of Head of the Party Chancellery, but not Deputy Führer. As the title ceased with Hess it seems clear that Hitler did not believe anyone else could – or should – step into his old friend's shoes.

The British interviews

Meanwhile, in Britain, the lengthy process of interviewing the distinguished prisoner had begun.[26] Ivone Kirkpatrick and the Duke of Hamilton visited Hess at Buchanan Castle shortly after midnight on 13 May. Kirkpatrick reported that the prisoner began a long speech outlining the reasons why he had come, starting with something of a history lecture on British foreign policy from 1904 onwards. He also stressed that, in Kirkpatrick's words, 'the Führer had never entertained any designs against the British Empire, nor had he ever aspired to world domination', and that Hitler 'would sincerely regret the collapse of the British Empire'. He warned Kirkpatrick that Britain would lose its independence to the USA, and offered 'proposals for a settlement whereby Germany should have a free hand in Europe and the British Empire should be left intact save for the return of the former [German] colonies'.[27]

Kirkpatrick brought the conversation round to the subject of Germany's plans for the Soviet Union – obviously suspecting that this figured largely in Hess's agenda. The prisoner told him that 'Germany had certain demands to make of Russia which would have to be satisfied either by negotiation or war'[28] – but, according to Kirkpatrick, he denied that Hitler was planning an early attack on the Soviet Union. Kirkpatrick had two more lengthy meetings with Hess in the following days, one together with Hamilton and one alone. During the latter Hess named two German internees – Kurt Maass and Eduard Semelbauer – whom he wanted to assist him in the anticipated peace talks. Not only did Hess name them, but he was able to give their internment numbers and place of confinement.[29]

On 16 May Churchill sent a memo to Cadogan, asking him to make 'a fairly full digest of the conversational parts of Hess's three interviews [with Kirkpatrick]' so that he could use it to brief Roosevelt.[30] But, as Padfield asks,[31] what does 'conversational parts' mean? He suggests there might have also been 'documentary parts', involving written material, although there are no details of this. Another alternative is that these were the formal parts of the meeting.

Cadogan reported a telephone conversation with Kirkpatrick that went as follows:

> Mr Kirkpatrick suggested that it might be best if the Duke of Hamilton could move him to his own home which is now being used as a hospital and he further suggested that the Duke of Hamilton's brother, who speaks German well, might eventually be put in touch with him together with some other individual who might well play the role of a member of the Conservative Party indicated above [i.e. the anti-Churchill faction].[32]

This extraordinary suggestion does not appear in Kirkpatrick's report. In any case, Churchill clearly did not approve it: on 13 May he ordered that Hess be taken to a convenient and secure place near London, adding that it should be 'fitted by "C" with the necessary appliances' (presumably surveillance apparatus because transcripts were made of all the conversations). He gave instructions that Hess should be 'treated with dignity as if he were an important general who had fallen into our hands' and should be well looked after and allowed books – but strictly no access to newspapers or radio.[33]

Menzies was given the somewhat daunting task of finding a suitably secure location in which to keep Hess, finally settling on Mytchett Place, a country house conveniently situated in Surrey close to the garrison town of Aldershot. Churchill had also agreed with the War Cabinet that Hess should be classified as a prisoner of war and a prisoner of state, which meant that he should be kept in isolation and only allowed to see visitors who were approved by the Foreign Office (or, in reality, MI6). That is how the strange second life of Rudolf Hess began.

On the day after Churchill issued his orders about securing Hess in splendid isolation, Berlin radio made another announcement, which dropped something of a bombshell as far as the British were concerned: 'Hess believed that the Duke of Hamilton belonged to a group opposed to Mr Churchill, and the object of his journey was to explain his view of the real position of Britain and Germany. He hoped to be able to prepare the soil for an understanding between Britain and Germany.'[34] The fat was in the fire about Hamilton's involvement. As this was now very much in the public domain, being not only announced on German radio but featured in the American and Swedish press, there was only one feasible course of action for the British government: it admitted that Hess had asked to be taken to the Duke of Hamilton. A further German statement added insult to injury: 'It further transpires from Hess's notes that he was fully convinced of the success of his mission. He even believed that the necessary petrol for his return journey would be put at his disposal in Britain.'[35]

The Prime Minister wanted to make a lengthy statement to the Commons summarising the facts as they were then known, but was opposed by Eden and Cadogan. Fortunately, however, the original draft of Churchill's intended statement survives:

> He [Hess] is reported to be perfectly sane and apart from the injury to his ankle in good health, as indeed seemed probable from the remarkable flight which he had made.

From his statements he seems to have had the idea that there was a strong peace or defeatist movement in Great Britain with which he might negotiate, and that by convincing the British public of the overwhelming power of Germany to win the war he might bring about a peace on the basis that Great Britain and the British Empire should be left intact, apart from the return of the German Colonies, and that Germany under Herr Hitler should become unquestioned master of Europe.[36]

An intriguing note was scribbled in the margin: 'He has also made other statements which it would not be in the public interest to disclose.' As the announcement was based on Kirkpatrick's interviews with Hess, the records of which contain no such statements, we can only conclude that they were excised from the public record. However, we can safely assume that whatever he said was potentially explosive as far as the Churchill government was concerned. Oddly, perhaps, it was the Premier himself who again appears to have wanted to give the public more or less the true story, while Cadogan and Eden favoured keeping the Germans guessing – despite giving the clear initiative to Goebbels. Lord Beaverbrook, whom Churchill also consulted on this issue, joined in the dissenting voices, and a later attempt by the Prime Minister to make his statement was unanimously opposed by the War Cabinet. The only minister to support Churchill's position throughout was Sir Archibald Sinclair (who was not a member of the War Cabinet).

Churchill never delivered the speech; instead, a brief statement was made on 13 May simply confirming that Hess had arrived, with the promise of more details to come 'in due course'. A full statement was not given to the Commons until September 1943, although the Prime Minister did slip some remarks about the affair into his answer to a parliamentary question in January 1942.

Press speculation

Although no official explanation of Hess's arrival was forthcoming at the time, the Ministry of Information briefed the press unofficially, promoting the line that Hess had fled from Germany because of a split in the Nazi leadership, perhaps to escape another purge like the Night of the Long Knives. Clearly the government did not want to put an official stamp on such a fabricated story, but was only too happy to have the press do their work for them and spread the disinformation as widely as possible. The Ministry of Information was keen to stress that Hess had not brought any peace proposals with him; this was then faithfully reported by the media at their press conferences. The political correspondent of the *Glasgow Herald* wrote after one briefing in Whitehall on 15 May: 'It is strongly emphasised again to-night that Hess did not bring with him any peace proposals. That much is definite and irrefutable.'[37]

Perhaps because the government was seen to be protesting too much, rumours continued to abound that the Deputy Führer had come to talk peace, the first such reports appearing in the American press just three days after Hess's arrival in Scotland. When on 19 May a group of MPs urged Churchill to make a statement to scotch the rumours, the following statement was issued (as reported in the *Glasgow Herald* of 20 May 1941):

> An official denial has already been given to an earlier rumour that Hess brought peace proposals either on his own responsibility or on behalf of Hitler, but it has not succeeded in destroying what the Government is most anxious should be clearly understood – the illusion that the facts are otherwise or that the War Cabinet is contemplating a compromise peace.[38]

However, the following day Churchill merely announced to the Commons that he was not yet in a position to make a statement about Hess, and did not know when he would be. While not in any hurry to let the people know why Hess was in Britain, it was obviously deemed a matter of enormous urgency to make it clear what his mission was *not* about – even if that meant being parsimonious with the truth.

Meanwhile, there were other problems. Of course, the German statement had thrust the Duke of Hamilton uncomfortably into the spotlight. He had returned to London on 15 May, bringing Kirkpatrick's written reports for discussions at the Foreign Office and the Ministry of Information, and to brief the King at Buckingham Palace. He also had another, very short, meeting with Churchill on 16 May in the Prime Minister's car on the way from Downing Street to Buckingham Palace.

Hamilton was desperate to limit the already serious damage to his reputation. Although he claimed to know nothing about the flight before it happened, he realised that things were looking bad for him, especially after the German statement had specifically linked him with Hess's alleged peace mission. As he so evocatively expressed it to an amused Winston Churchill, 'What do you tell your wife if a prostitute throws her arms round your neck?'[39]

The Hamilton archives reveal that Hamilton kept the King fully informed during this time. There is a letter to the King's private secretary, Sir Alexander Hardinge, dated 19 May, which accompanied the delivery of a 'sealed box' containing several documents with 'certain information that is most secret',[40] and another letter to the King on the same day classified 'Secret' that outlines the Hess story.[41] Another member of the 'Hamilton circle' who was reporting to the King was Kurt Hahn, who, as we have seen, drafted *The Times* letter in October 1939. Hahn wrote a report for Churchill on Hess's arrival and its implications, a copy of which Hamilton gave to the King.[42]

Hamilton seemed doomed to become a wartime villain to the British, an appeaser, a friend of Hitler's friend. Something had to be done to save the reputation of Scotland's premier peer. After discussing the situation with the King, Churchill eventually agreed to prime an MP with a parliamentary question that would elicit a suitably reassuring reply from Sir Archibald Sinclair. On 22 May Sinclair made his statement, in answer to the parliamentary question about Hamilton's role in the Hess affair. He said that despite Hess and the German press's claims that the Deputy had met Hamilton during the 1936 Olympics, this was not the case, although it was possible that Hess had seen him there. Then, in a well-manicured piece of wording, he stated: 'Contrary to reports that have appeared in some of the newspapers, the Duke has never been in correspondence with the Deputy Führer. None of the Duke's three brothers, who are, like himself, serving in the RAF, has either met Hess or had correspondence with him.'[43]

The over-careful wording only succeeds in prompting more questions than answers. While it might be true that the Duke had never been in *direct* contact with Hess, the two had been in touch, through Albrecht Haushofer. And although Sinclair is careful to say that Hamilton's brothers had never met Hess, what about the Duke himself? Then again, if Hamilton had not met Hess at the Olympics, had he perhaps met him elsewhere, on other occasions?

Sinclair finished with this definitive statement: 'It will be seen that the conduct of the Duke of Hamilton has been in every respect honourable and proper.'

In his account of this time composed in 1952 for a further libel action (which, in the event, did not proceed), Hamilton wrote that in this statement Sinclair 'sailed very close to the wind'.[44]

The meeting with 'the Duke'

Officially, Hess remained in the military hospital at Buchanan Castle until he was taken to London on 16 May. However, there might have been at least one significant departure from this programme, as recounted to Peter Padfield by retired RAF Squadron Leader Frank Day, who at the time of Hess's arrival was a trainee Spitfire pilot officer at RAF Grangemouth, not far from Turnhouse. Day claims that on 13 May he and some of his fellow trainees were ordered to report to RAF Turnhouse where they were told they had been selected to make up a special guard detail:

> they were then driven – without being issued with arms – a short distance to a large Victorian house. Inside the front door was a curving flight of stairs. After mounting to the first floor, he and one other Pilot Officer were told to stand outside the middle door of about three on the landing. Presently two men in khaki uniform escorted a tall German officer in uniform with a leather flying jacket up the stairs and through the door Day was guarding; one of the escorts went inside with the German, and Day had a glimpse of an ante room leading into a large living room furnished with easy chairs and a settee. The other escort remained outside holding a paper bag; Day discovered it contained 'pills' the German had brought with him. Some five minutes later a ranking RAF officer came up the stairs with a civilian and both went into the room. Day learned from a manservant that the RAF officer was 'the Duke'. Later that evening Day was driven back to Turnhouse. Asked in the mess next day, which was buzzing with speculation about Hess, whether he had seen him, Day replied, 'For about thirty seconds.'[45]

This looks like a secret high-level meeting between Hess, 'the Duke' and a civilian (possibly Ivone Kirkpatrick), although officially Hess was incarcerated in Buchanan Castle at that time. But although Kirkpatrick and Hamilton had already met with the Deputy Führer there, Day's story suggests that there was something very different about this meeting and it raises several questions. Whose house was it? Were Day and his companions there in the capacity of a guard of honour, as is strongly implied by their being in full uniform and unarmed? And if so, for whose benefit was this – the distinguished prisoner's or 'the Duke's'? In either case, it was a sign of respect for someone, indicating that this was a top-level meeting. Yet surely Hess, as a prisoner of war, hardly warranted a guard of honour, and if 'the Duke' were Hamilton, as Day appears to have assumed, surely such formality would be completely out of proportion for an RAF officer of the rank of wing commander. Hamilton's diary, although it records all other meetings with Hess, records no such meeting for that day and even places the Duke elsewhere. So if the guard were not present in honour of either Hess or Hamilton, in whose honour were they there? Who was 'the Duke' – if not Hamilton?

It would be tempting to dismiss Day's account as self-aggrandisement were it not for certain independent evidence that Hess was not where he was supposed to be on 13 May. In August 1997, Robert Shaw, a retired professor of Business Studies, gave an interview to the *Scottish Daily Mail* recounting his memories of guarding Hess at Buchanan Castle as a young lieutenant. (He was to encounter him again as one of the British administrators at the Nuremberg Trials.) Shaw's memories of that time are very clear, but he includes a puzzling detail: while he was serving at Maryhill Barracks, one evening's leave was abruptly cancelled in favour of an urgent guard duty. The guard detail were to take their prisoner, a German airman, to the military hospital at Buchanan Castle – presumably on 11 May, although the *Mail* gives the date as the day before. Charged with guarding the Nazi at the hospital, the next day Shaw was told that two VIPs were coming to interview the prisoner. However, before they arrived, he heard the radio announcement about Hess's arrival in Scotland, and immediately realised the identity of his charge. He made a point of spending some time talking to the Deputy Führer, who told him (according to a letter Shaw wrote to the Glasgow *Herald* of 28 August 1997): 'it was only a matter of time until they [the Germans] would defeat the Allied Armies. He persisted it would be more sensible if Germany and Britain were to join forces against Russia and thus prevent the spread of Communism in the West.'[46] Shaw went on to describe how Ivone Kirkpatrick and the Duke of Hamilton arrived at the hospital just after midnight, which tallies with the official account. But then Shaw drops a minor bombshell, albeit apparently innocently: 'He was taken away the next day and I never saw him again until 1946 in Nuremberg.'[47] This puts Hess's departure from Buchanan Castle on 13 May, whereas the official account claims he stayed there until the 16th, when he was taken to London. If Shaw's memory is correct, where was Hess in the missing three days? If he was still in Scotland during this time, it would dovetail neatly with Squadron Leader Day's testimony – and it may be significant that it was on 13 May that the MI6 'guardians' took over Hess's custody.

Interviewed in September 2000, Shaw volunteered another valuable piece of information. Not only had Hess told him that he had met the Duke of Hamilton at the 1936 Olympics, but when breakfasting with Kirkpatrick and the Duke, Hamilton himself confirmed it.[48]

Circumstantial evidence

Apart from personal testimonies, there is abundant circumstantial evidence to suggest that Hitler's public reaction to Hess's mission was part of an agreed plan. Top of the list is the Deputy's love for his family – as a devoted husband and father he would never have abandoned Ilse and little Wolf to Hitler's wrath. He must have known, if anyone did, how terrible that prospect could have been. The Nazis had a policy known as *Sippenhaft* (literally 'group liability') which meant that the family and friends of a traitor were also punished, even if they had no knowledge of his treachery. Hitler had no compunction about enforcing this particular instrument of terror: in the aftermath of the bomb plot against him in July 1944, many people only vaguely connected with the conspirators were rounded up and often summarily executed. Yet very little action was taken against Hess's circle, despite Hitler's disowning of his old friend so publicly. Not only were Ilse and Wolf allowed to remain in their Harlaching villa, but Hitler personally ensured that she received a generous pension – as the dependant of one Luftwaffe Captain Horn![49] No action at all was taken against Ernst Bohle, Hess's head of the AO, even though he freely admitted that he had helped in the preparations for the flight and had translated the documents that Hess took with him. Others in Hess's circle found themselves at the receiving end of what amounted to a mere slap on the wrist. Albrecht Haushofer was summoned to the Berghof on 12 May, where he was instructed to write an account for Hitler of his contacts in Britain and the extent of his involvement in the flight. This note still exists: the list of British contacts is extremely telling. Unlike the list he gave Hess back in August 1940, with high-level diplomats such as Hoare, Lord Lothian and Owen St Clair O'Malley at the top, this one lists a separate group of people (although the names of those gentlemen are also tacked on at the end). The focus of his report is what he describes as a 'leading group of young Conservatives', most of whom were Scottish. The list includes: the Duke of Hamilton, Lord Dunglass (later Prime Minister Sir Alec Douglas-Home), Kenneth Lindsay MP, Lord Malcolm Douglas-Hamilton (whose wife, Haushofer noted, was related to the then Queen), the Duke of Northumberland and Lord Eustace Percy.[50] This is the very group that the Hamilton archives make clear were working together on the Hess peace initiative. That these names should have been listed by Albrecht Haushofer two days after Hess's flight demonstrates that the whole affair had been closely co-ordinated.

Although Albrecht Haushofer was detained by the Gestapo for some weeks, he emerged to admit that he had been treated in a 'thoroughly honourable form'.[51] He was then released and carried on as before. Karl Haushofer, too, was reported in the British and American press as having been arrested a few days after Hess's arrival.[52] If so, he was soon freed.

Dr Willi Messerschmitt's detention was, if anything, positively light-hearted. On the morning of 11 May he was ordered before Hermann Göring for questioning. According to an interview the aircraft designer gave in 1947, the Luftwaffe chief thundered at him: 'As far as you are concerned, I suppose anybody can come and fly off in one of your machines!' Taken aback, Messerschmitt pointed out that the particular 'anybody' in question was the Deputy Führer, to which Göring retorted: 'You should have known that this man was crazy.'

Taking his life in his hands, Messerschmitt replied: 'How could I be expected to know that one so high in the hierarchy of the Third Reich could be crazy? If that were so, Herr Reichsmarschall, you should have procured his resignation!' There must have followed a tricky moment when Göring could have reacted either way, but in the event he roared with laughter, saying: 'Messerschmitt, you are quite incurable! Go back to your factory and get on with your construction. I will help you out of the mess, if the Führer shall seek to make trouble for you.'[53] (Messerschmitt puts this interview on the morning of 11 May, saying he had been summoned the night before. Is this just a slip of memory, or is it evidence that Göring knew about the flight before Hitler?) Clearly, this was merely a token effort at interrogating the factory owner. Göring must have known that Messerschmitt was much more deeply involved – after all, the modifications to the Me-110 had to be made with his personal approval, and it could hardly have escaped his notice that they were intended for a long-distance flight. If nothing else, the fact that Hess had chosen a long-range aircraft normally crewed by two, and the addition of extra fuel tanks, should have given the game away.

Helmut Kaden, who had been so closely involved with the preparations for Hess's flight, was naturally terrified that the Gestapo would come knocking at his door. But they never did, and Kaden was not interviewed by anyone about his part in the Hess affair.[54]

Peter Padfield points out that even after the war those who had been closest to Hess – such as Ilse, Messerschmitt and Pintsch – would have had every reason to maintain the party line that Hitler knew nothing about the plan.[55] To deviate from the agreed story would have seriously jeopardised Hess's chances of acquittal at Nuremberg – and later, of an early release from Spandau. The revelation that he had acted with Hitler's blessing would have made his enemies realise that his mission was a key part of a conspiracy to secure a peace with Britain, effectively giving Germany an advantage in the offensive against the Soviet Union. This was specifically part of the case for the prosecution at Nuremberg.

Sensation, speculation and scandal

The sensational flight of Hitler's Deputy naturally caused a furore among the British public. Rumours, speculation and gossip were rife.

One problem for Churchill and his administration was that the censors – who kept an eye on the letters of the armed forces – reported that there was a popular idea that there had been some form of collusion between Hess and certain people in high places.[56] Many people thought that his arrival in Scotland was by no means as unexpected as it was claimed. As we have seen, a full eight months elapsed before Churchill made a statement on the matter. On 27 January 1942 he announced to the House of Commons:

> When Rudolf Hess flew over here some months ago, he firmly believed that he had only to gain access to certain circles in this country for what he described as 'the Churchill clique' to be thrown out of power and for a government to be set up with which Hitler could negotiate a magnanimous peace.[57]

Churchill was admitting that Hess had come with peace proposals in the expectation of joining representatives of a pro-peace, anti-Churchill faction. But, cleverly, the phrase 'he firmly believed' implies strongly that this clique existed only in the imagination of the German prisoner. This is the position that has been generally accepted ever since, with the exception of those who believe Hess had been deliberately encouraged in this delusion by misinformation planted by British intelligence.

Assuming that there was no smoke without fire, the public still cast around for likely Quislings. Top of the list had to be the Duke of Hamilton, whose life had rapidly become a misery because of all the rumour and innuendo. There is even a story that one outraged lady slapped his face at a society party. Matters threatened to get out of hand as more and more people expressed their anger about him publicly, leading to the two libel actions in which Hamilton defended himself. But in one sense at least the court cases worked in Hamilton's favour: apart from Sir Archibald Sinclair's statement in the Commons, the newspaper reports of the trials gave the public their first chance to hear his side of the story.

In February 1942 Hamilton sued members of the London District Committee of the Communist Party and their printers, and the authors, publishers, printers and distributors of an article in *World News and Views* over their allegations that he had plotted with Britain's enemies, had known Hess before the war and knew all about his flight. The case was settled when some, but not all, of the defendants issued a public apology, Hamilton only asking for costs. In legal terms there the matter ended with the Duke's honour intact, but it must be said that one of his sworn statements looks suspicious. Read out by his barrister, it claims that when he was informed that a German airman named Alfred Horn was asking to see him, he 'thereupon' went with his interrogation officer to interview the prisoner – implying he went immediately.[58] According to the standard version he waited until the next morning, but we have seen that there is good evidence that he *did* go at once – and now here is further evidence, from the man himself. Had he forgotten the party line? Or had he baulked at committing perjury, hoping no one would notice the implication of his well-chosen word?

Later in 1942 Hamilton also took out an action in the American courts against journalist Pierre van Paassen, who in his book *That Day Alone* (published in late 1941) described the Duke as a 'British Fascist' who had plotted with Hess.[59] This was also settled out of court in Hamilton's favour.

The Duke's success in these two cases is often cited as vindication of his position that he was innocent of having met Hess before and of having prior knowledge of his flight – but further research reveals that the trials were by no means as clear cut as most accounts would have us believe. To begin with, his submission for the first case was approved by the Air Ministry,[60] and it is also clear that the government was unhappy with the action, putting pressure on him to drop it – not surprisingly, perhaps, seeing that the Communist Party was threatening to call Rudolf Hess as a witness.[61] There is a letter from the Home Secretary, Herbert Morrison, to Sir Archibald Sinclair, dated 18 June 1941, that reads:

> Personally, I find it difficult to understand what advantage a libel action can bring him as his reputation has been entirely cleared by your statement in Parliament and I should have thought that even if he is entirely successful in his libel action he would gain little by it.
>
> Perhaps in the circumstances it might be worthwhile for you, whilst freely recognising his right to proceed, to sound him out on the question of whether he thinks it is necessary to go on with the case.[62]

The outcome, superficially, was that Hamilton won, only asking for an apology and costs. While this is true in broad outline, what is not usually reported is the amount he was awarded. There is correspondence in the Hamilton archives in which the Duke's American lawyers in the van Paassen case seek guidance from his British solicitors about the terms of the out-of-court settlement: we learn that he received just £110, which, the British solicitors confirm, did not even cover all his costs.[63] In other words, Hamilton was happy to settle for a compromise. We also learn from the archives that although he took out a suit for $100,000 against Pierre van Paassen and his publishers, he finally settled for the offending passages to be removed in subsequent editions and for the modest sum of $1,300 in costs – to be payable in instalments.[64]

However, there is one 'libel' that he took no action against, which has received considerably less publicity than the court cases. On 13 May 1941 the *Daily Express*, under the headline 'Boxer Marquis Dined With Hess', stated that Hamilton had met Hess several times before the war. After the Duke's solicitor met with the editor, Godfrey Norris, it seemed at first as if the *Express* was going to print a retraction, but the solicitor arrived at their second meeting to find Norris in conference with the *Express*'s proprietor, Beaverbrook himself. When he emerged, Norris was in no mood to back down, declaring that Sir Archibald Sinclair's Commons statement denying that Hamilton had ever met Hess before the war was 'false' and that the paper would, if necessary, defend its accusation in court.[65] At this point Hamilton backed down. Perhaps he knew that he had an almost uniquely well-informed adversary in Lord Beaverbrook, who had had his finger on the pulse of the Hess affair. (He was one of only four people who were given copies of Ivone Kirkpatrick's report on his meetings with Hess.) If Beaverbrook stuck to his guns in court, it could well have been a particularly bruising fight.

The evidence is overwhelming that Hamilton had met Hess in 1936, and that he knew he was coming in 1941. It also seems clear that immediately after Hess landed Hamilton had rushed to meet him that night, not the next morning as in the official accounts. This means that Hamilton's public statements were designed to conceal certain inconvenient facts. Although, as an honourable man, when under oath he carefully took refuge in ambiguous phrasing, he seems to have dissembled in order to toe the official line. Truth is the first casualty of war, and Churchill and his ministers had worked hard to present the image of a united government to the British public, desperate to conceal the fact that a substantial faction of the Establishment would have preferred to negotiate peace with Germany. In the highly charged atmosphere of wartime, where emotive issues are seen in black and white, the subtleties of a non-Nazi peace party would have been lost on the man in the street. As Hamilton discovered the hard way, even to be rumoured to have met Rudolf Hess years before the war made him a Quisling in the eyes of many patriots. Exposing the truth about the dramatic split in the Establishment would also have had a devastating effect on the morale of the public, who still looked to the ruling class for strong, unequivocal leadership. There was no room for argument – the very existence of a British peace party had to be denied. Hamilton's loyalties might have been divided up to a point, but he knew he had to comply with the agreed story. He also had to cover the tracks of his fellow peace group members. No doubt such a ploy would have been both distasteful and extremely stressful for him, but in the circumstances it seems he had no choice but to maintain the deception.

The Lord Provost speaks out

Someone else who made life uncomfortable for Churchill was Sir Patrick J. Dollan (1885–1963), a one-time miner and former editor of the *Glasgow Daily Herald*, then the Lord Provost of Glasgow. Although a conscientious objector in the First World War, he believed the current conflict against the Nazis to be a just war, and threw himself totally behind the war effort. A committed socialist, and no admirer of Winston Churchill, Dollan was known for his forthright views and equally forthright manner of expressing them.

He began by attacking the government for putting the people of Glasgow at risk by revealing that Hess was being held in the neighbourhood.[66] Dollan was furious, but his attack on the government had only just begun. Unconvinced by the reports that Hess had fled from the Nazi regime, he announced that he had discreetly made enquiries of 'friends' to discover the truth.[67] After waiting impatiently for four weeks for the government to come forward with the real reasons for Hess's mission, Dollan felt free to go public with the fruits of his own enquiries in a series of lectures given in the Glasgow area. This summary of what he said managed to slip past the censor, appearing in a local newspaper: 'Hess came here an unrepentant Nazi. He believed he could remain in Scotland for two days, discuss his peace proposals and be given petrol and maps to return to Germany.'[68] Dollan's phrase 'an unrepentant Nazi' may be a clue about his sources. Exactly the same phrase is used of Hess in the Duke of Hamilton's letter to the King of 19 May 1941.

Once fired up, there was no stopping the Lord Provost, as evidenced by the following newspaper summary of a lecture he gave in Dumfries on 29 April 1942:

> Hess, he said, thought it would be possible to get into touch with a small minority in this country with a view to starting a peace by negotiating with Germany. This was one matter the Government handled badly. It was believed that Hess had come as a friend of this country. He [Dollan] knew better. He waited for four weeks and then told the people of Britain what they should have been told earlier, that Hess came here as a friend of Hitler, the enemy of democracy, and that his mission to Britain was to set up a pro-Hitler party in Great Britain that would bring about negotiations that would secure peace which would represent a Hitler triumph.[69]

Dollan summarised what he believed Hess's terms to be. In the main they agree with other versions: Germany was to be given a free hand in Europe, Hitler established as President of a United States of Europe, and Germany allowed a 'free run' into Russia. However, Dollan's list also features terms that appear nowhere else: a reduction of the Royal Navy and the RAF, British withdrawal from the Mediterranean and – oddly – independence for Australia.[70]

Not surprisingly, Dollan's contentious statements caused a furore on both sides of the Atlantic, prompting questions in the House of Commons. On 19 June 1941, Rab Butler was asked if there was any truth in the Lord Provost's allegations: he replied that while the government had no wish to detract from his contribution to the war effort, his statements were unauthorised and, he supposed, based on 'surmise'.[71] (In this masterly piece of politician's evasion there is no actual denial.) Dollan retorted that his version of events was based on 'authentic information'.[72]

Dollan stressed the connection between the Deputy Führer's flight and Operation Barbarossa, saying in January 1942 in a speech at an

'Aid for Russia' meeting in Rutherglen that Hess offered peace provided that Britain agreed not to interfere with Germany's war with the USSR.[73]

When Churchill finally admitted, also in January 1942, that Hess had come on a peace mission and had expected to find an anti-Churchill clique awaiting him, Dollan lost no time in pointing out that this vindicated him, saying:

> This should silence those who derided me last June. I knew then, *on absolute authority* [our italics] that Hess came with the knowledge of Hitler, and with the avowed purpose of dividing this nation.
>
> Hess believed he could obtain the backing of a clique of reactionaries to negotiate a peace which would have made Hitler and Germany the bosses of Europe, Africa and certain parts of Asia . . .
>
> He expected to have a talk with some Quislings, and fly back to Germany within 48 hours. He was surprised and indignant when taken prisoner.[74]

On the question of who Hess was to meet, Dollan was suddenly evasive, saying: 'I have my suspicions, but no legal evidence'.[75]

Although broadly agreeing with the government's version, Dollan's words prove that he believed that there was a peace party; Hess had not imagined it. The Lord Provost also made two other significant claims: that Hess expected to return to Germany within forty-eight hours without the British public ever suspecting anything about it, and that he expected to be given fuel for his return journey. Although this fits Hess's remark to Ilse about 'certainly be[ing] back by Monday evening', there is one major problem with Dollan's version. As we know, Hess could only make the journey by carrying extra fuel in drop tanks under the wings, which he jettisoned during the flight. How was he to get back to Germany without them? Tanks compatible with an Me-110 would hardly be easy to find in Britain. Perhaps Dollan's information was incorrect, but where did he get it from? His close relationship with the Polish community is likely a key factor and should not be underestimated. Many Poles had been posted to Scotland, which was also the centre of the Polish government in exile. Dollan was happy to be a major player in maintaining warm Scots–Polish relations, writing two books on the Polish cause during the war. It is probable that the Poles were a useful source of intelligence. But Dollan may have had valuable informants in other areas, being very interested in aviation – in his opinion air travel was the way of the future – and having many contacts among pilots and ground crew in the Glasgow area.

The voice of America

The controversy over Hess was fuelled yet further by comments made by Brendan Bracken, the British Minister of Information, during a visit to the United States in August 1943. (He had replaced Duff Cooper as Minister of Information in July 1941.) He told American reporters that Hess had come to Britain 'expecting to find quislings that would help him to throw Churchill out and make peace' – also stating unequivocally that Hess had met the Duke of Hamilton before the war.[76]

In May 1943 the *American Mercury* carried an article entitled 'The Inside Story of the Hess Flight'. Although the writer was anonymous, the editors added their personal endorsement: 'The writer, a highly reputable observer, is known to us and we publish this article with full faith in its sources.' (The former editor of the *American Mercury*, Ralph de Toledano, told us that the source, if not the writer, was US intelligence agent Jack Clements.) The article includes details that prove the writer had inside information – for example, naming Ivone Kirkpatrick as the official who went to Scotland to see Hess, something that had not been made public at that point. The article also states authoritatively that Hess flew to Britain on Hitler's orders, and that he was expected in certain quarters – and although there is nothing new there, it did add something. While including some unlikely embellishments, such as Hess having an RAF escort over Britain and Hitler's first choice for the mission being Ernst Bohle, the article is intriguing nevertheless.[77] Claiming British sources, the writer states that Hess went with Hitler's approval as a 'winged messenger of peace' and a 'shining Parsifal' after several months of negotiations with Hamilton and several other highly placed members of the pro-peace party. The story went on that the communications from Hess had been intercepted by the British secret service, and it was they who sent the replies in order to lure Hess over to Scotland. The writer states that, while Hess was being arrested by the Home Guard, 'Meanwhile, *a kind of official reception committee composed of Military Intelligence officers and Secret Service agents was waiting at the private aerodrome of the Hamilton estate* [emphasis in original].[78] This was the first published version of the recent 'British intelligence lure' hypothesis, although the detail of the 'reception committee' waiting at Dungavel is a new element. However, it is, as we will see, extremely significant for reasons rather different from the author's intention.

The flight of a madman?

Was Hess's flight – as claimed by Hitler at the time and many others since – simply a result of his mental instability? Although his state of mind during his imprisonment in Britain will be discussed more fully in a later chapter, the subject of his mental health before the flight needs to be considered.

These days it is so unquestioningly accepted that Hess was mad that it comes as a surprise to realise that there are no indications that anybody who had dealings with Hess in Germany before the flight had noticed any signs of instability. Just as in the case of his alleged fall from grace, many stories surfaced after the event to support Hitler's public statements, but there were none before. There is even some evidence that once he had made the momentous decision to fly to Britain, his stress levels dropped. Ernst Bohle said in 1945: 'From the moment he had that idea . . . there was such an enormous difference in him, no more doubt, [he] was fresh and seemed to be enthusiastic about the whole affair, [it] made him a perfectly, absolutely quiet man, well spirited.'[79]

There are only two pieces of evidence that can be used to support the idea that Hess had suffered from mental instability prior to 1941. A report by one of the doctors who examined him in 1917 stated that Hess 'shows a tendency towards hypochondria' and 'sometimes he did not know what was going on around him and that worried him'.[80] Although some have seen in this evidence of schizophrenia, it was not an unusual response to trench warfare, particularly while recovering from a major injury. The second piece of evidence is a statement made to a Scottish journalist by Karl Haushofer in September 1945, just before the start of the Nuremberg Trials. After saying that Hess might be pleading insanity, Haushofer added: 'He has never been quite normal. As early as 1919 he showed suicidal tendencies and a lack of balance.'[81] Clearly, as Haushofer believed his old friend was about to plead insanity, these comments were intended to back this up.

The long months of careful preparation, and – as Churchill himself pointed out – the skill and concentration needed for the flight, argue against Hess being in a disordered and delusional state of mind. Many of those involved in his capture testified to his composure – indeed, commenting on the shambles surrounding his arrest, Gordon Stewart remarked: 'On the 10th May 1941 he was the sanest man in Renfrewshire.'[82]

Ilse claimed to have had a copy of the letter her husband left for Hitler, although – tantalisingly – it was lost when her house was hit by a bomb in the closing stages of the war. However, unsurprisingly, she remembered it word for word. Apparently it ended with: 'And if, my Führer . . . fate decides against me, there will be harmful consequences for you or Germany; you can always deny all responsibility – simply say I am insane.'[83] If Ilse's memory was true, then Hitler's statement about Hess's 'hallucinations' is seen to be part of a plan.

Who knew in Britain?

Hess's flight was meticulously planned well in advance, with the full knowledge of certain key people in Germany, almost certainly including Hitler himself. But what of the British side? Who was expecting him at the end of his journey? There are only two options: either, as certain researchers now claim, he had been lured over by the British intelligence services, with or without Churchill's knowledge, or he had come to meet representatives of a genuine peace party as pre-arranged.

Some – such as the American researcher Louis Kilzer – have theorised that Churchill himself was behind the deception that lured Hess to Britain. As we will see, the Prime Minister turned it to his advantage, but was this merely because of his characteristic opportunism or was it part of the plan? He knew about Hess's arrival some hours before he should have done, but perhaps it was Hamilton who told him in the early hours of 11 May – a fact that had to be hushed up for the sake of the Duke's cover story. But there was another possible conduit for the news, which emerged in November 1969 when the *Yorkshire Post* carried an interview with the retired trade union leader Albert Heal.[84]

In May 1941 Heal was Yorkshire Area Secretary for the Transport and General Workers Union, but, more significantly, before the war he had been intimately involved in the No More War movement – which helped Communists and trade union officials escape from Germany – and for which he had devised a code. On 9 May Heal was contacted by an old friend, Ernest Bevin, the Minister of Labour, who asked for an urgent meeting in his Leeds hotel that evening. (He was due to address a meeting in Sheffield.) In his room at the Queen's Hotel, the minister told Heal that he had received a coded message from one of his contacts in German industry, a former colleague of Heal's in No More War. His help was urgently needed because her message was in Heal's code, which Bevin was desperate to decipher. (The woman, although known to Heal, was not identified. He would only ever admit that she came from London but had since died.) Heal immediately realised the explosive nature of the message he had decoded – it disclosed Hess's flight plan in detail, including his intention to contact the Duke of Hamilton. Immediately Bevin telephoned Winston Churchill with the incredible news. When the two men met again at 9.30 the next morning, Bevin told Heal that Hess had now arrived in Scotland, swearing him to secrecy.

Although we only have Heal's word for this intriguing story, it was a strange thing to have made up. However, there is one anomaly: according to the *Yorkshire Post*, Heal decoded the message on 9 May; therefore, he could hardly have been told of Hess's arrival the next morning – several hours before he had even set off! To make the story work, Heal and Bevin must have met on the evening of 10 May, which is confirmed by Peter Padfield, who discovered that Bevin had addressed his public meeting *that* night.[85] (It transpired that the mistake was made by the *Yorkshire Post*'s reporter, not by Heal.) Another significant point is that Bevin told Heal the next morning that Rudolf Hess – not 'Alfred Horn' – had arrived in Scotland, yet we are told the airman only revealed his true identity to the Duke of Hamilton on that morning, and that this was not passed on to London until the afternoon. Heal's story also confirms that some people in Germany did know in advance about Hess's mission and its goal: Padfield speculates that the German contact was a worker at the Messerschmitt factory, which would make sense.

The intelligence 'sting'

The idea that Hess had been lured to Britain first appeared in the *American Mercury* article in 1943, although it had been hinted at in one of the early German broadcasts. Karl Haushofer also gave some credence to it during his interrogation by the OSS in 1945, when he said, 'We had been sending [British] friends private letters through Portugal and I assume that some of these were intercepted by the Secret Services which must have written the answers which induced Hess to fly to England for the expected peace conference.'[86] Note that Haushofer is only speculating, but as a key player presumably he knew what he was talking about. And it is interesting that he thought Hess was flying to a peace *conference*, in which case the question arises as to who the British delegates (real or invented) were to be.

The intelligence 'sting' theory has inspired a flurry of books in recent years, such as Padfield's *Hess: Flight for the Führer* (1991), John Costello's *Ten Days that Saved the West* (1991), Louis Kilzer's *Churchill's Deception* (1994) and Harris and Trow's *Hess: The British Conspiracy* (1999). It has to be admitted that this hypothesis appears to be plausible, especially as it supplies answers to many of the major questions surrounding the flight, and certainly explains the intense secrecy that has shrouded it ever since.

The basic hypothesis is that one of the British intelligence services – either MI5's XX Committee (Padfield and Costello) or SOE (Harris and Trow) – lured Hess over by inventing a pro-peace, anti-Churchill party.

The KGB files

When in 1990 John Costello put in a request to Moscow to see the KGB files on the Hess affair he had no real hope of ever actually seeing them – it was a routine researcher's request, nothing more than a long shot. So imagine his surprise when a Russian official turned up at his New York apartment clutching bundles of files, which had apparently been sent over from Moscow in a diplomatic bag! Clearly the Russians had decided it was time to give them an airing.

The KGB file on Hess contained reports made by two Soviet

agents in Britain. One of them was Kim Philby, then working for SOE, who submitted two reports a few days after Hess's arrival: the first was sent to the Moscow headquarters of the NKVD (the predecessors of the KGB) on 14 May 1941. It read:

> Information received from SONNCHEN ['Little Sun' – Philby's code-name] is that HESS arrived in England [sic] declaring that he intended first of all to appeal to HAMILTON who he had become friendly with in connection with their common interest in aviation competitions in 1934 . . . HESS landed near the castle of HAMIL-TON. KIRKPATRICK, the first person of the SAKALUK [codename for the Foreign Office] to identify HESS who tells him that he had brought peace offers. We do not yet know the terms of these peace proposals.[87]

NKVD agents in Germany and the United States were instructed to investigate further – especially with respect to the terms offered by Hess. They unanimously reported that he had flown to Britain with Hitler's approval in order to deliver peace terms.[88]

Following information from Tom Dupree of the Foreign Office's Press Department, Philby sent a further message on 17 May through his control in London. According to this, Dupree had told him that during 'conversations with officers of British military intelligence' Hess had stated that he wanted peace in order to end the war between the two leading 'Nordic' (i.e. Aryan) nations and to 'preserve the British Empire as a stabilising force' in world affairs. Dupree said that Hess believed there was a powerful anti-Churchill faction to which he could appeal. He also told Philby about Haushofer's letter of September 1940, which – after being intercepted by MI5 – *had been sent on to Hamilton six weeks later*.[89] Another significant comment in Philby's report was that Hess came 'to confirm a compromise peace'.[90]

Philby also reported that Churchill was afraid that the 'opposition faction' would somehow conspire with Hess, which is why he made the statement that 'Hess is my prisoner', making sure they knew who was in control of the situation. Philby made the interesting prediction that 'as the course of the war developed Hess could become the centre of intrigues for a compromise peace and would therefore be useful for the peace party in England and for Hitler'.[94]

To Philby, at least, it was clear that Hess could still be used by the anti-Churchill, anti-war faction, even though he was in the clutches of the Prime Minister at the time.

Dupree gave Philby another surprising piece of information: that within days of his arrival Hess had been visited by Anthony Eden and Lord Beaverbrook. Nothing about this has surfaced in any other account, although the newspaper baron is known to have interviewed Hess some months later in Aldershot, and Eden's biographer has admitted that, despite the lack of documentary evidence, such a meeting was certainly possible.[92]

Experts in the history of intelligence services, such as Professor Christopher Andrew of Cambridge University, acknowledge that Philby's access to the most highly classified intelligence, and the accuracy of the information he passed to Moscow, made him a formidable spy. However, they exclude one episode from this assessment: his reports on the Hess affair, which, they say, were based on little more than civil service gossip, coloured by his own preconceptions.[93] Such selectivity neglects an important aspect of Philby's career. When he was recruited by the NKVD in June 1934, as part of his insinuation into the relevant circles in Britain he was ordered to join the Anglo-German Fellowship – becoming editor of its journal, *Germany Today*. Because of this he met Albrecht Haushofer, and as the latter edited the Anglo-American section of the journal *Geopolitik* the two found themselves working closely together. Philby's first field operation for the Russians – as a journalist attached to General Franco's headquarters during the Spanish Civil War – was facilitated by a letter of recommendation from Haushofer and papers identifying him as a staff member of *Geopolitik*.[94] It was this posting that also brought Philby to the attention of MI6 and led to his recruitment.

After being recruited by MI6, Philby was transferred to SOE in its earliest days and also served on the XX Committee from January 1941.[95] This committee discussed Haushofer's letter to the Duke of Hamilton – which led to the approaches through air intelligence – the following month. Therefore, where the Hess affair was concerned Philby knew what he was talking about. (This also effectively disproves the idea that either SOE or the XX Committee lured Hess over to Britain. As somebody who knew Albrecht Haushofer and had been a member of the Anglo-German Fellowship, Philby would inevitably have been involved in such an operation, but clearly he knew nothing about it until after Hess arrived.)

The Russians' second source, apart from Philby, was Colonel Frantisek Moravec ('Moravetz' in the reports), the chief of the Czech military intelligence service in London. In October 1942 he sent an important report to Moscow which was immediately summarised by NKVD chief Lavrenti Beria for Stalin and Molotov:

> Long before his flight HESS had corresponded about his mission with the DUKE OF HAMILTON. In this correspondence was discussed, in detail, all the questions to do with the organisation of his flight. But HAMILTON was not himself a participant personally. All HESS's letters to HAMILTON did not reach him but were intercepted by the intelligence services where the answers to HESS in the name of HAMILTON were manufactured. In this way the British had managed to trick HESS into coming to England.
>
> Colonel MORAVETZ declared that he personally saw this correspondence between HESS and HAMILTON. According to MORAVETZ's declaration the HESS letters clearly represented that the plans of the German government were linked with their plans of their attack on the Soviet Union. The same letters set out the necessity of stopping the war between Britain and Germany.[96]

Intriguing though this may be, parts of Moravec's scenario are somewhat unlikely: for example, it seems incredible that Hess, the head of his own intelligence operation, should commit intelligence about the Nazi attack on the USSR to paper. It is suspicious that Moravec is the only person who claims to have seen the correspondence between Hess and Hamilton; and how he came to see it (if it existed at all) is not made clear. However, a report on the Hess affair by an unnamed member of the Vichy French intelligence services – which was promptly stolen by the NKVD – tells much the same story. The writer, who states he was well connected with British political and intelligence circles, claims he was told by an MI6 contact in New York that Hess had been lured to Scotland as part of a 'tremendous success' for British intelligence.[97] According to this source, Haushofer's letter to Hamilton was intercepted by British intelligence, who then kept up a correspondence in Hamilton's name. The idea of a strong peace movement and anti-Churchill conspiracy was invented, and a request made for a personal visit by a representative from the German side. According to this version of the story, the visitor turned out – much to the surprise of the intelligence services – to be none other than Rudolf Hess.

Too many problems

Although the 'sting' theory is still popular these days, it poses new questions of its own. What was the point of luring Hess – or any senior Nazi – over to Britain when as soon as he arrived he became a huge embarrassment and little of either intelligence or propaganda value was ever squeezed out of him? (However, Churchill managed to turn the situation to his advantage, as we will see.) And if Hess's arrival was the whole point of the operation, why was there such confusion surrounding his capture? If, as is claimed in the *American Mercury* article, a team from MI6 was waiting in Dungavel, Hess's landing some ten miles away can only have been a minor hiccup in the operation. Surely it was not beyond the means of the cream of Britain's intelligence services to locate their target and wrest him from the Home Guard! It would have been a simple matter to put the fear of God into them, ensuring their silence on the grounds of national security.

Another problem with the intelligence 'sting' theory is that its main advocates – such as Padfield and Costello – have to argue that the existence of a strong pro-peace and anti-Churchill faction within the British Establishment was a fiction devised by the intelligence services as bait for Hess. But all the evidence – including, ironically, Padfield and Costello's own material – argues for the real existence of such a faction. Their line of argument has to assume that figures such as Sir Samuel Hoare – who was certainly involved in the lead-up to the flight – were acting on behalf of the intelligence services as part of the deception. In other words, they were pretending to be open to the idea of peace. But Hoare at least seems to be genuinely, even passionately, set on ending the British–German war.

There is another point that seems to have eluded these theorists, which, while taking MI6's involvement into account, still puts a completely different complexion on the matter. What if *MI6 itself* was trying to end the war? What if, instead of luring Hess over for the vaguest reasons, it was acting independently of the Churchill government? And what if, to all intents and purposes, MI6 *was part of the peace party*? Philip Knightley, writing for the *Independent on Sunday*, considered this possibility in 1997.[98]

This is by no means as fanciful as it might first appear. The head of MI6 himself, Sir Stewart Menzies, was an influential member of the 'peace group' who believed passionately that Britain's best interests lay in making peace with Germany while allowing the Nazis to exhaust themselves in an intensive war with the Soviet Union. Hess's peace terms should have suited Menzies down to the ground. His biographer, Anthony Cave Brown, agrees that there is strong circumstantial evidence that Menzies was behind luring Hess to Britain. However, he still assumes this means that he was laying a trap for Hess.[99] But once Menzies' personal sympathies are taken into account, it becomes much more likely that he wanted Hess's mission to be a success. It is also clear that MI6 agents had already been involved in other genuine peace feelers. Payne-Best and Stevens, the two agents kidnapped in Venlo, were MI6, as was Malcolm Christie. There was no suggestion that their attempts at brokering peace were part of an intelligence stratagem – they appear to have been totally genuine.

And the desire for peace was not confined to MI6. When the powers of Defence Regulation 18b were extended on 22 May 1940 – within days of Churchill coming to power – those arrested under its terms included Sir Barry Domvile, former director of naval intelligence. And the director-general of MI5, Sir Vernon Kells, was dismissed from his post at this time. So could Menzies and his MI6 have been involved in their own peace conspiracy? This was certainly Stalin's view, based on the reports the NKVD had received from Philby and Colonel Moravec. Churchill records an interesting after-dinner conversation with Stalin during the Moscow conference of October 1944. The Russian leader told him that he believed Hess had been brought to Britain by British intelligence in order to negotiate a peace in advance of the German attack on Russia. Churchill testily remarked that when he made a statement of fact of something 'within his knowledge' – in this case, that Hess was not part of an MI6 plot – he expected to be believed. Stalin replied that 'There are lots of things that happen even here in Russia which our Secret Service do not necessarily tell me about'.[100] This story is often aired as evidence of the intelligence 'sting' theory, but that is not what Stalin was talking about: he was saying that he thought British intelligence wanted Hess over for genuine peace talks because its leaders believed that Russia was Britain's greatest enemy. Churchill himself wrote of this meeting in a memorandum to Sir Archibald Sinclair in April 1945 forbidding the Duke of Hamilton from making an official trip to the USA:

> The Russians are very suspicious of the Hess episode and I have had a lengthy argument with Marshal Stalin about it at Moscow in October, he steadfastly maintaining that Hess had been *invited over* [our italics] by our Secret Service. It is not in the public interest that the whole of this affair should be stirred [up] at the present moment. I desire therefore that the Duke should not, repeat not, undertake this task.[101]

Stalin's suspicions were not simply based on the reports he received from his British agents. According to John Walter, former CIA Inspector General, the head of Hess's own diplomatic intelligence network, Franz Pfeffer von Saloman, was a double agent, also passing infomation to the NKVD.

In the circumstances, it may well be that stories such as the *American Mercury* article were carefully planted to give the impression that MI6 had lured Hess to Scotland; after all, that would be considerably less treasonable than the truth of the matter. This idea is supported by Colonel Moravec's report to the NKVD. The usual inference is that Moravec was a double agent, passing secret information to Moscow, but this is incorrect. A staunch anti-Communist who was to flee the Soviet takeover of Czechoslovakia in 1948, Moravec was Czech intelligence's liaison with the Russians, supplying them with information with the knowledge of, and indeed under the instruction of, the Allies. Unlike Philby, any information that he passed to Moscow was likely to be what the British security services wanted the Soviets to have.[102] In other words, MI6 only began to spread the story that the capture of Hess was a 'tremendous success' to cover themselves once it had all gone horribly wrong.

The confusion surrounding Hess's capture may be explained by two opposing forces – one supportive of the peace bid, the other hostile to it – being involved. If so, and MI6 were on the pro-peace side, then it is reasonable to suppose that their opponents would be within

SOE. As we have seen, there was a serious political rivalry between the two outfits: MI6 was supportive of a negotiated peace with Germany, as it saw Communist Russia as the real enemy, whereas SOE was in favour of an alliance with Stalin against Hitler. As the Prime Minister's creation, SOE was naturally pro-Churchill. Its chiefs were aware of Albrecht Haushofer's letter because the censor had passed them a copy. Kim Philby of SOE was on the XX Committee when it decided to approach Hamilton about the letter in February 1941. Were they out to wreck the plan?

This is not idle speculation. It may be coincidence that, on the night of 10–11 May 1941, SOE's headquarters at Woburn Abbey played host to not one but two cabinet ministers: Anthony Eden and Hugh Dalton, the minister responsible for SOE, as well as the director general of the Political Warfare Executive, Robert Bruce Lockhart. But it seems beyond coincidence that, according to Lockhart's diary, one of the items on their agenda that weekend was a discussion of the extent of support for appeasement among Conservative MPs. Lockhart noted tersely in his diary: 'plenty of them'.[103]

Significant sectors of the British Establishment – the aristocracy, the City, various industrialists, Conservative politicians and even the Court itself – were, for a variety of reasons, in favour of a negotiated peace with Germany. Hess did not imagine a peace group, nor was it invented by MI6, but its existence at such a level would explain why so much about the Hess affair was – and continues to be – hushed up. However, the conspiracy of silence that has shrouded the Hess affair protects figures much higher up – indeed, at the very pinnacle of the British Establishment.

CHAPTER EIGHT

By Royal Appointment

Hess himself had come to Britain with an understanding that he was under the King's personal protection: throughout his imprisonment in Aldershot he repeatedly claimed this and requested that messages be taken to George VI. One of his MI6 'guardians', Major Frank Foley, reported at the end of May 1941:

> He raised again the question of the Duke of Hamilton and Mr Kirkpatrick. In his confused way he seems to think that they are outside the political clique or Secret Service ring which is preventing him from meeting the proper peace people and the King. He reiterated that he had come here of his own free will, trusting to the chivalry of the King.[1]

It is interesting that not only had Hess claimed to be under the King's protection but that he had told his guards in Scotland that he had expected Hamilton to take him to the King.[2] Even Churchill – although making light of the Hess affair – told Stalin in October 1944 that Hess had come to Britain on the expectation of having an audience with the King.[3] This is usually seen as evidence of Hess's slender grasp on reality, but what if it were true? What if there had been an arrangement that George VI would protect the Nazi leader, one that had to be abandoned the minute the mission foundered?

The possibility of a connection between Hess's mission and royal circles has been aired, but never fully explored, by other researchers. Peter Allen, in *The Crown and the Swastika*, theorised that it was part of an attempt to bring about peace between Britain and Germany and to re-establish the Duke of Windsor on the throne. This is based on the popular view that if anyone in the Establishment was involved in the Hess affair the most likely candidate would seem to be the 'black sheep' of the Royal Family, the Duke of Windsor. However, this ignores the fact that his point of view was largely shared by the rest of the Royal Family. Indeed, Windsor seems to have been used as a convenient scapegoat to deflect attention from this unpalatable fact. Scott Newton has established that there was a substantial pro-peace movement at Court, with Queen Mary – the King's indomitable mother – at its centre. And, of course, the Royal Family's best interests lay in peace with Germany for two reasons: the 1914–18 conflict had taught them what world wars could do to royalty; and they saw Bolshevism as their real enemy. The horror of the execution of the Tsar and his family was still fresh in their minds. Indeed, if there were a British peace party extending the hand of fellowship to Rudolf Hess, it would not be surprising to find it had a major connection with the monarchy. Initially, information from a retired senior intelligence source pointed us in the direction of two people: a Colonel W. S. Pilcher and 'the then Queen' – the present Queen Mother.

Apart from the fact that many different trails in this investigation lead to the Court, there is no specific evidence to implicate Queen Elizabeth the Queen Mother in the Hess affair. There is, however, an intriguing connection that emerged during a conversation with John Harris (co-author of *Hess: The British Conspiracy*, which theorises that SOE was responsible for luring Hess to Britain). Harris discovered that Queen Elizabeth's brother, David Bowes-Lyon – to whom she was extremely close – occupied an important but vaguely defined role in SOE, being described evasively as a 'liaison officer'. Harris mentioned this apparently innocuous piece of information in passing in the first draft of his manuscript – and was amazed to be asked by his publishers to remove it.[4] Perhaps it was seen as offensive in certain quarters.

However, we were able to establish at least that David Bowes-Lyon was also a pre-war supporter of the Anglo-German Fellowship. Although there is no evidence that he personally was a member, one company of which he was managing director (Lazard Brothers) and one of which he was on the board of directors (the Dunlop Rubber

Company) were corporate members.[5] It is unlikely that he did not also agree with the aims of the Fellowship.

Recently the extent of David Bowes-Lyon's sister's support for the pro-peace movement has been the subject of intense speculation in the British press. In March 2000 there was great excitement among historians at the prospect of the release of the papers of Walter Monckton, which were expected to contain significant revelations about the abdication crisis. However, at the very last minute, one box of papers was withheld because it contained letters written by the then Queen of a highly personal nature, specifically, it was said, with reference to Wallis Simpson. But the *Independent on Sunday* of 5 March 2000 reported that, according to insiders who had seen the papers, they were concerned not with Simpson but with the Queen's desire to avert war with Germany and for closer ties to be established between the two countries. (Her attitude to Churchill was also revealed to be at best lukewarm, at worst downright hostile.) The article went so far as to claim that the Queen would willingly have accepted a German occupation of Britain provided that the monarchy and her place within it were left intact. In our view, the *Independent on Sunday* is extrapolating much too far here: as we have seen, the attitude of the Royal Family generally was that their and the nation's best interests lay in averting a war with Germany and stemming the tide of Bolshevism. If they had their way there would have been no question of Nazi occupation.

What of the mysterious Colonel Pilcher? Researchers into the Hess affair, such as Scott Newton and Andrew Rosthorn, often come across his name, but beyond that it is very difficult to discover anything more about him. The only accessible information is in *Who's Who*, where – until 1943 – he appears as a successful but unremarkable army officer: Lieutenant-Colonel William Spelman Pilcher, DSO, was born in 1888 and spent most of his career in the Grenadier Guards, eventually commanding its 3rd Battalion. The only potentially significant part of his career was that he was involved in the British Military Mission to Poland in 1920–1. He retired in 1936. But then something odd happened: after 1943 he seems to have become an 'unperson' as far as the Establishment was concerned. The last *Who's Who* entry for him, in 1943, adds that he was 're-employed' (presumably by the army) in 1939. In 1944 his name disappears, but although it might reasonably be expected that it would then appear in the obituaries for that year, he is not recorded there either. (He did not die until 1970.[6]) Nor was his entry transferred, as is customary, into *Who Was Who*. His name is even missing from the general index of *Who's Who*, which is supposed to list everyone who has ever appeared in its hallowed pages. Whatever happened to Colonel W. S. Pilcher? Did he fall from grace, having committed some unforgivable crime, such as treason?

There may be some significance in the fact that Pilcher served with the Grenadier Guards during the First World War at the same time as the Duke of Buccleuch. Serving with that regiment was also a family tradition of the Percys (the Dukes of Northumberland), potentially providing Pilcher with contacts among the anti-war aristocracy.[7] In 1998, in an attempt to trawl for information on some of the more obscure points of research, we posted some material on the Internet, dropping a few names, including Pilcher's. In response, we received a letter from Kenneth de Courcy, the Duc de Grantmesnil, who had been involved in the peace initiatives of 1940 through Sweden that were backed by Lord Halifax and Rab Butler.[8] In his letter, De Courcy – a friend of Colonel Pilcher – said:

> Both [the Duke of Buccleuch and Colonel Pilcher] were very close friends of mine, and the latter disappeared suddenly without trace for nearly 40 years. That it was in some way connected with Hess I know. I was, in fact, officially questioned – but I knew nothing. I should greatly like to discover the truth. I went to the very highest levels at the time, but I was told it was a top state secret.[9]

Unfortunately, de Courcy died soon after writing this declaration, but it did establish that Pilcher was connected with someone who was involved in peace initiatives through Sweden.

Our major source of information from within the inner circles of Whitehall – our 'Deep Throat' – is a retired Ministry of Defence official who also has very good contacts in the Foreign Office. To preserve his anonymity, he will be referred to only as 'Alexander'. Throughout the course of this investigation he was able to give invaluable leads, information and, in some cases, copies of usually inaccessible documents.

Naturally, we asked 'Alexander' what he could find out about Pilcher. According to him, Pilcher had been held incommunicado on the orders of the Royal Family from 1941 until his death in 1970 in a remote cottage on the Balmoral estate. The reason for this was that, apparently, it was Pilcher who had signed a letter of safe conduct given to Hess in the King's name. Naturally, we have not been able to confirm this, but the existence of such a letter on Hess's person on the night of 10 May 1941 certainly would explain a great deal.

There were to be other clues, no less tantalising and suggestive. In 1995 Stephen Prior and Robert Brydon attended a dinner party at Charleton, the home of Baron St Clair Bonde in Fife, Scotland – which had also been the house of his grandfather, the Swedish diplomat and businessman, Baron Knut Bonde. In the after-dinner conversation the subject of Rudolf Hess came up, to which St Clair Bonde contributed a small bombshell to the effect that his grandfather had been closely involved in efforts to broker a peace between Britain and Germany – and that, 'My grandfather was instrumental in Hess's flight'. Unfortunately, when pressed, he would not elaborate. Perhaps he thought he had said more than enough already.

It is known that Knut Bonde was indeed a key player in peace initiatives through Sweden – to the point that, although a devoted anti-Communist and dedicated to bringing peace to Europe, he was regarded as a thorough nuisance by the Foreign Office. He travelled frequently between Sweden and Scotland during the war because, besides being married to a Scotswoman (to whom Menzies acted in the capacity of a favoured uncle), he had a house and business interests there. There is no doubt that he was involved in the peace talks started by Rab Butler,[10] but this was the first time that his name had been associated with the flight of Rudolf Hess. Again, it was intriguing, but ultimately no more than that. But fortunately other snippets of information were to prove more satisfying.

The Dungavel disaster

In 1975 Robert Brydon had a very interesting conversation with his friend, the American writer Elizabeth Byrd, at her Scottish home, Old Craig Hall in East Lothian. A former secretary to Lord Malcolm Douglas-Hamilton in the United States just after the war, she told him something completely new. She said that Lord Malcolm told her that after Hess arrived he had flown with the Duke in an Avro

Anson. He had been terrified at having to fly in such an antiquated training plane, which was so dilapidated that he could see the far-distant ground through holes in the floor. Not surprisingly, he described it as one of the most frightening experiences of his life. This story would appear to be corroborated by the two Czech pilots at Aldergrove who were scrambled to intercept Hess's flight but were called back: they had described how, later that night, two high-ranking RAF officers had arrived in an Avro Anson to interrogate them. Was this the occasion mentioned by Elizabeth Byrd? Were those two RAF officers the Duke of Hamilton and his brother Lord Malcolm?

Elizabeth went on to say that Lord Malcolm had implied that his brother had allowed himself to take the flak for the whole Hess affair in order to protect others even higher up the social scale. He had strongly hinted that the cover-up was necessary to protect the reputations of members of the Royal Family.

Shortly afterwards, Elizabeth introduced Robert to an elderly lady who also had some extraordinary information about the Hess affair: for reasons that will become obvious, she asked to remain anonymous, so will be referred to only as 'Mrs Abbot'. In May 1941 she had been stationed at Dungavel with one of the women's wartime services. She said that the house had an operational airfield that had been used by the Air Training Corps. Sometimes parked at the end of the landing field were the Bristol Blenheim training planes. Mrs Abbot added that Dungavel was also listed as an Emergency Landing Ground (ELG) for RAF pilots who could not return to their home bases (which we were able to confirm), being equipped with temporary lights that were switched on for landings at dusk.

Mrs Abbot said that late on the night of 10 May 1941, as they were leaving the kitchen in Dungavel House, she and a companion were taken aback when they saw that the airstrip landing lights had been turned on. They wondered whether they were being tested or whether a plane was coming in. With the recent Glasgow air raids and the blackout in mind, both women hoped that this was not the result of 'some infernal electrical fault that would attract Jerry raiders and get us all killed'. A few minutes later the lights were switched off. Soon afterwards the two women heard an aircraft coming over low – although not, Mrs Abbot thought, so low that it was trying to land – and for a moment half expected the lights to go back on again. But they remained off. A short time later the women heard an aircraft – presumably the same one – pass over again. On asking about this strange incident, Mrs Abbot was told that the lights had been switched on as the result of a phone call from Bowhill (the home of the Duke of Buccleuch), and that they had been turned off by a group of strangers who had entered the house.

Mrs Abbot's testimony appears to confirm not only that Hess was intending to land at Dungavel, but that there were people there that night who, perhaps for very different reasons, were expecting him. But (as always) it raises further questions. Who were the strangers who entered the house and, apparently, turned off the landing lights? Whose orders were they obeying that night?

Although Mrs Abbot has since died, we were able to trace one of her former colleagues who had been on duty that night. (Again, she requested anonymity, so we will call her 'Mrs Baker'.) During a meeting with Stephen Prior in early 1996 she was able to confirm that the landing lights at Dungavel had been turned on and off – at the same time as an unknown plane flew overhead. But she quite casually added two highly significant pieces of information. First, she said that during 1941 two packing cases bearing the marks of the Messerschmitt factory had been delivered to Dungavel and were stored in one of the hangars. She was told (but did not see this for herself) that the packing cases contained 'petrol tanks'.

As if that were not enough, Mrs Baker claimed: 'The Duke and his people were in the Kennels,' adding that this group included some Poles. (The Kennels is a small house close to the airstrip.) Of course, there is substantial documentary evidence that the Duke of Hamilton was at RAF Turnhouse when Hess landed, which would seem to challenge Mrs Baker's credibility. However, when Stephen questioned her further on this, she replied, astonishingly, 'Not the Duke of *Hamilton*. The Duke of *Kent*.' If the King's youngest brother had been involved, this would certainly explain the often impenetrable conspiracy of silence that has surrounded the Hess affair for all this time. Was Kent really at Dungavel that night – *waiting for Rudolf Hess*?

If true, this would explain many of the intractable puzzles surrounding the events of 10 May 1941, as well as the apparent confusion that surrounded Hess's capture and its aftermath. It would, for example, explain why Sir Patrick Dollan, while keen to expose the Hess plan, was so reticent about naming those behind it. (And it may be significant that he presented the clock from Hess's Me-110 to a royal visitor to Glasgow.[12] Although his identity is not mentioned, it is understood to have been the Duke of Kent.) But is there independent evidence to support Mrs Baker's claim?

Curiously, the status of Dungavel during the war has received little attention from other researchers, although it is well known that it was Hess's intended destination that night. It is usually assumed that the house was still the private property of the Duke and Duchess of Hamilton, even though they were then living in a house near RAF Turnhouse. However, most stately homes had been given over either to the armed forces or for use as hospitals for the duration of the war. Although Sir Alexander Cadogan, after his telephone briefing by Ivone Kirkpatrick, stated that Dungavel was a hospital at the time, it proved difficult to substantiate this. The current Duke of Hamilton finally clarified the matter in a letter to us by stating that, although it 'may' have been used as a hospital, parts of it were certainly occupied by various other organisations, including the Girls' Training Corps, the Women's Land Army, the Women's Royal Air Force – and the Red Cross.[13] This is extremely interesting for two reasons: first, it backs up our informants' stories of being stationed there along with the WRAF; second, the fact that an office of the International Red Cross was based in the house also means that it was effectively a small area of neutral territory. This made Dungavel the ideal place for a peace conference.

According to statements given to the Gestapo by one of Hess's adjutants, Emma Rothacker had expected the message concerning 'Alfred Horn' to come to her from the Red Cross. Hamilton claimed that Hess had asked him to send the telegram to his aunt, but said nothing about the Red Cross; in fact, he implied that the message was to be sent to her directly. Either Hamilton knew where to send it or the information is omitted from his report. The Red Cross theme seems to run through the intricate events of that time: Albrecht Haushofer met Carl Burckhardt, head of the International Committee of the Red Cross, in Geneva just a few days before Hess's flight. Burckhardt played an important role in co-ordinating the arrangements for the mission. As we now know that there was a Red Cross office in Dungavel, presumably the message was to be relayed from there to Geneva and then on to Hess's Aunt Emma. Clearly, the Red Cross had a central role to play in the drama of Rudolf Hess, but – like many other key parts of the story – it has been determinedly downplayed.

What of the telephone call that Mrs Abbot claimed came from Bowhill, the home of the Duke of Buccleuch? He had been under virtual house arrest on his estate because of his unrepentant pro-German views, so why should a significant phone call come from there? Hess's route across Scotland would have taken him directly over Bowhill: perhaps someone was warning Dungavel that he was on his way.

As we have seen, Hess deliberately changed course to fly within sight of Alnwick Castle, the seat of the Duke of Northumberland. The British leg of his journey took him within sight of Alnwick, Bowhill and Dungavel, all seats of prominent aristocratic pro-peace families who were also interrelated. (The Duke of Northumberland's sister was married to the Duke of Hamilton and the Duke of Buccleuch's eldest daughter subsequently married the Duke of Northumberland himself, while Buccleuch's sister Alice had married the King's brother, the Duke of Gloucester. Significantly, the Duke of Buccleuch wrote to the government at the beginning of June 1941 urging that he be allowed to meet with Hess.[14])

The delivery of the fuel tanks was even harder to believe than the royal involvement. Could it really be true that, in the middle of the war, drop tanks for an enemy plane could be delivered to Scotland, presumably directly from the Messerschmitt factory? It seems an extremely unlikely scenario, given the dangers involved, but the claim is supported by the fact that the German broadcast of 14 May claimed that Hess expected to refuel for his return journey. Sir Patrick Dollan confirmed this, based on his enquiries among 'friends' in Scotland. Significantly, the British government made no attempt to ridicule these suggestions, although it should have been very easy to do so simply by pointing out that as Hess's plane had jettisoned its drop tanks it would have been impossible to provide enough fuel for the return journey (the existence of the drop tanks suggests that he intended to return to Augsburg). But if tanks were delivered, the question remains as to how. The most obvious way was through Sweden – remember the testimony of Baron St Clair Bonde that Knut Bonde had been 'instrumental' in arranging Hess's flight. A respected citizen of a neutral country, Bonde had diplomatic privileges, besides having business interests in Scotland: it would have been relatively easy for him to have arranged for the tanks to be shipped over via Stockholm.

Gordon Stewart (one of the Home Guard contingent at Floors Farm) perhaps offered confirmation that the landing lights at Dungavel were turned on when he recalled seeing lights some distance away, which he was told comprised a 'decoy flare path'.[15] But a decoy for what? Sadly, Stewart's account gives no details of direction or timing, but it is interesting nevertheless. Was it possible he had mistaken the lights from Dungavel – some twelve miles away? Or was this a genuine decoy flare path, intended to lure Hess away from his destination, perhaps even to his death? The existence of a decoy unit near Eaglesham is confirmed by Inspector Hyslop's report, in which he lists members of that unit among the throng gathered around Floors Farm.[16] It should be remembered that Hess appears to have had a pre-arranged 'abort point' when he came within sight of Dungavel. Perhaps the signal he was waiting for from the ground was the switching on of the airstrip lights.

But what of the claim that there was any welcoming committee – with or without the Duke of Kent – waiting for Hess at Dungavel? This claim was made in the *American Mercury* article in 1943, although there it is described as a welcoming party of intelligence officers. Oddly enough, this is partly corroborated by a significant later omission by the Duke of Hamilton: in 1943 he was contemplating yet another libel action – although he did not proceed with it – this time against the London publisher of a pamphlet that quoted extracts from the *American Mercury* article. As part of the briefing to his lawyers, he had scribbled his own terse comments in the margin of the article in question: where it claims that Hess's plane was given an RAF escort, Hamilton wrote, 'Not true'; and where it makes the statement that Hess had been lured over by the British intelligence services, he wrote, 'Untrue'. However, when it comes to the statement about the 'welcoming committee' at Dungavel, he made no comment at all.[17]

Mrs Baker's aside about the fact that there were Poles among the Duke of Kent's entourage in the Kennels that night seems logical for several reasons. As the war had started over Germany's invasion of Poland, any attempt to negotiate a settlement would have to include Polish representatives. The Polish government in exile, headed by

General Sikorski, was based not far away near Edinburgh. If there were Poles in a peace group waiting for Hess to land at Dungavel, perhaps that explains why Roman Battaglia, the Polish diplomat, arrived unannounced at the Home Guard headquarters at Giffnock, and 'interrogated' Hess in German for fully two hours. His presence baffled MI5, who failed to discover who had called him out or how he had learned of the airman's arrival.

The most extraordinary claim by far, however, was that the Duke of Kent was waiting at Dungavel House for Rudolf Hess on the night of 10 May 1941. This at first seemed very unlikely, but interesting bits and pieces of information would seem to support it. There was an oblique reference to Kent right at the start of Hess's plan, when he first broached the subject of a peace initiative in his walk in the woods with Karl Haushofer at the end of August 1940. Haushofer, it will be recalled, reported:

> [Hess asked] Do you, too, see no way in which such possibilities could be discussed at a third [neutral] place with a middleman, possibly the old Ian Hamilton or the other Hamilton?
>
> I replied to these suggestions that there would perhaps have been an excellent opportunity for this in Lisbon at the Centennial, if, instead of harmless figureheads, it had been possible to send well-disguised political persons there.[18]

Haushofer implies that Hamilton was envisaged as a mediator between Hess and someone else, not as their ultimate contact himself. He also refers to the Portuguese celebrations of June 1940. Perhaps it is no coincidence that the British representative at the ceremony in Lisbon was George, Duke of Kent.[19]

Prince Georgie

Born George ('Georgie') Edward Alexander Edmund in 1902, the fourth (and youngest-surviving) son of George V and Queen Mary, this charming and glamorous member of the Royal Family was to die in very mysterious circumstances on a bleak Scottish hillside in August 1942. The present Queen's uncle, he was the first member of the Royal Family to have died on active service since the fifteenth century, yet curiously his name is rarely mentioned. Few members of the post-war generation have even heard of him, although they are familiar with the story of his eldest brother, the exiled Edward VIII.

Although born into supreme privilege, his was not a glamorous, sophisticated or even a well-adjusted family. Queen Mary's mantra, when tempted to cuddle one of her offspring, was 'I must remember that their father is also their king'. Edward, the heir, was a diminutive but attractive Peter Pan, whose youthful looks lasted well into middle age, but whose emotional and intellectual development also refused to mature. He was to shake the British Empire to the foundations when, as King Edward VIII, he abdicated in 1936 to marry the twice-divorced American Wallis Simpson. But there were other scandals, too, concerning allegations of money laundering and Nazi sympathies that refused to disappear and which, in these less reverent days, are surfacing more stridently than ever.

Edward's successor was his brother Bertie, a tongue-tied and stammering man given to wild rages of frustration, whose life had been a series of humiliations – often at the hands of his dashing elder brother, with whom he engaged in a lifelong sibling rivalry – except for two areas in which he shone. Prince Albert, later the Duke of York and later still King George VI, had reached the semi-finals of the men's doubles at Wimbledon, partnered by Sir Louis Greig. But this was nothing compared to his greatest triumph, which was to earn him the admiration and respect not only of the entire British Empire, but – more significantly, at least to him – of his parents. Incredibly for such a shy and immature man, he married the perfect woman – Lady Elizabeth Bowes-Lyon, of the ancient Scottish family of the Earls of Strathmore – in 1923 and fathered two perfect daughters, Princess Elizabeth, now Her Majesty the Queen, and HRH Princess Margaret.

But what of Prince Georgie, his mother's favourite child, whose sunny disposition and ready wit made him the most instantly likeable of all the Windsor children? Like his brothers, he was a relatively frail child, but, unlike them, exceptionally blessed with social graces. Charming and artistic, he was nevertheless forced to endure the rigours of naval training, although his keen mind meant that he, alone of all the Windsor boys, was trained in intelligence work while with the Royal Navy at Rosyth.[20]

After the navy, George expressed his burgeoning conscience by taking the novel step for a royal prince of becoming a factory inspector. He feared that if conditions did not improve for the working man the country would become Bolshevik.

However, George lived a double life: conscientious royal duke and champion of the masses by day and scandalously bisexual, cocaine-addicted playboy by night. His brother Edward, to whom he was always close, cured him of his drug dependency.[21]

In 1934 he married the glamorous Princess Marina of Yugoslavia, being created Duke of Kent at that time. They had three children: Edward, Alexandra and Michael. Marina's cousin, Prince Philip of Hesse, was intermediary between Hitler and Mussolini, and National Socialism interested both the Duke and Duchess of Kent greatly. Marina had ample opportunity to watch it develop at close quarters when staying with her sister – who was married to the Count Törring-Jettenbach – in Munich, Rudolf Hess's home town.

Always the dutiful son, George was made a Knight of the Garter in December 1923. On his shoulders also fell the burden of another kind of royal tradition: in 1928 he became a Freemason and on 19 July 1939 he was installed by his brother George VI as Grand Master of English Freemasonry at a ceremony at Olympia in West London.[22] His son is Grand Master today.

He might have upheld tradition as staunchly as the next royal prince, but George, Duke of Kent, was also very much a forward thinker, as his days of inspecting factories revealed. In his opinion the future belonged to aviation, in which he was passionately involved, having won his wings in 1929. He was the first member of the Royal Family to cross the Atlantic by air, and in 1936 became Grand Master of the Guild of Air Pilots and Air Navigators, which at that time, as we have seen, was organised on quasi-chivalric lines as befitted an association of 'knights of the air'. Of course, both his background and interests brought him into contact with the Duke of Hamilton frequently, but did his passion for flying – if nothing else – also bring him into contact with that other knight of the air, Rudolf Hess?

In fact, George and the Deputy Führer had much more than aviation in common. Because of his interest in industry and social problems such as unemployment, the Duke of Kent, like many of the British ruling class of the early 1930s, was attracted to the strength and success of German National Socialism. The Blitz and the Holocaust were in the future: all they could see was that Hitler had swept away unemployment, economic ruin and Communism. At that time, while not being everyone's political cup of tea, Hitler was widely seen as a worker of economic and social miracles – an example for others to follow.

Just before war broke out, it was planned that the Duke of Kent would become Governor-General of Australia, but the tense international situation put paid to that. Instead, he became an air vice-marshal, but – in a characteristic gesture – relinquished the rank in 1940 so that he would not be senior to more experienced officers, becoming a more lowly group captain and, in July 1941, an air commodore in the Welfare Section of the RAF Inspector General's staff. Basically his job consisted of exploiting his royal glamour in morale-boosting visits to RAF bases.

But George had another, less well-publicised duty. By far the most politically astute of the royal brothers, he was even briefly seen as a contender for the crown. When Edward VIII abdicated, he wanted to pass the throne to his youngest sibling, not Bertie, because he believed he would make the far better King.[23] Edward was by no means alone – many in the Establishment considered both Bertie and Harry, Duke of Gloucester, to be too weak, ineffectual and, essentially, boring.[24] George, however, was a blue-eyed, tanned and dashing glamour figure, with a gorgeous wife and – another major consideration – the only one of the brothers with a male heir. There was no real contest, of course: constitutionally Bertie had to become King, and duly did, with his hugely popular wife Elizabeth crowned by his side as Queen Consort. The Duke of Kent became his unofficial intelligence officer, a job he had been trained for when in the Royal Navy, and which he had performed for his father, George V, and for Edward VIII. Royal biographers never attach much significance to this, but it was undoubtedly the most important aspect of his life – and perhaps even the key to his untimely death.

During the abdication crisis the Duke of Kent acted as Edward's political adviser, together with Walter Monckton – who later, as Director of the Ministry of Information, seemed to know far more about the Hess affair than he should have done in the immediate aftermath of the flight.

The day after Kent's return from every one of his visits to his wife's sister in Munich, the Court Circular records that he dined with the King.[25] Was he briefing him about certain German developments? A superb linguist, he was frequently chosen as the Royal Family's political envoy. His trip to Lisbon in 1940 was by no means simply a courtesy visit. He took part in secret negotiations aimed at ensuring that the Portuguese leader, Antonio Salazar, remained neutral,[26] but it seems that was by no means his only role in clandestine deals of the highest importance. He had met Hess and Rosenberg, and dined regularly with von Ribbentrop.

In the name of the King

The flying fraternity was significantly involved in the movement to foster Anglo-German relations after the Nazis came to power. A major figure among them was Baron William de Ropp, who was both Alfred Rosenberg's envoy to Britain and the main contact in Berlin of Frederick Winterbotham of air intelligence. And, of course, Rosenberg was Hess's close ally, lunching with him on the day of his departure for Scotland. In his 1978 book *The Nazi Connection* Winterbotham writes of de Ropp's pre-war activities: 'Later, de Ropp was ordered to go to England to explain to the Duke of Kent the aims and objectives of the Nazis. The request had originally come from King Edward VIII, but it was thought advisable to make the contact through his brother.'[27] This is the only reference to the Duke of Kent in Winterbotham's book, but there is an intriguing note about another version of ten years before, *Secret and Personal*, written when he was still bound by the Official Secrets Act, long out of print and difficult to find. The earlier book, surprisingly, contains more information, rather than less: there is an entire chapter devoted to de Ropp's role as Rosenberg's liaison officer with the British Royal Family – specifically with the Duke of Kent – in the 1930s. Ten years later, this chapter had been dropped.

The relationship between the British monarchy and Hitler's regime went much deeper than has been suspected. When published in 1956, Rosenberg's diaries revealed an amazing situation, as can be seen from a particularly revealing entry for 21 January 1935, quoted by Winterbotham:

A few days ago Baron de Ropp came here again. Mysteriously; only for me and the Führer. His Majesty the King of England had expressed great astonishment to his political adviser that England's information about the true situation in the Saar[28] . . . has been very poor. The 'serious press', especially, had failed. The adviser in question applied to the Air Ministry, which has always been in contact with me, and asked for a detailed instruction about the situation in Germany. Whereupon Major Winterbotham called de Ropp and asked him to come to London. De Ropp is going to meet with the King's Adviser in a club in London to inform him about what is going on. Yesterday he left.[29]

When de Ropp arrived in London for the meeting, he discovered that the 'King's (George V's) Adviser' was the Duke of Kent.[30] The two men then engaged in deep discussion until the early hours. A report prepared by Rosenberg for Hitler in October 1935 reiterates Kent's political significance:

At the end of last year we were notified that the King of England had pronounced himself dissatisfied with the official press reports. The Duke of Kent's visit to Munich had only worsened the English King's opinion regarding official news reporting, and so one day we received the request from London to explain about National Socialism down to the last detail to the Duke of Kent for the purpose of informing the King of England. After careful consultation with me, de Ropp travelled to London where he unobtrusively had a three-hour conversation with the Duke of Kent, who then reported to the King of England. It may be accepted that this meeting contributed very greatly in strengthening the pressure for a reconstruction of the Cabinet and mainly towards beginning the movement in the direction of Germany.[31]

The Duke of Kent obviously had very real influence on political events. He was uniquely placed to act as intermediary between high-ranking Nazis and the movers and shakers of British society for the betterment of Anglo-German relations, an opportunity he seemed to relish. A Foreign Office report from 1937 notes the close relationship between the Nazi Ambassador in London, von Ribbentrop, and the Duke and Duchess of Kent.[32]

After one of their visits to Munich in February 1937, the Kents joined forces with the Duke of Windsor in Austria, where he was castle-hunting.[33] *The Times* noted that the previous weekend Walter Monckton had visited Windsor in his Austrian retreat. The pro-German sympathies of the two brothers were well known among leading politicians; once war broke out they rapidly came to be seen as a real threat. The Windsors were packed off to the farthest outpost of the British Empire, the Duke, with huge reluctance and resentment, taking over the governorship of the Bahamas. Churchill made strenuous efforts to keep the two brothers apart. When Kent was at the Portuguese celebrations at Lisbon, Windsor – who was in Madrid at the time – also planned to attend. British offi-cials in Spain were instructed to prevent Windsor from going to Portugal until Kent had left.[34] Again, when visiting the USA in September 1941, Kent intended to meet Windsor – due to make his first US tour as Governor of the Bahamas – but the British govern-ment deliberately delayed the Windsors' trip in order to keep the brothers apart.[35]

The Duke of Kent was considerably more than a leader of the Anglo-German peace group. He also took part in last-minute moves to avert the coming conflict, visiting his cousin Prince Philip of Hesse early in 1939 for top-level discussions.[36] In July 1939 he initi-ated a plan in which he would negotiate directly with Hitler; this plan had the support of the King, who put it to Chamberlain and Lord Halifax.[37] Although his official biographers acknowledge his role in the plan, it is now impossible to find any details of it.

The Duke of Windsor's alleged pro-Nazi sympathies are well known, but there are other connections that have attracted far less attention. It is acknowledged that, shortly after the end of the war, Anthony Blunt – later the Queen's art expert, who was notoriously unmasked as the 'Fourth Man' in the Burgess–Maclean–Philby spy ring in 1979 – was sent to the home of Prince Philip of Hesse to retrieve compromising letters that the Duke of Windsor had written to him. Philip's son, Prince Wolfgang, stated in an interview in the *Sunday Times* in 1979 that his father, an SA general who was arrested by the Allies in 1945, had unofficially conducted talks between Hitler and Windsor (then Edward VIII) and Prince George, Duke of Kent.[38] According to John Costello, in *The Mask of Treachery*, the letters collected by Blunt were written by *both* royal brothers.[39] (There is also a strong sexual element in this intrigue. Blunt is rumoured to have had an affair with the Duke of

Kent in the early 1930s, as Blunt later did with David Bowes-Lyon.[40])

As mentioned earlier, the seating plan of the 'round-table' meeting at the Foreign Office on 9 June 1939 in the Hamilton archives shows that not only was Hamilton (then the Marquess of Clydesdale) seated at the top table, but also present were General Walther von Reichenau and the enigmatic Group Captain Sir Louis Greig. The significance of the latter escaped us at the time, only becoming apparent with the publication in 1999 of his grandson, Geordie Greig's, book, *Louis and the Prince*, which describes the remarkable career of this strangely influential figure. Louis Greig was a great favourite of George V, who entrusted him with befriending Bertie, then Duke of York, with the hope that he would lose some of his extreme gaucheness (Greig was fifteen years older than the King's second son). This proved so successful that the two men became intimate friends, in addition to being Wimbledon doubles partners. Indeed, their relationship was so close that after the Yorks' wedding night, Bertie confided the details to his great friend Louis. Perhaps with more truth than was intended, Greig was appointed as comptroller of the Yorks' household. All seemed set for a lifetime of friendship and brotherly larks, but there was one problem: the former Elizabeth Bowes-Lyon, now the Duchess of York, did not like her husband's best friend. Shortly after the wedding, he was forced to resign.[41]

However, at the beginning of the 1930s George V found a new role for Greig, as personal assistant and – in Geordie Greig's words – 'sort of minder' to the Duke of Kent.[42] Greig became George's companion, right up to his death in 1942, accompanying him on his trips to the United States and Canada. Sharing Kent's political and social interests, he was also there when the Duke of Kent met with Rosenberg's representative, Baron de Ropp, in London in 1935.

Sir Louis Greig was in an almost uniquely powerful position within the British Establishment. On the outbreak of war he was posted to the Cabinet War Rooms, one of only a handful of people with the clearance to enter the Map Room, where all information on Britain's entire war effort was collected and co-ordinated. Louis held no formal position there, being more of an 'unofficial fixer'.[43] He worked closely with the intelligence departments (one of his daughters was with SOE), but he also fulfilled an important unofficial role as the King's eyes and ears in the Cabinet War Room. George VI wrote him a letter, marked 'Secret', with the request: 'If you hear of anything that may not come my way please let me know.'[44] In 1941 Greig was appointed personal secretary to Sir Archibald Sinclair, with responsibility for liaising with foreign heads of state, working particularly closely with General Sikorski. Geordie Greig describes his role at that time as 'political fixer on a grander international scale'.[45] Given these connections, the only possible reason for someone in Greig's position to have been at the 'summit' on 9 June 1939 – at which the Duke of Hamilton figured so prominently – was as the representative of the King, or of the Duke of Kent.

A clear picture of the Duke of Kent's role emerges: from the early 1930s he was definitely involved in fostering closer relations between Britain and Germany; as war loomed, he was a participant in moves to avert hostilities. That much is irrefutable, but what can also be deduced is that, once war had broken out, he would have been a prime mover in any serious attempt to end it.

At the beginning of the war, the Kents left their home in Belgrave Square to the Red Cross and moved up to Scotland, taking Pitliver House, at Charlestown, near Rosyth, in Fife. (They also had a house, the Coppins, at Iver in Buckinghamshire.) At Pitliver House they entertained General Sikorski in November 1939 – in all the Duke and the Polish leader would meet ten times between the outbreak of war and the Duke of Kent's death in August 1942.[46] His bond with the Polish community was particularly strong, perhaps because they had their eye on him for a very elevated task.

In 1972 an extraordinary revelation was made public for the first time. It emerged in newly released Foreign Office files that Sikorski had offered the Duke of Kent the Polish throne.[47] Kent had always been deeply interested in Poland's politics and affairs of state, having many friends among the Polish nobility whom he visited in 1937.[48] However, the British government was deeply unhappy about both the offer of the Polish throne and the Kents' interest in Poland in general, even 'advising' (more accurately, ordering) the Duke not to become patron of a charity he and Marina had set up for destitute Poles, on the grounds that 'it might become an embarrassment'.[49] The Polish connection gave the Duke of Kent an extra vested interest in pursuing peace and in the progress of the war. He would not have wanted to see the Russians win the forthcoming

Soviet–German war, because that would preclude his taking up the offer of the Polish throne. His personal interest lay in a German victory over the USSR, together with an agreement to make at least the non-German-speaking parts of Poland free. He and Sikorski would have been especially sympathetic to a peace initiative such as that of Rudolf Hess.

As we have seen, Mrs Baker claimed that the Duke of Kent was at Dungavel on 10 May 1941. Although it is difficult to trace his movements on that weekend, especially because all of his papers are embargoed – none of them have ever been released and historians are routinely refused access to them[50] – according to John Harris, he was in Scotland, at Balmoral, on the weekend of 10–11 May 1941.[51] On 9 May he was reported as having been at RAF Sumburgh in the Shetlands on one of his morale-boosting visits.[52] And two days after Hess's arrival he paid another such visit to RAF Wick at Caithness.[53] Was this a hastily devised reason for his being in Scotland at that critical time?

All this establishes that the Duke of Kent had the motive and opportunity for being involved in the Hess plan, but, apart from Mrs Baker's testimony, is there any evidence specifically to link him with the events of 10 May 1941, or with the 'Hamilton peace group' in general?

The answer to the second question is an emphatic 'yes'. The Duke of Hamilton's diary for January 1941 records two meetings with the Duke of Kent in a single week: on Monday, 20 January the entry reads: 'Duke of Kent. Lunch', and on Thursday, 23 January, 'Duke of Kent. Prestwick.' As we have seen, Hess made either an attempt to fly to Dungavel or a dummy run on the previous Saturday, 18 January. The week after Hamilton's two meetings with the Duke of Kent, he took ten days' leave which, according to his diary, he spent on the Duke of Northumberland's estate at Lesbury. Hamilton's movements coincided with a similar flurry of activity on the German side, most specifically Albrecht Haushofer's visit to Sweden. The timing of Hamilton and Kent's two meetings is, at the very least, intriguing. (Whether there were similar meetings at the time of Hess's first 'attempt' in December 1940 is unknown, as Hamilton's diary for that year is reported as missing.)

The royal archives at Windsor were able to supply us with details of the Duke of Kent's movements for that period. However, although his many public and private engagements for the week of 20–24 January 1941 are listed, there is no mention of his two meetings with Hamilton. And there is no information at all on Kent's whereabouts the following week, when Hamilton was on leave: after spending two days in Newcastle on 24–25 January, the next reference is to 4 February, when he was in London.[54]

More exciting confirmation of the Duke of Kent's involvement came from Mrs Elizabeth Adam, a retired Conservative Party agent in Scotland, now living in Cumbria. She is a descendant of the famous eighteenth-century architect and interior designer Robert Adam, and her family has always had strong connections with the Dukes of Northumberland. (Robert Adam established his reputation under their patronage, restoring Alnwick Castle and designing their house at Syon Park in Richmond, Surrey.) Elizabeth Adam's knowledge of the Hess affair comes from her late father, also Robert, who was directly involved.[55] He served with the Argyll and Sutherland Highlanders until the mid-1920s, and was recalled as a reservist in 1938. He became personal assistant to Major-General Douglas McConnel, Commander-in-Chief of southwest Scotland. According to Elizabeth Adam, her father was sent to the Dungavel area *in advance* of Hess's arrival, specifically because there was some uncertainty about exactly when the Deputy Führer would be coming. (This fits with the evidence that the flight was planned for 5 May, but delayed at the last moment.) Robert Adam was certainly part of a group that was supportive of the peace plan, but the pièce de résistance in Mrs Adam's testimony was what her father told her about the peace plan: 'It must have been pukka because of Kent's involvement. Kent was the youngest and brightest so it clearly came from him to give the royal blessing.' Adam said that in retrospect it was 'an attempt that might have helped, but in any event it gave Churchill the breathing space that he needed'. This summing up of the event was to assume greater significance in the light of our discoveries about how Churchill turned Hess's mission to his own advantage, as we will see.

As a former officer with the Argyll and Sutherland Highlanders – one of the most royalist of all regiments – Adam's involvement might explain the anomaly noted earlier in which that regiment was specifically ordered *not* to pick Hess up from the Home Guard, even though it was the nearest military unit. On the hypothesis that two opposing forces were trying to gain possession of the Deputy Führer, and that the Argylls were under the control of the peace party, could this be the reason for such a curious departure from standard procedure?

There is more, albeit circumstantial, evidence supporting the Duke of Kent's direct involvement in the Hess affair. We have seen that Squadron Leader Frank Day testified that he was called out to mount an unarmed 'guard of honour' at a large Victorian house near RAF Turnhouse on 13 May, for what appeared to be a meeting involving Hess. Day was not able to identify the house, but we have discovered evidence that not only does so but also supports his testimony. Remarkably, this is in a 1986 booklet produced by Army Headquarters, Scotland, on the history of Craigiehall House (where the HQ is based). The author, Major C. B. Innes, writes:

> There was a story about Hess, which I have been quite unable to substantiate. However, several officers have told me that there used to be a photograph in the Mess showing Hess arriving at Craigiehall under escort. I tend to believe that it may be true, that Rudolf Hess was brought to Craigiehall for interrogation on about 20th May 1941.[56]

Although the date is incorrect – by 20 May Hess was in London – Craigiehall, which is very close to RAF Turnhouse, matches perfectly the location and description given by Squadron Leader Day. (Innes's reference to the photograph in the Officers' Mess is tantalising, as it would have been the only one taken of Hess during his entire time in British custody.)

It will be recalled that Day said Hess was taken there to meet with a high-ranking RAF officer who was referred to as 'the Duke'. It has always been assumed that this was Hamilton, but he and Hess had already met twice before in the preceding days, both times without the need for a guard of honour. Although the Duke of Hamilton's diary records that he met Hess on 12 and 14 May, there is no mention of his meeting the Deputy Führer on the 13th – in fact, the diary entry explicitly has him somewhere else.[57] So 'the Duke' in question was almost certainly not Hamilton. Further evidence that that duke seen by Frank Day was not Hamilton – and that the circumstances surrounding Hess's arrival are markedly different from the official version – came from a conversation in Washington with Nicholas

Sheetz, the manuscript archivist at Georgetown University Library, in October 2000. According to Sheetz, he had been at a dinner party several years ago given by the Dowager Duchess of Hamilton, during which she reminisced about Hess having visited the house in which she and the Duke were living during the war. (She did not mention the Duke being present.) This was a revelation: there had never been any suggestion that the Duchess had met Hess. Was Sheetz perhaps mistaken? It seemed likely. However, we were able to confirm this – again, strangely, from an official government publication.

We found in the Hamilton Muniments that the Duke and Duchess were living in a fine old house called Millburn Tower, about ten minutes' drive from RAF Turnhouse. Then we found in the National Library of Scotland an official survey of historic Scottish buildings – made in 1987 for the Countryside Commission for Scotland and the Scottish Development Department – which states in its entry for Millburn Tower: 'During World War II . . . amongst its recorded visitors were Rudolf Hess and Amy Johnson'.[58]

Clearly, this supports what the Duchess told Nicholas Sheetz. The implication is that if Hess was taken to Millburn Tower it was on the way to Craigiehall House, presumably to wait until it was time for the meeting there. Therefore, if Hess was to meet the Duke of Hamilton, surely he would have done so at Millburn Tower and there would have been no need to have met him – with some attendant formality – at Craigiehall. And if so, another duke was involved. We are looking for another duke who was a high-ranking RAF officer. The obvious candidate, of course, is the Duke of Kent, who at the time held the rank of group captain.

There may be a further hint of the Duke of Kent's involvement in the apparently trivial quip of Churchill's, 'Hess or no Hess, I'm going to see the Marx Brothers.' This now famous comment appeared in Lord James Douglas-Hamilton's 1971 book, but the first published version was in 1948, and was based on what was reported to Harry L. Hopkins, President Roosevelt's special adviser. According to this version, the remark was not made in the evening, but when Brendan Bracken, Churchill's parliamentary private secretary, informed him of the telephone call from the Duke of Hamilton reporting Hess's arrival. To this Churchill reportedly replied, 'Will you kindly instruct the Duke of Hamilton to tell that to the Marx Brothers?', before giving instructions for the Duke to fly south to brief him in person.[59] This version is supported by Churchill's own account, published in 1950, in which he says that he was watching a Marx Brothers film when the telephone call came through.[60] Churchill was noted for his schoolboyish habit of giving people nicknames – so in this case, who were the 'Marx Brothers' (assuming they were not Groucho and his gang)? A source close to the Hamiltons revealed that the 'Marx Brothers' was an old joke referring to the royal princes that was shared between Churchill and the Duke of Hamilton. So, with this in mind, Churchill might have been instructing Hamilton to pass on the news of Hess's arrival to one or all of the royal brothers. Or did he want the Duke to tell them that he was flying down to brief the Prime Minister? In other words, was he making it abundantly clear who was now in charge: Winston Churchill?

The Duke of Kent's activities raise some profoundly unsettling questions, especially about the knowledge and involvement of his brother, the King. During the 1930s Kent had acted on behalf of three kings as go-between with Germany. It seems likely that he would be doing much the same with Hess.

Reconstruction

Hess's mission was intended to be the last move in the peace plan, not – as most believe – the first (remember that Kim Philby had reported to Moscow that Hess came to *confirm* a peace deal). He flew to Scotland for a face-to-face meeting with the principal members of the peace group, intending to return to Germany without his visit ever becoming public knowledge. Although only a small group of people in Britain were initiated into the plan, they were still able to secure a safe passage for Hess's plane through their contacts within the RAF and Air Ministry.

There was a delegation from the peace group waiting for him at Dungavel – which was partly occupied by the Red Cross and, therefore, as neutral territory, was an ideal venue for a peace conference. The welcoming committee included representatives of the exiled Polish government. General Sikorski could not have been among them, as he did not return from a month-long visit to the USA until the morning of 11 May;[61] however, the fact that he returned to Scotland within hours of Hess's arrival is significant, as it allowed him to be present at any negotiations. (Obviously, no talks would have taken place until Hess had had a good night's rest following his flight.)

MI6 were involved – just as they were in other genuine peace feelers in 1940 – but this was not a trap for Hess. The head of MI6, Sir Stewart Menzies, was a prominent member of the 'peace party', who believed that Britain's interests lay in a negotiated peace with Germany, in order to allow the Nazis (and MI6) to concentrate on the real enemy, the Soviet Union, at best leading to peace in Europe, at worst, a quasi-armistice while Germany and Russia fought each other to exhaustion.

All this begs the question of what would have happened if Hess had been successful, had landed at Dungavel, and had safely returned to Germany. Hess was clearly planning a two-day visit at the most. We also know that he would not have negotiated with either Churchill or his government, but does that mean that there were plans afoot to oust the British Prime Minister? It is only when Hess's flight is seen in the context of the political events in Britain leading up to the time of his mission that it begins to make sense. By May 1941, after a year as Prime Minister, Churchill was in serious trouble. Although still popular with the people, his management of the war and his autocratic style of leadership were the subjects of intense criticism in Parliament. Britain was losing the war: Greece had been lost to the Germans and Italians, Rommel was winning in North Africa, air raids were having a devastating effect on British cities, and the empire's shipping was being sunk by U-boats at an alarming rate. Matters came to a head on 7 May – just three days before Hess's arrival – when Churchill faced a rebellious Commons and a savage attack on his leadership. Significantly, the central figure in this campaign was David Lloyd George, who attacked both Churchill's competence and the fact that he surrounded himself with yes-men, refusing to countenance any form of criticism.[62] In a heated debate, Churchill contrived to counter Lloyd George's criticisms by insinuating that they amounted to anti-British defeatism, and with magnificent defiance called for a vote of confidence. He won easily – 447 for and just 3 brave souls against – but the vote did not represent the true feelings of the Commons. MPs knew that although they might criticise Churchill among themselves, they had to give the impression of unity to the outside world, for the sake of British morale if nothing else. In any case, those opposed to the Prime Minister would not vote against him until they were sure of having a majority. Lord Hankey wrote to Sir Samuel Hoare in Madrid about the vote of confidence, saying that although Churchill had won 'there is still a good deal of murmuring', and voicing the opinion that 'Although the façade is almost as strong as ever I fear that the structure behind is not quite as sound as it was'.[63] On 14 May Labour MP Richard Rapier Stokes wrote to Lloyd George to say that there was 'much more support for the views you expressed . . . than was apparent'.[64]

The House of Lords was also in revolt, with a steady build-up of pressure, not only against Churchill's leadership, but for a negotiated peace. On 10 May itself the pro-peace Duke of Bedford wrote to Stokes that Lloyd George should make a statement of the peace terms that would be acceptable to Britain.[65] Stokes's letter to Lloyd George four days later, after the Hess story had broken, said: 'What many of us hope . . . is that the criticisms of last week should not be allowed to fade out and that if the Hess visit holds out any opportunity of bringing the war to an early conclusion that opportunity should not be lost.'[66] And on 12 May Hugh Dalton, Minister for Economic Warfare (and minister responsible for SOE), wrote in his diary that several members of the House of Lords were openly advocating that Britain sue for peace with the Axis powers.[67] (This entry was not included in the published version of Dalton's diaries.)

We suggest that this mounting pressure on Churchill was no coincidence, but was an orchestrated campaign which was tied into the Hess mission, and aimed at forcing the Prime Minister from office. This does not mean that all the MPs and peers involved knew that a deal was about to be struck with Hess, but the campaign was orchestrated by those who did know. Two key figures in the peace group – Lloyd George and Sir Samuel Hoare – were holding themselves in readiness to form a government. Indeed, according to John Harris, who has seen Lord Beaverbrook's diary, on 10 May 1941 Lloyd George had an appointment with the 'kingmaker' at his house, Cherkley, in Surrey.[68] It should be remembered that Beaverbrook had also been behind the intrigue that surrounded the ousting of another popular wartime Prime Minister, Asquith, in 1916, which led to Asquith's replacement by Lloyd George.

Also significant is that – according to records in the Spanish Foreign Ministry archives discovered by Scott Newton – the day before Hess's flight, Sir Samuel Hoare was involved in a dispute with Spanish customs about the import of a large quantity of aviation fuel for his 'personal use'.[69] Newton points out that it was sufficient for a return journey to Stockholm. (Another event that cannot, surely, be coincidental is that telephone connections between Sweden and Germany were completely cut off for ten hours between 8 p.m. on 10 May and 6 a.m. on 11 May.[70])

It was within the King's prerogative to choose a new Prime Minister, although this power would only ever be exercised in the most extreme circumstances. Constitutionally, a general election was not required (after all, Churchill himself had not been elected to the office by the people). There was always the possibility that, faced with the open opposition of the King and a large proportion of the Establishment, Churchill could have been persuaded to stand aside. The public might never have known the truth about his removal. They would just know that they had a new Prime Minister.

Unlikely – even sensational – though that may seem, there is evidence that the situation really was balanced on a knife-edge. Of course, any such plan involving the King in peace deals with Germany would have been rigorously covered up with a secrecy that would be stringently maintained to this day. However, there is evidence that such a plan existed. Indeed, it was said in aristocratic circles that George VI feared that, if Churchill refused to leave office as part of the armistice with Germany, the situation might escalate into full-blown civil war. This is certainly what Lord Willingdon, one of the pro-peace members of the aristocracy, told Lord Wigram, equerry to the King (and to both preceding kings) and Keeper of the Royal Archives at Windsor.[71]

In this connection, it is surely not a coincidence that two days after Hess arrived, the Scottish Honours (the crown jewels of Scotland) were removed from Edinburgh Castle and clandestinely buried.[72] The secret of their whereabouts was entrusted to just three people, which did not include the Duke of Hamilton, despite the fact that he was their hereditary keeper. (Some leaders of the Scottish Nationalist Party advocated making a separate peace with Germany[73] and there were police raids on their premises in the days immediately before Hess arrived,[74] which suggests that the authorities were genuinely concerned at the prospect of trouble in Scotland.)

Another significant event was the sudden replacement of the Commander-in-Chief of Scottish Command (a post that carried with it the role of Governor of Edinburgh Castle) the day before Hess's arrival. The official reason was a new policy that 'younger general officers should hold the principal operational commands' – the new man, Lieutenant-General Andrew Thorne was, in fact, just three years younger than the outgoing commander, Lieutenant-General Richard Carrington. On the same day, the Commander-in-Chief of Eastern Command was also replaced.[75] Eastern Command was headquartered at the stately home of Luton Hoo in Bedfordshire, which, as we will see, has its own part to play in the aftermath of Hess's arrival. Why should the heads of these two Commands – and these two only – be suddenly changed the day before Hess arrived?

However, the plan came to nothing; something went badly wrong. But was this simply a matter of Hess's failure to find Dungavel and his arrest by the Home Guard? Surely it was not beyond the wit of such powerful figures as Hamilton, the Duke of Kent and Menzies to circumvent such inconvenient details.

Although this must remain a matter for speculation, it is probable that Churchill somehow learned of Hess's imminent arrival, possibly through the coded message deciphered by Albert Heal in Leeds, but more significantly maybe from Sir Archibald Sinclair, whose role is ambivalent. He seems to have been aware of Hamilton's activities in the months between receiving Albrecht Haushofer's letter and the flight itself. Sinclair was an intimate friend of both Churchill and Menzies – even acting as mediator between them – and therefore had a foot planted firmly in both camps.[76] And Sir Louis Greig was his assistant in May 1941.

From Daniel McBride's testimony, we know that all leave in the area was suddenly cancelled on the afternoon of 10 May, and there were other signs that there was a flap on that night. Mrs Abbot told how the landing lights went on without warning at Dungavel and that they were turned off again. Was someone trying to wreck Hess's mission by making it impossible to land at Dungavel? Or were they on the side of the peace party, acting swiftly as soon as they realised something had gone wrong with their plans? Much of the confusion is explained if there were two opposing forces in operation in Renfrewshire that night: one was the peace group and the other sent by those who wanted to scupper the plan, and who were quite happy for Hess to be taken into custody by the Home Guard. This scenario would explain the presence of Roman Battaglia, the Pole who 'interrogated' Hess for two hours at Giffnock. Was he really warning the prisoner that something had gone wrong, and perhaps concocting a story for him to stick to? Was this also the reason for the meeting between Hess and the Duke of Hamilton on the road to Maryhill Barracks later that night?

This scenario would explain why the British government failed to exploit the propaganda value of Hess's arrival – in the event it tried to keep the affair as low key as possible. This was obviously Churchill's initiative: while some ministers wanted to exploit the situation, he expressly forbade it, going to the opposite extreme, even wanting to make an announcement that confirmed the German position. Although the only member of the Cabinet who supported him in this was Sir Archibald Sinclair,[77] Churchill was soon to reinforce his position. The failure of the Hess mission did not just devastate the conspiracy to remove the Prime Minister from office; with characteristic adroitness, Churchill managed to turn the situation so dramatically that it ensured his political survival – and much else besides.

CHAPTER NINE

The Secret Armistice

After the drama and confusion of the immediate aftermath of the flight, Hess's British captors now had to find the best way to deal with their VIP prisoner. His ankle healing, the Deputy Führer was taken southwards by train to London, where he was taken in a closed vehicle to the Tower of London.

The guard who logged Hess into the Tower wanted a souvenir of what was even then regarded as a historic event, and asked him to sign the back of a sheet of notepaper. Having obligingly written his name, Hess turned the paper over and, seeing the Tower's letterhead, realised where he was. The framed signature can now be seen on the wall of the Yeoman Warders' Club, where the members proudly draw attention to it. It is not hard to imagine Hess's emotions – as an Anglophile, knowing of the Tower's history, he may have felt rather apprehensive, although it might also have dawned on him that at least his accommodation reflected his eminence. He was held in the officers' quarters of the Governor's House.

Hess was imprisoned in the Tower only while his intended place of confinement was being prepared – Mytchett Place, a Victorian country house just outside the garrison town of Aldershot in Surrey, which had to be specially equipped, on Churchill's orders, with state-of-the-art security features. The whole place was wired for sound: nothing the prisoner said, even to himself, was to be lost. Hess was given the codename 'Jonathan', while Mytchett Place was known as 'Camp Z' in official reports.

The protection – and isolation – of the Deputy Führer was taken very seriously. In all, some 120 Coldstream and Scots Guardsmen were engaged in guarding the house. The outer perimeter, continually patrolled by Military Police, was protected by earthworks and gun emplacements, and an inner barbed-wire perimeter was equipped with guns and floodlit at night. A sentry posted at the main entrance meticulously checked the identity of all visitors, who had to be personally approved by Sir Stewart Menzies; all passes were issued by the Foreign Office and signed by Sir Alexander Cadogan, and visitors also had to pass a second security check when entering the house. There were armed guards and orderlies stationed inside the building, which was partitioned off by wire screens into areas to which the prisoner was allowed access, and those that were forbidden to him. Churchill was taking no risks: doctors who visited wrote of the danger of tripping over machine-guns sprouting from under sofas, where they were kept at hand in case of a surprise attack by Nazis or their British sympathisers.[1]

The Deputy's quarters were on the first floor, and consisted of a sitting room, bedroom and bathroom. This part of the house was sealed off by a wire grille, with a locked metal door flanked on either side by armed guards. There were hidden microphones in Hess's quarters, all conversations being listened to and recorded in another room. Although there is no direct evidence that Hess was aware of this surveillance, it is likely that he would have been suspicious – after all, he had run his own intelligence unit and knew how they operated.

While at Mytchett Place, Hess was closely supervised by a team of three MI6 officers: Colonel Thomas Kendrick (listed as 'Colonel Wallace' in the official records), a senior MI6 officer who had been Head of Station in Vienna until the outbreak of war; an unidentified officer with the cover name of 'Captain Barnes'; and their commanding officer, Major Frank Foley. What was not known at the time is that one of the men tasked with listening to and transcribing Hess's conversations was a Communist agent.[2] (Those posted to Camp Z were screened for Nazi sympathies only.) Although the identity of this agent is not known, perhaps this explains why 'Captain Barnes' has never been identified. And surely it is no coincidence that some of the reports of Hess's conversations were passed on to the Communist Party in London, no doubt leading to their allegations that Hess had come to negotiate with right-wing elements in the British Establishment: the accusations that led to Hamilton's libel action.

The involvement of Major Frank Foley in Hess's confinement at Mytchett Place is significant. An important figure in British intelligence, he has recently achieved posthumous fame as 'Britain's Oskar Schindler', receiving the Righteous Gentile award at a solemn ceremony in Jerusalem in 1999 for his humanitarian action in helping Jews to escape from Germany before the war. Attached to the British Embassy in Berlin as passport officer, he had arranged that as many as 10,000 Jews had passports so that they could emigrate to Palestine.[3] Foley was specifically recalled from his other duties because he knew Hess relatively well, having met him several times before the war. But there was something else that made Foley in particular the man for the job at Mytchett Place: his main duties since the outbreak of war had been concerned with gathering intelligence on Germany's atomic bomb project. In 1940 he had been part of an MI6 team that made a daring escape from embattled France with quantities of heavy water from the French A-bomb project.[4] Since then Foley had continued to gather information about German atomic weapons research. He was now in charge of Rudolf Hess, who, as Commissar for All Technological Matters and Organisation, was in ultimate command of the Nazis' atomic bomb project.

Behind closed doors

If we are to believe the official story, very little of importance happened at Mytchett Place. There seem to have been no serious attempts to interrogate the prisoner, or prise any of Germany's secret plans out of him in any way. There was only a casual kind of debriefing, in which he was engaged in – admittedly somewhat leading – conversations with Foley and his colleagues. The report that went to 'C' (Menzies) and then on to Churchill claimed, astonishingly, that the Deputy Führer knew very little of military or political value.

Although Hess was visited by two government officials – Lord Simon (the Lord Chancellor) in early June and Lord Beaverbrook at the beginning of September – we are led to believe that these were simply half-hearted attempts to discover something interesting about the Nazis' intentions towards the USSR. Beaverbrook, then newly appointed 'Minister of State', was about to leave for a series of meetings with Britain's new ally, Stalin, in Moscow, so no doubt any extra intelligence from the enemy would have been very welcome. Both Simon and Beaverbrook were known to have supported the pro-peace lobby before the war, which may have persuaded Churchill that they were particularly suited to the task of dealing with Hess. What is notable about this period is that there was no attempt to extract the least bit of propaganda value from his capture, prompting Goebbels to ask in his diary why the British were not inventing statements and attributing them to Hess.[5] Who, except for high-ranking Nazis, would know the difference? Even Major Desmond Morton, Churchill's personal intelligence adviser, urged that the government should 'cash in on this windfall' for propaganda purposes.[6] It never did – although, as we will see, it did use Hess in other ways.

Within weeks of Hess's arrival at Mytchett Place the first reports of his mental deterioration began to circulate, resulting in his being placed under a team of army psychiatrists led by Colonel (later Brigadier) John Rawlings Rees and Major Henry Dicks. They reported that he was suffering from paranoia – complaining his food was being poisoned and that his captors were trying to drive him insane by interrupting his sleep. They also noted his extreme mood swings, one day appearing perfectly rational and the next confused and eccentric. Things appeared to come to a head on 15 June when the prisoner, dressed in his Luftwaffe uniform, rushed out of his cell and threw himself over the first-floor bannister. Although he only succeeded in breaking his left leg – confining him to bed on traction for several weeks – it seems he had intended to kill himself.

Throughout this time Hess had made repeated requests to be put in direct contact with George VI, claiming (with some justification, it seems) that he had been assured of the King's protection. He complained that his guards were part of the 'Churchill clique' who were preventing him from meeting the people he had come to see, and kept stressing that he should be treated as befits a peace envoy. In his early days at Mytchett Place he also asked several times to see the Duke of Hamilton, but was told that the Duke would not be given permission to see him. Significantly, the administrator of Camp Z, Lieutenant-Colonel Malcolm Scott, recorded in his diary that Hess had told one of the guards that 'members of the government' had known about his flight in advance.[7] Of course, all his claims and requests to see the King were regarded by the authorities as proof of his madness.

Behind the cover story

Our investigation was to uncover information that cast considerable doubt on the official version of what happened at Mytchett Place. Very early on we realised that there is a basic problem with the government's version of events. If we are correct, and the story of the lone madman had to be concocted to conceal the truth about the involvement of leading figures in suing for peace with Germany, then obviously all subsequent official records about Hess had to be tailored to follow the party line.

One of the earliest puzzles about Hess's period of captivity in England was what happened while he was in the Tower of London. Charles Fraser-Smith, who was responsible for supplying special equipment and uniforms to the intelligence services, records in his autobiography that he was summoned to London by MI5, who asked him to organise the making of a copy of Hess's Luftwaffe uniform while the Deputy Führer was lying drugged in his room.[8] Obviously this shows that Hess was, at least on one occasion, deliberately drugged by his captors. Apart from one episode in early 1945 – when he was given a 'truth drug' supposedly as a treatment for amnesia – Hess's allegations that he was being drugged have always been denied, even being used as proof of mental instability. And here we are told that he was drugged so that a copy of his uniform could be made. Why should the British security services want an exact copy of his uniform?

The main sources for this period of Hess's life are papers now lodged in the Public Record Office at Kew and elsewhere, plus the reminiscences of his guards that occasionally surface in the press, and the book written in 1947 by John Rawlings Rees.

Where the Mytchett Place phase is concerned, 'Alexander' supplied us with two sets of documents: the first comprised original papers relating to Hess's psychiatric assessment, many of which have never been published – and which will be dealt with later. The second, however, is of much more immediate significance: it reveals that – despite claims to the contrary – Hess was giving valuable information to his captors.

The Admiralty document

Among the key documents that 'Alexander' passed on to us was a report from the Foreign Office to the Admiralty containing a transcript of a conversation with Hess that took place on 22 May 1941 – twelve days after his arrival, and the day after he arrived at Mytchett Place. Dated 28 May, the report is stamped 'MOST SECRET' and 'BY HAND: NOT TO PASS THROUGH ANY REGISTRY'. There is a circulation list that contains the names of senior Admiralty officials, including the First Sea Lord and the director of naval intelligence – and, we were delighted to note, our copy boasts a handwritten note to the director, saying, 'I'd like to talk to you about this', from his PA, Ian Fleming. The report is summarised: 'Extracts from conversation on 22.5.41 with Hess. Views on German construction of submarines and submarine warfare.' The transcript is a translation of talks between Hess ('J') and two of the MI6 officers at Mytchett Place, 'F', the camp commandant (clearly Major Foley) and 'B', presumably the mysterious 'Captain Barnes'. Hess explains the Nazis' aim of starving Britain into submission through U-boat blockades, a typical carrot-and-stick approach. He is trying to soften up the British by first convincing them that resistance is useless, then hitting them swiftly with the offer of mutually acceptable terms. He points out how close Germany came to succeeding in this objective in the First World War, and how it is in a much stronger position this time. Whereas before, he explains, the U-boat bases were confined to Germany and were vulnerable to Royal Navy attacks when trying to find their way through the Channel, now there were bases on the French Atlantic coast. Remarkably, Hess backs up his warning with details about the size of the U-boat fleet and Germany's strategy for using it, clearly trying to convince the British that he is not making idle threats, and that the facts are on his side. He even outlines Hitler's strategy in detail:

> What the Führer has announced, the U-boat war, *that* will come. And secondly, there is the whole Air Force as a weapon against shipping, which he hadn't got at all before. Thirdly, there is the attack on your shipyards by the Air Force; fourthly the attack on the ports, unloading facilities, etc., by the Air Force, the destruction of stores, warehouses, raw materials, foodstuffs, etc. by the Air Force . . .

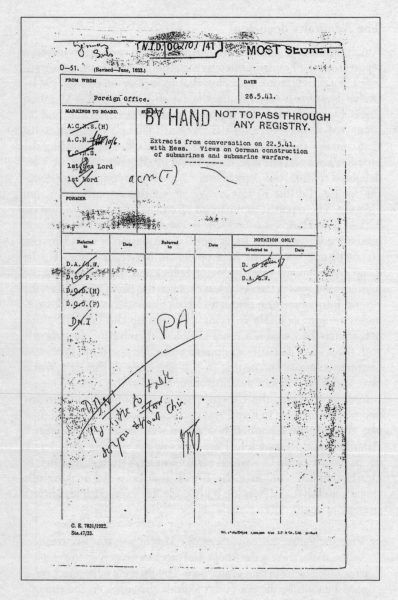

Pages from the transcript of the discussions with Hess on 22 May 1941, later passed to the Admiralty.

MOST SECRET

~ date

ROUGH TRANSLATION

J: I <u>know</u> - by my intimate knowledge of these things
I can guarantee you - that within a certain time, though I
should not like to give the definite date, you will come to
the point where you have the choice either to accept these
limitations and put up with them, or to see England starve.
Judging from the whole situation, I feel sure that it will
come to that.   And above all, England's prestige will then be
severely hit - <u>now</u> it would not be hit so hard; because now
there is an <u>opportunity</u>, just because I am here - here is an
opportunity to be seized: on the other hand, if a day must
come when England must capitulate, then, at the same time,
England's prestige is mortally damaged.

F: You see, we cannot see ourselves beaten.

B: We can't believe that we can be beaten.

J: You may not believe it, but in this case History will
decide.   But I <u>know</u>, with absolute certainty: I should not
have come otherwise, if I didn't know it so exactly.   In 1917,
as a result of the U-boat war, England was nearly at the point
of having to give in.   But compare the situation then and now.
At that time we had thickly mined the German Bight, the
Heligoland Bight that was continually being mined, and it became
a base out of which hardly a ship could emerge.   We couldn't
get through the Channel, we could hardly get to the other side
of it, and long cruises were therefore impossible; while now
we are securely based from the northern point of Norway right
down to Spain, with countless U-boat bases, from which of course
we cannot be turned out.   Secondly, we have the Channel.
Even if it were mined, we are established on the other side;
we have our U-boats on the other side - thirdly, entirely
leaving aside the number of U-boats we possess, when the Führer
sets about such a problem - whether it may be the Siegfried
Line or rearmament in the air or anything else, then he does it
in a big way.   And so, too, there is no comparison in the time
that's coming - the U-boat war has not yet begun in the way
the Führer ....

F: The U-boat war hasn't yet begun?

J: Not properly.   What the Führer has announced, the
U-boat war, <u>that</u> will come.   And secondly, there is the whole
Air Force as a weapon against shipping, which he hadn't got at
all before.   Thirdly, there is the attack on your shipyards
by the Air Force; fourthly the attack on the ports, unloading
facilities, etc. by the Air Force, the destruction of stores,
warehouses, raw materials, food stuffs, etc. by the Air Force.
I've been to see the factories.   During the winter the only
trouble our factories had was what to do with the finished
machines, because there was simply nowhere where they could be
used.   The losses, compared with the aircraft we possessed,
were comparatively slight.   In one, two days we made up a
month's losses.   Everything that was turned out in the other
28 days had to be stored somewhere because, you see, the crews
were not yet trained.   Because the Führer is almost exaggerat-
edly foresighted, the crews get an almost endless training.

                                        You've no ...

I should like to emphasise that I'm not talking propaganda, but that I'm speaking from inner conviction when I converse with you about these questions; that we must discuss together absolutely openly and without any exaggeration, so that we can get a true view of the state of affairs from both sides and get a picture of what it really is; and only then can we perhaps look for a reasonable way to reach a conclusion.

Hess boasts of the rate of U-boat production, the training of their crews and the building of underground bases – obviously trying to impress his questioners by confirming their worst fears about Germany's military capabilities. At that time, Britain's shipping losses were colossal, far outstripping production. If the USA had not entered the war, Hess's grim prophecy would almost certainly have come true. But there is another serious implication: Germany had no intention of invading Britain – indeed, Hess said as much to Lord Simon, telling him that Germany did not want the complications of looking after an occupied Britain. The extract ends:

I assure you, I have come here purely in a spirit of *international* humanitarianism, because I feel that it is crazy, since it is not at all necessary, so that one must try to prevent it. That which is now going to happen on the basis of the new aeroplanes and trained crews we are going to bring into action – there will be attacks, compared with which the former ones are nothing but minor preludes. This is *horrible*. Then, in addition, there are new bombs with more powerful explosive, etc.

Clearly, Hess – expressing himself lucidly and intelligently – believed he was negotiating with the British representatives. This is obviously just one report of many that were distributed to various military and government departments, showing that Hess's arrival in Britain was taken seriously to the extent that what he had to say was brought, albeit in the utmost secrecy, to the attention of the relevant people.

Hess's plan

Officially, Hess met only two senior government figures – Lords Simon and Beaverbrook – during his time in Britain. (The meeting with 'the Duke' and a civilian official, possibly Ivone Kirkpatrick, on 13 May was strictly unofficial.) As we have seen, Kim Philby was told that Hess had seen Anthony Eden and Lord Beaverbrook within days of his arrival, but we have found no hard evidence for this. Certainly Simon and Beaverbrook visited Hess under direct orders from Churchill, and there are official transcripts of their conversations (which were secretly recorded). But in both cases some parts are missing. It is possible that even the written record might have been doctored.

There is also an intriguing memo in the official files from one of Churchill's staff, J. M. Martin, to the Foreign Office, dated 18 May, reporting that a BBC technician had confirmed that it would be possible to wire the Cabinet Room or Churchill's office in the Cabinet War Rooms for sound, should Hess be interviewed there.[9] This shows at least that a meeting between the Prime Minister and Deputy Führer was being considered.

The reason for Beaverbrook's visit, on 9 September 1941, is clear enough. He was about to leave for meetings with Stalin in Moscow, and needed to see the Deputy beforehand because the Soviet dictator would be bound to ask about him. However, the reason for Lord Simon's earlier visit, on 9 June – a month after Hess's arrival – is more obscure. It seems to have been an attempt to draw more information out of him by pretending to take his peace offer seriously: after all, as Lord Chancellor, Simon had enough status to impress the Deputy Führer, but because he was not a member of the War Cabinet Churchill could always deny that either he or his cabinet had ever negotiated with Hess – technically, at least. From the outset Churchill obviously planned to make Hess believe that his proposals were being taken seriously. This strategy was suggested in Kirkpatrick's report of 15 May 1941,[10] and Cadogan's diary for 19 May records the Prime Minister's agreement to the plan that they should pretend to negotiate using Simon.[11] Further confirmation that Simon was being used in this way comes from a memo dated 20 May 1941 from Anthony Eden to Churchill:

> I saw Simon yesterday and I think he will be willing to undertake the task of which we spoke. He has asked for 24 hours to consider the matter. We are agreed that he should make it plain that the Government know of the interview but that it would be unwise for

him to indicate close collaboration with you and me – rather the reverse. Simon will be fully briefed before he goes to the interview and I propose to write him a letter saying that you and I would be glad if he would undertake this task.

All this will be kept most secret and only Cadogan and I in this office are aware of the project.[12]

If, as seems most likely, the meeting with Simon was a sham, it was carried out with great aplomb. He was accompanied by Ivone Kirkpatrick, who acted as interpreter, plus a small team of notetakers. For his part, Hess was allowed an assistant, an interned German named Kurt Maass. Although the word is carefully kept out of the official records, in Foley's reports Simon is referred to as the 'negotiator',[13] while the meeting itself is called a 'conference'.[14] Clearly, Hess was being led to believe that these were serious peace negotiations. (Indeed, the presence of Kirkpatrick, who had been an interpreter for Chamberlain in the 1938 Munich talks, would have encouraged Hess to believe his mission was being taken seriously.)

Tight security surrounded the visit. Simon and Kirkpatrick went under the guise of Drs Guthrie and Mackenzie, respectively – apparently for the benefit of the guards and staff at Mytchett Place. One of the guards records in his diary that he had accidentally discovered the real identity of Lord Simon by seeing it in the prisoner's papers,[15] so Hess knew who was coming to see him, although attempts were made to keep his guards in the dark. Most of the personnel were kept out of the way when the distinguished guests arrived so that they would not even catch a glimpse of them.

Hess told Simon – as he had Hamilton and Kirkpatrick – that Germany would, sooner or later, defeat Britain and outlined the reasons why: there would not be an invasion, but using the might of its U-boats and the Luftwaffe, the Nazis would blockade the British Isles and starve the country into submission. Hess repeated that Hitler had never wanted a war with Britain and saw no reason for it to continue. And he outlined the terms for a mutually beneficial settlement: Germany was to have a free hand in Europe, Britain in its empire; German colonies confiscated after the First World War were to be returned; the British would leave Iraq and make an armistice with Italy.[16] When Simon asked whether Hess had come with Hitler's knowledge, the Deputy replied in English, 'Without his

102

MOST SECRET   Translation.

Rudolf Hess.

Statement

As I have been asked to give my opinion on the eight point declaration of the President of the U.S.A. and the English Prime Minister, I make the following statement:

The basis for an understanding between Germany and England, which I gave to the English Government with the object of reaching a lasting peace was a very fair one.

The declaration under reference is a kind of answer. It mentions Nazi tyranny. It contains a demand for the disarmament of agressor nations, which according to Mr. Rosevelt (sic) and Mr. Churchill are Germany and Italy.

As long as a declaration contains insults, I must refuse to make a statement even on a single point of such a declaration.

I welcome it from the point of view of its effect on the peoples concerned.

The German people have not forgotten the experiences which they made over a period of fifteen years when they faced, unarmed, their adversaries who retained their arms in breach of the Treaty of Versailles. Those experiences were weighed all the heavier as Germany was in those days not an

105

England, 21.8.41.
Rudolf Hess (Sgd.)

Document from PRO file WO 208/4471 showing that Hess was being asked for his views on important diplomatic developments – and therefore being misled about his true position – as late as August 1941.

knowledge,' then added, '*Absolut!*' ('Absolutely!'). He then spoiled
the effect slightly by laughing, although saying emphatically, 'This
which I have written down is what the Führer told me in several
conversations.' Simon moved on to ask him about how the Nazi
proposal would affect other countries such as Norway and Greece, to
which Hess replied stiffly: 'The Führer has not pronounced', which
obviously implies that he had 'pronounced' about the other matters
they had discussed.

Documents in the PRO make it clear that the meeting with Lord
Simon was presented to Hess as a formal negotiation. Moreover,
there is a copy of the transcript with corrections, annotations and
clarifications in Hess's hand bearing the date of November 1941 –
showing that, even then, Hess still believed that it was worthwhile.[17]

When Churchill read Lord Simon's report about his conversation with Hess he was quick to call the German proposals 'the
outpourings of a disordered mind',[18] glibly condemning the prisoner
to a lifelong reputation as a madman. Hess's statement about the
imminent U-boat blockade that would starve Britain into submission
might have been brushed aside by Churchill, but it was an accurate
summary of Britain's vulnerability at the time: annotations on the
document confirm that what Hess said was known to be true.
Although Churchill might not have wanted to hear the truth, it was
strangely perverse to deny the reality that Britain's Achilles' heel was
her need to import vital supplies by sea.

The mysterious internees

The treatment of the German witness to the Lord Simon conference, Kurt Maass, and his companion Dr Eduard Semelbauer shows
the lengths to which the British authorities went – and continue to
go – to preserve the secret of Hess's mission. As we have seen, Hess
asked for these two internees at his first meeting with Ivone
Kirkpatrick in Scotland. Semelbauer, a chemist, was born in Munich
and settled in Liverpool in the 1930s. Although not a member of the
Nazi Party, he was reported to be a 'wholehearted supporter of Hitler'
at his internment interview in November 1939.[19] Kurt Maass is
more interesting. Born in Hamburg in 1905, he had been a member
of the Nazi Party and Hess's Auslandorganisation since 1935. From
1926 he had lived in Liberia, West Africa, where he worked for a

German export firm and was a senior figure in the AO.[20] He was interned in Huyton Camp near Liverpool in December 1939, but curiously even the official report on him drawn up for the Foreign Office following Hess's request ends: 'We do not appear to have any information as to how he came to be interned in this country.'[21] Equally curiously, Sir Alexander Cadogan wrote in the margin of Kirkpatrick's report in which Hess requested the two internees: 'I believe Maass was lately released. If so, it looks as if he might to be [sic] put back.'[22] This shows that the civil service head of the Foreign Office was familiar with Maass's name on 19 May (he dated the margin note), and begs the question of why he believed that a senior AO member and Nazi had been released from internment.

Maass and Semelbauer were brought to an army camp at Ham Common, near Aldershot, in readiness to assist Hess at any meetings, although there is evidence that only Maass was used. Following that meeting both Germans were placed in solitary confinement at Ham Common pending, as one official memo ominously put it, a decision 'as to what their fate is ultimately to be'.[23] A week or so later it was agreed that the two men could be confined together, but with the injunction that they must not mention Hess in the hearing of their guards. (Their cells were bugged, but a report of 25 July notes with frustration that, because of the injunction, the two dropped their voices when discussing Hess and so could not be heard.[24]) They were refused contact with either the Red Cross or Swiss Legation, and were at first even deprived of letters sent through the Red Cross, although these were later allowed after passing through the censor.[25]

On 3 August 1941 Maass and Semelbauer wrote a petition to the authorities complaining about their treatment, and stating that they had been drawn into the Hess affair through no fault of their own.[26] Later that month Churchill decided that they should be returned to internment after signing an undertaking never to disclose anything of their part in the Hess story.[27] Significantly, Churchill's memo states that, as the Home Secretary (who was responsible for internees) had not been informed that they had been removed from internment, there was no reason for him to be told of their return – demonstrating that decisions concerning Hess were being taken by Churchill and Eden, not the Cabinet. But despite the Prime Minister's instructions, the records show that Maass and Semelbauer were still in isolation at Ham Common in February 1942. The last reference to them is a memo stating that it had been decided that they would be sent to a camp on the Isle of Man in which (in a no doubt euphemistic turn of phrase) 'non-returnable Nazis' were held.[28]

When we asked the International Committee of the Red Cross in Geneva to check their records for the two internees, a highly significant fact emerged. According to their records, Maass and Semelbauer were transferred just days before Hess's flight. On 7 May Semelbauer was moved from a camp at Lingfield in Surrey and the following day Maass from Huyton Camp: both being dispatched to Knapdale Camp at Lochgilphead in Scotland – about an hour's drive from Dungavel.[29] It is surely too much of a coincidence that the two Germans asked for by Hess should have been moved into the area just days before his arrival. The Red Cross records also show that Semelbauer was still in the camp at Ramsey, Isle of Man, in October 1945, but the last information on Maass is his transfer to that camp, which is undated. Nothing of their subsequent fate is recorded, and the testimony of these two vital witnesses (particularly that of Maass) has never emerged. What became of them is a mystery.

The peace document

During his research, Peter Padfield was introduced to a source who asked to remain anonymous, even refusing to allow Padfield to identify his job. From his own knowledge of his informant's credentials, and the inherent persuasiveness of the story, Padfield took his claims seriously.[30]

The source revealed that Hess had brought detailed written peace proposals with him. He knew about this because shortly after Hess's arrival he was asked to join a team of translators formed by Ivone Kirkpatrick to work on the document at the BBC headquarters in Portland Place, central London. The document was originally in both German and English, but apparently the government wanted to make its own translation. For security reasons, each member of the team was only given one section, although Padfield's source managed to see the whole document on one occasion. Kirkpatrick reported on the work to John Colville, Churchill's private secretary; he, as we have seen, was one of the few privy to the full Hess story from the very beginning.

Padfield's informant stressed that the document was taken very seriously. It was no vague list of demands or threats, but a detailed set of proposals intended to form the basis of a treaty between the two countries. It set out Germany's plans for eastward expansion and conflict with Russia and defined the respective spheres of influence of Germany and Britain. Although many of the proposals are by now familiar, there were others concerning areas other than the British Empire, such as the Suez Canal. Apparently, the document recognised that there were parts of the world where their respective interests could come into conflict, and made it clear that Hitler regarded the USSR as being within Germany's sphere of influence. This is particularly significant because it was an issue that had pre-occupied Hess's early questioners: both Kirkpatrick, during the first interviews in Scotland, and Simon, during the Mytchett Place 'conference' in June, wanted to know whether Hess considered that Russia was in Europe or Asia – whether Hitler and Hess thought that it came automatically within Germany's sphere of influence.

Padfield's source remembers one phrase in particular, which was used to describe the attitude that Britain was to adopt in the coming Russo-German war: it was 'benevolent neutrality' (*wohlwollende Neutralität*).[31] Significantly, this phrase also occurs in both André Guerber's story of the papers discovered in Berlin in 1945 and in the 1943 *American Mercury* article.

But what happened to the detailed peace proposals that Padfield's informant claims Hess had with him? It appears to have been a somewhat bulky document, and there were both English and German versions – not something that would have been easy to magic away in the pockets of a flying suit. Although it is suspicious that the inventory of Hess's belongings is still withheld, Daniel McBride makes no mention of such a bulky document either, nor is there so much as a passing reference to anything like it in any of the other accounts of the events of 10 May. We know that Hess took off with a briefcase containing documents, but as it presumably did not survive the crash and fire, it is unlikely to have contained the document in question. It is possible that the document had already been sent to Scotland – perhaps through the Red Cross – and was waiting for Hess to arrive and pick it up. On the other hand, it might have arrived later, after he had arrived safely: this scenario would shed some light on a cluster of three mysterious incidents that followed in the wake of Hess's arrival.

The first happened three days after he arrived, when a parachutist dropped down near a wood in the vicinity of London Colney in Hertfordshire, just north of London, early in the morning of 13 May.[32] Shortly afterwards, he was arrested (by sheer fluke) by a local constable and found to have £500, $1,000 in cash, a map of East Anglia and a compass on his person. Found to be a Sudeten Czech named Karel Richter, he was tried, convicted and sentenced to death as a spy, and duly hanged in Wandsworth Prison on 10 December 1941. The hangman later noted that of all the condemned he had dispatched, Richter put up the most ferocious fight.[33]

Richter himself never gave any reason for his arrival in Britain, but it is officially recorded that he had brought money to pay members of the German spy network. However, there is more than just the date to connect him with the Hess affair. Not only was Richter an Obersturmbannführer in the SS, but he was an adjutant to the Nazi Gauleiter of the Sudetenland, Konrad Henlein, who, before the German occupation, had been head of the Sudeten Deutsche Partei (the German Party of Sudetenland) which agitated for independence from Czechoslovakia. Henlein, an old friend of Karl Haushofer, was a Hess man, funded directly – 8 million crowns a year – under the Deputy Führer's personal authority.[34]

On 20 May 1941 – ten days after Hess's arrival – a Dornier 217 took off from the Luftwaffe base at Aalborg, Denmark. Astonishingly, in a move that had clearly been pre-arranged with the British, it flew unmolested to the RAF airfield at Lincoln, where the pilot, Heinrich Schmitt, handed over a package to a waiting RAF officer before returning to Aalborg.[35] Schmitt, later, in the war, presented the RAF with a prize possession when he defected to Britain in a Junkers Ju-88 bomber fitted with a new type of radar. However, when interviewed in the 1970s, Schmitt stated that the 1941 flight was actually an official Luftwaffe mission, adding, 'It was all part of the grey war that existed at the time. I wasn't the only German pilot to land, by arrangement, in Britain, and several British pilots made landings in Germany which were known to the people who mattered on our side. It was well known that Hitler was prepared to pay a high price to make peace with Britain, and the secret flights were only ended when we attacked Russia, and Britain and Russia became allies.'[36] Schmitt was not told what was in the package, but the timing suggests that it may well have been the peace document.

The third peculiar incident first came to light in 1979, when Colonel John McCowen related something that occurred in May 1941.[37] At that time he was a major on the staff of the commanding officer of No. 11 Fighter Group, Air Vice-Marshal Trafford Leigh Mallory. On the night of 27 May, Mallory summoned McCowen and told him that a message had been received from Germany for No. 11 Group[38] – which meant that it had not been intercepted but was *intended* for Mallory's group. The message advised of the landing of SS parachutists near Luton, Bedfordshire, under cover of an air raid. McCowen was ordered to move an anti-aircraft unit and searchlights into the area to intercept them, as, he was told, they were planning to assassinate Hess.

Shortly before 3 a.m. on 28 May the raid happened according to plan. Two men dressed in civilian clothes and carrying sidearms were dropped by parachute close to Luton Hoo and were duly arrested. Luton Hoo and Dungavel were marked on their map.[39] According to McCowen, they were subsequently executed as spies without trial.

Like Albert Heal's story, this is an extremely puzzling incident, but there is no obvious reason for McCowen to have made it up, and it is equally unlikely that he was mistaken. On the other hand, unlike the case of every other apprehended German spy, there is no record of the trial or execution of these men. Either the capture and execution of the two Nazis has been covered up with almost unique success – which begs the question of why – or they were never executed. We only know what McCowen was told later.

Perhaps the parachutists had arrived in Britain in a desperate attempt to discover the whereabouts of Rudolf Hess. But why should they choose to parachute in close to Luton Hoo? The Georgian mansion owned at that time by the family of businessman Sir Harold Wernher, Luton Hoo may well have been a focus for the peace group. Wernher was chairman of the British branch of Electrolux Limited, which was owned by Birger Dahlerus, and had been one of the organisers of the August 1939 peace conference with Göring. He also had close connections with both British and European royalty – being a good friend of Queen Mary – besides the great aristocratic houses (his granddaughter is the current Duchess of Westminster). Sir Harold was married to Lady Anastasia Torby, niece of the last Tsar of Russia, who was related to virtually every royal family in Europe. His status is underlined by the fact that Princess Elizabeth and Prince Philip spent their wedding night, in November 1947, at Luton Hoo. In May 1941, the house was the headquarters of Eastern Command – whose Commander-in-Chief was, as we have seen, replaced the day before Hess's arrival – although the Wernher family still occupied part of it.[40]

Maybe the parachutists were not attempting to find Hess at all but rather represented a further attempt to contact members of the British peace group at Luton Hoo – after all, thanks to Churchill's shroud of secrecy, Germany was still pretty much in the dark about what had happened to Hess. Once again, however, the British authorities foiled the plan.

Any of these events could have been the delivery of the document seen by Padfield's informant; such a document certainly seems to have existed. In any case, it is acknowledged that Hess himself gave a specific set of proposals to end the war between Britain and Germany. Whatever the terms – and leaving aside the question of whether they could, or even should, have been accepted – the important point is that Churchill took the unilateral decision to turn them down, without putting them to his Cabinet, let alone Parliament.

Churchill takes action

Undoubtedly, in the two months following Hess's arrival Churchill's political position strengthened enormously. From the concerted opposition he had faced at the beginning of May 1941, by July – although that opposition was not totally silenced – he felt secure enough to indulge in what Andrew Roberts describes as a 'Churchillian Night of the Long Knives' in which he purged his administration of those who did not support his policies, and replaced them with yes-men.[41] Roberts has linked Churchill's decision not to exploit Hess's capture for propaganda purposes with his fear that it might cause the pre-war peace group to re-emerge.[42] However, we believe that the evidence shows that the peace group had never gone away. But Hess was now under Churchill's control. He had foiled the peace group's plans for a negotiated settlement with Germany and its bid to oust him, and –with considerable skill and subtle gamesmanship – was to turn the situation still further to his own advantage.

First came the 'stick' approach, in which he used Hess as a weapon against his opponents, as demonstrated in his extraordinary performance in the House of Commons some ten months after Hess's arrival, when once again he was facing stiff opposition. This was the occasion when Churchill for the first time let slip some of the details of the Hess affair, and the context in which he did so was extremely telling. In January 1942, after returning from a conference with his new ally Roosevelt, Churchill had headed off his critics who were accusing him of selling Britain out to the United States by calling for another motion of confidence in himself and his government. While calling for the motion and imposing a three-line whip, he quite unexpectedly dropped Rudolf Hess into his statement, saying that he had come expecting to find an anti-Churchill faction that wanted to make peace with Hitler. Not only was this the first time it had been made public, but the subtext was clear: it was a warning to the peace group. Effectively Churchill was saying to them: 'I know all about you and the Hess plot, so let's do a deal. Vote in my favour now (and continue to back me) and you can stay where you are. Step out of line and you can expect no mercy.' He knew that, to certain prominent figures, the very name Rudolf Hess – coming from him in this context – would be perceived immediately as the threat it undoubtedly was.

When the Prime Minister announced the confidence vote, he also took care to point out that any suggestion that Parliament was not fully behind him would be 'flashed all over the world' and exploited for propaganda purposes by the enemy.[43] He was hinting heavily that even if MPs did not agree with his policies, they should restrain themselves when it came to the vote for the good of Britain. Even more significantly, he continued to play the Hess card for all it was worth to maintain his own position, once again implicitly threatening the peace party. Replying to a question from the left-wing MP Emmanuel Shinwell as to whether it would be a genuinely free vote (in which the MPs could vote according to their consciences), the Prime Minister said no, it was a matter for the whips. He went on:

We have also to remember foreigners' views of our country and its way of doing things. When Rudolf Hess flew over here some months ago he firmly believed that he had only to gain access to certain circles in this country in order for what he described as the Churchill clique to be thrown out of power and for a Government to be set up with which Hitler could negotiate a magnanimous peace . . . I can assure you that since I have been back in this country I have had anxious enquiries from a dozen Governments and reports of enemy propaganda in a score of countries all turning upon the point whether His Majesty's present Government is to be dismissed from power or not. This may seem silly to us, but in those mouths abroad it is hurtful and mischievous to our common interests and our common effort. I am not asking for any special personal favours in these circumstances, but I am sure the House would wish to make its position clear, and therefore I stand by the ancient constitutional parliamentary doctrine of free debate and faithful vote.

The members of the peace group were left in no doubt where they stood. On the other hand, Churchill took no reprisals against those involved in the Hess plan. Indeed, he gave key figures, such as Lord Beaverbrook, important roles in the aftermath of the flight. Both Hamilton and the Duke of Kent were promoted in July 1941 (to group captain and air commodore, respectively). Churchill also handed Hess over to the care of Sir Stewart Menzies.

But what was Hamilton up to in the days and weeks after Hess arrived? Denis C. Bateman[44] points out that he did not resume his post at RAF Turnhouse until 1 June 1941, while Hamilton's own account states that he was attached 'to the Air Ministry on special duties'[45] in this period. The Duke's diary in the Hamilton archives reveals that he spent the next two weeks flying around the country in a Hurricane. Tracing these journeys suggests he was making contact with members of the aristocracy who were implicated in the peace plan. Returning to London on 15 May with Kirkpatrick's report, he dined with his brother Nigel ('Geordie'), Kenneth Lindsay and an unknown associate, one 'W. W.'. The next day he had lunch with the King and stayed at Albury near Guildford in one of the Duke of Northumberland's properties. On 18 May he flew to the airfield at Old Sarum, Salisbury. His diary for that day records 'Leigh Mall.', which can only refer to a meeting with Air Marshal Sir

Trafford Leigh Mallory – who, we have seen, nine days later received a message from Germany informing him of the arrival of two SS men at Luton Hoo. Hamilton then dined with 'W' and 'B', probably – from the context – 'Winston' and 'Brendan' (Bracken). After staying at the Dorchester Hotel for two nights, he flew up to RAF Acklington, close to Alnwick, breaking his journey at Church Fenton near York, where his brother David was stationed, and at Woolsington, near Newcastle, where Lord Eustace Percy lived. He stayed at Lesbury, on the Duke of Northumberland's estate, for eight days, before returning to RAF Turnhouse.

It seems clear that Hamilton was flying around the country, contacting members of the peace group, presumably to brief them on the Hess situation. At this stage, this could only have been done with Churchill's full knowledge. It is likely that Hamilton was delivering a message on behalf of the Prime Minister, but was it a threat of the imminent implementation of Regulation 18b? Strangely enough, probably not. Churchill's strategy seems to have been not to confront his opponents head on, but rather to leave the threat of Regulation 18b hanging in the air while also trying to persuade them that he might be about to engage in serious peace negotiations with the Deputy Führer. So it was not just Hess who was being fooled into believing Churchill would play ball, but the peace group, too. And this gave the Prime Minister time to consider his next move. In effect, Churchill had 'turned' the Duke of Hamilton so swiftly and completely as to have made the XX Committee green with envy.

The Barbarossa connection

Churchill also used Hess to his advantage beyond the domestic situation. He exploited him to achieve one of his major aims, the all-important alliance with Stalin's Soviet Union, the way for which was paved by Hitler's Operation Barbarossa.

The accepted story has it that the flight and Barbarossa were not connected in any way – how could they be, if Hess knew nothing of the plans for Russia? Yet an objective reading of the facts reveals that the two events were intimately connected. Lord Beaverbrook stated unequivocally several times after the war that Hess had come to negotiate a peace with Britain specifically in order to allow Germany to attack the USSR.[46] He told Stalin as much during his visit to

Moscow in November 1941, when he presented the Soviet dictator with a copy of a document on the Russian situation written by Hess at Mytchett Place.[47] This view was also shared by Sir Stewart Menzies, head of MI6.[48] If anyone in Britain knew the whole truth about the Deputy's mission, it was Beaverbrook and Menzies. It is hard to escape the conclusion that the flight and Barbarossa were part of the same plan.

Many historians have argued that Hess knew nothing of Barbarossa because of his 'fall from grace': he was effectively an outsider in whom Hitler no longer confided. But the 'fall' never happened: not only did Hess represent Hitler himself on the six-man War Council that planned the whole of Germany's war effort, but two of the men closest to Hess – Alfred Rosenberg and Martin Bormann – were initiated into the top-secret plans for Barbarossa in at least early April.[49] As Bormann was Hess's deputy, it is unthinkable that Hess was not also aware of the plans.

As soon as Hess arrived in Britain, the Churchill government made it a priority to try to find out what he knew about Hitler's precise plans for the USSR because the opening of the second front would prove a lifeline to war-battered and increasingly desperate Britain. Ivone Kirkpatrick went to interview Hess in Scotland with this very much in mind, as did Lord Simon in Mytchett Place on 9 June. Kirkpatrick is said to have reported that Hess had denied that Hitler was about to launch an early attack on the Soviet Union, but he had admitted that Germany had 'certain demands' to make of Stalin which – if not settled by negotiation – would have to be settled by war.

The planning for Barbarossa involved a massive campaign of deception – replicated later in the war by the Allies in advance of D-Day – to conceal the build-up of troops for what was to be the greatest offensive in military history. Part of this colossal campaign of deception was, as we have seen, the alleged preparations for the invasion of Britain, Operation Sea Lion. Another strand of the plan – which had assumed a greater importance by the time of Hess's mission – was the planting of misinformation that appeared to show that Hitler intended to try to negotiate with the Russians before blasting his way into their homeland.[50] Incredibly, Stalin fell for this trick, which is why – despite many warnings – he was taken by surprise by Barbarossa.

An important question is whether, as some researchers believe, Hess was persuaded to give anything away to the British – specifically the date of the launch of Barbarossa? It seems highly unlikely, for several good reasons. What advantage would it give Hess? If Churchill knew for certain that the USSR was going to be attacked, surely he would be discouraged from making peace, rather than the opposite. But perhaps Churchill had no need of Hess's inside information: it seems that, based on deciphered German signals, he had personally second-guessed Hitler's intentions as early as March 1941, realising that the offensive had been intended for May but deferred until June.[51] As B-Tag approached, British intelligence sources firmed up on the German plans until they were confident that the offensive would begin on the weekend of 21–2 June. (The British Ambassador to Moscow, Sir Stafford Cripps, was giving 22 June as the most likely date as early as 24 April – six days before Hitler himself decided on it.[52]) If Hess had given anything away it would have served only to confirm what the British already knew, or at least strongly suspected – thanks not to a crystal ball but to Churchill's uncanny understanding of the way Hitler's mind worked. Both caught up in a sense of their own historic destiny, Churchill saw that 22 June had a certain powerful resonance for his opposite number: as well as being Nordic Midsummer's Day, it was on that day in 1812 that Napoleon attacked Russia.

David Irving has argued that the date of Barbarossa was leaked to the British and Americans in early June – by Hermann Göring through his Swedish go-between, Birger Dahlerus.[53] This is based on the fact that on 1 June, immediately after Hitler had briefed him on Barbarossa, Göring met with Dahlerus in Berlin: according to Irving, the Swede had then warned British and American diplomats of the impending attack. If true, this is astounding – why would Göring of all people have wanted to tip off the British, knowing that they would then warn Stalin? American historian Barton Whaley has been able to clarify the issue, demonstrating that what Göring gave Dahlerus was a list of the demands that would supposedly be given to Russia before military action was taken.[54] In other words, Dahlerus received misinformation. This was exactly the same line that Hess took when he was interviewed by Kirkpatrick, suggesting strongly that he and Göring were working to the same agenda.

Although Churchill was certain that the Germans planned to attack Russia in summer 1941, encouraging Hitler to believe that Hess's peace proposals were being taken seriously would likely ensure that the Führer went ahead with the attack. The fact that Hess had been captured and his mission made public knowledge threatened to make Hitler have second thoughts; after all, despite his disowning of Hess, the Soviets might be alerted to the danger that was awaiting them. Churchill desperately wanted the offensive to go ahead as soon as possible in order to take the heat off Britain. If Hitler was wavering, it would help him make up his mind if he really believed that Britain was taking the peace proposals seriously. Whether Hitler would have pressed ahead with Barbarossa no matter what the circumstances must remain an open question. Given his grim focus on his ambition to destroy Bolshevism and all Slavs with it, it seems unlikely that he would have been deterred from seeking his ultimate goal (although Barbarossa might have been delayed). But perhaps Churchill's cunning use of Hess clinched the matter.

However, there is one area in which there is no doubt that his flight had a profound effect.

The American game

The other major development on which Churchill's whole game plan depended was at least greater commitment to Britain's cause from the USA in the concrete form of more armaments and, ideally, its wholehearted entry into the war as an ally. From the outset, Britain had been dependent on a supply of military hardware and other wartime essentials from America. But if Britain was to secure further American assistance, there was one monumental obstacle to overcome first: the American people were resolutely isolationist. They failed to see why they should be involved in other people's problems and were still smarting from the loss of many of their young men in the First World War. Indeed, two years after Hitler's war began to rage in Europe – in October 1941 – a Gallup poll found that only 17 per cent of all Americans favoured going to war with Germany.[55] So pervasive was the isolationist mood that Congress had passed a series of restrictive measures, the Neutrality Acts, forbidding any form of trade whatsoever with any nation that was engaged in war. In 1937, however, on Roosevelt's initiative, this was amended to a ban on the supply of munitions only. So the moment that Britain declared war on Germany, the supply of American armaments ceased. Fortunately for the British war effort, Roosevelt again managed to push through changes that this time enabled America to supply munitions.

Matters came to a head in October 1940 when the Treasury reported to Churchill that within three months the country would have no more money to buy from America.[56] In response, Roosevelt then pushed through the Lend–Lease Bill, which was made law on 11 March 1941. This ensured that the USA would provide munitions and other supplies on credit – at a price. Britain had to agree to hand over $50 million of gold from South Africa, and sell one of its most successful American-based companies, American Viscose (a subsidiary of Courtaulds), to a consortium of bankers. They wasted no time in selling it on for a handsome profit.[57]

Many politicians were suspicious about the Americans' motives. Lord Beaverbrook let his frustration with the situation boil over in a memo to Churchill, on 20 February 1941, saying:

The contractors in the United States have immense armaments orders in hand for us. We cannot be expected to pay beyond our resources.

These American manufacturers have been led to believe that they will be paid by the American Government when the 'Lease and Lend' Bill is passed by Congress. That being so, the American Government has its own manufacturers to contend with. It is not possible for them to hide behind financial difficulties.

The argument which Lord Halifax put forward had, in one form or another come up in all our dealings with the United States.

We were told that if we agreed to the twelve-mile limit off the American coast, all would be well. We did agree. But all was not well.

We were told that if we stopped the export of drink from the Empire to the United States, there would be a wonderful improvement in our relations with America. There was not.

If we made peace with Ireland, we were to enjoy for ever and ever the favour of America. We did as we were told. But it brought us no comfort in Ireland and little credit in America.

If we only settled the War Debt, even at five cents in the dollar, we should have the complete approval of the United States. We settled, and earned ruin in England and abuse in America.

We were incited by the Americans to break the alliance with Japan. We did so. And look where it has taken us! The Japanese are our relentless enemies. And the Americans our relentless creditors.

Now we are told by Roosevelt and [Wendell] Willkie [Roosevelt's political opponent turned special envoy] that if we only stand up to Germany, all will be well. We are doing so. But we would stand up better if we knew there would be something left to provide sustenance for our people in the day of hardship.

If we give everything away, we gain little or no advantage over our present situation.

Stand up to the Democrats![58]

After Dunkirk, Churchill made a speech in which he said Britain would fight on 'until in God's good time, the New World, with all its power and might, steps forth to the rescue and the liberation of the Old'.[59] For 'God' read 'Roosevelt'.

By May 1941 Britain was floundering in her darkest hour with resources running dangerously low: the need for American support was more desperate than ever. In particular Churchill wanted the US Navy to provide an escort for the British convoys bringing supplies across the Atlantic, since German U-boats were exacting a terrible toll (as Hess never wasted an opportunity to point out to his captors). Not only would America's involvement help to make the way safer for the convoys, but if US ships were sunk it might increase the chances of the USA entering the war – just as the United States had almost joined the Allies in the First World War after the sinking of the *Lusitania in 1915*.

Churchill's desperation is revealed by a cable he sent to Roosevelt on 3 May 1941, just a week before Hess's arrival, in which he positively pleaded with the President to commit his country to Britain's aid:

Mr President, I am sure that you will not misunderstand me if I speak to you exactly what is in my mind. The one decisive counterweight I can see to balance the growing pessimism in Turkey, the Near East, and in Spain, would be if the United States were immediately to range herself with us as a belligerent power. [emphasis as in the original][60]

Perhaps it is Churchill's pride or patriotism that prevents him from admitting the 'growing pessimism' considerably nearer to home.

The reaction of the American industrial and financial circles to Hess's arrival was one of blank dismay. In Irving's words, Wall Street 'shivered'.[61] A significant proportion of American industry was geared up for the supply of armaments, tanks, ships, planes and other essential war *matériel* to Britain. If the war between Britain and Germany ended the effect on the American economy would be catastrophic. Industrialists were expressing their fears forcibly to Roosevelt, and British officials in America reported their sentiments to London, ensuring that Churchill was fully aware of them. Dated 19 June, one official cable read as follows:

> The cessation of all news of the whereabouts of Hess, the decision of the Prime Minister to make no public statement, the secrecy of [US Ambassador] Winant's visit to Washington, the temporary suspension of air-raiding by both sides and the private visit of Kirkpatrick to Ireland[62] have combined in the public mind to create out of the Hess case a series of steps towards a negotiated peace.
>
> The most serious result has been the introduction into the minds of some industrialists the doubts of the advisability of vast plant expansion lest this rumoured peace negotiation prove a reality.[63]

The same cable refers to the 'feeling of apprehension and uncertainty' caused by the possibility that peace was about to be made.

We have seen that Roosevelt was scheduled to make an important speech on 14 May – the pre-publicity for which gave rise to speculation about an imminent Act of Union between Britain and the USA. However, on 12 May – two days after Hess's arrival – Roosevelt cancelled the speech. An examination of the events of the war around that time reveals nothing that had substantially changed the picture or would in any way have accounted for a major change of heart . . . except that Hess had arrived. The *New York Times* reported that the cancellation of the speech was directly related to Hess's arrival in Britain, because Roosevelt needed time to consider what change, if any, this would mean in the direction of the war.[64]

Two days after, Roosevelt cabled Churchill to ask him if Hess was talking and, if so, what he was saying, particularly about America.[65] Churchill instructed the Foreign Office to prepare a summary of the 'conversational part' of Kirkpatrick's interviews with the Deputy, which Churchill then used as the basis for his reply three days later. Churchill stressed that Hess showed 'no ordinary signs of insanity' – which is obviously intended to counter the German announcements and to imply that Hess should be taken seriously. He reported that:

Impression created by Hess was that he had made up his mind that Germany must win the war but saw it would last a long time and involve much loss of life and destruction. He seemed to feel that if he could persuade people in this country that there was the basis for a settlement that might bring the war to an end and avert unnecessary suffering.

This told Roosevelt that Hess offered a choice between an end to the war or a struggle that could go on for several more years. Of course, the latter would be the preferred option of American industry.

Churchill then developed the idea that a peace settlement might be achieved despite his personal opposition: 'If he is to be believed he expected to contact members of a "peace movement" in England whom he would help to oust the present Government.' Although Churchill laughs this off in his cable, he knew that Roosevelt was aware that the peace movement was a reality – he had been told as much by his officials in London. In December 1940 the US Military Attaché had reported to the President that the City was 'ready for appeasement at any time'.[67] Now, with Hess's arrival, this 'appeasement' seemed – at least as matters were depicted by Churchill – to be a real possibility. The clear implication is that if he were ousted, the next government might not be nearly so pro-American.

Churchill makes much of what Hess said about the U-boat 'blockade' of the British Isles: 'U-boat war with air co-operation would be carried on till all supplies to these islands are cut off. Even if these islands capitulated and Empire continued to fight blockade of Britain would continue even if that meant that the last inhabitant of Britain died of starvation.' This reinforces Churchill's contention that it was imperative that the US Navy help defend the British convoys.

Of Hess's statements about America, Churchill adroitly only reports that he had made 'some rather disparaging remarks about your country and the degree of assistance that you will be able to furnish us'. Hess, it will be remembered, had told Kirkpatrick that

America did not want Britain to make peace with Germany because it was in America's interests for the war to continue, and warned that the USA wanted to 'inherit' the British Empire, whereas Germany wanted Britain to keep it.[68]

The day before receiving Churchill's cable, Roosevelt gave a press conference at which he stated that the USA had fought many 'undeclared wars' when its interests had been threatened – a clear hint that another such 'undeclared war' was about to be undertaken against Germany.[69] The President finally made his rescheduled speech on 27 May. Earlier in the day he had cabled Churchill: 'I hope you will like the speech as it goes further than I thought it was possible to go even two weeks ago and I would like to hope that it will receive general approval from the fairly large element which has been confused by details and allow them to see the simple facts.'[70]

Roosevelt's speech marked a watershed in America's support for Britain and opposition to Germany, committing his country unequivocally to both moral and material support of Britain. His first major initiative was to declare an 'unlimited national emergency' which gave him full powers – short of declaring war, which only Congress can sanction. However, it did enable him to put the armed forces on a war footing, which he did immediately.[71]

To overcome the American public's opposition to closer involvement in the European war, Roosevelt argued (taking a line that would become a favourite with his successors) that if America did not help in the war in Europe, its own territory would eventually be threatened:

> Our national policy today is this. First, we will actively resist, wherever possible and with all our resources, all attempts by Hitler to extend Nazi domination to the Western hemisphere or to threaten it. We will actively resist every attempt to gain control of the seas. We will insist on the vital importance of keeping Hitlerism from any point in the world which it could use, and would use, as a base for attack against the Americas.

And then he made a dramatic leap in American policy: For no apparent reason, other than the threat of peace breaking out in Europe, he gave in to several of Churchill's hitherto consistently refused demands:

From the viewpoint of strict military and naval necessity we will give
every possible assistance to Britain. Our patrols are now helping to
ensure delivery of needed supplies to Britain and all additional measures necessary to deliver the goods will be taken.

The delivery of needed supplies to Britain is imperative. This can
be done. It must be done. It will be done.

Unsurprisingly, many in America regarded Roosevelt's speech as a
'virtual declaration of war' on Germany. The *New York Times* wrote:
'Roosevelt made it absolutely plain that he proposes to wage war
against Germany, Italy, and Japan if he deems it necessary.'[72]

This momentous *volte face* can only have been due to the arrival
of the Deputy Führer in Britain. Nothing else had happened, mili-
tarily or politically, to cause Roosevelt to cancel his planned speech
and begin work on his historic announcement. The next day the
President sent another cable to Churchill, announcing his approval
of the shipping of 75,000 tons of freight to North Africa.[73] This
included 200 tanks, 490,000 rounds of ammunition for Howitzers,
700 trucks and huge quantities of heavy ammunition and other military equipment. Churchill replied:

We are uplifted and fortified by your memorable declaration and by
the far-reaching executive measures involved in the state of emergency you have proclaimed. Pray accept, Mr President, my heartfelt
thanks. It was very kind of you to let me know beforehand of the
great advance you found it possible to make.[74]

Roosevelt's speech – one of the greatest in his career – managed to
swing the support of the American public behind the British war
effort. It cleared the way for military involvement in the future, and
increased the supply of military hardware to Britain. In December
1941, with the Japanese attack on Pearl Harbor, Churchill finally
had what he wanted: the triple alliance between Britain, Russia and
America was complete.

The second phoney war

Many have argued that it was no coincidence that Hess's flight happened on the last night of the Blitz on London. As well as the last it

was also the heaviest the British capital was to suffer throughout the war: 1,436 people were killed and some 12,000 made homeless.[75] The next day one-third of the roads in central London were impassable and among many historic landmarks the Houses of Parliament were hit and the Commons debating chamber – the central symbol of British democracy – was destroyed. Historian Martin Gilbert summed up the impact on public morale of this single raid: 'Londoners were apprehensive that morning, as they had not been since the previous December.'[76]

It is interesting to note that American war correspondents based in London, such as Walter Lippmann, bluntly declared that the Battle of Britain ended on 10 May 1941, not in October of the previous year.[77] Vincent Sheean, writing in 1943, described the period of April to June 1941 as marking 'the lowest ebb in British spirit . . . There seemed nothing for it but . . . to hang on like grim death, hoping for some event to change the state of the world . . .'[78] After a series of bludgeoning raids on London, with the most terrifying on 10 May, it seemed as if the hell would go on for ever. 'But', as Sheean wrote, 'there were no more: May 10 was the end, the end of a great epic. There is still time for the Germans to strike at London of course, but when and if they do all the conditions will have altered and the results cannot be the same.'[79] Like many others, Sheean was puzzled by the sudden cessation of the Blitz on London: there seemed no reason for the Nazis to choose to abandon a course of action that was successfully flattening the British capital and sapping its citizens' morale.

Although there were a few raids on other cities – and even they ceased for ever six days later – the sudden silence over London was very odd. Many at the time saw a connection between this phenomenon and Hess's arrival. As James Murphy wrote in July 1941: 'The fact that Hess's melodramatic appearance in Scotland was timed to coincide with the mass raid on London is another example of the Nazi technique in using dramatic surprise as an instrument of psychological aggression.'[80]

While a great deal of attention has been paid to the connection between the end of the London Blitz and Hess's arrival, far less has been accorded to the changes in the British bombing of Germany. We have seen that one of the reasons for the American industrialists' fear that a peace settlement was about to be made was 'the temporary suspension of air-raiding by both sides' following Hess's arrival. The RAF significantly reduced the number of raids on Germany in the early summer of 1941.[81] Although strategic targets and factories were still being bombed, the attacks on civilian targets in Germany stopped, not to be resumed until May 1942, and even then in a limited way until 1943. What is particularly significant is that less than a year earlier Churchill had declared that once Germany turned east, the RAF would inflict cataclysmic air raids on the enemy. But now that Germany was about to turn east, Churchill did the opposite. This curious reversal caused Sir Charles Portal, Chief of the Air Staff, to write a memorandum to Churchill complaining 'Since the Fall of France the bombing offensive had been a fundamental principle of our strategy, and had been fully backed by the Prime Minister.'[82] What, he asked, had changed? Churchill responded testily that he had changed his mind, and now believed that 'It is very disputable whether bombing by itself will be a decisive factor in the present war'.[83] Another RAF leader who was surprised and angry about Churchill's change of heart was Air Chief Marshal Sir Arthur 'Bomber' Harris, who, when asked by an American counterpart in June 1943 about the effects of bombing Germany, replied sarcastically, 'I don't know. Why don't we try it some time?'[84] As the leading British correspondent Douglas Reed wrote in 1943: 'The long delay in bombing Germany is already chief among the causes of the undue prolongation of the war.'[85]

The change in Britain's bombing policy led us to consider whether this was also in some way connected with Hess. The idea came from a comment made to us by a senior army figure who had a great deal of knowledge of the Hess affair. He told us that Hess's arrival had brought about a 'virtual armistice'. An examination of what Britain did in the following year reveals that although his phrase is something of an exaggeration, the term 'second phoney war' does not seem totally inappropriate. In Europe the whole theatre of war had shifted to the east, where the titanic struggle between Hitler's Germany and Stalin's Russia made other fronts of the Second World War seem mere skirmishes by comparison. Although Britain was face-to-face with the Germans in North Africa, she was involved in no other major military action against Germany at that time. After December 1941 Britain's main war effort shifted to the Far East and the war with Japan.

Coming so soon after Hess's arrival and the cessation of the Blitz, this state of affairs might seem more than coincidental. We would go further, and suggest that it was the result of an arrangement between Churchill and Hitler. This is not to suggest that they communicated directly, or through any kind of official channel. They had their go-betweens: the Hamilton group in Britain and the Haushofer group in Germany. In Britain the Duke of Hamilton seems to have been co-ordinating the peace group – and convincing them that Churchill was running with their agenda – under the Prime Minister's instructions in the weeks following Hess's arrival; in Germany Albrecht Haushofer was ordered to brief Hitler in person. While Hess's arrival had failed to bring about the peace he sought, it had succeeded in effecting a kind of unofficial truce that was to last in Western Europe until the beginning of 1943, when, with the German campaign floundering after the siege of Stalingrad, it became apparent which way the conflict was going.

From Churchill's reactions in the aftermath of Hess's arrival it seems that he was trying to give the impression that the Deputy Führer's mission was not yet dead in the water, and that Hitler also entertained the idea that it could be resurrected. On the very day that Barbarossa began – 22 June 1941 – Goebbels recorded an extraordinarily significant conversation with Hitler: 'The Führer has high hopes of the peace party in England. Otherwise, he claims, the Hess affair would not have been so systematically killed by silence.'[86] This is indisputable evidence that Hitler believed that the peace group was still active and influential in Britain, and implicitly that Hess's mission had not yet failed. The fact that he was giving voice to such sentiments on the very day that German forces began their offensive against Russia shows that he was confident that there would be no distraction from Britain. Something from the British side must have encouraged Hitler in this belief, perhaps a tacit gesture such as the scaling down of RAF raids on Germany.

Also interesting in this regard is the fact that when members of Hess's staff were arrested by the Gestapo, Martin Bormann pressed for them to be put on trial, but on 27 July Hitler decided there would be no trials until he 'has reached a decision on the Rudolf Hess case'.[87] Even at that late date he was still clearly keeping his options open.

It was a tricky situation. When Hitler attacked Russia, and the

Soviets joined the Allies, Churchill's government walked a diplomatic tightrope. Stalin wanted Britain to open a second front against Germany, taking some of the pressure off the Russian defenders. He was deeply suspicious that Churchill would not do this, fearing that – at any moment – Britain would either pull out of the war, concluding a compromise peace with Hitler, or would even form an alliance with Germany against him. (Churchill's own pre-war antipathy towards Bolshevism was hardly a secret.) The Prime Minister was therefore keen to reassure Stalin of Britain's commitment to the alliance, while protesting that she was in no position to open a second front. (That, at least, was true.) It seems that, in the aftermath of Hess's arrival, Churchill played a cunning game by fostering Hitler's belief that his Deputy's proposals were being seriously considered. The reduction of British air raids on Germany might have been, like the German cessation of the Blitz, a gesture of 'good faith'. This ensured that the Führer felt able to concentrate on the USSR in the belief that Britain would no longer be a problem.

The importance for Britain of the German–Soviet conflict was summed up in 1942 by Victor Cazalet MP, who worked alongside General Sikorski and accompanied him on visits to the USSR:

> Russia is winning the war for themselves and incidentally for us. The Germans are being killed in vast numbers. If, after victory, we continue to live in England in even a relatively free condition it will be because millions of so-called Communists have died to help us defeat the Germans. No-one has yet suggested how we should ever have won the war until Russia had been attacked by Germany.[88]

It is no exaggeration to say that, until the spring of 1943, Churchill let the Russians fight the European war on Britain's behalf while he waited to see which way that titanic struggle went.

It is interesting that the Soviet judges at Nuremberg argued that Hess's mission had been 'undertaken in the hope of facilitating the realization of aggression against the Soviet Union by *temporarily restraining* England from fighting [our italics]'.[89] This seems to be referring not to Hess's aims – which the Russians always maintained were to *end* conclusively the war with Britain – but to what actually happened as a result of his mission.

The Mytchett Oracle

Although documentary evidence for Churchill's exploitation of the Hess affair is hard to come by, it is possible to extrapolate some of the details.

Once Hess was in the hands of the authorities Churchill acted quickly to ensure that he and he alone controlled access to him. Only he and Menzies saw the reports from Foley's team and the transcripts of Hess's 'conversations' with the MI6 men. Only then would he make the decision that extracts could be circulated to other departments – as in the case of the 'Admiralty document'. Other heads of state, such as Roosevelt and Stalin, were entirely dependent on him for information about the Deputy Führer and what he was saying about his reasons for the flight and about the German war effort. And, of course, if – as seems to be the case – Hess had come to see a highly influential peace group, then that, too, put Churchill in a unique position at home. Those who had 'conspired' with Hess were, if the Prime Minister so pronounced, liable to imprisonment under Regulation 18b. He was in a supreme position to blackmail his opponents.

Historians acknowledge that, despite his popularity with the people, Churchill was in an extremely weak position politically. He failed to enjoy the confidence of the King, the House of Lords or much of the Conservative Party. At that stage in the war, even MPs who agreed with his policies tended to question his judgement and decision-making. Yet somehow he managed to cling on to power long enough for the tide to turn in his favour. It seems that Churchill owed much of his continuing power to his control of Hess: what Hess said while at Mytchett Place was irrelevant, it was what Churchill *said* he was saying that was important. We have already seen how he used this tactic while convincing Roosevelt to throw more resources behind Britain. He did the same with Stalin – letting it be known that Hess had come to make peace with Britain as a prelude to Hitler's attack on Russia, but simultaneously making the Soviet leader consider that such a peace could still be a possibility. And he let both leaders know that there was a faction in Britain that wanted to negotiate for peace – making it imperative that they supported his leadership. It was a very clever game in which the essential moves always seemed to revolve around Rudolf Hess.

Churchill turned Hess into the 'Mytchett Oracle', whose utterances – at least during those months which brought the USSR and the USA into the war – the Prime Minister could invoke as it pleased him. After all, who could check whether he was telling the truth? The concept of the Mytchett oracle explains some of the puzzles that arose in the wake of Hess's arrival. For example, we know it is very unlikely that Hess gave away the date – or other specific details – of Operation Barbarossa. Yet some researchers – most notably John Costello – believe he did, and produce a certain amount of circumstantial evidence to back this up. In late October/early November 1941 both American and Russian agents in London reported that Hess had talked. Reasonably enough, Costello concluded that this must have been the case.[90] However, not only did this information reach the American and Soviet governments after the event, but both reports can be traced back to the same source – none other than Major Desmond Morton, Churchill's personal intelligence adviser. The American report, dated 5 November from Captain Raymond E. Lee, does not identify his source, specifically requesting his chiefs in Washington not to distribute it too widely in order to protect his identity; but Lee's diary reveals it to be Morton.[91] The Russian NKVD report, from Colonel Moravec, also declines to identify its source, but admits the information was given during a lunch on 26 October. Costello points out that the wording of Moravec's report is so similar to that of Lee that the information must have come from the same source, and might even have been dropped during the same lunch.[92] But would Churchill's personal intelligence adviser really be so indiscreet? Almost certainly his apparent gaffe was a deliberate tactic, intended to convince Washington and Moscow that reliable information had come from Hess. Indeed, the American Ambassador to London, John G. Winant, remarked after reading Lee's report that he had wondered how Churchill had known of the German attack in advance, but now realised he must have got it from Hess.[93] But it had not originated with Hess: Churchill's information had come from German signals that had been intercepted and deciphered by British intelligence – and in any case, he had known about Barbarossa before Hess had even arrived, a fact that he carefully omitted to tell his allies.

Between May and July 1941 Churchill had achieved the seemingly impossible. He had changed Britain's fortunes from a no-win situation into one in which she had, at last, the possibility of winning and, provided the Russians were not swiftly defeated, was now unlikely to lose. Much of this arose out of the Prime Minister's highly devious exploitation of Hess's mission, which far from being the amusing sideshow to which it is usually relegated, can now be seen as one of the pivotal events in the entire Second World War.

The Canadian commentator Pierre van Paassen had come to similar conclusions within a few months of Hess's arrival in Britain. He writes in his *That Day Alone* (published in late 1941) that Churchill had pretended to negotiate with Hess in order to bring about the end of the Blitz, to ensure that Hitler attacked the Soviet Union and to strengthen ties with the USA.[94] Hess's arrival in Britain was nothing short of a windfall for the beleaguered Prime Minister.

Churchill's only public pronouncement of his own feelings on the Hess affair came in the third volume of his *The Second World War*: 'Reflecting upon the whole of this story, I am glad not to be responsible for the way in which Hess has been and is being treated . . . He came to us of his own free will, and, so without authority, had something of the quality of an envoy.'[95] On the other hand – apart from this bizarre denial of responsibility – it seems as if the very name of Hess had some intrinsically humorous connotation for him. In January 1942, when he was in America, he was depressed because matters were not going smoothly for him. His physician, Lord Moran, attempted to cheer him and recalled: 'To get him in a sunnier mood, I asked him about Hess, whereupon the PM, throwing off his ill humour, launched out into a description of Hess's motives.'[96] Clearly Hess's motives had become an in-joke among the Churchill circle.

CHAPTER TEN

Sanity and Insanity

Leaving aside the reports of Hess's changes of mood and inconsistent rationality, any truly objective view of his behaviour during the months following his capture makes it obvious that not only was he remarkably self-possessed, but he appeared to have been working to a plan. In the transcripts of his meetings with Lords Simon and Beaverbrook, his lucidity and sharp intelligence come over very strongly. The same is true of the letters he wrote from Mytchett Place (although he waited for a month before writing his first letter home, possibly because he believed he would shortly be going back to Germany). Judging solely from his letters and conversations with visitors, there seems no doubt that he was sane and alert. He was even capable of running rings around his captors when it suited him. Major Shephard, who commanded the guard that took Hess to London, reported that he was 'cunning, shrewd and self-centred'.[1]

We have seen that Hess had concocted in advance a 'dummy' flight plan to cover his use of the German radio beacon at Kalundborg in Denmark, and to account for the extra hour that it took him to get to Scotland. Sticking to his story – according to Major Shephard – he whiled away some of the journey southwards by giving the details of his flight, although at the time his captor thought he was simply boasting about his navigational skills.

Then, while at Mytchett Place, on 8 August 1941, Hess drew the route on an atlas. (Because of the impression given by the authorities, this map is generally thought to have been drawn much later, while

Hess was in Abergavenny. However, in the documents supplied by Alexander, there is a photograph of the original, which Hess had clearly dated '8.8.41'. As we will see, the claim that the map was drawn later was not a simple error but part of a radical cover-up.) The map – together with a description of the flight in one of Hess's letters to his son– has been accepted as accurate ever since. However, we now know that this was disinformation cunningly thought out by Hess before his mission. In this, at least, he remained sharp enough to outwit his captors. He was also trying to pull the wool over their eyes about the German attack on the Soviet Union, keeping to the line that Hitler would attempt to negotiate first.

Lord Beaverbrook wrote to Hess on 1 September, reminding him about their last meeting in the Reichschancellory in Berlin, and suggesting they have 'some further conversations'. With immense irony, he concludes: 'So if this is convenient to you, perhaps you could tell me where and when you would like the meeting to take place.'[2] (In the circumstances, they were unlikely to have met at the Savoy Grill.) Intriguingly, a transcript of the secretly recorded conversation is among the Beaverbrook Papers in the House of Lords Record Office, where it is listed as 'No. 98', implying there were at least another ninety-seven such transcripts of earlier conversations.[3] In this report – in which Beaverbrook appears under the pseudonym of 'Dr Livingstone', while Hess is 'Jonathan' – Beaverbrook's main purpose seems to have been to collect a lengthy document that Hess had prepared about the Russian situation. As neither of them mentions this in the letters they exchanged in order to arrange the visit, they must have had another means of communication.

At 'Dr Livingstone' and 'Jonathan's' meeting, Beaverbrook opened by telling Hess how much he was against the war, and Hess replied, 'I know it.' The Deputy then says he has been asking to see the Duke of Hamilton, only to be told that the Duke would never receive permission. He calls Hamilton 'the only man who is, so to speak, a friend of mine, even though I don't know him very well'. (Even this challenges Hamilton's position, which was that they had never met.) He informed Beaverbrook that since 'jumping down' (the stairwell) he has been allowed newspapers and a wireless, which he was previously refused. At one point he tells Beaverbrook that he is teetotal – perhaps a minor point at the time, but one that was to assume a greater significance later. He also speaks with knowledge of the build-up of Soviet armaments, and has clearly been following the course of the war against Russia, expressing the belief that the war will make Bolshevism even stronger, even if Russia itself is beaten.

Hess refers to a two- or three-page 'protocol' that he prepared for Lord Simon, which apparently discussed the reasons why the war started and his reasons for coming. This document has never emerged in the public domain. However, we are in no doubt what Hess thought of fighting the British, as can be seen from the following exchange:

DR. L: You know my views on the Germans.
J: You have the best men and we have the best men.
DR. L: Certainly.
J: And one kill other, and I think for nothing.

Beaverbrook collected the 'memorandum' written by Hess, and a few weeks later handed a copy to Stalin – basically in an attempt to allay the Soviet leader's suspicions by saying, yes, Hess did come to make peace so that Hitler could concentrate on you, but we have refused his offer.

For a 'memorandum' it was rather comprehensive, being a thirty-two-page document entitled 'Germany–England from the viewpoint of war against the Soviet Union', of which a carbon copy exists, together with a (particularly bad) translation, in the Beaverbrook Papers in the House of Lords Record Office.[4] Hess had carefully written in German 'Handed to Lord Beaverbrook 9.9.41' on the top right-hand corner. He begins by setting out Germany's position on the war with Britain. (Some minor corrections have been made to the punctuation):

> Germany, for her part, wishes a 'reasonable' peace. She is ready to conclude this without victory over England, that is on the basis of an understanding with England.
>
> I believe it can be taken for certain that the Axis-partner Italy has the same desire.
>
> Both states are ready to forgo a final victory in the interests of a lasting peace for Europe. They wish to spare the belligerents on all sides further sacrifices, and to make possible the early task of reconstruction.

> The question which England must put to herself is:
>
> Is the distinction between what England on her side, and the Axis on their sides, understand as [being] a reasonable peace, so far one from the other as to justify the continuation of the war by all means possible by England to secure a victory?

This tortuous question manages to penetrate to the very heart of the Hess mission, effectively putting Britain on the spot. Should Britain's leaders have seriously considered his proposals, rather than refusing even to think about them? Hess goes on to describe the destruction and loss of life that will inevitably follow. He says he is convinced that Germany will eventually triumph, setting out his reasons in considerable detail, including Germany's ability to defend the existing fronts and her acquisition of new sources of raw materials from the occupied territories. He emphasises – basing his arguments on figures published by the British government – that Britain could not hope to sustain the current rate at which ships are being lost. He repeats that the U-boat war will be intensified and reiterates his warning that the devastating air raids will only increase, using new and even more terrible weapons. He continues:

> I openly admit that the anticipation of this, which would involve real frightful conditions here, has recently strengthened the decision I took to dare the flight to England. We National Socialists deplore not only the unnecessary bloodshed of the German people, but also that of the English. My arrival represents an attempt to prevent it from going any further.

After issuing these warnings and developing his theme for several closely argued pages, Hess then devotes a section to what the end result would be, even if Britain should win the war. In view of what did happen, his assessment is remarkably astute. Concluding that 'a victory for England would be a victory for Bolshevism', he points out that Russia has huge resources – of land, people and raw materials. He anticipates that the USSR will attempt to spread Communism throughout the world, bringing it into conflict with the British Empire, especially as the people of the poorer countries were attracted by the Communist message. He also points out that Communism will increasingly influence the working class in Britain.

The only major outcome that Hess fails to predict is the effect of the post-war American presence in Europe and the subsequent descent of an Iron Curtain. He believed that the USSR would conquer the rest of Europe, if not through military might then through its ideology, arguing that the USSR posed a far greater long-term threat than did Germany to Britain and her empire. Hess also delivered another home truth: 'It must not be forgotten that the longer the war lasts, the more will the balance of power between England and America move in favour of the latter.'

In Section IV of his document, Hess outlines the conditions on which Germany would be willing to make peace:

> The only important condition – besides the return of her colonies – which Germany puts forward is a genuine understanding between the Axis and Great Britain that would eliminate all causes of friction.
>
> Germany thereby wishes to eliminate by all means all causes of future war between the participating states.

The main points of Hess's terms are by now familiar: Britain must agree the respective spheres of influence with Germany, must return the German colonies lost in the First World War, and both governments must compensate those on the opposing side who had suffered 'loss of life, health or possession' (pointing out that this would cost a fraction of what was already being spent on making war), and a similar peace should be made with Italy. These are not remotely the ramblings of a delusional madman. On the contrary, Hess marshals his arguments intelligently, producing detailed facts and figures. He quotes from a strategic study by the British Commander Grenfell, Admiralty statistics and the opinions of American experts on Britain's naval position. Clearly Hess and his intelligence network had done a great deal of homework for his mission. But although still maintaining that Hitler knew nothing about it, he explicitly states that he is speaking on behalf of Germany, repeatedly referring to the conditions that his country would find acceptable. He states: 'Germany's conditions are known to me through innumerable conversations with the Führer, and often emphasised by him', to which he added the footnote: 'The contents [of the peace conditions], but not their formulating, come from the Führer. The points were formulated through me.'

From the moment of his arrival at Mytchett Place, the standard account has it that Hess's state of mind was deteriorating badly. And yet, the records in which Hess's own voice is heard – such as the transcripts of the Beaverbrook interview – give a very different impression. With Beaverbrook he discusses the developing situation in the Soviet Union, von Ribbentrop's unpopularity in Britain before the war and much else besides – even correcting the other's mistakes: when the press baron says that the British Expeditionary Force numbered some 500,000 men, Hess points out immediately that in fact there were nearer 300,000 (which is correct). He even cracks the occasional joke – telling Beaverbrook that when he heard the British Ministry of Information had suffered a direct hit by the Luftwaffe, he told Göring that he shouldn't be bombing such a good ally.

The sanity question

The impression Hess gives in these discussions is that of a lucid and rational man, in sharp contrast to the image portrayed, for example, in Brigadier J. R. Rees's 1947 book of a confused, disordered and delusional mind. The idea of Hess as a madman has come to taint all subsequent investigations into his story – but is it the true picture? Because of the numerous contradictions and discrepancies in the available material, we need to go back over his behaviour from his arrival in Britain onwards and cast a completely new eye over it.

Immediately after he arrived in Scotland, nobody seems to have noticed anything odd about his behaviour. Presumably the first doubts were engendered by the German announcements about Hess having suffered from hallucinations. Churchill seemed to seize – perhaps gratefully – on this, asking those who had seen Hess in Scotland for their impressions of his mental state. The commander of the guard detail that took Hess to London, Major Shephard, reported: 'At times I have been doubtful of his mental stability and I have formed the opinion that he is controlled in some degree by some form of mental influence.'[5] However, the only evidence he offers is that, although Hess was relaxed and open in casual conversation, if asked about anything deeper, 'he immediately averts his gaze and his eyes take on a strange and distant look, and he is then very cautious in his replies'.[6] In the circumstances, perhaps it is not surprising that he guarded his tongue. We know that he was with-holding information – about the exact plans for Barbarossa and much else besides – so he would hardly be likely to speak freely on serious matters. The only peculiar point is that Shephard expected him to do so. Then, immediately, there appears to be a contradic-tion: Lieutenant-Colonel Gibson Graham, the Royal Army Medical Corps doctor who looked after Hess at Drymen Military Hospital, said in his first report: 'He looked well, and while guarded in his conversation, did not strike me as being mentally of unsound mind.'[7]

Presumably in order to limit the number of people who had con-tact with Hess, Graham was ordered to accompany him to London and then on to Mytchett Place, where he was initially in charge of the prisoner's health. In a later report, he said Hess was: 'Quite sane, certainly not a drug-taker, a little concerned about his health and rather faddy about his diet, quite ready to chat . . . even about the origins of the war.'[8]

Interestingly, Churchill himself told Roosevelt four days after Hess's arrival that he was 'perfectly sane', but later in the war the British government admitted to Stalin that they were keeping Hess's mental deterioration a secret, because otherwise they would have to repatriate him.[9] Of course, Hess could have arrived sane and then rapidly deteriorated, but that would raise disturbing questions about whether his treatment at the hands of the British actually contra-vened the terms of the Geneva and Hague Conventions.

In the first few days at Mytchett Place, however, Lieutenant-Colonel Graham began to be concerned about his patient's behaviour. He wrote in his final report: 'He showed marked hypochondriacal, paranoid tendencies, apprehension and delusions of persecution.'[10] Of course, some might think that being impris-oned alone in a country with which you were at war might be enough to make a man feel apprehensive and persecuted. However, Hess did seem to exhibit classic signs of paranoia, claiming that his captors were trying to poison him and swapping his plates with those of his guards (meals were taken communally). He sometimes insisted that others taste his food or drink before he began to eat, and also began to secrete samples of food and medicine in his quarters, which he would then press on visitors with the request that they have them analysed for him.

Hess also complained about the noise. He said he was being subjected to almost constant sirens and the noise of motorcycles from outside, and the banging of doors inside. At least he was not deluded about this: Mytchett Place was situated next to a Military Police motorcycle training school and a machine-gun firing range, and the continual racket got on the nerves of others at Camp Z as well.

The situation was complicated by the involvement of Colonel John Rawlings Rees, the Royal Army Medical Corps' chief psychiatric consultant who was brought in to assess the prisoner's mental competence on 30 May. (Rees, from London's Tavistock Clinic, had been an army consultant since 1938. He would eventually become director of the World Federation of Mental Health.) Hess told him he was depressed and had difficulty sleeping, and complained about not being allowed any news and about being locked up, 'which he evidently feels are unseemly for a man who has "come with a flag of truce" and who is "of flag rank"'.[11] Rees reported:

> I think this suspicious tendency is pathological and not entirely to be explained by his unusual circumstances. He showed what was to me an extraordinary lack of insight and failure to realise his position. He also seemed to have no obvious appreciation of the impossible nature of his self-imposed task. He twice said to me 'the King of Britain would never let these things happen', and he was clearly surprised that the Duke of Hamilton had not forthwith arranged for him to talk to the King and that he could not see the Duke of Hamilton and Mr Kirkpatrick whenever he wished. Though he did not say so to me, the implication was that he was in the hands of the 'war-mongers'.[12]

Rees bases his diagnosis on Hess's 'failure to grasp his position' – implying that, at least in this respect, his hold on reality was weak. But did Rees himself know what Hess's true position was? He only knew the official line: for him there was no peace party, so Hess's continuing belief in it was obviously a sign of his delusional state.

The Deputy was clearly confused by the mixed signals he was receiving from his captors: on the one hand, he was given the impression that he was being taken seriously, as can be seen from the detailed conversations of the 22 May transcript and the later talks with Lord Simon; on the other hand, he found himself under lock and key and denied access to news of the outside world. Worse, it seems clear that he had not been informed of his status as a prisoner of war, so as he had no idea of his position, the fact that he failed to appreciate it can hardly be taken as evidence of delusion.

Rees also took Hess's belief that there was a realistic chance that he would be taken to see the King as a sign of instability, but once again it was Rees's personal understanding of the political situation that led him to those conclusions, which were – as we know – based on faulty assumptions. All the evidence points to Hess's expectations about being taken to Hamilton, Kirkpatrick and even the King as being quite reasonable; it was Rees who was ignorant of the true situation.

Rees concluded:

> While this man is certainly not to-day insane in the sense that would make one consider certification, he is mentally sick. He is anxious and tense; he is of a somewhat paranoid type, i.e., he has suspicions for which there is no sufficient indication in his situation and which persist despite very full explanation . . . He is obviously an intelligent man, and the consequent impression is of a somewhat confused condition in which there are both hysterical and paranoid tendencies.[13]

Rees's final diagnosis was that Hess was 'a psychopathic personality of the schizophrenic type'.[14] There is no doubt that Hess was anxious, tense, confused and suspicious, but if his symptoms can reasonably be ascribed to his situation, then it is hard to agree with Rees's diagnosis.

Considering that the prisoner needed to be monitored by a psychiatrist, Menzies swiftly replaced Graham with one of Rees's team, Major Henry Dicks, who was bilingual in English and German (having been born of an English father and a German mother in Estonia in 1900) and had worked as an interpreter for British intelligence just after the First World War.[15] Hess was not told that Dicks was a psychiatrist, only that he was replacing Graham, who had to return to his army posting.

If Hess ever had hopes of getting through to Dicks, they must have been dashed immediately. As for Dicks' impression of the prisoner, he claims his 'first glimpse' convinced him that he was a 'typical schizophrenic', which can hardly be considered an objective scientific appraisal.[16] In his account of his time in charge of Hess (which is in Rees's book), he catalogues a series of episodes that, to him, confirm Rees's diagnosis. It has to be said that some of his criteria for deciding on the prisoner's mental state are at least as bizarre as Hess's reported behaviour. According to Dicks, Hess was quite clearly out of touch with reality because he had never played tennis and had no idea how to keep the score . . . and he did not know the names of common flowers in the garden.[17] Another example was that Hess 'stubbornly refused' to drink wine (provided by the Brigade of Guards' Officers' Mess).[18] Dicks seems to be linking teetotalism with mental instability. Hess was well known for not drinking: Major Donald of the ROC even claimed to have recognised him from this one fact. According to Dicks' highly personal criteria, a further sure sign of Hess's confused mental state was the fact that his underwear was not of a compatible standard with his high status, not to mention his unostentatious taste in watches.[19]

Dicks' complete lack of objectivity can be seen from his first impression of Rudolf Hess:

> He was gaunt, hollow-cheeked, pale and lined; whereas the full face produced an impression of baleful strength, the profile disclosed a receding forehead, exaggerated supra-orbital ridges covered by thick bushy eyebrows, deeply sunken eyes, irregular teeth which tended to be permanently bared over the lower lip in the manner of 'buck' teeth, a very weak chin and receding lower jaw. The ears were misshapen and placed too low in relation to the height of the eyes . . . The whole man produced the impression of a caged great ape, and 'oozed' hostility and suspicion.[20]

Dicks seems to have taken the precepts of the phrenologist, rather than the psychiatrist, to heart in his depiction of this caged Neanderthal. Perhaps all is explained by the fact that Dicks was Jewish,[21] which would explain the hostility on both sides. Whatever the reason, both patient and doctor had what appear to be insuperable problems in dealing with each other. Perhaps this was some kind of black joke on someone's part – Foley, Menzies or even Churchill himself – but if so it was pointless, effectively ensuring that the prisoner would never open up or divulge any useful information to his psychiatrist.

Particularly telling for Dicks was Hess's 'fixed idea' that

> his confinement as a prisoner was due to a narrow clique of war-mongers centred on Winston Churchill which kept him from establishing contact with a large movement for peace and friendship with Germany. This large movement, he thought, permeated the chivalrous Court circles around the throne, of which he had made the Duke of Hamilton the symbol.[22]

In other words, the fact that Hess believed a peace movement, even involving the Court, existed was proof that he had lost his grip on reality. Once again Hess had the advantage of his doctor.

Dicks gave as his reasons for agreeing with Rees's diagnosis:

1 The existence of a paranoid attitude towards his present surroundings only partly accounted for by reality, and of a long-standing hypochondriacal preoccupation with his own health and internal bodily processes for which he sought cranky rather than ordinary treatment.

2 The existence of a fixed division of his environment into evil persecuting forces and good and helpful forces, notable for the *a priori* nature of such beliefs.

3 The general fantastic background to his thinking.

4 The curious mixture of official haughtiness and anxiety to maintain status on the one hand with personal modesty and simplicity on the other hand.

5 The general impression of having his mind fixed on some far-away inner topics which was apt to produce a series of withdrawnness and lack of contact with reality, except in certain narrow segments of experience in which his inner and outer worlds fused.[23]

Dicks' apeman analogy was somewhat rattled when he gave his patient an intelligence test – and his results put him in the top 10 per cent of the population.[24] Even so, Dicks diagnosed that Hess was developing symptoms of paranoia, which had probably existed for some time but had been exacerbated by his current predicament. But Dicks did not get everything his own way. As late as 20 July, Colonel Scott recorded in his diary: 'one begins to wonder if Col. Rees & Major Dicks were right in their diagnosis that he is "permanently insane." '[25] Although this is admittedly not a medical opinion, Scott did see Hess every day and knew him well by then.

At the end of his talks with Lord Simon on 10 June, Hess asked to speak to him alone, and the rest of the negotiating team were dismissed. However, their exchange was recorded, and appears in the transcript. In English, Hess began: 'I have come here, you know, and I appealed to the gallantry of the King of England and the gallantry of the British people and I thought that the King and the Duke of Hamilton would take me under their protection.'[26] After saying that he had been well treated in Scotland and the Tower, he complained of the noises that kept him awake in his new location and his suspicion that his food was being drugged. Simon assured him that his claims were unfounded, and that such things simply weren't done in England. Hess – his English becoming increasingly fractured as he became more desperate – repeated that he believed that the new doctor, Dicks, was trying to drive him insane, perhaps even to suicide. Finally he handed Simon his photographs of Ilse and Wolf and implored him: 'Please save me for them. Save me for peace and for them.'

The most dramatic development was his suicide attempt, five days after Lord Simon's visit. In the days before he had written two suicide notes, one to Ilse and one to '*Mein Führer*'. The latter ended: 'I die in the conviction that my last mission, even if it ends in death, will somehow bear fruit. Perhaps my flight will bring, despite my death or indeed partly because of my death, peace and reconciliation with England.'[27] In the early hours of 16 June Dicks was woken to be informed that Hess was asking for him because he was unable to sleep. When the iron door to the 'cage' separating Hess's quarters from the rest of the house was opened and the guard stood aside to let Dicks pass, he got more than he bargained for: Hess stood at his bedroom door, dressed in his Luftwaffe uniform and 'The expression on his face was one of extreme despair, his eyes staring, his hair dishevelled,' Dicks reports.[28] Then Hess rushed towards him. Dicks thought he was about to be attacked, but at the last moment Hess swerved and leapt over the bannister. Although he later claimed he had tried to jump head first – and make a good job of it – he landed on his back, breaking his leg on a lower handrail as he fell. Rees came to examine the prisoner that evening, reporting that he found that Hess's 'delusional tendencies' had worsened, and had developed into 'true psychosis'.[29]

In this context it is interesting that while a prisoner in the Tower of London, Hess wrote a letter to the Duke of Hamilton, which was never delivered – perhaps understandably, given the circumstances.[30] In it he said that he had given Hitler his word that he would not commit suicide. Clearly the letter was an attempt to pre-empt any untimely accident befalling him while in British custody, or to prevent the British government having him killed and passing it off as suicide. But then we are told that he did try to kill himself.

Was Hess mad?

In trying to reach a conclusion about the true state of Hess's mental health, there are four possibilities that need to be taken into account:

1 That the reports of Hess's psychological condition are accurate. In that case, the British statement to Stalin about deliberately withholding the fact of his insanity in order to prevent his being repatriated is true. There is proof that Churchill issued an order to this effect. In the papers relating to Hess's psychological condition given to us by 'Alexander' is a letter from Rees to his Canadian colleague W. Clifford Scott, who had written a paper on Hess, dated 11 June 1958, which contains the following admissions:

> we were forbidden by the highest authority in this land at the time to regard him or speak of him as a psychiatric patient, because he might then be liable to repatriation . . .
>
> Churchill's comment in his book to the effect that of course Hess should have been treated as a patient . . . [ignored] his own written instructions that on no account was he to be in a mental hospital or to be treated as a patient.[31]

Although this supports the traditional view of Hess the madman, it is important to note that Churchill gave this instruction in advance, before knowing what Rees's diagnosis would be. In other words, Rees was told, 'Don't find him insane, whatever you do!'

With supreme irony, in the published account, the Geneva Convention is used – in a twisted way – to justify aspects of the British treatment of Hess. Dicks explains that Hess was never given any medical treatment because 'he was still technically a sane and responsible person, and that under the Geneva Convention and medical ethics it was difficult to force drugs or other treatment on an unwilling prisoner, especially one in his mental condition'.[32] This is extremely tortuous reasoning: Dicks claims he couldn't treat Hess because the Geneva Convention would not allow a mentally ill prisoner to be forcibly treated, but that same prisoner can't be repatriated under the Geneva Convention because it is officially denied he is insane . . .

2 **That Hess was completely sane**, but Churchill concocted the idea that he was mad as a cover story. In this case, the reports of Hess's bizarre behaviour are false. However, despite Dick's unproffessional reasoning, it is not possible to dismiss all such reports.

3 **That Hess could have been deliberately acting in bizarre ways in order to get himself repatriated**. This is supported by the letter he left for Hitler that, according to Ilse, ended with the suggestion that if he failed then the Führer should denounce him as mad. In this scenario, we have a Hess who was successfully duping the army psychiatrists.

4 **That Hess was, as he claimed, being drugged by his captors.** As we have seen, the British reports of his odd behaviour where food, drink and medicine were concerned say that he was suffering from the delusion that he was being poisoned. However, Hess himself never claimed he was being poisoned. He claimed he was being *drugged*. While in bed, on traction, after his suicide attempt, he produced an eleven-page 'Statement of Evidence and Protest', with two appendices for the British authorities.[33] Once again, it is an ordered and clear exposition of his complaints. On 23 October 1941 Hess sent a copy of this to Lord Beaverbrook, with the request that he pass on his complaints to the British government. Translations of the protest and Hess's covering letter are in the Beaverbrook Papers. Hess's first point is:

A short time after my arrival in my present quarters I was given in food and medicines a substance which had a strong effect on brain and nerves. The symptoms of this substance are, as far as I think I have been able to observe them, as follows:

A short time after taking it a curious feeling of warmth rising over the back of the neck to the head. In the head feelings similar to headache. Afterwards, over long periods of time an extraordinarily rapid tiring of the brain. After taking the substance the negative reaction to the initial feeling of well-being was so strong that I became convinced that I should become insane if further quantities were successfully administered to me. Although from that time onwards I fed only from common dishes, I was once careless and took another larger quantity, of which I was aware as soon as I had taken it.

I had to expect that the ensuing negative reaction would break my nerve completely. In view of my position in Germany, I considered I should not offer such a picture to foreigners. I decided, therefore, that I should quit this life voluntarily while I was still able to take a decision, should the same results appear.

My farewell letters show that I acted in complete calm and with deliberation. When, during the night, it became evident that results similar to the first were appearing, I jumped into the well of the house with the intention of ending my life. Although I jumped head first, I only broke my thigh and received no other injuries. The explanation is that my leg hit the lower banister.

During the following days, I was given further quantities of the unknown substance; I could clearly feel it. After the administration of the substance had been stopped the dangerous effect appeared in a milder form only. Each new quantity delayed the negative reaction and prolonged the feeling of well-being.

Usually Hess's suicide attempt is dismissed as either a consequence of his mental disturbance or as an attention-seeking ploy. Yet here he gives his own reason: he tried to kill himself because he feared he was being fed some kind of mind-destroying drug. Rather predictably, Dicks brushes this aside, preferring to ascribe Hess's suicide attempt to 'the expression of self-punishment urges at his own inadequacy in relation to the Messianic peace-bringer role which he had assumed'. Hess's stated reason is dismissed as 'an attempted rationalisation-projection of his own inner destructive tendencies, but in line with his persecutory delusions'.[34] Yet Hess had described a specific set of physical symptoms and emotional reactions after he had eaten, which Dicks does not even address. It is possible, of course, that they could have marked the onset of a serious mental condition that Hess incorrectly associated with his meals. But the physical symptoms, such as the rising warmth, do sound more like the effects of sodium pentathol, the classic 'truth drug', which was in use in 1941. Sodium pentathol is morphine based, and Hess's description sounds very like the symptoms of morphine ingestion. (We can speak from experience. One of us has experienced the use of sodium pentathol, and can vouch for the fact that this is a perfect description of the effect of this drug.)

Hess cites Lieutenant-Colonel Graham as a possible witness to the first administration of the drug: 'After the visit of an officer, who, I think, came from the War Office, he [Graham] was obviously perturbed. I think I was given a small amount of the substance the same evening.' As the visitors to Mytchett Place – of which there were few – were meticulously recorded, it is not difficult to work out who this 'officer' was: Sir Stewart Menzies, 'C' himself, who visited Camp Z on 25 May.[35] (However, the purpose of this visit, and what he did there, are not recorded.) It seems suspicious that Menzies' visit should coincide with the onset of the prisoner's symptoms, which led within a few days to his being placed in the charge of Major Dicks, who had – it must not be forgotten – been appointed by Menzies. Was this a ploy to replace Graham with Dicks in Mytchett Place? The former had ended up in charge of the prisoner's health by accident, simply because he had been at Drymen. In other words, between the team led by Foley and Dicks as the medical officer, MI6 now had complete control of the Deputy Führer. It seems that Dicks was part of the plot because, writing in his history of the Tavistock Clinic in 1970, he states that his secondment to Mytchett Place marked the beginning of a period – which continued after his involvement with Hess – during which he was taken into the 'hush-hush realm' of MI6.[36] So Dicks was not looking after Hess as an officer of the Royal Army Medical Corps, but as an officer of MI6.

Note that Hess complains in his protest that the symptoms of narcotic administration increased when Dicks took charge. He also complained of intimidatory tactics by Foley, Dicks and the other MI6 men. There were veiled threats: sometimes he was asked whether his family were provided for should he not return home. He also complains of deliberate sleep deprivation saying: 'In my present quarters and until my crash, my sleep was constantly disturbed by the officers on duty, who were under orders to flash a light in my face several times during the night.' This is tacitly admitted in the official reports. They say that – allegedly because of his mental state – he was frequently checked on in the night.[37] Hess also complains that he had not received any letters from relatives or friends in Germany since his arrival, and that (until his suicide attempt) he was not allowed access to any news – except bad news where Germany was concerned, such as the sinking of the *Bismarck* on 27 May 1941. Another complaint concerns an attempt by Dicks and a Lieutenant Atkinson-Clark of the Scots Guards to introduce a catheter into his penis (in order to help him urinate) without an anaesthetic while he was laid up with a broken leg. According to Hess, Atkinson-Clark told him that 'We are only treating you as the Gestapo treats people in Germany.'

If Hess was madly accusing his captors then he was remarkably selective. He was convinced that only certain people in the house were involved in a conspiracy against him, naming Dicks and Foley. He praises many others in the house for their kindness and helpfulness – hardly a typical paranoiac's trait. Significantly, he doubts whether Rees is one of this group, although he says he may be 'partly initiated'.

Hess ends: 'I hereby protest to the British Government against the treatment which I have received.' He adds that he should be treated as befits his position as a minister of the Reich and Reichstag Deputy: 'There can be no doubt that the British Government recognised my character as a Parliamentary. They sent me one of the highest dignitaries of the land [the Lord Chancellor] with instructions to listen to the proposals which caused me to come here.' Hess demands that he be treated as the unarmed peace envoy that he was, and petitions the government – who he is prepared to accept know nothing of his treatment – as follows:

- That an investigation is held into his claims, and that if found true those responsible should be punished.
- That there should be no repetition of these acts.
- That steps should be taken to reduce the external noise to which he is subjected, if necessary by being moved to another location.
- That the wire cage that seals off his quarters, and the barbed wire that prevents his access to the garden, be removed.
- In return, he undertakes that he will not try to escape, or make further suicide attempts.

The main petition concludes: 'Of course I shall not allow the German public to know of the treatment I have received. It would contradict the meaning of my flight to England which was undertaken to improve and not to worsen the relations between our two countries.'

The first of the two appendices deals with allegations of cruelty in German concentration camps, which will be discussed below. In the second appendix, Hess enlarges on his admission that the majority of the personnel at Mytchett Place treated him well, and that he believes that some of them – if allowed to testify freely – would support his claims. Only Dicks, Foley and Kendrick are, he believes, involved in drugging him and in other attempts to influence him.

Ironically, the very fact that Hess made this formal protest was deemed to be proof that he was mentally unsound. Sir Alexander Cadogan stressed this in a letter to Beaverbrook on 1 November 1941:

> I need hardly say that Hess's accusations that we have been deliberately maltreating him are without the slightest foundation. Though his condition varies from day to day, he is suffering from a marked form of paranoia and some of his delusions have become a complete obsession.[38]

The British diagnosis relies on his accusations being completely untrue, so the only alternative is paranoia. But we believe that Hess's version is correct for the following reasons: Hess's description of his symptoms is consistent with his having been given a drug – one that causes a 'high' followed by depression. Also, the way in which the whole episode has been distorted in the official accounts strongly suggests that the authorities were deliberately diverting attention from something: we see this in the way they chose to ignore Hess's stated reason for attempting to commit suicide, and his claims of being drugged were changed to claims of being 'poisoned', which carries a much more obviously paranoid connotation. Most important of all, however, is the testimony of Lord Beaverbrook – the man to whom Hess sent his protest. In 1962 he not only told James Leasor that he believed Hess to be sane, but claimed that it was he who suggested to Churchill, during a walk in the gardens outside the Houses of Parliament, that they invent the cover story that Hess was insane.[39] He had told Churchill that most people automatically assume that anyone in the care of a psychiatrist must be insane, so all they had to do was hand Hess over to one. Beaverbrook told Leasor that it was his idea to put the prisoner in the care of two psychiatrists (Rees and Dicks) because he was sure that no two psychiatrists could ever agree on a diagnosis! This was not as flippant as it sounded: the suggestion was made in all seriousness as it would give Churchill, at a later date, a choice of diagnoses to believe. Leasor told Ilse Hess that the idea for his book – the first about Hess since Rees's – originated with Beaverbrook who, in effect, commissioned Leasor to write it. And since there is no reason for Leasor to have lied, we can only assume that he was telling the truth.

Wolf Hess told us that Leasor told his mother that Beaverbrook had been so distressed at the way Hess had been treated in Britain – describing it as 'the darkest point in my life' – that he never spoke to the Duke of Hamilton again. (The rift between Beaverbrook and Hamilton is confirmed in biographies of the press baron, but other reasons for it are given.[40])

However, even if it is true that Beaverbrook initiated the psychiatrists cover story, there is no doubt that Hess was behaving strangely: either he had cracked up, or his claims of being drugged were not delusions, but reality. This is exactly what Beaverbrook said. In September 1943 Robert Bruce Lockhart of SOE's Political Intelligence Department recorded in his diary a conversation with Beaverbrook in which the latter told him that he believed Hess had been given drugs to make him talk.[41] However, only the three MI6 officers and Major Dicks were in on the plot at Mytchett Place itself, while, outside, Menzies, as head of MI6, would obviously have known about it, and it seems likely that Churchill would have at least given his approval. Rees was probably unaware of the situation, and on the few occasions that he examined Hess came to what he believed was a correct diagnosis – given that he gave no credence to Hess's claims of being drugged. It seems never to have occurred to him that the prisoner was simply telling the unvarnished and somewhat bleak truth.

The most obvious justification for feeding Hess a truth drug was to discover more about his mission or about Germany's war secrets. But there could have been another motive: sodium pentathol only works as a truth drug in small quantities. Used regularly, it dramatically increases suggestibility. Major Foley had written a report to Menzies proposing that they try to 'turn' Hess by playing on his hatred of brutality and cruelty: if he could be convinced that unjustified atrocities were being committed in Germany, his faith in Nazism might be undermined to the point where he would turn against it.[42] Foley would have known the basic concept of brainwashing: fanatics are always the easiest to convert; if they can believe totally in one system, then all that energy and devotion can be turned into an equally fanatical belief in exactly the opposite. The 'don't knows' of the world, the people who have no overwhelming beliefs, are the most difficult to brainwash because they have nothing to 'turn', no basic template of strong beliefs. Foley and Dicks continually impressed upon Hess the brutalities that were being carried out in Nazi concentration camps. Hess refers to being given 'reports of alleged witnesses' to the horrors and also a book by an Austrian describing the camps.[43]

In the first appendix to his protest, Hess dealt with this issue, promising to hold an investigation when he returned to Germany, but stating that the details he was given were one-sided, dwelling only on the Nazi horrors and ignoring the Bolsheviks' atrocities (for which he provides precise details from memory). He writes:

I shall not undertake this investigation – I wish to emphasise the point – because of the curious treatment I have received in England or because England desires it.

As British subjects are not concerned, I refuse England the right to deal with the question of the treatment of the prisoners in Germany.

Otherwise I have to ask for the same right for Germany. Germany would then like to make it her business to investigate the English treatment of the Irish in Ireland, of Indians in India, or Arabs in Palestine.

Then he quotes – presumably from memory – from J. A. Farrar's *England under Edward VII*, even citing the page number.

If, as someone told me, the closing of concentration camps in Germany is one of England's war aims, Germany would have to make one of her war aims a guarantee that England would never again create concentration camps for women and children, which she did a generation ago . . . during the Boer War. (During the Boer War 26,000 women and children died on account of conditions that prevailed in concentration camps. Germany has never sent women and children to concentration camps.)

This demonstrates not only that Hess's ability to marshal a logical argument using facts, figures and quotations was unimpaired, but that he was under systematic pressure from the MI6 team, who were clearly trying to convince him of the uniqueness of Nazi atrocities, as proposed earlier by Foley. If they were trying this preliminary brainwashing tactic while he was in a heightened state of suggestibility due to drugs, it would have stood a greater chance of success.

Last days at Mytchett Place

Major Dicks left Mytchett Place on 17 July, passing on the responsibility for Hess to Captain M. K. Johnston of the Royal Army Medical Corps, although the reason for this is unclear. Rees's explanation that it was no longer thought necessary to have a German-speaking psychiatrist in charge of the prisoner makes little sense. Two of the MI6 team were also withdrawn, Foley alone remaining. Perhaps they felt that – with the attack on the Soviet Union – Hess's usefulness was coming to an end.

The new man, Johnston, summed up his patient's state of mind, writing: 'He [Hess] was liable to long periods of moody self-absorption, and spent much time staring into the corner of his room, but refusing to discuss his thoughts. He is secretive and difficult to approach.'[44] Like Dicks, Johnston thought these signs were symptomatic of acute mental disturbance. He also noted that the prisoner spent most of his time writing, giving a lengthy document to one of the officers to pass on to his father, who was an MP. Johnston wrote: 'On translation the document was found to be the typical effusion of a paranoiac, with its persecutory delusions and bizarre ideas of poisoning and torture.'[45]

When Dicks told Hess that the German attack on the Soviet Union had begun, he had replied, 'So they have started after all.'[46] The course of the war, from which he was now so completely removed, was increasingly to occupy his thoughts. In the covering letter he sent to Beaverbrook with his protest on 23 October 1941, there is a noticeable tone of resignation and sadness about another development: Hitler had made a speech in which he made it clear, for the first time, that Germany would fight on until victorious. Hess wrote to Beaverbrook:

> That which I felt for some time would come has now happened.
>
> As I have heard through the German news service, the Führer – certainly in agreement with the Axis partners – has said publicly that the war will be fought to a clear victory.
>
> I know the Führer too well not to understand what that means. Just as tenaciously – in spite of negative experiences – as he held fast to the idea of an understanding over a period of years, just as tenaciously will he now maintain the new decision.
>
> It means a fight to the death.

After reiterating that he is certain of a German victory, he goes on:

> Nevertheless I am not happy about this development.
>
> I admit openly that until quite recently I had not given up hope that reason would come in England and that an understanding between the two peoples would be brought about.
>
> But the Führer could not do more than he has done, i.e. stretched out his hand over and over again. And I staked everything as far as I was personally concerned.
>
> It was not to be apparently.[47]

The disillusionment is palpable. Here Rudolf Hess is admitting finally that his mission had failed. His leg mended, he was allowed out of bed in early November 1941, but his mind was more burdened than ever. Then, in December, he suffered another blow when he heard that his father had died, but he did not give in to complete depression, still trying to get messages to those who might be able to help him. On 12 December, at his own request, he was visited by Walther Thurnheer, the Swiss Minister to Britain, and in his presence wrote a letter to the King which he asked Thurnheer to deliver to the Duke of Hamilton so that he could give it to George VI. Unfortunately, when Hamilton was approached he refused to take the letter, but Thurnheer honourably kept trying, finally handing it over to the King's private secretary.

A draft of a letter Hess wrote to the King emerged in 1981 in papers taken by one of his guards at Nuremberg, although it is not certain that it is the same letter that was delivered to George VI, since it is dated 13 November 1941. Reasonably supposing that this draft at least echoed the sentiments of the letter he gave to Thurneer, it is interesting to note what is said in it. Mostly it consists of complaints about his treatment, although he takes care to add: 'Today I still believe in the fairness ['fairness' is in English, although the rest is in German] of the English people. Therefore, I feel certain that the treatment I have suffered is not in accordance with their wishes. I have no doubt that only a few people are responsible for it.'[48]

While Hess stewed in Mytchett Place, Churchill and other British powers continued to weave plots around him. Soon he would be on the move again, although under circumstances he was unlikely even to have imagined, except perhaps in his darkest and most confused hours.

CHAPTER ELEVEN

From Decoy to Doppelgänger

On 25 June 1942 Hess was moved again. This time his home was Maindiff Court, just outside Abergavenny in Wales, where – officially at least – he was to remain until being taken back to Germany to stand trial at Nuremberg in October 1945. Before the war, Maindiff Court had been the admission hospital for the County mental hospital, but it was given over for the duration of the war to the treatment of wounded soldiers. There were no mental patients there when Hess arrived.

For some reason, one of the official specifications for Hess's new billet was that it should be a hospital 'where officers and Service personnel were actually undergoing treatment',[1] although why this stipulation was made is unknown. It certainly wasn't so that the prisoner could fraternise: once again, he was put in splendid isolation with a whole wing to himself, guarded by a detachment of thirty soldiers. This ring of steel, however, seemed curiously at odds with the relaxed – almost lax – air in which the prisoner now found himself. His life at Maindiff Court was very different from the tense and troubled time at Mytchett Place. Nevertheless, mysteries abound about the Maindiff Court period, even beginning with the journey there.

Hess was driven there in an army estate car, accompanied by Captain Johnston and another officer, but no escort.[2] However, there was no suggestion that the Deputy Führer was smuggled into a top-secret location: Maindiff Court's domestic staff actually lined up to witness his arrival.[3] Indeed, it seemed as if all the locals knew he was coming – and what was even more perplexing was the fact that officialdom did not seem remotely bothered about it.

Once in Abergavenny, Hess was under a considerably less stringent regime, being allowed out for walks and picnics in the countryside with his guards. Yet one thing had not changed: he was still in the charge of a psychiatrist, a Dr David Ellis Jones, although at first he hardly seems to have needed such attention. When Hess first arrived at Maindiff Court, it was reported that: 'His condition was such that the account given of his mental state at Mytchett was almost incredible.'[4] Perhaps he was just happy to be out of that repressive and intimidating regime. However, Rees reports that towards the end of September 1942 the paranoid behaviour returned, followed by the onset of hysterical amnesia.

There is something incongruous about the whole Maindiff Court episode. Even the reason for Hess's transfer there is by no means satisfactory. It might be assumed that he was taken to a low-security location because there was no need to tie up valuable resources in continuing to guard and monitor him. Of course, by the summer of 1942 the military situation had changed and there was no point in pretending that vital military secrets were still being squeezed out of him, although he could still come in useful if it became apparent that Britain was going to lose the war. However, the official reason for Hess's move is rather more bizarre. In May 1942 there was apparently real fear that – for all the tight security around Mytchett Place – Hess might be kidnapped by a group of Poles. On 28 May an official wrote that word had been received that certain Poles were planning to break into the camp, kidnap Hess and beat him up in revenge for Nazi atrocities in Poland.[5] Two days later, Major Loxley, Sir Alexander Cadogan's private secretary, wrote expressing his concern about this plot.[6] Matters take an even odder turn, however, when around the same time tensions rose about a 'mysterious, loitering man' on a bicycle who rode past the camp. It is reported that, when stopped and questioned, 'His explanation to [sic] various questions we regarded as unsatisfactory'.[7]

Are we to believe that the cream of the British Army at Aldershot would really be so nervous about a rumoured plot by a few Poles and the activities of one man on a bicycle? And was it really beyond the authorities to discover the cyclist's business? But if they were so worried about these threats while Hess was held in circumstances of the highest possible security, why was he then moved – without an escort or any form of guard – to a much less secure facility, where he was allowed to roam the countryside?

There are other anomalies. News of the celebrity prisoner's new location was leaked to the press: a major story appeared in the *Daily Mail* on 1 September 1943, headlined 'THE DAILY LIFE OF HESS IN PRISON CAMP'. It is said that one of the guards, who was subsequently court-martialled, had given the information to the press.[8] But it is frankly inconceivable that, given wartime censorship, it could have happened like that without the government's tacit approval at some level. (Rees states that this was the only time during Hess's wartime captivity that any information about him was leaked to the press.[9]) Surely the *Mail*'s staff would have known better than to risk official displeasure by going public with such a story in those hypersensitive times? And the fact that this appeared in a national newspaper is telling: the local Abergavenny newspaper, for example, made no mention of Hess until it announced his move to Nuremberg.[10]

Incredible though it may seem, it looks as if the British government wanted the public – and the Germans – to know or believe that Hess was at Maindiff Court. And, we were to discover, the publicity surrounding his sojourn in Wales was by no means the only mystery about that time.

We are told that Hess devised a method – simple but effective – of fooling his censors. Every time he wrote a letter to friends or family in Germany he submitted it to his captors, who then deleted passages where necessary. But the next time he wrote to the same person, he enclosed a copy of his last letter, which got past the censors because they assumed it was the edited version.[11] So Hess was able to get information about his location (among, one must suppose, other interesting details) back to Germany. Certainly, from descriptions of the local hills (and even the soil) Karl Haushofer was able to deduce that he was being held somewhere in the Abergavenny area.[12] It might be tempting to put this down to extraordinary incompetence on the part of Hess's jailers, were it not for the other signs that – for whatever reason – the British wanted his location to be known: they seemed to be drawing attention to Abergavenny, not keeping it secret.

There is something else. In Rees's book, there is a photograph of the page of the atlas on which Hess drew his supposed route from

Germany. The caption reads: 'Route and timing of his flight, drawn by Hess later while at Maindiff.' However, among the documents Alexander supplied was the map, on which, as mentioned earlier, Hess had written, in the top right-hand corner the date on which he had made the sketch: it is '8.8.41.' – when he was at Mytchett Place. But this had been carefully cropped off for Rees's book, and the caption stresses that it was done '*later . . . while at Maindiff*'. In other words, officialdom wanted the public to think of Hess at Maindiff at certain, perhaps critical, points in his captivity. But what possible reason could they have for this apparently pointless deception?

The Scottish rumour

On 4 May 1942, Reinhard Heydrich sent von Ribbentrop a report from one of his agents in Britain, which stated that Hess was being held in a villa in Scotland.[13] Although much of this report seems to be unlikely – it has Hess spending four days roaming freely around London with the agent (disguised with dark glasses) – the suggestion that the Deputy Führer was being held in Scotland is rather more plausible.

We were to discover that there are many stories about Hess being kept in a house near Fort William in the western Highlands. We interviewed Alec Kennedy, now living in East Lothian but brought up during the war in Fort William. He remembers his parents, who owned a newsagents in the main street, frequently talking about Rudolf Hess. They believed he was kept at an isolated address, Inverlair House, near the town, where he was interrogated by intelligence officers who lived opposite their shop in a building called Granite House. According to Kennedy's parents, these officers were driven to Inverlair House every day to continue their interrogation of the Deputy Führer. Professor Peter Waddell found other Fort William people who tell a very similar story, prompting him to construct a theory based on Hugh Thomas's 'doppelgänger' hypothesis.[14] Inverlair House was to surface again when Alexander told us that it was where Colonel Pilcher was held for a while. Perhaps Pilcher was being held there because of his role in the Hess affair. Or perhaps both Pilcher and Hess were kept there.

If Hess really was in Scotland, what was going on at Maindiff Court? If he was not there in the period between June 1942 and

October 1945, what about the carefully stage-managed 'public appearances': the drives in the country, the picnics and the walks?

There may be a simple, if apparently fantastic, explanation.

The disappearing scars

As we have seen, the military surgeon Dr Hugh Thomas based his theory that the prisoner in Spandau was not Rudolf Hess on the observation in 1973 that he did not bear the scars from Hess's First World War gunshot wound on either his chest or his back. Thomas also failed to find any signs of scars on his left hand and arm caused by shrapnel in June 1916. Although they usually receive less attention than the more dramatic gunshot wounds, they are just as important. As Dr Thomas stresses, scars might fade with time, but they never disappear.

Thomas claims that of the fifty-eight doctors who examined the prisoner after 1941, not one reported his gunshot wounds. Admittedly, many of the examinations were simply carried out to ascertain Hess's general health, so the reports would not necessarily list old scars, but some are still rather suspicious. Perhaps in some ways the most compelling is the extremely detailed description given by US Army medic Captain Ben Hurewitz, who gave the Deputy Führer a thorough check-up when he arrived at Nuremberg. Even though Hurewitz listed every wart and blemish on the prisoner's body, including a very faint half-inch-long scar on one of the fingers, and a quarter-inch papilloma (wart) on the chest, there is no mention of either the bullet wound or the 1916 shrapnel wounds.[15] The doctor also reported that the scalp was 'essentially normal', whereas Hess had a scar on the back of his head, together with a small bald patch, from one of the beer hall skirmishes in the 1920s. Understandably, Thomas was puzzled by these omissions, so he tracked down Hurewitz and questioned him. The doctor remained adamant: he had seen no such scars.[16]

After his tour of duty at the British Military Hospital in Berlin (BMH), Thomas took time to dig deeper into Hess's medical background. In the Berlin Document Centre, he unearthed a copy of Hess's medical file covering the period of his active service in the First World War, which stated he had been: 'Severely wounded in the storming of the Ungüreana (rifle bullet – left lung).'[17] The file reveals that Hess spent four months in various hospitals, followed by a further six weeks' convalescent leave. Because the brief report gives few details, especially on the exact location and size of the wounds, Thomas had to make several assumptions about the extent of the internal and external damage. For example, as the bullet would have been extremely unlikely to go through the chest and out of the back without hitting a rib, he assumed it had. And if it had, the bone would have splintered, not only causing serious damage internally, but making the exit wound larger than the entry wound. Thomas also assumed that because lung wounds almost always require some surgery – to clean them properly or draw fluid from the lung – there would be some degree of scarring from that, too. On this last point, Thomas had been led up a blind alley by Major Dicks' reporting, as quoted in Rees's book,[18] that Hess had been operated on by the renowned chest surgeon Ferdinand Sauerbruch, with whose work Thomas was familiar. (In the First World War Sauerbruch had pioneered a technique for treating gunshot wounds to the chest that often entailed the partial removal of a rib in order to drain the lung, a procedure that always left extensive scarring.) Why Dicks thought Sauerbruch was involved is unclear, because in the light of new evidence, it appears he was wrong.

The medical file Thomas had found in Berlin contained only a summary of a much more comprehensive version, which, according to the Berlin Document Centre, was 'missing'. However, in 1989 a BBC Scotland journalist, Roy McHardy, found a copy of it in the Bavarian State Archives in Munich. This sparked a great controversy, because it was claimed by some to discredit Thomas's doppelgänger theory. This file includes several descriptions of the wound to Hess's left lung by different doctors who examined him in the months immediately after he had been shot. One, from 12 December 1917 – the last examination before he was sent to convalesce – is typical: 'Three fingers above the left armpit, a pea-sized, bluish-coloured, non-reactive scar from an entry wound. On the back, at the height of the fourth dorsal [thoracic] vertebra, two fingers from the spine, a non-reactive exit gunshot wound the size of a cherry stone.'[19] In other words, the bullet went in about one and a half to two inches above Hess's left armpit, therefore near the collarbone, and came out about an inch from the spine at about the level of the middle of the shoulder blades. This is confirmed by a letter that Hess sent to his parents while in hospital recuperating, in which he describes the injury as 'a clean through-shot, in under the left shoulder, out at the back'.[20]

So, unfortunately for Thomas, the Munich file reveals that the scarring was less extensive than he had surmised, and that the wounds were in different places. The summary's terse phrase 'Rifle bullet – left lung' gave the impression that Hess had been shot more or less from straight in front, with the bullet entering the chest cleanly and exiting out of the back almost in a straight line. But the reports in the Munich file show a complication: apparently – presumably because Hess was either lying down or crouching, perhaps because he was taking aim with his rifle at the time – the bullet had entered just above the left armpit and travelled more or less horizontally through the body, exiting between the spine and the left shoulder blade. He had been very fortunate: the bullet managed to miss his spine, ribs and shoulder blade, limiting the damage. There was no spin on the bullet as there would have been if it had struck bone, and no complicating splinters of bone. The records also make it clear that no operation had been necessary.

Faced with this, Thomas's theory clearly requires closer examination. Perhaps because the scars were smaller and in a different place from where he thought them to be, had he simply not seen them? However, Thomas was adamant to us that he would have noticed them, on both the front and back.[21] Given his trained eye, it seems unlikely that he would miss even the smallest scar. And, of course, it is still true that none of the other detailed medical reports dating from between 1941 and 1987 mention them. The new evidence might cast doubt on some of Thomas's original deductions, but his initial suspicions remain. And strangely, the discovery of the Munich file does more to discredit his critics than it does Thomas himself.

When Thomas's book first appeared in 1979 it caused quite a stir, even prompting questions in the House of Commons and the West German Bundestag. Unsurprisingly, both governments were insistent that the prisoner in Spandau was the real Rudolf Hess, although they simply took the word of the British Military Hospital on the matter.

However, that was by no means the end of the doppelgänger theory. After Hess's death in 1987, Thomas found yet more evidence from the autopsy reports. Although there were two post-mortem

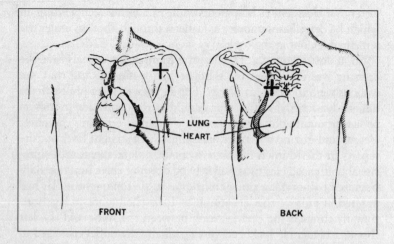

The position of the entry and exit wounds from Hess's First World War injury, according to the medical file discovered in Munich in 1989.

examinations – the official one conducted by Professor J. Malcolm Cameron (the doctor in the infamous Australian 'dingo baby' case, also known for his studies of the Turin Shroud) and the independent autopsy arranged by the Hess family – neither report mentioned bullet scars.[22] (When confronted with the puzzle of the missing scars by Thomas, Cameron confirmed he had not seen them.[23]) Yet both of them described other scars on the chest – two parallel scars close together, according to the independent autopsy, or a single one, according to Cameron – over the heart. Both Hurewitz and Thomas himself had also noted them: they were the result of a so-called suicide attempt in 1945, when Hess had skewered a fold of skin with a bread knife.[24] At least these scars prove that the man who died in Spandau was the same man who was in Maindiff Court in 1945, but that is all they prove.

It is difficult to argue against Thomas's conclusions: even the British government found it hard to discredit them. A senior Ministry of Defence source revealed – with amusement, stemming from interdepartmental rivalry – that when, after the death of Prisoner Number Seven, the Foreign Office set out to prove he was Rudolf Hess, they were unable to do so. But, stung into action by

Thomas's conclusions, they tried hard: in November 1988, the Foreign Office announced that there was: 'a fibrous, irregular, roughly circular old scar typical of an exit wound . . . in a posterior position on the left side of the chest'.[25] As this was over a year after Prisoner Number Seven's death and burial, the 'finding' seems a trifle suspicious. Why hadn't this information been provided when they had the body? And if this description is correct, why had no previous examination noted the scar?

To confuse matters further, in August 1988, when Thomas persuaded Dr David Owen to write to Foreign Secretary Sir Geoffrey Howe on the subject, the latter replied that the chest scar noted by Cameron had been identified as the bullet scar in question.[26] That was simply not correct: that scar, over the heart, was not in the place described in the Munich medical file. If Sir Geoffrey Howe was correct, Hess would have been shot in the heart and killed outright.

Clearly, Hess's medical records at the British Military Hospital where he had been treated for over twenty years did not record either the front or back scar. Either they were astonishingly inefficient, or the scars simply did not exist.

Strangely, while it should have been easy enough to debunk Thomas because the scars were in the wrong place to fit his theory, the British government failed to do so. The fact is that until the discovery of the Munich file in 1989 *nobody knew where the scars were*. Before then, the injury was known about only from vague descriptions in biographies of his having been shot 'through the lung'. Moreover, the prisoner in Spandau himself seemed to have been under the same misapprehension.

Intriguingly, in an interview with Wolf Rüdiger Hess he told us that after Thomas's book came out he asked the Spandau prisoner about the bullet wounds. He replied, 'I can't see the scars on my back, but I see the ones on my chest every day.'[27] Yet, according to the medical reports of Hess's First World War injuries, the scar in question was not on the chest: it is just above the armpit. It seems that not even 'Hess' himself knew where the scar was supposed to be.

When faced with an account of Thomas's doppelgänger hypothesis in his latter days, Hess's reaction was very interesting. He had struck up a relatively cordial relationship with Pastor Charles A. Gabel, whose book, *Conversations interdites avec Rudolf Hess*, based on his diary of day-to-day dealings with the prisoner between 1977

and 1986, otherwise tells us very little. Even the spiritual adviser was
not allowed to discuss any of the 'forbidden' subjects such as the war
and the flight, so the book concentrates on conversations they had
about such matters as current events. Its main interest is that Gabel
was at Spandau when Thomas's book was published, so he could
record Hess's reaction.

Despite the reporters camped at the prison gates and the feverish
speculation in the media, Gabel felt reluctant about bringing up the
subject of Thomas's doppelgänger theory with Hess. However, on
visiting the prison on 16 May 1979 – a couple of weeks after
Thomas's book had appeared – Gabel discovered that Hess had seen
an article about it in a newspaper that had somehow got past the
censors. (Normally anything connected with the war, Hitler or Hess
himself was cut out of all reading material before he received it.)
Having seen the piece, Hess asked the pastor what it was all about,
and Gabel – to his relief – finally felt able to fill him in on what he
knew about Thomas's theory:

> Rudolf Hess then laughed heartily in recounting to me that two
> English doctors, the director of the military hospital and a surgeon,
> had come to see him the day before and had examined the famous
> scars, which they had finally discovered, although they were not very
> visible! They had themselves spoken to Hess about Thomas's book,
> and had said that the doctor had been thrown out of the army [which
> is untrue]. I asked him how he had been wounded on the Romanian
> Front during the First World War. He recounted to me that a bullet
> had passed right through his chest, brushing the heart and exiting
> under the left shoulder blade. He had only very small external scars,
> and nearly nothing visible internally as a result.[28]

This may have convinced Gabel – and even Prisoner Number Seven
himself – but we know that *it is wrong*. Thanks to the medical file we
know that the bullet went in above the left armpit, coming out
between the shoulder blade and the spine and not 'brushing' the
heart. The real Rudolf Hess would have known this.

The last British governor of Spandau, Lieutenant-Colonel Tony le
Tissier, in his book *Farewell to Spandau* (1994), also stated that the
army doctors had found the 'missing' scars. (According to le Tissier,
the examination took place on 16 May – not on the 15th, as Hess

told Gabel – and it happened at the British Military Hospital, not in Spandau – easy mistakes for le Tissier to make as it happened before his time.)

However, we were able to obtain a copy of Spandau's medical log, which shows that the examination took place at the end of *April* 1979 – there are no entries for either 15 or 16 May. The entry, signed by Richard E. George (the only time his name appears in the log) reads:

> 2.5–3.0 cm. transverse scar & adjacent suture scars noted in 4 inter-costal space centred 6.5 cm to left of centre line . . . Note this wound lies immediately anterior to his heart.

This is clearly not the bullet wound, but the scar from the 1945 'suicide' attempt.

In trying to debunk Thomas's theory, le Tissier also makes a fundamental error, writing:

> Although there was no trace of a wound on any of the chest X-rays taken between 1965 and 1979, this was explained by the wound path being so close to the mid-line that any fibrosis present would have been obscured by the heart shadow.
>
> Following examination of Hess made at the BMH on 16 May 1979, the CO reported that all the entry and exit scars that Dr Thomas denied existed were there, just as expected.[29]

However, the file found in Munich in 1989 shows that these statements are mutually exclusive. The bullet did not pass near the heart, so its proximity is not the reason why the track fails to show up on the X-rays. And if the British Military Hospital examination had found the scars where the Munich file indicated them to be, le Tissier would have known this.

Wolf Rüdiger Hess, in a BBC radio interview in 1991, stated:

> My mother tried to approach this [the doppelgänger] story by asking my father whether he is still suffering from the shot in the lung and already when my mother started this line to approach the question she was interrupted [by the guards] and not allowed to continue with this item.[30]

An equally bizarre episode occurred in Maindiff Court in early 1944, when Hess was given sodium pentathol (according to the official records, this was the only time) as a treatment for his amnesia. It was this session that was to lead to the later confusion about whether Ferdinand Sauerbruch had operated on Hess. While under the influence of the drug, the patient was asked a series of questions about his past in order to stimulate his memory: Major Dicks took the lead, although Dr Ellis Jones, Dr Phillips and two RAMC officers were also present. Hess apparently failed to recognise the names Haushofer, Willi Messerschmitt – even Adolf Hitler. It is only towards the end of the session that he begins to respond:

JONES: Haushofer – he was your dear friend. And Sauerbruch, the great surgeon, who operated on your wound? Remember your wound?
PATIENT: (*no reply, but Phillips and Jones note a quick gleam of recollection at these two memory-jogging stimuli*)
JONES: But at least, who are you? And your wife?
PATIENT: (*confidently repeats his name*) 'And your wife? [Bizarrely, Hess repeated the question back to the doctors.]
He then sat up and asked for water and some food.[31]

Interestingly, Hess seems to react to the question about his First World War wound, but there is something very strange about it. The questioners ask the prisoner if he can remember having been operated on by Sauerbruch, but why they thought this surgeon had been involved is a mystery, since the medical file gives no indication either of his involvement or even of any operation. In any case, why would such an eminent surgeon have operated on just another casualty from the Romanian Front? (Sauerbruch became President von Hindenburg's personal surgeon, and even operated on Hitler, although he later joined the conservative opposition to the Nazis.[32])

The significance of this exchange is not so much about the involvement of Sauerbruch as what it reveals about the true identity of the prisoner. Majors Dicks and Ellis Jones, as well as the others present, were clearly under the impression that Hess bore the scars from major chest surgery. However, we now know that there were none from such an operation – only minor scarring from a clean through-shot on the upper chest and back. Surely the doctors who had looked after the prisoner for roughly three years knew that their patient had no operation scars. In which case, why did they ask him about the wound? Were they trying to catch him out or test him in some way?

Suspicion upon suspicion

According to Thomas, the physical marks of past injury were not the only evidence of a doppelgänger. He cites the odd behaviour of Hess and his treatment by the British government as being very suspicious from the outset: for example, within days of the Deputy Führer's arrival, it was expressly forbidden to take photographs of him. Bizarrely, the official reason given by Harold Nicolson, the parliamentary secretary to the Minister of Information – was that 'such ignominy should not be put on this fundamentally decent man'.[33] As the British were unlikely to depict him handcuffed, craven and sporting a black eye and bruises, why publishing new photographs of Rudolf Hess would be considered ignominious must remain a mystery. (Perhaps Hess should have called Nicolson as a character witness at Nuremberg.) But, remarkably, this injunction held. Not a single photograph of Rudolf Hess exists from the moment of his arrival in Scotland in 1941 until he was taken to Nuremberg in October 1945. Even the relatively lax regime at Maindiff Court upheld this rule.

There were other possible anomalies. According to Thomas, the teetotal and vegetarian Hess began to drink alcohol and eat meat on his arrival in Britain. Of course, stress can do odd things to people: even quite strict teetotallers and vegetarians can lapse when removed from their everyday routine, but did this happen to Hess? And although Thomas is wrong to claim that Hess was an absolute abstainer – he did drink occasionally, but always abstemiously – surely his alleged taste for alcohol at Maindiff Court is completely at odds with his refusal to take wine with his meals at Mytchett Place.[34]

As we have seen, the Hess at Nuremberg went through some very curious – and profoundly pitiable – mental contortions. He claimed to be suffering from amnesia (although at one point in the trial he also declared he had only been pretending) and that he could not recognise any of his former colleagues, even senior Nazis like Göring. He even claimed not to know Karl Haushofer, when the professor was taken to the prison specifically to jog his memory.[35] He also failed to recognise both of his former secretaries, one of whom broke down in tears.[36] If this were not really Hess, this amnesia act was certainly a very convenient way of avoiding making any slip-ups.

Thomas also points out that on several occasions Hess gave the wrong year of his birth: 1899 instead of 1894 (although he got the day and month right).[37] Then there is the fact that he refused to see his much-loved wife and son for an astonishing twenty-four years. In fact, he chose not to receive any visitors at all until 1965, and then only his lawyer, Dr Alfred Seidl (who had defended him at Nuremberg, but had not known him in pre-war Germany).

Thomas claims that he has a letter – which he is prevented from publishing because of the Official Secrets Act – from Lord Willingdon to the Canadian Prime Minister William Mackenzie King, discussing Hess and referring to 'the problem we have with the double'.[38]

The publicly available records on Hess contain two dental charts from the war years, one from Mytchett Place dated 30 September 1941 and the second from Maindiff Court, dated 21 April 1943.[39] As with all documents that should prove that it was the same man, these are frustratingly inconclusive. The fillings and bridgework are similar, though not identical, but two prominent features of the earlier chart are missing in 1943: a crown and a gold tooth. David McLean described the Deputy Führer's gold tooth on 10 May 1941, but – if the 1943 dental chart is to be believed – the tooth apparently grew back some time after September 1941. This could, of course, be due to sloppy record-keeping, but once again we find records that should demolish the doppelgänger theory do not. When we showed the charts to a leading British consultant dentist, Dr Paul Aronow, after studying them carefully he declared: 'Assuming the charts to be correct, the chart dated 21 April 1943 cannot be of the same person who had the work done in September 1941.' In 1987 David Irving attempted to check the 1941 chart against the Spandau prisoner's dental records, but was refused permission by the British Military Government in Berlin.[40]

Problems and confusions

Because of its sensational nature, Hugh Thomas's doppelgänger theory is difficult to swallow, even though his medical evidence

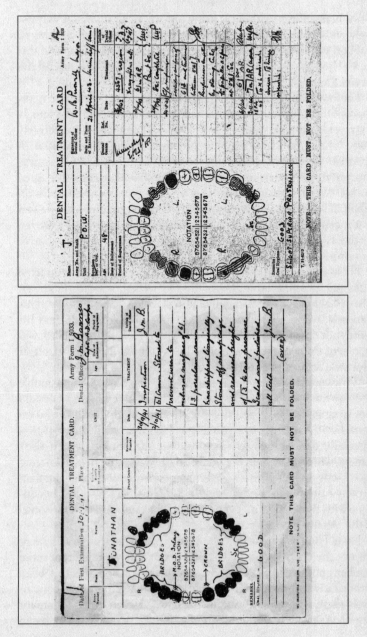

Hess's dental charts from September 1941 and April 1943.

seems compelling. Although many are sceptical, many are surprisingly persuaded, including the leading intelligence historian M. R. D. Foot, who wrote in *The Times:* 'Enormous difficulties attend this view [Thomas's hypothesis]; yet still more enormous ones attend the received version.'[41]

The most difficult part of the hypothesis to accept is the near-impossibility of persuading the double to accept Rudolf Hess's fate. It was a very long time from 1945 to 1987, and much of it was actively nasty (the American guards at Nuremberg and the Russians in Spandau were particularly unpleasant), while the rest of it was uncomfortable, lonely and desolate. Why should an impostor agree to this? What man would choose to grow old so unpleasantly on behalf of someone else? Yet even with this glaring problem, we feel that it cannot be denied that Thomas is on to something. However, his theory is much less plausible when it comes to providing a motive for using a double, and when the substitution was made.

Thomas's reconstruction is as follows: the real Hess took off from Augsburg, possibly intending to fly to Sweden, not Scotland, but other Nazi leaders – probably including Göring – had discovered his plan and, wanting to thwart his attempt to make peace, had his plane shot down. A second Me-110, with a lookalike on board, was then sent from Aalborg in Denmark, and it was this doppelgänger pilot who arrived in Scotland.

Why would Hess's enemies, having shot him down, want a double to complete the journey? What would that achieve? And how did they arrange for a doppelgänger with such piloting skills to be on stand-by at Aalborg? How could they have dealt with the logistics, especially details such as ensuring that the double carried Ilse's camera, which Hess borrowed only on the day of the flight? Thomas also claims that the British government soon realised that the man in their custody was not the real Rudolf Hess. So why did they continue with the deception, even allowing the double to be imprisoned in the Deputy Führer's name?

Then Thomas claims that the plane that took off from Augsburg was not the one that crashed at Eaglesham, having a different serial number and identification code. However, not only has this been authoritatively challenged by aviation experts,[42] but most conclusively there is also the testimony of Helmut Kaden, who is adamant that Hess's plane bore the identification code VJ OQ[43] (which can be seen on the section of fuselage displayed today in London's Imperial War Museum).

Some of the other points that Thomas raises are even easier to refute. For example, he asks why Hess brought only photographs with which to identify himself[44] – and no formal identification. But surely this was the sensible thing to do, considering he was supposed to be 'Alfred Horn' until he reached Dungavel. If he had fallen into the wrong hands – as, indeed, he *did* – a quick body search would soon have revealed his true identity.

Another piece of evidence that Thomas cites to support his theory that it was the double who arrived in Scotland is that, when the airman was X-rayed as part of the medical examination in Drymen Military Hospital within days of his arrival, the doctors found no internal damage to the left lung. However, they did report a 'small calcified area in the upper right zone'.[45] Damage to the upper part of the lung would match what we now know about the rifle-shot wound, but this, of course, should have affected the left lung, not the right. Could it be that the doctor at Drymen was simply looking at the X-ray the wrong way round? Unlikely though this may seem, the same report also mentions that the patient's heart was unusually small and centrally placed, which would make it easier to look at the X-ray from the wrong side.

Professor Waddell largely follows Thomas's theory, but, based on information that Hess was executed on Churchill's orders in Scotland in 1942, argues that the real Hess was kidnapped by SOE in Sweden and then taken to Scotland.[46] In order to prevent reprisals against British prisoners of war, an SOE agent impersonating Hess was made to parachute out over Scotland. Again, this seems unnecessarily convoluted and very unconvincing. And why would a British agent subsequently be willing to accept Hess's fate for the rest of his life?

Both theories assume that it was the double that landed at Eaglesham: but if the substitution was made *after* Hess's arrival in Britain, a great many puzzles and anomalies are immediately eliminated.

Only Peter Allen, author of *The Crown and the Swastika*, who accepts the medical aspects of Thomas's theory, has considered the possibility that the substitution happened in Britain.[47] Allen also cites Charles Fraser-Smith's testimony. Fraser-Smith was the model for 'Q' in the James Bond films (his group of technicians and other experts were known as the 'Q Force' and the special pieces of equipment they produced were 'Q Gadgets') who worked under the cover of a civil servant in the Clothing Department of the Ministry of Supply, but who was really responsible for meeting 'special orders' for the various intelligence departments. In his memoirs, Fraser-Smith recalled how he was called in by MI5 a few days after Hess's arrival and asked to assemble a team of textile and tailoring experts in order to make an exact copy of his uniform. The team had to work quickly, as Fraser-Smith was told that, 'We've given Hess something to ensure that he doesn't wake up until the morning.'[48] Although this happened in MI5 headquarters, other intelligence departments were involved: MI6 sent the car for Fraser-Smith, and the tailor he brought in was from SOE.

Fraser-Smith was never told why a copy of Hess's uniform was needed, but his own speculation is very interesting:

> I sometimes wonder if we intended sending somebody back in the copied outfit to try to penetrate the Nazi high command . . . The risk of having a double – what the Germans might call a *doppelgänger* – occupying the role of deputy to our leading antagonist would almost certainly have been worth a man's life.[49]

Clearly, the only reason that Fraser-Smith could think of for secretly copying Hess's uniform was that they intended someone else to wear it, presumably someone masquerading as the man himself. Indeed, it is hard to come up with any other reason. This story provides evidence that the idea of a substitute occurred to the British very soon after Hess had arrived.

Indeed, in January 1990 Fraser-Smith went further, telling the *Guardian*'s Richard Norton-Taylor that he had always believed that a 'phoney Hess' had been kept in Britain.[50] Fraser-Smith also claimed that doubts about the prisoner's identity were held at the very highest level, saying that in 1975 the head of MI6, Sir Maurice Oldfield, had convened a meeting 'to discuss releasing the whole story about Hess, about whether it was Hess or not'.[51] This was four years before the publication of Hugh Thomas's book.

The substitution of the double by the British would also account for the peculiar prohibition on taking photographs of Hess while in

Britain. Allen speculates that the substitution happened at the Tower, and that the fake Hess was incarcerated in Mytchett Place and in all the other places afterwards, the real Rudolf Hess having been shot. However, if true, then it is hard to explain what the Mytchett Place period was all about. And it is certainly difficult to see anyone but the real Hess being able to produce such a lengthy document about the Russian situation as the one given to Lord Beaverbrook or to participate in the various high-level meetings.

Why would the British have wanted a Hess double so soon after he arrived? Perhaps he was intended as a decoy in case of a German assassination attempt. But there is another possibility that fits the 'Mytchett oracle' hypothesis: in order to impress the British peace group and his overseas allies, Churchill wanted Hess to be seen to be co-operating. One of the Scots Guards who guarded Hess from 22 June 1941 and who was later taken prisoner by the Germans, told his interrogators that on the day of Barbarossa Hess had been moved back to the Tower, and for two weeks was taken for daily meetings at 'the intelligence centre in Whitehall'. Around 25 or 26 June Churchill had a meeting with Hess there – officially Hess was being kept at Mytchett Place during this time. Officers stationed at the RAF Military Police Headquarters at Hitcham House, Burnham in Berkshire, also claimed that Churchill had met Hess there.[52]

Given all the facts, while a lookalike might have been used from time to time earlier, it seems that the most obvious time for a decoy to take over would have been at the time of the transfer to Maindiff Court: indeed, the various discrepancies and anomalies already listed seem to point to something untoward going on precisely then. There is the strange insistence that Hess was being moved for security reasons, and then the fact that they moved him, unescorted, to a low-security establishment while positively inviting the world and his wife to know about it. In fact, this was a perfectly logical thing to do. It may be that the concern about the Poles was that they were intending not to attack Hess, but to rescue him (as the Poles' fears for the future of their country had grown with the British alliance with Russia). In MI5 files released in 1999 there was a puzzling reference to a report by Kenneth de Courcy of a gun battle between Polish soldiers and the guards at Mytchett Place, although what lies behind this is a mystery.[53] If the government was worried about the safety of the real Hess, it made sense to employ a decoy, although, as we have seen the plan to create one may well date back to Hess's stay in the Tower.

In order to work out the details of the plot, we need to establish if, or how, Hess's behaviour changed between Mytchett Place and Maindiff Court. The problem here, however, is that there is very little information about the Maindiff Court phase. For example, Rees's book devotes just thirty pages to the forty months he spent there, as opposed to forty-one pages on the thirteen months he was at Mytchett Place. And the majority of the chapter on Nuremberg is taken up with the events of 1944–5, when Hess was suffering from amnesia, supposedly because life was more eventful there at that time. In any case, what documentation does exist may well be deliberately misleading – as with the 'reassigning' of the flight map that Hess drew in Mytchett Place to the time of his stay at Maindiff Court.

Similarly, the letters allegedly written by Hess during this period might have been forged. If his 'evasion' of the censors was, as we believe, really a misinformation ploy to mislead key people in Germany as to his whereabouts, the letters could well have been written by specialist forgers from a department such as the XX Committee. Suspicion only increases when 'Hess' writes to Ilse in 1944 that, because of his amnesia, he can only write to her about subjects she first brings up.[54] Even Wolf Hess, who does not accept the doppelgänger theory, admits that at least one of the letters written from Nuremberg – describing the flight to Ilse – contained so many errors that it had, at the very least, to have been written under pressure.[55]

Intriguingly, we were told by the International Committee of the Red Cross in Geneva (who keep all records of prisoners of war and internees) that, although the Red Cross was allowed to see Hess when he was in Mytchett Place, it had been refused permission to see him while he was at Abergavenny.[56] Instead, the British government arranged for Hess to have a medical examination and sent the results to the London headquarters of the Red Cross. Arguments about changes in diet or attitudes to beer are one thing, but refusing to let the Red Cross anywhere near the prisoner is highly suspicious.

Bizarre though it might seem, the doppelgänger theory does appear to provide explanations for much of the anomalous behaviour of both the prisoner and the authorities in the Maindiff Court phase of the story. As we have seen, there appear to have been two Hesses at the same time – one in Wales and one in Scotland – although, because of the deliberate focus on the former by the authorities, one can surmise that the Maindiff Hess was a decoy, aimed at the public, at German intelligence, and possibly also at the Poles. And Hugh Thomas's post-war evidence would suggest that it was the decoy who ended his days at Spandau. But in that case, what happened to the real Hess? Is Professor Waddell right: was he secretly executed by the British?

A little girl's historic encounter

Exciting confirmation that the substitution was made at the time of the transfer to Abergavenny came from the testimony of Evelyn Criddle, who was a child there at the time. Evelyn is the daughter of William Flint, whose mother was a member of the ancient Herbert family, that of the Earls of Pembroke. She recalls, as a four-year-old in the early summer of 1942, going from their home in Surrey to stay in the lodge in the grounds of the Herberts' wartime residence of Cae Kenfy House in Abergavenny. The first surprise was that they were greeted by armed soldiers, who at first refused them access. She remembers: 'I gathered from the atmosphere something very dramatic, something very big was happening – and it wasn't Christmas.'

> My father put me to bed that night, and he said, 'In the morning I'm going to show you a man, and nobody's ever going to believe you've seen him. When you get older, after the war, I will tell you who he is.' The next morning we stood by the rhododendron bushes, and I can see him now. This very tall man appeared from Cae Kenfy House, flanked each side by soldiers who only came up to his shoulders. He passed down the path – my father and I were looking at him – and he sort of half smiled at me.
>
> Years after the war my father told me who he was. He was Hess. And he said, 'Nobody's ever going to believe you.'[57]

Mrs Criddle says that, being so young at the time, she would have forgotten the incident, had her father not continued to remind her of it over the years. He took pains to impress its significance on her, saying: 'You must remember, because in years to come people will want to talk about it.'

According to Mrs Criddle, although soldiers were present, Cae Kenfy House was not heavily guarded. She believes – based on what she now knows of the Hess story – that he was there while Maindiff Court was being prepared, and was subsequently moved there. However, contemporary accounts make it clear that he was taken directly to Maindiff Court from Mytchett Place. If so, who was the man in Cae Kenfy House?

Mrs Criddle's testimony suggests that the substitution took place at Abergavenny, with the real Hess being driven there from Surrey and being kept at Cae Kenfy, while the double was installed at Maindiff Court. However, there is another layer of intrigue to this story. Why was the Herbert family chosen to shelter the Deputy Führer? Although this is the family of the Earls of Pembroke, one of the oldest noble families in the country, it is surely more relevant that, in 1942, the son and heir to the earldom, Sir Sidney Herbert, was the *equerry to the Duke of Kent*.

The fact that Hess was no longer being held in a government building like Mytchett Place but in a private aristocratic house suggests that there is more to this part of the story than might first appear. As the family who were sheltering him were so closely connected to the Duke of Kent, could this mean that the peace party had managed to gain control of the Deputy Führer?

An astonishing discovery

Repeatedly, the Hess story seems to be drawn back to Scotland. In May 1993, Stephen Prior had dinner in Thurso, Caithness, with Lord Thurso (Robin Sinclair, now sadly deceased), the son of Sir Archibald Sinclair, whose family own a large estate in the area. When the conversation turned to our Hess research, Lord Thurso made the astounding statement that, as a wartime teenager, he remembered Hess being kept in a hunting lodge called Braemore Lodge on the adjoining estate of the Duke of Portland, not far from Dunbeath in Caithness. He remembered this as being in 1942, or at least for part of that summer. Although he had not seen the Deputy Führer himself, he had been told about it, and his mother had also told him that Hess had been kept 'for a short time' in Lochmore Cottage, on his father's estate, on the shore of Loch More.

Another Caithness connection surfaced when Robert Brydon was discussing recent Hess research at the Edinburgh exhibition soirée of an artist friend, Marianna Lines. During the course of their conversation, she remembered that some time before, one of her clients, Lady 'Bunty' Gunn, wife of Sir James Gunn, from Caithness, revealed that Rudolf Hess was once held captive in her local area – or so a persistent local rumour went. The story had come from her elderly mother-in-law, who had lived in Caithness during the war. Lady Gunn had then added a bizarre twist to the already tantalising story when she claimed that Hess had been kept in the same cottage on the Duke of Portland's estate *that the Kaiser had been kept in after the First World War*.

There is no record of the German leader ever being held on British soil. However, when Kaiser Wilhelm was sent into exile in Holland, he was given a château that belonged to Count Godard Bentinck, who comes from the same family as the Cavendish-Bentincks – the Dukes of Portland. So it is conceivable that while his new residence was being prepared, he might have found a temporary home in another house belonging to the same family, although for security reasons it was in an isolated – and unlikely – area, and the location was kept secret. Obviously, this ruse was highly successful: apart from a few locals, nobody ever got to know about it from the end of the First World War to the present day. And if it worked once with such a high-security prisoner, why not try it again, this time with Rudolf Hess?

Obviously, the challenge was to discover any clue as to where the Kaiser was kept. By a stroke of luck, we found it in the letters page of the *Scotsman* dated 12 September 1985. Our find was a letter from Tom Sinclair, writing about a story told to him by a friend who had been in an RAF maintenance unit during the Second World War. He had been sent to remove the wreckage of an aircraft from a nearby mountain, being billeted on the Duke of Portland's estate, where he rapidly befriended the Duke's gamekeeper and his elderly bedridden mother. At tea one Sunday, she told them that she used to look after 'Kaiser Wullie' when he was kept there after the First World War while his future residence in Holland was being prepared. When they asked where he was housed, with a fine sense of the dramatic, she drew back the curtains and pointed to 'a substantial stone-built house nearby'.[58]

When we successfully located the gamekeeper's cottage, which is on the edge of the hamlet of Braemore, we saw that the only lone substantial stone-built house within sight is Braemore Lodge. As this is the very house in which Lord Thurso said that Hess was kept, it means that, ultimately, both Lord Thurso's and Lady Gunn's testimonies pinpoint the same place.

If Hess was at Braemore Lodge, what was he doing there, and who was responsible for him? Was he being kept 'on ice' by the British government on Churchill's orders or had the peace group somehow managed to seize him and keep him out of the Prime Minister's clutches for its own ends?

There may be clues in the very location where he was kept. As we noted earlier, Braemore Lodge is on the estate of the Dukes of Portland – the Cavendish-Bentinck family. (The present Queen Mother's mother was Cecilia Cavendish-Bentinck.) Victor Cavendish-Bentinck (who later became the 9th Duke of Portland) was the wartime chairman of the Joint Intelligence Committee of the Chiefs of Staff, which oversaw and co-ordinated all British intelligence departments, and of which the heads of all intelligence agencies (such as Menzies) were members. If Hess was hidden away on the Portland estate, it must have been his doing.

And if the real Rudolf Hess was hidden away in the wilds of Scotland while his double attracted attention down in Wales, what happened to him? While the double went on to become – as far as history is concerned – the one and only Rudolf Hess, it seems that the man himself simply disappeared.

CHAPTER TWELVE

Death on Eagle's Rock

Today a stone cross marks the spot where the Sunderland flying boat that carried the Duke of Kent and fourteen (or fifteen, see below) other men crashed into a remote hilltop on 25 August 1942. This cross, raised by the grieving Duchess, is the only memorial to the Duke, despite the fact that he was the first member of the Royal Family to be killed on active service for 500 years. There is also no mention of his death in the RAF Museums at Hendon, north London, and Duxford, in Cambridgeshire, even in connection with the exhibits of Sunderland flying boats. Right from the beginning of our research we realised that there was something about his death that marks it out as being in some way suspicious.

The accepted story is as follows: the Short Sunderland flying boat left Invergordon, on the east coast of Scotland, carrying the Duke of Kent and three members of his staff. About sixty miles after take-off, the plane ploughed into a hill called Eagle's Rock in the Caithness area in low cloud. All but one of those on board were killed.

The exact circumstances surrounding the death of the Duke of Kent have long been acknowledged to be one of the great aviation mysteries of the Second World War. Robert Brydon, who in the 1980s was one of the first to realise that there *was* a mystery – and who had operated with and flown on Sunderlands during his National Service – was quick to note certain anomalies. How did the plane, flown by the cream of RAF pilots, crash into a hillside? And what was this flying boat doing over land at all?

The Short S-25 Sunderland Mk III was essentially a military version of the classic Empire flying boat – and it was huge: just over 85 feet (26 m) long, it had a wingspan of nearly 113 feet (34 m), with a maximum speed of 210 mph, a cruising speed of 178 mph and a minimum flying speed of 78 mph. Its normal range was an impressive 1,800 miles. One of the most successful flying boats ever produced, it was relatively easy to manoeuvre, but its major disadvantage was that it was very heavy and sluggish when climbing – especially when heavily laden, as it was on the Duke of Kent's flight. Sunderlands were also extremely well equipped – even boasting sleeping quarters and cooking and toilet facilities – almost living up to their slightly exaggerated description as a 'mobile workshop with all the conveniences of a two-storey flat'.[1]

Designated W4026, the Duke of Kent's Sunderland was part of Coastal Command's 228 Squadron, stationed at Oban on the west coast of Scotland. It was almost brand new, being delivered only in March of that year. Officially, the Duke was on a morale-boosting visit to RAF personnel stationed in Iceland. British troops had moved in as soon as the Nazis took over Norway because Iceland had supreme strategic importance, as a base both for transatlantic convoys and for defence against U-boats. Convoys bound for Russia also made use of Iceland. There were regular seaplane flights between the west coast of Scotland and Kaldadarnes, near Reykjavik.

The crew of the doomed Sunderland were hardly run-of-the-mill airmen. They were the best Coastal Command could supply. The captain, twenty-six-year-old Flight Lieutenant Francis ('Frank') Mackenzie Goyen was specially selected because he was one of the top Sunderland pilots in the RAF. (He had also been chosen to fly Sir Stafford Cripps, Ambassador to the Soviet Union, to Moscow in 1941.) Several other members of the hand-picked crew had previously crewed VIP flights.[2] Like many wartime teams, they were pitifully young – the grand old man being thirty-year-old Sergeant Edward Blacklock, from the Royal New Zealand Air Force, and the baby of the crew being twenty-one-year-old Flight Sergeant Andy Jack, who was the sole survivor of the crash.

The Duke took an impressive entourage with him on the fateful flight: his private secretary, thirty-two-year-old Lieutenant John Arthur Lowther, Royal Naval Volunteer Reserve, grandson and heir of a former Speaker of the House of Commons (Viscount Ullswater);

his equerry, Pilot Officer Michael Strutt (twenty-eight), son of Lord Belper and brother of the Duchess of Norfolk; and a valet, John Hales. Only Lowther of those accompanying the Duke was normally part of his entourage: Strutt had replaced one of his usual equerries, Squadron Leader P. J. Ferguson, who was said to be ill, and another equerry, Sir Sidney Herbert, was also absent, although no reason was given; Hales was a replacement supplied by Oban.[3] Two other members of the Duke's regular entourage who did not – unusually – accompany him that day were Group Captain Sir Louis Greig and Detective Sergeant Evans, his personal detective, who was on leave at the time.[4]

It was normal practice for a Sunderland to have three pilots on board – a captain and a first and second pilot. On this particular flight they were, respectively: Goyen, Wing Commander Thomas Lawton Moseley, the commanding officer of 228 Squadron, who joined the flight at the last minute for reasons unknown, and Pilot Officer Sydney Wood Smith of the RAAF. The navigator, Pilot Officer George Saunders, was also a pilot. In all, this flight had an embarrassment of aviation skill: no fewer than four pilots and four navigators on board. But of all its highly trained team, the story focuses on just three of them: Goyen, Moseley and Jack.

Flight Lieutenant Goyen, an Australian, had flown over 1,200 hours in Sunderlands, many while in Coastal Command (having previously served in Alexandria and Malta) escorting convoys or on lookout patrols for U-boats. Joining the RAF in 1938, he was greatly respected by his colleagues for his skill, courage and coolness. One story illustrates this perfectly: in May 1942 he had to land a badly damaged Sunderland at Oban. As the ambulances and crash wagons gathered to greet the stricken plane, one of Goyen's colleagues said, 'Oh, they'll be OK. Frank's there.' Goyen made a textbook landing, later saying – in the stiff-upper-lip tradition that Hess would have admired so much, 'Well, yes. It was rather a shaky do. After all, Sunderlands cost a lot of money.'[5] He was no gung-ho exhibitionist, however, being very aware of his responsibilities and a consummate professional. He would never have endangered the lives of his passengers or crew in any circumstances – even if ordered to do so by a superior. As captain of this flight, Goyen was in overall command, irrespective of the fact that his commanding officer and an air commodore – the Duke of Kent – were on board.

Wing Commander Moseley, also an Australian, had been the commanding officer of 228 Squadron since the previous April. One of the RAF's most experienced pilots – by the time of his death he had completed 1,449 flying hours – he was a navigation specialist, a former instructor at the School of Air Navigation, chief instructor at the General Reconnaissance School and (immediately before his posting to Oban) on the Air Ministry's navigation training staff.[6] His expertise was a critical element in the unfolding crash drama.

The last of our trio was the youngest member of the crew. Flight Sergeant Andrew ('Andy') Jack was the son of a semi-professional footballer (who played for Falkirk). Jack inherited his father's athleticism, being a strapping six-foot-tall Scots lad who also boasted his fair share of brains. He had been all set for a university education – quite an achievement for a working-class boy at that time – and planned to resume his studies after the war.[7]

The Kent flight

W4026 flew from Oban to Invergordon on the east coast of Scotland two days before the crash. It took the usual route, following the Caledonian Canal and the line of lochs – including the spectacular long stretch of silver water that is Loch Ness – to ensure that it remained over water as much as possible.

The Duke of Kent and his party travelled to Invergordon on the morning of 25 August, joining the plane shortly before take-off after lunching in the Officers' Mess. W4026 took off from Invergordon at 1.10 p.m., launching its great bulk from the calm waters of the Cromarty Firth: too calm, as it turned out. That day the sea was so tranquil that the plane needed an unusually long run-up – around three miles – to get airborne. (Sunderlands are more efficient at take-off in waves because they help to bump them up into the air.) It set off on a northeasterly course along the coastline.

Being a flying boat, its standing orders were to fly over water, only crossing land when absolutely unavoidable. For this reason, it was usual to follow the coastline to Duncansby Head – the northernmost tip of Scotland near John o' Groats – and then turn northwest over the Pentland Firth towards Iceland. The whole journey should have taken about seven hours, well within the Sunderland's twelve-hour range. Later that afternoon – the exact time is, as we will see, a matter of dispute – the Sunderland crashed into a hillside some two and a half miles inland, about three and a half miles from the town of Dunbeath and slightly further from the village of Berriedale. This is about sixty miles from the starting point of Invergordon.

The plane crashed into a hill known as Eagle's Rock or Eagle's Crag, overlooking the valley carved by Berriedale Water, on the Duke of Portland's estate. Despite its dramatically craggy name, the crash site is not particularly rocky, although it is certainly bleak, and is covered in peat bog and heather. The Sunderland crashed into the hill behind the peak of Eagle's Rock, where the crest is a little over 650 feet. Travelling in a northerly direction, the Sunderland struck the gently rising hillside at a shallow angle, somersaulting on its nose to land on its back. It disintegrated on impact, scattering the wreckage over a wide area. Its 2,500 gallons of fuel, carried in the wings, exploded. Most of the wreckage was scattered over the rise, in the direction of travel. As the plane crashed down on its back, the tail section broke free and was thrown over the brow of the hill, coming to rest in the peat bog on the other side, escaping the full blast of the explosion. Because of this, the only survivor – Andy Jack – escaped with relatively minor burns to his face and hands. The wreckage continued to burn after impact. The fuselage and wings were made of aluminium, which has a fairly low melting point, adding to the almost total destruction of the plane. Apart from Jack, the tail-gunner, all those on board died instantly as a result of the impact, rather than the fireball. Several of the bodies – including Kent's – were thrown from the wreckage and escaped the conflagration, although those in the cockpit were badly burned.

The aftermath

The crash was heard by local people who immediately organised search parties. As we will see later, inaccurate newspaper reports and other problems of recall have introduced inconsistencies that make it difficult to reconstruct a full picture of the aftermath of the crash.

Nobody claims to have seen the Sunderland crash – which is not surprising, considering the remoteness of Eagle's Rock – but several people heard it. Two of those, sheepfarming father and son David and Hugh Morrison, are usually credited with raising the alarm. Out rounding up stray sheep (being the first day of sheep dipping), they heard what they described as two explosions in quick succession – probably either the impact itself followed by the fuel going up, or each of the two wing tanks exploding separately. Hugh Morrison jumped on his motorcycle and roared off to raise the alarm. The police and local doctor, John Kennedy from Dunbeath, were alerted, and a search party hastily cobbled together from what David Morrison described as 'local people and military personnel' from the hamlet of Braemore, some two and a half miles from the crash site.[8]

They found the still-burning wreckage about an hour and a half after the crash. Shortly afterwards two special constables from Dunbeath, Will Bethune and James Sutherland, arrived on the scene, followed by another party including the doctor, John Kennedy. (Most of the early reports confusedly have the aged doctor being the first to arrive on the scene at the head of the search party. It seems unlikely that even the hardiest Scot would have been quite so nimble over that kind of terrain at the age of seventy. Perhaps the reporters had to make someone their hero, and who better than the district's well-respected doctor?)[9]

The various parties searched the wreckage and found no survivors. There are conflicting accounts about who was the first to identify the Duke of Kent as one of the victims. Some of the local farmers from the first search party said it was them, while Special Constable Bethune and Dr Kennedy made the same claim. Bethune found the Duke's identity bracelet (which read: 'His Royal Highness, the Duke of Kent, The Coppins, Iver, Bucks'),[10] while Dr Kennedy said he identified the body from a monogrammed cigarette case and the inscription on the Duke's wristwatch.[11] But – although he did take the watch to make sure it was returned to the Duke's family – he had arrived after the policemen and fails to mention the identity bracelet. Bethune seems to be the winner in that sad little tussle for personal glory.

Of the Duke's injuries – after having been thrown violently from the plane – Bethune would only ever say: 'He was hit in the head. More than that I don't say.'[12] More intriguingly, in a 1985 radio interview, the then elderly Bethune added another little item, which has curiously failed to attract much attention. He said that handcuffed to the Duke's wrist was an attaché case that had burst open, scattering a large number of hundred-kroner notes over the hillside.[13] Of course, the kroner is the currency of Iceland, where they were allegedly heading.

Some time in the late afternoon or early evening a team from RAF Wick – the nearest airfield, some twenty-five miles from the crash site – arrived to examine the wreckage. With them were policemen from Wick (regular police, not specials like Bethune and Sutherland). As night began to fall, it was decided to postpone removing the bodies until the next day, and a guard was posted to watch over the wreck. The next morning, when it was known that a member of the Royal Family was among the victims, a party of more senior RAF and naval officers visited the scene, and the bodies were finally removed in a small fleet of ambulances. The Duke's remains were taken to Dunrobin House, a curious Victorian château belonging to the Duke of Sutherland, then partly converted to a wartime hospital. The other bodies were taken to Wick.

At Balmoral, George VI was dining with the Queen and the Duke and Duchess of Gloucester when the dreadful news came through from Sir Archibald Sinclair, Secretary of State for Air. Shocked and shaken to the core, the King passed the news on to his mother, Queen Mary, who said immediately: 'I must go to Marina.'[14] Meanwhile, at the Kents' family home, The Coppins, Marina's old nurse Kate ('Foxy') Fox took the call. Mrs Fox had nursed the Duchess as a baby, and had come out of retirement to look after Prince Michael, then just seven weeks old. Very much part of the family, it broke her heart to have to tell Marina of Georgie's tragic death.[15] Marina collapsed in shock, from which she was slow to emerge. The months that followed were utterly wretched, although gradually she came to take great comfort from her family, and from her royal duties. Her long widowhood was finally over in 1968. Collapsing on the twenty-sixth anniversary of her husband's death, she was to die of an inoperable brain tumour just one day later.

The mystery of the tail-gunner

The first news stories reported that everyone on board the Sunderland had been killed. This was also the official version –

telegrams were duly dispatched to the next of kin of all members of the crew. But there was a dramatic twist to the story: in the early afternoon of the next day Andy Jack turned up very much alive at a crofter's cottage at Ramscraigs, a scattered hamlet near the coast between Dunbeath and Berriedale, and about two miles from the crash site.

It turned out that Andy Jack owed his life to Lady Luck. Before take-off he had tossed a coin with one of the other crewmen, Flight Sergeant Lewis, to decide who should take the unpopular turn in the rear gun turret, where it was both cold and cramped. Jack lost the toss.

Although there are some inconsistencies and unanswered questions about Jack's actions after the crash, it seems that he regained consciousness not long after the plane exploded. Some accounts say that he then dragged some of the bodies free of the burning wreckage, which is how he burned his hands. However, Jack himself never claimed to have pulled any of the bodies clear, although he did say he found and recognised the Duke's body because of his uniform, with its distinctive air commodore's insignia. He also realised that everybody else was dead, although whether he recognised and counted the bodies is uncertain. He then set off to find help, in direct contravention of standard procedure – which was always to remain with the wreck – although quite why he chose to do so is not clear. Certainly, he would have been in no fit state to be thinking with any clarity, especially after the trauma of seeing the bodies scattered around the hillside, some of whom were close friends, and one of whom was a senior member of the Royal Family. But, strangely, Jack's own account of his wanderings that day does not smack of delirium; if anything it showed considerable presence of mind. Of his decision to leave the crash site, he said only: 'All along, I had been trying to get help. I knew help was useless, they were all dead.

'But I felt someone ought to be told. I think that's why I walked away and went on wandering, though the best thing I could have done from my own point of view was stay near the wreckage.'[16]

Jack had left the scene by the time the first search parties arrived. Alone and – it can be imagined – in considerable distress of both mind and body, he wandered that evening around the area, following a small stream, hoping it would lead him to human habitation.

The soles of his flying boots had been all but ripped off, so at some point he discarded them, along with his badly ripped trousers. Before leaving his trousers behind on the hills, in his own words 'being a proper Scot', he counted the money in the pockets – a little over five shillings. Several weeks later he received a postal order for that amount from the police: apparently a shepherd had found the trousers with the money and, realising where they came from, handed the coins over to the authorities.[17] He clearly had abandoned his jacket, too, otherwise he would have transferred the coins to his jacket pockets.

When night fell, Jack dug into the bracken to sleep, waking to a beautiful summer day. He continued to wander about, eventually deciding to climb a hill in order to get a better idea of his surroundings. From there he saw a crofter's cottage and headed towards it, arriving at about 1.30 p.m. The owner, Mrs Elsie Sutherland, alerted Dr Kennedy at Dunbeath by telephone. Kennedy immediately left his lunch, rushing to attend to the injured airman, who was then taken to a hospital in Lybster.

As far as Jack's relatives were concerned, he was a dead man, his sister Jean in Grangemouth having already received the telegram informing them of his death. When he turned up alive, a second telegram was hurriedly sent to try to overtake the first; it ultimately just failed, arriving a matter of minutes later, to Jean Jack's great joy.[18]

Reactions to Kent's death

Not surprisingly, the press coverage of the tragedy was huge the next day, and expressions of sympathy flooded in. The Court went into mourning for four weeks (more was considered bad taste in wartime, when so many other families were also bereaved). Winston Churchill made a speech in the Commons, calling the Duke of Kent 'a gallant and handsome prince'.[19]

After being kept for two days at Dunrobin House, the Duke's body was taken to London by train and lay in the Albert Memorial Chapel in Windsor Castle until the burial on the Saturday after the crash – 29 August. Kent was finally laid to rest in the vaults of St George's Chapel in Windsor Castle – the chapel of the Order of the Garter – in the presence of a galaxy of royal mourners, many exiled from their own countries by Nazi occupation, and other friends, including Noel Coward and Douglas Fairbanks, Jr, then serving with the US Navy in Britain. Although Winston Churchill was not present, a separate service was held for MPs at Westminster Abbey a few days later.

Of the many tributes and messages of condolence received from other countries, one of the most effusive came from General Sikorski. In a special dispatch to all Polish troops in Britain, he called the Duke 'a proven friend of Poland and the Polish armed forces'. This was read out to all units at the first morning parade after the crash.[20] The dispatch also said that Kent was to have visited the Polish Army on 8 September 'to declare his sympathy to the Polish cause', and ended: 'The British Empire has won a new and eloquent example of the understanding of duty to the Motherland on the part of one of its highest representatives.'[21] Nicholas Bethell, writing of this incident in 1972, put into words what many have thought: 'It was of course unusual for a country to react so strongly to the death of a foreign prince.'[22] But the full circumstances that underpinned Kent's special relationship with the Poles were not known then; particularly the fact that he had been offered the Polish throne.

In 1968, when Marina was interred in the royal burial ground at Frogmore, Windsor, Kent's coffin – as she had requested many years before – was moved to lie next to hers. The other British crewmen were buried in their local churchyards, while the four crewmen from the empire – Goyen, Moseley, Blacklock and Smith – were buried in Pennyfuir Cemetery in Oban.

The forgotten prince

Although the death of the King's brother made headline news around the world, the burial was notably low key – officially because the King did not want it to appear that a royal casualty of war was treated as more important than a commoner. Laudable though that may be, it does not seem to be the real reason why Kent's memory has been so neglected since the end of the war. As mentioned earlier, no official memorial has ever been erected, and the only outward and visible sign of Kent's passing was the stone cross set up on the hillside by Princess Marina. The inscription reads:

IN MEMORY OF
AIR CDRE. H.R.H. THE DUKE OF KENT
K.G., K.T., G.C.M.C., G.C.V.O.
AND HIS COMPANIONS
WHO LOST THEIR LIVES ON ACTIVE SERVICE
DURING A FLIGHT TO ICELAND ON A SPECIAL MISSION
THE 25TH OF AUGUST 1942
'MAY THEY REST IN PEACE'

What was their 'Special Mission'? Surely not merely flying to Iceland to boost the troops' morale, as claimed. A similarly odd choice of words was made by Marina in a telegram of condolence to the mother of Flight Sergeant Lewis on 9 September: 'Your dear son lost his life on active service together with my husband for the same fine cause.'[23] What 'fine cause'? And why the stress on active service? All military personnel are on active service, even if engaged on routine duties.

A minor mystery concerns the reaction of the Duke of Windsor – who, despite the trauma of his abdication, had remained very close to his brother the Duke of Kent. Most biographies of Windsor suggest that he behaved callously towards Marina by omitting to send her any word of condolence after her husband's death. Certainly, no such letter has emerged from any royal papers, including Marina's. But Philip Ziegler, in *The Official Biography of King Edward VIII* (1990), quotes a letter from Windsor to Queen Mary expressing his sorrow at Kent's death – describing him as 'in some ways, more like a son to me' – and including the sentence 'I have written to Marina'.[24] If he had, Marina seems not to have received it. Ziegler comments: 'Perhaps the letter was blown away by some wind of war.'[25] The 'wind of war' must have blown exceedingly cold if that letter – apparently an innocent expression of sympathy – was intercepted by an unknown hand.

The official findings

A court of inquiry was held, although the full dossier of its findings has disappeared. However, a summary of the details of the crash and the court findings is in the archives of the Air Historical Branch of the Ministry of Defence. A statement of the findings was

EXTRACT FROM RAF FORM 1180 (ACCIDENT RECORD CARD)

Aircraft : SUNDERLAND III   Date   : 25 · 8 · 42

Serial : W4026   Approximate Time
                             of Accident   : 1400

Engine : PEGASUS 18   Location   : Dunbeath, NW Berridale
                                                Caithness
Serial(s): 240435   Flight Duration : (?)

        : 240647   Duty   : TRANSIT FLIGHT
                                                (Invergordon – Iceland).
        : 240608

        : 240631

                Capt : FL FM GOYEN
Pilots : P1 : WgCdr TL MOSELEY   Unit   : 228 Sqn
          P2 : P/O S.W. SMITH
Casualties: 14K , 1 I   Group   : 15 Grp

Damage   Command : Coastal
Category : E (TOTAL WRITE-OFF)

"A/c CRASHED INTO HILL IN CLOUD NEAR BERRIDALE"

C of I :- "ACCIDENT DUE TO A/c BEING ON WRONG TRACK AT
          TO LOW ALTITUDE TO CLEAR RISING GROUND ON
          TRACK...." "CAPT. OF A/c CHANGED FLIGHT-PLAN
          FOR REASONS UNKNOWN & DESCENDED THROUGH
          CLOUD WITHOUT MAKING SURE HE WAS OVER WATER,
          AND CRASHED."

AoC in C :- "CONCURS FINDINGS. CONSIDERS WEATHER
            CONDITIONS PRESENTED NO DIFFICULTIES TO A CREW
            OF SUCH EXPERIENCE."

This Department is prohibited, by the Ministry of Defence Legal Department,
from providing facsimile copies of Form 1180 Accident Record cards. It is
hoped this transcript will suffice.

*The official summary of the findings of the court of inquiry, giving the time of
the crash as 2.00 p.m. and no duration of flight.*

also given in the House of Commons by the Secretary of State for Air, Sir Archibald Sinclair, on 7 October 1942, and was duly recorded in *Hansard*. The court of inquiry summarised its findings thus: 'Accident due to aircraft being on wrong track at too low altitude to clear rising ground on track. Captain of aircraft changed flight-plan for reasons unknown and descended through cloud without making sure he was over water and crashed.' The 'AoC in C' adds, 'Concurs findings. Considers weather conditions presented no difficulty to a crew of such experience.' In other words, the Sunderland appeared to have deviated from the official flight path and was flying too low.

Sir Archibald Sinclair's statement in the House of Commons adds a few other details. The cause of the disaster was not mechanical failure: the official investigation concluded that not only were all four engines working properly at the time of the crash but they were on full throttle; nor were any navigational aids found to be faulty. Sinclair's statement omitted one significant point. According to an account of the crash on the Royal Air Force Station Oban website, 'The aircraft's engines were examined after the crash and found to be set at full throttle with propellers at coarse pitch, thus indicating that the aircraft was *still climbing* [our emphasis] when it hit the obstruction and not in cruising configuration. This fact was not made clear at the inquiry but was noted by members of the 63rd Maintenance Unit whilst clearing the debris.'

Sinclair also delivered a devastating blow to one particular bereaved family, saying: 'the responsibility for this serious mistake in airmanship lies with the captain of the aircraft [Goyen].'

In the absence of first-hand testimony – Andy Jack, isolated in the rear turret, would not have known what was going on in the cockpit – most commentators have reconstructed the following sequence of events. Shortly after leaving Invergordon, the Sunderland entered low cloud, obscuring the navigator's view of their position. Therefore, the pilot took the plane down in order to regain visual contact with the coastline, but failed to realise that they had drifted off course and were no longer over the sea but over ground that was swiftly rising to meet them. At first glance this might seem reasonable enough, but there are a great many problems with this interpretation.

At the time and for many years afterwards, the story of the Duke of Kent's death was regarded as one of the war's many tragedies, all the more poignant because it was the result of an avoidable accident. However, we began to realise that there are many unanswered questions about the crash, particularly the official response. Vital documents have vanished – the most important being the flight plan filed by Goyen before take-off. And although the court of inquiry's report should have been made public after fifteen years, it is still unavailable sixty years later. No one can even find it: in 1990, Roy Conyers Nesbit attempted to find the records in the Public Record Office at Kew, but drew a blank.[27] The PRO suggested that they might have been transferred to the royal archives at Windsor Castle, but the registrar told him that the file was not there now and had never been there.

The summary gives only the conclusions of the court of inquiry, not the evidence that led to them. Even so, it shows certain inconsistencies. It is known that W4026 took off from Invergordon at 13.10, which would have been logged by the flight controllers at the base. (Take-off time for a Sunderland was judged to be the moment its hull left the water.) To arrive at the crash site – some sixty miles away – would only have taken about twenty minutes, but the inquiry report gives the crash time as 'approx. 14.00'. Yet more curiously, against the heading 'Duration of Flight' there is only a question mark.

One of the most glaring anomalies was that the only survivor, Andy Jack, *was not called to give evidence*. He gave a statement but – as we will see – this only manages to muddy the waters further.

Then there is also the matter of the difficulty of reconciling statements about the cause of the crash. Although the inquiry laid the blame squarely on the captain, Goyen, this conflicts with its own findings. The standard interpretation is that, realising the plane was off course and wanting to get his bearings from a sighting of the coastline, Goyen took the plane down through the cloud, thinking he was still over the sea. But was it really Goyen's fault? The responsibilities of pilot and navigator were sharply defined: the navigator was responsible for ensuring that the plane stayed on course, and for keeping the pilot informed of any corrections necessary. In this case it would have been the navigator who would have asked the pilot to descend through the cloud so that he could check their position. So responsibility for the crash lay not with Goyen at all but, if it was anyone's fault, with his navigator. The pilot would never have made such a descent unless requested to do so by the navigator and assured it was safe to do so. Therefore, by all the normal rules, the conclusion should have been 'navigator error'. The only possible reason for blaming the pilot would be if he had overruled the navigator, but since no one knows what happened in the cockpit during the last minutes of the flight, the court of inquiry had no justification for its verdict.

Add to this anomaly the strange treatment of Andy Jack. When he arrived at Lybster Hospital the day after the crash he had difficulty speaking because his face was tight with burns. It had been arranged for members of his family to visit him, including his sister Jean, his brother Robert, a corporal with the Scots Guards, and his sister Nancy, a leading aircraftwoman. Jean reports an odd incident on the Saturday, four days after the crash (the day of the Duke of Kent's funeral). When she and other family members visited him in hospital, they found two senior officials – one from the RAF and another from the Admiralty – at his bedside. They asked Jean and the others to leave the room. Jack was in the process of struggling to sign a document, which is said to have been a statement (although some researchers believe it to be the Official Secrets Act) with his burned hands. If it *was* a statement, then he could not have dictated it, because, as Jean made clear, his family could barely understand what he was saying. He later explained that the two officers had had to guide his hand so that he could sign the mystery document.[28]

In 1985, Jean Jack (then Mrs Auld) was most emphatic in an interview, saying: 'I think he was sworn to secrecy.'[29] She went on to say that her brother never revealed what was in the document he signed, and from that moment on he would never speak about the crash, even to his own family.

On 12 September Jack was moved to a hospital between Edinburgh and Glasgow, possibly to prevent the King from visiting him when he made his 'pilgrimage' to the crash site two days later. It would have been natural for George VI to want to talk to the only survivor of the terrible tragedy that carried off his dashing younger brother.

Presumably because of the document he signed, Jack never said much about the official response to the crash – certainly nothing contentious – although he did make it known that he was incensed by the court of inquiry blaming Goyen for the disaster. The local story in Grangemouth is that he was so angry about it that he refused the medal he had been about to receive.

After recovering from his visible injuries, Jack was posted elsewhere, and after the war to Gibraltar. While he was there he was visited several times by the Duke of Kent's widow, Marina, who saw him as often as she could. Obviously there are no records of their conversations, but strangely it seems that they shared a feeling of being outcasts.

Then, astonishingly, having remained reticent (even with his family) for nineteen years, Jack suddenly gave his own account of events to the *Scottish Daily Express* on 18 May 1961, his one and only public statement about the crash. Not only was this completely inconsistent with his virtual silence before and after, but the fact that there are inconsistencies in his story and that he was still serving in the RAF suggest that he went public under orders, presumably to corroborate the official version. Certainly, if anyone was expecting new revelations then they were to be sadly disappointed. So why, after nearly twenty years of silence, did Jack suddenly talk to the press?

The answer lies in an event of the previous day. The Duchess of Kent and her children had made their first pilgrimage to the site of the crash, awakening interest in the tragedy. So to circumvent any awkward questions about what was largely a long-forgotten incident, Jack seems to have been thrust forward. The newspaper story took the form of an article by Jack himself, not an interview, giving his words an added gloss of authority. But although his account appears to keep to the official line, there is a subtext hidden between the lines. He described how, following the usual practice, he took his position in the tail turret about ten minutes into the flight. Then he made a routine test of the intercom link to the cockpit, stating that after this 'I had no conversation with any other member of the crew or captain again',[30] which seems a strange way of saying he spoke to nobody again. Jack then describes flying into low clouds about twenty minutes into the flight – adding, 'I can't recall exactly' – then feeling the plane descending. He says, 'I didn't know any more until I woke up and found myself on the ground.'[31] In other words, Jack can say nothing about the crash or what caused it. So why go to the press, especially so long after the event?

(Jack never sought to pick up his promising academic career from

MOD

MAJOR C. B. INNES

Top: The aircraft hangar and outbuildings (known as the 'Kennels') at Dungavel House, the Hamilton family residence. Although Hamilton had moved out for the duration, evidence suggests that highly placed persons, including a royal duke, *were* there that night, waiting for them. *Above*: Craigiehall House, the Scottish Army Command Headquarters, scene of a clandestine meeting between Rudolf Hess and 'the Duke' three days after the Deputy Führer's arrival.

George, Duke of Kent – the King's youngest brother, and the favourite of the Duke of Windsor – and his wife Marina. They were the epitome of glamour in the pre-war years. Interested in Hitler's economic policies, they often visited relatives in Munich, Hess's hometown.

Above: coded 'M-for-Mother', this Sunderland flying boat pictured at Oban, Scotland, in 1942 may be the actual plane in which the Duke of Kent and his companions died. *Right:* Captain Frank Goyen and members of the doomed crew with (*inset*) the Sunderland's boxing kangaroo motif.

The sole survivor of the crash, tail gunner Andy Jack, stands second from the left.

THIS DAILY SKETCH PHOTO WAS CENSORED BY THE MINISTRY OF
INFORMATION THREE DAYS AFTER THE CRASH
OF D of K's PLANE AT EAGLES CAIRNIE.

NOT to be

16
NOT
TO BE PUBLISHED

THIS WRECK IS NOT ON IRISH GROUND
but was about 600 feet.

Top: the mysterious Kent mission lies in ruins on a bleak Caithness
hillside known as Eagle's Rock. Among the many puzzles of the
crash is the central question of why a flying *boat* should have been
over land at all. *Above:* this photograph of the crash site – with the
Sunderland's propeller bleakly upright – was immediately censored by the authorities.

Wreckage of the Duke of Kent's Sunderland strewn over 400 yards of the lower part of Eagles Rock, in Caithness, Scotland. The photograph was taken the day after the crash by Captain Fresson, on the mail plane run to the Islands. The evidence suggests that, from mid 1941 to summer 1942, there were two 'Hesses' in Britain: the real Deputy Führer and a decoy, understudy or double.

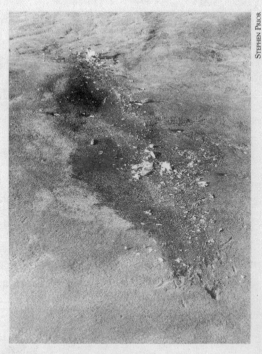

New evidence puts one of them at Cae Kenfy House, Abergavenny in Wales (*bottom left*) and the other at Braemore Lodge, near Loch More, in Scotland (*bottom right*). Which of them went on to life imprisonment in Spandau Prison – and what happened to the other one?

IN MEMORY OF
AIR CDRE. H.R.H. THE DUKE OF KENT
K.C., K.T., G.C.M.G., G.C.V.O.
AND HIS COMPANIONS
WHO LOST THEIR LIVES ON ACTIVE SERVICE
DURING A FLIGHT TO ICELAND ON A SPECIAL MISSION
THE 25TH OF AUGUST 1942.
"MAY THEY REST IN PEACE."

This is the only memorial to the Duke of Kent, raised by his widow, close to the crash site. The wording may be significant: why is 'active service' stressed, and just what was the 'special mission'?

Below: the last photograph of the Duke, taken in August 1942. An Air Commodore, he was on a morale-boosting visit to an air force base.

Right: 21 September 1946: Hess rambles incoherently in the dock during the Nuremberg War Trials. His behaviour was so bizarre that it amused and embarrassed his fellow Nazis (Göring, on the left, barely suppresses his laughter). Certainly, his demeanour was by no means normal (*below*), but was this because 'Hess' was – as the evidence may indicate – a double, controlled and bewildered by mind-altering drugs administered by British psychiatrists? Was his 'amnesia' a convenient cover for the double's ignorance of the real Hess's past?

HULTON GETTY

GOERING
Successor Designate to Hitler

DOENITZ
C-in-C. of the German Navy

RAEDER
Inspector of the German Navy

SCHIRACH
Nazi Youth Leader

HESS
Deputy to Hitler

RIBBENTROP
Nazi Foreign Minister

KEITEL
Chief of the High Command

BRIGADIER D. MURPHY

Above: the last inmate of Spandau, aged ninety-three, walks in the grounds shortly before his death, allegedly from suicide, on 17 August 1987. *Right:* Wolf Rüdiger Hess and lawyer Dr Alfred Seidl wait outside the prison, hoping to see the body of Prisoner Number Seven. They were denied permission. *Below:* the memorial erected by the Rudolf Hess Society at Eaglesham. Widely deemed an affront to decent feeling, it was soon destroyed. It has not been replaced.

THIS STONE MARKS THE SPOT
WHERE BRAVE, HEROIC
RUDOLF HESS
LANDED BY PARACHUTE
ON THE NIGHT OF
10th MAY 1941
SEEKING TO END THE WAR
BETWEEN
BRITAIN AND GERMANY

where he had left it at the outbreak of war, staying in the RAF and receiving his commission in 1945. He retired at the statutory age in 1964, when he became a telephone engineer. But he was a broken man, deeply unhappy about the crash, suffering from depression and taking to drink to blunt the edge of the pain – cirrhosis of the liver was one of the causes of his death, aged just fifty-seven, in Brighton in 1978.[32])

More evidence of a cover-up

The meteorological conditions around Caithness on 25 August 1942 are, of course, critical to the credibility of the official version of the crash. So we were intrigued to discover that a former WAAF, Dorothea Grey, remembered that the civilian meteorologists at Oban who had issued that day's weather forecast were immediately drafted into the RAF and thus made subject to military jurisdiction.[33] She added that many at the time believed there was a cover-up.

There are many other scattered clues that suggest a cover-up. One George Gilfillan, an RAF engineer officer at Oban, says that he was awoken abruptly on the night of the crash and ordered to take all documentation about the flight to Kerrera, near Oban.[34] In the days following the tragedy, newspapers were forbidden by the censors from publishing photographs taken at the crash site, although no reason was given. Unusually, the order was given to clear the site of all wreckage, despite the enormous difficulty of doing so in such a remote location. The task ultimately took about-three weeks – everything having to be hauled by hand to the nearest road, some one and a half miles away. The hills of Caithness are a graveyard for aircraft, with a scattering of many wrecks, both from war and peacetime, which are customarily left where they are, only human remains being removed. A book for aviation enthusiasts, *High Ground Wrecks* by David J. Smith, gives detailed directions for those who wish to visit such sites, but in only one case does it note that there is no point in making the trip, as none of the wreckage remains.[35] Of course, this could – at least in part – be accounted for by the Royal Family's abhorrence of souvenir hunters, but there is still something curious about the alacrity and thoroughness with which the authorities cleared that particular site.

Another apparent act of censorship concerns the memoirs of Captain E. E. Fresson, a pioneer of the airmail service linking the islands of Scotland. A well-known aviator, at that time he was working for Scottish Airways, and on the day of the crash was actually in the air over Caithness, making a run between Inverness and Kirkwall in the Orkneys. He was in the same area as the doomed W4026 at the time of the crash, although he was much higher, above the clouds. The next day, which was beautifully clear, Fresson was asked to make an aerial reconnaissance of the crash site, because at that time its location was apparently not certain. So he ended up taking the only aerial photograph of the wreckage – a picture that has never been published before and which has several secrets to reveal.

In 1963 Fresson published his autobiography, *Air Road to the Isles*. In it one historic event is conspicuous by its absence: Chapter 11 ends in October 1940 (when he flew the Duke of Gloucester over Caithness), while Chapter 12 picks up the story on New Year's Day 1944. There is no mention whatsoever of any events in between. However, Fresson *did* write an account of the Kent crash – presumably to go in his book – because it was published by his son, Richard A. Fresson, in 1985 in the *Scotsman*, after a previous article had raised questions about Kent's death. This account suggests possible reasons why it had originally been censored.

Why was there a cover-up?

Because it is quite clear that there was – and still is – a cover-up about the Kent crash, several theories have been put forward to account for the conspiracy of silence and the obviously doctored official accounts.

It has been suggested that the crew and passengers were drunk, having partied before and even during the early stages of the flight.[36] This is based on the fact that various bottles of alcohol, including champagne, were found in the wreck. However, the more likely explanation is that these were gifts from the Duke for those at his intended destination. And although it seems that the Duke and his party had been drinking at their lunch at Invergordon just before take-off, there is no evidence that any of the crew had indulged. It would have been totally against regulations, the crew were highly professional, and Goyen in particular was known to be a stickler for discipline.

Another theory to account for the cover-up is that the Duke of Kent was at the controls when the plane crashed,[37] but there is no evidence for this, and indeed some against it. First, those in the cockpit, bearing the full brunt of the impact, would have been the most severely damaged, but, apart from a severe head wound, the Duke's body was not badly mutilated or burned. His wounds suggest he had been in the wardroom in the belly of the plane and was thrown clear. And he had an attaché case handcuffed to his wrist, which would have made piloting difficult.

The very nature of cover-ups often means that the answers to even the most basic questions need to be painstakingly pieced together, no more so than in this case. The first question is why was a flying boat used when Liberators routinely flew from Prestwick to Reykjavik?[38] But then, a flying boat having been chosen, why did W4026 leave from Invergordon, when Oban was the logical choice when departing for Iceland, being nearer and ensuring a safer route? The west coast was also where 228 Squadron was based: the Duke's plane had to fly from there to Invergordon on the east coast two days before the doomed flight. There was a very good reason why the squadron was based at Oban – the west coast of Scotland was out of range of most German fighter–bombers, whereas the east coast was much more exposed to their depredations. Surely such a risk was completely unnecessary, especially for a plane carrying such a VIP? Yet no explanation has ever been given for this anomaly, except the vague assurance that it was more 'accessible' for the Duke to join the flight at Invergordon.[39]

Not only were Greig, Ferguson, Herbert and Evans not on the flight, but the last-minute addition of Wing Commander Thomas Moseley has never been explained. And there was a curious incident in which Goyen gave Andy Jack a signed photograph of himself, just before take-off, on which he had written: 'With memories of happier days.'[40] Often taken as a poignant example of strange coincidence, or even some psychic foreshadowing of the tragedy, it may well have indicated that there was something different, possibly especially risky, about this particular trip. One recalls the wording of Marina's memorial: this was, in some way, a 'special mission'.

Of course, the big questions are how and why the plane crashed. Officially, the tragedy happened because the crew made two errors in abandoning the course of their original flight plan: they were flying

over land and not water, and were far too low, descending to the fatal
height of just 650 feet. The usual interpretation is that, enshrouded
in cloud, the plane had drifted off course, going below the cloud line
in order to reconnect visually with the coastline. But if the pilot
knew he was off course, he would not have gone down so low, precisely because they might have been flying over land (and in any
case, there were better alternatives). On the other hand, if he had
failed to realise he was off course, there was absolutely no reason to
take the plane down in the first place. So the reason for the devia-
tion has never been satisfactorily explained – even the official
summary admits to bemusement.

The mystery is compounded by the fact that there was certainly
no shortage of navigational expertise on board, yet to have reached
the point where it crashed, the plane would have had to drift a huge
15 degrees off course from its point of departure. Two different scenarios have been put forward to explain this. The first is that the
plane was gradually moving off course more or less from take-off,
either because of a compass error or because of crosswinds blowing it
sideways, steadily pushing it west without the pilot realising. In this
scenario, the plane was flying straight, but the track was wrong. The
second scenario is that the Sunderland was following its intended
course parallel to the coast, but then turned inland, which would
have necessitated a sharp turn, making it impossible to account for
in terms of instrument malfunction or crosswinds. To have crashed at
that spot, the pilot must have deliberately changed course. The first
scenario may be easily discounted because there were no crosswinds
strong enough to blow a heavy plane like a Sunderland sideways on
that particular day.[41] Moreover, it would have meant that the plane
approached the crash site on a course that would have taken it safely
over much higher hills before crashing (a very unlikely scenario).
This also disregards the findings of the court of inquiry that the pilot
changed the flight plan, not that the plane was off course. So the
plane seems to have deviated from its course quite deliberately for
some reason.

One explanation is that the pilot believed they were many miles
further on than they were, thinking they had passed Duncansby
Head, where he should have made the northwest turn towards
Iceland.[42] This seems very unlikely because it would have required a
major blunder on the part of the navigator for him to think the

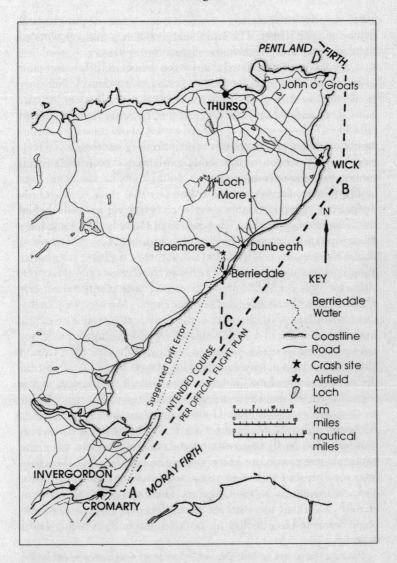

The flight plan of the Duke of Kent's flying boat, according to the official version. However, the plane crashed many miles from this course, prompting theories that the pilot changed direction at point C (thinking he was at point B) or that the plane drifted badly off-course.

plane was fifty miles ahead of where it was – twice the distance and flying time – and even if he had made such a major miscalculation, there was no reason to bring the plane down so low.

It has also been speculated that Goyen deliberately flew over land to save time by cutting across that corner of Scotland.[43] Not only would that have been in direct contravention of all safety instructions, it would have saved only a matter of minutes. An experienced pilot like Goyen would have realised that it would have been tantamount to suicide to attempt this at an altitude of less than 5,000 feet. And, more to the point, there would have been a compelling reason for him not to descend, because he would know he was flying over land, and mountainous terrain at that.

Another suggestion is that the plane's compasses were affected by local magnetic anomalies,[44] but although the area does sometimes cause weird navigational problems, they only affect compasses when planes fly over them – they don't lure them off course from miles away. Equipment malfunction – either in the navigational aids or the altimeter – has been put forward as an explanation of the crash, but while it cannot be totally ruled out (the inquiry found no fault in the instruments that were recovered, but some had been destroyed), it would have required a very unlikely set of circumstances. If, for example, the altimeter gave a false reading so that the pilot had no idea how low he was, why was the plane also off course? And why did the pilot take the plane low in the first place? Few accounts of the tragedy mention that the Sunderland was fitted with a new form of air-to-ground radar, a mark II anti-surface vessel (ASV) radar.[45] Although primarily designed for detecting enemy ships, it was also routinely used by flight navigators to find the coastline. So if the navigator had needed to know where the coastline was, he could have used his state-of-the-art radar, and not simply taken the plane down, as the official account suggests. There was also a radio beacon at RAF Wick that was used for navigation and which a navigator could have used to establish his position, rather than taking visual bearings.

Finally, there is Captain Fresson's evidence, which was excluded from his memoirs and only published in 1985. He states that he left Inverness on the morning of 25 August on his regular mail run to Kirkwall, from where he was returning at the time of the crash. He details the weather report he was given before leaving, which forecast bad weather across Caithness, but clear weather over the Pentland Firth. This was absolutely accurate – once he reached the northern coast of Scotland there was no cloud. Fresson commented: 'I have never understood what possessed that captain to take such unnecessary risks. He only had to fly on course for another ten minutes and he would have had the whole of the Pentland Firth in view.'[46]

Goyen would have had exactly the same weather forecast as Fresson, plus the benefit of knowing what the actual conditions were, as he took off much later. So if he was uncertain of his bearings he would have known that all he had to do was continue on course for another ten minutes to reach an area of perfect visibility, and take bearings from the coastline. Once again, then, there was no reason for him to descend. Robin Macwhirter discussed this with Group Captain Geoffrey Frances, the commanding officer at Invergordon at the time of the crash, who told him that if the navigator became disoriented in cloud, the standard procedure was to climb, specifically because of the risk of drifting over land, and to wait until he was certain that he was well clear of land before descending again.[47]

None of the theories as to why the plane was in that area and flying so low makes sense. However, the court of inquiry's summary makes a comment that sheds some important light on the issue: 'Captain of aircraft changed flight-plan for reasons unknown and descended through cloud without making sure he was over water and crashed.' Notice the wording: the Sunderland had not *deviated* from its flight plan, which is what the summary should have said if sticking to the standard line. Rather, it clearly implies that Goyen had deliberately chosen to fly in a new direction, changing the flight plan, and in doing so had signed his own death warrant. Indeed, the change of flight plan might explain why Moseley was on board: only he had the authority to change it while the plane was in the air; otherwise Goyen would have had to radio back to base.

In reconstructing the circumstances of the crash, the weather plays a vital role. Some of the search parties' reports claim that visibility was down to fifteen feet, but this is extremely unlikely. The weather was not that bad. According to Air Chief Marshal Sir Charles Portal in a report he sent to Winston Churchill the day after the crash, the cloud at Invergordon was at 1,000 feet, and even in that visibility was three miles.[48] Admittedly, there was a 'bad patch off Wick' (out at sea) where cloud was as low as 300 feet, but the crash site is about twenty-five miles from Wick. Certainly, beyond the north coast of Scotland – as reported by Captain Fresson – the weather was clear.

It seems that the Sunderland crashed in cloud, but visibility was not that bad – possibly even as much as a mile. This is supported by the court of inquiry, which stated: 'weather conditions presented no difficulties to a crew of such experience'. But even so, why did the navigator take the plane down? The only evidence that appears to support the official version is a remark said to have been made by Andy Jack in the statement presented in his name to the court of inquiry (although, as the papers have vanished, it is impossible to verify this). He is alleged to have said that he heard the pilot say on the intercom: 'Let's go down and take a look.'[49] But it would have been unlikely for Jack, in the tail, to have overheard any remark in the cockpit, because the pilot only pressed the intercom button when he had something specific to say.

Why did the plane crash on Eagle's Rock?

There are also problems with the position of the crash. The opposite side of the valley to Eagle's Rock – immediately to the south – is a peak known as Donald's Mount, which at a height of about 1,300 feet is considerably higher and marks the end of the massive ridge of the Scaraben, over 2,000 feet at its highest point. It seems very strange to have successfully cleared such a height before crashing into lower land. This has given rise to bizarre statements, such as Audrey Whiting's: 'The flying boat had just cleared the summit of a 900-foot hill known locally as Eagle's Rock, but the Sunderland did not clear the deep, narrow valley which separated it from the next rise.'[50]

The official version is that W4026, for reasons unknown, had turned inland and was following the course of the valley, although nearer to Berriedale the valley is too narrow for a Sunderland. Perhaps the plane had dropped – by sheer fluke – through the clouds into the wider valley near Eagle's Rock.

Comparing Fresson's aerial photograph with those taken on the ground and observations made on the site, it is clear that the wreckage was scattered in a north-northeast direction. Using the Fresson photograph and other censored pictures, together with the aid of metal detectors, we have been able to map the crash site and confirm this (there are still many small fragments of the plane embedded in the ground). We have also checked the impact marks on the ground – still visible after nearly sixty years. Fresson's photograph clearly shows the marks caused by the belly of the Sunderland, the two wing floats and the leading edges of the wing. The impact marks show that the plane hit the hillside with a glancing blow, skipping off the ground before somersaulting on its nose and crashing down on to its back – clearly shown on the aerial photograph. There is a gap of some yards between the scars caused by the belly and wing floats and the field of debris. In other words, the plane hit the ground, bounced once and then smashed into the hillside with enormous force.

The direction the Sunderland was taking can be worked out relatively easily from the marks made by the wings and floats on the ground. The port float and wing hit the ground slightly before the starboard float and wing, suggesting either that the plane was not quite level (although at the point of impact, the ground was) or that it was banking to port at the time. It is also clear that the Sunderland was flying on a northeasterly course at the moment of impact. This can be worked out because the wreckage lies in a north-northeast path and as the port wing hit the ground first and the engines were on full power, the plane would have been pulled round several degrees to port before the main body of the aircraft crashed into the ground. Therefore, the wreckage would have scattered along a path in a slightly more northerly direction than the track of the aircraft.

So the Duke of Kent's plane did not approach the hill directly from the south but was turning into Eagle's Rock from a more westerly direction. However, there are problems with this. First, if the pilot had come up the valley, he would have had to turn to port to end up where he did, in which case the plane would have been travelling in a northwesterly direction, not northeast. And it would mean that he had turned towards *higher* ground, whereas continuing in a straight line would have enabled the plane to pass safely over the lower end of Eagle's Rock. On the other hand, if the Sunderland had approached from the south, there is a problem with the angle at which it hit the ground and the pitch of the propellers. Directly south of the crash point, on the other side of the valley, is the much higher Donald's Mount, some 650 feet higher than the crash site. In

order to have cleared Donald's Mount but hit Eagle's Rock, the plane
would have had to come in at a very steep angle, but in that case it
would have ploughed into the hillside leaving an impact crater, and
not skipped off it. And the pitch of the propellers showed that it was
climbing, not descending. The same problem applies if the plane was
banking, as the evidence of the port wing suggests. Although it is
impossible to gauge how steeply the plane banked or how tightly it
turned, it must have been turning to port, meaning that it was
approaching from somewhere west of south, which would have
brought it in over the even higher ridge of the Scaraben, again
demanding a steep angle of approach. But in that case where is the
impact crater one would expect?

Taken with the standard line, the evidence makes no sense. There
are too many problems, too many glaring inconsistencies to make it
work. But the data does fit, as we will see, an alternative explanation,
which radically changes the picture and raises some new questions
about Kent's 'special mission'.

Inside the doomed flight

Several researchers have raised the question about who was flying
the plane when it crashed. According to Corporal Tim Wilson, who
had served with Andy Jack in Oban and later met him when he
passed through RAF Aldergrove in Northern Ireland in 1943, Jack
told him that Wing Commander Moseley was in the number 1 seat,
Goyen in the number 2 position, while the Duke of Kent stood
between them.[51] This must have been the scene as Jack saw it before
moving to the rear turret just after the plane took off, so it is unlikely
that Kent was still standing there when it crashed.

The number 1 seat (on the left looking from the door) is customarily taken by the pilot, with the co-pilot in the number 2 position
to his right.[52] If Moseley was in the number 1 seat, it suggests that it
was he rather than Goyen who was flying the plane. In 1961 Jack
stated that, ten minutes into the flight, he made a routine test of the
intercom from the tail turret to the cockpit, adding the carefully
chosen words: 'I had no other conversation with any other member
of the crew or captain again.' Did he talk to someone else on board,
someone who was neither a crew member nor the captain?

However, according to Corporal Wilson, Jack *did* say that he had called the cockpit again, after dropping some smoke flares to check the wind direction, but that it was Moseley, not Goyen, who replied.[53] As Moseley was the squadron's commanding officer, he was neither the captain nor a member of the crew – so was *he* the person with whom Jack so cunningly implied he had had a conversation? But if he was flying the plane at the time of the crash, why does the official account so obviously not want us to know about it?

There are also major problems with the timing of the crash. As we have seen already, the court of inquiry's report introduces some uncertainty, noting the time as approximately 2 p.m. Instead of an estimate of the duration of the flight, there is that evasive question mark. The squadron's record book, which has all the details of every flight, also gives the time of the crash as 1400 hours.[54] Since there is no doubt that the Sunderland took off at 13.10, if the plane crashed at 1400 hours, why not record the duration of the flight as approximately fifty minutes? It seems simple enough, after all. But, of course, had the entry been made, it would have drawn attention to a glaring anomaly: at the outside, the crash site is only twenty-five minutes from Invergordon – so there are between twenty and twenty-five minutes unaccounted for.

Most published accounts state that the Sunderland crashed between 1.30 and 1.40 p.m.. This is said to be based on the fact that both the cockpit clock and the Duke's watch stopped at the moment of impact, freezing the time for ever. Dr Kennedy, believing it to be useful evidence, had handed over Kent's wristwatch to the authorities, but neither his account nor any contemporary report says what time the watch was showing. As Robin Macwhirter has pointed out, it was simply assumed that it and the plane's clock had stopped around this time after the flying time required to reach the site had been worked out.[55] In fact, nobody has ever stated the time at which the timepieces stopped, although many accounts report that the Morrisons and other local people – for example, at Langwell House on the Portland estate – heard the plane overhead at 1.30 p.m. But it transpires that, once again, this is based on an assumption that they *should* have heard it then.

However, we have unearthed local press reports from the *Caithness Courier* and the *John o' Groat Journal* – both very reliable sources for details of the tragedy, given that their reporters were members of the tightly knit communities in the area – which tell quite a different story. On the Friday after the crash, the weekly *John o' Groat Journal* carried an interview with David Morrison (the elder of the two farmers who heard the crash and raised the alarm), who said that the crash occurred at 2.30 p.m. – half an hour later than the approximate time given by the authorities and a whole hour later than most accounts.[56] And the 2.30 p.m. time can be shown to be consistent with the rest of Morrison's testimony. He says that, after they heard the explosion, his son Hugh rushed off on his motorcycle to raise the alarm in nearby Braemore, about two miles away. After Hugh returned with 'local inhabitants and military personnel',[57] who formed a search party, his father said it took them an hour to locate the wreck, and that they found it at about four o'clock. Allowing half an hour for Morrison to raise a search party, contact the constabulary and telephone the doctor in Dunbeath, the timings tally perfectly. Whatever the later accounts claimed, it is clear that the local reporters were all working on the understanding that the crash happened at 2.30 p.m.: for example, Andy Jack is reported as turning up at Mrs Sutherland's cottage twenty-three hours after the crash – at 1.30 the next afternoon.[58] The court of inquiry tacitly acknowledges the problem by giving a time between when the plane should have crashed and when it was reported as having crashed, effectively splitting the difference. And by neglecting to give the duration of the flight, the inquiry reveals it was aware of the anomaly.

This sort of evasion is typical of the mentality of officials. Such people are very wary of lying directly in official documents, knowing it may well come back to haunt them one day. Instead they depend on their skilful use of words – a technique honed by generations of British civil servants over the centuries. To this mindset, a crash time of 'approximately' 1400 hours can be justified as meaning anywhere between 13.30 and 14.30, whereas baldly giving a flight duration of fifty minutes would risk drawing attention to the anomaly. The question mark is a safer bet – at the very least, there are likely to be fewer comebacks. The official report is, in its own way, a small masterpiece: there are no direct lies in it, only the most adroit evasions.

Other information supports the locals' timing. In an interview with Robert Brydon in 1985, Dr Kennedy's daughter Louise recalled that the telephone call about the crash had been received at 'about two-thirty'. (Hugh Morrison rode two miles to Braemore on his motorcycle to raise the alarm. Although the sole telephone in the hamlet, in the gamekeeper's cottage, only connected to Langwell House, and the message had then to be relayed through the public exchange, this could not have taken more than fifteen minutes.)

The Prime Minister's papers in the Public Record Office include a note – timed at 9.55 p.m. – by the person who received the call from the Air Ministry breaking the news of the Duke of Kent's death. This states that the Sunderland had taken off at 1.30 p.m. (incorrect, of course) and that it had crashed 'one hour later'. (It also records 'Local weather not bad as a whole' and that patrols had been flying.)[59]

As Robin Macwhirter wrote in 1985: 'If the crash did not occur till 2 p.m. then the machine was taken somewhere to do something specific in the intervening time.'[60] And, of course, there is even more time unaccounted for if the crash happened half an hour later. Where was the Sunderland during that time?

In the 1961 newspaper article, Andy Jack is also evasive. He says that the plane was 'probably' airborne for about twenty minutes before it ran into low cloud, adding, 'I can't remember exactly.' Although this seems, at first glance, to corroborate the official version, he is careful to give only the time before the plane entered the cloud. He does not relate the time that elapsed before the crash. In fact, Jack denies all knowledge of what was happening to the plane, because he was too isolated in the rear turret to be aware of what was going on in the cockpit. However, in another account, he says 'in another two minutes we would have been over the sea'. This is more than a little bizarre. Jack must have known that, according to the official reports, the Sunderland was heading inland – *away* from the sea – when it crashed. Had it continued on that course it would have had to cross the whole of Caithness – some twenty-five miles – to reach the Pentland Firth, taking a minimum of ten minutes, not two. Had Jack stuck to the official line, he would never have made such an elementary mistake, which suggests he had a shrewd idea of where the plane was and its intended course. But, given the direction of flight, how could he have thought they would be over the sea in two minutes?

The body count

However, there is one anomaly that eclipses even the mystery of the missing hour. The initial accounts make it clear that there was *one body too many in the wreckage*. When W4026 took off, there is no doubt that there were fifteen people on board: ten crew, their commanding officer, the Duke of Kent and three members of his entourage. The Air Ministry's announcement of the evening of 25 August stated 'All the crew of the flying-boat lost their lives'. The first newspaper reports, the next morning, said that everybody on board had been killed, fifteen in all, but the next day, when Andy Jack turned up, they hastily adjusted the total to fourteen dead with one survivor.

This was not merely a mistake. The reporters were not speculating, but basing their articles on the official announcement. For example, the *Glasgow Herald* of 27 August, reporting the survival of Andy Jack, said: 'Previously it had been *officially stated* [our emphasis] that all the crew and passengers, said to number 16, had perished.'[61] Confusion was setting in: the day before all aboard had been killed, fifteen in all, but now the *Herald* is trying to reconcile this by assuming that sixteen were on board, of whom fifteen were killed.

The Air Ministry informed the press that there were no survivors and that fifteen people were on board – which is surely inconceivable without first checking the number of bodies. By that time many people had visited the site, including the district doctor, the police and an RAF team from Wick. And although some of the bodies were terribly burned, none had been torn apart, which is what normally presents difficulties in counting bodies at the site of a major disaster. When the team from RAF Wick arrived at the scene, it is unlikely that they knew anything about the flight, but by the evening they would have been in contact with Invergordon and been fully put in the picture. They would have known how many people were on board and they would have counted the bodies. Even if, through some peculiar incompetence, they had miscounted, the next morning a more senior group of RAF and Admiralty officials visited the site and would surely have corrected them. Not only that, but the bodies were removed that morning by ambulances before Andy Jack turned up unexpectedly. This would have required a certain amount of organisation, giving them plenty of time to familiarise themselves with the number of bodies – yet nobody had, apparently, realised that they were one body short. This is confirmed by a report in the *Evening Citizen* of 26 August – the situation as it was understood on the evening of the day after the crash – which makes no mention of Jack's survival, probably because it went to press before the news came through. It said: 'The other occupants of the plane [besides the Duke] were also killed, *and it is now known that all the bodies have been recovered from the wreckage* [our emphasis].'[62]

While it is inconceivable that no one would have checked the number of the crew against the number of bodies, surely it is also inconceivable that a telegram was dispatched to Andy Jack's next of kin telling them he had died if there had been any room for doubt. Although some of the bodies were unrecognisable, the telegram would not have been sent before all the bodies had been accounted for, if not identified.

News stories continued to be confused. One newspaper report of the Duke of Kent's funeral states that (besides his body) those of ten airmen had been sent south by train, and four others taken to 'a Scottish town'[63] – a typically coy wartime reference to Oban, where the four Commonwealth casualties were buried. This brings the total to fifteen. To add to the confusion, another report refers to the bodies of five airmen being taken to Oban.[64] But the local Caithness newspapers are the most insistent on the number of bodies – so insistent that it seems they go as far as they can to score a point against the official censors. The weekly *John o' Groat Journal*, which appeared every Friday, had as its headline on 28 August (two days after Jack's appearance):

DUKE OF KENT KILLED IN AIR CRASH
TRAGEDY IN THE NORTH OF SCOTLAND
FIFTEEN DEAD IN WRECKED PLANE
SURVIVOR DISCOVERED ON FOLLOWING DAY

The following week, on 4 September, the newspaper was still referring to Jack as 'the sole survivor of the plane crash in which the Duke of Kent and 14 others lost their lives'. To the *Journal*, at least, there was no doubt that there had been sixteen on board. Then, on 18 September, reporting the visit of George VI to the crash site four

days earlier, it said that the crash 'resulted in the death of 15 out of
16 occupants'. It also ended the report by saying: 'The King asked
about the finding of *all* 15 victims of the crash, and before he left he
made special enquiries about the progress of Flight Sergt. Jack, the
only survivor [our emphasis].' It must not be forgotten that these
reporters had advantages over their colleagues on other papers: not
only did they know the local gossip, but they would have had contacts among people who had been members of the search parties
and recovery teams.

A local history book published in Wick in 1948 (and reprinted in
1994), *Caithness – and the War, 1939–1945* by Norman M. Glass
and compiled from local newspaper archives, states that Kent 'set out
for Iceland on the afternoon of Tuesday, August 25, 1942, in a
Sunderland flying boat carrying 16 in all' and that, when the search
parties arrived at the crash site 'All the occupants (15) were dead'.[65]

There is no room for doubt. There was one more person on the
plane when it crashed than when it took off. But whose was the extra
body and where did it come from?

Conclusion

The crash that killed the Duke of Kent is an acknowledged aviation
mystery, but the mystery has always centred on the cause, why the
plane crashed where it did, the 'missing time' and the fact that the
official records are obviously covering up something. That is why
most of the speculation to date has focused on questions such as
whether Kent himself was flying the plane, or whether the pilot –
whoever he was – had been drinking. In fact, until Robert became
interested in the mystery in the 1980s, nobody, to our knowledge,
had even realised the anomaly of the extra body. And nobody has
ever questioned other aspects of the flight, such as why the party
chose not to go on the regular Liberator run from Prestwick, and why
the flying boat took off from Invergordon, instead of the usual – and
safer – Oban. Certainly, no one has asked whether this flight was
anything other than what it was supposed to be – a routine transit
flight carrying a member of the Royal Family on a morale-boosting
visit to Iceland. But there are clues that there was something else
going on, something that the authorities still do not want us to
know. Why did Marina insist that the memorial describe the flight as

a 'special mission'? And is it a coincidence that that was the very same phrase used by Rudolf Hess to describe his own flight?

There are other hints and clues as to what was really going on. Sir Samuel Hoare made a speech to his wife Maud's Madrid 'Knitting Party' (who provided socks and other woolly comforts for internees in Spain) in October, stating that: 'I knew the Duke of Kent very well. In fact, it was due to me that he undertook the duties in the Air Force which he was carrying out at the time of his death.'[66]

What was Kent's 'special mission'? And what is its connection to the Rudolf Hess story?

CHAPTER THIRTEEN

Reassembling the Pieces

A major turning point in our investigation was the moment, in May 1993, when Lord Thurso told Stephen Prior about Hess's detention at Braemore Lodge. However, he proved he had yet more crucial evidence to impart. He particularly remembered the crash that killed the Duke of Kent because it happened practically on his own doorstep. The search party that found the wreck had been mustered from 'locals and military personnel' from the hamlet of Braemore – not far from Braemore Lodge. Thurso, who was then nineteen, had more reason than most to remember the circumstances surrounding the tragedy, not least because on answering the door of his home, Dalnawillan Lodge (the main house on the Thurso estate) one day in 1942, who should he find there but the King. (Presumably this was at the time of the latter's 'pilgrimage' to the crash site.) This was interesting, but not as relevant as his next recollection. In the context of the King's visit and the Sunderland crash, he casually mentioned that his father, Sir Archibald Sinclair, occasionally used to travel back from London to his Caithness estate at weekends by flying boat, landing on Loch More (from where it was only a short walk or two-minute drive to Dalnawillan Lodge). To have evidence of a flying boat on Loch More – *any* flying boat – was a revelation.

When Robert Brydon first began researching the crash, he realised that the principal conundrums relating to the Kent crash revolved around why his flying boat was over land at all, where it had been for the missing hour and why there was one body too many on board.

Could the plane have landed on an inland body of water – a loch, for example? Checking the map, he found that there were three possible landing sites, but only one of them was on the land of Sir Archibald Sinclair: Loch More. So when Lord Thurso told Stephen Prior about Hess being kept at Braemore Lodge and briefly at the lochside, suddenly both researchers had a blinding revelation: there seemed to be an explosive link between the Kent and the Hess mysteries. Could it be that the answer to one of these mysteries would prove to be the key to the other, too? Could the Duke of Kent's Sunderland have put down on Loch More *in order to pick up Rudolf Hess?*

Sounding out Loch More

Loch More lies about eight miles to the north of the crash site, where the hills give way to the flat moorland and pine forest that characterise the northeastern tip of Britain. There is a private, unsurfaced road, which runs from Braemore through the hills and down the valley of Strathmore Water to Loch More itself. The two cottages mentioned by Lord Thurso – Braemore Lodge and Lochmore Cottage – are on the same road (although only nine miles apart as the crow flies, the road winds for fifteen between them). It makes sense that Hess would have been kept in the larger Braemore Lodge, and taken to Lochmore Cottage to be kept out of sight while waiting for the flying boat.

But was it possible for a large seaplane like a Sunderland to land and take off from Loch More? Although Thurso said that his father used flying boats on the loch, he didn't say what type, although it is likely to have been something smaller and more easily manoeuvrable than a Sunderland – a Catalina, for example. Using a large boat just to fly one man (albeit a senior cabinet minister) home for the weekend would have been considered an excessive waste of resources, especially in wartime. Loch More is one of the largest of the many lochs in that area, some two miles long by about a third of a mile wide at its broadest point, stretching almost exactly north–south, although it bends at the southern end, where it is joined by Strathmore Water. A heavily laden Sunderland can take off within three-quarters of a mile and land in even less.[1] Unlike the other lochs near by, Loch More is isolated from the public gaze, being in the middle of the Sinclairs' private estate. The nearest village – Westerdale – is some

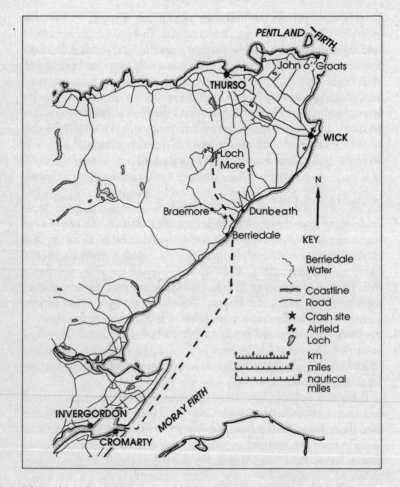

This is the authors' reconstruction of the course that the Duke of Kent's flying boat took in order to set down on Loch More.

five miles away. Nor is it overlooked: unlike the crash site, this part of Caithness is flat.

Lochmore Cottage, a small bungalow, is situated at the north end of the loch, where the River Thurso flows out, eventually to join the sea at Thurso. There is a small dam and sluice, which controls the level of the loch, and from there a road winds through the Sinclair estate.

The Sunderland would have approached from the southern, shallower end, landing towards the deeper end where the cottage is. After picking up its passenger, it would then turn round and take off in a southerly direction. (The pine forest at the north would have been too high to clear.) At this point, where Strathmore Water feeds the loch, it is extremely marshy, which in itself would provide another mile of take-off water. A Sunderland that has already partly risen from the water can move relatively well over marsh – indeed, it would help by giving it the necessary 'bounce' to make it airborne.

So, although it would have been tricky, it was certainly possible for an experienced pilot to put a Sunderland down on Loch More and take her up again. But assuming that all went to plan, what happened next? Apart from accounting for the missing hour, can this hypothesis about the plane diverting to Loch More tell us anything about the crash itself?

It is possible to reconstruct the course that the plane would have taken to arrive at Loch More, and – more importantly – how it travelled to the crash site at Eagle's Rock. The most direct approach to Loch More takes it over the same route as the one favoured by most investigators – turning in from the coast and following Berriedale Water. However, taking this route would have entailed the risks that were discussed earlier, flying over the peaks of the Scaraben range while descending through low cloud. A more logical and safer option would have been to continue along the coast, turning inland after Berriedale once the hills had been passed. (The flying boat had been reported being heard at Langwell House at 1.30 p.m., but it could just as easily have been flying along the coastline as inland along Berriedale Water.)

However, taking off would have presented more difficulty. Of necessity, the Sunderland had to take off heading south, and would then have headed directly for the hills, specifically the wall of the Scaraben some nine miles away. A fully laden Sunderland is a sluggish climber, although the climb rate depends on several factors, including the weather: it was probably as little as 200 feet per minute.[2] With a full load, a Sunderland has to get up to at least 80 miles an hour to take off, covering perhaps one and a half miles per minute, and taking about six minutes to reach the Scaraben, when it would have climbed to around 1,200 feet. Loch More itself is a little over 400 feet above sea level, and the highest points of the Scaraben are around 2,000 feet, so there is a question as to whether the Sunderland could have gained enough height in time. Even if it could, the pilot was unlikely to risk it in low cloud, since heading into the hills with limited visibility and such a small safety margin would be tantamount to suicide. In the circumstances, even if the plane could have climbed higher, it would have been sure to stay below the cloud so that the navigator could find his way to the sea by keeping an eye open for landmarks.

Ideally, the pilot would – as soon as possible into the flight – have turned to port (east), towards the coast, before reaching the hills. But even this would have taken them into significantly higher ground, varying between 600 and 850 feet, before they had managed to gain much height. (When banking to turn, a Sunderland always loses height.) The pilot would have wanted to keep as straight as possible, to gain as much height as he could – but still wanting to turn to port before reaching the hills. Given all these difficulties, the most logical course of action would have been to gain as much height as possible while turning into a valley that would lead towards the open sea and safety.

Captain Fresson's aerial photograph at first glance seems to provide confirmation of this reconstruction. From the way the wreckage lies, it appears as if the plane was indeed flying in the opposite direction to the official version: the tail section is in the north and the engines lie with their propellers facing towards the south. Perhaps the official line, which has the plane flipping on to its back on impact, was an invention to cover up the dangerous fact that it was coming from the wrong direction. However, it is not that simple.

On the aerial shot the marks on the ground caused by the various parts of the plane – belly, floats and leading edges of the wing – were to the southwest of the field of debris, meaning that the plane came in from that direction, hit the hillside and did a somersault on to its back. The plane *had* been travelling in a northeasterly direction when it crashed, and yet, if the reconstruction that the Sunderland had taken off from Loch More is correct, it should have been heading south. The theory looked fatally flawed, but then another explanation presented itself. Heading south from Loch More, with

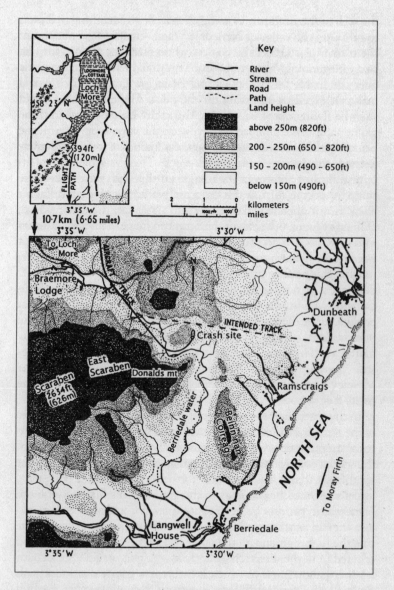

Authors' reconstruction of the actual, compared with the intended, course of the Duke of Kent's flight after leaving Loch More.

the wall of the Scaraben looming ahead, the logical thing to do was to turn into the valley of Berriedale Water – much wider and flatter there than it is nearer the coast – while planning to turn into an eastward-running valley to the sea. This would have taken the plane over the hamlet of Braemore, and Braemore Lodge, which would make an excellent landmark for the pilot. The Sunderland would then be flying southeast, making the relatively easy turn into the valley. Ahead the pilot would have seen the impassable ridge of the Scaraben to starboard, while to port was a series of lower hills interspersed with valleys – and Eagle's Rock. There is something of an optical illusion, however: looking down the Berriedale Valley, the sharp 90-degree turn as the river and valley bend around Eagle's Rock is not apparent. Once past Eagle's Rock, the steep side of Donald's Mount – the end of the Scaraben range – suddenly rears up into view. Faced with this abrupt, insurmountable obstacle, the pilot would immediately turn to port, banking sharply and therefore losing height. But at that point the valley turns a little more than 90 degrees, as if turning back on itself. To avoid hitting the side of Donald's Mount, the pilot would have to take them in the tightest possible circle. There was only one way out, over the lower ground behind Eagle's Rock, which would require an almost impossible manoeuvre – going into a virtual U-turn before immediately straightening up again. The pilot – probably Wing Commander Moseley – almost made it, failing to clear the ridge by just some thirty feet.

In the absence of eye-witness testimony, the precise circumstances of the Kent crash must remain a matter for speculation, although this reconstruction does fit. If the plane had made a tight turn in from the southwest and failed to straighten up in time, that would account for the fact that it was travelling northeast, and that the port side – as demonstrated by the scars in the ground – hit first, because the plane was in the process of straightening up from banking. It would also explain how the plane came in from that direction without hitting the higher ground on the other side of the valley, because it had entered from the direction of Loch More. This would also account for the shallow angle at which it hit. It is similarly consistent with Andy Jack's apparently bizarre statement that 'another two minutes and we would have been over the sea'. If the standard version is correct, this is nonsense. But if Jack knew the plane was coming from another direction entirely, heading for the coast, it makes perfect sense. Finally, this version also explains the curious wording of the court of inquiry's conclusions that the pilot 'changed the flight plan for reasons unknown', implying that it was a deliberate act on the part of the pilot.

However, the question remains as to why the plane was in the valley in the first place. There are two possible scenarios: either Moseley failed to get the plane any higher or he deliberately chose to take that route. If the latter, perhaps he planned to make a turn between the peaks of Cnoc na Feadiage at 1,050 feet and Eagle's Rock, at 850 feet. The valley between them would take the plane directly to the coast and safety. In other words, he intended to turn before he reached Eagle's Rock, but, looking along the Berriedale Valley, he failed to distinguish between the two very similar-looking peaks. He could simply have missed his turning (it seems obvious on the map, but from the cockpit would be far less so). On the other hand, if the plane simply failed to gain sufficient height, was this because of mechanical failure or deliberate sabotage? Was the Kent crash engineered? Were those on board the Sunderland murdered?

Sabotage?

Any direct evidence of sabotage would have been scrupulously cleared from the site with the rest of the wreckage almost immediately. Conveniently, the report of the investigation into the crash promptly disappeared. On the other hand, perhaps such evidence was never found. There were tried-and-tested methods of sabotaging aircraft that are very difficult to spot, especially in a total wreck like that of W4026. In the absence of any physical or documentary evidence, two questions may be asked: how likely is it that sabotage could have resulted in this kind of crash? And was there anything particularly suspicious either before or after the crash?

There are some striking parallels with the Kent crash. Perhaps the most relevant – and eerily similar – was the mysterious death of Kent's great friend General Sikorski on 4 July 1943. Returning in a Liberator from a visit to Polish forces in Egypt, he had stopped to refuel in Gibraltar. Within minutes of taking off the plane crashed into the sea, landing upside down in thirty feet of water. As with the

Kent crash, there was only one survivor, this time the Czech pilot, Flight Lieutenant Edward Prchal. (Of all those on board, he alone had put on his life jacket, but not, as was the usual practice, under his parachute harness, perhaps implying that he expected to crash into water rather than bail out from high in the sky.) An RAF court of inquiry found the immediate reason for the crash but not its cause: the elevator controls had jammed shortly after take-off, but the inquiry could not establish why they had jammed.[3] Although the court concluded that it was an accident, not sabotage, many had their doubts: the Polish government in exile asked how the court could be so sure, if the cause could not be established;[4] and Sumner Welles, the US Under-Secretary of State, explicitly called Sikorski's death an 'assassination'.[5]

The suspicion of sabotage is compounded by the fact that eight months before, in November 1942, Sikorski had been involved in a similar incident that *had* been declared to be sabotage by both the US and British governments. Going to the USA for a meeting with Roosevelt, after first flying across the Atlantic to Montreal, he boarded a Lockheed Hudson to complete his journey. On take-off, when the plane was only thirty feet in the air, both engines cut out. The pilot made a successful emergency landing; Sikorski escaped unhurt.[6]

If Sikorski was assassinated, who was responsible? Although the Germans might seem to be the prime suspects, at that stage of the war the Polish Prime Minister had other potential enemies – some rather surprising. He was regarded as something of an obstacle by Winston Churchill, who (together with Anthony Eden) had already agreed to allow the Soviet Union, after the war, to keep at least some of the Polish territory they had occupied in 1939.[7] Understandably, Sikorski was furious. On the other hand, Stalin was also unhappy with Britain's support for the exiled Polish government. This maelstrom of suspicion and plotting culminated in Sikorski's apparent assassination, and at least one person seems to have had no doubts about who was responsible: Sikorski's widow pointedly shunned Churchill ever afterwards.[8]

A very similar incident happened with General de Gaulle, although it was not made public until 1967. In the spring of 1943, the Free French leader was due to visit Glasgow, and although he hated flying, he was persuaded to travel by plane. At the suggestion of the Air Ministry (and, therefore, of Sir Archibald Sinclair), de Gaulle was to go from RAF Hendon in north London to Abbotsinch near Glasgow by Wellington bomber. But – just as in the Sikorski tragedy – on take-off the plane's elevators failed to respond. On this occasion the flight was instantly aborted and no harm befell the French leader. A secret RAF investigation found that the control rods had been eaten through with acid – clearly a deliberate act of sabotage – and hastened to lay the blame squarely on German infiltrators.[9] However, as recently released files make abundantly clear, this happened at a time when Churchill had come to regard de Gaulle as a nuisance to be 'eliminated'.[10]

In his book on the Sikorski crash, *Accident* (1967), David Irving makes the point that the British had both the motive and the opportunity to sabotage Sikorski's plane. He also makes the following observation, which could equally apply to the Kent affair: 'To the layman, perfect sabotage is when an aircraft disappears without trace in mid-Atlantic; but any country trying to dispose cleanly of a General so publicly important as Sikorski would *have* to make his death seem accidental, and impossible to prove as otherwise.'[11] In other words, there has to be a wreck and bodies, precisely to allay any doubts.

Of the three examples just discussed, two demonstrably involve tampering with elevator controls to prevent the plane from gaining height. In the case of the de Gaulle attempt, had the plane crashed, the cause might never have been established. How would the investigators have spotted the insidious work of acid on elevator rods in a total wreck, especially in those wartime days, when forensic science was still relatively unsophisticated and not all accidents were thoroughly investigated?

There seems little doubt that the British – presumably certain elements in SOE – were responsible for both the Sikorski assassination and the attempt on General de Gaulle's life, which suggests that their preferred method for ridding themselves of troublesome VIPs was by air 'accident'. None of this proves that the Kent crash was also due to British sabotage, but it is certainly a serious possibility. SOE, infiltrated by Philby and other Soviet agents, served two masters: Churchill and Stalin. Both had reasons for sabotage in all these incidents.

Suspicious circumstances

Just ten days after the Kent tragedy, there was another Sunderland crash. This flying boat – also from 228 Squadron – crashed off Tiree on 4 September 1942, killing respected Glasgow journalist Fred Nancarrow. The official verdict was that the plane had run out of fuel. While possible, it seems somewhat strange that such a thing could have happened. (Both the ground crew and the pilot would have had to have made one of the most fundamental errors possible – an extraordinary coincidence.)

Among journalistic circles in Glasgow it has long been thought that there was something very suspicious about Nancarrow's death, but no explanation has yet been forthcoming.

Nancarrow was the only reporter to cover both Hess's arrival and the Kent crash, because he was Scotland's leading aviation journalist. After the Battle of Britain he wrote a history of Glasgow's 602 Squadron, with a foreword by Sir Patrick Dollan, the outspoken Lord Provost of Glasgow, a close friend. Nancarrow's obituary in the *Glasgow Herald* said that at the time of his death he was working on a 'revised and enlarged' edition of that book.[12] As Dollan was very interested in the true story of the Hess mission (particularly the existence of the British 'peace group'), had he engaged – or at least inspired – Fred Nancarrow to investigate it? After all, the journalist would have had some very interesting contacts, especially in the aviation world, who might have been willing to talk to him but not to others. Had he stumbled on some secret connected with the Hess affair? Was this why Nancarrow had to die?

His death is by no means the only 'extra' mystery surrounding the Kent crash. Who were the 'military personnel' at Braemore who, together with the locals, joined the search party? What they were doing there – even which unit they belonged to – has never been revealed. It is tempting to speculate that they were part of Hess's guard. And why did this group of military men fail to leave a guard at the crash site? Special Constable Bethune testified that when he and his companion were almost there, they met members of the first search party on their way back down. He specifically stated that they tried to dissuade him from going on to the site because, as everyone on the plane was dead, there was no point, but he insisted it was his duty to see for himself.[13] While it might be understandable that the local people – civilians – would not think of leaving a guard at the site, surely a group of soldiers would.

It is also intriguing that there was a team of army sabotage experts in the area that day – at Berriedale. This was what was known as an 'Oxen Unit' (so called because their cover was that they were cattle inspectors) which toured Scotland training local volunteer groups – called Auxiliary Units – in guerrilla tactics to be used in the event of an invasion.[14] These Auxiliary Units were linked to SOE as they had been set up by Brigadier Colin Gubbins, later its head.[15] However, this Oxen Unit was unlikely to be the 'military personnel' just mentioned, because, although Berriedale is only some five miles from Braemore, there is no direct road between them, only a footpath, so they could not have joined the hastily assembled search party at Braemore within, at most, half an hour of the crash.

Another puzzle concerns the RAF unit that so thoroughly cleared the wreckage from the crash site – No. 63 Maintenance Unit, which also happens to be the one that cleared the wreckage of Hess's Me-110.[16] Their use in the earlier crash made sense, for they were based at Carluke, near Glasgow, but why were they used to clear the Kent crash, roughly 200 miles away from base? Surely there was a similarly qualified unit much closer to Eagle's Rock, such as at RAF Wick, just twenty-five miles away.

Behind the scenes

As we have seen, wartime British intelligence operations were characterised by a simmering feud between MI6 and SOE. Although both of them were represented on the Joint Intelligence Committee, Victor Cavendish-Bentinck (later the Duke of Portland) allied himself more closely with MI6, which earned him SOE's displeasure and distrust. He was so unpopular with them that he claimed: 'SOE would gladly have murdered me.'[17] That this was no mere figure of speech is shown by the fact that Cavendish-Bentinck went on to say that he arranged with an MI6 scientist reporting directly to Menzies that if he died suddenly the scientist should conduct the post-mortem examination on his body.

If Hess was on the Portland estate, it seems likely he was there because of the intervention of Cavendish-Bentinck. Kim Philby had predicted in May 1941 that the peace group would still try to use

Hess in the future, which would make sense. As long as the Deputy Führer was still in the country, as far as they were concerned it was a case of 'where there's life, there's hope' – in itself enough to prove fatal for the real Rudolf Hess.

We have seen that Hess was also said to be at Loch More on the Sinclair estate, which implies the knowledge, support and participation of Sir Archibald Sinclair, although his personal allegiances are frustratingly hard to pin down. On some occasions he appears to belong to the peace group, while on others he comes across as strictly a Churchill man. This dichotomy is exemplified by the fact that he was close to both the Prime Minister and Menzies, between whom there was notoriously no love lost. Indeed, Sinclair seems to have acted as something of a mediator between the two, suggesting that – truly neutral friends being extremely rare, especially where such opinionated politicians were concerned – both men regarded him as being ultimately on their side. (Interestingly, Menzies was often invited to join the shooting party on the estate, so he was familiar with its layout.[18]) However, it is entirely possible that Sinclair – who was in London on the day of the crash – knew nothing about it. But there was one person who linked him with the Duke of Kent: Group Captain Sir Louis Greig. In 1942 he had not only been part of Kent's entourage for many years, but was Sinclair's private secretary.[19] He was therefore bound to have been familiar with the Sinclair estate and probably even organised Sinclair's flights home by flying boat. It has often been remarked that Greig was a very lucky man because he always accompanied Kent on his foreign travels. Why he failed to do so on this fatal occasion has never been explained.

'Like a white bird'

If the Duke of Kent picked up Hess from his lochside cottage and took him off – as it happened, to his death – what were these two apparently ill-matched VIPs up to? What was the real nature of the 'special mission' so carefully mentioned on the Kent memorial?

Since the Hess affair had often involved Sweden, it seems logical that the Sunderland's true destination was somewhere in that neutral country. If it was heading for somewhere other than Iceland – its official destination – the pilot would have requested weather reports for that area, which would explain why the flight plan disappeared and the meteorological personnel were press-ganged into the forces and made to sign the Official Secrets Act. If Kent's destination were really Sweden, it would also explain why he took off from Invergordon, on the east coast, rather than the more logical Oban, where the plane was based and which is nearer to Iceland. Although the initial stages of the journey would be the same, flying parallel to the coast as far as Duncansby Head, for Iceland they should then have turned northwest, and for Sweden in a more easterly direction. Coincidentally, the distances (and therefore flying time and amount of fuel needed) from Invergordon to Reykjavik and Stockholm are almost the same – about 750 miles.

Andy Jack's sister, Jean, recalled that on the Saturday before the crash she had visited her brother in Oban, and had been taken to see the Sunderland being prepared. It was in the process of being painted white, looking 'like a white bird'.[20] Pieces of the wreckage we brought back from the crash site confirm this, showing that the customary olive and brown camouflage had been covered over with white paint. This was odd because in 1942 Sunderlands were painted camouflage olive and brown, although early in 1943 they were ordered to be painted white.[21] (This was because they were fitted with a new type of depth charge which meant that they had to fly lower, and so needed to be less visible.) However, during the war, flights between Britain and neutral Sweden were painted white. Lieutenant Colonel Ewan Butler, in his 1963 book *Amateur Agent*, describes how Dakotas that made the run from Scotland to Stockholm bore special identification codes and, in particular, a black bar on the tailplane, and were painted white to highlight this marking so that German patrols would spot them from a distance and leave them alone.[22] Hughie Green – best known as a television personality, but also a wartime aviator – described to Michael Bentine how he had made such a diplomatic flight to Sweden in a white-painted Catalina flying boat. Is this why Kent's Sunderland was specially painted for this trip? Now the official censorship of newspaper photographs of the crash site makes sense. In the photographs taken a few days afterwards there are tarpaulins covering various objects on the ground. As the bodies had been taken away at that stage, what were they covering up – signs that would have identified it as a neutral flight?

Other anomalies begin to make more sense. Special Constable

Will Bethune, who was the first to reach the Duke of Kent's body, said that a suitcase chained to his wrist had burst open, scattering a large number of kroner notes over the hillside. Although the kroner is the currency of both Sweden and Iceland, at that time, as Iceland was occupied by Britain and the USA, its own currency was virtually valueless, while the mighty dollar held sway. In those circumstances there seems to be no reason for the Duke to have been carrying large amounts of Icelandic kroner, although he may have had every reason to be taking currency to Sweden.

Andy Jack and after

Andy Jack behaved oddly after the crash – leaving the site, discarding his trousers and so on. It was almost as if he believed he was in enemy territory. Not only did he put as much distance between himself and the crash as he could, but by shedding his trousers (and, because he had no pockets in which to put his money, presumably his jacket as well) he was effectively getting rid of his uniform, or of any sign that he had been in a plane. According to Jack's account, he spent the night after the crash in the heather, waking to a glorious summer morning, quite unlike the weather on the previous day. He had then walked uphill, in order, he said, to get his bearings. It was when he reached the top that he realised he was near human habitation. But there are problems with this story. The hillside is on the other side of the valley from Eagle's Rock: on a beautiful summer's day, he would have had a clear view of the crash site, which was then teeming with people. There was no way he could miss them, but not only is the scene conspicuous by its absence in his account, he also failed to do the most logical and natural thing and try to make his presence known. He did not signal to them or go back to the crash site; he just carried on up the hill.

Even if Jack had no knowledge of the real purpose of the mission in advance, he must have been informed, with the others, that they were not going to Iceland but to Sweden. That was unusual enough, but supposing he had also recognised the extra passenger, the one the official records deny ever existed, the tall man with the bushy eyebrows in the Luftwaffe uniform? Even with the involvement of the King's brother, it would have been obvious that this mission was not sanctioned by the government, making it virtual treason.

Physically shocked and injured he may have been, but all Jack's actions immediately after the crash suggest that he wanted no part of it. And as the only survivor, he may even have feared for his life. Certainly, when Dr Kennedy arrived, Jack refused to give his name, although that is often put down to the fact that his burns made it difficult for him to speak.

The 'special mission'

What were Kent and Hess up to? And who would have wanted to stop them with such explosive and brutal finality? If they were going to Sweden on a 'Special Mission' for peace, they would have been a very tempting target for both the Soviet Union and the USA, as well as for those in Britain opposed to peace with Germany.

Hess had stressed that he had flown to Britain under the King's protection, which has always been dismissed as naïve romanticism on his part. But what if it were *true*? What if Kent was acting on behalf of his brother and doing his chivalric duty by allowing the Deputy Führer – a peace emissary who came under a white flag – to return in accordance with the Geneva Convention? Perhaps Kent was acting on his own initiative, or perhaps it was part of a much grander plot on the part of the peace group to bring Britain's involvement in the war to an end.

If the members of the peace party had lain low since Hess's capture, it is only to be expected that they would regroup at some point. And it made perfect sense for that point to be the summer of 1942. Their objectives would remain unchanged, except perhaps in that they had become more focused on the anti-Bolshevik issue since Britain had now allied herself with the USSR. There was also another influential factor: Poland. The pro-Polish faction would have been extremely alarmed at the Soviet alliance, as it implied (correctly, as history was to prove) that after the war Poland would remain in the Soviet sphere of influence. For anti-Bolsheviks there was now more reason than ever to try to make peace with Germany. And among those with a vested interest in seeking peace was, of course, the Duke of Kent himself, not only a great friend of Poland in general, but a close associate of General Sikorski, who had offered him the Polish throne (which would never become his if the Soviet Union was on the victorious side in the war).

The political imperative of the peace group applied equally to the pro-empire people, such as Beaverbrook. It was clear that Britain's alliance with the USA would only increase its economic and political dependence on America, and inevitably lead to the break-up of the British Empire – indeed, Roosevelt had already tried to insist upon Indian independence.[23] There was also concern about the effects of American involvement in the European war – what would the influence of Uncle Sam do to the political map of Europe afterwards? The American generals were pushing hard for the opening of a second front (the invasion of France) in the summer of 1942, in order to relieve the Soviets.[24] This was resisted by the British Chiefs of Staff on practical strategic grounds: the Allies simply were not prepared for such a big push, and would not be ready until 1944. Many were worried that a 'half-successful' offensive against the European mainland would open the way for Soviet domination. If the Western Allies did manage to gain a foothold in Europe, successfully dividing Germany's forces, but were then unable to advance, a Russian victory in the East would allow them to sweep into Europe and capture Germany, and then, in the aftermath of war, sow the seeds of revolution in the rest of Europe.

The anti-Bolsheviks were even more alarmed when, on 11 June 1942, Eden announced in the Commons that, seventeen days earlier, the British government had concluded a treaty with the Soviet Union that not only confirmed a twenty-year alliance but committed the two nations to closer co-operation after the war. Molotov had secretly flown to London on 21 May to sign the treaty, which was signed on the British side by Churchill, Eden, Clement Attlee and Sir Archibald Sinclair.[25]

For all those reasons, the anti-Bolshevik, pro-empire people saw that Britain was in a no-win situation: either Britain would lose the war or it would win at the cost of increased Soviet influence, increased dependence on the USA and the end of the empire. In any case, Britain was still not winning the war: although the Blitz had stopped and the threat of invasion (if ever there was one) had lifted, Britain was now engaged in – and losing – a bloody war in the Far East, a further drain on precious resources, besides doing badly in North Africa. Both Britain and America were still losing colossal amounts of shipping to the depredations of U-boats in the Atlantic. In 1942 Britain's losses exceeded the production of new ships by about 1 million tons: it was not until May 1943 that production tipped the scales the other way.[26] There was another problem. It was not yet clear what the outcome would be in the Russo-German war. Although the Nazis had suffered setbacks in the winter of 1941–2, the decisive breaking of the German offensive was still in the future, with the siege of Stalingrad. Indeed, in August 1942 it looked as if the Germans would win.[27]

Churchill's position at home was not too certain, either. Although still generally popular, criticism of his conduct of the war was once again escalating among Britain's movers and shakers. As we have seen, in January 1942, after returning from a conference with Roosevelt, he had headed off his critics by calling another motion of confidence and using Hess's name as a threat. Despite winning the vote, his position continued to slide during 1942 as a result of more military disasters. February of that year saw the debacle of the fall of Singapore, which Churchill himself described as: 'The worst disaster and largest capitulation in British History.'[28] Then came the devastating news of the fall of Tobruk in North Africa on 20 June. As Churchill's physician, Sir Charles Wilson (later Lord Moran), wrote: 'The loss of Tobruk was the rallying point for those who had lost confidence in Churchill's leadership.'[29] (Significantly, at that time all by-election candidates with the Prime Minister's backing were utterly routed at the polls.) Although today it may seem incredible that so far into the war Churchill's position was so insecure, Wilson wrote: 'He [Churchill] himself has told us that in September, 1942, his position was more vulnerable than at any other period in the war.'[30] It is significant that in his speech at the Liberal Party conference on 4 September 1942, Sir Archibald Sinclair felt it necessary to appeal to his party to support Churchill and the coalition government.[31] Why bother to do this if there was no opposition? Given the ugly mood of many politicians towards him at that time it is less credible to assume there was *no* anti-Churchill party who wanted to end the war than to assume there was.

In the shadows

Certain key players in the peace group – Lords Beaverbrook and Halifax and Sir Samuel Hoare – were exchanging some particularly interesting letters around this time. Beaverbrook and Hoare had kept in close contact throughout 1941 and 1942: Beaverbrook keeping his old friend in Madrid up to date with the intrigue in Whitehall, especially the toings and froings of those opposed to the Churchill government. On 17 February 1942, in a letter marked 'Private and Personal', to which Beaverbrook added by hand '& Secret', he wrote: 'We are in the midst of political crisis in Britain. The newspapers made it. But the Prime Minister keeps it alive.

'It appears probable that this phase in the crisis will pass away. What the next one will be I know not. But I am bound to say that there is no sign of the agitation coming to an end.'[32] In February, after a series of furious rows with Churchill, Beaverbrook resigned from the government. Churchill offered him the post of either Ambassador to Washington or Lord Privy Seal but he refused both. It was agreed that it should be said that Beaverbrook had resigned because of ill health. In his letter of resignation to Churchill, he – ironically, perhaps – saluted him as 'the saviour of our people and the symbol of resistance in the free world'.[33] But as A. J. P. Taylor noted, the real reason why Beaverbrook gave up power was in order to wield influence.[34]

In the months following his resignation, Beaverbrook met with other politicians to try to organise the opposition to Churchill. The most significant meeting was with Ernest Bevin, who claimed that Beaverbrook had sounded him out about replacing Churchill as Prime Minister. In the words of his biographer, Alan Bullock, Bevin told his staff that he believed that Beaverbrook was proposing to 'do for Bevin what he had done for Lloyd George in the earlier war'. Bevin refused the offer and threatened to tell Churchill, to which Beaverbrook laughed and retorted that Churchill wouldn't believe him.[35]

Most commentators believe that Beaverbrook's attempt to oust Churchill foundered because of reactions such as Bevin's, but there was one Prime Minister-in-waiting who continued to maintain a close relationship with Beaverbrook at this time: Sir Samuel Hoare. Others, too, were keeping Hoare abreast of developments, with hints that they were looking to him to take over if Churchill was ousted. On 12 March 1942 Lord Hankey – Minister without Portfolio in Chamberlain's War Cabinet, but since sidelined by Churchill – wrote to Hoare:

I warned you when you were home last autumn that I did not think the Government would last long. They are now very rocky indeed. One hears nothing but abuse of Winston wherever one goes – in Clubs, Government offices, Parliamentary lobbies, Fleet Street, private houses, and I am told even in the Services. Absolutely the only thing that keeps the Government in office is the difficulty of finding a successor to the Prime Minister.

After some discussion of events in the war, the typewritten letter goes on: 'I think, however, that we shall very soon have a change, and I hope we will get a better and more reliable Government.' But Hankey adds a handwritten postscript: 'I should not be surprised if the situation blew up at any time. Feeling is very strong. If I can foresee the date I will drop you a line.'[36]

Even though tucked away in Madrid, Hoare still had both influence and supporters in London, and was following political developments carefully. On 21 May, Halifax wrote to him from Washington, ending his letter with these apparently innocent words: 'We think of going back to England in a month or so at the end of June or early July. Cannot you make a trip at the same time? I would like to see you.'[37] On 12 June, Beaverbrook wrote to Hoare:

There is a growing recognition here of what you have accomplished and of how much this country owes to you.

All the same, I think you should come home now. It is a mistake to stay abroad too long . . . And certainly many changes are taking place in political life. Values here are altering all the time and the old party divisions are getting blurred.

The course of the war determines the popularity of the Administration. It can survive with ease criticism and even condemnation of its conduct of affairs provided the military news is satisfactory. But a conjunction of bad news from abroad with mismanagement in domestic affairs would, in my view, at this stage bring about a crisis which might well be fatal to the Government as at present constituted . . .

I should like so much to see you again and to discuss all these matters with you . . .[38]

The very same day, Beaverbrook wrote to a less intimate friend, the

American author Damon Runyon: 'In the dark days after [the fall of] Singapore there was criticism and perhaps a waning confidence in the Government. But now all that has changed . . . Churchill's prestige in the country is immense. He is the unchallenged leader without a rival to his place.'[39]

What was Beaverbrook up to? The only possible answer is that he was playing a double game, watching his own back while waiting to see which side came out on top.

On 25 June 1942, Hoare replied to Beaverbrook's letter: 'My present plan is to try to come back to England for a time, probably in August.' He ends with what is a clear statement of his intention to return to Whitehall politics – with a little help from his friend Beaverbrook:

> . . . many people in England, including some of my constituents, have been wondering what I have been doing in Spain, and some of them have been frankly critical. Do you think you could infiltrate from time to time into the *Express* and the *Evening News* a few paragraphs to circumvent this kind of attitude? After all, if, as you suggest, I am to come back to England, it is important to have the ground gradually prepared.[40]

Hoare is obviously planning to return for more than a brief holiday. It is almost as if he can smell something promising in the air, the imminent advent of a major change that will sweep him (and others) back to power.

In the meantime, Churchill had become suspicious that Beaverbrook was plotting against him. In July 1942 the Prime Minister faced a major challenge: a vote of no confidence in his leadership was called in the Commons. Not surprisingly, Churchill expected Beaverbrook to side with his critics, but Beaverbrook not only backed the Prime Minister but actually hailed him as the unrivalled leader of Britain.[41] What was he up to?

If there was an attempt to oust Churchill – some kind of very British coup – Beaverbrook would have been the key player. After all, he had already been behind one 'palace coup' that had removed a Prime Minister in the middle of a war – and he was unreservedly proud of the fact. The official line in his biographies is that, in the summer of 1942, he was fully behind Churchill –

indeed, one of his main defenders – as well as a staunch advocate of the second front and the alliance with the Soviet Union.[42] However, was that really his position? Might he have been attempting to lull Churchill into a false sense of security? He wrote to Hoare on 10 July, giving the details of the no confidence motion, adding that Churchill won because his critics 'were never able to convince that they or anyone else could be an alternative to the present administration'. The thought of an 'alternative' seemed much on his mind. He went on:

> Yet the Government's stock is not high with the public. There is a widespread demand for the scrapping of Committees . . . The Coalition's stock of goodwill may be nearing exhaustion. And in by-elections it is the man of ability who wins the seat, whatever his label.
>
> Shipping and the Russian military situation dominate the news at the moment. Both are acknowledged to be critical. Yet they bring no immediate threat of danger to the people here . . . In fact it might be said that the swing of the war eastwards has removed the sense of urgency as well as of danger from this country.[43]

Reading between the lines, Beaverbrook is telling Hoare that the time is right, both from the point of view of political opposition to Churchill, of the public mood and with the military position, to take a stand. And so the scene was set. Halifax and Hoare made sure they were both back in London during August. Halifax had an audience with the King on the 11th,[44] returning to Washington on the 23rd, the same day that Hoare arrived in London via Lisbon. He, too, had an audience with the King, on the 28th.[45]

Interestingly, in the first half of August rumours were circulating among the British community – and among Spanish journalists – in Madrid that Sir Samuel Hoare was involved in secret peace negotiations with the German and Italian Ambassadors. The rumours became so insistent that, precisely at that time, Lady Maud Hoare, in a speech to the 'Knitting Party' written by her husband, had to deny them, calling them 'moonshine', but taking care to add that 'the Germans see that this would be a first class moment for peace and they know in their innermost hearts that they will never get such a chance again'.[46]

Suspicious movements

In the critical month of August 1942 the conspirators had another factor in their favour: Churchill himself was out of the country. Stopping off at Egypt on the way, he visited Moscow for a conference with Stalin on 12 August. Although for security reasons the visit was not made public until the 18th, obviously the cabinet and senior parliamentary figures at home would have known about it for some time beforehand. The purpose of the trip was for Churchill to break the bitter news that there would be no Allied second front that year, although he did throw in the sweetener of Operation Torch, the joint British/US offensive in North Africa, planned for November.

A successful conference would – and did – enormously strengthen Churchill's position both at home and abroad, and of course commit Britain to a much deeper alliance with the Soviet Union, much to the horror of the anti-Bolsheviks. If ever there was a time for the peace group to act, this was it.

It seemed odd at the time that Churchill specifically chose an American pilot named Vanderkloot to fly him, prompting the Premier's doctor, Sir Charles Wilson, who went with him, to write in his diary: 'I wondered why it was left to an American pilot to find a safe route to Cairo – but that did not seem a profitable line of enquiry.'[47] Perhaps, not knowing whom he could trust, Churchill dared not entrust himself to an RAF pilot at that critical time.

There are other intriguing oddities. Churchill arrived back earlier than scheduled – on 24 August – by Liberator bomber, travelling in the uniform of an air commodore (the same rank as the Duke of Kent), saying to reporters, 'Call me Mr Bullfinch,' which seemed to amuse him greatly.[48] He was then taken by train to Paddington Station, arriving at 11.25 p.m., where he was met, on his own specific instructions – despite the late hour – by a very distinguished gathering, including the leaders of the three major political parties, Eden, Attlee and Sir Archibald Sinclair; all the members of the cabinet; the American and Soviet Ambassadors; and representatives of the General Staffs of all the armed forces, including Lord Louis Mountbatten.[49] Was this impressive turnout some kind of test of loyalty, had Churchill ordered them there just to keep his eye on them, or did he perhaps simply wish to assert his power? It is interesting to note who was *not* there: there was not a single representative of any

European royal family, including that of Britain (excepting Lord Louis Mountbatten, who was there because of his position in the General Staff); and there was no Polish representative.

And why did he choose to call himself 'Mr Bullfinch', apparently much to his private amusement? We could find nothing to explain it until, as a last resort, we looked in a 1940s encyclopedia of birds. The entry on bullfinches says that although they are usually regarded as a menace by fruit-growers because they feed on the buds that develop into fruit, this is a fallacy, because the bullfinch prunes – or *culls* – rather than destroys, only picking off the rotten buds to the benefit of the whole tree. Had Churchill called himself 'Mr Bullfinch' because he was about to nip something in the bud? Or perhaps the question should be, *who* was he about to 'cull'? The very next day the Duke of Kent's plane crashed and, with him, it seems, Rudolf Hess, the jewel in the crown of the anti-Churchill peace group. No wonder 'Mr Bullfinch', pruner and culler, chuckled to himself.

There are question marks over the Duke of Kent's movements immediately before his fatal flight. The standard account is that he left The Coppins in Buckinghamshire the previous day, drove himself to London, and then took the overnight train to Scotland, from which he was taken direct to Invergordon. However, palace-approved biographer of the Kents, Audrey Whiting, has the Duke departing from The Coppins on 23 August, leaving a day unaccounted for.[50] However, one of the exiled foreign royals, Prince Bernhard of the Netherlands – a German count by birth and an early member of the Nazi Party – has stated that he was the last person to dine with Kent, at Balmoral the night before the crash, and one biography of the Queen Mother confirms that Kent had stayed with his parents at Balmoral before the flight.[51] Although there would be nothing odd about Kent breaking his journey at Balmoral, clearly it is deemed too sensitive to admit it, presumably because of the meeting with Prince Bernhard, whose presence has never been explained.

There is also something evasive about the gathering of British and foreign royalty at Balmoral that night. It is clear from the accounts that the visit of George VI and Queen Elizabeth was unscheduled.[52] The Duke of Gloucester and his wife Princess Alice (sister of the Duke of Buccleuch) also made what is described as a spur of the moment visit to Balmoral.[53]

History being written by the victors, hard evidence of an attempted coup has long since disappeared, but all the circumstantial evidence points to the culmination of a sensational plot in August 1942. Everything suggests a dramatic gesture to bring the war to an end: a 'palace coup' in London to remove Churchill from office and replace him with Hoare, while Kent and Hess made a joint appearance in Stockholm to announce a peace deal. Or perhaps Kent was simply doing what he saw as his chivalric duty, as a fellow knight of the air, and taking the Nazi aviator/peace envoy to freedom. He may even have been taking him out of harm's way as the expected battle between the pro- and anti-Churchill factions raged. It is unlikely that we will ever know the full truth.

On 3 October a Nazi-backed newspaper in Stockholm called for the lifting of the veil of secrecy that still enshrouded the Deputy Führer. It stated that his mission had been part of Hitler's policy of forming an alliance with Britain, and that Hess was supposed to offer a deal in advance of the German attack on Russia. The report emphasised that Churchill had rejected Hess's offer without consulting Parliament or informing the British public, saying that he had made the decision to turn down the offer – and imprison Hess – after consulting Roosevelt. The article then stated that the American President opposed the terms of the offer because he did not wish Europe to become too powerful or prosperous. A European war would conveniently prevent either of those possibilities becoming a reality.[54]

Furthermore, it is odd that, in the following months, after having been virtually forgotten, Hess should suddenly become the subject of renewed interest on the part of the Soviet government, while speculation about his mission intensified once more. Stalin's questions about where Hess was and how he was being treated prompted the report of November 1942 referred to earlier. At the same time articles appeared in Russian newspapers accusing Britain of harbouring war criminals like Hess, suggesting that Britain was about to do a deal with Germany.[55]

Then the German Ambassador to Portugal, Baron Oswald von Hoyningen-Huene, sent a telegram to von Ribbentrop on 5 December 1942, which read:

As the Embassy has learned, confidentially, the death of the Duke of Kent has been discussed recently in the innermost circles of the

British Club here. The gist of the talk being that an act of sabotage was involved. It is said that the Duke, like the Duke of Windsor, was sympathetic towards an understanding with Germany and so gradually had become a problem for the government clique. The people who were accompanying him were supposed to have expressed themselves along similar lines, so that getting them out of the way would also have been an advantage.[56]

CHAPTER FOURTEEN

The Hamlet Syndrome

We are convinced that in the summer of 1942 there were two Hesses, one in Scotland and one at Maindiff Court, Abergavenny, Wales. Given the way in which attention was drawn to the Maindiff Hess, and the fact that this was the only Hess as far as officialdom was concerned, it seems that he was a decoy to cover up the fact that the real man was elsewhere. But by the end of the war – and probably from August 1942 – there was only one Hess, and he was in Abergavenny. Stories about Hess being in Scotland are specific to the summer of 1942 and there is no evidence of a second Hess after this, in Scotland or anywhere else.

We have placed the real Hess in northern Scotland, at Caithness, specifically on the estate of the Duke of Portland in Braemore Lodge and (briefly) at Lochmore Cottage. We have linked this with the plane crash in the same area in August 1942, which killed the Duke of Kent, and in which we are certain there was one body too many.

Of course, there is one major, glaring problem with the doppelgänger theory. Even though it seems to fit the evidence perfectly, it has to be admitted that the mind skids on the thought that any man would allow himself to be tried and sentenced in Hess's name, not to mention continuing with the deception for the rest of a very long life in the harshest and most hopeless of conditions. And why would the British authorities have allowed a substitute – who might at any moment choose to reveal his secret – to be incarcerated in Spandau, or, for that matter, to stand trial in the first place? Why not arrange for an 'accidental' death, or claim he had suffered a fatal heart attack? During the war they might have thought twice about such a drastic action because of the probable reprisals against British POWs. But why keep the double when the war was over?

One thing at least is clear: if the 'Hess' who was sentenced at Nuremberg was a double, then he must have colluded in the deception. It is possible to conceive of scenarios in which this could happen. Greg Iles, in his 1993 novel based on the doppelgänger hypothesis, *Spandau Phoenix*, has the double (really Alfred Horn) going along with the deception because the lives of his family are threatened – which, because of the Nazi *Sippenhaft* policy, he readily accepts. This was the explanation also favoured by M. R. D. Foot.[1] (There are other possibilities, too, which we will discuss later in this chapter.)

Another obvious question is who was the hapless double? Unfortunately, this must remain one of the most tantalising questions of the entire Hess affair: any documentary details have long been destroyed. All that can be said with any degree of certainty is that he was most likely to have been a German – as this was his first language – and presumably a devoted Nazi. He may have been a prisoner of war in Britain, already singled out by the British authorities because of his uncanny likeness to the Deputy Führer. Indeed, Charles Fraser-Smith's story of the copy being made of Hess's uniform just a few days after his capture suggests that they already had a double in mind for the job. But beyond such speculations, the trail is cold.

Is there anything that reinforces – or discredits – the idea that it was not the real Hess in Spandau? And is there anything that might help explain why a fake Hess had, willingly or unwillingly, accepted such a strange and bleak fate?

It might be assumed that only the real Hess could have written the letters he sent from his various prisons over the years. However, while at Mytchett Place, Hess is reported to have spent a great deal of his time writing, although none of it has ever been made public. The details of his life and innermost thoughts contained in these works could easily have been recycled by those behind the double. In 1954 Sir John Wheeler-Bennett, the biographer of George VI, wrote to the Duchess of Hamilton offering her a copy of the memoirs Hess had written while in Britain.[2] Indeed, some of his letters read very much as if they are extracts from a book. Even Wolf Hess – who rejects the doppelgänger idea – accepts that at least one of the letters written from Hess's cell at Nuremberg contains such errors and unlikely details that it must have been written under the orders of his captors. And if one was, why not more?

The psychiatric puzzle

As we have seen, Rees's book – apart from the occasional guard's reminiscence in the press – is the only source of information about Hess's personal life while at Maindiff Court, and it largely glosses over 1942 and 1943. Indeed, after describing Hess's arrival at Maindiff, there is only one extract for the period in which we believe there were two Hesses, from 4 August 1942, when Rees notes that the prisoner's previous delusions seem to have disappeared.[3] Then nothing until 29 September – after we believe the real Hess had died – and even then there is only a handful more until the psychiatric story resumes fully at the beginning of 1944. And, as we have seen, the Red Cross were refused permission to see Hess in early 1943 and throughout the remainder of his captivity.

According to Rees, from September 1942 Hess's mental condition at Maindiff Court returned to the same pattern as at Mytchett Place, with phases of paranoid delusions (accusations that his keepers were poisoning him and so on), alternating with more rational periods. But at the beginning of 1944 a new symptom is said to have emerged: hysterical amnesia. Although Hess was reported to have had one bout of memory loss while at Mytchett Place, this was quite different: while the earlier problem was put down to general mental confusion,[4] these later bouts are something else entirely.

The first period was reported on 3 February 1944 (although Rees's book gives it as 1943, perhaps accidentally). Rees notes that this symptom had appeared since his last examination at the beginning of October 1943. He adds: 'His condition is . . . an hysterical amnesia, very comparable to the state which is developed by many soldiers in war-time, and by not a few civilians when confronted by situations which they feel it is impossible to face. A loss of memory is in these cases a self-protective mechanism.'[5] Rees ascribes its onset to the increasingly bad news for the Nazis from the Eastern Front. He also claims that

> if the prisoner were an ordinary civilian . . . [it] is practically certain that we could recover the whole of his memory in a very short time either by the use of hypnosis or by what is called narco-analysis, i.e., by the use of an anaesthetic given intravenously. Unfortunately, even if it were thought justifiable to use hypnosis, he would be very resistant to that and some objection has previously been raised by the Foreign Office to the use of drugs, which I suppose still holds.[6]

It needs to be stressed that – as Rees himself notes – paranoid delusions and hysterical amnesia are symptoms of two quite separate psychological conditions. One does not lead to the other. And interestingly, the reported onset of amnesia brought about the return of Major Dicks, who had left Mytchett Place in July 1941, leading to what is supposed to be the only time during which Hess – with his permission – was administered with drugs. He was given sodium pentathol, the 'truth drug', in an effort to reawaken his memory. As we have seen, even under the influence of the drug, Hess appears to remember nothing, except when asked about the chest wounds. Suddenly he seemed to snap out of his amnesiac fog and become alert once again, asking for a glass of water. It was exactly as if he had been brought back from a hypnotic trance by the chest wound question. Significantly, when writing to Ilse about the same episode from Spandau in 1947, he stated that he had only ever pretended to have amnesia, even managing to maintain the play-acting when given the truth drug.[7] It is odd, however, that the thought suddenly occurred to him – surfacing in a letter to Ilse – at exactly the time that Rees's book was published.

It is interesting to note that in his 1958 letter to the Canadian psychiatrist W. Clifford Scott, Rees refers to this episode as involving the use of 'Pentathol and suggestion'.[8] In other words, Hess was drugged *and* hypnotised in order to put him into a more suggestible state. And since Major Dicks had been brought from London specially for this session, the implication is that he was a trained hypnotist.

Back on 21 January 1944, Hess wrote to Ilse and told her he had lost his memory: 'that is the reason why I cannot, in fact, write you a reasonable letter; for that purpose one wants a memory more than one believes. It is another matter when one has letters to answer which supply one with material and suggestions.'[9] This seems to be an attempt to avert suspicion by explaining why he only writes about subjects that his wife brings up first.

The alleged amnesia lasted for several months. On 4 February 1945 there was the second of Hess's so-called suicide attempts, when he skewered a fold of skin on his chest with a bread knife.[10] Although he claimed to have plunged the knife in to the hilt, all he had done was push it through a fold of skin, resulting in two parallel slits that subsequently scarred over. Even though the wound required just two stitches, these scars have been put forward as the bullet scars sustained by Hess in the First World War – by Sir Geoffrey Howe and, of course, by the prisoner himself, among others. It is tempting to speculate that this was why 'Hess' made them in the first place. If he was a double and knew he was supposed to be a man who had scars on the chest (although he had no idea of their true position), perhaps he was trying to ensure that he had them.

At Nuremberg the behaviour of the man known as Rudolf Hess was extraordinary. Although leaving the indelible impression of a man in extreme mental (and sometimes even physical) distress, it was – either by design or accidentally – a very clever, even a bravura performance. Through his 'mad' behaviour, including his refusal to see his wife, failing to recognise former close colleagues such as Hermann Göring and his own secretaries, and refusing to sign his name, he was effectively pre-empting the possibility of being unmasked as an impostor. And, of course, this scenario demands that the double was actively colluding with the pretence. On the other hand, it is hard to dismiss the evidence of one's own eyes: the newsreels show what seems to be a genuinely confused and tormented man, irrespective of whether he was the former Deputy Führer. In one respect Hess's mental condition calls to mind the great literary debate about Hamlet: was he mad or was he just putting it on for his own purposes? Unfortunately, for much of the time, Hess's version of what might be termed the 'Hamlet syndrome' seems just as intractable as the Prince of Denmark's condition. Nothing is clear cut about Nuremberg-Hess's behaviour. Although the psychiatrists who examined him concluded that his amnesia was genuine, the result of a hysterical condition, he claimed that he was only pretending to have lost his memory, both when speaking from the dock and in later letters to Ilse. The other major paradox is that only the British psychiatrists report him to be suffering from paranoia, based on his history, whereas others examining him for the first time found he was presenting no such symptoms.

The paradoxes in Hess's behaviour prompted some strangely illogical statements. When, towards the end of the trial, the court asked another psychiatrist, Dr G. M. Gilbert, to make an assessment of Hess, he reported:

> There can be no doubt that Hess was in a state of virtually complete amnesia at the beginning of the trial. The opinions of the psychiatric commissions in this regard and with respect to his sanity have only been substantiated by prolonged subsequent observation . . .
>
> On the day of the special hearing in his case, November 30th, 1945, Rudolf Hess did, in fact, recover his memory. The cause of his recovery is an academic question . . .'[11]

Gilbert then goes on to speculate that Hess might have recovered his memory as a 'face-saving device' to prevent himself being excluded from the proceedings, but fails to say how a genuine amnesiac could arrange to do this.

There is another major anomaly. The Hess who went to Spandau suddenly recovered from both paranoia and amnesia without ever being given any form of treatment for either. Indeed, Prisoner Number Seven was quite normal mentally – not even showing any signs of senile dementia until shortly before his death, at the age of ninety-three. How does a man who has allegedly been a paranoid schizophrenic spontaneously become totally normal, especially in highly stressful and traumatic circumstances?

Among the documents supplied by Alexander was a report by Maurice N. Walsh, consultant in neuropsychiatry to the US Army, about an examination carried out on Hess in Spandau on 25 May 1948 – the first psychiatric evaluation of the prisoner after he began his sentence. It is definitely genuine (it came with private correspondence between Rees, Dicks and Walsh, who discuss it). Walsh's conclusions are very significant:

> In the first place, it is my definite opinion *that Rudolf Hess is not psychotic at the present time* [emphasis in original]. No evidence of hallucinatory, delusional or illusional trends were secured . . . No

evidence of paranoid colouring of Hess's mental content was encountered. His intelligence is obviously superior. Although Hess believes that his memory is intact at the present time, he totally failed to remember the occurrence of two amnesic [sic] episodes which had occurred in England, thus reinforcing the impression created by reading Brigadier Rees's book *The Case of Rudolf Hess* that these were of hysterical origin.[12]

Once again, this part of Walsh's diagnosis is based solely on statements made in Rees's book – he himself had seen no evidence of Hess's amnesia. However, on the basis that Rees's report was accurate, Walsh concludes that Hess must have been amnesiac because he couldn't remember it. Walsh goes on:

Hess obviously made great efforts to impress the undersigned with his sincerity and normality. He was most courteous and responsive, frequently looking directly into the eyes of the interviewer whilst speaking. He did not give the impression of being grandiose or of overestimating his own importance but rather an impression of some humility and considerably quiet self-assurance was gained.

Walsh asked Hess about his two suicide attempts, to which he replied that both were the result of depression, arising from the failure of his mission. However, we know that the first 'suicide' was not attempted for that reason, but because he feared he was being drugged. It is also doubtful whether the second occasion – the breadknife episode – qualifies as a suicide attempt. Then, when Walsh broached the subject of his early life in Alexandria, Hess 'answered that he recalled nothing of his early life in Egypt, except dim details of the family dwelling and his immediate family'.

Walsh's report ends:

In summary the impression was gained that Rudolf Hess is an individual of superior intelligence with schizoid personality traits, and that he has no psychosis at the present time, but there would appear to be adequate evidence that he has experienced at least two episodes of hysterical amnesia and of depression with suicidal attempts, both of which occurred only at a time when he was exposed to strong emotional stress.

Walsh's report is highly significant. It tells us that, less than nineteen months after his antics at Nuremberg, Hess was essentially completely normal. And that is how he remained. Another psychological evaluation in 1964 concluded that the prisoner was 'An alert man who reveals no disturbance of thought, memory or orientation at this time'.[13]

Lieutenant-Colonel Tony le Tissier, the last British governor of Spandau – appointed in 1981 – records in his book *Farewell to Spandau* that he never saw any signs of mental illness in his elderly inmate, writing: 'This curious behaviour [exhibited at Maindiff Court and Nuremberg] . . . had ceased long before I came into the picture.'[14] Indeed, when Hess was taken to the British Military Hospital in Berlin suffering from pneumonia at the end of April 1987 – some four months before his death – the doctors reported that they detected the first signs of senile dementia creeping in. At this, le Tissier called an emergency meeting of the directors, because they had never even considered this possibility and its implications and needed to decide how they would cope with the demands of looking after a senile prisoner.[15]

The minds of objective researchers find themselves more than a little frayed by the problems implicit in Hess's Hamlet syndrome. For example, if he was only pretending to be mad at Nuremberg, was he also pretending in Britain? If he was feigning amnesia at his trial, what about the earlier loss of memory at Maindiff Court? Presumably that was all part of the act because all such delusions disappeared immediately the trial was over. However, he was reported as having made similar statements before: in particular, on the day of his second 'suicide attempt' – the bread-knife incident – he had, according to Rees, produced a list of people whom he claimed were under the mental control of the Jews.[16] It included Churchill, Eden (on the grounds that he had once been rude to Göring at a banquet), the entire Bulgarian government – and even one 'Rudolf Hess' . . . It is sheer lunacy, but perhaps that is the point. Perhaps its surreal quality hides the fact that it has been concocted by a sane person who wants people to think he is mad. But if he was not delusional – as Peter Padfield points out, the letters he was writing at the same time were perfectly normal, if somewhat stilted[17] – then what was the 'suicide attempt' really about?

A clue as to what was really going on lies in the identity and background of the psychiatrist the Americans chose to evaluate the prisoner, and who, as we saw in Chapter 1, was asked by Allen Dulles specifically to try to identify him. This was Dr Donald Ewen Cameron, a pioneer in what became known as brainwashing techniques. A Scots-born Canadian, since 1943 Cameron had been head of a psychiatric research centre, the Allen Memorial Institute, which had been set up by McGill University with funds from the Rockefeller Foundation. Although it is well known that later, in the 1950s, Cameron rose to the heights of his profession, becoming president of both the American Psychiatric Association and the World Psychiatric Association, it is less well known that from at least 1957 his work was also funded by the CIA as part of their infamous MKULTRA programme, channelled secretly through a conduit called the Society for Investigation of Human Ecology. MKULTRA was authorised by the then CIA director, Allen Dulles.[18]

Cameron's original interest – indeed obsession – was in finding a cure for schizophrenia (which makes it all the more significant that he failed to note any signs of it in Hess), but his driving professional ambitions could make him very difficult as a person. One member of the Rockefeller Foundation wrote that he had 'a need for power which he nourishes by maintaining an extraordinary aloofness from his associates'.[19] Becoming disenchanted with psychoanalytical methods for curing schizophrenia, he turned to the now largely discredited electroshock therapy and also the use of drugs: his method involved first wiping the patient's memory clean by applying intensive electric shocks combined with virtually twenty-four-hour-a-day drug-induced sleep, resulting – as may be imagined – in total amnesia. Although Cameron himself had not invented this traumatically radical – perhaps even soul-destroying – technique, he had worked intensively with it since at least the 1940s. But perhaps more important is the fact that the electroshock therapy part had been originally recorded by two British psychiatrists, L. G. M. Page and R. J. Russell, who published a paper about it – after many years of intensive experimentation – in 1948.[20] Another major inspiration was the British psychiatrist William Sargent, whom Cameron considered to be the leading expert on Soviet brainwashing techniques.[21] Cameron took this work and used it for what he called 'depatterning'. He believed that after inducing complete amnesia in a patient, he could then selectively recover their memory in such a way as to change their behaviour unrecognisably. If 'depatterning' has a bleak Orwellian ring to it, then 'psychic driving' – which Cameron invented in 1953 – takes us into an even more terrifying world. He discovered that once a subject entered an amnesiac, somnambulistic state, they would become hypersensitive to suggestion. If a statement was repeated to them over and over again (for example, on a tape loop), it would penetrate so deeply into their subconscious mind as to change their behaviour completely; their personality would undergo such a radical metamorphosis that they essentially became someone else. Such a powerful tool was not going to remain exclusively in the hands of therapists for long: soon the CIA became interested in the extraordinary potential of Cameron's 'psychic driving'.

There was no doubting its value to them. This sinister technique could be used to implant all manner of ideas in the mind of either a willing or an unwilling subject. For example, an agent on a secret mission could have his cover identity mentally implanted, not only enabling him to recall all the details of his assumed identity much more fluently than if he merely learned them off pat, but effectively turning him into that person. To all intents and purposes he would *become* his cover. However, the technique was by no means foolproof: there was always the danger of mental conflict between the real and induced memories, possibly resulting in bizarre and unpredictable behaviour.

Perhaps Cameron's work was directly responsible for changing the course of history. Although he was responsible for 'programming' several American agents through psychic driving in the late 1950s, the most notable was certainly Lee Harvey Oswald before his 'defection' to the USSR in 1959. Psychic driving was, as may be guessed, the first step in the creation of '*Manchurian Candidate*' assassins, whose usual human scruples about committing murder had been wiped away with their real personalities. As American researcher John Marks writes: 'By literally wiping the minds of his subjects clean by depatterning and then trying to program in new behaviour, Cameron carried the process known as "brainwashing" to its logical extreme.'[22]

Could the mind of the man known as Rudolf Hess have been subjected to such a process? Could this explain his bizarre behaviour? After all, the technique requires that a psychiatric team has the subject under its control for several months – and Hess was at Maindiff

Court for three years. The first stage is to induce amnesia, and then implant the suggestions that bring about the change in behaviour. With this in mind, it is particularly interesting that in 1944 it was seriously proposed that Hess should be hypnotised and sent back to Germany to assassinate Himmler – essentially as a 'Manchurian candidate'.[23] This was proposed by SOE planners (who did not have access to Hess and had to drop the plan because they were forbidden to see the files on him) and was based on the apparent success of an 'American Officer stationed in Ireland' in this field. The most significant aspect of this proposal was that those who made it clearly considered it to be a viable option at that relatively early date and presumably knew that Hess was being subjected to hypnosis.

Research into this area where the British are concerned is severely hampered by the lack of freely available documentary evidence. Indeed, it was only with the passing of the American Freedom of Information Act in the 1970s that the world first learned of the full horror of MKULTRA and other mind-control projects perpetrated against American citizens. Undoubtedly, however, experimental work was already well advanced by the time Rudolf Hess was taken into captivity. Techniques for wiping memory were definitely known by 1945, and those for implanting a new personality were being discussed and explored – although allegedly not perfected until Cameron's work in the 1950s. Despite the paucity of official records on British mind-control experiments, a certain amount of information on the subject has been pieced together by researchers. Significantly, one of the names most frequently encountered – without any reference whatsoever to his involvement in the Hess affair – is that of Brigadier John Rawlings Rees. Before the war Rees, an enthusiastic advocate of eugenics, studied methods of artificially inducing psychosis, which he believed could be used for social control.[24]

In any case, as far back as the 1930s, the notorious Moscow show trials gave ample evidence that the Russians had reached a high standard with their brainwashing techniques. Many observers noted that the defendants seemed to be under the influence of drugs or hypnosis, sitting glassy-eyed and indifferent to their surroundings and then making – as one writer later described – 'unbelievable confessions in dull, cliché-ridden monotones'.[25] It was precisely this that inspired secret British and American research into this field.

If Hess were under some form of mind control it would explain almost all of his erratic and otherwise puzzling behaviour at Nuremberg. But what was the background to brainwashing Hess? And what did 'they' hope to gain by it?

If it was the real Hess, then the doctors had tampered with his memory in order to eradicate what would otherwise prove to be – at least to the Churchill legend and the Establishment – the aspects with the most potential to embarrass and undermine. They would have attempted to erase from his mind issues connected with the Duke of Hamilton, the Royal Family and anything else that might have seriously rocked their boat. If it was a double at Maindiff Court, the intention would have been more ambitious. But could they actually make the double believe he really was Rudolf Hess? Perhaps. But the human mind is far too complex and tricky for that to be a safe and reliable option, and there could have been no guarantee that any apparent success would be lasting. It is, however, possible through the use of drugs and hypnosis to reinforce suggestions that bypass the brain's critical faculties. As the double would seem to have been a German, and presumably a Nazi, he could have been conditioned with the belief that it was a matter of necessity that the world believed he was Hess. They could have impressed on him that, as a good Nazi, it was his duty to play the part to perfection. But surely this is easier said than done. How on earth do you convince someone of reasonable intelligence and normal mentality of this? The easiest way to do this would be to reinforce the idea – and keep reinforcing it until it became an obsession – that one day the Nazi Party would rise again, and that when it did they would need a figurehead from the old days. It was necessary for the sake of the Fourth Reich that the deception be maintained. Indeed, in this light it is interesting that, based on his conversations with Hess in his cell at Nuremberg, Major Kelley writes: 'He considers himself to be the only standard-bearer left of the Nazi Party, and will continue true to his adolescent ideals to the end.'[26]

The schooling of a double may help explain the 'suicide attempt' at Maindiff Court. Not only was it not a genuine suicide attempt, but nor was it a classic 'cry for help'. The way in which Hess stabbed himself – sticking the bread knife through a pinch of skin – posed no threat to his life at all. But if this were a double, constantly impressed with the idea of being Hess, he would know that the real man was supposed to have scars on his chest, and the lack of them would have troubled him greatly. Anything that challenged his new identity would have to go. We know that Hess was reminded of this while drugged: under the influence of sodium pentathol, Dr Ellis Jones asked him if he remembered his First World War wound. It seemed to be this question that brought Hess out of his drugged state, because it bothered him so much. Did he then, in the state of dissociation caused by his 'treatment', decide to give himself a scar, although incorrectly assuming that it should be in the centre of the chest?

It may also be significant that during the last months of his stay at Maindiff Court he never left the hospital, something that Rees mentions only in passing in his book.[27] In other words, after the relative fanfare of his arrival in Abergavenny, Hess was shut away and no longer seen by the local people.

With this in mind, it is instructive to look at the often derided speech that Hess gave in his defence at Nuremberg. As we saw in Chapter 1, it was a rambling monologue in which he blamed the atrocities committed by German concentration camp guards, and even Hitler's actions, on unknown mind controllers. However, close study of the content suggests that, while at times confused and unclear, the defendant at Nuremberg was trying to convey a message.[28] (It should be noted that the president of the tribunal ordered Hess to end his defence speech on the grounds that the defendants were allowed a maximum of twenty minutes. Reading Hess's actual words from the trial proceedings – even allowing for hesitancy and slowness of speech – it is difficult to make them last much more than ten minutes.)

Hess begins his speech by saying that he predicted before the trial that witnesses would make untrue statements that would incriminate the defendants. He then goes on to compare this with the behaviour of the accused during the Moscow Show Trials of the 1930s. At this point, he lets drop a surprising fact: that during his captivity in Maindiff Court he had access to pre-war issues of the *Völkischer Beobachter* (which he used to refresh his memory about the Moscow trials). Why should Hess, whose access to newspapers and reading material was restricted, have been allowed to have back copies of the Nazi Party's official newspaper, for which he had written articles on party policy? Could this have been part of the schooling of a double?

Hess goes on to suggest that the German concentration camp guards, and the scientists who experimented on the inmates, were under a similar form of control as the Moscow defendants, and even that Hitler's reported mental abnormalities in the final years were due to an external cause. He then describes how he began to think along these lines because of the behaviour of his guards and doctors in Abergavenny:

> Some of them – these persons and people around me – were changed from time to time. Some of the new ones who came in place of those who had been changed had strange eyes. They were glassy and like eyes in a dream. This symptom, however, lasted only a few days and then they made a completely normal impression. They could no longer be distinguished from normal human beings.

It is usually suggested that these confused ramblings about 'mental influence' were an attempt to argue that Hitler and the Nazis were not responsible for their actions. However, it is clear that all this is simply a preamble in which he is trying to establish in the court's mind that such things are possible (although admittedly not making a particularly good job of it with the examples he picks). It is equally clear that he is building up to some revelation concerning himself. After giving his examples he stresses the importance of what he is going to say next:

> Obviously it would have been of the utmost importance if I had stated under oath what I have to say about the happenings during my own imprisonment in England. However, it was impossible for me to persuade my defence counsel to declare himself willing to put the proper questions to me . . . But it is of the utmost importance that what I am saying be said under oath. Therefore I now declare once more: I swear by God, the Almighty Omniscient, that I will speak the pure truth, that I shall leave out nothing and add nothing . . . I ask the High Tribunal to give all the more weight to everything which I declare under oath, expressly calling God as my witness.

Having stressed at such length the importance of what he is about to say next, Hess then begins his revelation: 'In the spring of 1942 . . .' *It is at this point that the president interrupts*, telling him that he is at the end of his allotted twenty minutes. What was it that Hess was about to reveal about something that happened in the spring of 1942 – around the time of his transfer to Maindiff Court?

Assuming that Hess had been brainwashed in order to prevent him giving a good account of himself at Nuremberg, surely the British government was taking two astonishing risks: first, by allowing him to stand trial and, second, by letting him become a long-term prisoner? After all, his new conditioning could give way at any time, and his old self return, perhaps even in the witness box. Maybe the reason why he was permitted to stand trial was that the government had changed: Churchill had been ousted by a Labour landslide in the General Election of 5 July 1945. Churchill, together with a few trusted associates, had personally directed the management of the Hess affair, so anything connected with the former Deputy Führer was a matter of great secrecy. It is perhaps significant that the only doctor to argue that Hess was incapable of standing trial was Lord Moran, Churchill's personal physician. Why Moran, who was not a psychiatrist, was a member of the three-doctor team to evaluate Hess is otherwise a puzzle – indeed, the whole episode is conspicuously absent from his memoirs. The only explanation is a comment by Rees in one of his personal letters that Moran 'wished himself'[29] on to the team – i.e. it was Moran's own initiative to take part. Strangely enough, if Hess had not stood trial because of insanity, he would not have gone free. Instead, he would have been incarcerated in a top-security mental institution somewhere in Britain (as he was still in British custody). Is this why Churchill's man alone argued for such a diagnosis?

A friend indeed?

Although the real Hess could have easily feigned not being able to recognise the other Nazi leaders and his former secretaries at Nuremberg, surely his reaction to the news of the deaths of his best friends, Karl and Albrecht Haushofer, would have been well beyond his acting talents. (Unfortunately, there is no record of his reaction to the news of Hitler's death.) It was Karl Haushofer himself who told Hess of Albrecht's death, yet the reaction was merely one of formal sympathy, with not a shred of the personal feeling that even the emotionally disciplined Hess must surely have shown. On 23 April 1945, with the Allies just streets away, Albrecht Haushofer was killed, apparently by the SS, in Berlin, taking all his secrets – including his part in Hess's flight – to the grave with him. Imprisoned by the Gestapo since the bomb plot against Hitler of July 1944, there are indications that even then he was in some measure protected by Himmler and others in high places. But then, without warning, that protection came to an end. It is a strange story: the Gestapo had released Haushofer and fourteen others when an SS unit arrived at the prison and demanded custody of them. They were taken outside – ostensibly to be moved somewhere else – lined up against the wall and shot in the back of the head.[30] What this SS unit was, why it killed the prisoners and on whose orders it was acting have never been explained.

Having barely reacted at all to the news of Albrecht's death, Hess's response to that of his former 'second father' and mentor, Karl Haushofer, is equally strange. Karl and Martha Haushofer committed suicide in April 1946. After leaving a note for their other son Heinz, they went into the woods near their home and took poison. Hearing of this, Hess's only recorded reaction was to say that the professor had been due to testify on his behalf,[31] behaviour hard to reconcile with the honourable and unselfish man who had felt privileged to be the Haushofers' friend.

CHAPTER FIFTEEN

Free at Last

Although Hess had largely been forgotten by the British public, his imprisonment remained a hot issue in Germany to the end of his days. The lone prisoner of Spandau had in some ways become a symbol of what the Cold War meant for Germany. After the fall of the Nazi regime, the country had been partitioned between two opposing blocs: the USSR controlling East Germany, while West Germany was under the protection of NATO. In 1987 Berlin itself was still – although well inside East Germany geographically – neither east nor west politically. The city was divided into four sectors, each controlled by one of the Four Powers, with its own military government. While the East Berlin Soviet Military Government worked almost as one with the East German government, the other three in Berlin were completely independent from each other and even from the West German government. Sitting in his cell in Spandau, Hess had become the living embodiment of the reasons for Germany's divisions. Even out of the sight of the German people, Hess was rarely out of their minds.

Entering the fortress

After sentence was passed at Nuremberg, seven former Nazi leaders stepped into the gloom of Spandau. They were: Walter Funk, Minister of Economic Affairs; Admiral Karl Dönitz, Commander-in-Chief of the German Navy and Hitler's last-ditch successor as Second Führer of the Third Reich; Erich Raeder, Commander-in-Chief of the

Navy until 1943; Baldur von Schirach, former leader of the Hitler Youth and Governor of Vienna; Constantin von Neurath, Protector of Bohemia and Moravia; Albert Speer, former Nazi Minister for Armaments and War Production; and finally, there was the man known as Rudolf Hess, sentenced to life imprisonment, which in his case – and of all the prisoners, his alone – was to mean just that. Prisoner Number Seven was the last one of the condemned Nazis to enter Spandau, and was to be the last one out.

Designed to instil in the inmates a sense of repressive guilt and hopelessness, the Spandau regime was unforgiving and even draconian, especially at the very beginning. Yet somehow Prisoner Number Seven managed not only to stay alive but to be interested in life: throughout his long Spandau existence he was to read voraciously and tried to maintain a fitness regime. The harsh conditions imposed by the Allies, particularly by the hate-fuelled Russians, failed to break him. It is just as well that he had no conception of how long his life sentence would be, and how hard the hearts of his Soviet enemies would remain. Of the four governors, one from Britain, France, the USA and the Soviet Union, it was the last who insisted on enforcing the prison regulations to the letter in order to inflict the greatest punishment on the seven Nazi leaders. Each nation took it in turns to supply the guards, who watched over the exterior of the prison. They were forbidden to mix with the internal warders, who were all on permanent postings. There was also a small ancillary staff – cooks, cleaners and so on – made up of specially vetted non-German civilians.

The bleak nineteenth-century building was chosen because it was virtually impregnable. Its high wall, electrified fence and six manned watchtowers, bristling with armed guards, sent a clear warning to any faction who might have thought it worth their while to storm the building, attempting perhaps to free its infamous inmates and carry them off to some secret Nazi outpost to spearhead the rise of the Fourth Reich.

There was to be no such attempt. In the end, the whole of the Nazi war machine had come down to just seven tired, increasingly elderly men shuffling through the yawning days as best they could under the gaze of indifferent, unsympathetic or downright hostile jailers. Life was tough because it was meant to be. The prisoners were to be denied every tiny shred of comfort, joy or humanity. They were always called by their number, never their name. Even when it was finally agreed that they might while away the endless hours by cultivating garden plots, it was decreed that they must grow vegetables, not flowers (for their colour and scent might be too uplifting).[1] Visits were severely restricted and visitors were forbidden even to shake hands with the prisoners on the grounds that this would constitute 'physical comfort'. The Russians in particular made sure that this rule was obeyed, even when Hess was the sole prisoner.

The main record of Hess's imprisonment is comprised of the many letters that he wrote to his family, and the records of his – considerably fewer – meetings with his wife and son. The subject of his flight – indeed any mention of Hitler or the war – was *verboten*, but Hess does sometimes refer to events from before 1941. Certainly Ilse Hess never seemed to have any doubts that the man in Spandau was her husband; nor did Albert Speer, who had known Hess before 1941 and was imprisoned with him for twenty years. (Wolf Rüdiger Hess was only three and a half years old when his father left for Scotland, and – like his mother – did not see him again for twenty-eight years.)

The Hess whom Speer describes in Spandau is as maddeningly elusive as ever, remaining largely aloof from the others, never really trying to forge anything other than the most formal relationship with them. At times his behaviour irritated his companions, sometimes provoking outright hostility, particularly where Baldur von Schirach was concerned – which is perhaps not so surprising, considering that Hess was supposed to testify in his defence at Nuremberg but had suffered a bad memory day at the time.

Although mentally fit, Hess had frequent bouts of hypochondriacal illness, especially complaining about stomach pains, but often ruined the effect by not even bothering to put on a particularly good performance. Declaring he was ill seemed almost a hobby with him. He also claimed occasional periods of memory loss, but even then told Speer that he was just pretending. Other old obsessions surfaced, such as the belief that his food was being contaminated – yet even then he seems to have been playing some kind of game. One day in 1954 in the prison garden when he told Speer that he had realised his suspicions in that respect were incorrect, Speer asked if his obsession was now cured. Hess bared his long yellow teeth in what approximated to a smile and said, 'No, of course not.

If it did, it wouldn't be an obsession.'[2] Was this just his warped sense of humour or was he trying to convey something else? Speer also describes an incident in 1957 when one of the other prisoners mentioned the name of Alfred Leitgen, Hess's chief adjutant in 1941. Immediately Hess ostentatiously – and apparently unconvincingly – claimed he had never heard it before, saying he must have lost his memory again.[3] Discussing Hess's amnesia, Speer records that he 'has amazingly detailed memories when he wants to',[4] yet there is very little in Speer's diary to back this up. When the two men do discuss the past, it is only in generalities. Speer records only one full conversation with Hess, on New Year's Day 1959.[5] Hess reminisced about how Hitler had personally paid Unity Mitford's hospital expenses after her suicide attempt on the day war broke out, going on to tell an anecdote about the Führer flying into a rage when he saw that a favourite cinema had changed its name. The Mitford story was well known in Nazi circles anyway, and there were no other witnesses to the cinema incident. A double could easily have sounded the part.

In 1960 an article in *Die Welt* on the forthcoming publication of the 'sequel' to *Mein Kampf* caused hot debate among the prisoners. Hess denied that such a book existed, claiming that if Hitler had written anything else, he – as his secretary – would certainly have known about it.[6] And yet we know that the manuscript – published as *Hitler's Secret Book* – evidently *did* exist, dating from the time when Hess was the Führer's secretary (1928), and, as with *Mein Kampf*, some of it even appears to have been written by him.

The mystery of the veto

Hess watched as the other 'lifers' left Spandau for the outside world. Erich Raeder was released in 1955, followed by Walter Funk in 1957: both on the grounds of ill health.

The story goes that all attempts to have Hess released were always vetoed by the Soviet Union, which has become part of the accepted story of Spandau-Hess. It is believed that the Russians wanted him to suffer because of their anger at his – or so they thought – conspiring against them and having cheated the death penalty. Besides, having a presence at Spandau gave them a valuable, if small, foothold in the British sector of Berlin. However, Wolf Rüdiger Hess argues that the British government simply used the Russian veto as an excuse, effectively hiding behind it for their own purposes. He points out that the other Allies had no reason to allow the Russians to remain in Spandau after 1948 when the USSR walked out of the joint Allied command set up for Germany as a whole.[7] Why permit the Soviets to maintain a foothold in Spandau, particularly when they left the Allied Kommandatura that controlled Berlin? Wolf Hess is emphatic that there must have been a reason why at least one of the other three powers wanted the USSR to maintain a presence in Spandau. According to Wolf Rüdiger Hess and Hugh Thomas, there was even one occasion, in 1957, when a request was made for Hess's release that the Soviets did not veto. When this happened, the British director, acting under instructions, hastened to veto the release on the grounds that the Soviet Union must have forgotten to do so and that it would be unfair on the prisoner, as he could not cope with life outside Spandau.[8]

It is now known that the secret rules governing the administration of Spandau included a clause to the effect that if any one of the Four Powers decided to withdraw from it, the prison would be closed and the prisoners returned to the power that had originally arrested them.[9] In other words, at any time Britain could simply have declared the prison closed and taken Hess into its sole charge. The fact that this did not happen, and that Britain allowed vast resources to be squandered on looking after a single frail prisoner for twenty-one years after the others had left, shows that all the governments perceived that there was some advantage in maintaining Spandau.

Spandau diary

Of the many anomalies surrounding Hess's Spandau years, surely the most intriguing was his blanket refusal to receive any visitors for nineteen years after his arrival there, even though he had been a prisoner since 1941. It was only in 1965 that he agreed to a visit – not from his wife or family as might be expected, but from his lawyer, Dr Alfred Seidl, who had defended him at Nuremberg. It was not until Christmas Eve 1969, and only then because he had an illness he believed to be terminal, that he agreed to see Ilse and Wolf for the first time in twenty-eight years. He had previously refused visits from them on the grounds that it would be undignified.[10]

Prisoner Number Seven was allowed to send and receive one letter of at most 1,300 words each week. Both outgoing and incoming mail was strictly censored, as were any enclosures such as newspaper cuttings. He was forbidden from mentioning anything to do with his flight and the war generally. In Spandau, life became a battle for trivial victories: if the censor missed something, Hess would be delighted for days. Visits were similarly strictly controlled. He was allowed one visit of thirty minutes a month, which had to be approved well in advance, and was rigorously supervised. Visitors were searched before entering the prison, and no physical contact of any sort was allowed; nor were they permitted to hand anything to the prisoner. All four directors had to be present. Whispering, making signs and any other 'non-interpretable actions' were forbidden. All visitors had to sign an agreement not to reveal anything about their visit to the press. Breaking any of these conditions made the visitor liable to arrest under military law.[11]

Even before finally gaining access to his client, the tenacious Dr Seidl had been working steadily on his behalf, trying to secure his release or even win small concessions, such as permission to wear a watch or to take a bath whenever he wished (rather than the stipulated once a week) and to decide for himself when his light was switched off each night. He was unsuccessful in all of this until 1970, when the prisoner was seventy-six years old.[12]

In 1974 Dr Seidl became a state secretary in the Bavarian Ministry of Justice, ceasing (at his own request) to represent Hess, although never failing to maintain his relationship with the family and his support for the Free Rudolf Hess campaign. But nothing connected with Rudolf Hess runs smoothly or fails to startle in some way: the appointment of his replacement, Dr Ewald Bucher, a former Minister of Justice, provoked yet another Kafkaesque episode. Once Wolf Hess had secured his father's approval for changing lawyers, Bucher made an application to visit his new client; after considering it for a month, the governors refused. When Bucher protested against this denial of Hess's basic human rights, they replied that they would have preferred him to be represented by a lawyer who was less dedicated to his release. As Wolf Hess comments dryly, 'All that was lacking was for them to tell the family to choose a lawyer for Rudolf Hess who was *opposed* to his release!'[13] Hess was never allowed to sign power of attorney over to

Bucher – effectively depriving him of legal representation, in breach of every international convention.

Alone in Spandau

In 1965 the new British Military Hospital in Berlin was finished, complete with a 'Hess suite' on the third floor, where their most prized prisoner would be taken for medical treatment – surely a sign that they intended to keep Prisoner Number Seven in Spandau for a very long time. (Hess's medical care was always the responsibility of the British.) The suite was designed for maximum security: one account describes it as a 'mini fortress',[14] with steel shutters at the doors and windows, and its own private lift.

A year after the opening of the hospital, on 30 September 1966, the last of Hess's fellow prisoners – Albert Speer and Baldur von Schirach – were released into the outside world. Hess's leave-taking of his former colleagues could hardly have been less effusive. As Speer writes:

> Hess did not come out of his cell for supper either. I went to him, but he waved me away. I took his hand; it was as lifeless as his face. 'Make it short,' he said.
>
> 'Goodbye, Herr Hess,' I said, 'You know—'
>
> He interrupted: 'No! No! No! It's – Oh, let it go.' Shortly afterwards, Hess asked the guard to have the light in his cell turned out.[15]

The Free Rudolf Hess Campaign

Started in 1966 by Wolf Rüdiger Hess and the devoted Dr Seidl, the Hilfsgemeinschaft Freiheit für Rudolf Hess (Freedom for Rudolf Hess Support Association) ran into a problem immediately, from a somewhat unexpected source: Rudolf Hess himself. He steadfastly refused to ask for his release – or have others seek it – for humanitarian reasons, so his supporters had to campaign for his freedom on the grounds that his sentence had been unjust and that he was, in effect, falsely imprisoned. Again there is a weird sense of collusion between Hess and his captors (particularly the British), which seems almost designed to keep him in Spandau. Hess was adamant not to be seen to beg for mercy, while his jailers were equally emphatic that he would *only* be released on humanitarian – not legal – grounds. This was made clear in a letter from Margaret Thatcher's private secretary to Dr Seidl dated 21 December 1979:

> As you will be aware . . . the British Government, together with the Governments of the United States and France, have for the last 12 years expressed themselves in favour of the unconditional release of Herr Hess on humanitarian grounds. The Prime Minister has asked me to assure you that the British Government for its part is continuing to press for agreement among the Four Powers for his release.
>
> I should say, however, that in Her Majesty's Government's view, the arguments which you put forward relating to Hess's trial and conviction are likely to reinforce the Soviet Union in their opposition to Hess's release and to make it less likely that they will reconsider their firmly held position.[16]

There was an increasing clamour for Hess's release at this time. The most vociferous and highly placed campaigners included Airey Neave. His widow, Baroness Airey of Abingdon, continued her husband's ten-year campaign to free Hess after Neave's murder. To the campaigners, the continuing imprisonment of an old man whose guilt was, at best, circumstantial and speculative, was nothing short of barbaric. While being – on the whole – opposed to the evils of Nazism, the campaigners saw Hess as a scapegoat, an increasingly elderly whipping boy for the vengeful anger of the victorious powers.

Other distinguished supporters (though not necessarily members) of the Free Hess Campaign included, in Britain alone, the historian A. J. P. Taylor, the Tory Prime Minister Sir Alec Douglas-Home, the prominent Jewish journalist Bernard Levin and Lord Chalfont . Even the British prosecutor at Nuremberg, Lord Shawcross, added his voice to the increasing clamour for Hess's release, while the famous Nazi hunter Simon Wiesenthal expressed the view that Hess should be released on medical grounds. In July 1986 West German Chancellor Helmut Kohl wrote a personal letter to the leaders of the four nations – Mikhail Gorbachev, Ronald Reagan, François Mitterand and Margaret Thatcher – appealing for Hess's release as 'a dictate of humanity'.[17]

Hess himself refused for a long time to make any appeals for his release. In letters to Ilse and Wolf he explained that it would seem like capitulation: he might have lost everything else, but he still had his pride. (In 1966 he reprimanded his son for writing to the heads of state of the Four Powers and to the Pope demanding his release.) However, in 1979, at the age of eighty-five, he finally asked for release on the grounds of ill health. His appeal was refused.[18]

Three years after he had become the solitary soul in Spandau – at the end of November 1969 – Hess was diagnosed as having a perforated duodenal ulcer, which is potentially life-threatening, particularly at seventy-five years of age. On 8 December, while in his 'mini fortress' in the hospital, he finally requested a visit from his wife and son, asking that it might take place in private on Christmas Eve. He promised not to allow them to touch him, even to shake hands.[19] The visit was subject to the standard rules for visitors: Ilse and Wolf were to be searched, were not to attempt any physical contact with the prisoner, and were to undertake not to make any statement to the press about the visit (or they would be refused further visits). They were still, even at this late date, liable to arrest if they contravened these rules.[20]

Because of the rules, this momentous meeting appears to have been somewhat stilted – although admittedly most people would have found the circumstances hardly conducive to spontaneity or merriment; and, in any case, these were highly disciplined, controlled people who had never been emotionally demonstrative. We know that one of the first things Hess said to Ilse was to tell 'Freiburg' (his secretary, Hildegard Fath, who was also a close family friend, having been engaged to a cousin who died) that he was sorry to have distressed her at Nuremberg in 1945 by pretending not to recognise her. Clearly this had preyed on his mind ever since.[21]

When finally reunited with her husband, Ilse commented to him that his voice was lower than it used to be. This is very interesting because – as Dr Thomas points out – it is very rare for a man's voice to grow lower with age: if anything, it usually gets higher.[22]

Bird's book and after

A guard at Spandau in 1947, Eugene K. Bird, became its American director in the late 1960s. His book, *The Loneliest Man in the World*, published in 1974, was based on his many conversations with Prisoner Number Seven. Bird claimed that in 1970 a box of papers written by Hess in Nuremberg was 'discovered' in Spandau and handed over to him as director, either to keep or destroy.[23] They included Hess's diary and an account of his flight, together with a paper outlining the foundation of a new German government (with himself as Führer) and details of its political programme. Bird claims Hess gave him permission to publish the papers, along with recordings of their conversations, although he takes care to point out that this was strictly against the rules. Wolf Rüdiger Hess has expressed his reservations about the documents since neither he nor his family was allowed to see the originals.[24]

Bird claimed that Hess had not only approved the book, but had also signed over the copyright on some of his personal writings. Wolf Rüdiger Hess retorted that his father wanted to stop publication as Bird had promised to publish only after Hess's death, but Dr Seidl was unable to secure the authorities' permission to allow Hess to sign a power of attorney that would enable him to secure an injunction. There was also the further complication that although Hess had specified that none of his writings should be altered in any way – as Wolf points out – since it was impossible to see the originals, and his father was unable to read Bird's book, it cannot be determined whether they have been changed. Prisoner Number Seven was not the only loser in all this, however, because, according to Lieutenant-Colonel Tony le Tissier, the British governor of Spandau at the time of Hess's death, Bird was dismissed from his post for writing the book.[25] (Indeed, given the inordinate restrictions that surrounded everything connected with Spandau, it is amazing that the book was ever published or that the authorities in effect sanctioned its publication by not allowing Hess to bring an injunction against Bird.)

The release that never was

In May 1979 rumours circulated that the USSR was considering allowing Hess to be released; certainly, the matter was the subject of high-level communications between the Soviet and German governments at that time. It was understood that the Soviets would agree to his release provided that he undertook to make no public statements. This flicker of early *glasnost* also included an agreement that would allow Wolf Hess to have a private meeting with his father. Hopes were relatively high when this optimistic message was relayed to Hess's son through a German minister of state, who said he had received word personally from 'the highest in the Soviet Union'. Naturally, then, Wolf Rüdiger Hess was unpleasantly surprised when in August his application for a private meeting was refused: he was allowed to see his father but under the usual restrictive rules, which suggests that another of the Four Powers – not the Soviet Union– had vetoed it. He made another application for a private visit on 4 September, but once again was granted only a restricted one. However, at that meeting Wolf told his father that attempts were still being made to arrange a private visit. Perhaps he should have kept quiet: while he was on the plane returning home, Rudolf Hess was rushed into the British Military Hospital. No reason was given. He was returned to Spandau six days later, after undergoing unspecified tests.[26]

On 21 September the British director, G. P. T. Marshall, telephoned Ilse to say that Hess was refusing to have an operation on his prostate gland, which he needed urgently. Marshall explained that there was a grave risk of complete blockage of the urinary tract and serious infection. Although naturally concerned over Hess's health, both his wife and son agreed to abide by his decision, refusing to allow the operation to go ahead. In the end it did not take place, but – strangely, after all the dire prognostications – Hess's health did not deteriorate.

When Wolf next visited his father, on 2 October 1979, he learned that Hess had been forbidden from discussing either the proposed operation or his reasons for refusing it. The letter Hess sent his family beforehand – which Wolf believes referred to the operation – was confiscated by the prison authorities. The Four Powers also refused Hess's son permission to see the relevant medical documents. Finally, when the story was leaked to the press in November of that year, the British government dismissed reports of Hess's ill health and the need for an operation as 'pure speculation'.[27]

What was this peculiar episode all about? As Wolf Hess points out, September was 'British month' at Spandau, which suggests that the British might have become alarmed by the softening of the Soviet attitude to Hess's release, and rushed him into the 'mini fortress' of the Hess suite at the British Military Hospital so that he was on indisputably British territory until the whole business blew over. There is an even more sinister possibility. Was the story of the need for an emergency prostate operation preparing the way for his sudden demise, if it should become expedient?

The strange death of Prisoner Number Seven

On 17 August 1987 the British military authorities in Berlin announced that Rudolf Hess was dead. It was a bald announcement, giving no cause of death – that had to wait until the authorities had carried out their post-mortem examination. It was only then that they stated that Hess had hanged himself in a small hut in the prison garden, using an electrical cord. The official account has it that Hess, after waking from his customary afternoon nap, went for a walk in the garden, accompanied, as always, by one of the warders. But at about 2.30 p.m. the warder – unnamed in the reports but we now know him to be an American named Anthony Jordan – was called away to take a telephone call, and when he returned he found his elderly charge lying crumpled in the garden hut with an electrical flex wound tightly round his neck. (The hut was originally used for storing gardening materials but in later years Hess was allowed to use it as a shelter.) The warder called for help, and frantic attempts were made to resuscitate the old man, while the British Military Hospital was alerted by the codewords designated for such emergencies: 'Paradox' and 'Xerox'. It dispatched a military ambulance, which arrived back at the hospital around four o'clock – but to no avail. Prisoner Number Seven was declared dead at 4.10 p.m. The man known as Rudolf Hess was finally free, although his story was by no means over: if nothing else, the manner of his death ensured its future status as a great mystery.

Two days later the post-mortem was carried out by J. Malcolm Cameron, Professor of Forensic Medicine at the University of London and chief pathologist of the British Army. His report concluded that the cause of death was suspension – death by hanging. At 6 p.m. on 19 August an official statement by the British Military Government in Berlin affirmed that Hess had committed suicide, although it concluded – confusingly – that it was unclear whether the suicide attempt 'was the actual cause of death'.[28]

A full version of events was not made public for another month.

On 19 September part of the official statement read: 'Investigations have confirmed that, on the 17th of August, Rudolf Hess hanged himself from a window latch in a small summer house in the prison garden, using an electrical extension cord, which had for some time been kept for use in connection with a reading lamp.'[29] It was reported that a suicide note was found in a jacket pocket. Written on the back of a letter from Wolf Hess's wife Andrea (the prisoner's access to paper had been strictly controlled), it began: 'Written a few minutes before my death . . .'

Perhaps conveniently, according to the rules of the British Military Government, there was no need for an inquest.

Even after their statement of the circumstances of the prisoner's death, the authorities maintained an incomprehensible secrecy. When researching an article for *After the Battle* (which appeared in November 1987), Denis C. Bateman asked the British Military Government exactly where Hess had died, only to be told that it refused to say where the garden house was situated 'as it was agreed by the Four Powers that such information would not be made public'.[30]

The original procedures and regulations for Spandau had decreed that, on the death of any of the prisoners, they should be cremated and their ashes scattered in secret (which is what happened to those who were executed or died by their own hand at Nuremberg). However, in October 1982 Wolf Rüdiger Hess managed to persuade the four directors to agree that, in the event of his father's death, they would hand his body over to the family for burial in their plot at Wunsiedel. This agreement was kept secret on the insistence of the directors[31] – so secret that apparently neither the Foreign Office nor the intelligence services were informed.

On Thursday, 20 August, the body was flown by RAF Hercules from Berlin to the USAF base at Grafenwöhr near Munich, and handed over to Wolf Hess and Dr Seidl. The priest who had replaced Charles Gabel in 1986 came with the four directors to officiate at the burial but Wolf Hess refused to allow him to do so, having already arranged for Gabel to officiate. Everything was done in the greatest secrecy – it was in everyone's interest to keep the burial arrangements from leaking out. The family hated the idea of a media circus, while the Bavarian government – Wolf Hess had managed to secure its support for a private burial – did not want it to provoke neo-Nazi (and anti-Nazi) demonstrations.

Wolf Hess and Dr Seidl delivered the body to a funeral parlour and then went to a meeting with the mayor of Wunsiedel, the Bavarian Ministry of the Interior and the police to discuss arrangements for the secret burial and the provision of a police escort. It was on their way back that they came up with the idea of a second, completely independent autopsy, which was arranged by Seidl with the eminent pathologist Dr Wolfgang Spann of Munich University's Institute of Forensic Medicine.[32] The second post-mortem was carried out on the following day.

Plans had been made for a clandestine burial at night in a graveyard at Wunsiedel: Wolf Hess alone was supposed to deliver the body to a group from the Bavarian Interior Ministry at a secret rendezvous. But clearly the whole business took a dreadful toll: on the afternoon of 21 August he suffered a stroke and had to be rushed to hospital where he was put in intensive care. Andrea Hess had to take over, delivering the body as arranged. At four o'clock the next morning she received a phone call saying simply: 'It's done.'

The following April, without any fuss, the body was reinterred in a grave in the family plot. The gravestone bears the simple epitaph, in German: 'I dared.'

Was it murder?

It took over a year for an eye-witness to give his story – Abdallah Melaouhi, a Tunisian who had been Hess's nurse from 1982. The only other version of what happened in the garden hut that day was given by Lieutenant-Colonel Tony le Tissier. Le Tissier took pains to debunk Melaouhi's account, presenting a more briskly prosaic version, so in the end it is a matter of Melaouhi versus le Tissier. However, it must be remembered that le Tissier was not present, so his account is therefore unattributed hearsay, whereas Melaouhi was there – his is the version that would be acceptable in a court of law. But is it possible to discover whose version tells the truth about the death of Prisoner Number Seven?

Melaouhi's version was first made public in a BBC *Newsnight* programme in 1989 – and in later statements and an affidavit, copies of which are in our possession.[33] He said he left the prison at 11.05 a.m. Before leaving, as always he checked the first-aid box to ensure that everything was in order in case of emergencies, noting that the seal was intact, and checked the emergency oxygen cylinder. While in the mess having a late lunch, at around 2.00 p.m., he received a telephone call recalling him urgently to the prison. But when he arrived at the main gate, the American guard refused to let him in, saying: 'It's all over. You don't have a job any more. Be happy.'

However, when the gate was opened to let an American in, Melaouhi took advantage of it, and slipped in with him. Realising that – at that time of day – Hess would be in the garden, he tried to get there the quickest way, through the prison block, but found the door unaccountably locked. So he took the other route, through the garden, which entailed talking his way past another reluctant American guard at another locked gate – eventually arriving at the garden hut at about 2.45.

An astonishing scene greeted Melaouhi. Hess was lying on his back on the floor. Present were two men in US Army uniforms and Jordan, the American warder, who – according to Melaouhi – was standing, his shirt and tie dishevelled, shouting, 'The pig is finished!' Jordan seemed surprised to see Melaouhi. According to the nurse, the hut was in chaos and, most tellingly, the reading lamp – its flex supposedly the means of Hess's suicide – *was still plugged in*. He saw no electric flex attached to the window latch. Three men were in the hut – he recognised Jordan, but not the other two. Unfamiliar figures, dressed in American uniforms, they should not have been there. Although this was during the Americans' tour of duty – their turn to supply the guard – it was against regulations for them to be in the grounds.

Melaouhi alleges that it was impossible for Hess to have killed himself in the way the authorities claimed because of his disabilities. Although, thanks partly to his self-discipline – he had still tried to maintain a regime of physical exercise – Hess had reached old age relatively healthily, by the 1980s his years had finally begun to take their toll. He had suffered a mild stroke in the early years of the decade; his eyesight was poor, especially in the left eye; his arms and hands were weak – again, especially on the left side, where his grip is reported to have been as weak as a six-year-old's. He also had a frozen left shoulder, preventing him from raising his arm horizontally. He walked with a stick and could not climb stairs unaided. His balance was bad, and he stooped – the result of arthritis in the spine.[34] How could an old man with so many disabilities have had the strength to kill himself with electric flex?

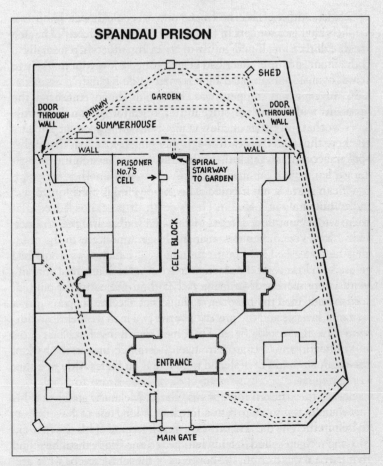

Plan of Spandau Prison, Berlin. Hess's body was found in the summerhouse.

Several other aspects of the death of Prisoner Number Seven cast doubt on the official verdict. Melaouhi and others familiar with the layout of the prison and its day-to-day routine have pointed out that the hut was the worst place for Hess to choose to kill himself – it would have been far more logical, and easier, to do it in his cell late at night.

If correct, was the chaos in the garden hut a sign that Hess had put up a fight? Although Melaouhi and others believe it was, surely it is unlikely that two soldiers in the prime of life would have had much trouble with a weak and infirm man in his nineties, especially if they surprised him. If there had been a struggle it was more likely to have involved Jordan. Had he returned while a putative assassination attempt was happening? This would have presented the 'assassins' with a problem, since if they killed Jordan too the suicide story would look rather unconvincing. Is it significant that Jordan – the key witness to the death of Prisoner Number Seven – has never spoken about it, and that the testimony that he gave to the investigation has never been made public?

Of course, to some it could raise the possibility that Jordan was more intimately involved in Hess's death. It is acknowledged that there was a great deal of friction between Jordan and the prisoner; Hess had severe difficulties with the black American, to the point that he had asked for him to be removed, but the governors had refused.[35] However, other factors make it more likely that Jordan's words were merely descriptive rather than indicative of guilt. If Jordan had killed the prisoner, it would not account for the signs of a titanic struggle and the presence of the two men in American uniform. The fight could not have involved Hess himself, because of his infirmities; in any case, apart from a mysterious bruise on the back of the head, no marks of violence were found on Hess's body in either post-mortem.

Seeing the stricken form of his charge, Melaouhi states that his first thought was to try to resuscitate him, asking one of the strangers to help, which he did. He says he asked Jordan to fetch the first-aid box and oxygen cylinder, but when he returned with them he found that the seal was broken, the contents of the kit tampered with, and the cylinder empty. According to Melaouhi, Jordan had also alerted the British Military Hospital, which sent a vehicle that arrived soon afterwards. Melaouhi travelled with the body to the hospital and was there when Hess was declared dead.

The nurse adds a macabre touch. He claims that, at the hospital, the British, American and French directors (there were no Russians present) met in the next room and opened a bottle of champagne and that someone in British Army uniform went up to him, telling him to 'Keep your mouth shut, if you know what I mean'. He asked him to sign a document, but Melaouhi refused, and as soon as he left the hospital he went straight to a West Berlin police station, where he told his story in the belief that he was reporting a murder. He claims he was plagued by telephone calls in the following weeks, warning him not to say anything about what he had seen.

As a result of Melaouhi's statement, the West Berlin State Prosecutor opened a murder file, but as the death had happened on territory under British control, it was beyond his jurisdiction.

The version according to le Tissier

Le Tissier was not in the prison that afternoon but at a meeting at the Soviet HQ about a minor issue of protocol, not returning to his office at the British Sector HQ until about four o'clock, when he was told he was required urgently at the prison. (Intriguingly, whoever called him failed to tell him why. Did the caller assume that he already knew?) On his way out of the building he encountered a colleague who told him that Hess was probably dead.[36]

Coincidentally, a Military Police Special Investigation Branch (SIB) team – led by Major J. P. Gallagher, an old colleague of le Tissier's from a previous posting – happened to be in the barracks next to the prison, investigating another case. So it was convenient, to say the least, for someone to order an immediate investigation into the death – so immediate, in fact, that the four governors not only failed to authorise it, but were completely unaware that it had started.[37]

According to le Tissier,[38] Jordan had accompanied Hess out to the garden at about 2.10 p.m., going ahead to the 'hut' – although variously described as a 'gardener's shed', 'garden house' and 'a small cottage in the garden', it was an elderly Portakabin – before going off on other business. According to some accounts, he was called to the telephone. A few minutes later he checked the hut and found Hess slumped against the wall, having apparently looped the cable around his neck using a simple knot, then slid down the wall, fatally tightening the loop around his neck.

Le Tissier's version has it that Jordan removed the cable (and, if we are to believe Melaouhi, plugged it back in again) and then went to the main prison block to raise the alarm, ensuring that the British Military Hospital was alerted. Meanwhile, a soldier in one of the guard towers, seeing Jordan's alarm, had alerted the guardroom.

Going to investigate, the commander of the guard unit found that Hess still had a pulse, if a very weak one. He called for the two medical orderlies from the guard unit, one of whom arrived shortly before Melaouhi appeared on the scene, and together they attempted to resuscitate the old man. They were joined by the second of the US medical orderlies a few minutes later. According to le Tissier, these are the two mysterious men in US Army uniform whom Melaouhi encountered in the hut. The director implies that the nurse knew full well who they were. Another discrepancy is that Melaouhi says that both these men were already there when he arrived.

The ambulance from the hospital arrived at 3.12 p.m., Hess was loaded aboard, and efforts to revive him continued during the drive to the hospital. They arrived at around 3.50 p.m. Roughly fifteen minutes later Hess was declared dead.

Clearly, le Tissier believes that Melaouhi is under the impression that he witnessed a state-sponsored killing:

> I was simply astounded by Melaouhi's presentation [on *Newsnight*]. When the SIB had tried to obtain a witness statement from him during the course of the investigation, he had refused to co-operate, appealing to me in an almost hysterical manner to be excused, and saying he was just a nurse and wanted nothing to do with the police. This had happened on three separate occasions as the SIB vainly tried to obtain a statement from him . . . I found this attitude at the time of Hess's death, and the SIB investigation completely out of character, utterly inexplicable.
>
> Having seen the *Newsnight* programme I concluded that the ideas now being expressed had either entered, or been fed, into Melaouhi's mind before the SIB approach, and that he must have thought that he was being asked to co-operate in the cover-up of a crime committed under state auspices![39]

Melaouhi has never said that he thought it was a state-initiated crime. Was this perhaps a conclusion Lieutenant-Colonel le Tissier felt Melaouhi had reached for himself? It is difficult to see how Melaouhi could have been 'fed' ideas such as seeing the signs of a struggle and two men in US Army uniforms whom he had never encountered before. However, even the governor's account makes it clear that right from the start Melaouhi was a frightened man, who

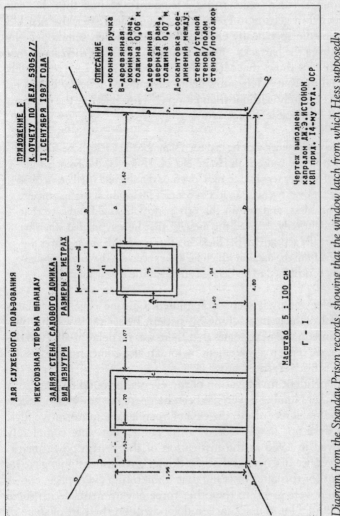
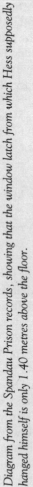

Diagram from the Spandau Prison records, showing that the window latch from which Hess supposedly hanged himself is only 1.40 metres above the floor.

believed he had witnessed something very disturbing and had gone straight to the West German police to report it.

There is a discrepancy in le Tissier's apparent attempt to discredit Melaouhi's story, concerning Melaouhi's claims that he was obstructed in getting to Hess. According to le Tissier, the first US Army medic specifically checked his watch when summoned (by radio) from the barracks – it was 2.40 p.m. Le Tissier then states that the gate's log shows that Melaouhi was booked in at 2.45, reasonably concluding that 'Melaouhi's claim of imposed lengthy delays en route is entirely without foundation'.[40] However, on the previous page of his book le Tissier writes:

> Melaouhi claimed that he had been summoned by telephone from his lunch in the canteen in House No 24. However, the French Duty Chief Warder reported to his Governor that he had tried unsuccessfully for over twenty minutes to contact Melaouhi at his apartment, at the Mess, and within the prison, which would indicate that Melaouhi only received the message that he was wanted when he eventually appeared at the Mess. In other words, his absence over this period from the areas in which he was expected to be found substantially contributed to his delayed arrival at the Portakabin.[41]

Le Tissier's analysis seems convoluted. On one page he explains Melaouhi's delay in reaching his patient by saying it was his own fault, and on the next argues that there was no delay at all. And the nearest we have to a statement by Jordan also comes from le Tissier, which is not very satisfactory.

Independent investigation of the events surrounding the death of Prisoner Number Seven has been hampered by the lack of access to the official records. In the case of Spandau's administrative files, these were not simply closed to the public, but were completely destroyed in 1988 at the instigation of the British government. However, we discovered that the Soviet government only gave its consent for this after insisting that it microfilm every page, copies of which were given to the other three governments. With some effort, and a lot of assistance and goodwill on the part of some of our foreign contacts, we were able to gain access to these records, which shed intriguing light on the immediate aftermath of Hess's death.

Foul play?

The official autopsy was performed, as we have seen, on the morning of 19 August by Professor J. Malcolm Cameron, who had been on stand-by for this task for several years. Originally it was intended that he should make a post-mortem report exclusively for the British Military Government in Berlin, but when the moment came he was told he was now required to make a report for the other powers, the Hess family and, ultimately, the public.[42]

No photographs were taken during the autopsy, ostensibly to prevent neo-Nazis from peddling macabre souvenirs. The operation was relayed by CCTV to a room outside where the directors could watch the proceedings, if they wished – although at the insistence of the Russians no video recording was made. Cameron concluded that the cause of death was:

(1) Asphyxia
due to (or as a consequence of)
(2) Compression of the neck
due to (or as a consequence of)
(3) Suspension.

To the question on the Death Certificate 'Was the death due to natural causes?' Cameron answered, 'No'.

There is a discrepancy between different accounts about the time that the body was stripped – this is important because it has a bearing on both the question of the identity of the deceased and the validity of the 'suicide note'. Dr Hugh Thomas discovered that orders were given – against standard procedure – that the clothes should not be removed from the body before the post-mortem, which meant that X-rays were taken (incredibly) of a fully clothed corpse.[43] The presence of the clothes seriously threatened to confuse the issue: bits of dirt and debris on the trousers, picked up from the floor of the hut, showed up as spots which were, at one stage, thought to be possible 'gun-shot residue'. (Obviously Hess had meant to make a thorough job of it.)

The second, independent post-mortem, performed for the Hess family by Dr Spann, challenged both Professor Cameron's findings and the suicide verdict. According to Spann, death was not due to suspension, which kills by constricting the windpipe. Prisoner Number Seven had been killed by forceful closure of the two carotid arteries – in other words, *by strangulation*. The tell-tale clue is the pattern of the marks caused by the cord on the back of the neck: hanging makes V-shaped marks that rise to a peak at the point of suspension. But those on Hess's neck made an unbroken horizontal line, indicating that the cord had been placed around his neck and then tightened, strangling him.

Despite the official line that Hess was supposed to have hanged himself with a tightly wound electric flex, Cameron's report *mentioned no marks on the back of the neck at all*. Referring to the omission, Professor Spann later stated in an interview for BBC's *Newsnight*: 'We were astonished at that . . . Not only must they [the marks] have been there at the time of the first autopsy, they must have been observed then, too. They simply weren't recorded.'[44]

Spann's conclusion, that the marks on Hess's neck – being straight rather than V-shaped – are more consistent with throttling than suspension, has been disputed by Professor Bernard Knight, a pathologist at the University of Wales, who claimed that there are cases of hanging that produce a horizontal mark.[45] But even so, such marks are atypical and should at least have been noted at the first post-mortem. As we've seen, Cameron makes no mention of any marks on the back of the neck. Professor Spann writes in his report:

> Professor Cameron, in reaching the conclusion that the cause of death was asphyxiation caused by compression of the neck due to suspension, appears to have neglected to consider the other method of strangulation, namely throttling . . . Making this distinction would have required examination of the course of the ligature mark. The precise course of the mark is not reported in Professor Cameron's autopsy report.[46]

It is virtually impossible even for an able-bodied person to strangle himself in the manner described because the grip is relaxed as soon as unconsciousness intervenes. But Hess was far from being able-bodied: he was ninety-three, extremely frail and crippled with arthritis. He could only walk with a stick, needing help to get up out of a chair. Not only was he manifestly incapable of even tying his own shoelaces – and therefore had no hope of being able to twist the flex around his own neck – but he was also unable to raise his arm to shoulder level. It seems highly unlikely that he could even have fixed the cord to the latch of the relatively high window, as officially claimed.

The suicide note

The scrawled note – written on the back of a recent letter from Hess's daughter-in-law Andrea – seemed to be Hess's farewell to the world. It said:

> Would the Governors please send this home. Written a few minutes before my death.
>
> I thank you all my loved ones for all that you have done for me. Tell Freiburg that I was infinitely sorry that I had to behave ever since the Nuremberg Trials as if I did not know her. There remained nothing else for me, otherwise all attempts to free me would have been in vain. I had looked forward to seeing her again. I have received photographs of her as well as of all of you.
>
> Your Big One [*Euer Grosser*][47]

There are problems with virtually every sentence, but the most glaring is the reference to 'Freiburg'. At his first meeting with Ilse in 1969 this seemed to be uppermost in his mind. But the note is unlikely to have been written in 1987 because, having got the Freiburg business off his chest way back in 1969, he had not denied knowing her since. Similarly, what was the point of mentioning as late as 1987 that he had received photographs of her – surely his family would have known that by then?

Wolf and Andrea Hess believe the note to be a forgery, although probably based on a genuine letter written by Hess in 1969, when his life was hanging in the balance due to the perforated ulcer – prompting him to ask to see Ilse and Wolf for the first time.[48] Apart from the oddity about Freiburg, Wolf also points out that certain phrases in the note were characteristic of Hess in the late 1960s – as with most people, his personal catchphrases changed with time. He had not used the '*Euer Grosser*' sign-off for many years, preferring by 1987 to conclude simply with '*der Eure*' ('Yours'). The Hesses were also surprised that the note contained no reference to his grandchildren, who featured prominently in his letters in the years immediately before his death.

If the Hesses are right and it is a forgery, the original note must have been copied on to the back of the more recent letter to give the appearance of authenticity. There were other anomalies: there is no date on the note, despite the fact that Hess – and Prisoner Number Seven – obsessively dated everything. Wolf and Andrea Hess also point out that, although incoming mail was stamped by the prison authorities, the letter on which the note had been scrawled bore no such stamp, raising the question of whether he had ever received it. However, from the Spandau records we found that the prison had become lax in this regard by 1987, and not all letters were stamped.

Hugh Thomas was told that the note was not found until the body was stripped for the post-mortem two days after Hess's death, which allowed an opportunity for a forgery to be placed in his pockets.[49] Le Tissier, however, claims it was among the personal effects taken from the body on 17 August and placed in an envelope which was opened by the four directors at an emergency meeting that evening.[50] The Spandau records support le Tissier – but introduce more questions.

The minutes of the meeting that took place at 19.55 on 17 August do indeed show that the envelope was opened in the presence of the four directors, and that in addition to handkerchiefs, spectacles and pens, it contained '1 letter'. However, no significance is attached to this, and there is nothing about it being a suicide note – which surely the four officials would have noticed. However, by the time a second meeting was convened at 12.30 the following afternoon to discuss the wording of the press release, the fact that it was a suicide note written on the back of a letter from his daughter-in-law was known, and the question of whether it should be released to the family was debated. And yet there was clearly some doubt in the minds of one of the four powers about the exact circumstances of the discovery. The Russian director objected to the wording of the press release and – at a further meeting at 18.55 after he had consulted his superiors – insisted that the words 'A note was found in his pocket' be deleted from the statement. Why did the Soviet representative object to such an innocuous phrase?

At a meeting of the directors after handing over the body to Wolf Hess on 20 August, le Tissier proposed that, in view of the letter's

```
                        BERLIN        GERMANY

                      SPECIAL MEETING              AP/SM(87)3

                         M I N U T E S             20th August 1987
```

of an extraordinary meeting of the Governors of Spandau Allied
Prison held at the request of the Acting Soviet Governor at 1855
hrs on Tuesday, 18th August 1987.

Present: Mr KEANE   USA   Presiding
                Lt Col LE TISSIER   UK
                M PLANET   FR
                Mr KOLODNIKOV   USSR Acting Governor

1.   The Soviet Acting Governor informed the Governorate that the
purpose of the meeting was to announce that the Soviet Element was
now prepared to approve the proposed Western Powers press statement
providing two changes were made. The first change to remove the
wording "investigation by authorities of the four powers" and the
second change "A note was found in his pocket." to be removed.

     All Governors noted the Soviet Element's approved version and
expressed satisfaction with the new wording.

     The American Chairman Governor stated that this special meeting
was now adjourned at 1925 hrs.

```
!!!!!  [signature]        [signature]       [signature]    [signature]

       USA                UK                 FR              USSR
    Mr KEANE        Lt Col LE TISSIER      M PLANET      Mr KOLODNIKOV
```

*Minutes of meeting of Spandau's directors on 18 August 1987, giving the
Soviet objections to the proposed press release.*

importance, a forensic expert be brought in from London to authenticate it. According to le Tissier's published account, the expert, P. A.
M. Beard, was (apparently) by his own admission unfamiliar with
German script, although we are told that he was able to authenticate
the note using samples of Hess's writing (supplied by the prison
directors) which were later destroyed.[51] Beard's report was not seen
by anyone other than officials in Spandau and the British Military
Government. Besides this, although Wolf and Andrea Hess were
assured that forensic tests had proved that the note was written with
the same ink as that in the fountain pen in Hess's pocket, there was
no way they could confirm this as the pen had been destroyed.[52]

So if the note was a forgery, the question is why would the British
want the public to believe that Hess killed himself? The answer
seems clear enough: if he did not commit suicide, he was murdered.

The bungled investigation

The initial investigation of Hess's death was, by anyone's standards unsatisfactory, to say the least. Although normal procedure in a case of suspicious death is to secure the scene, in this case it was not done: various people were free to tramp in and out of the Portakabin as they pleased. Any evidence that might have been there was presumably soon obscured, irretrievably lost or deliberately removed. The SIB team was not allowed to take fingerprints from the body when they saw it at the British Military Hospital,[53] an essential procedure to eliminate a victim's own prints from a crime scene. Moreover, their report has never been made public, although, in any case, it would have been impossible to corroborate because all the evidence had been either accidentally lost or deliberately destroyed.

In what must be one of the most emphatic acts of overkill in modern times, the entire edifice of Spandau was razed to the ground within just six weeks of the prisoner's death. Every last brick was deliberately pulverised into dust by bulldozers and crushing equipment. There was not to be the tiniest fragment for the determined Nazi memento hunter to pocket.

Then finally, on 18 December 1987, in the presence of all four directors, the last Spandau building, the Portakabin, was crushed by a bulldozer, doused in petrol and burned away to nothing. Le Tissier himself threw all Hess's clothing (including the historic flying suit) and walking stick on the pyre – along with the electric cable (recovered from the Military Police) with which he had supposedly killed himself.[54]

Because of questions raised by the Hess family, Dr Hugh Thomas and *Newsnight*, a review of the case was ordered in 1989. The task fell to Detective Superintendent Howard Jones of Scotland Yard, who submitted a report to the Director of Public Prosecutions at the beginning of July. It was reported in the press that he had concluded that there was sufficient evidence to warrant a murder investigation;[55] the Labour MP Rhodri Morgan claims Jones also told him this at a meeting on the terrace at the House of Commons. (Subsequently the First Minister for Wales, Morgan has long been interested in the Hess affair.) According to Morgan, Jones had been horrified at the apparent incompetence of the original investigation, and the way vital evidence had been destroyed – including, incredibly, the X-rays from the official post-mortem.[56] Morgan claims that Jones came back to him later, clearly worried about his previous words. Morgan had the distinct impression that the policeman might have been warned off from talking about his report.[57] We have learned that Jones also told reporters that he had recommended that a formal investigation be instigated, with witnesses being questioned under caution – specifically naming Melaouhi, Jordan and le Tissier.

Ultimately, however, the Director of Public Prosecutions decided not to act. The reasons for this were given in November 1989 by Solicitor General Sir Nicholas Lyell in reply to a parliamentary question from Rhodri Morgan. He said that Jones's inquiries 'have produced no cogent evidence to suggest that Rudolf Hess was murdered, nor, in the view of the Director of Public Prosecutions, is there any basis for further investigation'.[58]

Morgan asked twice – in 1989 and 1992 – that a copy of Jones's report be placed in the House of Commons library, but was told both times that such reports are always confidential, and therefore could not be disclosed.[59] In a response to a request from researcher Alfred Smith to see the report in April 1993, Jones stated: 'The subject matter is confidential between the Metropolitan Police Service and the office of the Director of Public Prosecutions on whose behalf the inquiry was conducted, and is covered by Public Interest Immunity.'[60] This is a legal device preventing the disclosure of evidence if it is deemed that the public interest in its concealment outweighs the public interest in its release – something necessitating the signature of a government minister. This is usually only done if the interests of the state are likely to be compromised. Jones's reply surely amounts to an admission that the facts about Hess's death might in some way embarrass the British government.

An uncertain registration

The Spandau records show that, on the evening of 17 August, Colonel Hamer-Philips of the British Military Hospital issued a preliminary death certificate giving the cause of death as 'Cardiac Arrest secondary to Asphyxia (Unknown)' – significantly leaving the cause of the asphyxia open.[61]

Then a second death certificate was issued after the official post-mortem, with the death officially registered by Major Frank Crabtree, registering officer for the British forces in Germany and Northwestern Europe, giving 'asphyxia due to compression of the neck due to suspension' as the cause of death. On 24 April 1995, on the basis of the second autopsy, Wolf Rüdiger Hess applied to the British Office of Population, Censuses and Surveys (OPCS) to have the cause of death on the register amended from 'due to suspension' to 'due to throttling'. The British authorities' reaction was very odd: after several months of dithering they cancelled the registration and have never issued a replacement, inadvertently creating a weird scenario. Without a valid registration, Rudolf Hess is still – officially – alive.

The reason the British authorities gave for taking such a step was that, as a result of looking into Wolf Hess's request, they realised that his father's death had been registered incorrectly and therefore – technically – illegally. They claimed that the British Army registrar in Berlin did not have the legal authority to register the death. Yet the Certificate of Competence issued to him by the British Military Government – which defined his responsibilities – gave him authority officially to register 'all deaths occurring to members of the British Forces and civilians accompanying, sponsored and otherwise with the British Forces and to all persons for which the British Forces have a responsibility under national and international laws, treaties and protocols'.[62] This comprehensive sweep clearly included the lone prisoner of Spandau. However, the OPCS now declared that the only law under which the death could have been registered – the Registration of Births, Deaths and Marriages (Special Provisions) Act 1957 – did not bestow such authority on Major Crabtree. That Act, they claimed, only applied to members of the armed forces serving overseas, civilians employed by them and 'certain welfare organisations'. It did not extend to persons for whom the British forces have responsibility under national and international laws. So, as it was deemed that Crabtree had no authority to register Hess's death, the registration was duly cancelled.

Writing to Wolf Hess's British solicitors on 10 December 1996, the Ministry of Defence's legal adviser, Anthony Inglese, stated:

> our researches have failed to discover how and why the decision was taken to register Hess's death in the United Kingdom . . .

We have made further enquiries but no records have been traced to explain why the death of Hess was registered in the UK. We do not know why the Service Registering Officer's certificate of competence was drafted in terms wider than the Registration of Births Deaths and Marriages (Special Provisions) Act 1957 . . .

It is common ground that the 1957 Act does not apply in this case and we are not aware of any other power under which the death could correctly be registered. The question of a recommendation to the OPCS, as requested in your letter of 19 July, therefore does not arise.

We have done our best to discover the answers to your queries and to answer them as far as we confidently can. We now leave it to you to pursue your enquiries in other directions.[63]

So the MoD washed its hands of the whole affair, effectively saying, 'It's some other department's responsibility, but we don't know which one and frankly we don't care.'

At the end of January 1997, the official line on the registration was confirmed in a House of Commons written reply by Armed Forces Minister Nicholas Soames to a question raised by Rhodri Morgan.[64] And that is the way it has stayed ever since.

The authorities claim that as it was nobody's responsibility to register the death, the cause of death on the original registration cannot be changed – which is very convenient because it prevents the key word 'throttling' from appearing on any official documents and forestalls any attempt to reopen the case of Rudolf Hess's death.

Release plans

All this adds up to a convincing case that the death of Prisoner Number Seven was, to say the least, suspicious – but is it proof of murder? Wolf Hess and Dr Hugh Thomas not only have no doubts that it was homicide, but are certain who was responsible. They believe that everything points the finger at the British government, and having sifted through the evidence, so do we. But what possible motive would the British government have for killing off the old man? Why decree that he had to die then, when he could have only had a few more years to live anyway?

We believe he was killed because he was about to be released.

In February 1987 *Der Spiegel* reported that Mikhail Gorbachev was considering approving Hess's release after an appeal from West German President Richard von Weizsäcker – who attracted some controversy by comparing Hess's imprisonment with that of Russian dissident Andrei Sakharov and Nelson Mandela – and a few months later Moscow radio announced that Hess's release was being seriously considered.[65] This made sense, fitting in with Gorbachev's programme of fostering closer relations with the West and of *glasnost*, or greater openness. It was time to make a goodwill gesture to Germany – a sign that the war was finally over and that the post-war tension between the USSR and West Germany could be forgotten, and both countries could look forward to an amicable future as economic allies, not military enemies.

Expectations grew: in April the West German newspaper *Bild* reported that Hess was to be released on his ninety-third birthday on 26 April 1987.[66] Did the prisoner know that his release was imminent? Obviously, if he did, then for the first time in decades he would have had something to look forward to, effectively demolishing the idea that he committed suicide. Melaouhi was in no doubt, claiming that his imminent release had made the old man fear for his life: Prisoner Number Seven had specifically said that 'the English will kill me'.[67] In any case, according to le Tissier, in July he asked to see a copy of the Nuremberg judgement against him – the first time he had done so. He was given a copy on 17 July, a month to the day before his death.[68]

Dr Hugh Thomas claims he has evidence that the British government had given a five-point veto on his release to Gorbachev, which was taken to Moscow in early 1987 by Sir Christopher Mallaby (Deputy Secretary to the Cabinet Office at the time).[69] Even so, had the Russians really been adamant about releasing Hess they would have got their way, with or without a British veto. During their next 'month' they could simply have removed their guards and let it be known that they wanted Hess to be freed. And the British government, which had always claimed it would approve his release on humanitarian grounds if only the intransigent Soviets would stop vetoing it, would have been in a rather embarrassing position.

It is clear that if Hess was killed, it was because whoever was responsible had no intention of ever allowing him to be released, presumably because they did not want him to speak in public. So what were they afraid of?

A case of murder

Wolf Hess believes that his father was murdered because the British government did not want him to reveal the terms of the peace proposals he took with him in 1941. If they became widely known, even after all this time, gravely disquieting questions would be asked about why they had not even been seriously discussed, let alone accepted, thus exposing Britain to four more terrible years of war. After all, there were many families, on both sides, whose tragic losses in the years 1941–5 would ensure the issue would not go away. There might even be talk of legal action and compensation.

Although disagreeing on the identity of the prisoner, since 1987 both Wolf Hess and Dr Hugh Thomas have campaigned tirelessly for the file on Hess's death to be reopened. Thomas updated his book to include the death and the so-called 'suicide', the official autopsy and the investigation.

It was too intriguing for us not to ask Alexander what he could find out about the true circumstances of the old man's death. After several months, he came back with arguably the most sensitive piece of information he had ever given us. He claimed that Hess had indeed been murdered, and that the perpetrators were a team of three members of the elite Special Air Service (SAS), who had been infiltrated into the prison in American Army uniforms and who, after completing their mission, had returned to the UK on an RAF Hercules that had been dispatched from RAF Lyneham some seventeen and a half minutes after the prisoner had been declared dead. Obviously this had been a most secret operation, ordered at the highest level, with a 'need-to-know' policy strictly enforced.

Hugh Thomas's and Wolf Hess's investigations came to the same conclusions. Thomas and other researchers believed they had uncovered the existence of a secret plan connected with Hess's death called Operation Royston.[70] However, Alexander revealed that, although Op. Royston certainly existed, there was nothing particularly sinister about it. It was the Foreign Office contingency plan according to which, immediately after the old man was declared dead, a Hercules plane was to leave RAF Lyneham to collect the body and return it to Britain for disposal. Ex(ercise) Royston had been drawn up many years before to be put into practice in the event of Hess's death and was specifically concerned with the rapid retrieval and disposal of the body in accordance with the rules for all the Spandau prisoners – cremation and the scattering of the ashes in secret. It appears that those in charge of the Op. Royston contingency file were not informed of the agreement with Hess's family in 1982 for the body to be given over to them for burial. So Royston appears to have nothing to do with the killing of Rudolf Hess, except to suggest that the method of death was chosen on the understanding that there would be a controlled post-mortem immediately followed by cremation, and except that the SAS seem to have availed themselves of the flight in order to make a swift escape from Berlin.

Two sources in US intelligence (one ex-CIA, the other ex-naval intelligence) told us that they believe the British were behind Hess's death and claim that some of the American military were extremely angry because it happened during their tour of duty.

Alexander also told us, cryptically, to find the 'Sandman Telegrams' – whatever they are – and although we have failed to do so, we now realise that the clue may not be so difficult to crack after all. In earlier decades people talked of 'The Sandman' bringing sleep: did he bring one last long sleep to Rudolf Hess?

Rhodri Morgan has stated on a film for a Dutch television documentary that he was told by Group Captain Geoffrey Osborne – formerly the Air Attaché at the British Embassy in Bonn – that Hess had been 'bumped off by the Brits'. This extraordinary disclosure came his way when both of them were in a party of MPs flying to a conference in Bonn in 1988. Morgan and the others attended a reception at which President von Weizsäcker and Lynda Chalker, the number two at the Foreign Office, were present. While circulating, Morgan was approached by a British diplomat, who brought up the subject of Morgan's interest in Hess, becoming 'quite aggressive'. Perhaps this incident was connected with the fact that on the flight back to London Osborne told Morgan he had been mistaken to say Hess had been murdered by the British, as he had since spoken to Foreign Office people in Bonn who had assured him that it was not the case.[71]

Morgan has tried to raise several questions – both verbal and written – in the House of Commons on the subject, but they were mostly either blocked or evaded. It appears that the reason why Morgan's questions were blocked was that MPs are not allowed to ask about matters concerning the security services. But Morgan had only asked about the death of Rudolf Hess, which officially has no connection whatsoever with the security services.

Reactions

It should be pointed out that – despite the impression given by his detractors – Dr Hugh Thomas is no anti-Establishment maverick. He may be forthright in his opinions and unwilling to compromise his principles, but he has always maintained a close relationship with the security services because of his former role in Northern Ireland.

Revelations about Rudolf Hess are rarely trouble-free. Following the publication of Thomas's updated book in 1988, there has been a concerted attempt to discredit him and his theories. While there are signs that Thomas was under surveillance after the earlier edition of his book, the campaign against him intensified after the revised edition, which dealt with Hess's death.

In 1988 Thomas was in Amsterdam and, realising that he needed certain documents from his files at home for a meeting with his German publisher, he telephoned his wife and asked her to send them urgently. She duly arranged for them to be taken by rail via the Red Star parcel service from Cardiff to Slough, where they could be collected by a courier. The package never arrived, which was bad enough, but things became decidedly worrying when further enquiries revealed that, alone of all the Red Star packages, it had been stolen from the train. Thomas believes that his telephone call was monitored and that whoever was behind it stole the documents that they knew would be on a specific train.[72]

While this was going on, the media was also criticising Thomas's theories. A BBC *Timewatch* documentary was broadcast on 17 January 1990; originally inspired by BBC Scotland researcher Roy McHardy's discovery of Hess's medical file in Munich, the programme set out to explore some of the questions raised by the Hess affair without necessarily coming to any conclusions. However, during the making, the programme lost its way, arguably turning into little more than a hostile debunking of Dr Thomas's theory.

When the presenter, Cambridge historian Professor Christopher Andrew, and the BBC crew interviewed Thomas at his home in Cardiff, they presented him on camera – for the first time – with a copy of the translation and the original of the Munich medical file, so that they could film his reaction. Thomas claims the translation he was given was incorrect. It stated that the exit wound was on the level of the fourth lumbar vertebra, whereas the correct translation was the fourth dorsal (or thoracic) vertebra, which is much higher on the back. The significance of this is that Thomas has a photograph of the latter area taken during the second autopsy which shows, in his words, 'no vestige' of the scars. Apparent evidence that the scar was in quite another place on the back would have undermined faith in Thomas's theory. However, his German was good enough to spot this error, which he pointed out on camera, but regrettably this sequence was not transmitted.[73]

Shortly after the *Timewatch* programme a puzzling and disturbing episode took place. Involving claims of forged letters, it attracted widespread coverage in the British press, leading to calls for a police investigation.[74]

Five copies of a letter purportedly written by Professor Andrew were sent from Cambridge on 1 February 1990 to Hugh Thomas, Rhodri Morgan and three journalists with an interest in the Hess affair. They appeared to be in Andrew's handwriting, on his college notepaper and, bizarrely, there were two versions in circulation at the same time. The one received by Thomas was a photocopy of a letter allegedly written by Andrew discussing the mistranslation of the Munich file to make it less favourable to Thomas's case. Whoever sent the copy to Thomas had written in the top left-hand corner: 'Original sent Rhodri Morgan MP.' However, this is not the letter that Morgan and the other three actually received. Moreover, when Rhodri Morgan made enquiries of the Royal Mail he found that all four copies of this version (unlike the first) had passed through the main London sorting office at Mount Pleasant in London, and that they had apparently been removed from the post at that point, resealed, restamped and then returned to the mail system. As tampering with the Royal Mail is a serious offence, Morgan asked the police to investigate, but they were unable to do so because they only usually act on a complaint by the *senders* of letters, and as these were anonymous they claimed they were powerless to act.

What was going on? Both versions appear to be forgeries, and Andrew categorically denies not only writing either of them but that he has any connection with the intelligence services (which is implied in the letter). He believes that someone managed to get hold of his private correspondence about his research into the Hess affair and then used a cut-and-paste method to concoct a letter that made him appear to say something he had never said. But who was this enterprising mail thief? The fact that they had access to Andrew's private correspondence and were able to breach the security of the Mount Pleasant sorting office to intercept the mail suggests that it was more than a prank. Such action can only be taken on a warrant signed by the Home Secretary – then Michael Howard – which is only issued in case of a matter of national security. Did the Home Secretary grant such a warrant, and if so, on whose request? The whole affair looks suspiciously like a professional job, a typical intelligence exercise with the purpose of spreading confusion.

Dynamite

During our conversations with Alexander about the death of Prisoner Number Seven, he had brought up the name of Ian Gow, the Conservative MP and Margaret Thatcher's private secretary at the time of Hess's death. Alexander claimed that Gow had told Hugh Thomas that in return for the latter's dropping of his allegations that Hess was murdered, the government would be prepared to admit that there was doubt about the identity of the prisoner. We were able to confirm this. In a television documentary made by a Dutch production company in 1998, Thomas stated that a few months before Margaret Thatcher was ousted as Prime Minister in 1990, he was approached by a group of right-wing MPs representing Ian Gow.[75] They told him that because of the bid to replace the Prime Minister, Gow wanted to 'clear the cupboard of skeletons' first. Thomas entered into a dialogue with this group that went on for several months, but – wary of possible skullduggery – covered himself by telling several journalists and historians what was going on. The group told him that they were prepared to admit that there was some doubt about the identity of the prisoner in Spandau, but only on the condition that he dropped the murder allegation. They said that the British government had been concerned about the identity question for a long time, but it had been ameliorated by the acceptance by the Hess family of the old man as the real Rudolf Hess. (Presumably this was around 1969, when the prisoner first met Ilse and Wolf.) When Thomas refused to make such a deal with them, the negotiations ended. A few months later Ian Gow was killed by a car bomb, which was attributed to either the IRA or INLA. The murder remains unsolved to this day.

Thomas's account is significant. Not only does it back up what 'Alexander' told us, but it also raises some important questions. If correct, why should Gow want to clear this particular 'skeleton' out of the cupboard? It implies that he may have been in some way involved in planning or covering up the murder: if he succeeded in becoming Prime Minister or achieving a Cabinet position, this would be the last thing he would want to leak out into the public domain.

Evidence upon evidence

Further evidence which tends to support the murder theory comes from an affidavit sworn before notaries in Pretoria, South Africa, by a lawyer who worked for the South African National Intelligence Service, Hans H. Hain. In the affidavit he states that he was given details of the killing of Hess the day after it happened by a contact in the Israeli intelligence service, Mossad. The affidavit, dated 22 February 1988, includes the following statements:

> Reich Minister Rudolf Hess was murdered at the instigation of the British Home Office (Ministry of the Interior). The murder was committed by two members of the British SAS (22nd SAS Regiment, SAS Depot Bradbury Lines, Hereford, England). The SAS ('Special Air Service') is answerable as military unit to the British Home Office (*not* to the Defence Ministry). The responsible planning and management of the murder mission was done by MI5 (usually responsible for the 'internal' security of Great Britain; secret service, military actions outside Great Britain fall within the competence of MI6). The secret service action was so hastily planned that it was not even given a code name, which is absolutely unusual.

Other initiated services were the American, the French and the Israeli service. KGB and GRU [the Soviet military intelligence service] and the German services were *not* informed.

The murder of Rudolf Hess had become necessary because the government of the USSR intended to release the prisoner in July 1987 (in connection with the visit of the Federal President v. Weizsäcker to Moscow), but Federal President v. Weizsäcker negotiated a prolongation of the date until the following Soviet guard period in November 1987.

The two SAS men had been in the Spandau prison since the night of Saturday to Sunday (August 15/16, 1987). The US secret service gave concurrence for carrying out the murder on Monday (August 17, 1987).

During the afternoon walk of the prisoner in the prison grounds, the two men lay in wait for the prisoner in the summer house located in the prison grounds, and attempted to throttle him with an approximately 1.50m long cable, then a suicide through 'hanging' was to be feigned. But since Reich Minister Rudolf Hess resisted and also called for help, and at least one US soldier from the guard squad became aware of the assault, the attempt was broken off and an ambulance from the British Military Hospital was called. The unconscious Reich Minister Rudolf Hess was brought in an ambulance to the British Military Hospital; the two assassins left the Spandau prison with the same vehicle and completed the attempt during the trip.

I received the above information in the case orally and personally from an officer of the Israeli service on Tuesday, August 18, 1987 at around 08.00 a.m., South African time. I have known this employee of the Israeli service officially and personally for four years. I am completely convinced that he is sincere and honest and I have no doubt of any nature concerning the truth of what he told me. The purely private character of the conversation with me is equally without doubt.[76]

It should be pointed out that the SAS does not, as claimed in the affidavit, usually come under the auspices of the Home Office. However, some very special units used in counter-terrorism do and it is not unknown for SAS units to be temporarily placed under the direct authority of the Home Office. There is also the apparent contradiction of Melaouhi's statement that he travelled in the ambulance, while here it is stated that the assassins went with the body to the hospital, completing their grisly task in the ambulance. However, this may not be such a discrepancy as it seems: whatever happened beforehand, the fact remains that Hess was not certified dead until he reached the hospital.

If the scenario given by Mossad to Hain is substantially correct, it is further corroboration of a murder hypothesis – which we share with many, including Dr Hugh Thomas, Wolf Hess and reportedly former German Chancellor, Helmut Kohl, who is said to have privately expressed his belief that Hess was murdered, probably on the orders of the British government. The statement about the assault being interrupted by one of the internal staff (clearly Jordan) supports the suggestion that this is what caused the signs of the struggle noted by Melaouhi.

Apart from this affidavit, Hain has claimed on record that further enquiries revealed that the murder had been planned at the highest level and that only the smallest number of people possible were initiated into the conspiracy. All orders were given orally so that there were no awkward documentary records to come back and haunt them (except perhaps the elusive 'Sandman telegrams'). Hain was also told that the 'suicide note' was a forgery, originating in a 'London laboratory'.[77]

All of the evidence points towards homicide, possibly instigated at the highest levels of the then British government, and carried out by agents of the security services, possibly the SAS. Although much of this evidence comes from confidential sources and – of necessity – secret contacts, at least it makes a prima facie case for reopening the investigation into the death.

Hess's family are currently proposing to bring an action against the British government with demands that include the reopening of the investigation into Hess's death, as proposed by Detective Chief Superintendent Howard Jones, and the re-registering of Hess's death. At least then the former Deputy Führer would be officially dead.

This then, is what we have been able to reconstruct of the story of Rudolf Hess, with all its dark undercurrents, sensational claims and counter-claims, and far-reaching historical implications. The official story, from 1941 onwards, is riddled with so many contradictions, anomalies and evasions that suspicions of a cover-up are unavoidable. These suspicions have been compounded by the excessive official secrecy that continues to this day. Files are still withheld. Although some had trickled out over the years, the majority of the all-important Foreign Office files dealing with the arrival and arrest of the Deputy Führer were to be closed to the public until 2017, under a special seventy-five-year rule. However, under pressure from MPs, especially Rhodri Morgan, the government agreed to release the bulk of them in 1992. (When it was suggested to the then Prime Minister, John Major, that the non-release of the files was only fuelling suspicions, he replied incredulously: 'If there's been a cover-up, it has been covered up from me, as well.')[78] When these papers were released researchers such as Peter Padfield expressed surprise that they had been withheld for so long: they contained nothing new and certainly nothing contentious. Indeed, many were copies of material that had been disclosed much earlier. But some files were still withheld. Foreign Minister Douglas Hurd told the House of Commons that he had kept at least one file back because it contained 'certain records which still pose a risk to national security'.[79] What threat could a fifty-year-old file possibly pose to twenty-first-century Britain? (It must be remembered, too, that the files released were those dealing with the wartime period. Records for the Spandau years are subject to the normal thirty-year rule, which means that anything relating to the death of Prisoner Number Seven will not be released until 2017.)

Without a British Freedom of Information Act how can one know what files exist? And without that knowledge, how can one ever be certain that all the information has been released? For example, in January 1999, MI5 opened its Hess files, which came as a surprise to researchers because they had not even known of their existence. There is also the problem that the Foreign Office files (which include MI6's material) have almost certainly been 'weeded'. Some historians acknowledge that this was the case where the released files are concerned, and this is apparent from the files themselves: documents listed in the indexes are missing (such as the reports by Sergeants McBride and Morris on their role in the events of 10 May 1941) and there are gaps in the sequence of numbered documents in several files. Astonishingly, Sir Maurice Oldfield, head of MI6 from 1973 to 1978, is known to have removed one of the Hess files and handed it over to a historian in order to prevent it being 'weeded'.[80]

Now safely in Holland, the file is reported to include a full (as opposed to an edited) transcript of Hess's meeting with Lord Simon.

Even the information that is publicly available has, as we have seen repeatedly, been ruthlessly distorted and manipulated. At every step of the story, history has been coldly and deliberately rewritten to create a myth that would effectively distract attention from unpalatable facts about the highest echelons of the British Establishment, the activities of the Allies and the course of the Second World War. Now that the twentieth century is over, surely it is time to face the facts.

CHAPTER SIXTEEN

The Hess Alternative

The evidence strongly suggests that Hess's flight represented the end of a period of negotiation, not the beginning – a final gesture of goodwill to prove that he meant what he said. Whatever the terms were that he brought, they appear to have been broadly acceptable to the peace group, although, because the details have never been made public, the questions of whether the peace terms should have been accepted must remain open. Even after the plan failed and he had fallen into Churchill's hands, the Prime Minister had the option of putting the terms to his Cabinet or Parliament (in secret session), but took it upon himself to prolong the German expectation of a deal until long after the Americans were in the war.

It seems likely that had Hess not baled out some way from his intended destination and been taken prisoner by the Home Guard, he could have come and gone, having clinched the negotiations. Everyone's life would be very different: instead of this book, the investigation would have been into the conspiracy that had ousted Winston Churchill, replacing him with Sir Samuel Hoare, and the unexpected armistice between Britain and Germany in May 1941.

Although the what-if game is usually only academic, it is particularly thought-provoking where the story of Rudolf Hess is concerned. What would have happened if his mission had been successful? What if the war, as far as Britain was concerned, had ended in May 1941? Most obviously, Germany would have gone to war with the USSR without having to watch its back. But would the

Germans have won the war in the East or – as Menzies advised Churchill and certain historians still maintain – would both countries only have succeeded in exhausting themselves, effectively removing them both as threats to the rest of Europe? Although, of course, this argument could go on for ever, it is likely that the end result would have been either a German victory or an eventual armistice with German occupation east of the Ukraine. Either way, the Soviet domination of Eastern Europe – and therefore the Iron Curtain and the Cold War – would not have happened, but at the cost of a surviving and thriving Germany.

Undoubtedly, Hess's arrival in Britain had a profound effect on history, though hardly the one he wanted. Indeed, it must be said that as far as his own objectives were concerned, it would have been considerably better if he had stayed at home. We have seen how Churchill used his arrival to ensure that Germany launched its offensive against the Soviet Union, which led Britain to forge an alliance with Stalin, precisely the opposite of what Hess wanted to achieve. Churchill also used Hess's arrival to strengthen Britain's ties with the USA – again, diametrically opposed to the result Hess envisaged: he had come with a warning about the Roosevelt administration's designs on the British Empire.

So far we have only considered what effect Hess's presence in Britain had on subsequent events: we have not looked at what happened because of his *absence* from Germany – which we would argue is equally important.

There is no doubt that Hess exercised a uniquely moderating influence on Hitler. Post-war commentators may have come to a very different conclusion, but those who were there at the time, including Konrad Heiden, James Murphy and, of course, Karl Haushofer (who would know if anybody did), are all agreed. The anti-Nazi Konrad Heiden wrote in an article just a few months after Hess's flight:

With Rudolf Hess, Adolf Hitler's better half disappeared from Germany. The two had become intellectually conjoined to a degree that is possible only in abnormal personalities. Indeed, they had in a way grown into one personality consisting of two men. If Göring had fled, one might say: 'The Third Reich has blown up!' Hess's flight meant that Hitler himself had gone to pieces.[1]

A prime example of the result of Hess leaving Hitler was what happened in the months immediately after Operation Barbarossa. In June 1941, in the first wave of Operation Barbarossa, German troops poured into the Ukraine. Many of the people of the Ukraine – hostile to Stalin because of his policy of enforced starvation – welcomed the Nazis as liberators. In scenes that prefigured the liberation of Paris by the Allies three years later, cheering crowds turned out *en masse* to greet the German tanks, throwing flowers before the conquering heroes.[2] With the Ukraine occupied, Hitler had to decide how his new territory would be ruled. SS Lieutenant-General Erich Koch, who was appointed Reich Commissar of the Ukraine in October 1941, believed that Germany should rule directly and that its racial policies should be applied with full force to the Slavic population. That meant that Slavs became *Untermenschen* – 'subhuman' – and, Koch argued, should be treated accordingly. On assuming power, his first act was to close all the schools – after all, to the Nazis with their perverted mentality, education is wasted on 'subhumans'. The population was left with no doubts how they were to be treated when Koch delivered a speech in which he said: 'We are a master race, which must remember that the lowliest German worker is racially and biologically a thousand times more valuable than the population here.'[3]

This terrifying attitude was not without its opponents, even in Nazi Germany. Ironically, one of the most vociferous was Alfred Rosenberg, the man whose racial ideas underpinned the whole Nazi creed. Appointed Minister for the Occupied Eastern Territories in July 1941, he became administrator of the Ukraine when it was invaded. He wanted to make the occupied regions into semi-autonomous states, ruling themselves but still subservient to Germany in matters of foreign policy and defence. (Something like Vichy France.) The Ukraine was to form one of the 'buffer' states between Germany and the Soviet Union – Karl Haushofer's original concept of *Lebensraum*. The Slavic states would not be completely subjugated, but would be semi-independent regions whose populations would pour taxes into the German exchequer and supply valuable raw materials, agricultural produce and cheap – but not slave – labour for German industry.[4]

When the clash between the ideas of Rosenberg and Koch came to a head in the autumn of 1942, both men appealed to Hitler. Rosenberg wrote a series of reports expressing outrage at the conditions in the Ukraine and Koch's brutal treatment of its population, but Hitler overruled him, choosing to accept Koch's ideas instead, largely because Koch was supported by Himmler, Göring and Bormann, whereas Rosenberg stood alone.[5]

Of course, Rosenberg did not advocate indirect – and therefore more lenient – rule of the Ukraine for humanitarian reasons: he was also an 'unrepentant Nazi'. His reasons were purely practical: the Ukrainian Army had many divisions that were prepared to fight alongside Germany against the Bolsheviks – and in any case the people largely regarded the Germans as liberators and sought to co-operate willingly with their new masters. Rosenberg wanted to harness and capitalise on that mood. But in the event he lost the argument to Koch and as a result the reign of terror the Nazis unleashed on the 'subhuman' population only resulted in a hostile people and the depredations of bands of partisans, effectively tying up resources that could have been deployed against Stalin's troops.

As Hess and Rosenberg were ideologically and politically very close, there is no doubt that had the Deputy Führer still been in office, he would have supported him against Koch. And there is equally little doubt that Hitler would have listened to him.

The consequences of Hitler's backing Koch over Rosenberg go far beyond the suffering of the Ukrainians. It is generally accepted that the Führer's fatal mistake was launching his offensive against the Soviet Union in the first place, but had he taken a different line in the Ukraine – winning the backing of the people and particularly those divisions of Ukrainian troops – there was a real possibility that his Russian campaign would have been victorious. The importance of Hitler's fatal decision to back Koch cannot be exaggerated: arguably it cost him the war. And it is a decision he was unlikely to have made if Hess had still been by his side to advise him. Hess's mission backfired badly: effectively it brought about the destruction of Hitler and Nazism.

There is another what-if scenario that must be discussed. If Hess's mission had been successful, would the Final Solution have happened? The group in Britain with whom Hess chose to make contact had effectively declared their position on this issue at the start of the war in the *Times* letter signed by the then Marquess of Clydesdale. This was a clear signal to Germany that there were circles in Britain who were willing to talk, and that Clydesdale was their front man. The letter itself presented the Germans with only two subjects for discussion, one implicit and the other explicit. The first was that they were only willing to talk once 'honourable men' had come to the fore – implying that Hitler was not one of them – and the second was that any peace settlement would have to take account of the plight of Germany's Jews. As this letter was partly drafted by the German Jewish refugee Kurt Hahn, they clearly viewed this matter both seriously and honourably. With this in mind, the reaction of the Jews of the Warsaw Ghetto when news of Hess's arrival in Scotland broke is significant. According to one survivor, 'people went wild' at the news, as they believed it would mean the end of the war and their liberation. A rhyming tribute to Hess did the rounds: '*Mit Hess iz geshen a ness*' ('With Hess has come a miracle').[6]

Given the Hamilton group's constitution and demands and the fact that Hess's go-betweens were Karl and Albrecht Haushofer – whose wife and mother, respectively, was half Jewish – it is hard to believe that whatever proposals Hess brought with him did not in some way address the question of Germany's Jews.

We know that Hess was opposed to violent action against the German Jews – as at Kristallnacht, when his active displeasure prevented a recurrence of such vandalism – preferring the option of enforced emigration. The Nuremberg Laws were (like previous laws in Poland[7]) designed to make life so uncomfortable for the Jewish population that they would be only too willing to emigrate. The problem was that too many other countries refused to accept them. Britain in particular was afraid that many Jewish immigrants would end up in Palestine and add to Britain's problems there. We have seen that in February 1939 – four months after Kristallnacht – both the British Foreign Office and George VI put pressure on Germany to restrict emigration. Even in 1944 Churchill's government – Eden and Cadogan in particular – opposed plans for the release of Jews from the Bergen-Belsen concentration camp in case they made their way to Palestine. Because of this, the Nazis turned to alternatives. Even in the early stages of the war, the favoured solution was the Madagascar Plan, in which the Jews of Germany and its occupied territories would be settled on this island in the Indian Ocean. The plan was not new: it originated in Bismarck's day and the idea of Madagascar as the Jewish state was first put forward by the Zionist leader Theodor

Herzl.[8] The Polish government had also carried out a feasibility study of establishing such a settlement on Madagascar in 1937.[9] Although by the outbreak of war the Madagascar Plan was well advanced, it had to be abandoned in the late summer of 1940 because the first phase required that peace be made with France (as Madagascar was a French colony) and with Britain.[10] This was because of Britain's control of the Mediterranean and the Suez Canal. As historian Norman M. Davies writes: 'At this stage of the war [1939–40] the Nazi leaders were intent on herding the Jews into reservations, and subjected them to innumerable indignities and violences . . . They still entertained fanciful schemes of settling them on an unspecified island of the British Empire, of auctioning them off to the highest bidder, or of deporting them to Central Asia . . . They were not faced with the problems of disposing of the inhabitants of the reservations until those earlier schemes were invalidated by the emergence of the British–Soviet–American alliance of mid-1941. It was at that moment, and no earlier, that the Final Solution was finalized.'[11]

Perhaps it is significant that the first use of the term *Endlösung* – 'final solution' – in an official Nazi document came in a directive from Göring on 20 May 1941, which stopped all further Jewish emigration from Germany or its occupied territories, including France.[12] Coming just ten days after Hess's departure, the timing is suggestive. Could this have been a move to put pressure on the British peace group, in the belief that Hess was negotiating with them? Or could it be that it was part of the 'virtual armistice' effectively agreed between Churchill and Hitler, which led to the end of the Blitz and the suspension of RAF raids on German cities? Churchill and his government remained vehemently opposed to Jewish emigration to Palestine, and therefore did not welcome further enforced emigration from Germany. The 20 May 1941 directive suspended Jewish emigration pending the agreement of a 'doubtless imminent final solution'. This seems to indicate that a number of options were being considered, perhaps including the reinstatement of the Madagascar Plan. And it is significant that Göring seemed to believe a solution was forthcoming, presumably because he thought negotiations were afoot.

The first systematic exterminations of civilians began during the eastern campaign when special SS divisions – made up not only of Germans but of Ukrainians and fiercely anti-Soviet Russians – followed behind the advancing German forces, rounding up and executing groups whose existence was deemed an ideological menace.[13] This was aimed initially chiefly at Communists, but because of the Nazis' warped association of Communism with Jews, it also included the latter. At first they were executed by firing squads, but eventually Himmler had to admit that the conveyor-belt execution of old men, women and children had a debilitating effect on even his most fanatical SS troops, and so sought a less personal method of dispatching their victims. This eventually led to the gas chambers. The first mass killings using gas also took place during the eastern campaign using mobile units. It was at the infamous Wannsee Conference of January 1942 – presided over by Reinhard Heydrich – that approval was given for the building of permanent extermination camps in the conquered territories of the East. All this, of course, came after Hess's flight. He was exonerated of any complicity in these crimes against humanity at Nuremberg.

If Hess brought proposals concerning the question of Germany's Jews – a reinstatement of the Madagascar Plan, perhaps, which, odious though it was, would by that time have been acceptable to those such as Kurt Hahn who were concerned with saving their fellow Jews from an even worse fate – this would be one explanation for why there has been such a cover-up. That certainly seems to have been the Israeli governments's suspicion: a senior Mossad source in Israel told us that his government made several requests over the years to the British for permission to interview Hess in Spandau about his peace proposals, but were consistently refused. It is difficult to see any other reason for the Israelis' interest or any other explanation for the British Government's constant refusal.

An alternative 1941 scenario

If Hess's mission had been successful, and a peace had been concluded between Britain and Germany in mid-1941, what would the results have been? Apart from the saving of many thousands of British lives, Britain would not have ruined itself economically by owing such a monumental debt to the USA, would have retained the economic advantage of empire and Churchill would have been removed from office. But what would have happened on the German side? There is one possibility that – seen from the viewpoint of the early twenty-first century – may seem quite unthinkable.

Of all the sympathetic British contacts listed by Albrecht Haushofer in 1940, Hess chose to make contact with what may be described as the 'Hamilton circle' – those behind the *Times* letter in October 1939. The underlying message of the letter was that Britain would be willing to negotiate with Germany – *but not under Hitler*. This was known to be Neville Chamberlain and Lord Halifax's position, as well as that of Sir Samuel Hoare, who is reliably reported to have told a German intermediary that peace was impossible while both Churchill and Hitler remained in power. It is also significant that both the Haushofers had expressed their unease at the way things were going in Germany under Hitler's leadership. Therefore, the groups in both countries who were involved in Hess's mission shared the same view: that Hitler, too, had to be removed from office before a peace deal could be made. And it is inconceivable that Hess, as the most high-ranking go-between, was not aware of this.

So the apparently extraordinary question has to be asked: did Hess's proposals include the removal of Hitler? Given the accepted image of him it seems absurd, but we know that, as the man who created the Führer, he specified as early as 1921 that the leader to restore Germany to greatness would, when his task was done, actually stand aside to act as an adviser to a new, more moderate government. As Hitler's secretary in 1925 Hess had also written that he would not always be beholden to his Führer. Just as he deemed it necessary for Germany that Hitler should become leader, he might just as easily have advocated his standing down if he believed it to be in Germany's best interests.

Perhaps that adds an extra significance to Hess's denial to the British that he had come on Hitler's orders, or even with his knowledge. Was he really saying that he was very much his own man and did not need Hitler to approve his plans? Remember that in his negotiations – for example, with Lord Simon at Mytchett Place – Hess stressed that he was not speaking for Hitler, but for Germany. Is it possible that had his mission been successful, *Rudolf Hess himself would have taken over as Führer*? Is that why the German press had so enthusiastically built up his importance and success in the weeks leading up to the flight?

On the other hand, as we know, all the evidence points to the fact that Hitler *did* know about and approve Hess's mission. On the face of it, it seems outrageous to suggest that Hitler might have colluded in his own removal from office. But there is no doubt that Hess must have known that those with whom he discussed his peace proposals in Britain would have demanded the removal of Hitler. Perhaps Hess had come to formulate some kind of compromise – such as making Hitler the figurehead President of Germany, while he took over as Chancellor. (Although Hitler had assumed presidential powers on the death of President von Hindenburg in 1934, he had never actually taken the title.) Unfortunately, this must remain one of the most imponderable aspects of the whole Hess affair.

Haushofer's European vision

It is ironic that, sixty years on, a resolutely anti-Nazi Europe appears to have largely achieved the Hess/Haushofer vision. Karl Haushofer's ideas – presented as the concept of *Lebensraum* by Hitler in *Mein Kampf* – can be summarised as follows:

The aim was to make the states to the east and north of Germany quasi-autonomous – that is, independent except for their foreign and defence policies, but tied to Germany politically and economically, supplying raw materials, agricultural produce and cheap labour to Germany and the rest of Western Europe. Germany would then be the dominant force in a United States of Europe, which would eventually adopt a single currency (the Reichsmark) and share a European defence force. The German-led United States of Europe would have special trading arrangements with Britain and its empire, although Britain itself would not be part of the European federation. The role of the pan-European defence force would be taken by the SS, which in its later manifestations had moved away from the original concept of a Teutonic elite to include divisions recruited from the occupied states or those allied to Germany. There was even a British SS unit, recruited from the POW camps, which fought with a Union Jack insignia on its uniforms, although it is unlikely to have numbered more than sixty men.[14] There were also SS divisions from the eastern states and France, Holland and Belgium. (French SS troops were among the last fanatical defenders of the Hitler bunker.[15]) Some of the phrases used by the later SS strike a startlingly modern note: the monthly journal of the French SS, *Devenir* (*Becoming*), was subtitled *Journal de combat de la Communauté Européenne* ('The Fighting Journal of the European Community') and one 1944 edition includes an article that declares: 'We are for a federalist Europe.'[16]

At the beginning of the twenty-first century we find ourselves with a united Europe (on paper at least) and a single currency – initiated by the Bundesbank and stabilised by the Deutschmark – in which Britain is not involved but with which it has a special relationship. A common defence policy – and even joint armed forces – is now seriously being considered.

Because of the collapse of the USSR, Poland, Hungary and Romania are already in NATO, and the Baltic states are also protected by that body. These states have a trading relationship with the EU and seek full membership in the long term. Because of their EU involvement and NATO membership, their defence and foreign policies are largely decided at the centre of Europe: in practice, despite the American involvement in NATO, the decision-making process on European affairs is largely led by Germany, France and the UK.

There is more to ponder. The fact of effectively having two borders – the eastern edge of the European Union now lies well within the borders of the NATO countries – is jokingly referred to in MoD and Foreign Office circles as the *Lebensraum* policy; while that of part inclusion of the eastern states in the EU – tying them economically to Europe while creating a further barrier against eastern refugees – is known as *Wirtschaftsraum* ('economic space').

For these plans to succeed, the EU's policies on refugees and immigration will inevitably have to toughen up considerably, but that is already happening. As an economic sop to the satellite 'Lebensraum' countries, special arrangements will have to be made for short-term emigration (in other words, short-term imported labour), as must the greater use of cheap labour within those countries. This is the *Wirtschaftsraum*.

The comparison between Europe's current situation (and the direction in which it is inexorably moving) and the vision of Karl Haushofer and Rudolf Hess is remarkable. The analogy is not perfect and many circumstances have changed: France has a much stronger role in the EU than Haushofer and Hess ever envisaged, and

Britain – without its empire – is much more closely tied to Europe than they could have anticipated. But nevertheless, in all the essentials, their plans have come to fruition. This is not to suggest that the development of the EU has somehow been directed by a 'Fourth Reich' hidden away in some sinister *Schloss*. It is simply that the ideas formulated by Karl Haushofer at the beginning of the last century as the best thing for Germany and Europe have now been accepted – quite independently but for the same reasons – by the leaders of a Europe that is no longer held back by the Cold War chains of the USA and the USSR, right-wing totalitarianism, or, looking further back, by those of the old imperial dynasties.

The face of the twentieth century

To the children of the liberal post-war years, it is an unpalatable fact that if any one man embodies the history of Europe in the twentieth century it is Rudolf Hess. Born in one of the old imperial colonies, his ideology sprang from the chaos of post-First World War Germany, particularly the left against right struggle that raged with extraordinary hatred and bitterness. He was the major force in constructing the Nazi Party, and more than any other figure in that organisation embodied its tensions and paradoxes between thuggery and discipline and between the most evil brutality and a highly ordered state. In his failed peace mission he personified all the complexities that lie behind the simplistic standard history of the time: the American ambition, the Soviet threat and the realities of the Anglo-German war. And whether he was the real Hess or a double, Prisoner Number Seven came to personify the Cold War in the heart of Europe.

The treatment of Prisoner Number Seven raises fundamental questions about the very purpose of war crimes trials, now relevant because of the former Yugoslavia, and even about the basic notion of punishment and guilt. Various governments still fall over themselves to investigate and prosecute any alleged Nazi war crimes (as indeed, they should), but where is the similar desire to bring to book those responsible for Soviet genocide and war crimes such as the Katyn Forest massacre of over 14,000 Polish officers – for which a Russian apology seems to have sufficed?[17] The apportioning of guilt can seem extraordinarily selective.

And of the many guilty men who will probably never be made accountable for their crimes, who will answer for the deaths of Prince George, Duke of Kent, General Władisław Sikorski – and Deputy Führer Rudolf Hess, not to mention lowly Prisoner Number Seven?

Afterword

As the result of the publicity surrounding the publication of the first edition of this book in April 2001, new information has come to us from enthusiastic readers – or because *Double Standards* actually prompted certain major public disclosures. And our own ongoing research continues to shed more light on the many mysteries surrounding Rudolf Hess.[1]

The Eagle's Rock tragedy

The material on the flying-boat crash on Eagle's Rock in which George, Duke of Kent, died drew a keen response from the public – it was particularly exciting to be contacted by relatives of the crew of Sunderland flight W4026. Peter Brown, the nephew of Pilot Officer George Saunders, told us that his mother Sarah (Saunders' sister) recalls that Pilot Officer Saunders had been given special, unexpected leave a few days before the flight, which he spent with his family in Sheffield. Saunders told them, 'I'm just on leave for a couple of days. I'm going on a most important mission, very secret. I can't say any more.' Clearly, this special leave suggests that there was something more to it than a simple VIP flight from which he would return in a few days – something even more dangerous than 228 Squadron's usual missions searching for U-boats over the north Atlantic, and certainly more secret and dangerous than a 'routine transit flight to Iceland'.

We were also contacted by Nick Goyen, nephew of Lieutenant

Frank MacKenzie Goyen, the pilot of the doomed flight He confirmed that his family always believed that there had been an official cover-up, and that his father (Goyen's brother) tried for many years to penetrate the veil of secrecy surrounding it, but to no avail

Margaret, Lady Thurso (the widow of the 2nd Viscount Thurso, Robin Sinclair), told us that there was something that might be of significance in the visitors' book for Dalnawillan Lodge, the main house on the Sinclairs' Caithness estate. The first signature in the book after the crash was that of the Duke of Hamilton, on 23 September 1942. (However, Lady Thurso believes that Hamilton must have signed the book at the Sinclairs' other Caithness home, Thurso Castle, as Dalnawillan Lodge was empty during the war.)

After reading *Double Standards*, members of the Sinclair family made enquiries among the families of estate workers, who remembered flying boats landing on Loch More during the war, confirming what we had been told by Robin Sinclair. Unfortunately, they could not recall the type of flying boat.

Moreover, new evidence for our reconstruction of the Kent crash came from an unexpected source – a primary school project. In 1996 the children of Hillhead Primary School in Wick produced a book, *Wings over Wick*, drawn from the memories of people who had lived in the area during the war. One of the accounts they received was from James Swanson, a former sergeant with the Military Police at RAF Wick. The first from the base to reach the crash site, he recalled two significant points. Because RAF Wick had 'no knowledge' of any military flight that day, it was assumed at first that it was a civilian plane that had crashed. More intriguingly, as Swanson was one of those who guarded the site overnight, he confessed he was still mystified by the fact that before Andy Jack was found alive they had been told that all the bodies of the crew were accounted for.[2] This is important support, from someone directly involved, for our contention that one body too many was recovered from the wreck of flight W4026.

The death of Prisoner Number Seven

Since the publication of the first edition, we have located Major Alfonso J. Ahuja, one of the men in US Army uniforms encountered by Hess's nurse, Abdallah Melaouhi, when he arrived in the garden hut in Spandau where the prisoner lay stricken, and whose apparently inexplicable presence was described in Chapter 15. In August 1987 Major Ahuja, who is now serving at West Point Military Academy, was a lieutenant in charge of the American guard at Spandau. He confirmed to us that he was one of the soldiers in the hut, and the other was the company medical officer. Ahuja had been alerted by one of the watchtower guards to whom the warder Anthony Jordan had called out, and went to the hut. Finding the prisoner apparently dead (there was no discernible pulse), he radioed for the medic, who arrived in the hut a few moments before Melaouhi.

Although this evidence provides an explanation for one of the many suspicious elements surrounding Hess's death, it does not discredit Melaouhi – whose brush with hostile guards en route had clearly reduced him to a nervous wreck – and in any case, the normal rules forbade the exterior guards from entering the prison grounds. Melaouhi's suspicions were only exacerbated by the thick veil of secrecy that was allowed to shroud the incident, in which the presence, let alone the identities, of the US soldiers was not acknowledged. (Indeed, it took us some time to discover their identities.) More tellingly, Major Ahuja's account reveals that Melaouhi's testimony is essentially accurate.

In particular, Ahuja (who accepts the official version of how Hess died) describes the scene when he arrived at the hut. 'The cord was right next to him. It was attached to a lamp. From what I gathered, he used the lamp cord by attaching it to the window knob and then wrapping it around his neck and letting himself [go] . . . Again, I didn't see this.'[3]

However, according to the official version it was an *extension* lead, not the flex of the lamp itself. And the official 'scene of crime' photographs, supposedly of the untouched hut, shows the extension cord tied to the window latch and *not* attached to the lamp.

Closer examination of the secret Spandau records (see Chapter 15), which only came into our possession as the first edition of this book was going to press, revealed many more anomalies on the afternoon of Hess's death. An unsuccessful attempt was made to contact the governors by bleeper, as described in the Emergency Medical Procedure. Neither Major Ahuja's involvement nor that of the medical officer is recorded. In fact, scant details of the decisions made

that day and the actions taken in response to the emergency are
given in the Duty Chief Warder's logbook. All that the log records is
that an 'incident' took place that led to the prisoner being taken to
the British Military Hospital, where he was declared dead. The
entries were made by two warders as there was a change of shift in
the middle of the emergency.[4]

There are problems in reconciling the various accounts of the
sequence of events. In particular, why did it take one hour twenty
minutes to get Hess to the British Military Hospital from the moment
his body was discovered? The records of previous emergencies (which
were meticulously logged) show that the total journey time for the
ambulance – there and back – was just thirty-five minutes.

In Chapter 15 we discussed the interest of Rhodri Morgan, First
Minister for Wales, in the Hess affair. When we had our national
launch in Cardiff Castle on 10 April 2001, the press seized on this,
even managing to obtain an extraordinary admission from him.
Although Rhodri Morgan denied our suggestion that his involvement in the Hess mystery was the reason that his original candidacy
for First Minister was vetoed by the Blair government,[5] he added
that he was 'still strongly of the opinion that Hess was murdered by
the British secret service'.[6] For someone in such a position, this is
quite astonishing. (And surely it is naive to believe that holding such
a view would not deem him a security risk?)

During the day of our Cardiff launch, HTV Wales' evening tele-
vision news programme also asked the Prime Minister's office at
Number 10 Downing Street for its comments on this matter.
Number 10 refused to comment, on the grounds that the Prime
Minister never discusses the advice received from the security serv-
ices on ministerial appointments.

One satisfying reaction to the publication of this book was that it
prompted the Foreign Office to release more of its documentation on
Hess – abruptly and without warning on 10 April 2001. This related
to the period in which Hess was hospitalised from November 1969 to
January 1970, presumably being made public because it seems to
indicate that the British government – or at least some Foreign
Office officials – was trying to get Hess released. Because of the
adverse publicity they feared might result from returning the elderly
and ailing prisoner to Spandau, the officials suggested ways of overcoming the Soviet veto. One idea was simply to keep him in the

British Military Hospital when he recovered; another was to allow the USSR to build a trade centre in West Berlin if they would agree to Hess's release. However, the files prove nothing: the significant point is that these proposals were not accepted by their superiors either in the Foreign Office or the government. No doubt those who proposed them did not know that there were other reasons for Hess to be kept in prison.

Other files, too, were suddenly made public as a result of this book. After the Scottish launch – in Edinburgh Castle – the media picked up on the possible nationalist connection, particularly the concealing of the Scottish Honours just two days after Hess's arrival (see Chapter 8). While some greeted this connection with scepticism, a few days later, on 8 May 2001, MI6 released files showing that as late as 1943 some Scottish Nationalists were in contact with the Nazi regime (through the German legation in neutral Eire), offering assistance in the event of a German invasion of England, in return for which Scotland would be given its independence. While not directly relating to the Hess affair, these files might explain some of Churchill's paranoia about why Hess had chosen to arrive in Scotland and why there were raids on Scottish Nationalist premises just before 10 May 1941.

The ultimate hiding place

In Chapter 15 we saw that when the Foreign Office finally released its files relating to Hess's flight in 1992, Foreign Secretary Douglas Hurd kept one back on the grounds that it contained 'records which still pose a risk to national security', and we asked what risk a fifty-year-old file could possibly pose to modern Britain. Since the first edition, we have been informed by a senior Foreign Office source with access to this file what really lies behind Hurd's curious statement. The 'file' is in fact a box of several individual files, each of which contains a single sheet of paper stating that the contents have been transferred 'on permanent loan' to the Royal Archives in Windsor Castle.

Obviously, we have not been able to verify this for ourselves, but if true it has enormous implications. Unlike government records, the release of material in the Royal Archives at Windsor is not covered by Public Records legislation, but can be made public only on the personal instruction of the Queen. What better way to keep compromising information out of the public domain, and to prevent any future government from releasing it? (One significant implication of hiding away uncomfortable documentation deep in the Windsor vaults is that the practice could easily be used to circumvent any future British Freedom of Information Act.)

What is in these files? Could they include the document detailing Hess's peace proposals? Or the papers delivered to the King by the Duke of Hamilton a few days after Hess's arrival? Or perhaps the King's guarantee of safety, said to have been signed by the unfortunate Lieutenant-Colonel Pilcher (see Chapter 8)?

Our informant also tells us that the documents missing from the Foreign Office files are kept in a special section of the Windsor Archives, together with other documents relating to the activities of the Royal Family before and during the Second World War, such as the letters retrieved from Germany by Anthony Blunt in 1945. These include letters written by the Dukes of Windsor and Kent – and others, such as government minister Duff Cooper – to Hess, Göring and diplomat Franz von Papen, and their replies, together with letters to the Dukes from Hitler, written on his gold-embossed notepaper – and even Christmas greetings from him!

We have no way of verifying what our informant told us because the other source of information, the Foreign Office files, are also resolutely closed to the public. The very existence of such carefully cultivated black holes for compromising material is nothing less than a scandal in today's allegedly open and democratic society. Those in power who pour scorn on 'conspiracy theories' have a very simple means at their disposal for killing them off for good: open the files . . .

Notes

Chapter One: Judgement Day

1 Persico, p. 134.
2 Hugh Thomas, *Hess: a Tale of Two Murders*, p. 152. The letter was written in January 1946.
3 Padfield, *Hess*, p. 305.
4 J. R. Rees, p. 170.
5 Ibid., p. 171.
6 Order of IMT, 24 November 1945. (This order, and the request that Hess be examined by psychiatrists from a neutral country, is omitted from the official British publication of the trial proceedings, but is included in the American version.)
7 J. R. Rees, pp. 140–141.
8 In his book (p. 143) Rees does not name the dissenting member, but in a letter to a Canadian colleague, W. Clifford Scott, dated 11 June 1958 (a copy of which is in our possession), Rees says that Lord Moran 'violently opposed the recommendation' that Hess was fit to plead.
9 J. R. Rees, p. 217.
10 Ibid., p. 223.
11 Ibid., pp. 211–213.
12 International Military Tribunal, vol. I, pp. 305–306.
13 J. R. Rees, p. 181.
14 Ibid., pp. 181–182.
15 Gordon Thomas, pp. 167–168.
16 Ibid., p. 168.
17 Neave, p. 346.
18 J. R. Rees, p. 169.
19 G. M. Gilbert, p. 89.

20 International Military Tribunal, vol. I, p. 31.
21 Ibid., vol. I, p. 48.
22 Ibid., vol. VI, p. 151.
23 Ibid., vol. VI, p. 163.
24 Ibid., vol. X, pp. 60–67.
25 See p. 100.
26 International Military Tribunal, vol. X, pp. 132–133, 157 and 214.
27 Ibid., vol. IX, p. 632
28 Ibid., vol. XXII, pp. 384–385.
29 Ibid., vol. XXII, pp. 487–488.
30 Ibid., vol. XXII, pp. 540–541.
31 Bradley F. Smith, pp. 181–182.
32 Dzelepy, p. 7 (our translation).

Chapter Two: Behind the Myth

1   Wistrich, p. 105.
2   Winterbotham, *The Nazi Connection*, p. 64.
3   Ibid., p. 157.
4   Ibid., p. 67.
5   Wolf Rüdiger Hess, pp. 39–40.
6   Schwarzwäller, p. 91.
7   Hutton, p. 42.
8   Quoted in Schwarzwäller, p. 81.
9   Quoted in ibid., p. 88.
10 Ibid., p. 78.
11 Winterbotham, *The Nazi Connection*, p. 65.
12 Schwarzwäller, p. 34.
13 Heiden, 'Hitler's Better Half', p. 74.
14 Deighton, p. 29.
15 Passant, p. 155.
16 Wolf Rüdiger Hess, p. 30.
17 The map is displayed in the Duke of Hamilton's current residence, Lennoxlove House in East Lothian.
18 The Treaty of Versailles took the South Tyrol from Austria and gave it to Italy. Because of the potential conflict with his ally Mussolini, this was the one territorial claim that Hitler did not push, although the region did revert to Austria at the end of the war. Various documents in the Hamilton Muniments (Bundle 5027) in the Scottish Record Office attest to the Duke's interest in this question. In Bundle 5023 there is a letter, dated 16 July 1946, to the Duke from the South Tyrolese People's Party thanking him for his help.
19 Schwarzwäller, pp. 41–42.
20 Cavendish, pp. 90–91.

21 Bentine, pp. 93–94.

22 Quoted in Heiden, *Der Fuehrer*, vol. I, p. 191.

23 Michael Smith, p. 160.

24 Andrew Sinclair, p. 191.

25 Picknett and Prince, pp. 258–263.

26 Gordon, Jr, pp. 94–96; Padfield, *Hess*, p. 18.

27 Quoted in Heiden, *Der Fuehrer*, vol. I, pp. 84–85.

28 Quoted in Heiden, 'Hitler's Better Half', p. 86.

29 Ibid.

30 Quoted in Padfield, *Hess*, p. 16.

31 Wistrich, pp. 46–47.

32 Padfield, *Hess*, p. 16.

33 OSS/CIC records, US National Archives, Maryland: 'Interview with Prof. Karl Haushofer, Major General, Retired, 27 September 1945' (document ref. XL22853).

34 Heiden, *Der Fuehrer*, vol. I, p. 73.

35 Ibid., pp. 25–26.

36 Ibid., p. 74.

37 Deighton, p. 85.

38 Heiden, *Der Fuehrer*, vol. I, p. 50.

39 Kurt Lüdecke, quoted in Padfield, *Hess*, p. 14.

40 Originally the *Münchner Beobachter*, the paper had been acquired by the Thule Society in 1919. In 1921 it had heavy debts, and von Epp bought it on behalf of the fledgling Nazi Party.

41 Schwarzwäller, p. 62.

42 Manvell and Fraenkel, p. 24.

43 Schwarzwäller, pp. 61–62.

44 Deighton, p. 43.

45 Manvell and Fraenkel, p. 23.

46 Schwarzwäller, p. 90.

47 Ibid., p. 63.

48 Heiden, *Der Fuehrer*, vol. I, p. 162.

49 In a letter to his parents dated 4 December 1923, Hess tells how he had been individually briefed by Hitler on his part in the putsch, and that he had 'promised unconditional silence' on his instructions (Padfield, *Hess*, p. 18).

50 Schwarzwäller, p. 68.

51 Padfield, *Hess*, pp. 20–21.

52 Schwarzwäller, p. 69.

53 Padfield, *Hess*, p. 21.

54 Ibid., p. 18.

55 Schwarzwäller, p. 74.

56 Van Paassen, *That Day Alone*, p. 508.

57 Murphy, p. 9.
58 'Testimony of Karl Haushofer, taken at Nurnberg, Germany, 5 October, 1945, by Colonel Howard A. Brundage, JAGD, OUSCC'. Our copy of the transcript supplied by the US National Archives, Washington, DC.
59 Schwarzwäller, p. 73.
60 Conversations with Wolf Rüdiger Hess, Munich and Hindelang, November 1999.
61 J. R. Rees, p. 10.
62 Wolf Rüdiger Hess, p. 35.
63 Heiden, *Der Fuehrer*, vol. I, p. 220.
64 Ibid., p. 221.
65 Padfield, *Hess*, pp. 55–56. Hess's importance in building the relationship between the Nazi Party and industrial and financial circles is confirmed by Thyssen (p129).
66 Heiden, *Der Fuehrer*, vol. I, pp. 281–282.
67 Deighton, p. 85.
68 Scharzwäller, p. 78.
69 Ibid., p. 79.
70 Translator's Introduction to *Rudolf Hess, Germany and Peace*, p. 2.
71 Heiden, 'Hitler's Better Half', p. 80.
72 Manvell and Fraenkel, p. 48.
73 Ibid., p. 40.
74 Wistrich, p. 105.
75 International Military Tribunal, vol. VI, p. 149.
76 Imperial War Museum archives, FO 645, Box 155.
77 Padfield, *Hess*, pp. 61–62.
78 Ibid., p. 62.
79 Van Paassen, *That Day Alone*, p. 509.
80 Steinert, p. 14.
81 Schwarzwäller, p. 93.
82 Ibid.
83 Translation supplied by the 15th Duke of Hamilton.
84 Schwarzwäller, p. 92.
85 Ibid., pp. 97–98.
86 Levene.
87 On Churchill's racism, see Roberts, *Eminent Churchillians*, Chapter 4.
88 Ibid., pp. 211–212.
89 Ibid., p. 212.
90 Steinert, p. 113.
91 Manvell and Fraenkel, p. 35.
92 Schwarzwäller, p. 87.
93 Ibid., pp. 108–109.

94 Murphy, p. 36.

95 Heiden, *Der Fuehrer*, vol. I, p. 85.

96 Van Paassen, *That Day Alone*, p. 508.

97 Heiden, *Der Fuehrer*, vol. I, pp. 285–286.

98 Ibid., p. 285.

99 Ibid.

100 Heiden, 'Hitler's Better Half', p. 73.

101 Padfield, *Hess*, p. 68.

102 Schwarzwäller, pp. 99–100.

103 The claim was first made by Hess's former personal physician (1936–9), Dr Ludwig Schmitt, when interviewed by an American journalist (*New York Times*, 21 May 1945).

104 Padfield, *Hess*, p. 69.

105 Ibid., pp. 66–67.

106 Ibid., p. 69.

107 Schwarzwäller, p. 102.

108 Padfield, *Hess*, p. 68.

109 Ibid.

110 Schwarzwäller, pp. 109–110.

111 Irving, *The War Path*, pp. 44 and 94. Hitler's decree of 7 December 1934 (reproduced in Manvell and Fraenkel, pp. 223–224) specified that, in the event of his death or incapacity, Hess should be responsible for the running of the Nazi Party and its relationship with the German state, and that Göring should be responsible for 'all other matters of state government' – essentially the same relationship as that between Hitler and Hess.

112 Public Record Office (PRO), file HO 199/482: Foreign Research and Press Service, 'Rudolf Hess', confidential report dated 19 May 1941.

Chapter Three: Journey into Conflict

1 Hitler, *Mein Kampf*, p. 189.

2 Ibid., p. 88.

3 Ibid., p. 87.

4 Bloch, *The Duke of Windsor's War*, p. 223.

5 Costello, *Ten Days that Saved the West*, Appendix 6.

6 Griffiths, pp. 307–317.

7 Van Paassen, *Days of Our Years*, p. 165.

8 Newton, p. 185.

9 Ibid., p. 166.

10 Haxey, p. 165.

11 Newton, p. 152.

12 Ibid., p. 170.

13 Warwick, *Princess Margaret*, p. 162.

14 Newton, p. 153.
15 Norton-Taylor and Jolliffe.
16 Charmley, 'The King of Appeasers'.
17 'Queen Mother hoped for Peace with Hitler', *Independent on Sunday*, 5 March 2000.
18 Roberts, *Eminent Churchillians*, p. 13.
19 Charmley, 'The King of Appeasers'.
20 Hoare's account of his experiences during the Russian Revolution are in his *The Fourth Seal*.
21 Newton, pp. 183–184; Inglis, p. 223.
22 Hoare's speech was published by the Union of Conservative Associations as *Ourselves, the World and Peace*.
23 Cadogan, p. 287.
24 Newton, p. 168.
25 Ibid.
26 A. J. P. Taylor, p. 164.
27 Ibid., p. 80.
28 Ibid., pp. 99–100.
29 Ibid., p. 102.
30 Chisholm and Davie, pp. 371–372.
31 Ibid., p. 372.
32 A. J. P. Taylor, p. 163.
33 Ibid., p. 231.
34 Ibid., p. 164.
35 Chisholm and Davie, p. 347.
36 Davies, vol. II, p. 393.
37 Brown, *The Secret Servant*, pp. 14–15.
38 Ibid., p. 14.
39 Newton, pp. 142–143.
40 Winterbotham, *Secret and Personal*, p. 79.
41 Hamilton Muniments, Bundle 5001.
42 Shepherd, p. 138.
43 Murphy, p. 31.
44 Shepherd, p. 204.
45 Ibid., p. 214.
46 Ibid., pp. 1–5.
47 Henderson, p. 224.
48 Newton, pp. 124–127.
49 On the Wilson–Wohltat and Dahlerus initiatives, see Watt, Chapter 21.
50 Newton, p. 123.
51 Roberts, 'The Plot to Betray Poland'.
52 PRO, FO 800/316: Letter from Lord Buxton to Lord Halifax (undated, but with covering memo dated 12 July 1939).

53 Ibid.: Memo from Sir Nevile Henderson to Lord Halifax, 31 August 1939.
54 Davies, vol. II, p. 433.
55 Deighton, p. 113.
56 Lamb, p. 124.
57 Ibid.
58 Ibid., p. 125.
59 Davies, vol. II, p. 397.
60 Carr, pp. 313–314.
61 Davies, vol. II, p. 423.
62 Ibid.
63 *The Times*, 25 March 1937.
64 Davies, vol. II, p. 430.
65 Ibid., p. 393.
66 Ibid., pp. 259–260.
67 Ibid.
68 *The Times*, 21 July 1999.
69 Davies, vol. II, pp. 431–432.
70 Newton, pp. 133–134.
71 Ibid., p. 142.
72 Costello, *Ten Days that Saved the West*, p. 65.
73 Padfield, *Hess*, p. 125.
74 *The Times*, 9 September 1965.
75 Costello, *Ten Days that Saved the West*, p. 61.
76 Padfield, *Hess*, p. 111.
77 Newton, p. 147.
78 Ibid., citing PRO file CHRS 180/1/28.
79 Cambridge University Library: Templewood Papers, Part XIII, File 18: Memo from Hoare to Cadogan, 6 March 1941.
80 Padfield, *Hess*, p. 167.
81 Ibid., p. 175.
82 Ibid.
83 Ibid., p. 154.
84 Ibid., pp. 154–155.
85 Colville, p. 141.
86 Costello, *Ten Days that Saved the West*, pp. 46–47.
87 Ibid., p. 47.
88 Charmley, 'The King of Appeasers'; see also Roberts, *Eminent Churchillians*, Chapter 3.
89 Churchill, vol. I, p. 599–600.
90 Gilbert, *In Search of Churchill*, p. 215.
91 Stafford, *Churchill and Secret Service*, pp. 11–12.
92 Foot, *Churchill and the Secret Services*, p. 7.

93 Stafford, *Churchill and Secret Service*, pp. 5–6.

94 Foot, *Churchill and the Secret Services*, p. 13. On Churchill's 'moles', see Stafford, *Churchill and Secret Service*, Chapter 8.

95 Costello, *Ten Days that Saved the West*, p. 158.

96 Foot, *Churchill and the Secret Services*, p. 173.

97 See Foot, *SOE*, pp. 202–206. SOE was closed down with just forty-eight hours' notice in January 1946 by Prime Minister Clement Attlee, on the grounds that he 'had no wish to preside over a British Comintern [Communist International]' (ibid., p. 355). See also Deacon.

98 Interviewed for the TV series *Churchill's Secret Army* (produced by Martin Smith and James Barker, Carlton Productions for Channel 4, 2000).

99 Bloch, *The Duke of Windsor's War*, p. 36.

100 Costello, *Ten Days that Saved the West*, p. 175.

101 Liddell Hart, *The Other Side of the Hill*, p. 139.

102 Ibid.

103 Ibid., p. 141.

104 Ibid.

105 Liddell Hart, *History of the Second World War*, p. 80.

106 From conversations with Wolf Rüdiger Hess in Surrey (October 1999) and Munich and Hindelang (November 1999).

107 Churchill, vol. II, p. 70.

108 Moran, p. 318.

109 Ciano, pp. 266–267.

110 Wilmot, p. 26.

111 Hitler, *My New Order*, p. 666.

112 Kieser, pp. 265–270.

113 Ibid., p. 265.

114 Whaley, pp. 247–251.

115 Ibid., p. 254.

116 Ibid., pp. 252–253.

117 Ibid., pp. 136–137.

118 Ibid, p. 229.

119 Ibid.

120 Roberts, *Eminent Churchillians*, p. 161, citing diary of Cecil King of the *Daily Mirror* for 4 June 1940.

121 Sheean, p. 54, citing articles by Churchill in the *Daily Telegraph* in January 1939.

Chapter Four: The Network is Activated

1 The correspondence between Hess and the Haushofers relating to the origins of the plan was captured by the British at the end of the war, and returned to the West German government in 1958 after

microfilm copies were placed in the Public Record Office. Translations were published in *Documents on German Foreign Policy (1918–1945)*, Series D, vol. XI.

2 *Documents on German Foreign Policy (1918–1945)*, Series D, vol. XI, pp. 15–18 (original document ref. C109/C002185–7).

3 Wootton, Chapter XXIX.

4 OSS/CIC records, US National Archives, Maryland: 'Interview with Prof. Karl Haushofer, Major General, Retired,' 27 September 1945 (document ref. XL22853).

5 Padfield, *Hess*, p. 114.

6 McBlain, p. 16.

7 Entwhistle, p. 12. (Our thanks to John Harris for supplying us with a copy.)

8 *Documents on German Foreign Policy (1918–1945)*, Series D, vol. XI, pp. 78–81 (original document ref. C109/002190–4).

9 Owen St Clair O'Malley, a vehement anti–Bolshevik, was Ambassador to Hungary at the outbreak of war, and played a vital role in evacuating Polish troops to Britain through that country. When Britain declared war on Hungary in December 1941 O'Malley became Ambassador to Sikorski's Polish government in exile.

10 British Ambassador to the USA until his death in November 1940. Before the war Lothian had been a supporter of Anglo–German co-operation, and after the fall of France made overtures to the German Embassy in Washington about possible peace terms. Although his actions were backed by Lord Halifax, Churchill ordered him to discontinue the contact (Padfield, *Hess*, pp. 126–127).

11 *Documents on German Foreign Policy (1918–1945)*, Series D, vol. XI, pp. 60–61 (original document ref. C109/002188–9).

12 Whaley, pp. 18–19.

13 *Documents on German Foreign Policy (1918–1945)*, Series D, vol. XI, p. 129 (original document ref. C109/002197).

14 Quoted in *Daily Record and Mail*, 12 May 1941.

15 Churchill, vol. II, pp. 164–165 and 180–183.

16 Rudolf Hess, p. 14. Hess's speech was translated and disseminated in Britain. Although this is now widely regarded as a propaganda exercise – aiming to defuse British and French fears about Germany's ambitions – there is little doubt about the sincerity of the personal sentiments expressed in the quoted passages.

17 Ibid., p. 13.

18 PRO FO 1093/1: Translation of transcript of meeting with Lord Simon, 9 June 1941.

19 *Documents on German Foreign Policy (1918–1945)*, Series D, vol. XI, p. 162 (original document ref. C109/002203).

20 PRO, FO 1093/1: Translation of transcript of meeting with Lord Simon, 9 June 1941.

21 Hamilton Muniments, National Register of Archives, Scotland.

22 Douglas-Hamilton, *The Truth about Rudolf Hess*, p. 68.

23 Ibid., p. 73.

24 Ibid., pp. 74–77.

25 Reproduced in ibid., pp. 94–96.

26 Ibid., p. 99.

27 Hamilton Muniments, Bundle 5012.

28 Douglas-Hamilton, *Motive for a Mission*, p. 72.

29 Hamilton Muniments, Bundle 5019: Handwritten statement by Duke of Hamilton, in papers relating to his November 1943 legal action against J. Redfern Collins.

30 Douglas-Hamilton, *The Truth about Rudolf Hess*.

31 Padfield, *Hess*, p. 88.

32 Costello, *Ten Days that Saved the West*, p. 407, citing Channon's diary for 13 May 1941.

33 Stated by W. Gallacher MP during debate in House of Commons, 27 May 1941. (House of Commons, vol. 371, col. 1702).

34 Reported in, for example, the *Scotsman*, 23 September 1943.

35 Hamilton Muniments, Bundle 5026: Letter from Duke of Hamilton to Richard Collier, 13 March 1959.

36 Ibid., Bundle 5019: Statement by Duke of Hamilton (see note 29).

37 Douglas-Hamilton, *The Truth about Rudolf Hess*, pp. 71–72.

38 Hamilton Muniments, Bundle 5021.

39 Ibid., Bundle 5019: Statement by Duke of Hamilton, (see note 29).

40 Ibid., Bundle 5000: Letter from Lieutenant Colonel T. C. R. Moore to Marquess of Clydesdale, 27 June 1935.

41 Ibid., Bundle 5002: Letter from D. Conwell Evans, Ph.D., to Marquess of Clydesdale, 11 May 1938.

42 Ibid., Bundle 5019: Annotation in Hamilton's hand to his November 1943 statement (see note 29).

43 Ibid., Bundle 5000: Memorandum by anonymous author dated 31 July 1939. The covering letter from Mr Hurd to Lord Nigel Douglas-Hamilton, written on the notepaper of the Union Bank of Scotland and dated 14 August 1939, describes the writer as 'an old acquaintance who was one of the founders of the Anglo-German friendship movement'.

44 Ibid., Bundle 5012: Memo from Lord Halifax to Clydesdale, 3 May 1938.

45 PRO, WO199/3288B: 'Special Report of [*sic*] Prisoner of War' by Colonel R. A. Lennie, Officer Commanding, Drymen Military Hospital, 13 May 1941.

46 Hamilton Muniments, Bundle 5001: Letter from Lord Malcolm Douglas-Hamilton, written from No. 12 Flying Training School, RAF Grantham (Lincolnshire), to 'Douglo', 9 November 1939. Letter from 'Mac' dated 30 October 1939 enclosed.

47 Ibid., Bundle 5019: Undated statement by Duke of Hamilton on his connection with Albrecht Haushofer.

48 Ibid., Bundle 5019: Statement by Duke of Hamilton (see note 29).

49 *Daily Express*, 18 May 1941. This is also confirmed in Kurt Hahn's report on the Hess affair (Hamilton Muniments, Bundle 5005).

50 *Daily Telegraph*, 10 March 1939.

51 *The Times*, 4 June 1936.

52 Hamilton Muniments, Bundle 5001: Draft enclosed with letter from Lord David Douglas-Hamilton to Marquess of Clydesdale, 22 September 1939.

53 Ibid.: Letter from Clydesdale to Lord Halifax, 30 September 1939.

54 Ibid.: Letter from Lord David Douglas–Hamilton to Clydesdale, 22 September 1939.

55 Ibid.: The letter from Lord David on 22 September 1939 states that 'Hahn is seeing Ogilvie of the BBC to make sure that it is given the fullest possible publicity in Germany'. In a letter to the current Duke and Duchess of Hamilton dated 9 August 1967, Hahn quotes from a letter of 11 October 1939 from Sir Frederick Ogilvie, director-general of the BBC (1938–42): 'You may like to know that Lord Clydesdale's letter was quoted in the 10.15 p.m. German news on the 6th October.' Hahn comments: 'I had previously sent him a German translation of the letter.'

56 Ibid., Bundle 5017.

57 Ibid., Bundle 5001. For a full list of attendees, see authors' website, www.pharo.com.

58 For a summary of von Reichenau's career see Snyder, pp. 283–284.

59 Padfield, *Hess*, p. 33.

60 Winterbotham, *The Nazi Connection*, pp. 81–88.

61 Harris and Trow, p. 162, quoting correspondence in the possession of the Haushofer family.

62 *Documents on German Foreign Policy (1918–1945)*, Series D, vol. XI, pp. 129–132 (original document ref. C109/002197–202).

63 Colville, p. 134.

64 Ibid.

65 Haxey, p. 199.

66 *Documents on German Foreign Policy (1918–1945)*, Series D, vol. XI, pp. 129–131 (original document ref. C109/002198).

67 Ibid., pp. 162–163 (original document ref. C109/002204–5).

68 It was not until 1992, when a photographic copy was released to the Public Record Office as part of file FO 1093/12, that the original letter was made public. Until then, the contents were known from a draft found in the German Foreign Ministry records, a translation of which was published in *Documents on German Foreign Policy*, Series D, vol. XI., pp. 131–132 (original document ref. C109/002202).

69 PRO, FO 1093/11: Censor's report dated 6 November 1940.

70 Ibid.: Letter from War Office (name of writer censored) to Henry Hopkinson of the Foreign Office, 22 November 1940.

71 Ibid.: Letter from Henry Hopkinson to War Office, 7 December 1940. (Parts of this letter have been censored.)

72 *Bulletin and Scots Pictorial*, 15 May 1941.

73 PRO, WM 142(42)2. (The report is reproduced in Douglas-Hamilton, *Motive for a Mission*, p. 292.)

74 Duke of Hamilton's statement, November 1943 (see note 29).

75 Padfield, *Hess*, p. 146.

76 Ibid., p. 156.

77 Hamilton Muniments, Bundle 5011.

78 Ibid.: Letter from Group Captain F. G. Stammers to Duke of Hamilton, 28 March 1941; reply from Hamilton, 6 April 1941.

79 Ibid.: Telegram, Group Captain Stammers to Duke of Hamilton, 18 April 1941.

80 Douglas-Hamilton, *The Truth about Rudolf Hess*, p. 129.

81 Hamilton Muniments, Bundle 5011: Letter from Duke of Hamilton to Group Captain D. L. Blackford, dated 28 April 1942. Hamilton appears to have backdated his letter, as it contains the text suggested by Lord Eustace Percy in his letter of 29 April (see note 84).

82 Ibid.: Letter from D. L. Blackford to Duke of Hamilton, 3 May 1941.

83 Ibid.: Letter from Duke of Hamilton to D. L. Blackford, 10 May 1941.

84 Ibid.: Letter from 'Eustace' (Lord Eustace Percy) to Hamilton, 29 April 1941.

85 PRO, KV235.

86 Day, p. 36.

87 Imperial War Museum archive, FO 645, Box 155.

88 Goebbels, p. 377.

89 Padfield, *Hess*, p. 156.

90 Wolf Rüdiger Hess, pp. 79–80, citing notes written by Stahmer in 1959.

91 Newton, pp. 183–184.

92 Padfield, *Hess*, p. 156.

93 Douglas-Hamilton, *The Truth about Rudolf Hess*, p. 195.

94 Padfield, *Hess*, p. 178.

95 Harris and Trow, p. 165.

96   Douglas-Hamilton, *The Truth about Rudolf Hess*, pp. 60–61.

97   Hamilton Muniments, Bundle 5002.

98   Harris and Trow, p. 142.

99   Reitlinger, p. 164.

100 Ibid.

101 One of Haushofer's pupils was arrested as part of the Rote Kapelle Ring (Reitlinger, p. 163). In addition, one of the Haushofers' contacts is referred to discreetly in Karl Haushofer's letter of 31 August 1940 (see note 2 above) as 'the American from Wisconsin'. This is either Arvid Harnick of the Ministry of Economics, who had studied at the University of Wisconsin, or his American wife Mildred, whom he met and married there. Both were convicted as members of the Rote Kapelle Ring (Reitlinger, pp. 231–232).

102 Reitlinger, pp. 163–164.

103 US National Archives, Washington DC: 'Testimony of Karl Haushofer, taken at Nurnberg, Germany, 5 October, 1945, by Colonel Howard A. Brundage, JAGD, OUSCC'.

104 OSS/CIC records, US National Archives, Maryland: 'Interview with Prof. Karl Haushofer, Major General, Retired,' 27 September 1945 (document ref. XL22853).

105 Papers of Father Edmund A. Walsh, Georgetown University Library, Washington, DC: Letter from Dr Karl Haushofer, 7 February 1946.

106 Costello, *Ten Days that Saved the West*, p. 457.

107 Ibid.

108 Wolf Rüdiger Hess, p. 81, citing notes written by Stahmer in 1959.

109 Newton, p. 188.

110 Ibid.

111 PRO, FO 371/26945.

112 PRO, PREM 3/219/7: 'Report on Interview with Herr Hess by Wing Commander the Duke of Hamilton, 11 May 1941'.

Chapter Five: Into the Unknown

1   Ilse Hess, p. 16.

2   Two events suggest that Göring knew in advance of Hess's flight. The first is the testimony of Adolf Galland, the First World War ace who was commanding a Luftwaffe fighter group on the Channel coast. Galland asserts that he received an urgent telephone call from Göring at about ten o'clock on the evening of 10 May, saying that Hess had gone mad and had stolen a plane which he was flying to Britain. Göring ordered Galland to send up fighters to shoot Hess down, and Galland says that – disbelieving the story but unwilling to argue with his superior – he sent up a token force. Galland's account clashes directly with the official Nazi line that none of the leaders knew about the flight until they were

summoned to the Berghof by Hitler the following evening. Yet if Göring *did* know the evening before, what was the purpose of the call to Galland – which was in any event far too late for any action to be taken, as by that time Hess was approaching the British coast? (Baker, p. 162).

The second piece of evidence is that Willi Messerschmitt claimed that he was interrogated about the flight personally by Göring on the *morning* of 11 May, again before he is officially supposed to have been told (see Chapter 6).

3 Murphy, p. 48.
4 *New York Times*, 20 September 1942.
5 Imperial War Museum archives, FO 645, Box 155.
6 PRO, KV237: Translation of intercepted cable, 14 May 1941.
7 Padfield, *Hess*, p. 212.
8 Manvell and Fraenkel, pp. 89–90.
9 The following details are taken from the text of Kaden's lecture, published by the Rudolf Hess Gesellschaft. Our thanks to Tina Metz for the translation.
10 PRO, FO 1093/1: Translated transcript of interview with Lord Simon, 9 June 1941.
11 Padfield, *Hess*, p. 184.
12 *Sunday Dispatch*, 30 September 1945.
13 Newton, p. 127. Sir Horace Wilson discussed this proposal of Chamberlain's with Fritz Hesse, a German press attaché in London, in the summer of 1939.
14 See note 2 above.
15 RSHA Protokolle, Institut für Zeitgeschicht, Munich. Copies and translations supplied by Wolf Rüdiger Hess.
16 Padfield, *Hess*, p. 185.
17 Hitler, *My New Order*, pp. 754–765. For the full text of the speech, see the authors' website, www.pharo.com.
18 Ibid., p. 662.
19 Shortly after the Hess incident, Pintsch was transferred to the Russian front, where he was taken prisoner. When his captors found out that he had been part of Hess's staff, Pintsch was tortured to make him reveal what he knew about his former chief's flight to Britain. He was imprisoned in Russia until 1955 when he was released and returned to Germany.
20 Padfield, *Hess*, pp. 185–186.
21 Ibid., p. 191.
22 Hutton, p. 31.
23 PRO, FO 1093/1: Letter from Hess to 'Buz', 10 June 1941.
24 Kaden.

25 Hess left Augsburg at approximately 17.45 Central European Time (CET) and his plane crashed at Eaglesham at 23.09 British Double Summer Time (BDST, which is GMT + two hours). (CET and BDST were synchronised at that time, so times were the same in Britain and Germany.) His journey therefore took about five and a half hours. The direct distance between Augsburg and Eaglesham is around 900 miles, and as the Me-110 had a cruising speed of 250 mph the journey should have taken, at most, four hours. However, the 'killing time' manoeuvres added another 200 miles, bringing the journey time nearer to five hours. (For a more detailed account of Hess's flight, see the authors' website, www.pharo.com.)

26 Ramsay, vol 1, p. 126.

27 Ashbee, p. 530.

28 Ilse Hess, pp. 18–19.

29 Kalundborg is approximately 540 miles from Augsburg and almost exactly 600 miles from Glasgow, a total of 1,140 miles.

30 Nesbit and van Acker, p. 44.

31 RSHA Protokolle, Institut für Zeitgeschicht, Munich.

32 Both Heydrich's widow and one of his agents, Hans-Bernard Gisevius, stated after the war that he had been flying over the North Sea that evening (Padfield, *Hess*, p. 196).

33 Ashbee, p. 530.

34 The British radar reports are summarised in Nesbit and van Acker, Appendix E.

35 PRO, HO 199/482: File note written by K. S. Tollit states, 'Plotted as raid 42J, made landfall at ALNWICK, Northumberland, at 22.17' (emphasis in original).

36 PRO, AIR 16/1266: 'RUDOLF HESS. Flight on May 10th, 1941, Raid 42J', report by Royal Observer Corps.

37 PRO, INF1/912: 'Additional Notes on the Hess Incident by Group Captain the Duke of Hamilton', undated.

38 House of Commons, vol. 371, col. 1591–1592.

39 Nesbit and van Acker, p. 62.

40 Costello, *Ten Days that Saved the West*, pp. 7–9.

41 Rosthorn.

42 Ibid.

43 Ibid.

44 Ibid.

45 MacLean, pp. 138–139.

46 Anonymous, p. 523.

47 McBride, 'Alias Alfred Horn', p. 2.

48 Wood, p. 2.

49 Ibid.

50 Padfield, *Hess*, pp. 355–356, citing letter from former Brigade Intelligence Officer Dennis Rose, 16 June 1992.

51 Ibid., p. 356, citing letter from Dennis Rose, 23 June 1992.

52 PRO, AIR 16/1266: 'RUDOLF HESS. Flight on May 10th, 1941, Raid 42J', report by Royal Observer Corps.

53 Padfield, *Hess*, p. 356.

54 Douglas-Hamilton, *Motive for a Mission*, p. 285.

55 MacLean, pp. 137–140.

56 PRO, AIR 16/1266: Major Donald's report, 11 May 1941.

57 David J. Smith, *Action Stations*, p. 20.

58 Harris and Trow, p. 187.

59 Statements were taken from various Eaglesham residents, and are now in the records of the Renfrew County Constabulary. Our thanks to Andrew Rosthorn for supplying us with copies.

Chapter Six: The Capture of Alfred Horn

1 PRO file WO (War Office) 199/3288A. This file was released to the PRO in the 1970s, but the companion file, 3288B, was closed until 2017, fuelling speculation that this contained more sensitive material that would answer some of the major questions about the Hess affair. However, 3288B was released in 1992, and to the consternation of researchers proved to contain no startling new information or anything to explain why it had been withheld for so long.

2 *Daily Record and Mail*, 12 May 1941.

3 Interview by the BBC, 13 or 14 May 1941. (This interview was not broadcast at the time, and remained untransmitted until 1991.)

4 *Glasgow Herald*, 15 May 1941.

5 Anonymous, 'The Inside Story of the Hess Flight', p. 523.

6 PRO, PREM 3/219/7: From the preamble (from the wording, not written by Hamilton) to 'Report on Interview with Herr Hess by Wing Commander the Duke of Hamilton, 11th May, 1941'.

7 *The Bulletin and Scots Pictorial*, 13 May 1941.

8 Ibid.

9 Ibid.

10 McBride, p. 4.

11 Stewart, p. 155.

12 *Edinburgh Evening News*, 13 May 1941.

13 *Glasgow Herald*, 13 May 1941.

14 *Edinburgh Evening News*, 13 May 1941.

15 PRO, KV235.

16 PRO, WO 199/3288A: 'Report by O.C. 3rd Battalion Renfrewshire Home Guard of the Incidents of the Night of 10th, 11th May, 1941'.

17 PRO, WO 199/3288A: A memo dated 22 May 1941 from Headquarters, 3rd Anti-Aircraft Corps, to Headquarters, Scottish Command, states, 'Herewith copy of statements from the two O-Rs [other ranks] concerned in the arrest of Herr Hess', but the statements are not attached. The reply from Scottish Command, dated 25 May 1941, acknowledges receipt of the statements from '2510157, Sgt. McBride and 2595648, Sgt. Morris'.

18 Hutton, p. 7.

19 Ibid., p. 8.

20 McBride Papers: Letter from Daniella Royland to Ilse Hess, 14 June 1978.

21 McBride, 'This is the Story of the Man who Caught Rudolf Hess'. The paper also carried a headline story about McBride the previous day.

22 This and the following quotes are from McBride, 'Alias Alfred Horn', unpublished typescript in the McBride Papers.

23 Stewart, pp. 154–155.

24 Hutton, Chapter 13.

25 PRO, WO 199/3288A: Memo from Scottish Command, 4 June 1941.

26 PRO, KV237.

27 McBride Papers: Letter from W. B. Howieson to Daniel McBride, 8 May 1974.

28 Interview with Wolf Rüdiger Hess, Surrey, October 1999. Also various correspondence between Wolf Rüdiger Hess and Daniella and Eddie Royland in the McBride Papers.

29 Stewart, p. 156.

30 Ibid.

31 The Home Guard report (see note 16 above) states that when Hess was searched an inventory was made of the items found and that a copy was attached to the report. It has never been released to the public. Padfield (*Hess*, p. 207) speculated that this was in the companion, 'B' file (see note 1 above), and that, since it might list a letter to the Duke of Hamilton (or someone else of even greater importance) this was the reason that the file had been embargoed for seventy-five years. However, when the 'B' file was released in 1992 it did not contain the inventory.

32 Hutton, p. 11.

33 Padfield, *Hess*, p. 358.

34 Wood, p. 4.

35 PRO, AIR 16/1266: Report by Major Graham Donald, 11 May 1941.

36 Douglas-Hamilton, *Motive for a Mission*, pp. 284–285. (Donald's 1942 *Royal Observer Corps Journal* article is reproduced in Appendix I of Douglas-Hamilton's book.)

37 Ibid., p. 285.

38 PRO, AIR 16/1266: Report by Major Graham Donald, 11 May 1941.

39 *Sunday Dispatch*, 16 April 1950.

40 Hamilton Muniments, Bundle 5034.

41 PRO, FO 1093/11: 'The Interrogation of Rudolph Hess by Roman Battaglia', Lt. J. Mair, 30 May 1941.

42 PRO, KV235: Memo from Major P. Perfect, MI5 Scottish Regional Office, Edinburgh, to A. S. MacIver, MI5 Oxford, 17 May 1941.

43 PRO, FO 1093/11: 'The Interrogation of Rudolph Hess by Roman Battaglia', Lt. J. Mair, 30 May 1941.

44 PRO, WO 199/3288A: Memo from Colonel Firebrace, Scottish Area Command, 18 May 1941.

45 Ibid.: 'German POW Captured Night 10/11 May 41 – Report by Night Duty Officer', Captain Anthony C. White, Glasgow Area Command.

46 PRO, WO 199/3288A, 'Report by O.C. 3rd Battalion Renfrewshire Home Guard of the Incidents of the Night of 10th, 11th May, 1941'.

47 Douglas-Hamilton, *Motive for a Mission*, p. 283.

48 PRO, WO 199/3288A: 'Report by O.C. 3rd Battalion Renfrewshire Home Guard of the Incidents of the Night of 10th, 11th May, 1941'.

49 Ibid.: 'Extract from Duty Officer's Report for Night of 10/11 May 1941, 14 (H.D.) Bn., A. & S. H HQ Paisley' (Lieutenant W. H. Cowie).

50 Padfield, *Hess*, pp. 208–209, citing article by Hector MacLean in *Air Mail*, Winter 1987.

51 PRO WO 199/3288A: 'German POW Captured Night 10/11 May 1941 – Report by Night Duty Officer', Captain Anthony C. White, Glasgow Area Command.

52 Padfield, *Hess*, p. 208, citing letter from Donald to Harry Greer, 19 May 1941.

53 PRO, WO 199/3288A: Colonel Firebrace's memo to Glasgow Area Command, 18 May 1941.

54 Ibid.: Lt. Cowie's report (see note 49 above).

55 Ibid.

56 PRO, AIR 16/1266: Letter from A. D. Warrington-Morris to Major Donald, 18 May 1941.

57 *Glasgow Herald*, 16 May 1941.

58 MacLean, p. 138.

59 Padfield, *Hess*, p. 354.

60 PRO, WO 199/3288A: Captain White's report (see note 45 above).

61 Ibid.: Report by Lieutenant F. E. Whitby, 11th Battalion Cameronians (Scottish Rifles), 11 May 1941.

62 Ibid.: 'Report on the Arrival of Hauftmann [*sic*] Alfred Horn to Maryhill Barracks on 11.5.41' by Second Lieutenant B. Fulton.

63   Ibid.: Home Guard report (see note 48 above).

64   Bateman, p. 13.

65   Padfield, *Hess*, p. 356.

66   Ibid., p. 357.

Chapter Seven: The Aftermath

1   PRO, PREM 3/219/4.

2   PRO, FO 371/30920.

3   PRO, PREM 3/219/7: 'Report on Interview with Herr Hess by Wing Commander the Duke of Hamilton, 11th May 1941'.

4   Conversation with Wolf Rüdiger Hess, Munich, November 1999.

5   See Chapter 5, note 14.

6   Douglas-Hamilton, *Motive for a Mission*, p. 178.

7   Colville, p. 457.

8   Ibid., pp. 458–459.

9   Costello, *Ten Days that Saved the West*, pp. 416–417, based on Lawford's unpublished diary.

10   PRO, INF 1/912: 'Additional Notes on the Hess Incident by Wing Commander the Duke of Hamilton'. (Report written in 1945 for submission to the International Military Tribunal.)

11   Hamilton Muniments, Bundle 5019.

12   Churchill, vol. III, p. 43.

13   Costello, *Ten Days that Saved the West*, p. 417.

14   Douglas-Hamilton, *Motive for a Mission*, p. 180.

15   Padfield, *Hess*, p. 219.

16   Ibid., p. 235.

17   Ibid., p. 358.

18   Ibid., p. 239.

19   Gestapo reports in RSHA Protokolle, Institut für Zeitgeschicht, Munich.

20   Schwarzwäller, pp. 171–172.

21   Wolf Rüdiger Hess, pp. 343–344.

22   PRO, INF 1/912.

23   PRO, PREM 3/219/4: Undated draft of statement by Winston Churchill.

24   Cadogan, pp. 379–380.

25   PRO, INF 1/912.

26   Kirkpatrick's reports on his three meetings with Hess were first made public for the Nuremberg Trials. The original reports were released to the PRO in 1992, in file FO 1093/1.

27   PRO, FO 1093/1: Ivone Kirkpatrick, 'Record of an Interview with Herr Rudolph Hess, May 13'.

28   Ibid.

29 Ibid: Ivone Kirkpatrick, 'Record of a Conversation with Herr Hess on May 15th, 1941'.

30 PRO, FO 1093/11: Memo from Prime Minister to Sir Alexander Cadogan, 16 May 1941.

31 Padfield, *Hess*, pp. 377–378.

32 PRO, PREM 3/219/7: Report by Sir Alexander Cadogan, 13 May 1941.

33 Ibid.: Memo from Churchill to Eden, 13 May 1941.

34 PRO, PREM 3/219/4.

35 Ibid.

36 Ibid.

37 *Glasgow Herald*, 15 May 1941.

38 Ibid., 20 May 1941.

39 Douglas-Hamilton, *Motive for a Mission*, pp. 194–195.

40 Hamilton Muniments, Bundle 5005: Letter from Duke of Hamilton to Sir Alexander Hardinge, 19 May 1941.

41 Ibid.: Letter from Duke of Hamilton to George VI, 19 May 1941.

42 Ibid.: Report by Kurt Hahn.

43 House of Commons, vol. 371, cols. 1591–1592.

44 Hamilton Muniments, Bundle 5019.

45 Padfield, *Hess*, pp. 374–375.

46 *The Herald*, 28 August 1997.

47 Fullerton.

48 Interviewed in Edinburgh, 13 September 2000.

49 Conversation with Wolf Rüdiger Hess, Munich, November 1999.

50 Douglas-Hamilton, *The Truth about Rudolf Hess*, pp. 193–194.

51 Padfield, *Hess*, p. 233, quoting Martha Haushofer's diary for 22 May 1941.

52 *New York Times*, 1 June 1941.

53 Ilse Hess, p. 18.

54 Kaden.

55 Padfield, *Hess* p. 220.

56 Costello, *Ten Days that Saved the West*, p. 433, citing PRO, INF 1/912.

57 House of Commons, vol. 377, cols. 594–595.

58 *Glasgow Herald*, 18 February 1942.

59 Van Paassen, *That Day Alone*, p. 518.

60 Hamilton Muniments, Bundle 5019.

61 Ibid. and PRO, AIR 19/564.

62 Hamilton Muniments, Bundle 5019: Letter from Home Secretary to Secretary of State for Air, 18 June 1941.

63 Ibid.: Cable from Hiram Todd (US lawyer) to McKenna & Co. (UK solicitors), 28 January 1943, requesting details of settlement, and reply on same date; cable from Todd to McKenna & Co., 29 January 1943, asking whether this covered the Duke's costs; reply of 30 January 1943 confirming that it did not.

64 Ibid.: Cable from McKenna & Co to Hiram Todd, 10 March 1943, confirming Hamilton's acceptance of the terms; cable Todd to McKenna & Co., 20 March 1943, confirming that the case has been settled.

65 Chisholm and Davie, pp. 409–410.

66 *Edinburgh Evening News*, 14 May 1941.

67 Dollan, 'The Dollan Story'.

68 *Bulletin and Scots Pictorial*, 12 June 1941.

69 Dollan, 'Premier and Hess'.

70 *Dumfries and Galloway Standard and Advertiser*, 29 April 1942.

71 *Bulletin and Scots Pictorial*, 20 June 1941.

72 Dollan, 'Premier and Hess'.

73 *Glasgow Herald*, 10 January 1942.

74 *Bulletin and Scots Pictorial*, 30 January 1942.

75 Ibid.

76 Reported, for example, in the *Scotsman*, 23 September 1943.

77 The *Mercury*'s claim about Bohle may be a garbled version of genuine information, as a few days after the flight, Bohle told Goebbels that at one stage it was intended that he accompany Hess (Goebbels, p. 377). Bohle also told his American interrogators that Hess had told him that 'if he took anyone it would, of course, be Bohle'. (US National Archives, Maryland, 'Notes of Interrogation of Ernst Wilhelm Bohle by W. Wendell Blancke, 5–8 September 1945', document ref. 19613).

78 Anonymous, p. 523.

79 Imperial War Museum archives, FO 645, Box 155.

80 Munich medical file (see Chapter 11, note 19).

81 Mann.

82 Stewart, p. 157.

83 Wolf Rüdiger Hess, p. 86.

84 Pithers.

85 Padfield, *Hess*, p. 212.

86 See Chapter 4, note 104.

87 Costello, *Ten Days that Saved the West*, p. 436.

88 Ibid., pp. 436–437.

89 Ibid., pp. 441–442.

90 Ibid., p. 441.

91 Ibid., p. 442.

92 Blitz and Kiley.

93 Andrew and Gordievsky, p. 239.

94 Brown, *Treason in the Blood*, pp. 180–185.

95 Ibid., pp. 250–254.

96 Costello, *Ten Days that Saved the West*, p. 453.

97 Ibid., pp. 452–453.

98 Knightley, 'Surely it's Time for the Truth?'

99 Brown, *The Secret Servant*, pp. 349–350.

100 Churchill, vol. III, p. 49.

101 PRO, PREM 3/219/7: Memo from Churchill to Sir Archibald Sinclair, 6 April 1945.

102 Decorated by the British and Americans, Moravec was working at the Pentagon at the time of his death in 1969. See Moravec's memoirs.

103 Lockhart, vol. I, p. 98.

Chapter Eight: By Royal Appointment

1 PRO, FO 1093/11: Report no. 16 from 'Camp Z', 30 May 1941.

2 PRO, WO 199/3288A.

3 Nesbit and Van Acker, pp. 121–122.

4 Conversation with John Harris, March 1999.

5 Haxey, p. 230.

6 See 'A close observer' (probably written by Kenneth de Courcy).

7 Both the 8th and 9th Dukes of Northumberland – respectively the father and brother of the Duchess of Hamilton – served with the Grenadier Guards.

8 On this and de Courcy's other activities, see Costello, Appendix 11. From 1934 de Courcy ran the Imperial Policy Group, described by Costello as a 'right-wing lobby of Conservative MPs', which pressed for closer ties with Germany in order to counter the threat of Communism and to preserve the empire.

9 Letter from Duc de Grantmesnil (Kenneth de Courcy) to Jeffrey Simmons (author's agent), 5 May 1998.

10 Padfield, *Hess*, pp. 154–155; Costello, p. 62.

11 David J. Smith, *Action Stations*, p. 20.

12 Stewart, p. 158.

13 Letter from His Grace the Duke of Hamilton to Stephen Prior, 7 November 1999.

14 PRO, KV237: Note from Roger Fulfort of MI5 Division B4A to Captain Guy Liddel, 8 June 1941.

15 Stewart, p. 159.

16 PRO, KV237: Report by Inspector Thomas Hyslop, 15 May 1941.

17 Hamilton Muniments, Bundle 5019.

18 *Documents on German Foreign Policy (1918–1945)*, Series D, vol. XI, p. 16.

19 Whiting, pp. 97–98.

20 Macwhirter.

21 McLeod, pp. 121–124.

22 *The Freemason and Masonic Illustrated*, 22 July 1939.

23 Whiting, pp. 90–91.

24 Holden, p. 269.

25 *The Times* reports visits to Munich by the Kents on 6 August 1936,

16–17 April 1936, 23–25 February 1937, 18 January 1938 and 15 September 1938. The Duke and Duchess visited Paris, Geneva and Italy in the five weeks before war broke out.

26 Whiting, pp. 97–98.

27 Winterbotham, *The Nazi Connection*, pp. 24–25.

28 The Saar Basin – a major coal-producing area – had been handed over to France by the Treaty of Versailles, but was returned to Germany in 1935 by a plebiscite of the population (of which over 90% voted in favour).

29 Winterbotham, *Secret and Personal*, p. 76.

30 Griffiths, pp. 122–123.

31 Winterbotham, *Secret and Personal*, p. 81.

32 Newton, p. 83.

33 *The Times*, 25 February 1937.

34 Bloch, *The Duke of Windsor's War*, pp. 81–83.

35 Ibid., p. 204.

36 Whiting, p. 97.

37 Ibid.

38 Costello, *The Mask of Treachery*, p. 448.

39 Ibid., p. 460.

40 Ibid., pp. 465–467.

41 Greig, pp. 209–210.

42 Ibid., p. 285.

43 Ibid., p. 278.

44 Ibid., p. 279.

45 Ibid., p. 282.

46 Bethell.

47 Ibid.

48 Ibid.

49 Ibid.

50 Riddell, p. 40.

51 Interview with John Harris, September 1999.

52 David J. Smith, 'The Death of the Duke of Kent', p. 29.

53 Glass, p. 154.

54 Letter to Lyndsay Brydon from Allison Derrett, Assistant Registrar of the Royal Archives, 30 August 2000.

55 Elizabeth Adam, interviewed in Cumbria, 15 May 2000.

56 Innes, p. 76.

57 Apart from the enigmatic entry (perhaps significant in the light of the Millburn Tower episode, below) 'At Turnhouse. Arriving?', the Duke's diary records 'Battle over HMS *Victorious*' – meaning he was flying a Fairey Battle over the destroyer, which was berthed in the Clyde – and dinner with the new Scottish Command chief, Lieutenant-General Thorne.

58 Land Use Consultants, vol. 5, p. 171.
59 Sherwood, pp. 293–294
60 Churchill, vol. III, pp. 52–53.
61 Sikorski's diary for 1941, in the Sikorski Museum and Historical Archive, London.
62 Roberts, *Eminent Churchillians*, pp. 204–205.
63 Quoted in ibid., p. 205.
64 Day, p. 184.
65 Ibid.
66 Quoted in ibid.
67 Ibid., citing Dalton's diary in the Dalton Papers, London School of Economics.
68 Interview with John Harris, September 1999.
69 Newton, p. 190.
70 *Daily Telegraph*, 12 May 1941.
71 Andrew Rosthorn, additional comments to Hugh Thomas, 'Hess, "Hess", Timewatch'.
72 Duncan McCallum, Senior Steward of Edinburgh Castle, telephone interview, 22 November 2000.
73 Calder, pp. 72–74.
74 Reports in *Glasgow Herald* and *Bulletin and Scots Pictorial*, 14 May 1941, on police raids of 3 May 1941.
75 Reported, for example, in the *Daily Record*, 10 May 1941.
76 Stafford, *Churchill and Secret Service*, pp. 84–85.
77 Cadogan, p. 380.

Chapter Nine: The Secret Armistice

1 J. R. Rees, pp. 26–27.
2 Padfield, *Hess*, pp. 254–255. After the publication of his 1962 book about Hess, James Leasor received a letter from this agent.
3 See Michael Smith's recent biography, *Foley: The Spy who Saved 10,000 Jews*.
4 Newton, p. 174.
5 Goebbels, pp. 361–365.
6 House of Lords Record Office, Beaverbrook Papers, file D/443: Copy of letter from Major Morton to Henry Hopkinson of the Foreign Office, 13 June 1941.
7 Padfield, *Hess*, p. 277, citing Colonel A.M. Scott's diary in Imperial War Museum archives.
8 Fraser-Smith, McKnight and Lesburg, pp. 135–138.
9 PRO, PREM 3/219/7: Memo from J. M. Martin, 10 Downing Street, to W. I. Mallett of the Foreign Office, 18 May 1941.
10 PRO, FO1093/1: Record of telephone conversation with Kirkpatrick

by Henry Hopkinson, in which Hopkinson notes Kirkpatrick's suggestion that they 'put someone in the role of negotiator who could question him [Hess] about his proposals'.

11 Cadogan, p. 380.

12 PRO, PREM 3/219/7: Memo from Eden to Churchill, 27 May 1941.

13 Michael Smith, p. 229.

14 For example, a note in PRO file FO 1093/12, dated 30 July 1941 and signed 'A', of a conversation between Hess and a new duty officer states: 'Jonathan began by revealing the identity of Dr Guthrie and by offering the minutes of the conference.'

15 Malone.

16 PRO, FO 1093/1: Translation of transcript of interview with Lord Simon.

17 Ibid.

18 Ibid: Memo from Churchill to Eden, 14 June 1941.

19 PRO FO1093/11: Interrogation report by 'ERH', 13 November 1939.

20 Ibid.: 'MAASS, Kurt: Information derived from German documents found in his possession', report dated 23 May 1941.

21 Ibid.

22 PRO, FO1093/1: Cadogan's margin note to Kirkpatrick's 'Record of a conversation with Herr Hess on May 15th, 1941.'

23 PRO, KV237: Memo to 'B2', 13 June 1941.

24 Ibid: Note by Major Stephens, 25 July 1941.

25 Ibid.: Various correspondence and file notes.

26 Ibid.: Petition by Maass and Semelbauer, 3 August 1941.

27 Ibid.: Report, 29 August 1941.

28 Ibid.: Report, 26 February 1942.

29 Letter to authors from International Committee of the Red Cross archives, 28 July 2000.

30 Padfield, *Hess*, pp. 368–370.

31 Ibid., p. 370.

32 West, pp. 259–260.

33 Pierrepoint, pp. 138–141. (Pierrepoint, writing in 1968, was not permitted to reveal Richter's name, and he therefore appears under the pseudonym 'Otto Schmidt'.)

34 Snyder, pp. 141–142.

35 Hill, p. 170.

36 Ibid. Schmitt's quote is from an interview in the *Bild am Sonntag*.

37 Padfield, *Hess*, p. 252.

38 Hamilton Muniments, Bundle 5034: Manuscript of Leasor's *Rudolf Hess: The Uninvited Envoy*, pp. 149–150.

39 Douglas-Hamilton, *Motive for a Mission*, pp. 177–178. Douglas-Hamilton was told about the map by an (unnamed) intelligence officer who was involved in the capture of the SS men.

40 Details from the official guide to Luton Hoo.
41 Roberts, p. 207.
42 Ibid., pp. 205–206.
43 House of Commons, vol. 377, pp. 594–595.
44 Bateman, p. 14.
45 Ibid.
46 Padfield, *Hess*, p. 368.
47 Ibid.
48 Brown, *The Secret Servant*, p. 348.
49 Whaley, p. 80.
50 Ibid., p. 181.
51 Ibid., pp. 60–61.
52 Ibid., p. 63.
53 Irving, *Göring*, pp. 326–327.
54 Whaley, pp. 117–118.
55 Calder, p. 48.
56 Dimbleby and Reynolds, p. 184.
57 Ibid., pp. 132–133.
58 House of Lords Record Office, Beaverbrook Papers, file D/416: Memo from Beaverbrook to Churchill, 20 February 1941.
59 Dimbleby and Reynolds, p. 125.
60 Kimball, vol. I, p. 182.
61 Irving, *Hess: The Missing Years*, p. 90.
62 Kirkpatrick's family home was in the Irish Republic.
63 PRO, PREM 3/219/7: Cable from Acting British Consul, New York, to Ministry of Information, London, 19 June 1941.
64 *New York Times*, 15 May 1941.
65 Kimball, vol. I, p. 187.
66 Ibid., p. 188.
67 Newton, p. 185.
68 PRO, FO1093/1: Ivone Kirkpatrick, 'Record of a conversation with Herr Hess on May 15th, 1941.'
69 Reported, for example, in *Edinburgh Evening News*, 17 May 1941.
70 Kimball, vol. I, pp. 196–197.
71 From report in *Edinburgh Evening News*, 23 May 1941.
72 *New York Times*, 22 May 1941.
73 Kimball, vol. I, p. 197.
74 Ibid., p. 198.
75 Gilbert, *Second World War*, p. 182.
76 Ibid.
77 Lippmann, p. 12.
78 Sheean, p. 245.
79 Ibid., p. 248.

80 Murphy, p. 7.

81 Churchill did not inform his Air Staff of the real reason for his change of heart, but resorted to delaying tactics. The 'area bombing' of German cities – intended, as with the Blitz on Britain, to undermine civilian morale – had been carried out by the RAF in late 1940, but at the time of Hess's arrival Bomber Command's priority had been switched to attacks on naval targets. At the beginning of July 1941, the Air Staff ordered the resumption of area bombing (Levine, p. 30), but surprisingly Churchill did not support the change, and (in the time-honoured way of politicians playing for time) established an inquiry under economist David Butt to evaluate the effectiveness of RAF bombing. Butt's report concluded that the raids were not achieving the desired results. Nevertheless, in September the air chiefs got their way, and the decision was made to concentrate on area bombing – but Churchill ordered a cessation of raids on the grounds that resources needed to be conserved for a big push the following spring (Delve, p. 101), delaying implementation of the new strategy until May 1942. Even then, 'The bombing of Germany began in earnest only in 1943' (Delve, p. 98). (Sources: Argyle; Terraine; Levine; Delve.)

82 Terraine, p. 295

83 Ibid.

84 Reed, p. 331.

85 Ibid.

86 Goebbels, p. 424.

87 Ibid., p. 480.

88 Cazalet, p. 34.

89 International Military Tribunal, vol. XXII, p. 541.

90 Costello, *Ten Days that Saved the West*, Chapter 17.

91 Ibid., pp. 447–448.

92 Ibid.

93 Ibid., p. 447.

94 Van Paassen, *That Day Alone*, p. 522.

95 Churchill, vol. III, p. 58.

96 Moran, p. 37.

Chapter Ten: Sanity and Insanity

1 PRO, PREM 3/219/7: Major J. J. Sheppard, 'My Impressions of "X" (Herr Rudolph Hess)', 21 May 1941.

2 House of Lords Record Office, Beaverbrook Papers, file D/443: Letter from Beaverbrook to Hess, 1 September 1941.

3 Ibid.: Transcript of meeting.

4 A copy of Hess's memorandum is in ibid.

5 PRO, PREM 3/219/7: Major Sheppard's report.

6 Ibid.
7 Quoted in J. R. Rees, p. 15.
8 Quoted in Padfield, *Hess*, p. 244.
9 PRO, FO 371/30920. The report is reproduced in Douglas-Hamilton, *Motive for a Mission*, Appendix III.
10 J. R. Rees, p. 21.
11 Ibid., p. 23.
12 Ibid., pp. 23–24.
13 Ibid., p. 24.
14 Ibid., p. 25.
15 Irving, *Hess: The Missing Years*, p. 114.
16 J. R. Rees, p. 28.
17 Ibid., p. 29.
18 Ibid., p. 31.
19 Ibid., p. 29.
20 Ibid., pp. 28–29.
21 Irving, *Hess: The Missing Years*, p. 133.
22 J. R. Rees, p. 30.
23 Ibid., p. 32.
24 Ibid., pp. 37–38.
25 Irving, *Hess: The Missing Years*, p. 165.
26 PRO, FO 1093/1: Translated transcript of interview with Lord Simon, 9 June 1941.
27 PRO, FO 1093/1.
28 J. R. Rees, pp. 47–48.
29 Irving, *Hess: The Missing Years*, p. 148.
30 PRO, FO 1093/11.
31 Letter from Rees to W. Clifford M. Scott, 11 June 1958.
32 J. R. Rees, p. 45.
33 House of Lords Record Office, Beaverbrook Papers, file D/443: Rudolf Hess, 'Statement of Protest and Evidence' (translation), 5 September 1941, with covering letter to Beaverbrook dated 23 October 1941.
34 J. R. Rees, p. 55.
35 Padfield, *Hess*, p. 251.
36 Irving, *Hess: The Missing Years*, p. 114.
37 J. R. Rees, p. 34. With characteristic circular logic, Dicks dismisses Hess's complaints about interrupted sleep with the remark 'He did not apparently resent the frequent inspection visits of the night duty officer'.
38 House of Lords Record Office, Beaverbrook Papers, file D/443: Letter from Sir Alexander Cadogan to Beaverbrook, 1 November 1941.
39 James Leasor, letter to *The Times*, 20 August 1987.
40 Chisholm and Davie, p. 410. The reason given was that Hamilton refused to support Beaverbrook's economic policies.

41 Lockhart, p. 255.
42 Michael Smith, pp. 232–233.
43 House of Lords Record Office, Beaverbrook Papers, file D/443: Rudolf Hess, 'Statement of Evidence and Protest', Appendix I.
44 J. R. Rees, p. 60.
45 Ibid.
46 Ibid., p. 52.
47 House of Lords Record Office, Beaverbrook Papers, file D/443: Letter from Hess to Beaverbrook, 23 October 1941.
48 'The Day Hess Appealed to the King', *Sunday Telegraph*, 13 December 1981.

Chapter Eleven: From Decoy to Doppelgänger

1   J. R. Rees, p. 67.
2   Hugh Thomas, *Hess: A Tale of Two Murders*, pp. 127–128.
3   Abergavenny Museum, display on Hess and Maindiff Court.
4   J. R. Rees, p. 68.
5   *The Times*, 3 July 1992.
6   Ibid.
7   Ibid.
8   Padfield, *Hess*, pp. 296–297.
9   J. R. Rees, p. 6.
10 Abergavenny Museum, display on Hess and Maindiff Court.
11 Hutton, pp. 121–122.
12 Ibid., p. 122.
13 Padfield, *Hess*, p. 290, citing Heydrich's report of 4 May 1942 in Foreign and Colonial Office Library (document 434005).
14 Kelly.
15 Quoted in J. R. Rees, pp. 136–137.
16 Hugh Thomas, *Hess: A Tale of Two Murders*, p. 15.
17 Ibid. pp. 27–29.
18 J. R. Rees, p. 89.
19 Military Doctor's Certificate, 12 December 1917, in Hess's medical file in the Kriegsarchiv, Munich. Copies and translation supplied by Andrew Rosthorn.
20 Quoted in Padfield, *Hess*, p. 9.
21 Telephone conversation with Hugh Thomas, 3 September 1999.
22 Hugh Thomas, *Hess: A Tale of Two Murders*, Chapter 12.
23 Ibid., p. 192.
24 J. R. Rees, p. 71.
25 Hart-Davis, 'The Curious Case of the Reappearing Scar'.
26 Hart-Davis, 'Reign of Silence at the Foreign Office'.
27 Hugh Thomas, *Hess: A Tale of Two Murders*, pp. 169–170.

28 Gabel, pp. 73–74 (authors' translation). The phrase used by Gabel to describe the near miss to the heart is '*frôlant le coeur*'.

29 Le Tissier, p. 45.

30 BBC Radio broadcast, 10 May 1991.

31 J. R. Rees, pp. 87–89.

32 Snyder, p. 307.

33 House of Commons, vol. 372, cols. 640–641.

34 There are references to Hess asking for whisky at Mytchett Place to help him sleep, but it is stressed that it was well watered down (e.g. PRO, FO1093/11, report by Second Lieutenant W. B. Malone, 29 May 1941).

35 Imperial War Museum archives, FO 695, Box 157.

36 Ibid.

37 Hugh Thomas, *Hess: A Tale of Two Murders*, pp. 172–173.

38 Andrew Rosthorn, additional comments to Hugh Thomas, 'Hess, "Hess", Timewatch'.

39 The 1941 chart was found by David Irving in Hess's RAMC medical files, which were transferred to the US Federal Records Center, Maryland, after the Nuremberg Trials. The 1943 chart is in PRO file FO 1093/5.

40 Irving, *Hess: The Missing Years*, p. 183.

41 Foot, 'Hess doubts that refuse to die'.

42 Nesbit and Van Acker, pp. 137–138.

43 Kaden.

44 Hugh Thomas, *Hess: A Tale of Two Murders*, p. 93.

45 J. R. Rees, p. 18.

46 Kelly.

47 Peter Allen, pp. 238–239.

48 Fraser-Smith, McKnight and Lesburg, p. 137.

49 Ibid., p. 138.

50 Andrew Rosthorn, additional comments to Hugh Thomas, 'Hess, "Hess", Timewatch'.

51 Ibid.

52 OSS intelligence report, November 1944.

53 PRO, KV237.

54 Letter to Ilse Hess, 21 January 1944, quoted in J. R. Rees, p. 79.

55 Wolf Rüdiger Hess, p. 145.

56 Letter to authors from Martin Morger of the International Committee of the Red Cross Archives Division, 13 February 1999, enclosing letters from H. de Pourtalès of the Red Cross, London, to the Foreign Office, 12 January 1943, and to Max Huber, ICRC President, 2 February 1943. (It should be noted that Walter Thurnheer, the Swiss Minister who saw Hess at Mytchett Place, was allowed a brief visit to Maindiff Court in August 1942).

57 Interviewed in Abergavenny, 5 September 2000.
58 Tom Sinclair, letter to the *Scotsman*, 12 September 1985.

Chapter Twelve: Death on Eagle's Rock

1 Bowyer, p. 114.
2 The crew of flight W4026 were: Flight Lieutenant Francis McKenzie Goyen (26); Pilot Officer Sydney Wood Smith (24); Pilot Officer George Saunders (31); Flight Sergeant William Royston ('Roy') Jones (28); Flight Sergeant Charles Lewis (27); Flight Sergeant Edward Hewerdine (24); Flight Sergeant Andrew Jack (21); Sergeant Edward Blacklock (30); Sergeant Arthur Catt (24); Sergeant Leonard Sweett (22). The Duke of Kent's entourage was: Lieutenant John Arthur Lowther (32); Pilot Officer Michael Strutt (28); Leading Aircraftman John Hales (25).
3 *Glasgow Herald*, 27 August 1942.
4 Greig, p. 286. The file on Evans at the PRO (MEPO 3/1899) gives no information on why he did not accompany the Duke.
5 Personal tribute by 'L.H.', *The Times*, 28 August 1942.
6 From Moseley's obituary in ibid..
7 Macwhirter.
8 *John o' Groat Journal*, 28 August 1942
9 By one of the more remarkable coincidences that has surrounded our personal investigation, Dr Kennedy was, in a very indirect way, responsible for us coming together as a team. He delivered Niven Sinclair, who acted as a catalyst for this investigation. It was through Niven that Stephen and Bob first met, and he who introduced Stephen to the research group through which he met Lynn and Clive. It was also Niven who introduced Stephen to Lord Thurso, whose testimony provided the key to unravelling the mystery of the Duke of Kent's death.
10 Will Bethune, interviewed by Robin Macwhirter for the BBC Radio Scotland *Portrait* programme 'The Crash of W-4026', broadcast on 26 August 1985.
11 Louise Kennedy (Dr Kennedy's daughter), interviewed by Robin Macwhirter for 'The Crash of W-4026', 1985.
12 Will Bethune, BBC interview. (op. cit.).
13 Ibid.
14 Warwick, *George and Marina*, p. 128.
15 Ibid.
16 Jack.
17 Ibid.
18 Jean Auld, interviewed by Robin Macwhirter for 'The Crash of W-4026' (op. cit.).
19 House of Commons, vol. 373, cols. 77–78.

20 Bethell.
21 The *Scotsman*, 27 August 1942.
22 Bethell.
23 Scott.
24 Zeigler, p. 184.
25 Ibid.
26 Royal Air Force Station Oban website (freespace.virgin.net/ paul.sclyde).
27 Macwhirter.
28 Jean Auld, interviewed by Robin Macwhirter for 'The Crash of W-4026' (op. cit.).
29 Ibid.
30 Jack.
31 Ibid.
32 Nesbit, 'A Travesty of the Truth'.
33 Hughes, p. 19.
34 Ibid.
35 David J. Smith, *High Ground Wrecks*, p. 3.
36 Malcolm Spaven, letter to the *Scotsman*, 5 September 1985.
37 Alderson.
38 Gander, p. 75.
39 Whiting, p. 102.
40 Macwhirter.
41 Nesbit, 'What *Did* Happen to the Duke of Kent?', p. 93.
42 David Angus, letter to the *Scotsman*, 5 September 1985
43 David J. Smith, 'The Death of the Duke of Kent'.
44 Barker, p. 69.
45 Poolman, p. 97.
46 Extract quoted in Richard A. Fresson, letter to the *Scotsman*, 7 September 1985.
47 Macwhirter.
48 Nesbit, 'A Travesty of the Truth', p. 28.
49 Fraser, p. 98.
50 Whiting, p. 102.
51 Nesbit, 'A Travesty of the Truth', quoting letter from Wilson.
52 Details from Air Ministry, *Sunderland III Pilot's and Flight Engineer's Notes*.
53 Royal Air Force Station Oban website (freespace.virgin.net/ paul.sclyde)
54 PRO, AIR 27/1415.
55 Robin Macwhirter, letter to the *Scotsman*, 12 September 1985.
56 *John o' Groat Journal*, 28 August 1942.
57 Ibid.

58 All press reports (e.g. *Glasgow Herald*, 27 August 1942) based on interviews with Mrs Sutherland give the time of his arrival at her cottage as 1.30. However, accounts vary on how long after the crash this was: 23 hours (Fraser, p. 93), 'almost 24 hours' (Aberdeen *Press and Journal*, 27 August 1942) or 22 hours (e.g. Glass, p. 153). It is clear that, at the time, all reporters were working on the understanding that the crash happened at between 2.00 and 2.30.

59 PRO, PREM 4/8/2A: File note signed 'AB', 25 August 1943.

60 Robin Macwhirter, letter to the *Scotsman*, 12 September 1985.

61 *Glasgow Herald*, 27 August 1942.

62 *Evening Citizen*, 26 August 1942.

63 *John o' Groat Journal*, 4 September 1942.

64 *Glasgow Herald*, 29 August 1942.

65 Glass, p. 153.

66 Cambridge University Library, Templewood Papers: Part XIII, File 15.

Chapter Thirteen: Reassembling the Pieces

1 From trials shown in the video *The Last Sunderland Flying Boat*, produced by Patrick Kempe, 1993.

 2 Wilson, p. 63.

 3 Irving, *Accident*, p. 143.

 4 Ibid., p. 144.

 5 Ibid., pp. 148–149.

 6 Ibid., pp. 158–162.

 7 Cadogan, pp. 449–454.

 8 Irving, *Accident*, p. 168.

 9 Ibid., pp. 163–166.

10 Lichfield.

11 Irving, *Accident*, p. 175.

12 *Glasgow Herald*, 7 September 1942.

13 Will Bethune radio interview (op. cit.).

14 R. M. Jones, letter to *After the Battle*, August 1986, pp. 51–52.

15 University of Edinburgh's Scots at War Project website, www.saw.arts.ed.ac.uk/secret/auxiliary.html. An Auxiliary Unit was established at Berriedale in 1940 but was later transferred to Golspie in Sutherland.

16 David J. Smith, 'The Death of the Duke of Kent', p. 32.

17 Howarth, p. 175.

18 Stafford, *Churchill and Secret Service*, pp. 84–85.

19 Greig, p. 282.

20 Jean Auld radio interview (op. cit.).

21 Bruce Robertson, 'Coastal Colours', in John W. R. Taylor (ed.).

22 Butler, p. 91.

23 Moran, pp. 46–48.
24 See, for example, Bryant, pp. 323–430 (based on the diaries of Field Marshal Viscount Alanbrooke).
25 Coates and Coates, pp. 709–719.
26 Details from Grove (ed.).
27 Werth, pp. 441–443.
28 Moran, p. 42.
29 Ibid., p. 54.
30 Ibid., p. 97.
31 *Evening Citizen*, 5 September 1942.
32 Cambridge University Library, Templewood Papers: Part XIII, file 19.
33 A. J. P. Taylor, p. 518.
34 Ibid., p. 520.
35 Bullock, *Life and Times of Ernest Bevin*, vol. II, p. 177.
36 Cambridge University Library, Templewood Papers: Part XIII, file 17.
37 Ibid.: Part XIII, file 4.
38 Ibid.: Part XIII, file 17.
39 A. J. P. Taylor, p. 535.
40 Cambridge University Library, Templewood Papers: Part XIII, file 19.
41 A. J. P. Taylor, pp. 536–537.
42 Ibid., Chapter 21.
43 Templewood Papers: Part XIII, file 19.
44 Court Circular, *The Times*, 11 August 1942.
45 Ibid.
46 Templewood Papers: Part XIII, file 4.
47 Moran, p. 66.
48 *The Times*, 25 August 1942.
49 Ibid.
50 Whiting, p. 102.
51 David Sinclair, p. 151.
52 Ibid.
53 Princess Alice, pp. 127–128.
54 Reported in *Glasgow Herald*, 5 October 1942.
55 Werth, p. 487.
56 Macwhirter.

Chapter Fourteen: The Hamlet Syndrome

1 M. R. D. Foot, 'Hess doubts that refuse to die'.
2 Hamilton Muniments, Bundle 5008: Letter from Sir John Wheeler-Bennett to Duchess of Hamilton, 11 December 1954.
3 J. R. Rees, p. 74.
4 Ibid., p. 64.
5 Ibid., p. 78.

6   Ibid.

7   Letter to Ilse Hess, 10 March 1947, quoted in Leasor, p. 181.

8   Letter from Rees to W. Clifford M. Scott, 11 June 1958.

9   J. R. Rees, p. 79.

10 Ibid., p. 71.

11 Quoted in ibid., p. 189.

12 This and the following extracts are from Maurice N. Walsh, 'Interview with Prisoner #7 – 25 May 1948', report dated 27 May 1948, p. 6. (Unpublished, copy in authors' possession.)

13 Wolf Rüdiger Hess, p. 362.

14 Le Tissier, p. 42.

15 Ibid., p. 68.

16 J. R. Rees, pp. 70–71.

17 Padfield, *Hess*, p. 303.

18 On Cameron's career, and the background to his brainwashing research, see Marks, Chapter 8.

19 Ibid., p. 133.

20 Ibid., pp. 134–135.

21 Krawczyk, p. 93.

22 Marks, p. 141.

23 Public Record Office, *Operation Foxley*, pp. 26–27.

24 See, for example, various articles on the American Almanac website (members.tripod.com/~american–almanac).

25 Marks, p. 125.

26 J. R. Rees, p. 174.

27 Ibid., pp. 72–73.

28 International Military Tribunal, vol. XXII, pp. 381–383. The full text can be found on the authors' website, www.pharo.com.

29 Letter from Rees to W. Clifford M. Scott, 11 June 1958.

30 Reitlinger, pp. 337–338, based on the account of Haushofer's death in the book by (in Reitlinger's words) his 'disciple' Rainer Hildebrandt, *Wir sind die Letzten*.

31 Tusa and Tusa, p. 294. However, according to Haushofer's son Heinz, the professor had been told that he would not be required as a witness. This was a major factor in the timing of Haushofer's suicide, as he considered himself relieved of his duty to his friend and protégé. (Heinz Haushofer, 'Explanation of the Reasons Leading to the Suicide of my Parents, Karl and Martha Haushofer', 14 March 1946, Papers of Father Edmund Walsh, Georgetown University Library, Washington, DC.)

Chapter Fifteen: Free at Last

1   This stricture was removed in later years, and the prisoners created a small flower garden.

2   Speer, *Spandau*, p. 255.
3   Ibid., pp. 305–306.
4   Ibid., p. 331.
5   Ibid.
6   Ibid., pp. 356–357.
7   Wolf Rüdiger Hess, pp. 300–302.
8   Hugh Thomas, interviewed for the Dutch television documentary *De Duppelganger van Spandau* (Quercus, 1989, written by Hans von Kampen and produced by Karel H. Hille); Wolf Rüdiger Hess, conversation in Munich, December 1999.
9   Wolf Rüdiger Hess, pp. 304–305.
10 Ibid., p. 276.
11 PRO, FO 1023/14: 'Prison Regulations for Spandau Allied Prison, Berlin–Spandau, Germany', 20 March 1952.
12 Wolf Rüdiger Hess, pp. 292–293.
13 Ibid., pp. 313–314.
14 Bateman, p. 21.
15 Speer, *Spandau*, pp. 448–449.
16 Quoted in Wolf Rüdiger Hess, pp. 298–299.
17 *The Times*, 2 August 1986.
18 Wolf Rüdiger Hess, pp. 326–327.
19 Ibid., p. 281.
20 Ibid., pp. 282–283.
21 Ibid., p. 286.
22 Hugh Thomas, *Hess: A Tale of Two Murders*, pp. 172–173.
23 Bird, pp. 2–3.
24 Wolf Rüdiger Hess, pp. 322–324.
25 Le Tissier, p. 44.
26 Wolf Rüdiger Hess, pp. 315–319.
27 Ibid., p. 319.
28 *Daily Telegraph*, 19 August 1987.
29 Schwarzwäller, pp. 1–2.
30 Bateman, p. 23.
31 Ilse Hess made the formal request on 10 May 1982. The agreement between the Four Powers and Wolf Rüdiger Hess was signed on 4 October 1982 (information supplied by Wolf Hess).
32 Interview with Wolf and Andrea Hess, Munich, November 1999.
33 Melaouhi swore two affidavits, on 10 January 1989 and 1 December 1989, both in Berlin. We are grateful to Wolf Rüdiger Hess for supplying us with copies.
34 Hugh Thomas, *Hess: A Tale of Two Murders*, p. 172.
35 From Melaouhi's affidavits, and conversations with Wolf Rüdiger Hess, Munich and Bavaria, November 1999.

36 Le Tissier, p. 72.

37 Ibid.

38 Ibid., pp. 72–75.

39 Ibid., p. 102.

40 Ibid., p. 103.

41 Ibid., p. 102.

42 Hugh Thomas, *Hess: A Tale of Two Murders*, p. 182. A copy of the autopsy report, supplied by Wolf Rüdiger Hess, is in our possession.

43 Ibid., p. 183.

44 Prof. Wolfgang Spann, interview for BBC's *Newsnight*, 28 February 1989.

45 Le Tissier, p. 108. Knight made his comments in the BBC *Timewatch* programme, 'Hess: An Edge of Conspiracy', produced by Roy Davies, directed by Paul Ashton, broadcast 17 January 1990.

46 Spann and Eisenmenger's autopsy report, 21 August 1987. (Copy supplied by Wolf Rüdiger Hess.)

47 Copy of original and translation supplied by Wolf Rüdiger Hess. The German reads:

'*Bitte an die Direktoren dies heimzuschicken. Geschrieben ein paar Minuten vor meinem Tode. Iche danke Euch allen, meine Lieben, für alles was Ihr mir Lieben angetan.*

Freiburg sagt, es hat mir maißlos Leid getan, daß ich so tun mußte seid dem Nürnberger Prozeß als kenne sie nicht. Es blieb mir nichts anderes übrig, sonst wären alle Versuche unmöglich gewesen in die Freiheit zukommen.

Ich hatte mich so darauf gefreut sie wiederzusehen, ich bekam ja Bilder von ihr wie von Euch allen.

Euer Großer'

48 Conversations with Wolf Rüdiger Hess, Munich and Hindelang, November 1999.

49 Hugh Thomas, *Hess: A Tale of Two Murders*, p. 184

50 Le Tissier, p. 76.

51 Ibid., pp. 77–78.

52 Conversations with Wolf Rüdiger Hess, Munich and Hindelang, November 1999.

53 Hugh Thomas, *Hess: a Tale of Two Murders*, p. 180.

54 Le Tissier, p. 90.

55 *Guardian*, 12 August 1989.

56 Letter from D. Keefe of the Western European Department of the Foreign Office to Wolf Hess, 11 February 1991.

57 Rhodri Morgan, interviewed for the Dutch television documentary *Rudolf Hess: The Appalling Truth*, 1998, produced by Karel H. Hille (as yet untransmitted).

58 On-line *Hansard* (House of Commons Daily Debates), www.publications.parliament.uk: vol. 159, column 670.

59 Morgan's questions were asked on 9 November 1989 and 9 June 1992. The reply to both questions was the same, word for word (ibid., vol. 159, column 711 and vol. 209, column 75).

60 Letter from DSI Jones to Alfred Smith, 21 April 1993.

61 Minutes of special meeting of physicians of Spandau Allied Prison held on 17 August 1987 (minutes dated 24 August 1987).

62 Copy supplied by Wolf Rüdiger Hess.

63 Letter, Anthony Inglese to Wolf Rüdiger Hess, 10 December 1986.

64 On-line *Hansard* (Written Answers to Questions) www.publications.parliament.uk: vol. 289, column 348.

65 Padfield, *Hess*, p. 328.

66 *Bild*, 21 April 1987.

67 Abdallah Melaouhi, interview for BBC *Newsnight*, 28 February 1989.

68 Le Tissier, p. 71.

69 Hugh Thomas, interviewed for the documentary *Rudolf Hess: The Appalling Truth*.

70 Hugh Thomas, cited in Gray.

71 Rhodri Morgan, interviewed for the documentary *Rudolf Hess: The Appalling Truth*.

72 Hart-Davis, 'The Curious Case of the Reappearing Scar'.

73 Telephone conversation with Hugh Thomas, 3 September 1999.

74 *The Times*, 17 February 1990.

75 Hugh Thomas, interview in documentary *Rudolf Hess: The Appalling Truth*.

76 Hans H. Hain, affidavit sworn before Justice of the Peace, in Pretoria, 22 February 1988. (Copy on file.)

77 Various correspondence between Hain and Wolf Rüdiger Hess (on file).

78 On-line *Hansard* (House of Commons Daily Debates), www.publications.parliament.uk: vol. 208, column 944.

79 Ibid.: vol 208, column 823.

80 Kelsey.

Chapter Sixteen: The Hess Alternative

1 Heiden, 'Hitler's Better Half', p. 73.

2 See Laurence Rees, pp. 86–87.

3 Wistrich, p. 142.

4 See Krawchenko Bohdan, 'Soviet Ukraine under Nazi Occupation, 1941–4', in Boshyk (ed.).

5 Wistrich, p. 212.

6 Martin Gilbert, *The Holocaust*, p. 152.

7 Davies, vol. II, pp. 244–245.
8 Van Lang and Sibyll, p. 65.
9 Ibid., p. 68.
10 Snyder, p. 219.
11 Davies, vol. II, p. 264.
12 Ibid. The term *Endlösung* in relation to the German Jews was first used in the *Völkischer Beobachter* in 1920.
13 Ibid., Chapter 12.
14 Masson, p. 1733.
15 See Mabire.
16 Reproduced in Mabire and Demaret.
17 In the aftermath of the Soviet invasion of Poland, 15,000 officers 'disappeared' from camps run by the NKVD. In April 1943, after capturing the area around Smolensk, the Germans discovered the mass graves of some 4,400 Polish officers in the forest of Katyn. Although Stalin claimed that they were the victims of German forces, it is clear that the Soviets were responsible. In the interests of the stability of the Triple Alliance, Britain and America chose to ignore this war crime both during and after the war.

Afterword

1 The results of our ongoing research and information supplied by others will be posted on the world wide web, at www.Pharo.com.
2 Hillhead Primary School, pp. 73–4.
3 Email from Major Ahuja to the authors, 1 March 2001.
4 A copy of the logbook and a detailed analysis, as well as the official photographs of the garden hut and cable, can be seen on www.Pharo.com.
5 In 1999 Morgan – the grassroots favourite – was blocked by Tony Blair in the Welsh Labour Party leadership contest, which would have made him First Minister for Wales. However, following a vote of no confidence in First Minister Alun Michael in February 2000, Morgan was voted in as his successor.
6 Mason.

Bibliography

Main entries are the editions cited in the text. Where this is not the first edition, details of first publication (where known) are given in brackets.

Air Ministry, *Coastal Command*, HMSO, London, 1943
—— *Sunderland III Pilot's and Flight Engineer's Notes*, second edition, HMSO, London, 1943
Alderson, Andrew, 'Did Champagne Down the Duke of Kent's Last Flight?', *Sunday Times*, 24 March 1996
Allen, Martin, *Hidden Agenda: How the Duke of Windsor Betrayed the Allies*, Macmillan, London, 2000
Allen, Peter, *The Crown and the Swastika: Hitler, Hess and the Duke of Windsor*, Robert Hale, London, 1983
Alice, Princess, Duchess of Gloucester, *The Memoirs of Princess Alice, Duchess of Gloucester*, Collins, London, 1983
Andrew, Christopher, *Secret Service: The Making of the British Intelligence Community*, Heinemann, London, 1985
Andrew, Christopher and Oleg Gordievsky, *KGB: The Inside Story of its Foreign Operations from Lenin to Gorbachev*, Hodder & Stoughton, London, 1990
Anonymous, 'The Inside Story of the Hess Flight', *The American Mercury*, vol. LVI, no. 233, May 1943
Argyll, Christopher (ed.), *Chronology of World War II*, Marshall Cavendish, London, 1980
Ashbee, Felicity, 'The Thunderstorm That Was Hess', *Aeroplane Monthly*, October 1987
Avon, The Earl of, *The Eden Memoirs: Facing the Dictators*, Cassell, London, 1962

Baker, David, *Adolf Galland: The Authorised Biography*, Windrow & Greene, London, 1996

Barker, Ralph, *Great Mysteries of the Air*, Chatto & Windus, London, 1966

Bateman, Denis C., 'Rudolf Hess', *After the Battle*, no. 58, Autumn 1987

Bentine, Michael, *Doors of the Mind*, Granada, London, 1984

Bethell, Nicholas, 'When Kent Nearly Went to Poland', *Sunday Times*, 3 November 1972

Bird, Eugene K., *The Loneliest Man in the World: The Inside Story of the 30-Year Imprisonment of Rudolf Hess*, Secker & Warburg, London, 1974

Blitz, James and Sam Kiley, 'KGB Claims British "Plot" to Lure Hess', *Sunday Times*, 18 May 1990

Bloch, Michael, *The Duke of Windsor's War*, Weidenfeld & Nicolson, London, 1982

—— *Operation Willi: The Plot to Kidnap the Duke of Windsor, July 1940*, Weidenfeld & Nicolson, London, 1984

Boshyk, Yuri (ed.), *Ukraine during World War II: History and its Aftermath, A Symposium*, University of Alberta, Edmonton, 1988

Bowyer, C., *Short Sunderland*, Aston, London, 1988

Boyle, Andrew, *The Climate of Treason*, Hutchinson, London, 1980

Brown, Anthony Cave, *Bodyguard of Lies*, W.H. Allen, London, 1976

—— *The Secret Servant: The Life of Sir Stewart Menzies, Churchill's Spymaster*, Michael Joseph, London, 1988

—— *Treason in the Blood: H. St John Philby, Kim Philby and the Spy Case of the Century*, Robert Hale, London, 1995

Bryan III, J. and Charles J. V. Murphy, *The Windsor Story*, Granada, London, 1979

Bryant, Arthur, *Turn of the Tide 1939–1943*, Collins, London, 1957

Bullock, Alan, *Hitler, A Study in Tyranny*, revised edition, Pelican, Harmondsworth, 1962 (Odhams, London, 1952)

—— *Life and Times of Ernest Bevin*, 3 vols, William Heinemann, London, 1983

Butler, Ewen, *Amateur Agent*, Norton, New York, 1964

Cadogan, Sir Alexander (ed. David Dilkes), *The Diaries of Sir Alexander Cadogan, O.M., 1938–1945*, Cassell, London, 1971

Calder, Angus, *The Myth of the Blitz*, Jonathan Cape, London, 1991

Carr, William, *A History of Germany 1815–1945*, Edward Arnold, London 1972

Cavendish, Richard (ed.), *Encyclopedia of the Unexplained: Magic, Occultism and Parapsychology*, Routledge & Kegan Paul, London 1974

Cazalet, Major V. A., *With Sikorski to Russia*, privately published, London, 1942

Charmley, John, *Duff Cooper: The Authorized Biography*, Weidenfeld & Nicolson, London, 1986

—— 'The King of Appeasers', *Sunday Telegraph*, 8 December 1996

Chisholm, Anne and Michael Davie, *Beaverbrook: A Life*, Hutchinson, London, 1992

Churchill, Winston S. *The Second World War*, 6 vols, Cassell & Co, London, 1948-1954

Ciano, Count, *Ciano's Diary 1939–1943*, William Heinemann, London, 1947

Clark, Alan, *Barbarossa: The Russian–German Conflict (1941-1945)*, Papermac, London, 1985

'Close Observer, A', 'The Hess Story: The Background', *Special Office Brief*, no. 249, June 1984

Clydesdale, Marquess of, and D. F. McIntyre, *The Pilot's Book of Everest*, London, 1936

Coates, W. P. and Zelda Coates, *A History of Anglo-Soviet Relations*, Lawrence & Wishart, London, 1943

Colville, John, *The Fringes of Power: Downing Street Diaries 1939–1945, Vol. One: September 1939–September 1941*, Sceptre, London, 1986 (Hodder & Stoughton, London, 1985)

Cooper, Duff, *Old Men Forget*, Rupert Hart-Davis, London, 1954

Costello, John, *The Mask of Treachery*, Collins, London, 1988

—— *Ten Days that Saved the West*, Bantam Press, London, 1991

Dalton, Hugh (ed. Ben Pimlott), *The Second World War Diary of Hugh Dalton, 1940–45*, Jonathan Cape, London 1986

Davies, Norman M., *God's Playground: A History of Poland*, 2 vols, Columbia University Press, New York, 1982

Day, David, *Menzies and Churchill at War: A Controversial New Account of the 1941 Struggle for Power*, Oxford University Press, Oxford, 1993

Deacon, Richard, *A History of British Secret Service*, Granada, London, 1969

Dear, I. C. B. (ed.), *The Oxford Companion to the Second World War*, Oxford University Press, Oxford, 1995

de Groot, Gerard J., *Liberal Crusader: The Life of Sir Archibald Sinclair*, Hurst & Company, London/New York University Press, New York, 1993

Deighton, Len, *Blitzkrieg: From the Rise of Hitler to the Fall of Dunkirk*, Triad/Granada, London, 1981 (Jonathan Cape, London, 1979)

Delve, Ken, *The Sourcebook of the RAF*, Airlife Publishing, London, 1994

Dicks, H. V., *Fifty Years of the Tavistock Clinic*, Routledge & Kegan Paul, London, 1970

Dimbleby, David and David Reynolds, *An Ocean Apart: The Relationship between Britain and America in the Twentieth Century*, BBC Books/Hodder & Stoughton, London, 1988

Documents on German Foreign Policy 1918–1945, Her Majesty's Stationery Office, London, 1961

Dollan, Sir Patrick, 'Britain, Hess and Russia', *Glasgow Daily Bulletin*, 30 October 1941

—— 'The Dollan Story', *Evening Citizen*, 20 March 1953

—— 'Premier and Hess', *Glasgow Daily Bulletin*, 7 February 1942

—— 'The Truth about the Hess Affair', *Glasgow Daily Bulletin*, 30 January 1942

Douglas-Hamilton, James, *Motive for a Mission: The Story behind Rudolf Hess's Flight to Britain*, Macmillan, London, 1971

—— *The Truth about Rudolf Hess*, Mainstream Books, Edinburgh and London, 1993

Dzelepy, E. N., *Le Mystère Hess*, Editions Raisons d'Etre, Paris, 1946

Entwhistle, C., *Undercover Addresses of World War II*, Chavril, 1992

Fleming, Peter, *The Flying Visit*, Jonathan Cape, London, 1940

Foot, M. R. D., *SOE: An Outline History of the Special Operations Executive 1940–46*, Mandarin, London, 1990 (BBC, London, 1984)

—— 'Hess Doubts that Refuse to Die', *Times*, 19 August 1987

—— *Churchill and the Secret Services*, Churchill Society for the Advancement of Parliamentary Democracy, 1989

Fraser, Donald M., *Scottish Mysteries*, Mercat Press, Edinburgh, 1997

Fraser-Smith, Charles, with Gerald McKnight and Sandy Lesburg, *The Secret War of Charles Fraser-Smith*, Michael Joseph, London, 1981

Fresson, Captain E. E., *Air Road to the Isles*, David Rendel, London, 1967

Fullerton, Tom, 'I Heard a Report on the Radio and Knew my Prisoner Was Rudolf Hess', *Scottish Daily Mail*, 29 August 1987

Gabel, Pasteur Charles A., *Conversations interdites avec Rudolf Hess 1977–1986*, Plon, Paris, 1988

Gander, Leonard Marsland, *The Long Road to Leros*, MacDonald & Co., London, 1945

Gilbert, G. M., *Nuremberg Diary*, Eyre & Spottiswoode, London, 1948

Gilbert, Martin, *The Holocaust: The Jewish Tragedy*, Collins, London, 1986

—— *Second World War*, Weidenfeld and Nicolson, London, 1989

—— *In Search of Churchill: A Historian's Journey*, HarperCollins, London, 1994

Glass, Norman N., *Caithness – and the War, 1939–1945*, North of Scotland Newspapers, Wick, 1994 (first edition 1948)

Goebbels, Josef (trans. and ed. Fred Taylor), *The Goebbels Diaries*, Hamish Hamilton, London, 1982

Gordon Jr, Harold J., *Hitler and the Beer Hall Putsch*, Princeton University Press, Princeton, 1972

Gray, Iain, 'Mystery of Spandau's Prisoner No. 7', *Glasgow Herald*, 4 April 1998

Greig, Geordie, *Louis and the Prince: A Story of Politics, Friendship and Royal Intrigue*, Hodder & Stoughton, London, 1999

Griffiths, Richard, *Fellow Travellers of the Right: British Enthusiasts for Nazi Germany 1933-39*, Constable, London, 1980

Grove, Eric J. (ed.), *The Defeat of the Enemy Attack on Shipping, 1939–1945*, revised edition, Ashgate, Aldershot, 1997. (first edition, 1957)

Grunberger, Richard, *A Social History of the Third Reich*, Penguin, London, 1987

Harris, John and M. J. Trow, *Hess: The British Conspiracy*, André Deutsch, London, 1999

Hart-Davis, Duff, 'Reign of Silence at the Foreign Office', *Independent*, 11 August 1988

—— 'The Curious Case of the Reappearing Scar', *Independent*, 10 November 1988

Haxey, Simon, *Tory MP*, Victor Gollancz, London, 1939

Heiden, Konrad, *A History of National Socialism*, Methuen & Co., London, 1934 (*Geschichte des Nationalsozialismus: Die Karrier einer Idee*, Berlin, 1933)

—— 'Hitler's Better Half', *Foreign Affairs*, 1941

—— *Der Fuehrer: Hitler's Rise to Power*, Victor Gollancz, London, 1944 (*Adolf Hitler: Das Zeitalter der Verantwortungslosigkeit*, 2 vols., Zurich, 1936–7.)

Henderson, Sir Nevile, *Failure of a Mission: Berlin 1937–1939*, Hodder & Stoughton, London, 1940

Hess, Ilse, *Prisoner of Peace*, Britons Publishing Co., London, 1954

Hess, Rudolf, *Germany and Peace: A Soldier's Message*, Berlin, 1934

Hess, Wolf Rüdiger, *My Father, Rudolf Hess*, W.H. Allen, London, 1986 (*Mein Vater, Rudolf Heß*, Langen Müller Verlag, Munich, 1984)

Hill, Robert, *The Great Coup*, Corgi, London, 1978 (Arlington Books, London, 1977)

Hillhead Primary School, *Wings over Wick*, Hillhead Primary School, Wick, 1996

Hitler, Adolf, *Mein Kampf*, single-volume edition, Hurst & Blackett, London, 1939 (Munich, 1925 and 27)

—— *My New Order* (ed. Raoul de Roussy de Sales), Angus & Robertson, Sydney, 1942

—— *Hitler's Secret Book*, Grove Press, New York, 1961

Hoare, Sir Samuel, *The Fourth Seal: The End of a Russian Chapter*, William Heinemann, London, 1930

—— *Ourselves, the World and Peace: A Survey of World Problems*, National Union of Conservative Associations, London, 1935

—— *Ambassador on a Special Mission*, Collins, London, 1946

Holden, Anthony, *Charles, Prince of Wales*, Weidenfeld & Nicolson, London, 1979

House of Commons, *Parliamentary Debates – Fifth Series*, vols 371–377, HMSO, London 1941–2

Howarth, Patrick, *Intelligence Chief Extraordinary: The Life of the Ninth Duke of Portland*, Bodley Head, London 1986

Hughes, Mike, *The Hebrides at War*, Canongate Books, Edinburgh, 1998

Hutton, J. Bernard, *Hess: The Man and his Mission*, David Bruce & Watson, London, 1970

Inglis, Brian, *Abdication*, Macmillan, London, 1966

Innes, Major (Retd.) C. B., *Craigiehall: The Story of a fine Scots Country House*, Army Headquarters, Scotland, Edinburgh, 1996

International Military Tribunal, *Trial of German Major War Criminals: Proceedings of the International Military Tribunal sitting at Nuremberg, Germany, 20th November 1945 to 1st October 1946*, 22 vols, HMSO, London, 1946–51

Irving, David, *Accident: The Death of General Sikorski*, William Kimber, London, 1967

—— *The War Path: Hitler's Germany 1933-9*, Michael Joseph, London, 1978

—— *Hess: The Missing Years, 1941-1945*, Guild Publishing, London, 1987

—— *Göring: A Biography*, Grafton Books, London, 1991 (Macmillan, London, 1989)

Jack, Andrew, 'The Day the Duke Died: Now – at last – the Lone Survivor Tells his Story', *Scottish Daily Express*, 18 May 1961

Judd, Dennis, *King George VI*, Michael Joseph, London, 1982

Judd, Terri, 'Secrets of the Trunks Entrusted to the Man from Corpus Christi', *Independent*, 13 September 1999

Kaden, Helmut, *Vortrag von D. Helmut Kaden zu den Flugvorbereitungen von Rudolf Heß*, Rudolf Hess Gesellschaft, Munich, 1989

Keegan, John, *Who's Who in World War II*, Routledge, London, 1995 (Bison Books, London, 1978)

Kelly, Susie, 'Hess Claim Shot Down', *East Kilbride News*, 23 June 1999

Kelsey, Tim, 'A Stolen File, the Spy Chief and Churchill: Latest Twists to the Riddle of Rudolf Hess', *Independent on Sunday*, 28 October 1990

Kershaw, Ian, *Hitler, 1889–1936: Hubris*, Allen Lane/Penguin Press, London, 1998

Kieser, Egbert, *Hitler on the Doorstep – Operation 'Sea Lion': The German Plan to Invade Britain, 1940*, Arms & Armour Press, London, 1997 (Bechtle Verlag, Munich, 1987)

Kilzer, Louis C., *Churchill's Deception: The Dark Secret that Destroyed Nazi Germany*, Simon & Schuster, New York, 1994

Kimball, Warren F. (ed.), *Churchill and Roosevelt: The Complete Correspondence*, 3 vols, Princeton University Press, Princeton, 1984

Kirkpatrick, Ivone, *The Inner Circle: Memoirs of Ivone Kirkpatrick*, Macmillan & Co., London, 1959

Knightley, Philip, 'Hess: Half a Century of Secrets', *Scotsman*, 10 May 1991
—— 'Surely it's Time for the Truth', *Independent on Sunday*, 24 August 1997

Krawczyk, Glenn, 'Mind Control', *Nexus New Times*, vol. 2, no. 11, January 1992

Lamb, Richard, *The Ghosts of Peace, 1935–1945*, Michael Russell, Salisbury, 1987

Land Use Consultants, *An Inventory of Gardens and Designed Landscapes in Scotland, vol. 5: Lothian and Borders*, Countryside Commission for Scotland/Historical Buildings and Monuments Directorate, Scottish Development Department, July 1987

Lane, B. M. and L. J. Rupp, *Nazi Ideology before 1933*, Manchester University Press, Manchester, 1978

Leasor, James, *Rudolf Hess: The Uninvited Envoy*, George Allen & Unwin, London, 1962

le Tissier, Tony, *Farewell to Spandau*, Ashford, Buchan & Enright, Leatherhead, 1994

Levene, Abigail, 'Swiss Laws on Sterilisation Inspired Nazi Horrors', the *Scotsman*, 28 August 1997

Levine, Alan J., *The Strategic Bombing of Germany, 1940–1945*, Praeger, Westport, 1992

Lichfield, John, 'Friends and Allies, but Churchill Loathed de Gaulle and Wanted him Eliminated', *Daily Mail*, 6 January 2000

Liddell Hart, B. H., *The Other Side of the Hill: Germany's Generals – Their Rise and Fall, with Their Own Account of Military Events 1939–1945*, Cassell & Co., London, 1948
—— *History of the Second World War*, Pan Books, London, 1973 (Cassell & Co., London, 1970)

Lippmann, Walter, *US War Aims*, Hamish Hamilton, London, 1944

Lockhart, Sir Robert Bruce (ed. Kenneth Young), *The Diaries of Sir Robert Bruce Lockhart*, 2 vols, Macmillan, London, 1973 and 1980

Mabire, Jean, *Mourir à Berlin: les SS français, derniers défenseurs du bunker d'Adolf Hitler*, Fayard, Paris, 1975

Mabire, Jean with Pierre Demaret, *Les S. S. Français: la brigade Frankreich*, Fayard, Paris, 1973

McBlain, John, *Rudolf Hess: The British Conspiracy*, Jema Publications, Moulton, 1994

McBride, Daniel, 'Alias Alfred Horn', unpublished typescript in McBride Papers, c. 1946
—— 'This is the Story of the Man who Caught Rudolf Hess', *Hongkong Telegraph*, 6 March 1947

McLeod, Kirsty, *Battle Royal: Edward VIII and George VI, Brother against Brother*, Constable, London, 1999

MacLean, Hector, *Fighters in Defence: Memories of the Glasgow Squadron*, privately published, Glasgow, 1999

Macwhirter, Robin, 'The Tragedy at Eagle's Rock', *Scotsman*, 24 August 1985

Malone, Barney, 'Z: The Private Hell of Rudolf Hess', *Observer*, 13 September 1987

Mann, Erica, 'This Is Why Hess Flew to Scotland', *Evening Citizen*, 20 September 1945

Manvell, Roger and Heinrich Fraenkel, *Hess: A Biography*, MacGibbon & Kee, London, 1971

March, Daniel J. (ed.), *British Warplanes of World War II*, Aerospace Publishing, London, 1998

Marks, John, *The Search for the 'Manchurian Candidate': The CIA and Mind Control*, W. W. Norton & Co., London, 1979

Mason, Toby, 'Intelligence service "gave Rhodri black mark"', *Western Mail*, 11 April 2001

Masson, Philippe, 'The SS: Warders of Hitler's Europe', *History of the 20th Century*, vol. 4, 1968

Moran, Lord, *Winston Churchill: The Struggle for Survival 1940–1965*, Sphere, London, 1968 (Constable, London, 1966)

Moravec, Frantisek, *Master of Spies*, Bodley Head, London 1975

Murphy, James, *Who Sent Rudolf Hess?*, Hutchinson, London, 1941

Nancarrow, F. G., *Glasgow's Fighter Squadron*, Collins, London and Glasgow, 1942

Neave, Airey, *Nuremberg: A Personal Record of the Trial of the Major Nazi War Criminals in 1945–6*, Coronet Books, London, 1980 (Hodder & Stoughton, London, 1978)

Nesbit, Roy, 'The Flight of Rudolf Hess', *Aeroplane Monthly*, November and December 1986

—— 'What *Did* Happen to the Duke of Kent?', *Aeroplane Monthly*, January and February 1990

—— 'Hess's Last Flight', *Aeroplane Monthly*, August 1995

—— 'A Travesty of the Truth', *Aeroplane Monthly*, September 1996

Nesbit, Roy Conyers and Georges Van Acker, *The Flight of Rudolf Hess: Myths and Reality*, Sutton, Stroud, 1999

Newton, Scott, *Profits of Peace: The Political Economy of Anglo-German Appeasement*, Clarendon Press, Oxford, 1996

Norton-Taylor, Richard and Jill Jolliffe, 'Kaiser Edward', *Guardian*, 13 November 1995

Padfield, Peter, *Himmler: Reichsführer-SS*, Macmillan, London, 1990

—— *Hess: The Führer's Disciple*, Weidenfeld & Nicolson, London, 1995 (revised edition of *Hess: Flight for the Führer*, Weidenfeld & Nicolson, London, 1991)

Passant, E. J., *A Short History of Germany 1815-1945*, Cambridge University Press, Cambridge, 1959

Peis, Günter, *The Mirror of Deception: How Britain Turned the Nazi Spy Machine against Itself*, Weidenfeld & Nicolson, London, 1977 (*So ging Deutschland in die Falle*, Econ Verlag, 1976)

Persico, Joseph E., *Nuremberg: Infamy on Trial*, Reader's Digest Association, London, 1995

Picknett, Lynn and Clive Prince, *The Stargate Conspiracy: Revealing the Truth behind Extraterrestrial Contact, Military Intelligence and the Mysteries of Ancient Egypt*, Little, Brown, London, 1999

Pierrepoint, Albert, *Executioner: Pierrepoint*, Harrap & Co., London, 1974

Pithers, Malcolm, 'The Man Who Broke the Secret News that Hess Was Coming', *Yorkshire Post*, 4 November 1969

Poolman, Kenneth, *Flying Boat: The Story of the Sunderland*, William Kimber, London, 1962

Public Record Office, *Operation Foxley: The British Plan to Kill Hitler*, PRO Publications, Richmond, 1998

Ramsay, Winston G. (ed.), *The Blitz Then and Now*, 3 vols, Battle of Britain Prints International, London, 1987

Reed, Douglas, *Lest We Regret*, Jonathan Cape, London, 1943

Rees, J. R. (ed.), *The Case of Rudolf Hess: A Problem in Diagnosis and Forensic Psychiatry*, William Heinemann, London, 1947

Rees, Laurence, *War of the Century: When Hitler Fought Stalin*, BBC, London, 1999

Reitlinger, Gerald, *The SS: Alibi of a Nation, 1922–1945*, Arms & Armour Press, London, 1981 (William Heinemann, London, 1956)

Riddell, Mary, *The Duchess of Kent: The Troubled Life of Katharine Worsley*, Sidgwick & Jackson, London, 2000

Roberts, Andrew, *Eminent Churchillians*, Weidenfeld & Nicolson, London, 1994

—— 'The Plot to Betray Poland', *Sunday Telegraph Review*, 8 August 1999

Rosthorn, Andrew, *Sunday Telegraph*, 21 February 1999

Schonfield, Hugh J. (ed.), *The Treaty of Versailles: The Essential Text and Amendments*, Peace Book Club, London, 1940

Schwarzwäller, Wulf, *Rudolf Hess, the Deputy*, Quartet Books, London, 1988 (*Der Stellvertreter des Führers: Rudolf Hess, der Mann in Spandau*, Wien, 1974)

Scott, Vernon, 'Royal Family Shared in a Mother's Grief', *Western Telegraph*, 12 November 1981

Sheean, Vincent, *Between the Thunder and the Sun*, Macmillan & Co., London, 1943

Shepherd, Robert, *A Class Divided: Appeasement and the Road to Munich, 1938*, Macmillan, London, 1988

Sherwood, Robert E., *Roosevelt and Hopkins: An Intimate History*, Harper & Brothers, New York, 1948

Sinclair, Andrew, *The Sword and the Grail*, Crown Publishers, New York, 1992

Sinclair, David, *Queen and Country: The Life of Elizabeth, the Queen Mother*, Futura, London, 1980 (Dent, London, 1979)

Smith, Alfred, *Rudolf Hess and Germany's Reluctant War, 1939–1941*, Book Guild, Lewes, 2001

Smith, Bradley F., *Reaching Judgement at Nuremberg*, André Deutsch, London, 1977

Smith, David J., 'The Death of the Duke of Kent', *After the Battle*, no. 37, 1982

—— *Action Stations, Vol. 7: Military Airfields of Scotland, the North-East and Northern Ireland*, Patrick Stephens, Wellingborough, 1983

—— *High Ground Wrecks: A Survey of Historical Aircraft Remains on Britain's Hills*, privately published, Bebington, n.d.

Smith, Michael, *Foley: The Spy Who Saved 10,000 Jews*, Hodder & Stoughton, London, 1999

Snyder, Louis L., *Encyclopedia of the Third Reich*, Robert Hale, London, 1976

Speer, Albert, *Inside the Third Reich*, Book Club Associates, London, 1971 (*Erinnerungen*, Propyläen-Verlag, 1969)

—— *Spandau: The Secret Diaries*, Collins, London, 1976 (*Spandauer Tagebücher*, Verlag Ullstein, Frankfurt/Main–Berlin, 1975)

Stafford, David, *Churchill and Secret Service*, John Murray, London, 1997

—— *Roosevelt and Churchill: Men of Secrets*, Little, Brown, London, 1999

Steinert, Marlis G., *Hitler's War and the Germans: Public Mood and Attitude during the Second World War*, Ohio University Press, Athens, 1977 (*Hitler's Krieg und Die Deutschen*, Econ Verlagsgruppe)

Stewart, Gordon, 'Rudolf Hess: The True Story of his Capture', *Scots Magazine*, May 1991

Taylor, A. J. P., *Beaverbrook*, Hamish Hamilton, London, 1972

Taylor, James and Warren Shaw, *A Dictionary of the Third Reich*, Grafton Books, London, 1988

Taylor, John W. R., *Aircraft 'Seventy*, Ian Allen, London, 1970

Taylor, Telford, *The Anatomy of the Nuremberg Trials*, Bloomsbury, London, 1993

Terraine, John, *The Right of the Line: The Royal Air Force in the European War 1939–1945*, Hodder & Stoughton, London 1985

Thomas, Gordon, *Journey into Madness: Medical Torture and the Mind Controllers*, Bantam Press, London, 1988

Thomas, Hugh, *Hess: A Tale of Two Murders*, Hodder & Stoughton, London, 1988 (revised edition of *The Murder of Rudolf Hess*, Hodder & Stoughton, London, 1979)

—— 'Hess, "Hess", Timewatch', *Lobster*, no. 20, 1990

Thyssen, Fritz, *I Paid Hitler*, Hodder & Stoughton, London, 1941

Tusa, Ann and John Tusa, *The Nuremberg Trial*, BBC Books, London, 1995 (Macmillan, London, 1983)

van Lang, Jochen and Claus Sibyll (eds.), *Eichmann Interrogated: Transcripts from the Archives of the Israeli Police*, The Bodley Head, London, 1983 (*Das Eichmann-Protokolle*, Severin und Siedler, Berlin, 1982)

van Paassen, Pierre, *Days of Our Years*, Hillman-Curl, New York, 1939

—— *That Day Alone*, Dial Press, New York, 1941

von Hassell, Ulrich (ed. Hugh Gibson), *The von Hassell Diaries, 1938–1944*, Hamish Hamilton, London 1948 (*Vom adern Deutschland: Aus den nachgelassenen Tagesbüchen 1938–1944 von Ulrich von Hassell*, Atlantis Verlag, Zurich, 1947)

Warwick, Christopher, *George and Marina, Duke and Duchess of Kent*, Weidenfeld & Nicholson, London, 1988

—— *Princess Margaret: A Life of Contrasts*, André Deutsch, London, 2000

Watt, Donald Cameron, *How War Came: The Immediate Origins of the Second World War, 1938–1939*, William Heinemann, London, 1989

Werth, Alexander, *Russia at War 1941–1945*, Barrie & Rockliff, London, 1964

West, Nigel, *MI5: British Security Service Operations 1909–1945*, The Bodley Head, London, 1981

Whaley, Barton, *Codeword BARBAROSSA*, MIT Press, Cambridge, Mass., 1973

Whiting, Audrey, *The Kents*, Hutchinson, London, 1985

Wilmot, Chester, *The Struggle for Europe*, Collins, London, 1952

Wilson, Richard, *Scotland's Unsolved Mysteries of the Twentieth Century*, revised edition, Robert Hale, London, 1995 (first edition 1989)

Winslow, T. E., *Forewarned is Forearmed: A History of the Royal Observer Corps*, William Hodge & Co., London, 1948

Winterbotham, F. W., *Secret and Personal*, William Kimber, London, 1969

—— *The Nazi Connection*, Weidenfeld & Nicolson, London, 1978

Wistrich, Robert S., *Who's Who in Nazi Germany*, Routledge, London, 1992 (Weidenfeld & Nicolson, London, 1982)

Wood, Derek, *Attack Warning Red: The Royal Observer Corps and the Defence of Britain 1925 to 1975*, MacDonald & Jane's, London, 1976

Wootton, Graham, *The Official History of the British Legion*, MacDonald & Evans, London, 1956

Zeigler, Philip, *The Official Biography of King Edward VIII*, Collins, London, 1990

Index

Index

Index